LAURENS COUNTY, SOUTH CAROLINA WILLS
1784-1840

By
Colleen Elliott

Please Direct All Correspondence and Book Orders to:

Southern Historical Press, Inc.
PO Box 1267
375 West Broad Street
Greenville, SC 29602-1267
or
southernhistoricalpress@gmail.com

----

southernhistoricalpress.com

ISBN #0-89308-606-1

FOREWORD

LAURENS COUNTY, SOUTH CAROLINA was created after the Public Law Act No. 1377 was passed 12th March 1785. Prior to 1785 the land was said to be in Craven or Berkley counties of Ninety Six District, which was created 25th May 1769. All colonial or pre-revolutionary records, if recorded, for the inhabitants in this specific geographical location would be filed in the Charleston County records.

The records of Laurens County are extant. Also housed with their records are the Washington District Equity Records recorded from 1808-1821 in the courthouse of Laurens County for district counties of Greenville, Laurens, and Newberry.

The settlement of today's Laurens County increased significantly in the 1760's as the overland migrations southwards continued steadily up to the revolutionary war. It is rare that the historian-genealogist has as complete a set of extant county records to research as these. The estate papers abstracted in this book will provide the reader with overwhelming documentations of the physical and economical status of the people living in Laurens County, listing many vital statistics and relationships hereunto unknown.

Ge Lee Corley Hendrix, C. G.

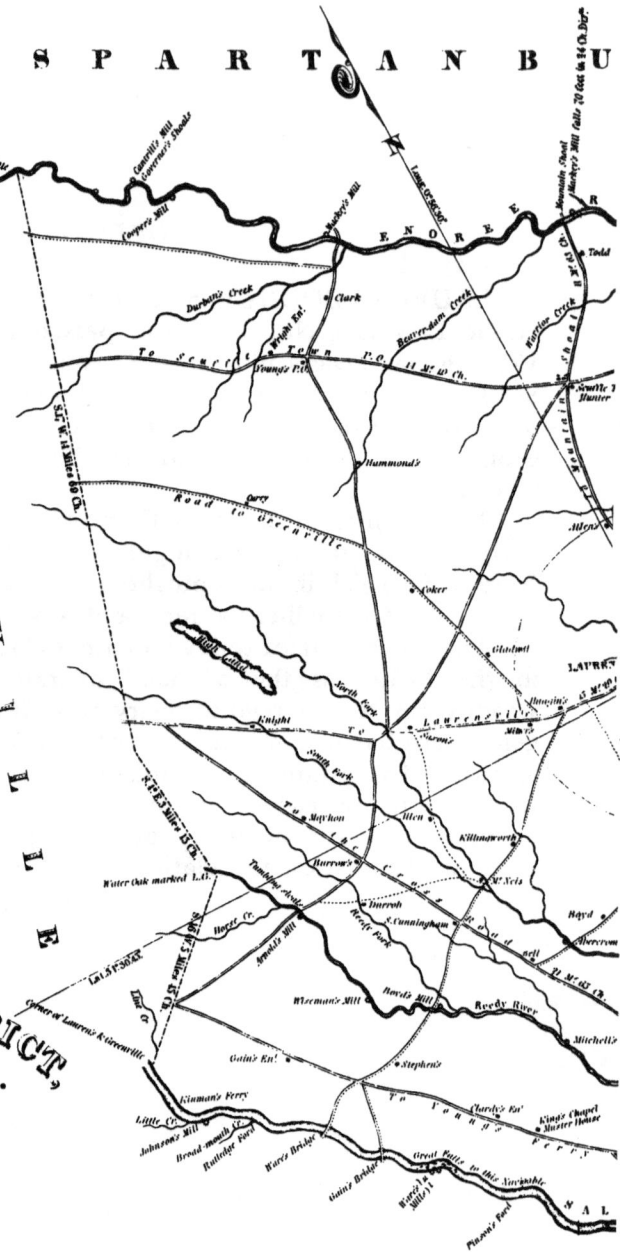

S P A R T A N B U

Corner of Laurens & Greenville

Greenville Mill
Governor's Shoals

G R E E N V I L L E

Cooper's Mill

Durban's Creek

Macksey's Mill

Lane Creek

ENOREE R.

Hunter's Mill H.W. 45 Ch.
Mountain Shoal
Calls. 70 Gen. to 84 Ch. Dist.

Todd

Clark

Wright En.

To Scuffle Town P.O.

Young's P.O.

Beaver-dam Creek

Warrior Creek H.W. 45 Ch.

11 M. to Ch.

Smiths
Hunter

Hammond's

Durey

Road to Greenville

Allen's

S.E.W. to Miller 60 Ch.

Coker

Glatfelt

LAUREN

Holly Cabin

North Fork

Knight

South Fork

To Laurensville

Shogin's 15 M.en.
Miles
Sirons

LAUREN

S.60 W. to Miller 65 Ch.

Water Oak marked L.D.

Maybon

Allen

Killingworth

To L.
Creek

Burch

Burrow's

Tumbling Shole

Reedy Fork

Mc Nels

Hogg Cr.

Arnold's Mill

S. Cunningham

Loyd
Abercrom

W.M. to 13

Wiseman's Mill

Powels Mill

Reedy River

Mitchell's

Gain's En.

Stephen's

Kinman's Ferry

Little Cr.

Johnson's Mill

Bread-mouth Cr.

Rutledge Ford

Ware's Bridge

To Younga

Clardy's En.

Kings Chapel
Muster House

Gain's Bridge

Ware's
Mill S

Great Falls Be able Navigable

SAL

Pinson's Ferry

LAURENS DISTRICT,
SOUTH CAROLINA.

SURVEYED BY HENRY GRAY D. S,
1820.

IMPROVED FOR MILLS ATLAS,
1825.

Eng. by H.S. Tanner & Assistants

Scale 2 Miles to an Inch.

Corner of Laurens & Greenville

A B B E

LAURENSVILLE.
Latitude North............. 34°.30'.45".
Longitude West.............
of Columbia.............. 0°.56'.30".

REFERENCE.
P. En! Public & Private Entertainment.
P.O. Post Office.

GEOLOGICAL POSITION.
This District lies within the upper
Boundary Line of the Granite region,
which extends to about 13¼ Miles N.E.
of Greenville Court House.

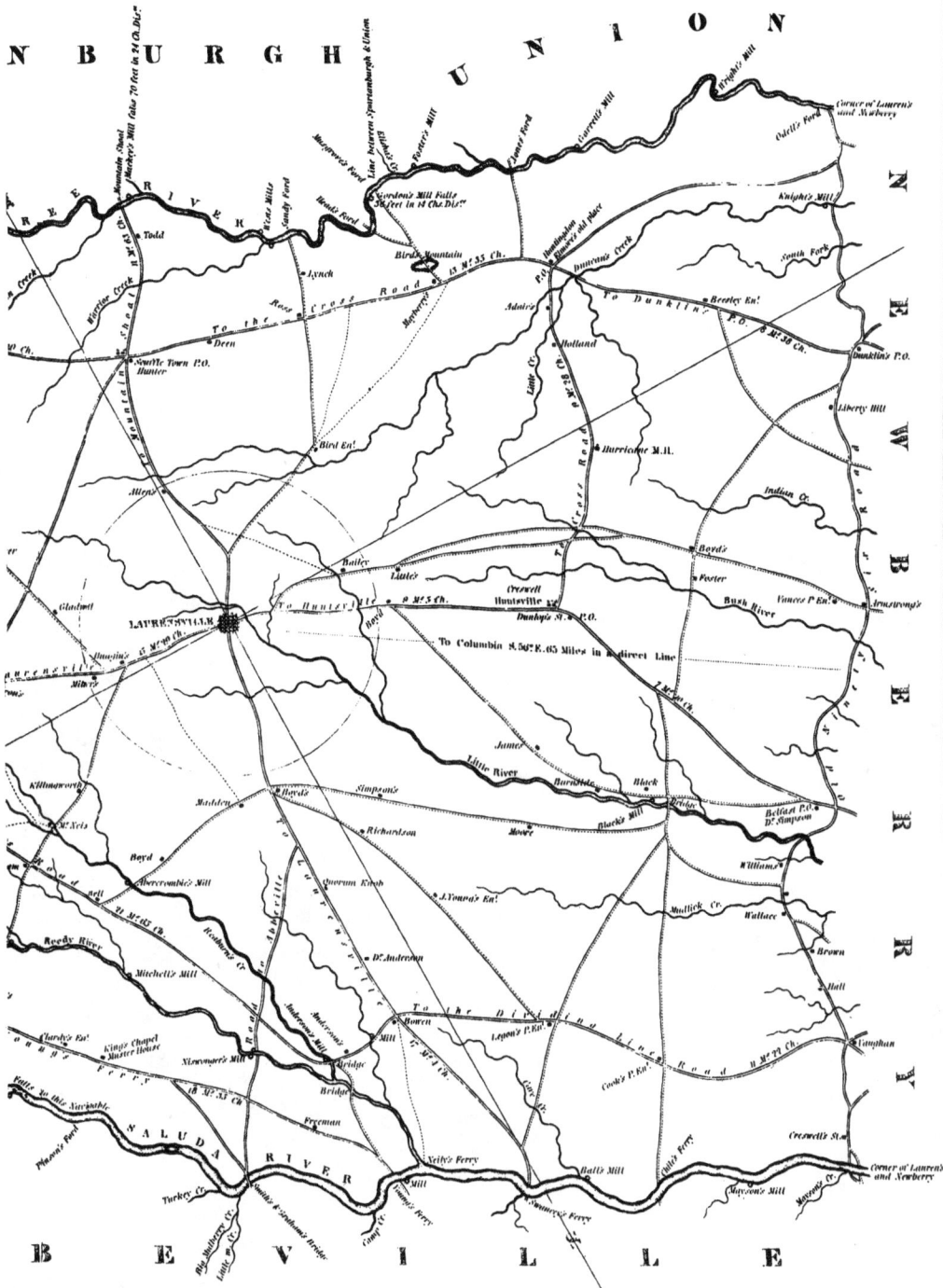

NBURGH UNION

NEWBERRY

LAURENSVILLE

SALUDA RIVER

ABBEVILLE

Mountain Shoal

Musgrove's Mill (alto 70 feet in 2d Ch. Dit.)

Line between Spartanburgh & Union

Poster's Mill

Garrett's Mill

Enoree Ford

Fripp's Mill

Corner of Laurens and Newberry

Odell's Fork

Knight's Mill

Gordon's Mill Falls 36 feet in 14 Che. Dist.?

Huntington Flowers old place

South Fork

RYE RIVER

Rice's Mills

Sandy Ford

Reeds Ford

Todd

Warrior Creek

Mt. 63

Birds Mountain

13 Mt 33 Ch.

Duncan's Creek

To Dunkin's P.O.

Beasley En!

8 Mt 30 Ch.

Dunkin's P.O.

Lynch

To the Cross Road

Mt. Creek

Mt. Ch.

Deen

Saville Town P.O.

Hunter

Adair's

Holland

Little Cr.

Mt. 26 Ch.

Liberty Hill

Bird En!

Hurricane M.H.

Cross Road

Indian Cr.

Allen's

Bailey

Little's

Boyd's

Foster

Vince's P En!

Armstrong's

Gladwel

Creswell

Huntsville

9 Mt 5 Ch.

Bush River

To Huntsville

Boyd

Dunlap's St P.O.

Mt 23 Mt Ch.

Laurensville 6 Mt 25 Ch.

Shaw's

Mile Cr

To Columbia S.56°. E. 65 Miles in a direct Line

Laurensville & Milledgeville Road

James

Little River

Black

Killingworth

Madden

Boyd's

Simpson's

Burnside

Black's Mill

Bridge

Bellah P.O.

Dr. Simpson

Mt Neil

Boyd

Richardson

Moore

Williams

Abercrombie's Mill

Mt Mt25 Ch.

Reedburg Cr

Quorum Kirk

J. Youra's En!

Mullick Cr.

Wallace

Reedy River

Mitchell's Mill

Dr. Anderson

Brown

Hall

To the Dividing Line Road

Clardy's En!

Kings Chapel Muster House

Newsonger's Mill

Anderson's Bridge

Bowen

Mill

Legon's P En!

Cook's P En!

Mt 77 Ch.

Vaughan

Phinny's Pond

18 Mt 33 Ch.

Bridge

Freeman

Camp Cr.

Creswell's St.

To the Navigable

Turkey Cr.

Little Cr.

Big Mulberry Cr.

Neil's Ferry

Mill

Ball's Mill

Cutt's Ferry

Magson's Mill

Mauros Cr.

Corner of Laurens and Newberry

BEVILLE

B E V I L L E

LAURENS COUNTY, SOUTH CAROLINA
Will Book A
ESTATE RECORDS

12 Dec. 1784. Estate of JACOB PENNINGTON, dec'd. Adm. and Exrs.:
Abraham Gray; James Bright, Charles King and Levy Caisey. Minor
legatees: Ruth Pennington, Neomi Pennington, Jacob Pennington,
Jr. Mentions Mary Gray. John Thomas, schoolmaster as witness
before J. R. Brown, JP of Newberry Co. Charles King and Levy
Caisey, joint guardians of minor children. Mentions: Absalom
Gray and Mary, his wife.

15 March 1786. Will of WILLIAM DREW. Ninety-six Dist., S. C.
Names: "beloved wife" (no name) as heir of plantation where
he lives with household goods, slave man, etc.; to his son,
William, property and slave; to son Langston, "freedom" of lands
joining ---- (torn); daughter Lucy, a negro; daughter Polly,
a negro boy; daughter Sarah, a negro girl; daughter Elizabeth,
a horse; the rest divided among the children as they come of
age. Names wife as Sarah and mentions Paul (no other reference).
Dated: 14 Feb. 1777. Witnesses: A. Rodgers, Jr., John Lucas,
and Edward Philpot. (Note: Elizabeth may be Osburn).
(Above record torn and some missing.) Exrs.: wife Sarah and
Daniel Osburn.

(No date) Appraisal of the estate of CHARLES EDWARDS by William
Bald (Bold?), Robert Fenney(?) and John Coal.

6 January 178_. Sale of estate of CHARLES EDWARDS. Purchasers:
Wm. Craig, Thos. Cason.

5 Aug. 1786. Will of JAMES MC CAIN. Ninety-six Dist. now called
Oxford Dist. Names legatees: son John McCain; daughter Mary;
to well beloved daughter (name torn) who is also executrix the
bulk of the estate. Witnesses: Richard Pugh, John Hollingworth,
and Henry Hollingworth. 16 Aug. 1788. Estate Inventory of JAMES
MC CAIN, dec'd. Appraised by: John Abercrombie, Geo. Hollingsworth and Marmaduke Pinson. Shows bond on John and Jane Hollingsworth.

(No recorded date) Will of JOSEPH KELLET, planter. Names wife:
Jennet; daughter Mary; son John to have land where he now lives
along the Indian line; son William to have land; daughters
Martha, Esther, Ann; sons James and Martin; land where Hugh
McHaffey lives to be sold and divided among the four youngest
children. Wife and son, William, executors. 9 Oct. 1785. Wit:
Martin McHaffy, Cornelius McMahon and Andrw. McKnight.

___ May 1788. Inventory of estate of JOHN SIMMONS, dec'd. Nancy
Simmons, adm. Appraised by: Joseph Simmons, John Simmons and
Robt. Simmons.

17 Jul. 1788. Appraisal of estate of Col. JAMES WILLIAMS, dec'd.
Ex.: Mary and Joseph Griffin. Appraised by: Robt. Gillam, Richd.
Griffin, Wm. Caldwell; certified by: Jno. Hunter, JP.

14 Apr. 1788. Will of HANSE (HANNCE) MILLER. Names youngest
son Joseph; daughter Betsey; sons John and Jacob; daughter Ellinor; beloved wife Susanna; son Jesse; sons-in-law: Jas. Gammer
and James Huddleston. Exr.: wife Susanna and friend, John Brown.
Wit: Joseph Adair, Thomas Ewings and James Adair.

(No recorded date). Will of WILLIAM MILLWEE. Ninety-six Dist. Yeoman. Son John Millwee; son-in-law John Entriean/Entrican; daughter Margaret Dunlap; son William Millwee; son James Millwee; beloved wife Sarah Millwee; grandson Wm. Hudgins (Sarah and William to be exrs. of Wm. Hudgins education). Exrs.: Sarah and Wm. Millwee. 26 Jan. 1784. Wit: George Rofs(Ross?), James Henderson and Wm. Irby.

2 July 1788. Will of WILLIAM HELLAMS. Beloved wife Constant Hellams; beloved grandson Jonathan Hellams, son of Jonathan Hellams; dearly beloved grandchildren, children of Wm. Hellams: Jonathan, William, Nancey and Rachael; dearly beloved daughter Rachel Allison and her son John Parker. Wit: John Childress, Richard Owings and John Hellams. (Note: the date of recording not available.) Appraisal of estate of Wm. Hellams, dec'd. 3 June 1789 by Robt. Coker, Saml. Dunlap and John Coker.

9 Mar. 1789. Will of JAMES ALLISON. Written 10 Nov. 1788. Dearly beloved wife Nancey; well beloved son James Allison, also exr.; James to have land where he now lives and the saw mill and grist mill; beloved daughter Polly Allison; beloved daughter Elizabeth Allison. Wit: Rolly R. Bowen, Saml. T. Campble and Joseph Lyon. Chas. Saxon, JP. Appraisal of estate of James Allison, dec'd. No date. Sale of estate of James Allison, dec'd. No date. Purchasers: widow, James Allison, Nancy Bowen, John Coker, Holloway Power, Saml. Means, Lewis Eakins, Peter Childress, Nathl. Marlow, John Brockman, Benj. Roberts, Geo. Berry.

28 Mar. 1789. Appraisal of estate of WM. MC DOLE(MEDOLE?), dec'd. Appraised by: Wm. Hall, James McCurley, Joseph Dean and Joseph Garsons(Parsons?).

(No recorded date) Will of WILLIAM PRATHER. Loving wife Mary, also Exr.; daughter Dorcas Prather (not yet of age). 3 Nov. 1788. Wit: Abraham Gray, John Lindsey and John Wallace.

8 June 1789. Appraisal of estate of WILLIAM SIMS, dec'd.; by A. Rodgers, Jr., Abel Boling and Thomas Babb.(1 rifle only)

(No date). Appraisal of estate of ROBERT RICHEY, dec'd.; by Samuel Wharton, Wm. Mitchell and Lewis Baylis(?). Household goods to Margaret Richey according to will of Robt. Richey, dec'd. Sale of estate of Robt. Richey: purchaser: William Goodwin 4 Aug. 1789. Second appraisal of estate of Robert Richey, dec'd. by Samuel Wharton, Lewis Banton(?) and Paul Phindley.

(No date). Appraisal of estate of GEORGE CARTER(?), dec'd. Mentions an account against the estate of Abraham Hollingsworth, dec'd.

(No recorded date). Will of DAVID LOGAN, Ninety-six Dist. Beloved daughter Cate Logan; dearly beloved son David Logan; beloved daughter Polly Hannah Logan (most of the estate being slaves). Exrs.: Angus Campbell, James Caldwell and Patrick Cuningham. 5 July 1789. Wit: Reubin Pyles, Jacob Gibson and Mary Gibson. Appraisal of estate of David Logan, dec'd. 3 Apr. 1790. By Richard Griffin, Jonathan Johnson and Alexander Snell. George Anderson, JP. Sale of the estate of David Logan, dec'd. 18 Aug. 1790. Purchasers: David Logan, Richard Griffin, and Gabriel Jones.

(No recorded date). Will of ANDREW MC NIGHT, SR. Dearly beloved wife Abigail; beloved daughters Abigail and Jennet; beloved

Will of ANDREW MC NIGHT cont'd:
sons Andrew and Archibald. Exrs.: wife Abigail and son Andrew.
8 Feb. 1789. Wit: Martin Huey, John Alexander and David Morton.

(No date) Appraisal of estate of JAMES LINDLEY, dec'd. By Jas.
Abercrombie, Geo. Hollingsworth, Thos. Cunningham and Jno. Abercrombie. Sale of estate, 12 Jan. 1790. Thomas Lindley, Adm.

(No recorded date) Will of JOHN CUNINGHAM, Ninety-six Dist.
now called Cambridge Dist., Laurens Co., S. C. Son: Thos. Cuningham; son Jas. Cuningham; dau. Ann Allison; dau. Margaret
and Wm. Hall; dau. Dorcus and David Allison; sons: John, William
and George Cuningham; grand-daughter Mary Allison; grandson
Samuel Allison; daughter Catherine and Joseph Dean; beloved
wife (not named); son Samuel Cuningham (where he now lives);
exrs.: wife and sons, Thomas and John. 15 Oct. 1788. Wit: David
Dunlap and James Dorrock (Dorrach?).

(No recorded date) Will of NEHEMIAH FORGUSON, planter. Beloved
sons John, William, Joseph, James and Thomas; daughter Elizabeth; beloved daughters Marget, Sarah and Mary; son Jeremiah
(in North Carolina?). Exrs.: sons Joseph and James Forguson.
9 Sept. 1789. Wit: Joseph Wood, Reubin Rolad and John Dalrymple.

(No recorded date) Will of JOSEPH ADAIR, cooper. 9 Jan. 1788.
Dearly beloved wife Susanna; sons Joseph, James and Benjamin;
daughter Jean Rammage; daughter Sarah Adair; daughter Mary Owens
and husband John Owens; son-in-law Robert Long. Exrs.: sons
Joseph and James Adair. Wit: James Montgomery, Wm. Bourlande
and James J. Greek(?). Appraisal of estate of Joseph Adair,
Sr., dec'd. (no date or appraisers shown).

(No date or appraisers) Appraisal of estate of JAS. WILLIAMS,
dec'd.

(No date) Will of JOHN RICHEY. Son John; daughter Mary; daughter
Ellinor; daughter Martah(?); son Robert Richey. Exrs.: wife,
Wm. McDonald and Saml. Dunlap. Wit: Wm. Paine and John McHaffy.
20 June 1778. Involves land bought from John Mehaffy (also note
other spelling McHaffy).

(No recorded date) Will of WILLIAM BAUGH, freeholder. 4 May
1787. Beloved wife Agness; sons John, William and David; daughter
Elizabeth; other children: Margaret, Jonathan, Mary and Agness.
Exrs.: wife Agness and son John. Wit: James Abercrombie, Wm.
Obannon and John Pinson.

1 Oct. 1789. Appraisal of estate of JOHN MURPHY, dec'd. (no
other names).

6 Mar. 1790. Appraisal of estate of BARNET KERNALL, dec'd. By
Alexander Deal, Clement Deal and Benj. Fooshee. Cert. by Angus
Cambpell, JP.

(No recorded date). Will of ELLINOR LEWIS. 11 Sept. 1789. Bro:
George Dalrymple; niece Ellinor Davis; niece Ellinor Dalrymple;
bro. John Dalrymple; sister Rachel Smith; Ellinor Dalrymple,
daughter of Samuel Dalrymple and her sister, Rosanna; nephew
Thos. Davis and his son, John Davis; niece Ellinor Smith. Exrs.
John and Geo. Dalrymple. Wit: Joshua Teague, David Mason and
John Hill. Appraisal of estate 22 Dec. 1789 by Joshua Teague,
Josiah East and John Miller. Sale of estate by exrs. (no date).

(No recorded date) Will of EBENEZAR STARNES, Ninety-six Dist. Son: Aaron Starnes, land on which he lives; eldest daughter Mary; daughters Anna and Rebekah; sons: Ebenezar and John Starnes land where I now live; beloved wife Anna, 1/3 of the farm lands plus stock, etc. Exrs.: wife Anna and son Aaron. 4 Nov. 1786. Wit: Samuel Wharton, John Field and Roger Murphy, Jr.

(No recorded date) Will of BENJAMIN MC DOWELL. 20 Aug. 1790. Wife Elizabeth (all estate except 50 acres in Georgia); land in Georgia to wife's daughter Patsey Jennings. Antony Jennings to receive all carpenters tools, saddle and wearing apparel. Wit: Reubin Pyles, John Tyner and Patrick Riley.

24 Aug. 1790. Appraisal of estate of ZACHARIAH SIMMS, dec'd. By David Anderson, Lewis Banton(?) and Saml. Wharton.

23 Nov. 1790. Appraisal of estate of JOHN WEST, dec'd. By David Anderson, Lewis Graves and Absalom Bobo.

24 Feb. 1791. Appraisal of estate of EPHRAIM SWINDLE, dec'd. By Lewis Graves, Absalom Bobo and Geo. Morgan.

(No recorded date) Will of EDWARD MUSGROVE of Enoree in Laurens Co. Loving son Edward Beaks Musgrove; loving little son William Musgrove my dwelling plantation, mill and all adjacent lands; daughter Rebecca Cannon; daughter Mary Berry; loving wife Ann the plantation and said mill; her seven children: William, Margarett, Ann, Hannah, Leah, Rachael and Liney. Exrs.: wife Ann and Thomas Crosby of Broad River. 25 Aug. 1790. Wit: George Gordon, John Hanna, Alexr. Morrison and John George. Appraisal of estate by Robt. Hanna, Benj. Adair and Roger Brown.

10 Sept. 1790. Appraisal of estate of WILLIAM TOLBERT, dec'd. By James Saxon, Chas. Simmons and Wm. Hunter. Sale of estate 20 Jan. 1791. Thos. Cason, Adm.

(No date) Appraisal of estate of ABSALOM GRAY, dec'd. By Edwd. Mitcheson(?), Eliss(?) Cheek, John McElroy and Thos. Malden. Sale of estate 1 June 1791. Purchasers: Mary Gray, John and Jacob Pennington, Thos. Farrow, Saml. Parsons, Isaac Gray, James McClintock and Eliza Spurgins.

4 June 1791. Will of JOHN FOWLER of Durbins Creek, Enoree River. Loving wife Molly; son Thomas Mitchell Fowler; (seven children with me at this instant); daughter Priscilla Stone; daughter Deborah Fowler; beloved son Mose Fowler; daughter Tabitha Fowler; beloved son Jesse; sons James, America, Joel. Exrs.: wife and Thomas Moore. Wit: Thomas Moore, William Fowler and John Fowler. Appraisal of estate 4 June 1791 by Thomas Parks, Holloway Power and James Allison.

(No recorded date) Will of JOSHUA ARNALL (ARNOLD). 5 Mar. 1791. Dear and loving wife Leanna; only daughter Martha Arnall; Joseph Millenor (land in Abbeville Co.); Joshua Arnall; Joshua Franks. Exrs.: Charles Smith and Samuel Franks. 5 Mar. 1792(?) Wit: N. Franks, Robert Franks and Poley Franks. 14 July 1791. Appraisal of estate by Nathan Barksdale, Charles Allen and Charles Smith. Cert. by Joshua Saxon, JP.

(No recorded date) Will of MOSES WALKER. Dearly beloved wife Elizabeth; brother Jatthrow (Jethro) Walker; mentions "my child when he is of age"; mentions mother and father; Elizabeth Walker

Will of MOSES WALKER cont'd:
and John Walker signed as agreeable to above terms. 1 June 1791.
Wit: Thos. East and James Bell. List of wearing apparel of dec'd.

(No recorded date) Will of JOSEPH ARMSTRONG. 30 Jan. 1790. Wife
Rhebeckah (Rebekah), his plantation on Mudlick Creek; eldest
son John (not of full age); son James; mentions land boundaries
of Maj. John Williams and James Burnside and Richard Griffin;
daughter Mary Ann Armstrong (plantation purchased from Benjamin
Carter). Exrs.: wife Rebekah Armstrong and Robert Gilliam, Sr.
30 Jan. 1790. Wit: James Burnside, Andrew Burnside and John
Butler. 25 Oct. 1790. Richard Griffin, Anthony Griffin and James
Burnside met at home of Joseph Armstrong, dec'd, appraised the
estate. Sale of same, 25 Oct. 1790. Purchasers: Rebekah Armstrong, Robt. Gillam, Samson Butler, James Goodman, James Williams, Isaac Grant, Thomas Farrow, Samuel Goodman and Samuel
Martin.

(No recorded date) Will of LEWIS AKINS. Daughters: Salley and
Fanny Akins; sons: John, Ezekiel, Archer and Frank Akins; son-
in-law Benjamin Kevil; grandsons William and Thomas Petty (both
minors); daughter Pattey Petty. Exrs.: son Ezekiel Akins and
son-in-law Benj. Kevil. 16 July 1791. Wit: Joab League, Thomas
Kevil and John Meador. Appraisal of estate by Hutson (Hudson)
Berry, John Brockman and Joseph Burchfield. 31 Dec. 1791.

(No recorded date) Will of RICHARD FOWLER. Beloved wife Elizabeth; son Richard Fowler, land on southside of Durbins Creek
where he now lives; son Joshua Fowler (land on northside of
Durbins Creek; children: Alas (Alice) Barton, Rebacker (Rebekah)
Barton, Richard Fowler, Ann Nevel (Nevil), Joshua Fowler, Elizabeth Flanigan. Exrs.: Richard and Joshua Fowler. 5 Oct. 1790(?).
Wit: Hutson Berry, Jos. Burchfield and John Armstrong.

(No recorded date) Will of SAMUEL DUNLAP. Beloved son John Dunlap, 100 acres on Raburn creek surveyed by a warrant of Ellen
Richey; beloved son James Dunlap, land adjoining the above;
beloved son Samuel Dunlap, land on which I live; beloved daughters Cathern (Catherine) and Suzanna Dunlap, 200 ac. on Laurel
Creek joining McDavid's land; dearly beloved wife Nancey and
3 youngest daughters Sarah, Nancy and Mary. Exrs.: friends Martin Dial, John Dunlap and Wm. Helums. 5 Feb. 1791. Wit: Martin
Diel (Dial), John Dunlap and Wm. Hellams.

(No recorded date) Will of THOMAS GARNER. 13 July 1791. Son
John, land at Rocky Mount; daughters Sarah Saffold and Molly
Roberts; beloved son Benjamin, plantation where I now live;
youngest daughter Elizabeth (minor); niece Sally Garner. Exrs:
David Anderson and Joseph Downs. Wit: Jonathan Downs, J. F.
Wolff and James Floyd. Appraisal of estate (no date): accounts
on Michael Purkle, Stephen Potter, Boling Byshop (Bishop), David
Madden, Anderson Arnold, Abraham Bolt, Wm. Rodgers, Wm. Kellet,
David Morgan, David McGladery, Wm. Burton, Jas. Downey, Chas.
Allen, Sarah Garner, Eliz. Wood, John Creecy, Wm. Thomas, Arch'd
McHurg, Benj. Camp, Calvin Coker, John Stone, Geo. Anderson,
Joseph Hughes, Mary Dunklin, Jas. Hughes, Wm. Davis, Lewis Saxon,
Joseph Downs, Jas. Saxon, Wm. Thomason, Jr. and John F. Wolff.

(No recorded date) Will of CHARLES SIMMONS. 7 July 1791. Sons:
John, Charles and William Simmons, land and plantation where
I live; daughter Sarah; youngest daughters Elizabeth and Jean
(minors); daughter Mary McCaa (McCade?); beloved wife Elizabeth.

Will of CHARLES SIMMONS, cont'd:
Exrs.: wife Elizabeth Simmons and son John Simmons. Wit: Joshua Downs, John Rodgers and James Floyd.

(No recorded date) Will of WILLIAM BAILEY. Beloved wife Ann; son William (land where he lives); son James (land where he lives); grandson William Bailey, son of David Bailey; all my children: John, Zachariah, Marjary, Mary, William, James, Lucey and Levicey. Exrs.: Zachariah, William and James Bailey. 27 Jan. 1787. Wit: A. Rodgers, Jr., Thos. Rodgers and John Rodgers. Appraisal of estate (undated). Note on Charles Bradford. Accounts against William Holdridge, William Boyce, William Dendy and Tandy Walker.

10 Feb. 1792. Appraisal of estate of USLEY BERRY, dec'd. By John Attaway, Seth Pettypool and Harley Attaway. Sale also not dated. Purchasers: George Berry, William Berry, Thomas Farrow, Joseph Deen, William Waldrop, Nicholas Brown. William Berry, Adm.

(No recorded date) Will of WILLIAM GRIFFIN, SR. 27 June 1791. Beloved wife Rachael Griffin; sons William, James and Joseph Griffin; mentions land adj. Wm. Freeman; land southwest side of Casons creek; daughter Jane and her daughters Caty and Peggy Griffin; brothers Richard and Anthony Griffin. Exrs.: Richard, Anthony and son James Griffin. Wit: Charles Griffin, James Leffan and Jane Dogharty.

(No date) Appraisal - estate of EDMOND CRADDOCK, dec'd.

(No recorded date) Will of JAMES MONTGOMERY. 17 Aug. 1791. Ninety-six Dist. Dear wife Margaret; daughters Rebeckah Adair and Isabella Ross; mentions 466 ac. in Greenville Co.; sons-in-law James Adair and George Ross (land in Laurens Co. on Enoree river called Harrold Branch, granted to Wm. Lacey and sold by him to Thos. Pearson, then purchased at sheriff's sale by Montgomery). Exrs.: wife and James Adair. Wit: Wm. Craig, John Craig and Isabella Craig.

(No recorded date) Will of ROBERT ALLISON. 5 Jan. 1791. Beloved wife Frances; beloved son James; daughters Nancy, Margaret and Mary; son Robert; daughter Jane; sons Willam and Joseph (land on Beaverdam creek); sons Samuel and Francis (land where Wm. Stone lives); daughter Ann; Ann's son Wm. Hellams; son Watson Allison; son Moses; daughter Bettey; son Lewis Allison (land where I live) and who shall maintain his mother; son Joseph and grandson James Allison. Exrs: wife Frances and son Joseph. 5 Jan. 1791. Wit: Wm. Turner, Emanuel York and Wm. Higgins.

(No date) Appraisal of estate of ROBERT BELL, dec'd. (No names of appraisers). Sale of same estate, 15 Aug. 1792. Purchasers: Isabella Bell, Patrick Scott, Nathaniel Cannon, Ann McClure, Evan Robards, James Rammage, Daniel Davis, Samuel Ewing, John Harris, Joseph Adair, son of James; Adam Bell, Gilbert McNary, James Pollock, John Roberson, Nathan Davis, John Owings, David Beazley, John Austen, Wm. Blackburn, Josiah East, Joseph Huddleston, John Adair, son of Joseph; Andrew McCrary, David Bailey, Wm. Price, John Calahan, Ann Craddock, John Archar Elmore, John Huston, Wm. Hunter, James Ramage, Wm. Gray, Saml. McConehey, John Willson, John Walker, Thos. Entrican, Thos. East, Sr., Thos. East, Jr., Saml. Eakins, John McCartney, John Duremple (Dalrymple?), Richard Bell, Charles Russell, John Robinson.

(No date) Appraisal of estate of WILLIAM PARKER, dec'd. (1 cutting knife). Appraised by Saml. Wharton, Wm. Hughes, Geo. Morgan and John Middleton.

(No recorded date) Will of LEWIS EAKINS. (See previous will of Lewis Akins).

12 Nov. 1791. Appraisal of estate of THOMAS MC CALL, dec'd. By Thomas Ewing, John Owings and Wm. Craig. Accounts due from: Gazaway Rodgers, Patrick Obrian, John Walker, Chas. Puckett and John Adair.

20 Feb. 1792. Appraisal of estate of JOHN BOYD, dec'd. By Ezekiel Griffin, Joseph Malcomb and Wm. Brown.

15 Feb. 1792. Appraisal of estate of JONATHAN PUCKETT, dec'd. By Hugh Abernathie, Wm. Nickles and Nathn. Nickles.

5 May 1792. Appraisal of estate of JOHN HALL, dec'd. By Geo. Rose, Jos. Patterson and Wm. Hutcherson. Notes on Tandy Walker, John Cargill, Robert Dicks, James Lindsee, Robt. Jacks and John McDowell.

26 June 1792. Verbal will of THOMAS BOYCE. Zachariah Bailey, Robert Shaw and Andrew Rodgers, Jr. duly sworn, they were at the house of the sd Boyce on 24th inst. and heard his verbal will as follows: divided among his children; Peggy Duram to have his two daughters; Mr. Wadsworth to have his son James; two younger sons, John and Jesse, to be educated; that Zachariah Bailey and Andrew Rodgers, Jr. be Exrs. Boyce died about 12 o'clock on the 25th inst. Sworn before Geo. Anderson, JP. Appraisal of estate of Thos. F. Boyce, dec'd. 3 Aug. 1792. Accounts on Richard Shackelford, Geo. Madden, John Garrett, Geo. Anderson, Steven Wood, Benj. Stone, Richd. Hancock, Geo. Watts, Elijah Burgess, John Adams, Wm. Crage, Wm. Chandler. Appraisers not named. Sale of estate held 23 Aug. 1792. Purchasers: Zachariah Carwile, Richd. Hancock, Abner Babb, Nath'l. Drummond, Andrew Rodgers, Drury Boyce, Claybourne Sims, John Hutchison, John Standfield, Danl. Blane, Natty Gear, Danl. Metheney, John Dacus, John Richey, Jos. Rodgers, Saml. Eakins, John Rodgers, Herusha (Kerusha?) Walker, Hugh Cromwell, Wilson Bryant, Zach. Bailey, David McCaa, Andw. Anderson, Wm. Anderson, David Anderson, John McMahan, Lewis Banton, Wm. Coleman, Wm. Whitehead, Peter Smith, Moses Madden, John Griffin, Patrk. Cuningham, John Arnold, John Dendy, Wm. Lowe, John Milam, David Cauldwell, John Fields, Ansel McGee, Wm. Culberson, Chas. Harvey, Amos Strange, Harley Shaw, Isaac Bailey, Wm. McFearson, John Hughes, Peggy Durham, Wm. Bailey, John Griffin, Wm. Donohew, Edmond Greenage, Jeremiah Green, Wilson Obrian, John Stevens.

(No recorded date) Will of MARTIN MAHAFFEY, SR. Wife Mary; son Martin Mahaffey, Exr. Wit: John McMahan and Elisha Hunt. Appraisal of estate 23 Mar. 1793 by Saml. Bolling, Wm. Choice and Alex. Paden. Sale of estate 23 Mar. 1793.

(No date) Appraisal of estate of WILLIAM DREW, dec'd. By Thos. Dandey, Saml. Powell and Zachariah Bailey.

(No recorded date) Will of JOSEPH COKER. Beloved wife Mary; dearly beloved and youngest son John Coker; well beloved sons Drury and Calvin Coker, who are also Exrs. 20 Mar. 1792. Wit: Wm. Hallams, Thos. Coker and Martin Dial.

(No recorded date) Will of THOMAS MC CRARY. Daughter Elizabeth
Young; son Matthew McCrary (land adj. John Watson); son Thomas
McCrary (land adj. David Batty and John Gray); son Charles Mc-
Crary; son-in-law John Greer, husband of daughter Jane (who
if she does not make up with John Greer will be taken care of
by her mother); son Moses McCrary (land adj. Andrew McCrary);
Moses and George to have two horses to sell to purchase land;
son Christopher McCrary; beloved wife Lettie; daughters Mary
and Catherine. 9 Jan. 1790. Exrs. Thomas Brandon, Lettie McCrary
and George Young. Wit: Geo. Bush and David Bailey.

(No recorded date) Will of ZACHARIAH GREEN, planter. 11 Feb.
1793. Wife (name not given); nephew Elisha Casey; beloved child-
ren James Green and Elizabeth Eastwood; Joel Johnson named.
Exrs. James Green and Elisha Casey. Wit: Wm. Hallums and Eliza-
beth Atkins. Appraisal of estate, 26 June 1793 by Wm. Hallums,
John Hallums and Martin Dial. Sale of estate, 10 Aug. 1793.
Purchasers: Thos. Matthews, J. F. Wolff, Mrs. Green, James Green,
James McKnight, Benj. Camp, Elisha Casey, David Green, Jane
Downan(?), Hugh Mahaffey, John Guthery.

6 July 1793. Appraisal of estate of SAMUEL MILLS, dec'd. By
Joseph Parsons, John McClintock and James Gidden. Sale of estate
23 Aug. 1793. Purchasers: Margaret Mills, John McClintock, Jas.
Parks, Wm. Burgess, John Crumton, Wm. Cheek, Robt. Ross, Jas.
McClintock, Wm. Power, Marshall Franks, Jas. Mills, Byrd Goldsby,
Jas. Hannah, Wm. Hutcherson, Alex. Mills, Thos. Ward, Wm. Mills,
Alex. Cochran, Alex. Taylor, Joseph Parsons, Wm. Fowler.

17 Jan. 1793. Appraisal of estate of WILLIAM DAVIS, dec'd. By
Joseph Adair, John Owens and Thos. Ewing.

27 Jun. 1793. Appraisal of estate of MARK GOODWIN, dec'd. By
Joseph Parsons and James Gidden.

14 Mar. 1793. Sale of estate of WILLIAM DAVIS, dec'd. Purchasers:
Jane Davis, Clement Davis, James Davis, William Davis, Littleberry McKinsey, Benj. Wilson, Samuel Ewing.

(No recorded date) Will of SHADRACH EAST, planter. Wife Mary;
children: Kesiah, John, Thomas and Ann; eldest son Allen East.
Exrs: Wm. East, Sr. and James Cook (planter). Wit: Saml. Henderson, Wm. Young (of Spartanburgh) and Thos. Wadsworth. 12 Nov.
1791.

(No recorded date) Will of ELENOR CRAGE (CRAIG). 17 Oct. 1785.
Beloved son William Crage (plantation where I live); beloved
son John (my other plantation); beloved son James (a colt).
Exrs: Thos. Logan and James Craig. Wit: Robt. Hanna, James Crage
and Thos. Logan.

17 Aug. 1793. Appraisal of estate of JAMES POLLARD, dec'd. By
Richard Turner and Richard Hatter.

(No probate date) Will of JOHN STEVENS. Beloved wife Mary; sons
John and James Stevens; John and James Steveson(?), their mothers
part; sons David and Solomon Stevens (land in George Co. in
the care of Thos. Black); daughters Janey, Elizabeth and Mary.
Exr: Mary Stevens. 8 Aug. 1793. Wit: Zachariah Bailey and Elisha
Wiles.

17 Mar. 1791. Sale of estate of JOHN SULLIVANT (SULLIVAN), dec'd.

Sale of estate of JOHN SULLIVAN cont'd:
Purchasers: Francis Sullivant, Moses Madden, Matthew Sullivant, with James Sullivant, Adm.

(No probate date) Will of GEORGE NEELY of Liberty Springs Congregation. 1 July 1793. Son James; daughter Agness; wife Ann. Exrs: Ann Neely and James Neely. Wit: Joseph Hollingsworth, Henry Hitt and John McCash.

19 Nov. 1793. Appraisal of estate of DAVID MC CULLOCH, dec'd. By John Brockman, Thos. Parks, Henry Fagin. Daniel Wright , Adm.

(No probate date) Will of JOHN JOHNSON, planter of Mudlick Creek Settlement, Laurens Co. Ninety-six Dist. Son Douglas (plantation, etc.); daughter Janet; daughter Agnes; daughter Mary; daughter Margaret. Exrs: son Douglas Johnson, G. McClintock and Charles Wilson. Wit: Wm. Fulton, James Wilson and John Wilson. 24 Nov. 1793.

23 Mar. 1793. Sale of estate of MARTIN MAHAFFEY, dec'd. Elisha Hunt, Adm.

(No probate date) Will of WILLIAM GOODMAN. Beloved wife Mary Goodman (all to her, but at her death to return to my brother); brother Clabourn Goodman; brother James Goodman; mother Mary Goodman. Exrs.: wife Mary Goodman, James Goodman and Clabourn Goodman. 28 Sept. 1793. Wit: Saml. Worton, Nicklous Vaughn, and Mary Goodman.

(No date) Appraisal of estate of JOHN JOHNSON, dec'd.

8 Mar. 1794. Appraisal of estate of GEORGE NEELY, dec'd. By John Watson, Peter Hitt and Drury Sims.

8 Mar. 1794. Appraisal of estate of ROBERT TEMPLETON, dec'd. By Robt. Hanna, James Adair and Thos. Logan.

13 Mar. 1794. Appraisal of estate of SHADRACH EAST, dec'd. Exr. William East. By Saml. Henderson, Wm. Barksdale and James Henderson.

10 Mar. 1794. Appraisal of estate of JACOB WRIGHT, dec'd. By John Henderson, John Baugh, Sr. and Robt. Freeman.

12 Nov. 1793. Sale of estate of JAMES POLLARD, dec'd. Purchasers: James Creswell, Jas. R. Mason, Saml. Bratcher, Richd. Pollard, Wm. Pollard, Jas. Caldwell, John Perry, Robt. Pollard, David Caldwell, Jonathan Childs, John Robertson, Wm. Mason, Nicholas Vaughn, Peter Smith, Wilson Sanders, Rich. Hatter, Danl. Duprey, Robt. Stewart, James Childs, Wm. Stone, Jas. Finney, Hiram Smith, Robt. Jason, David Gaines, John Jones, Benj. Allen, Jas. Cook, John Pulliam, Peter Hitt, Benj. Rowe, Benj. Cason, John Watts, Richd. M. Owen, Drury Sims, Benj. Hatter, John Dendy. Sale continued to 22 Jan. 1794. Purchasers: Richd. Pollard, John Grigby, Wm. Pollard, Wm. Sims, Jos. Bonner, Danl. Hitt, John Roberson, Henry Smith, John Carter, Benj. Peterson, James Creswell, Danl. Wood.

13 Mar. 1794. Appraisal of estate of WILLIAM GOODMAN, dec'd. By Saml. Warton, Paul Findley and Wm. Mitchell. Appraisal also made on 2 Nov. 1793 by Saml. Warton, Isaac Bailey, John Hughes.

(No date) Appraisal of estate of JOSEPH GRIER, dec'd. By Robt. McCarey (McCrary?), John Owens and Benj. Adair.

10-11 Mar. 1794. Sale of estate of DAVID MC CULLOCH, dec'd. Purchasers: James Saxon, Danl. Wright, James Russel, Benj. Warford, John Brockman, Wm. Warford, James Allison, Joseph Lyons, Joab League, Geo. Spillers, Wm. Parker, Wm. Arnold, John Childress, John Bowen, Bailey Lynsey, Stephen Thompson, Lewis Saxon, John Wright, Zadock Ford, Saml. Thompson, Robt. Hand, Joseph Allison, John Creasy, Denis Linsey, Rolley Bowen, John Coker, Asa Wright, Edward Pugh, Joel Harvey, Jacob Pennington, Isaac Morgan, Holloway Power, Joel Dean, Wm. Crow, Joseph Ellison, Joseph Howel.

18 July 1794. Sale of estate of WILLIAM SIMS, dec'd. Clayborn Sims, Adm.

15 Aug. 1794. Sale of estate of JOSEPH GREER, SR., dec'd. Purchasers: John Greer, Joseph Adair, Joseph Adair, Jr., John Hansel, Saml. McConnethy, Joseph Greer, Thos. McCrary, Robt. Greer, Wm. Hunter, Benj. Adair, Simon Ledford, Josiah Greer, John Logan, John Elmore, Manassah Wilson, Newton Higgins, C. Pucket, John Gray, Robt. Scott, John Rammage, John Owens, Hugh Skelton, Saml. Bishop, James Dillard, Josiah Rammage, Bazzel Prater, James Adair, Sr., John Watson, Wm. Price, Jonas Greer, Geo. Ross, Jane Davis, Joseph Parks, Wm. Gray. Certified 13 Oct. 1794 by Robt. Greer.

12 Aug. 1794. Appraisal of estate of MALACHIAH POWELL, dec'd. By Wm. Winn, (name not clear) and Joseph Rodgers.

(No probate date) Will of JAMES POLLOCK of Duncans Creek. 26 June 1793. Ann Pollock, dearly beloved wife; beloved daughter Gennet Henley; eldest son William Pollock; daughter Isabelle Pollock; son James Pollock; son Samuel's children; daughter Sarah Dalrymple (?); children of son John; daughter Elizabeth Gray; grand-daughter Ann Scott; Elizabeth Gray's son James Gray. Exrs: Patrick Scott and Robt. Long. Signed by James Pollock and Ann Pollock. Wit: Saml. McConehey, Alex. Adair and Joseph Grier.

27 Aug. 1794. Verbal will of EDWARD GARROT (GARRETT). Danl. Wright, JP. before whom appeared Nelson Kelly, Stephen Mullins and Stephen Garrett..that on Monday 25th inst. Edward Garrett was alive but on his death bed; expired soon after; his good wife mentioned; John Ashly (no relation given); son James Garrett in poor favor; Pleasant Sullivant had married a daughter of Garrett's and is now dead; Sullivant not to have a share in the estate but their child could have the value of 10 pounds and schooling; Stephen Mullins, son-in-law; wife Anny Garrett. Signed by Nelson Kelly, Anney Garrett and Mary (Maroh?) Garrett. Grandchild Garrett Sullivan.

(No probate date) Will of RICHARD HOLCOMB. 22 June 1794. Well beloved wife Sarah Holcomb (acreage on Durbins creek); Susana(?) Hays (very dim). Exr: beloved friend Jacob Robards. Wit: Elisha Holcomb, Reuben Higgins and Joseph Lyons.

(No date) Appraisal of estate of MATTHEW LOVE, dec'd.

28 Jan. 1795. Appraisal of estate of EDWARD GARRETT, dec'd. Sale of estate 14 Feb. 1795. Purchasers: John Ashley, John Gar-

Sale of estate of EDWARD GARRETT cont'd:
rett, Wm. Garrett, Nicholas Garrett, Jesse Garrett, James Garrett, Stephen Garrett, George Hughes, Stephen Mullins, Wm. Turner, Reuben Martin and Nelson Kelly.

(No date) Sale of estate of JEREMIAH HOLLAND, dec'd. Purchasers:
Nancy Holland, William Holland, Joseph Adair, Sampson Bobo,
Abraham Holland, Bas'c(?) Holland, Bessie(?) Holland, Richard
Holland. Sampson Bobo, Adm.

26 Dec. 1794. Appraisal of estate of WILLIAM GRIFFIN, dec'd.
By J. Dalrymple, Ambrose Hugens(?) and David Speers.

15 Feb. 1795. Appraisal of estate of JAMES POLLOCK, dec'd. Notes
on Estate of David Medlock, Zadock Wood, Saml. Neely, Thos.
Entrican, Robt. Richey, James Gammel, Jos. East, Wm. Milwee,
Ainsworth Middleton, Uriah Conner (insolvent), Estate of John
Pollock, James Phindley (out of state), Jno. Entrican (out of
state), Alexr. Bair (Adair?) (out of state), Estate of David
Simson (insolvent and out of state), John Calahan, Isham East,
Charles Russel. Accounts in books against Henry Costin, Jas.
Dillard, Isham East, Thos. East, Tarleton East, Jas. Greer,
Ambrose Johnson, Wm. Hunter, Geo. Aikens, Danl. McCarley, Wm.
Thetford, John Grier, Thos. Greer, Jno. Hunter, Mr. Giddens,
Jno. Burnett (Barnett?), Wm. Burland, Wm. Craig, Mr. Spence,
Robt. Richey, Robt. Ross, Jno. Walker, Alex. Adair. Appraised
by Benj. Wilson, John Owens and Saml. McConehey.

(No date) Appraisal of estate of DAVID SIMSON, dec'd. By Wm.
Neel, John Simon(?) and Wm. Cason.

(No recorded date) Will of PHILIP DAY, blacksmith. 9 Jan. 1793.
Beloved wife Frances; daughters Mary, Elizabeth and Jemima;
all my children: William, John, Amry, Philip, Nancy, Daniel,
Benjamin, Mary, Nathaniel, Elizabeth and Jemima. Exrs: Wm. Cason,
Jr. of Bush River and John Watts. Wit: Robt. L. Smith, Thos.
Wm. Fakes and Margaret Fakes.

(No probate date) Will of AINSWORTH MIDDLETON. Wife (not named);
sons Andrew, Thomas, Ainsworth, John and James; daughter Margaret
Hunter; daughter Ann Williams; daughter Judith; youngest daughters Sarah and Jane; mentions Wm. Anderson; Mathew Hunter. 1
Mar. 1795. Wit: Will Saxon, Thos. Roberts and James Cobb. Deliv-
ered to John Middleton, 15 Mar. 1795.

(No date) Appraisal of estate of MATTHEW MC CRARY, dec'd. Sale
of estate 13-14 Nov. 1794. Adm.: Saml. Dillard and Moses McCrary.
Purchasers: Andrw. McCrary, Benj. Lewis, Christopher McCrary,
Elizabeth Whitmore, Geo. Bush, Geo. McLain, Geo. McCrary, Jesse
Adair, Jas. Adair, Jos. James, Jos. Whitmore, Jos. Huddleston,
Jos. Gallegly, James Noteman, James Gibson, Lettice McCrary,
Richd. Ducket, Saml. Simson, Silas Garret, Thos. McCrary, Thos.
W. Satterfield, Wm. Dillard, Wm. Abrams, Wm. Polk(?), Wm. Gray,
Wm. Hunter, Robt. Scott, Thos. Elliot, Saml. Bishop, John Elmore,
Mary Baty, Nicholas Welsh, Danl. McCarty, James Dillard, James
Ray, James Lindsey, James Ducket, John Gray, Sr., John Gray,
Jr., John Biggs.

16 Mar. 1795. Sale of estate of EDWARD GARRETT, dec'd. Purchasers:
Ann Garrett, Stephen Garrett, John Garrett, Wm. Garrett, Jesse
Garrett, Nicholas Garrett, James Garrett, John Farrow, Thos.
Farrow, Zachariah Turner, James Kilgore, Jacob Pennington,

Sale of estate of EDWARD GARRETT, dec'd cont'd:
Benj. Wofford, Wm. Wofford, Lawrence Barker, Lazarus Hitt, Saml.
Parsons, Ebenezer Moss, Ezekiel Griffith, David Gibson, John
Ashley, Thos. Higgins, Reuben Martin, James Delong, Edw. Lindsey,
John Kelly, Geo. Berry, Geo. Hughes, Robt. Fleming, James Garrett.
Notes on Archibald Mcherg(?) and Stephen Marchbanks. Cert. by
Wm. Turner.

(No date) Appraisal of estate of JAMES GOODMAN, dec'd. By Danl.
Guin, Thos. Burnside and Stephen Harris.

17 Mar. 1795. Appraisal of estate of SAMUEL MURRELL, dec'd.
Mary Murrell, Admx. Appraised by John Wilson, John Templeton
and Wm. Craig.

(No date) Appraisal of estate of JOSEPH PINSON, dec'd. By James
Abercrombie, John Pinson and Geo. Hollingsworth.

2 May 1795. Appraisal of estate of SAMUEL MC CLERKEN, dec'd.
By Arch'd Owens, James Abercrombie, Geo. Hollingsworth and Isaac
Cook.

(No date) Accounts due by the estate of JONATHAN PUCKET, dec'd.
Wm. McMurtry, Exr. Receipts by: Robt. Swansey, Josiah Evans,
Wm. Rucks, James Pucket, Wm. Green, Lewis Saxon, Jonathan John-
son, Richd. Griffin, Joseph Hollingsworth, Joel Rucks, Agnes
Simson, Wm. Nichols, to Wadsworth for road, to Stedman, James
Ferguson, Alexr. Deal, to Bonner, John Sample, Danl. Perriman,
Jno. Simpson, to Mr. Ramsey for schooling, to Surveyor and Lawyer.
Wm. and Mary McMurtry, Adms.

23 May 1795. Appraisal of estate of PHILIP DAY, dec'd. By John
Dendy, Richd. Hatter and Robt. Smith.

(No date) Sale of estate of SAMUEL MURREL, dec'd, by Mary Murrel,
Admx.

7 July 1795. Appraisal of estate of AINSWORTH MIDDLETON, dec'd.
By Jas. Young, John Miller and Wm. Cason.

13 June 1795. Sale of estate of JOSEPH PINSON, dec'd. Purchasers:
Mrs. Mary Pinson, Marmaduke Pinson, Jr., Wm. Watkins, John Black-
well, Josiah Blackwell, James Box, Henry Box, Benj. Vaughn,
Berry West, Colwel Abercrombie, John Cochran, Stephen Potter,
Wm. McPherson, David Ross, Isom Histeloe. Adm.: John Blackwell
and Mary Pinson.

6 June 1795. Sale of estate of JAMES GOODMAN, dec'd. Jos. Goodman, Adm. Purchasers: Joseph Goodman, Charles Goodman, Timothy
Goodman, Clarband (Claiborn) Goodman.

(No date) Sale of estate of DAVID SIMPSON, dec'd. Purchasers:
Jane Simpson, Elizabeth Simpson, James Johnson, Jno. Gamble,
James Underwood, James Cobb, David Aston, Henry Johnson, Josiah
Leak.

(No date) Will of WILLIAM KELLET, planter. Beloved wife Anna
(Hannah?) Kellet, land in Greenville and Laurens Co.; beloved
mother Jennet Kellet (land); sisters Jennet and Margaret Kellet;
mentions fathers will; brothers and sisters, not named. Exrs:
Martin Kellet and John Kellet. 13 Aug. 1795. Wit: Edw. Scarbrough,
Hannah Kellet and Jane Kellet.

24 Aug. 1795. Verbal will of ANDREW HUNTER. Deposition of James Park who was at house of Robert Hunter on 22d inst. where Andw. Hunter lay near death. Deponant had difficulty understanding Hunter; brother Robert Hunter; sisters Elizabeth and Jane Hunter; Andrew Hunter, son of Matthew Hunter; Robt. Hutchison (who was called in to write down will but arrived after Hunter's death). Sworn to before John Hunter and James Park. Appeared Martha Millar to witness above conversation. Appeared Margaret Park to further witness above.

(No date) Will of HENDRICK ARNOLD. Beloved wife Ruth Arnold; son William Arnold; daughter Mary Arnold (land on Little Horse Creek, etc. bounded by John Johnson and Wm. Wood); daughter Nancy Arnold; son Ira Arnold. Exrs.: Ruth Arnold and Wm. Arnold. 15 July 1795. Wit: Benj. Arnold and Thomas Hamilton.

(No date) Will of JOHN MADDEN, freeholder. Beloved wife Susannah Madden; sons Charles, Abraham, William; land on Burris's Branch; sons John and David; mentions Madson(?) Madden. Exrs: Susannah Madden and son George Madden. 20 Aug. 1795. Wit: Richd Pugh and Ann Madden.

(No date) Will of ROBERT BOLT, JR. Sons: John and Lewis; wife (not named); daughters: Peggy, Sally and Polly. Exrs: wife and neighbor, Joseph Downs. 20 Oct. 1795. Wit: James Parker, Thomas Parker and Susannah McHarg.

(No date) Return on estate of JONATHAN PUCKETT, dec'd. Wm. Mc-Murtry, Adm. Shows payments from 1792 to 1795 to: David Cunningham, Surveyor; John Sample, Danl. Perryman, Evans, counselor's fees, E. Ramsey, Jos. Bonner for smithwork, John Wells for cost of suit, Stephen Wood, Jonathan Johnson, Alexr. Deale, Wm. Greene, Richd. Griffin, Richd. Grooms, John Simpson, Patrick Cunningham, James Ferguson, Wm. Rucks, W. Hart, James Puckett, Robt. Swanzy, Lem Saxon, John Carter, Jos. Hollingsworth, Angus Campbell, John McCash, Joel Rucks for maintenance of two of the children.

19 Mar. 1795. Appraisal of estate of HENDRICK ARNOLD, dec'd. Wm. Arnold, Exr. Appraisal by Reuben Pyles, John Jones and Nathan Camp.

14 Oct. 1795. Appraisal of estate of ANDREW HUNTER, dec'd. By Robt. Hutchison, David Speers and James Hunter.

12-13 Nov. 1795. Sale of estate of WILLIAM GOODMAN, dec'd. Purchasers: John Hazlet, Claybourn Goodman, John Carter, Henry Thompson, Lewis Banton, Robt. McCurley.

(No date) Legal demands vs the estate of DAVID MC CULLOCH, dec'd. Notes: Danl. Wright, Jacob Pennington, Dennis Lindsey, Thos. Holder, Saml. Thompson. Proven accounts: John F. Kern, Wm. Roundtree, Geo. Welch, John Wallace, Moses Holcomb, Wm. Bowen, John McDowel, John Brockman, James McDavid, Joseph Allison, Hudson Berry, Rolly Bowen, James Higgins, Elisha Holcomb, Wm. Hellams, Sally Stone, Robt. Hanna, Lewis Duvall, John Dukes, Thos. Holder, Benj. Wofford, Dennis Lindsey, Jos. Lyons, Patsy Wallace, Isaiah Shureen(?), Asa Wright, Holloway Powers, Burrel Thompson, Wm. Rodgers, Frank Teff(?), James Allison, John Young, Robt. Hand, Lewis Allison, Wm. Mitcherson(?), David Ross, Edw. Hooker. Danl. Wright, Adm.

(No date) For the estate of THOMAS BOYCE, dec'd. Payments by:

13

Estate of THOMAS BOYCE, dec'd cont'd:
John Hutchison, Andy Anderson, Wm. Lee, Wm. Culberson, Zach.
Carwile, David Caldwell, Jos. Rodgers, John Stephens, Danl.
Methany, Horatio Walker, John Martin, Peggy Durham, Paul Finley.
Payments to: Wm. Culberson, John Dunlap, Peggy Durham, John
Creecy; taxes; Wm. Dunlap, Danl. Levy, Danl. Methany.

15 Aug. 1795. Memorandum, sale of estate of AINSWORTH MIDDLETON,
dec'd. John Middleton, Exr.

(No date) Will of RICHARD PUGH. 10 June 1796. Wife Mary Pugh;
grand-daughter Nancy Cochran; four step-children: John McClanahan, Margaret Cochran, William McClanahan, and Samuel McClanahan. Exrs: Mary Pugh and step-son John McClanahan. Wit: Wm.
Boyd, Saml. Matthews and John Cochran.

2 Sept. 1796. Appraisal of estate of JOHN CALLAGHAN, dec'd.
By John Dalrymple, Benj. Wilson, Saml. Ewing and James Bond.
Margaret Simpson and John Simpson, Adms.

11 Oct. 1796. Payments to creditors of GEORGE CARTER, dec'd
for 1784 to 1795. John Carter, Adm. Funeral expenses paid to
Barbary Kinderman of East Florida Province; John Murphey of
E. Florida; John Adamson, merchant of Charleston; James Philpott of Laurens Co., S. C.; to Thomas Boyce; to Mary Durham
for raising and schooling two of Carter's orphans; to Sarah
Lucas, widow of John Lucas, Robt. Swanzy, Enos Stimson, James
Phinney, Patrick Cunningham, Richard Pugh - schoolmaster, for
recording lease from Richd. Carter to Geo. Carter, Cornelius
Cargill, Wm. Turk, Robt. Carter, Saml. Weathers, Saml. Wharton
(1784) and John A. Elmore (1795). Memo by John Carter, Adm.

5 Aug. 1796. Inventory of estate of RICHARD ROWLAND, dec'd by
Silvanus Walker, Joseph Box and Tandy Walker.

7 Nov. 1794. Adm of estate of MATTHEW MC CRARY, dec'd. Payments
rec'd by Moses McCrary, Adm. Wm. Hanna, Lettice McCrary, John
Thompson, Robt. Black, Joseph Huddleston, Jacob Frost, Wm. Gray,
Henry Davis, John Gray, John Gamlen, James Ray. Payments to:
Lettice McCrary for boarding children and burial expenses for
one child; John Gray, Geo. Whitmore, Mr. Dunlap for advice,
J. D. Kern, Alexr. Rosebrough (also shown as Alex. Rodger Brough)
Dated: 14 Nov. 1795.

11 Aug. 1796. Appraisal of estate of DOCTOR SMYTH, dec'd, as
shown by Mrs. Smyth, Adm. by Wm. Dunlap, James Little, John
Cason and J. Dalrymple. (Lists surgical equipment, medicine,
etc.)

28 Aug. 1795. Sale of estate of PHILIP DAY, dec'd John Watts,
Exr.

26 Mar. 1796. Sale of estate of JAMES GOODMAN, dec'd. Bond on
Meriah Goodman. Joseph Goodman, Adm.

(No date) Will of CHRISTOPHER ROWLAND. 29 Mar. 1796. Beloved
wife Mary; son Robert Rowland; mentions "all my children" but
not named. Exrs.: wife Mary Rowland and son Robt. Rowland. Wit:
Silv's Walker, Sr., Matthew Lefoy and Mary Rowland.

(No date) Will of PATRICK CUNNINGHAM. 22 Oct. 1796. Son William
Cunningham (money for schooling), beloved wife Ann; sons John

Will of PATRICK CUNNINGHAM cont'd:
and Robert Cunningham; tract lying on the Saluda and Reedy river
and land on Beaverdam creek; money for Robert's schooling. Exrs:
John Cunningham and William Cunningham. Wit: Lewis Graves, Menn.
Walker and Sarah Clarey.

5 Nov. 1796. Appraisal of estate of WILLIAM PRICE, dec'd by
Joseph Adair, Thos. Gammel and Patrick Briant. Sale of this
estate 15 Nov. 1796. Purchasers: Margaret Price, Mary Price,
Ruth Price, Sarah Price, Mary Cunningham, John Adair, Wm. McCoy,
Wm. Barksdale, James Adair and Joseph Adair.

9 May 1796. Administration of estate of MATTHEW MC CRARY, dec'd.
Debts paid by: Saml. Dillard, Saml. Simpson, Benj. Adair, J.
A. Elmore, Jas. Dillard, Joseph Adair, Jesse Dodd, Geo. Bush,
Joseph Jeanes, Robt. Scott, John Majors, James Ducket, Alse
Whitmore, Thos. Elliott, John Odle, Nicholas Welch, Mary Baty,
Danl. McCarty. Receipts: Patrick Scott for Robt. Scott, Eliza-
beth Whitmore. Paid: Jesse Dodd vendue master; J. A. Elmore,
Roger Brown, John Odle, Doctor Ross, Saml. Dillard (board for
2 boys 8 and 10 years of age). Saml. Dillard, Adm. Cert. 9 May
1796, Jos. Downs, JP.

24 Jan. 1797. Appraisal of estate of JOHN HURSKERSON(?), dec'd,
by John Henderson, John McGee and John Moor.

19 Dec. 1796. Appraisal of estate of JAMES A. GAINES, dec'd.
Thos. Gaines, Adm. By Michael Box, Charles Smith and Richard
Gaines.

17 Dec. 1796. Appraisal of estate of SAMUEL HALL, dec'd.

(No date) Will of MARGRET HENDRICK. 2 Jan. 1797. Sons Micajah
and William Win Hendrick; daughters: Fanny Turner, Peggy Forgy,
Rachael Hendrick, May Burgess, Elizabeth Wright and Martha Willard. Exr.: friend Lewis Graves. Wit: John Middleton, Jacob
Clemons and Elizabeth Sims.

(No date) Will of AARON PINSON, Minister of the Gospel. 21 Feb.
1794. Beloved wife Elizabeth Pinson; well loved sons Moses and
Isaac Pinson; daughters Jemimah Kennery, Mary Cole, dec'd (her
children); son John Pinson. Exrs: John and Moses Pinson. Wit:
John H. Kennery and Aaron Pinson, Jr.

18 Mar. 1797. Appraisal of estate of BENJAMIN MC CLELLAN, dec'd.
By John Davis, Benj. Byrd and Wm. Byrd.

18 Mar. 1797. Sale of estate of JOHN HUSKERSON, dec'd. Purchasers
were Mary Huskerson, widow; William Washington, Ansel McGee,
Saml. Mares (Maris?), Robt. Huskerson and Martin Norman.

6 May 1797. Appraisal of estate of STEPHAN POTTER, dec'd. By
Robt. McNeise, James Bumpass and Randal Cook.

15 Mar. 1797. Inventory of estate of STEPHEN EMBREY, dec'd.
App. by David Mason, John Dalrymple and Joshua Teague.

5 May 1797. Appraisal of estate of ROBERT SIMPSON, dec'd. By
John Monroe, Thos. McDonald, John Cason and Wm. Gallegly. Kitty
and John Simpson, Adm.

Administration of estate of JOSEPH PINSON, dec'd. For 1795-
1797.

8 May 1797. Estate of THOMAS FINEY BOYCE, dec'd. William White-
head, David McCaa, Wm. Bailey, Danl. Metheny, Edmond Granger,
Andrew Anderson, Wm. Crage. Payments to: Jesse Childers, John
Roling and Zach Bailey.

8 May 1797. Estate of GEORGE CARTER, dec'd. John Carter, Adm.
Receipts: John Richey, Elizabeth Burgess. Rents from Richd.
Hancock, Robt. Shaw. Payments to Ann Carter and Naomi Hodges,
orphans of Geo. Carter, dec'd. No rent paid by Joseph Hodges.

17 July 1795. Appraisal of estate of JAMES GOODMAN, dec'd. Sheriff's Books. By Thos. Burnside, Stephen Harris and Danl. McGin(?)

14 Nov. 1797. Sale of estate of JAMES A. GAINES, dec'd. Thos.
Gaines, Adm.

(No recorded date) Will of ANN SCURLOCK. 18 Sept. 1796. Daughters: Frankey Scurlock, Dolly Scurlock; Grand-sons: Reuben Scurlock and Joshua Scurlock. Exr.: trusty friend Lewis Banton.
Wit: Clabourn Goodman, Sarah Arrowwood and Easter Ware.

(No recorded date) Will of JAMES YOUNG. 23 May 1796. Cambridge
Dist., Laurens Co. Bulk of estate to two youngest children and
wife; other children already received their land. Exrs.: wife,
sons James Young and Robert Young and friend George Anderson.
Wit: Andrew Middleton and Abner Young.

17 July 1793. Estate of THOMAS GARNER, dec'd. Return of David
Anderson, Exr. Payments received from: Joseph Gallegly, Lydall
Allen, John Elmore, James Saxon, Saml. Saxon, David Dunlap,
Geo. Watts, David McCaa, Joseph Burton, David Maddon, Saml.
Wharton, Jas. Garner, G. Morgan, Saml. Parsons, J. T. Wolff,
Jos. Downs, Wm. Hunter, Woods & McHarg, Tomson & Hancock, J.
Martin, Benj. Camp. Payments made to: Ephraim Ramsey, Atty.
Clk. for Roder's suit; J. Raines, Jos. Downs, John Creecy, J.
McLaughlin, B. Saxon, B. Camp for board of two children 1793-
1797. Wadsworth & Turpin for supplies, etc. for children.

31 May 1797. Estate sale of STEPHEN POTTER, dec'd. Purchasers:
Jemima Potter, William Potter, John Potter, Ambrose Hudgens, Jas.
Bumpass, Nazia(?) Sumner. Jemima and John Potter, Adm.

2 June 1797. Appraisal of estate of MARGRET HENDRICK, dec'd.
By D. Anderson, Jno. Middleton and Robt. Freeman.

(No date) Appraisal of estate of STEPHEN EMRY (EMBRY?), dec'd
by John Dalrymple, Alex. Simpson and Thomas Horner. John Monroe,
Adm. Another appraisal was held on 10 June 1797.

3 June 1797. Sale of estate of SAMUEL MC CLURKIN, dec'd. Robt.
Haslet, Exr. John Cochran, Clk. Nancy Haslet, Admx.

11 Dec. 1796. Appraisal of estate of ROBERT ROSS, dec'd. by
Francis Ross, Sr. Mentions: Robt. Hutchison, David Speers; widow;
John Boyd; property in Greenville Co.; bond on Samuel Saxon;
notes on Francis Ross, William Ross, Wm. Rodgers, Jos. Gallegly,
John Cochran, Wm. Nicholl, John Martin, John Rodgers, Alex.
Menary, Gilbert Menary, Nathl. McCoy, J. Crumton. Reuben Pyles,
J.P.

6 June 1797. Sale of estate of ROBERT SIMPSON, dec'd. Purchaser:
Kitty Simpson. John Simpson, Adm.

(No recorded date) Will of RACHEL TURK, widow. Beloved brothers:
Archibald McDaniel and Matthew McDaniel (who are also the Exrs.);
two notes on Richard Puckett (one payable to brother on 25 Dec.
1799); beloved sister Margret McDaniel (one note on Puckett);
nephew Matthew O'Donal(O'Daniel). 16 July 1797. Wit: Matthew
Johnson and Archibald McDaniel.

(No date) Appraisal of estate of RICHARD TURNER, dec'd.

17 July 1797. Appraisal of estate of GEORGE HENDERSON, dec'd.
By Robt. Duncan, John Duncan and Wm. Duncan.

(No date) Appraisal of estate of WILLIAM FREEMAN, dec'd. By
Wm. Ragsdale, Robt. Hinton and Wm. Adkins.

29 Sept. 1797. Partial appraisal of estate of Capt. DANIEL HORSEY,
dec'd. by Edmond Kelley, James Kelley and Edw. Conaley.

(No recorded date) Will of ROBERT HINTON. 2 Oct. 1797. Son John
Hinton; grandson Robert Anderson; beloved wife Elizabeth Hinton
and her children; son Robert Hinton; daughter Hannah Moore;
daughter Elander Hinton; son Thomas Hinton. Exrs.: wife Elizabeth
and son John Hinton. Wit: Thad. Owen, Wm. Owen and Saml. Anderson.

31 Oct. 1797. Appraisal of estate of JAMES YOUNG, dec'd. By
John Miller, Matthew Hunter and William Underwood.

1 Nov. 1797. Sale of estate of JAMES YOUNG, dec'd. Purchasers:
Ann Young, Richard Jones, Joseph Young, James Young, Abner Young.
Exrs: Ann Young and James Young.

2 Nov. 1797. Appraisal of estate of JAMES HENDERSON, dec'd.
By Wm. Dunlap, Saml. Henderson, John Cargill (of Va.?) and Josiah
East. 4 Nov. 1797. Sale of the above estate. Purchasers: Ann
Henderson, Saml. Henderson, James Henderson, James Kelley, Wm.
Irby, Joel East, Jesse Motes, Wm. Henderson, Robt. Franks and
Wm. Hancock.

(No recorded date) Will of ANTHONY GRIFFIN. 20 Aug. 1797. Sons:
Asa Griffin, Abia Griffin, James Griffin; daughters: Betty Butler, Caty Cook, Sucky Griffin; well beloved wife Mary Ann Grif-
fin. Exrs: Richard Griffin, John Cole, Sr. and Mary Ann Griffin.
Wit: Robert Russel, Robert Cleland and John Armstrong.

(No recorded date) Will of JAMES BURNSIDE, SR. 17 Aug. 1797.
Daughter: Gennet Anderson; Sons: James Burnside, Andrew Burnside,
William Burnside, Thomas Burnside; daughters: Margaret Burnside,
Elizabeth Burnside, Martha Burnside, Ann Burnside, Jane Burn-
side, Hannah Burnside. Exrs:Wm. Burnside, Thomas Burnside and
Margaret Burnside. Wit: A. Rodgers, Jr., Wm. A. Rodgers and
James Cook.

(No recorded date) Will of JOHN CARTER. 14 Apr. 1798. Wife Rachel
Carter; son William Carter; son-in-law William McCrary; grandsons John McCrary and James McCrary. Exrs: wife Rachel Carter,
son William Carter and son-in-law William McCrary. Wit: John
Rowland, Jonathan Johnson and Robt. Carter.

(No recorded date) Will of WILLIAM JOHNSTON. 4 Apr. 1798. Wife
Salley Johnston; gifts to John Monroe, Elizabeth Guthrey, Salley
Monroe (Moore?), Larkin Shephard, Abraham Johnston. Exrs: John

Will of WILLIAM JOHNSTON cont'd:
Monroe and William Hardin. Wit: Thomas Dalrymple, James Gray
and Isabel Gray.

(No recorded date) Will of DRURY SMITH. 12 Aug. 1797. Beloved
wife Sarah Smith; son George Smith; son James Smith; son John
Smith has received his legacy; rest of my children: Elliott
Smith, Elizabeth Cheek, Mary Ford, William Smith and Sarah Smith.
Exrs: wife Sarah Smith and son John Smith. Wit: Daniel Ford
and Henry Vaughn.

11 May 1798. Appraisal of estate of ROBERT HINTON, dec'd. By
Robert Freeman and Samuel Freeman and Wm. Ragsdale.

1797. Administration of estate of MATTHEW MC CRARY, dec'd. Re-
turn of Samuel Dillard. Payments received of George Bush and
Jesse Dodd. 1797. On the same administration but return of Moses
McCrary. Payments received: Thomas McCrary, Thomas Wilson, Wm.
Potts, Andrew McCrary, George McCrary, Joseph Rammage, James
Scott. Payments to: George McCrary (3 coffins), to George Young,
Ex. of Lettice McCrary for boarding the children.

1798. Estate of THOMAS BOYCE, dec'd. Return of Zach. Bailey,
Exr. Payments received: Wm. Craig, John Ritchey, John Standfield,
Solomon Fuller. Payments to: John Roling, Tax Collector.

13 Mar. 1798. Appraisal of estate of WILLIAM TINSLEY, dec'd.
By Wm. Cason, Thomas Cason, Thomas Horner and Matthew Hunter.
Catherine Tinsley, Admx.

10 Nov. 1797. Sale of estate of RICHARD TURNER, dec'd. Purchasers
were: Robert Champ, Elizabeth James, Lucy Turner, John Davenport,
Richard Griffin, Harry Smith, Wm. Smith, Richd. Hatter, James
Creswell, Wm. Bell (Ball?), John Day, Robt. Griffin, Jas. A.
Williams, Fielding Turner, John Jones, John Roberson, John Watts.
Robt. Griffin, Adm.

3 Jan. 1798. Appraisal of estate of DAVID MC GLADERY, dec'd.
By David Dunlap, John Mitchell and Wm. South.

6 Nov. 1797. Appraisal of estate of DOCTOR THOMAS COFFEE, dec'd.
By Alexr. Simpson, John Blake, Daniel Griffin and James Simpson.
John Simpson, Adm.

20 Feb. 1798. Sale of estate of WILLIAM FREEMAN, dec'd. Robert
Freeman, Adm. Purchasers: Wm. West, James Ranes, Micajah Hend-
rick, Robt. Freeman, Danl. Walker, Martin Norman, Wm. Carson,
David Braden, John Alberson, Thos. Davenport, Danl. Cox, Thos.
Moore, Henry Hazle, Wm. Green, Zach. Carwile, John Savage, Jacob
Niswanger, Jas. Owen, Thos. Davidson, John Vinyard, Thos. Owen,
John Hinton, Robt. Moore, Wm. Ragsdale, Geo. Morgan, Saml. Free-
man, Robt. Hinton, Wm. Obannon, Robt. Walker, John Owen.

11 Nov. 1797. Sale of estate of DR. THOMAS COFFEE, dec'd. Pur-
chasers: John Simpson, Dr. Creecy, Dr. Jas. Davis, Dr. Kirk,
John Crawford, Wm. Satterwhite, Saml. Martin, John Gallegly,
Robt. Blake, Jas. McCrary, Jas. Lowery, Ezekiel Roland, Wm.
Ransom, David Greer, Joseph Neely, Joshua Nobels, John Monroe,
(lists medical and surgical equipment, etc.)

(No date) Appraisal of estate of WILLIAM BARD, dec'd. by Wm.
Dorrah, Jas. Dorrah and David Dunlap.

30 Oct. 1797. Sale of estate of GEORGE ANDERSON, dec'd. Purchasers: Lydia Anderson, Jacob Niswanger, Wm. Washington, John Hinton, Jacob Levy. Wm. Washington, Adm.

3 Apr. 1796. Appraisal of estate of PATRICK CUNNINGHAM, dec'd. by Lewis Graves, Wm. Harris and James Nickels. Lists various tracts of land; mentions Rev. Robt. Smith, J. B. Holmes, Edwd. Rutledge, David Madden, Danl. McCallister, John Mamxfield, Isaac Haynes, J. J. Schraum, Thos. Shirley, John Wells & Sons, David Whiteford, John McGowan, Wm. Caldwell, Wm. Harris, David Anderson, Jacob Bowman, Lewis Saxon, Maj. Downs, Geo. Forrest, Edw. Leavell, Mabra Madden, J. W. Cunningham, Robt. Cunningham, Moses Caldwell, Stephen Wood, Mr. Edwards. Large number of slaves. Shows seperate appraisal of cattle and stock.

(No date) Appraisal of estate of M. SULLIVAN, dec'd. by Wm. Simmons, Danl. Osborn, Joel Burgess and Charles Simmons. Z. Bailey, J.P. Sale of the same estate, but no date. Purchasers are John Manley, Sr., James Sullivan, Jr., E. S. Roland, Larkin Sullivan, John Todd, John Osborn, James Hughes, Noah Sullivan. E. S. Roland and Jas. Sullivan, Adm.

7 Mar. 1798. Appraisal of estate (tools) of MATTHEW SULLIVAN, dec'd. by Thos. Ross, Littleberry Bostick, Jonathan Beezley and John Hazel.

(No date) Sale of estate of WILLIAM ANDERSON, dec'd. Purchasers: John Middleton, Andrew Anderson, James Anderson, James Rains, Ambrose Anderson, John Duncan, Molley Anderson, Saml. Anderson, George Anderson, George Morgan, Randolph Mitchell, Robt. Young, James Clemons, Lewis Graves, Henry Hazel. James Anderson, Adm.

28 June 1798. Appraisal of estate of JAMES KING, dec'd. by James Powell, James Bumpass, and Aaron Clore. Reuben Pyles, J.P.

26 May 1798. Appraisal of estate of DRURY SMYTH, dec'd. by David Cowan, Reuben Martin and Reuben Kelley. 18 June 1798. Sale of the estate above. Purchasers: Sarah Smyth. Exrs.: John Smith and Sarah Smith (Smyth).

16 June 1796. Sale of estate of WILLIAM TINSLEY, dec'd. Purchasers: Catherine Tinsley, Joseph Gallegly, William Gary, Wm. Cason, Henry Johnston, James Neill, Abraham Tinsley, Robt. McAdams, John Entrekin.

11 July 1798. Appraisal of estate of TANDY WALKER, dec'd. by Danl. Osbourn, Thos. Cargill, Sr., Thomas Dendy, Sr., and Hardy Conant.

6 June 1795. Appraisal of estate of JAMES GOODMAN, dec'd. Include bonds on Meriah Goodman, Jon. Goodman.

9 June 1798. Appraisal of estate of WILLIAM JOHNSTON, dec'd. by Jacob Mason, David Mason, Thomas Dalrymple and Joseph Wood. Sale of the same estate, no date. Exrs: Wm. Harding and John Monroe.

Return on the estate of JAMES GOODMAN, dec'd. Payments to: T. W. Waters, Jas. Thurman, Jon. Younghusband, Wm. Caldwell, Danl. McGin, Robt. Gillam's estate, Thos. Burnside, Clerk fees at Laurens, Wadsworth & Turpin, Mariah Goodman. James Goodman, Adm.

Return on the estate of ABRAHAM GRAY, d ec'd. Payment of accounts to Thomas Farrow, Edw. Mitchuson(?), John Hudgens, Saml. Fleming, Joseph Adair, Gabriel Anderson, John Box, Robt. Scott, Jacob Duckett, Jos. Parsons, Jos. Burton, John Lindsey, John Pennington, Mary Gray (funeral charges). Mary Gray, Admx. 1781-1791.

33 Mar. 1798. Sale of estate of JOSEPH HUGHES, dec'd. Purchasers: William Hughes, Elizabeth Hughes, Thomas Hughes, Sally Hughes, John Hughes. Thomas Hughes and Wm. Hughes, Adm.

18 Feb. 1797. Return and settlement of the estate of JAMES POLLOCK, dec'd. Notes & Accounts: David McCulloch, Zadock Wood, Samuel Neill, Thos. Entrekin, Robt. Richey, Jas. Gambel, Jr. James Gambel, Sr., Josiah East, Wm. Millwee, Ainsworth Middleton, Uriah Conner, Chas. Russel, Jas. Findley, John Entrekin, David Simpson, John Callahan, Isham East, Henry Costen, Jas. Dillard, Thos. East, Jas. Greer, Tarleton East, Ambrose Johnston , Wm. Hunter, Geo. Aikin, Danl. McCarty, Mr. Thetford, John Greer, Thos. Green, John Hunter, Mr. Giddens, John Bennet, Wm. Bourland, Wm. Craig, John Land, Mr. Spence, Geo. Ross, John Walker, Alex. Adair, Mrs. Pollock. Payments to: Clerk's fees, Wm. Hunter, Adam Bell, Richard Bell, Andw. McCrary, Saml. Ewing, John Greer (coffin), J. D. Kern, John Robinson, Col. Robt. McCrary, Henry Johnston, Chas. Merril, Lettice McCrary, (includes three appraisals, three constables and payments to other legatees). Patrick Scott, Exr.

(No recorded date) Will of ALEXANDER FAIRBERN (FAIRBAIRN) of Duncan's Creek. 2 June 1798. Son James; daughter Geney Wood; wife Crissey; son James named Exr. Wit: Roger Brown, Samuel Laird, Basil Holland.

(No date) Sale of estate of WILLIAM BEARD, dec'd. Purchasers: Samuel Neighbors, Thos. Bradberry, Thos. Barde, David Dunlap, Wm. South, Job Thompson, Widow Berd, Thos. Berd, Wm. Norris, David Green, Mary Baird. Mary Beard, Exrx.

3 Sept. 1798. Sale of estate of JAMES KING, dec'd. Purchasers: Sally King, Polly King, Daniel Cook, Robt. Ross, John Stephens. Mary King, Adm. Reuben Pyles, J.P.

(No recorded date) Will of HENRY ATKINSON. 22 Apr. 1799. Instructions that the tract where he now lives should be sold immediately after 25th Dec. next and another tract purchased where his wife may so select; wife Mary Atkinson; eldest son John (not yet 21 years of age); youngest son William Alexander Atkinson; mentions "all my children" but does not name more. Exrs: wife Mary Atkinson, Drury Dupree and John Dacus. Wit: John Davis, Manfield Walker, Bartholomew Craddock.

(No recorded date) Will of WILLIAM HALL. 27 May 1799. Wife Mary Hall; sons Abram and Henry Hall; son William Hall; daughters: Eilzabeth Carter, Sarah Clardy, Mary Bailey and Frankey Carter. No exrs. shown. Wit: Tryparana Moore, Abram Hall and James Clardy

(No recorded date) Will of JESSE HOLDER.16 July 1798. First son Soloman Holder; son Jeremiah Holder; daughter Delilah Holder; daughter Rebecka Holder; daughter Martha Holder; daughter Sarah Holder; daughter Mary Holder; sons: Willie, Jesse and John Holder; youngest daughter Elizabeth Holder; father-in-law Solomon Langston; wife Mary (Langston) Holder. Exrs: Mary and Solomon Holder. Wit: Roger Brown, Henry Langston, Sarah Langston.

(No recorded date) Will of ROBERT HOOD. Daughter Jenny Cunningham; grandfather Kelly Cunningham; son Thomas Hood; mentions
lands of Patrick Cunningham, Richard Shackleford; horse received
from Dan Osbourn; cow due by Robert Todd; beloved wife Jane
Hood. Exrs: wife Jane and beloved son Thomas Hood, friend John
Cochran. 20 Aug. 1796. Wit: Thos. Richardson, Thos. Harris and
John Cochran.

(No recorded date) Will of JOHN TANNEY. 4 Sept. 1798. Wife:
Elizabeth Tanney; nieces: Penny Raney and Susannah Tanney. Exr.:
wife Elizabeth Tanney. Wit: Ambrose Johnson, Thomas Honor, John
Gamble.

(No date) Appraisal of estate of LEWIS DUPREE, dec'd. by Thos.
Rodgers, Wm. Oneal and Thos. Rodgers, Jr. Drury Dupree, Adm.

28 Feb. 1799. Return on estate of MATTHEW MC CRARY, dec'd. Payments: Wm. Dillard, John Martindell, Robt. Whitten, Philip Whitten, Geo. McClain, John Gry, Jas. Gibson, Jas. Lindsey, Saml.
Bishop. Moses McCrary, Adm.

10 May 1799. Appraisal of estate of ALEXANDER FAIRBERN, dec'd.
by Basil Holland, Jacob Miller and John Miller.

(No date) Sale of estate of ALEXANDER FAIRBERN, dec'd. Purchasers
were: Christian Fairbern, Jas. Fairbern, Jas. McCrary, Martin
Glidewell, Wm. Word (Wood?), Jas. Laird. Jas. Fairbern, Adm.

17 July 1799. Return on estate of ALEXR. FAIRBERN, dec'd. Payments from: Reuben Flanagan, David Grayham, Wm. Hanna. Expenses:
writing will, rum for funeral, clothing for interment, supplies
for making coffin; book accts paid to David Grayham, Alexr.
Morrison, Chas. Smith, Esq. Brown.

20 May 1799. Inventory of estate of JAMES GRIFFIN, SR, dec'd.
by John Miller, John Sinclair and Thomas Cason. Notes on hand
on John Floyd, Chas. Golding, John Golding. Wm. Barksdale, Adm.

27 Apr. 1799. Inventory of estate of MANASSAH WILSON, dec'd.
Shown by John and Ruth Dillard. App'd by Benj. Wilson, John
Owens, Robt. Long and James Bell.

15 July 1799. Return on estate of WILLIAM PRICE, dec'd. Payments
to Joseph Adams, Robt. Greer, Edw. Giddens, Francis Ross, Jos.
Downs, Jos. Huddleston, Jas. McDavid, John Owens, Chas. Merrill,
Wm. Dunlap. Margaret Price and James Cunningham, Adm. Appr'd
by Jas. Powell, Aaron Clore and Richd. Gains.

10 May 1799. Sale of estate of AGNESS MC CLAIN, dec'd. Andw.
McClain, Adm.

14 May 1799. Return on estate of THOMAS BOYCE, dec'd. Payments
received from: John Rodgers, Sr., John Rodgers, Jr., Danl. Metheney, John Stanfield, Solomon Fuller. Payments to: Benj. Saxon,
John Dunlap, John Roling. Zachariah Bailey, Exr.

20 July 1799. Return on estate of JAMES HENDERSON, dec'd. Pay-
ments to: Abraham Eddins, Thos. Wadsworth, John Harris, Wm.
Young, Chas. Smith. Legacies paid Jas. Henderson, Jr., Polly
Irby, Carter Irby, Wm. Irby, Wm. Hancock, Ambrose Hudgens. Ann
Henderson, widow and Samuel Henderson, Adm.

16 July 1784. Sale of estate of JOHN JONES, dec'd. Purchasers: John Adair, James Adair, James Dillard, Philip Harvey, Littleberry Harvey, Patrick Bryant, Saml. Ewing, Wm. Price, Thos. Donaldson, John Huston, John Owens, John Roberson, Jas. Saxon, Chas. Saxon, Saml. Saxon, John Rammage, Thos. Hughes, Reuben Pyles, Hance Miller, Wm. Brown, John Jones (Blacksmith), Julius Nichols. Patrick Bryant, Adm.

Return on the estate of JAMES GOODMAN, dec'd - indebted to James Goodman, Adm. Mentions courts at Laurens, Cambridge, Newberry re suits of Timothy Goodman, J. R. Brown, Jno. Haslet; trip to Georgia. (No date)

Return on estate of STEPHEN EMMORY (EMBREY?), dec'd. (1787-1798). Wm. Gallegly for expenses; Mrs. Emmory to doctor in North Carolina in 1790-1791; eight days riding to doctor in 1792; nursing and maintaining widow 1795-1798; also child Margaret Emmory.

30 Mar. 1798. Appraisal of estate of ANN SCURLOCK, dec'd. by John Middleton, David Anderson and James Hinson. Lewis Banton, Exr.

(No date) Return on estate of DRURY SMITH, dec'd. Payments to: widow, John Vaughn, Danl. Ford, John Smith, Wm. Smith, Sarah Smith, Austin Moore, Elliot Smith, Elizabeth Cheek. Sarah Smith, and John Smith, Exrs.

3 Oct. 1798. Return on estate of ROBERT BELL, dec'd. Payments to: Thos. Murdaugh, Geo. Ross, Thos. A. McCrary, Wm. Gray (for crying sale); John Robertson, Clerk for sale. Receipts of Isabella Bell from her father's estate, she is now wife of Robt. Scott. Wit: Robt. Long. Richard Bell, Adm. Proven: James Dillard, J. P.

(No date) Sale of estate of ANN SCURLOCK, dec'd. Purchasers: John Davenport, Hutchens Burton, John Middleton, Lewis Banton, Frances Scurlock, Thos. Reding, Joel Hughs, Thos. Hughs, David Nelson, Molly Anderson.

(No recorded date) Will of MARY TURK. 16 July 1799. Her sister's son Joseph Motes (given slaves); loving friend John Motes, son of Joseph Motes (named above); loving friend Mary Motes, daughter of Joseph Motes; loving sister-in-law, wife of my brother Benj. Collier (she is not named); sister Hannah Pitts; also gifts to sister Hannah's children (not named); brother Henry Pitts; brother James Bolen; sister Jean Bolen; also gifts to children of Jean Bolen (not named); brother Jonathan Motes; sister Ordery Motes, wife of Jonathan Motes; also to Ordery Motes' children (not named). Exrs: Ordery Motes, son Joseph Motes, nephew Joseph Motes and friend John Simpson. Wit: William Ranson, Zachariah Motes and Archibald Sayers.

6 Oct. 1798. Inventory of estate of JAMES FLOYD, dec'd. by Lydall Allen and Jesse Garrett.

10 Aug. 1799. Inventory of estate of EDWARD JONES, dec'd. by Richard Griffin, J. Burnside and John Meek. Angus Campbell, J. P.

23 July 1799. Appraisal of estate of WM. HALL, dec'd. by Claybourn Brown, James Bailey and Mark Moore.

23 Aug. 1799. Sale of estate of WM. HALL, dec'd. James Clardy, Adm.

3 July 1799. Inventory of estate of MANASSAH WILSON, dec'd. John Dillard, Adm.

(No date) Sale of estate of LEWIS DUPREE, dec'd. Drury Dupree, Adm.

14 Mar. 1800. Sale of estate of NEHEMIAH FRANKS, dec'd. Nancy Franks and James Bumpass, Adm.

20 Feb. 1800. Will of JAMES PUCKETT. 10 Feb. 1796. My children, Susannah Pinson, wife of John Pinson; their son Joel Pinson; daughter Jene (Jean) Beassley, her children Nancy and Chainey Beassley; John Beassley, husband of Jean; other children Richard, Dabney, Neeley, Lucy and James Puckett. Dabney Puckett and Neeley Puckett, Exr. Wit: William Ball, Martha Overby and Meshack Overby. Proven before David Anderson, Ord.

(No date) Appraisal of estate of JAMES PUCKETT, dec'd by Meshack Overby, Henry Hill (Hitt?) and Laurens Hitt.

17 Mar. 1800. Petition of Jeremiah Leek to adm. the estate of ROBERT MC NEIR(?), dec'd.

26 Feb. 1800. Petition of Frances Scurlock to adm. the estate of DOLLY SCURLOCK, dec'd.

3 Mar. 1800. Will of THOMAS DENDY, SR. proven by John Hunter and John Leek. Letters of test. to Mary Dendy and Wm. Dendy. (Also spelled Dendey).

3 Mar. 1800. Will of THOMAS DANDAY (DENDY), SR. Wife Mary Danday; daughter Elizabeth, wife of Samuel Powel; daughter Sarah and husband James Young; daughter Moley, wife of William Michel; bequeath to Martha Walker and Patsy Walker; sons: Cornelius, Thomas and William Danday. Exrs: Mary Danday and Wm. Danday. Wit: John Hunter, Wm. Danday and Saml. Leek.

9 Feb. 1800. Petition of John Harris to adm. estate of STEPHEN MORRIS, dec'd.

19 Feb. 1800. Inventory of estate of STEPHEN HARRIS, dec'd by Abner Pyles, James Cook and John Chandler.

3 Mar. 1800. Will of JAMES KIERK, planter. Son-in-law William Brison; son John Kierk; Sarah Brison, daughter of Wm. Brison; James Brison, son of Wm. Brison; also Robert Brison, John Brison and Jane Brison, children of Wm. Brison; cousin James Kierk; (he of North Carolina; name also spelled Keirk and Kirk); grand-son James Kierk, son of my son John Kierk; grand-daughter Sarah Kierk, daughter of John Kierk. Exrs: John Hunter and John Kierk. 30 July 1799. Wit: John Puckett, Agness Creswell, Danl. Chanle-ton. Will proven by application of John Hunter, oath of John Puckett and Agnes Creswell, 3 Mar. 1800. D. Anderson, Ord.

3 Mar. 1800. Inventory of estate of MARY TURK, dec'd. by Danl. McGinn, Anthony Golden and Wm. Morrow. Ex.: Joseph Motes.

Proven 17 Mar. 1800. Will of JOHN STONE, dec'd on application of Mildredge (?) Stone and Rolley Stone, by Danl. and Nansey

Will of JOHN STONE, dec'd cont'd: Wright.

17 Mar. 1800. Will of JOHN STONE. 25 Jan. 1797. Wife Milduge/Mil-drege(this name not clear); sons Rolley Stone, Lewis Stone, William Stone, Reuben Stone, Elias Stone; daughter Nansey Stone. Exrs: wife and son Rolley. Wit: Daniel Wright and Nansey Wright.

26 Apr. 1800. Application of John McLaughlin to adm. estate of WILLIAM HARRIS, dec'd.

28 Apr. 1800. Appraisal of estate of WILLIAM HARRIS, dec'd by Silvs. Walker, John Middleton and John Wait.

6 May 1800. Sale of estate of WM. HARRIS, dec'd. Purchasers: Braddock Harris, John Harris, Minyard Harris, Wm. Harris, James Clardy, Glanus Winn, Jas. Polley, Stephen Smith, John Burnes, John Milum, Isaac Medley, Jas. Holley, Wm. Nickels, Stephen Garrett, Joseph Griffin, Abner Teage, John Cureton, Moses Sanders and James Handcock.

12 June 1800. Application of Ann Peterson to prove the last W & T of JAMES PETERSON, dec'd. John Watts and Wm. Roberson, Wit.

2 June 1800. Will of JAMES PETERSON. 23 June 1799. Wife Ann Peterson; grand-daughter Patsey Peterson; grand-daughter Susanah Peterson; son Benjaman Peterson. Exr. Ann Peterson. Wit: John Watts and Wm. Roberson.

9 June 1800. Application of Nathaniel Vance, Exr. of last W & T of WM. MC TEER, dec'd. Wit: James Wallace and John Simpson.

20 Mar. 1800. Will of WILLIAM MC TEER. Wife and unmarried child-ren to be in care of Nathaniel Vance; daughters: Margret, Eli-zabeth and Frances; grandson Nathaniel McTeer, son of William McTeer; daughter Jean McClure(?). Exr.: Nathl. Vance and Chas. Griffin. Wit: John Simson, Jr., James Wallace and James Leffan.

23 May 1800. Sale of estate of WM. HARRIS, dec'd. Purchasers: Silvs. Walker, Jr., John Middleton, John Walker, Mrs. Harris, Chas. Harris, Wm. Harris, John Harris, Thos. Harris, Luke Demp-sey, John McLaughlin, James Vance, Thos. Cargill.

26 Mar. 1800. Appraisal of estate of THOMAS DANDY, dec'd. by John Hunter and Wm. Dunlap.

27 Mar. 1800. Sale of estate of THOMAS DANDY, dec'd. Purchasers: Thomas Dandy, William Dandy, Cornelius Dandy, John Milum, Joseph Young, Hennery Hall, Galanus Winn, Mansfield Walker, Jeremiah Curnant(?), John Milum, Jr., Robt. Pasley.

23 June 1800. Application of Elizabeth McDonnel to adm. estate of THOMAS MCDONNEL, dec'd (her husband).

21 July 1800. Application of Isabele Gray to adm. estate of her husband JOHN GRAY, dec'd.

30 July 1800. Application of Martha Crosson to execute will of THOMAS CROSSON, dec'd. Wit: John Wiseman and Joseph Reid.

30 July 1800. Will of THOMAS CROSSON. 1(5?) May 1800. Wife Martha

Will of THOMAS CROSSON cont'd:
Crosson; son Thomas Crosson, Jr.; mentions Benjamin Mauldin and Zimry Carter's land; daughter Mary Carter, wife of Zimry. Exr: wife and son Thomas, Jr. Wit: John Wiseman, Joseph Hollingsworth and Jonathan Reed.
Codicil: Wm. Nickal and Joseph Hollingsworth, Samuel Leaman and David Reed and George Hollingsworth to be counsellors in case of controversy in his family after his death.

22 ___ 1800. Petition for sale of estate of JOHN GRAY, dec'd by Isabel Gray.

28 July 1800. Appraisal of estate of JOHN GRAY, dec'd by Wm. Teage, John Munrowe, Jas. Simson, and Thos. Dalrymple, Sr.
7 Aug. 1800. Appraisal of estate of WILLIAM CARE, dec'd. by John Dandy, Thomas Dandy, John Milum and Thos. Cargill.

(No date) Petition of Sarah Care for order of sale of the estate of WM. CARE, dec'd in order to pay the legatees who are all of age.

12 Sept. 1800. Application of Baswell & Thos. Holland to adm. estate of ABRAHAM HOLLAND, dec'd.

14 Aug. 1800. Sale of the estate of JOHN GRAY, dec'd. Isabel Gray, Adm. Purchasers: John Simpson, David Littel, Isabel Gray, James Gray, James Lefan, Mikel Darumple (Dalrymple?), John Munroe, James Williams, Saml. Neil, James Littel, James McCrary, Thos. Gray, Catherine Gray. Mentions Mr. Moon(?).

13 Oct. 1800. Application of Thos. Goodwin and Elisha Holcom to adm. estate of JOHN YOUNG, dec'd.

13 Oct. 1800. Application of Thos. Mathis to adm. estate of MARTIN KELLET, dec'd.

19 July 1800. Appraisal of estate of THOMAS MC DONAL, dec'd. by Benj. Drake, John Cason and Silas Cason.

13 Oct. 1800. Will of JAMES GAMBLE. 40 Apr. 1799. Beloved son John Gamble; (part of the tract James Boyd now lives on); wife (not named). Exrs: William Fulton and John Williamson. Wit: Charles Watson and John Oneel. David Anderson, Ord.

13 Oct. 1800. Application of Benj. Wilson to adm. estate of MORGAN LAYSON, dec'd.

11 Oct. 1800. Appraisal of estate of MORGAN LAYSON, dec'd by John Owens, Alexander Adair and John Dillard.

23 Oct. 1800. Will of THOMAS EWING of Duncan Creek. 23 July 1800. Daughters Jane and Reach; Sons John and William; son David and daughter Margaret; son James; beloved wife Sarah. Exrs: wife Sarah and son John Ewing. Wit: Rodger Brown, John Finney and Manassah Finney.

17 Oct. 1800. Appraisal of estate of JOHN YOUNG, dec'd by Wm. Brown, Francis Allison and John Meador.

(No date) Appraisal of estate of JAMES GAMBLE, dec'd by Nathl. Nickell, John Bryce, James Hambleton. Anguish Campbell, J.P.

6 Nov. 1799. Inventory of estate of JETHRO WALKER, dec'd by Benj. Wilson, John Bowling and James Bell.

7 Nov. 1799. Sale of estate of JETHRO WALKER, dec'd. Purchasers: Susannah Walker, Tarleton East, Thomas Barton, James Bell, James Walker, William East, Evan Roberts, William Gray, Isaac Gray, John Walker, Ward Ferguson, Danl. Welch, John Dillard, James Johnston, John Lockeby. Susannah Walker and John Gray, Adm.

18 Oct. 1800. Inventory of estate of ROBERT MC NEIR, dec'd by Matthew Hunter, James Young and John Sinclair. Note against Joseph L. Griffin. Jer. Leek, Adm.

10 Aug. 1800. Appraisal of estate of WM. MC TEER, dec'd by James Leffan, John Simpson and Alexr·. Simpson. Nathaniel Vance, Exr.

31 Oct. 1800. Sale of estate of MORGAN LAYSON, dec'd. Benjamin Wilson, Adm.

31 Oct. 1800. Inventory of estate of THOMAS EWING, yeoman, dec'd. by John Owens, Alexander George and Wm. Craig, Sr.

28 Oct. 1800. Inventory of estate of ABRAHAM HOLLAND, dec'd by David Mason, Benjamin Byrd, Benjamin Adair. Baswill Holland and Thomas Holland, Adm.

11 Oct. 1800. Application of Joseph Downs for letters testamentary on the will of ROBERT BOLT, dec'd.

5 Nov. 1800. Appraisal of estate of ISUM ELLIOT, dec'd by John Yager, John Pringle and Wm. Simmons.

1 Nov. 1800. Application of Rebecca Elliot, wife of ISUM ELLIOT, dec'd to adm. his estate.

1 Nov. 1800. Inventory of estate of MARTIN KELLET, dec'd. Notes and debts due by: Joseph Avery, Solomon Hopkins, Samuel Bolling, Drury Boyce, James Kellet(paid), Joseph Reiley, James McNight, Laird Burns, Danl. Corder, GArsham Kelley, James Gilland, John McNight, Jane Kellet, Matthew Graydon, Abner Babb, Samson Babb, William Alexander, John Morton. Thomas Mathis, Adm.

9 Aug. 1800. Appraisal of estate of THOMAS CROSSON, dec'd by James Nickels, William Nickels and Samuel Leaman.

9 Dec. 1800. Application of Samuel Wharton for letters test. on will of EANUS (ENOS) STIMSON, dec'd; oaths of John Davenport, Thomas Davenport.

(No recorded date) Will of ENOS STIMSON. 7 July 1798. "The girl I brought into my house and known by the name of Mary Stimson." Exr.: Samuel Wharton. Wit: Thomas Davenport, Jno. Davenport, and Benj. Watson.

(No date) Sale of estate of ABRAHAM HOLLAND, dec'd. Purchasers: Esenor Holland, Baswell Holland, Thomas Holland, Reason Holland, William Holland, Richard Holland, Joseph Michel, James Adair, Elisha Adair, Joseph Adair, George Adair, Benj. Adair, James (son of Robt.) Hanna, Geo. Dillard, James Ensley, Abraham Tinsley, Michael Ferguson, Saml. Laird, Jas. Ford(?) John Kirk, John Cargill, Jas. Jones, Jas. Ramage, David Littel, Alex. Monroe, Mr. Wilkinson, Wm. Gray, John Miller, Bennett Langston, J. A.

Sale of estate of ABRAHAM HOLLAND, dec'd cont'd:
Elmore, Mr. Whitmore, John Pucket, John Ginn, James Brown, Thos.
Ensley, Joseph Gallegly, James Blakely, Wm. Jones, Wm. Rodgers.
Proven accounts: Sarah Lard (Laird?), John (?) Kern, John Weir(?)
Basil Holland and Thos. Holland, Adm.

1 Jan. 1801. Application of Elizabeth Manley and Joel Burgess,
Exrs. of the will of WILLIAM MANLEY, dec'd. Oath of John Cochran
and Joel Burgess.

(No recorded date) Will of WILLIAM MANLEY. 11 Sept. 1799. Beloved wife Elizabeth Manley; sons Joseph and Washington Manley;
beloved children: Ephraim, Jeremiah, Vincent, Joseph, Nancy
and Washington Manley; grand-daughter Deidamia Evans. Exrs:
wife Elizabeth and friend Joel Burgess. Wit: Joel Burgess, Thomas
Burton and John Cochran.

(No recorded date) Will of JOHN WILSON. 11 Dec. 1800. Estate
in part to mother (not named); land to William Wilson, James
Wilson, Jeane Grant and William Mare (More?). Exr. Wm. Mare
(More?). Wit: Edmond Learwood, Ma...(?) Learwood.

7 Jan. 1801. Application of Elizabeth Kirk to adm. estate of
her husband JOHN KIRK, dec'd.

Pr. 9 Jan. 1801.   Will of JAMES GRAY. Daughter Elizabeth's
two children; daughter Sarah's child, Agnes Kearnaghan; daughter
Phebe and her son, James Cochran; sons: Andrew, John and Robert
Gray; daughter Mary Lewers. Exrs: Andrew and John Gray, son-
in-law Thomas Lewers. Wit: Hiram Hollady(?), Joseph Downs.

(No recorded date) Will of HUGH O'NEALL, miller. Sons: Hugh,
Charles and Thomas Neel (note: O'Neall and Neel); mentions-
Patrick Ryley, Robt. Sims and Mary McDonal, wife of Thomas Mc-
Donal; daughters: Patience, Ruth, Ann and Rachel. Exrs: Mercer
Babb, Wm. Person and Elisha Ford. Wit: John Hunter, Thomas Wads-
worth and Patrick McDowell.

7 May 1788. Appraisal of estate of HUGH O'NEAL, dec'd by Saml.
Henderson, Wm. Cason and James Henderson. Notes, book accts.
etc on: Thomas Carter, James Henderson, Mary Griffin, Wm. Mil-
wee, Abraham Nabours, Joel Chandler, Saml. Akins, Martin Martin,
James Mauldin, Dr. J. A. Brown, Wm. Watson, Wm. Dunlap. Exr:
Mercer Babb and Elisha Ford.

9 May 1788. Sale of estate of HUGH O'NEAL, dec'd. Purchasers:
Wm. Haule, Thomas McDonal, Saml. Akin, Eldridge Fuller, Wm.
Johnston, John Coal, Joseph McDonal, John Perry, Claybourn Good-
man, Benj. Fuller, Jacob R. Brown, John Gray, Janet Griffin,
Elisha Ford, James Griffin, John East, John Wilkes, John Grigsby,
Thos. Wilkes, Meriah Goodman, Edmond Drake, Wm. Pollard, Chas.
Gray, Glanus Winn, Saml. Freeman, James M. Mason, James Williams,
James Creswell, Benj. Crosson, Wm. McDonal. Exrs: Mercer Babb
and Elisha Ford.

30 Jan. 1801. Application of Richard Shackleford and Wm. Bailey,
Exr. of will of JAMES ROBERTS, dec'd. Proven by Peter Roberts
and Zachariah Motes.

(No recorded date) Will of JAMES ROBERTS. 23 Jan. 1801. Daughter
Susanna Roberts; son James; son George; daughter Sally Fuller;
daughter Mary Ann Roberts; daughter Patty Bond. Exr.: Richd.

Will of JAMES ROBERTS cont'd:
Shackelford and William Bailey. Wit: A. Rodgers, Jr., Peter
Roberts and Zachariah Motes. Proven: 30 Jan. 1801.

8 Jan. 1801. Inventory of estate of JOHN KIRK, dec'd.

8 Jan. 1801. Application of Thomas O'Neal, minor about the age
og 18, Hugh O'Neal appointed guardian, whi with Levy Hilborn
gave bond.

10 Feb. 1801. Application of Emily* and Henry Brockman, Exrs.
of the will of JOHN BROCKMAN, dec'd. Proven by Robt. Burton
and Daniel Wright, Esq. (*may be Amelia)

13 Feb. 1801. Will of JOHN BROCKMAN. Wife Amely (Amelia?) Emily?)
Brockman; son Henry; other children Anney Parks, Mary Dean,
Franky Mullins; three children of dec'd daughter Lucy Owens
(Betsy, Amelia and John H. Owens, their father, John Owens;
son-in-law Thomas Mullins; grandson John Brockman, son of Henry
Brockman. Exr: Amelia and Henry Brockman. Wit: Daniel Wright,
Robert Burton and Asa Wright. 27 Nov. 1800.

23 Feb. 1801. Adm. of estate of JAMES LINDLEY, dec'd. List of
debts for Dec. 1777, also 2 Jan. 1778; Joseph Briton; proven
before John Rodgers 1795, Thos. Lindley, Adm.

23 Feb. 1801. Andrew Gray, John Gray and Thomas Lewers qualify
as executors of will of JAMES GRAY, dec'd.

22 Nov. 1800. Sale of estate of JOHN YOUNG, dec'd. Purchasers:
Wm. Brown, Jesse Wallis, David Green, Aaron Jones, Burrel Mosley,
Jonathan Wallace, John Wallace, John Howard, Joseph Brown, Joshua
Holcum, Elisha Holcum, Isaac Brown, Jacob Brown, Joel Marchbanks.
Adm.: Elisha Holcum and Thos. Goodwin. Return of same 21 Nov.
1800; notes of Thomas Goodwin, Elisha Holcum and James Dunlap.

3 Mar. 1801. Application of Elizabeth Sullivan, wife of FRED-
ERICK SULLIVAN, dec'd, with Littleberry Sullivan and Manoah
Sullivan, to adm. estate of sd dec'd.

(No date) Return of estate of STEPHEN EMMORY, dec'd. Notes of
Alexander Simson, Frederick Motes, John Gray planter, Wm. Gal-
legly, Ann Tinsley, Thomas Dalrymple, Thomas Wadsworth, Samuel
Crumton, Maj. John Simpson, Isaac Thomas, Robt. McAdams, J.
D. Kern, Alexr. Simpson, Evan Linvell, Zed. Wood. Payments to
Daniel Davis, Dudley Bonds, Robt. Gallegly, John Saxon, Wm.
Shaw for coffin, Wm. Neal, James Gallegly. Exr: John Monroe.

10 Mar. 1801. Mrs. Sarah Evans qualifies as executor of will
of JOHN EVANS, dec'd by John Thomas, Ord. of 96 Dist.

11 Oct. 1800. Sale of estate of WILLIAM MC TEER, dec'd. Exr:
Nathaniel Vance. Purchasers: Widow McTeer, Patsey McNeir, Nathan-
iel Vance, Richard Griffin, John Alton, Frankey McTeer, Daniel
McDaniel, Betsy McTeer, Charles Gray, John Leonard, Robt. Gal-
legly, Benj. Johnston, Mickel Dalrymple, James Vance, John Mason,
John McClure, James Wilson, John Gallegly, Robert Gaxston, Richd.
Waldrop, James Wallace, James Simpson, Wm. Hunter.

16 Mar. 1801. David Simmons, minor about 16 years of age, chose
Charles Simmons as his guardian who with John Manley and Benj.
Adkins gave bond. D. Anderson, Ord.

23 Mar. 1801. Charles Griffin and Jacob Crosswhite qualify as executors of the will of ANTHONY GOLDING, dec'd. Will proven by Jno. Leonard.

(No recorded date) Will of ANTHONY GOLDING. 27 Dec. 1800. Wife Isabel Golding; daughters Elizabeth, Rachel, and Permelia Nansey sons James Golding, John Read Golding, Anthony Foster Golding, Thomas Golding. Mention of land purchased from Douglas Johnston. Exr: Charles Griffin and nephew Jacob Crosswhite. Wit: James Tinsley, James Atwood Williams and John Leonard.

(No date) Appraisal of estate of FREDERICK SULLIVANT, dec'd by Thomas Burton, James Sullivan and James Wilson.

16 Mar. 1801. Will of DANNEL ABBETT. 3 Oct. 1800. Wife Alsey Abbett; daughter Betsy Pagett Abbett; sons Lewis Morgan Abbett, and William McClanahan Abbett, Daniel Marshall Abbett, James Smith Abbett; a soldiers claim to lands in Western Pennsylvania. Exr: Wife Alsey Abbett, Daniel Wright and Reuben Kelley. Wit: Austin Moore,Nelson Kelley and McElanahn(?) Stallard. David Anderson, Ord.

18 Mar. 1801. John Simson, Robert Hutcheson and William Hunter qualify to adm. estate of WILLIAM RANSOM, dec'd.

18 Mar. 1801. Sale of estate of JOHN KIRK, dec'd. Purchasers: Elizabeth Kirk, John Kirk, James Brown, James Parks, Abner Pyles, Samuel Malcolm, James Henderson, Wm. Blakely, Jesse Johnston, John Harris, Saml. Leake, Wm. Bryson, James Bryson, Joseph Vance, Wm. Hanna, Saml. Henderson, Wm. Taylor, John A. Cargill, Thomas Jones, Daniel Martin, John Cargill, Robert Black, John Danday, Alexander Henry, Hardy Connant, Robt. Creswell, John McLaughlin, John Stuart, Bartley Milum, Robt. Glidewell, Robt. Milam, John Creecy, James Griffin, James Golding, Wm. Carter, Polly Jones, James Ford, Wm. Underwood. Adm.: Elizabeth Kirk.

12 Feb. 1801. Appraisal of estate of JAMES ROBERTS, dec'd by A. Rodgers, Jr., Jacob Miller and James Bailey. Exr: R. Shackelford and Wm. Bailey.

16 Feb. 1801. Sale of estate of JAMES ROBERTS, dec'd. Purchasers: Isham Fuller, Peter Roberts, James Hamilton, James Roberts, A. Rodgers, Wm. Runnels, Jno. Creecy, Jas. A. Williams, Isaac Michel, Timothy Dunnaho, Zeb. Mathis, Jno. Riley, Geo. Roberts, Johnston Ball, Wm. Holdritch, Benj. Drummond, Jno. Wiseman, Lazarus Wood, Jas. Henley, Jno. Harris, Jas. Fuller, Danl. Layce (Lacey?), Joseph Rodgers, Wm. George, Archd. McCay, R. Shackelford, Jacob Miller, Danl. Whitehead, Jones Fuller, Edmond Roberts, John Morris, Wm. Ruson(?), Mary Roberts, Patrick Rodgers, John Shotwell, Stephen Trible, Moses Madden, Mary Ann Roberts, Patty Bond Roberts. Exr.: Richard Shackelford and Wm. Bailey.

Will of JAMES ROBERTS. (See page 27)

17 Mar. 1801. Mary Hughes, wife of CALEB HUGHES, dec'd. qualifies to adm. estate of same with Elisha Holcomb and John Meadow.

29 Apr. 1801. Appraisal of estate of CALEB HUGHES, dec'd by Elisha Holcomb, Joseph Layson and Benj. Brown.

4 May 1801. Nancy More, widow, qualifies to adm. est. of JOHN MORE, dec'd; security Geo. Mosely and Danl. Wright.

9 Apr. 1801. John Dandey (Dendy?) qualifies as executor of will of WILLIAM DENDY, dec'd. Bennett Hill and Jeremiah Saddler, Wit.

9 May 1801. Will of WILLIAM DENDY. Wife Clary Dendy; sons: John Dendy, William Dendy, Thomas Dendy, Daniel Dendy, James H. Dendy and Joel Dendy; daughters: Betsy Dendy, Priscilla Watts, Sally Motes. Exr: sons John Dendy, Joel Dendy and Wm. Dendy. Wit: Bennett Hill, William Smith, Jr. and Jeremiah Saddler. 12 Aug. 1800.

(No date) Appraisal of estate of DANNEL ABBOTT, dec'd as shown by Mrs. Alsey Abbott; by Peter Hammond, Austin Moore and James Bumpass.

16 Mar. 1801. Alsey Abbott qualifies as executrix of will of DANL. ABBOTT, dec'd. Austin Moore and Nelson Kelley, Wit.

24 Mar. 1801. Appraisal of estate of JOHN EVANS, dec'd by John Watts, David Whiteford and John McGowen.

11 Apr. 1801. Inventory of estate of WILLIAM RANSOM, dec'd by Wm. Hunter, Nathaniel Vance and Reubin Griffin.

(No date) Frances Scurlock received full satisfaction from Lewis Banton, Sr., Adm. of estate of DOLLY SCURLOCK, dec'd. Wit: Archibald McKay.

8 Dec. 1800. Sale of estate of MARTIN KELLET, dec'd. Purchasers: James Kellet, Moses Kelley, John F. Wolff, James McNight, James Johnston, Samson Babb. Moses Crofford, cryer. Adm.: Thos. Mathis.

15 Nov. 1800. Sale of estate of THOMAS MC DONNALD, dec'd. Purchasers: Elizabeth McDonnald, James Stewart, Giles Cason, Glanus Winn. Adm.: Elizabeth McDonnald.

25 July 1801. Elender Sutherland, widow of JOSHUA SUTHERLAND, dec'd. and Wm. Leake qualify as executors of will of sd dec'd. Wit: Martha Leake and Andrew Rodgers.

25 July 1801. Will of JOSHUA SUTHERLAND. 28 Apr. 1801. Wife Ellender Sutherland; beloved son Samuel Sutherland; mentions division between my whole family. Exrs: Ellender Sutherland, Wm. Leake and Andrew Rodgers. Wit: Elijah Edwards, Martha Leake and Andrew Rodgers.

2 May 1801. Inventory of estate of ANTHONY GOLDING, dec'd by Daniel McGinn, Ephraim Andres and Washington Williams. Mentions John Black.

20 June 1801. Sale of estate of WILLIAM RANSOM, dec'd. Purchasers were: Benj. Johnston, James Smith, James Hutcheson, John Gates, John Simson-merchant, John Galliga, Wm. Farrow. Adm.: John Simpson.

10 July 1801. In Livingston Co., KY, Dec. Court of 1800. David Bell, infant orphan of ROBERT BELL, dec'd. chose Richard Bell as guardian. Said guardian entered into bond with James McNabb and John Pounds as security. Cert. true copy by Enoch Prince, Clk. of Crt. Also certified that Wiley Davis and James McCobb are two of acting J. P. for Livingston Co. Also receipt: Rec'd of Richard Bell, Adm. of Robt. Bell, dec'd $10 my part in full

Guardianship of David Bell cont'd:
of the sd estate. Signed: James Bell. 11 July 1801 before Wiley
Davis, Esq. and James McNabb, Esq.

1 Aug. 1801. Appraisal of estate of JOSHUA SUTHERLAND, dec'd.
by Andrew Rodgers, Jeremiah Leake and George Leake. Note on
John Sims.

29 June 1801. Part of sale of estate of JOHN KIRK, dec'd. Pur-
chasers: Elizabeth Kirk, Thomas Jones, John Harris, Widow Vance,
Robt. Fleming, Sarah Tinsley, David Vance, Abner Teague, John
Munrow, Jas. Parks, Jos. Vance, Jas. Griffin, Joel Dendy, Benj.
Blakely, John Roberts, Capt. Wm. Rodgers, Jas. Brown. Adm: Eliz-
abeth Kirk.

27 June 1801. Sale of estate of CALEB HUGHS, dec'd. Ex.: Mary
Hughs.

(No date) Appraisal of estate of Maj. JOHN MORE, dec'd, by Wm.
Rowntree, Saml. Fleming and Thompson Farley.

19 Oct. 1801. Anderson More, minor, made choice of Archibald
Young as guardian, who entered into bond with Elisha Holcomb,
Daniel Wright and Wm. Bowen.

19 Oct. 1801. Application of John Hunter, Wm. Dunlap and Saml.
Henderson for letters testamentary to execute will of ANN HEND-
ERSON, dec'd. Pr. by Abner Pyles and Saml. Henderson.

16 Apr. 1801. Inventory of estate of JOHN BROCKMAN, dec'd by
Jacob Roberts, Wm. Bowen and Robt. Burton.

19 Oct. 1801. Application of Mary More to adm. estatee of AUSTIN
MORE, dec'd, her husband. John and Nicklus Garrett, security.

19 Oct. 1801. Will of ANN HENDERSON, widow of James Henderson,
dec'd. 25 Aug. 1801. Daughters: Fanney Henderson, Sarah Henderson, Polley Earby (Irby?), Patsey Henderson, Ritter Earby, Nancy
Earby; sons: James Henderson, Samuel Henderson and William Henderson; son-in-law William Hancock. Exr: John Hunter, Wm. Dunlap,
son Samuel Henderson. Wit: Abner Pyles, Saml. Henderson, Wm.
Dunlap. Codicil: 26 Aug. 1801. Money for boarding the scholars.
Wit: Abner Pyles, Saml. McNees, Saml. Henderson.

18 Dec. 1801. James Sims, minor, made choice of John Crecy
as guardian. Security: John Roberson and Silas Walker, Jr.

(No date) Inventory of estate of AUSTIN MORE, dec'd. by Wm.
Garret, John Garret and Nickles Garret. Mentions cash sent to
Saml. Vaughn.

19 Feb. 1800(?). Richard Pucket, Dabney Pucket, Neely Pucket
and James Pucket relinquish to Martha Pucket their claim and
title to two negroes and agree to furnish her a home on any
of land of James Pucket, dec'd. Milly and Lucy Pucket sign.
Wit: Nimrod Overby, Wm. Beazley, and Wm. Rucks. Anguish Campbell,
J. P.

23 Dec. 1801. James Mitchel, minor, made choice of Isaac Mitchel
as guardian. Elisha Mitchel and Wm. Bailey, security.

(No date) Appraisal of estate of ENOS STIMSON, dec'd by S. Adams,

Appraisal of est. of ENOS STIMSON, dec'd cont'd:
Thomas Davenport and James Findley. This also includes a note
on Vinson Sprouse.

(No date) Sale of part of the estate of ANTHONY GOLDING, dec'd.
Purchasers: William Cox, Samuel Neel, John Simpson, Robert Golding and William Ransom.

6 Oct. 1798. Inventory of estate of JAMES FLOYD, dec'd by Lydel
(Lyddall) Allen, Jesse Garret.

25 June 1801. Sale of estate of JAMES FLOYD, dec'd held at Mrs.
Susannah McHerg's; purchasers: Mrs. McHerg, Thomas Coker (who
bought a Bible and hymn book), J. F. Wolff. J. R. Wolff, Adm.

27 Nov. 1800. Inventory of estate of ROBERT BOLT, dec'd by James
Cunningham, Manfil (Mansfield?) Crisp and Jesse Garret.

9 Jan. 1801. Sale of estate of ROBERT BOLT, dec'd. Purchasers:
Leonard Dunkin, Col. J. F. Wolff, John McHerg, James Johnston,
John Nabours, Joseph Mathews, Abraham Bolt, Thomas Parkes, Samuel
Chew, Margaret Bolt, James Bumpass. Exr: Joseph Downs.

15 Nov. 1796. Sale of estate of WILLIAM PRICE, dec'd. Purchasers:
Margret Price, Mary Price, Ruth Price, Sarah Price, Mary Cunningham, John Adair, Wm. McCarty(?), Wm. Barksdale, James Huddleston,
and James Cunningham, Adm.

1 Mar. 1802. William Cato with Israel Teague and Thomas Entrekin
gave bond to adm. the estate of JESSE CATO, dec'd.

(No date) Application of Elnah Donaho and Peter Roberts to execute will of JOHN DONAHO, dec'd. Wit: Peter Roberts and Mary
Kellet.

23 Mar. 1802. Will of JOHN DONAHOE. 25 Dec. 1801. Wife Eleanor
Donahoe; mentions division of estate among children (not named).
Exr: wife Eleanor Donahoe and Peter Roberts. Wit: Peter Roberts,
Mary Kellet and Eliza Sarah Donahoe.

9 Aug. 1801. Sale of estate of Maj. JOHN MORE, dec'd. Purchasers:
Nancy More, Maj. Starling Tucker, David Cowan, John Hunter,
Joseph Allison, Ebenezer Morss, James Morss, Samuel Fleming,
Ezekiel Rowland, Archibald Young for Andrew More, William Round-
tree, James Garret, William Morss, Robt. Creswell. Adm.: Nancy
More.

19 Feb. 1802. Appraisal of estate of ANN HENDERSON, dec'd by
Abner Pyles, Samuel Henderson and William Dunlap.

(No date) Application of Isabel Ross, widow of GEORGE ROSS,
dec'd. and George Ross, son, to adm. the estate, bond with Alexr.
George and John B. Kennedy, Security.

8 May 1802. Application of Marey Hunter to execute the will
of WILLIAM HUNTER, dec'd with George Millar and Andrew Middleton.

9 Mar. 1802. Appraisal of estate of JESSE CATO, dec'd by John
Millar, David Mason and Elisha Teague.

18 Dec. 1801. Sale of estate of AUSTEN MORE, dec'd. Purchasers:
William Cheek, Marey More, James Garret, Hennery Martin, Alsa

Sale of estate of AUSTEN MORE, dec'd cont'd:
Abbot, Samuel Mason, James Vaughn, Obediah Morss, George Mossley, Thomas L. Duncan, Barret Roberson, John Ashley, Anna Garret, Mason Foley, Thos. Downs, John Garret, John Atwood, Marey Martin, Jacob Nabours, Bacon Guin, Lewis Devaule, Nicklus Garret, Wm. Garret, Harasha(Herusha?) Garret, John Garret. Mary More, Adm.

13 Feb. 1802. Manoah Roberson, William Roberson and Barnett Roberson assured contents, etc. in will of their father JOHN ROBERSON, SR., dec'd who frequently said he had made such a will and left it in the hands of Daniel Abbott. Danl. Wright, J. P.

23 Feb. 1802. Elsa Abbett, wife of DANIEL ABBETT, dec'd. says that the said will was left in the care of her husband and she destroyed it through mistake. Daniel Wright, J. P.

19 Nov. 1803. Deposition of John Roberson, son of JOHN ROBERSON, dec'd says his father willed a tract on Warrior creek purchased of Moses Sanders to Barnett Roberson, and a tract where he lived to Reuben and Toliver (Roberson?) to be equally divided between them at death of their mother Marah(?) Roberson; personal estate to be divided between Fanny Roberson, Peggy Roberson, Polly Roberson, Milly Roberson. Danl. Wright, J. P. 23 Feb. 1802.

8 May 1802. Will of WILLIAM HUNTER. 21 Mar. 1802. Wife Marey Roberson; children (not named) to be educated and have equal shares at death of mother. Exr: wife Mary, John Hunter, Mathew Hunter and Wm. Dunlap. Wit: Geo. Miller, Thomas Cason and Andrew Middleton.

END OF BOOK A

START OF BOOK C

1 Mar. 1802. Application of Nancy Neal, wife of JAMES NEAL, dec'd. to adm. estate. Security: Thomas Cason and George Roberson.

3 May 1802. Application of Benjamin Drake to adm. estate of EDMOND DRAKE, dec'd. Security: Bartley Brooks and Joseph Blakely.

28 June 1802. John Ross, minor, made choice of John B. Kennedy as guardian. Sec.: Robt. Creswell and John Hemphill.

28 June 1802. Will of THOMAS BURTON. wife Lillian Burton; land purchased of Isaac Rodgers; daughter Judah Burton; daughter Anna Burton; other children: Samuel Burton, Robert Burton, Benjamin Burton and Rebeca Ford. Exrs: wife Lillian Burton, Robert Criswell and Hennery Box. 4 May 1802. Wit: John Pucket, John Garlington and Thomas Grace.

18 Sept. 1802. Sale of estate of JOSHUA SUTHERLAND, dec'd. Purchasers not named.

(No date) Inventory of estate of Doctor GEORGE ROSS, dec'd, by Robt. Long, Wm. Craig and Rodger Brown.

1 Oct. 1802. Will of ANN STARNES, dec'd proven by wit. Peggy Middleton, Rachel Anderson. Exr: Aaron Starns.

28 Nov. 1800. Will of ANN STARNES. Sons: Aaron Starnes, Ebenezer Starnes, John Starnes; daughters: Milly Murphey, Ann Jones,

Will of ANN STARNES, dec'd cont'd:
Rachel Hughs and Rebeccah Sims. Exr: son Aaron Starnes. Wit:
Rachel Anderson, Peggy Middleton and David Anderson.

(No date) Appraisal of estate of JOHN DONAHO, dec'd by William
Coleman, Stephen Tribble and Wm. Hall.

18 Mar. 1802. Appraisal of estate of JAMES NEEL, dec'd by Israel
Teague, Elijah Teague and John Miller.

8 Apr. 1802. Sale of estate of JAMES NEEL, dec'd. Purchaser:
Nancy Neel (Neil). Adm: Nancy Neel.

6 July 1802. Appraisal of estate of THOMAS BURTON, dec'd by
Benjamin Adkins, Charles Simmons and Larkin Sullivan.

29 Sept. 1801. THOMAS BURTON, dec'd. Debts and unsettled accts.
on books: Wm. Godfrey, John Martin, Jr., Wm. Martin, Jr., Joel
Burgess, Sr., John Simmons, Sr., Capt. John Hughes, Robt. Ander-
son, Benj. Burton, Wm. Martin, Sr., Robt. Coil, David Madden,
David Kerns, Joel Burgess, Jr., Jesse Byram, Jno. Crooks, Jno.
Harper, Jas. Burnes, Jno. Manley, Alex. Dean, Nicklus Vaughn,
Danl. Martin, Jr., David Caldwell, Jas. Culberson, David McCaa,
Walker Burgess, Jno. Rodgers, Gina Madden, Danl. Osbourn, Jr.,
Wm. Hughes, Jeremiah Martin, Andrew Rodgers, Lazarus Wood, John
Willard, Wm. McCaull, Charles Garman, John Osbourn, Thos. Beedle,
Geo. Horner, David Craddock, John Rodgers.

24 Apr. 1800. John McLaughlin deposed that John Harris, son
of WILLIAM HARRIS, dec'd confessed that he did burn and destroy
the last W & T of his father, the sd. Wm. Harris, dec'd. Pro:
David Anderson.

9 Nov. 1802. Lard (Laird) Boyd and Nancy Boyd to adm. estate
of JOHN MOORE, dec'd. Bond by Jno. Boyd and Geo. Mosely.

1 Nov. 1802. Anderson Moore, minor, chose Laird Boyd as guardian.

1 Nov. 1802. James Moore, minor, chose Robert Creswell as guardian. Bond: Elihu Creswell and Jno. Watts.

11 Nov. 1802. Isaac George to adm. estate of AMBROUS GEORGE,
dec'd. Bond: Howard Pinson and Robt. Bradford.

8 Oct. 1802. William and Ira Arnold, heirs of HENDRICK ARNOLD,
dec'd - division of property on Horse creek and Cherokee county
by court order 9 May 1796. Jonathan Downs, D.S. Wit: Joseph
Downs and John Jones.

18 Oct. 1802. Judith Maddox, widow of JUSTIAN MADDOX, dec'd
granted letters of adm. on estate. Sec.: Joseph Blackeby and
John Simson.

(No date) Will of REZIN HOLLAND. Wife Mary Holland; sons: John,
Thomas, Jeremiah; daughters: Sarah, Elizabeth, Rachel and Marah.
Mentions unborn child. Exr: Mary Holland and Joseph Adair. Wit:
Wm. Saxon, Thos. Holland and Richd. Holland.
22 Nov. 1802. Letters of adm. to Rachel Goggins, widow and Benj.
Neel on estate of WILLIAM GOGGINS, dec'd.

30 Nov. 1802. Adm. of estate to Catherine Ross, widow of FRANCIS
ROSS, dec'd with Robt. Ross and John Ross, Sr. Security: David

Adm. of estate of FRANCIS ROSS, dec'd cont'd:
Glen and William Cowing.

4 Dec. 1802. John McClanahan qualified as executor of estate
of RICHARD PUGH, dec'd.

13 Nov. 1802. Appraisal of estate of AMBROUS GEORGE, dec'd by
Samuel Leaman, Ansel Godfrey and Moses Swafford.

27 Dec. 1802. Letters of adm. to Claybourn Goodman and Samuel
Goodman on estate of MARIAH GOODMAN, dec'd. Sec: Thomas Burnside and Charter Nickels.

6 Aug. 1802. Sale of estate of GEORGE ROSS, dec'd. Purchasers:
Isabelle Ross, George Ross, John Ewing, J. B. Kennedy, Joseph
Adair and son, James; Wm. Farrow, John Hitch, Dr. Button(?),
John Owens, Margaret Montgomery, Zaddock Adair, Aaron Starnes,
Wm. Dabbs(?).

6 Jan. 1803. Betsy Pasquet Abbet chose Samuel Vaughn as guardian.
Sec: David Cowen.

1 Jan. 1803. Return of estate of DANIEL ABBET, dec'd. Ex: Danl.
Wright.

13 Dec. 1802. Appraisal of estate of REZIN HOLLAND, dec'd by
Wm. Saxon, Thomas Holland and Richard Holland.

1 Jan. 1803. Inventory of estate of MERIAH GOODMAN, dec'd by
Thomas Burnside, James Cook, Thomas Wilks. Notes and accts.
against: Charles Goodman, Joseph Goodman, Samuel Goodman and
Timothy Goodman, Bartley Brooks, Zach. Carwile, Duke Williams,
dec'd; Mrs. Williams, dec'd. Adm: Clabourn Goodman and Saml.
Goodman.

9 Jan. 1803. Will of JOHN CURETON, dec'd proven by exr. Hannah
Cureton, Thomas Cureton and Edward Thweatt. Wit: James Young
and Stephen Jones.

31 Aug. 1802. Will of JOHN CURETON. Wife Hannah Cureton; sons:
John Cureton, Nathaniel Cureton, David Cureton; daughter Jeney
Payne; sons George Washington Cureton, Thomas Taylor Cureton;
Susannah(?) Cureton; son Daniel Cureton; daughter Elizabeth
Burnett Cureton. Exr: Hannah Cureton, Edw. Cureton, Thomas Taylor
Cureton and David Cureton. Wit: James Young, Blagrove(?) Glenn
and Stephen Jones.

12 Jan. 1803. Will of LAUGHLIN HUNTER. 24 Feb. 1798. Wife (not
named); daughters: Mary Hunter, Esther McDowall, Hatty Simpson,
Margarett Hunter, Abigail Hunter. Exr: Thomas McDonnald and
Giles Cason. Wit: James Young, Wm. Gallegly, and John Lyon.

12 Jan. 1803. Will of LAUGHLIN HUNTER, dec'd proven by James
Young and John Lyon.

17 Nov. 1802. Inventory of estate of JUSTINIAN MADDOX, dec'd
by John Munro, James Griffin and Giles Cason.

27 Nov. 1802. Sale of estate of JUSTINIAN MADDOX, dec'd. Purchasers: Judah Maddox. Adm: Judah Maddox.

17 Jan. 1803. Warrant of appraisal and sale to Giles Cason,

Warrant of appraisal cont'd:
exr. of will of LAUGHLIN HUNTER, dec'd.

30 Jan. 1803. Letters of adm. granted to Daniel Williams on estate of DANIEL WILLIAMS, dec'd. Sec: Ab. Griffin and Francis Lester.

30 Oct. 1802. Appraisal of estate of ANNA STARNS, dec'd by Silas Walker, Jr., John Richey, William Eddins and Jonathan Forgey.

4-5 Nov. 1802. Sale of estate of ANNA STARNS, dec'd Purchasers: George Wharton, Joel Walker, Jordon Mosley, John Newman, James Vance, Wm. Lowe, Joel Burgess, Geo. Madden, Ezekiel Rowling, John Hinton, Isaac Medley, John Creecy, Meredith Bryant, John Bell, Saml. Anderson, John Roberson, David Anderson, James Findley, Thomas Davenport, Wm. Sims, Stephen Tribble, Margaret McCurley, B. Brooks, Jones Fuller, Silvs. Addams, Silvs. Walker, John Osbourn, Henry Thomson, John Rodgers, John Martin, Danl. Matheny, John Rowlings, Gabl. Joel, Berry West, John Sims, Joel Sims, Henry Fuller, John Starnes, Wm. Sprouse, John Hughs, Jane Harris, Andrew Rodgers, Ebenezer Starnes, Robt. McCurley, John Milum, Thomas Gore, Wm. Runnels, Henry Box, James Roberts, Aaron Starnes, Benj. Garner, John Willard. Exr: Aaron Starnes.

8 Dec. 1802. Appraisal of estate of WILLIAM GOGGINS, dec'd by Thomas Dalrymple, Wm. Harding and Isaac Case.

9 Dec. 1802. Sale of estate of WM. GOGGINS, dec'd. Purchasers: John Dalrymple, Wm. Neale, Rachel Goggins, Mary Goggins, John Leopard, Jas. Goggins, John Johnston, Jas. Lefon, Thos. Goggins, Jno. Morrow, Jno. Blackburn, David Gray, Robt. Johnston, Thos. Dalrymple, Jas. Gray, John Neale, Abrum Harding, Jacob Gray, Benj. Neel, Wm. Harding, Prov. Williams, Saml. Neale, Isaac Case. Notes on: Jno. Thomas, Thomas Neale, Nicholas Harding. Adm: Benj. Neale and Rachel Goggin.

29 Jan. 1803. Administration of estate of ALEXANDER DEALE, dec'd granted to John Deale and Marey Deale. Sec: Anguish Campbell and John Cook.

27 Jan. 1803. Administration of estate of NATHANIEL ROOK, dec'd granted to Margaret Rook, widow. Sec: Thomas Motes and Elijah Watson.

(No date) Inventory of estate of NATHANIEL ROOK, dec'd by Elijah Watson, John Neeley and Daniel McGin.

29 Jan. 1803. Sale of estate of MERIAH GOODMAN, dec'd Purchasers: Clabourn Goodman, Joseph Goodman, Chas. Goodman, Saml. Goodman, Nancy Goodman, Bartlet Brooks, Jos. Gallegly, Abner Pyles, Wm. Young, Jas. Atwood, Andw. Rodgers, Jr., Jas. Caldwell, Wm. Caldwell, Wm. Dandey, David Greer, Minyard Harris, Glanus Winn, Jas. Henderson, Thos. Wilks, Wm. Leegon, Josha Chandler, Wm. Trap, Andw. Rodgers, Silvanus Addams, Jacob Millar, Woodson Leegon, Francis Lester, John Munrow, Richd. Williams, Jeremiah Glenn, Jas. McMahan, Geo. Watts. Adm: Samuel Goodman and Clabourn Goodman.

1 Feb. 1803. Adm. of estate of JOHN WILLIAMS, dec'd granted to Sarah Williams, widow. Sec: Aaron Clore and Robt. Gains.

(No date) Appraisal of estate of FRANCIS ROSS, dec'd by Samuel

Appraisal of estate cont'd:
Fleming, David Cowan and Francis Glenn.

21 Jan. 1803. Second appraisal of estate of MERIAH GOODMAN, dec'd by Thomas Burnside, James Cook and Thomas Wilks.

21 Feb. 1803. Adm. of estate of JAMES SULLIVANT, dec'd granted to John Boyd. Sec: Silvs. Walker, Jr. and John Middleton.

12 Feb. 1803. Inventory of estate of JOHN WILLIAMS, dec'd by Wm. Powell, Thomas Gaines and Richard Gaines.

2 Mar. 1803. Will of JOEL BURGESS, dec'd proven by Ezekiel Rowling and Thomas Babb. Exr: Elan and Joel Burgess.

11 Feb. 1803. Will of JOEL BURGESS. Wife Elen Burgess; son Elijah Burgess; son-in-law William Win Hendrick and his daughter Tabitha (when age 16); sons Walter Burgess, John Burgess (the youngest), Thomas Burgess, William Burgess; daughters Jenney and Salley Burgess; sons Rowling Burgess and Joel Burgess; daughters Betsey and Nelley Burgess. Exr: Elen Burgess, Rowling Burgess and Joel Burgess. Wit: E. S. Rowland, Thomas Babb and William Nelson.

24 Jan. 1804. Inventory of estate of JOHN CURETON, dec'd by Bartlett Brooks, James Young, Paul Findley and Mansfield Walker.

17 Feb. 1803. Sale of estate of JOHN CURETON, dec'd. Purchasers: Joseph Brownlee, Bartlett Brooks, Robt. Pasley, Robt. Newby, Clabourn Brown, Moses Butler, Jas. Young, Chas. Simmons, John Burkes, Danl. Fuller, Timothy Donaho, Jacob Millar, Saml. Mathis, Wm. Coleman, Wm. Huggins.

4 Mar. 1803. Will of JAMES BURNSIDE, dec'd, Exr: Anna Burnside; proven by Joseph and George Hollingsworth.

1 Dec. 1801. Will of JAMES BURNSIDE. Wife Anna Burnside; sons: John, William and James Burnside; mentions Cornelius Donaho; younger children (not named). Exr: wife, and son James. Wit: Joseph and George Hollingsworth.

21 Apr. 1800. Sale of estate of JAMES KIRK, dec'd. Purchasers: Saml. Vance, Wm. Bryson, John Kirk, Thos. Milam, Robt. Morgan, Jas. Underwood. Note by John Simpson, exr. of John Hunter, dec'd. This paper found just as it stands among the papers of John Hunter, dec'd.

(No date) Appraisal of estate of JOHN KIRK, dec'd. Includes same note as above.

10 Mar. 1803. Settlement of estate of JOHN YOUNG, dec'd. Adm: Thomas Goodwin, Elisha Holcomb. Pr: Chas. Allen, J.Q.(Will Bk A)

26 Feb. 1803. Will of JOHN HUNTER, dec'd. Exr: Sarah Hunter with John Hunter and John Simson before Wm. Neale.

11 Dec. 1818(?). Will of JOHN HUNTER. Wife (not named); son James and his son John B. Hunter; son John and his son William Hunter; son Samuel; son William Hunter; daughters Margaret Mc-Clintock and Nancy Hunter; mentions land from John McDaniel and Robt. Fleming; mentions Avery Leek, Wm. Donaho, Wm. Anderson; son Henry Hunter to study law under H. W. DesChamps; son Joshua Hunter; daughters Elizabeth Criswell and Sarah Hunter;

Will of JOHN HUNTER cont'd:

to Robert Creswell and Wm. Dunlap (tracts) granted to Matthew Hunter; daughter Mary Creswell; also John and William Dunlap. Exr: wife, son John Hunter, Col. John Simpson. Wit: John Colwell, Mary Johnson, Henry Hunter. Codicil: Wit: John Hunter, Matthew Hunter, Wm. Underwood.

26 Feb. 1803. Estate of JOHN VITELLO, dec'd. Adm. granted to wife Sarah Vitello. Sec: John Smith and John Edwards.

13 Jan. 1803. Sale of estate of DANIEL ABBET, dec'd. Purchasers: Saml. Vaughn, widow Abbet, Edw. Harris, John Atwood, Barnabas Robertson, Stephen Garret, Henry Feagins, Danl. Wright, Jas. Burks, John Robertson, Wm. Thomison, Wm. Clark, Anderson Arnold, Peter Hammond, Michael Willis, Wm. Grass. Exr: D. Wright.

9 Mar. 1803. Appraisal of estate of JOHN HUNTER, dec'd by Jas. Henderson and Matthew Hunter.

6 Apr. 1803. JOHN MEEK, dec'd. Elinor Meek qualified to execute will with Charles Neale and Wm. Owen. Pr.: John Cook and Drury Sims, Wit.

13 Dec. 1802. Will of JOHN MEEK. Wife Ellenor Meek; children: William Meek, Betsey Meek, Nancy Meek, Jinney Meek, Samuel Meek, John Meek, James Meek. Exr: wife, Charles O'Neal, Wm. Rowe. Wit: John Cook, Drury Sims and Benj. Croson.

21 Mar. 1803. Estate of WILLIAM ANGLIN, dec'd. Wife Kerenhappuch Anglin qualified to adm. Sec: Asa Wright and John Anglin.

21 Mar. 1803. Estate of WILLIAM COCKS (COX), dec'd.Wm. Cannon qualified to adm. Cit. pub. by John Brown. Sec: John Miles, and Joseph Lynch.

23 Mar. 1803. Estate of ROBERT BURTON, dec'd. Wife Sarah Burton qualified to adm. Sec: Henry Brockman and John Pugh.

25 Jan. 1803. Inventory of LAUGHLIN HUNTER, dec'd by John and James Simpson and David Greer. Exr: Giles Cason.

4 Feb. 1803. Sale of estate of LAUGHLIN HUNTER, dec'd.

23 Mar. 1803. Adm. of estate of ROBERT BLAKE, dec'd. David Dunlap applied for his daughter Jenet Blake to adm. the estate of her late husband she being unable to attend and the estate in a wasting condition. Permission granted to Jenet Blake by Wm. Neale, Esq.

12 Feb. 1803. Inventory of estate of ROBERT BLAKE, dec'd by James McQuerns, Alexander Simpson and John Blake.

1 Mar. 1803. Sale of estate of ROBERT BLAKE, dec'd. Adm: Jannete Blake.

11 Apr. 1803. Appraisal of estate of JOHN VITTELO, dec'd by Henry Hitt, Cornelius Puckett and John Beasley.

(No date) Sale of estate of JOHN WILLIAMS, dec'd. Adm: Sarah Williams.

28 Apr. 1803. Appraisal of estate of JOEL BURGESS, dec'd by E. S. Rowling, Jos. Brownlee, Thos. Babb and John Hughes.

22 Apr. 1803. Inventory of estate of ROBERT BURTON, dec'd by Thos. Parks, Nathaniel Powers and Edw. Pugh.

26 Feb. 1803. Inventory of estate of JAMES SULLIVANT, dec'd by Chas. Simmons, Edmond Wood and Larkin Sullivan.

19 Mar. 1803. Sale of estate of JAMES SULLIVANT, dec'd. Purchasers: Larkin Sullivan, Nancy Sullivan, Littlebury Sullivan, Jas. Sullivan, Joseph Brownlee, Richd. Duty, Chas. Simmons, Ezekiel Rowling, Saml. Whitlow, Saml. More. Adm: John Boyd.

14 May 1803. Application of Wm. Burnside and Thos. Babb to adm. estate of JOHN HUGHES, dec'd.

15 Feb. 1803. Sale of estate of NATHANIEL ROOK, dec'd. Adm: Margaret Rook.

5 Feb. 1803. Inventory of estate of DANNEL WILLIAMS, SR., dec'd by Elisha Watson, John Neely and Danl McGin.

17-18 Feb. 1803. Sale of estate of DANL. WILLIAMS, SR, dec'd. Purchasers: James Williams, Danl. Williams, Richard Williams, Wm. Williams, Davis Williams, Nancy Williams, Thomas Brown, Thos. Woodson, Wm. Ligon, Jacob R. Brown, Wm. Farrow, Thos. Farrow, Jas. Tinsley, Chas. Murphey, Francis Lester, Thos. Steel, Danl. Wood, Richd. Griffin, Maj. John Griffin, Wm. Fulton, Jas. Gates, Ephraim Knight, Jas. Chatwell, Jno. Charles, Jas. Charles, Jas. Caldwell, Danl. Pitts, Jas. Holley. Adm: Danl Williams, Jr.

2 June 1803. Appraisal and order of sale of estate of JOSEPH ARMSTRONG, dec'd. Exr: Robt. Gilliam, Jr.

25 May 1803. Appraisal of estate of JOHN MEEK, dec'd by John Cook, Richd. Griffin and John Watts. Angus Campbell, J.P.

12 Apr. 1803. Sale of estate of WILLIAM ANGLIN, dec'd. Purchasers were: Kerenhabbuch Anglin, Mikel Vickery, Ambrous Johnston, John Anglin, Benj. Lewis, John Gamble.

16 June 1803. Estate of JOHN MC CLINTOCK, dec'd. Adm. granted to Jas. McClintock. Sec: James and Alexander Mills.

30 Mar. 1803. Appraisal of estate of ELLEXANDER (ALEXANDER) DEAL, dec'd by John Cook, Patrick Todd, John Rusing. Notes and accounts of John Cook, Nathaniel Rooks, Stephen Bostick, Jas. Young. Amounts paid legatees John Deal and Jas. Cason.

10 June 1803. Estate of JAMES SAXON, dec'd. Adm. granted to wife Marey Saxon. Sec: Wm. Washington and Jos. Williams.

11 June 1803. Inventory of estate of JOHN MC CLINTOCK, dec'd by Jas. and Alexr. Mills and Joseph Dean.

1 Apr. 1803. Appraisal of estate of WM. COCKS (COX), dec'd by Henry Meredith, Solomon Langston, Henry Langston and Samuel Stiles. Adm: Wm. Cannon.

16 July 1803. Estate of JOHN ORZBOURN (OSBORN), dec'd. Adm.

Estate of JOHN OSBORN cont'd:
granted to Ezekiel S. Rowling. Sec: John Newman and Joel Hughes.

July 1803. Inventory of estate of JAMES SAXON, dec'd by Henry
Hazel, Michael Swindle and Jos. Williams.

21 May 1803. Inventory of estate of JAMES BURNSIDE, dec'd by
Nathaniel Nickels, Jas. Williams, Geo. Hollingsworth.

16 May 1803. Inventory of estate of JOHN HUGHS, dec'd by Jas.
Young, Jas. Culbertson, Paul Findley. Notes on James Shackelford,
John Roberson, Reynals and Madden, Clement Wharton, Joel Walker,
John Smith, Wm. Sims, Jas. Roberts, Jno. Creecy, Wm. Sprouse,
Joel Carter, Jno. Newman, Gabriel Joel, Benj. Garner, Silvs.
Walker, Jr., Robt. Pasley, Wm. Burnside, Jno. Fields.

8-9 June 1803. Sale of estate of JOHN HUGHS, dec'd. Purchasers:
Chas. Parks, Benj. Rodgers, Danl. Rodgers, Matheny Rodgers,
Danl. Matheny, Peter Roberts, John Rodgers, Nathan Neighbors,
Jas. Young, Zach. Bailey, Geo. Wharton, Clement Wharton, Doc.
Creecy, Wm. Michel, Richd. Duty, Wm. Huggins, Jas. Culberson,
David Madden, Wm. Love, Larkin Sullivan, Jno. Munrow, Jno. Mar-
tin, Jno. Hinton, Thos. Davenport, Thos. Hughs, Robt. Nickel,
Wm. Sims, Jno. Sims, Wm. Walker, Thos. Burgess, Jas. A. Williams,
Wm. Hazel, Herusha Walker, Jas. Findley, Elisha Michel, Geo.
Brown, Joel Walker, Jno. McMahan, E. S. Rowling, Jno. Powel,
Geo. Morgan, Wm. Borland, Wm. Drummond, Jones Fuller, Thos.
Babb, Ebenezer Starnes, Ahaiel Babb, Jno. Findley, Solomon Ful-
ler, Chas. Harris, Wm. S. Crisp, Jonth. Bailey, Dr. Hemphill,
Wm. Martin, Thos. Scott, Zeln. Mathis, David Bailey, Joshua
Wharton, Aaron Pinson, Jno. Walker, Wm. Burgess, Geo. Shackel-
ford, Robt. Brown, Robt. Pasley, Jno. Powell, Abner Teague,
Wm. Harris, Hardy Connant, Aaron Starnes, Silvs. Addams. Adm:
Wm. Burnside and Thos. Babb.

(No date) Sale of estate of JOHN MC CLINTOCK, dec'd. Purchasers:
widow McClintock, Saml. Lowe, Jos. Dean, John Dean, Jas. Mills,
Jas. McClintock, Jno. Taylor, Benj. Bray, Jas. Williford, Jno.
Hunter, Jas. Hunter, Jno. Crooks, Alex. Mills, Wm. Cheek, Obed.
Moore, S. Allen, Alex. Power, Wm. Pool, Jas. Howel, Spencer
Brown, Jon. Peterson, Robt. Fleming, Edmd. Craddock, Jos. Howel,
Saml. Fleming, Wm. Powers, Wm. Roberson, Wm. McNorton, Ebenezer
Morse, Jno. Attaway, Jas. Glenn, Robt. Fleming. Adm: Jas. Mc-
Clintock.

12 Aug. 1796. Will of JOHN MC CLINTOCK. Wife; sons James and
John McClintock; daughters Peggy Hunter, Mary Mills, Martha
McClintock, Betty Fleming, Nancy McClintock. Exr: wife and sons.
Wit: Margaret McClintock, James McClintock and John McClintock.

1 Aug. 1803. Will of JOHN MC CLINTOCK, dec'd proved by Jas.
McClintock and Jas. Hunter.

14 June 1803. Appraisal of estate of JOSEPH ARMSTRONG, dec'd
by Danl. Williams, Jas. Calwell and Drury Satterwhite.

21 June 1803. Sale of the above estate. Purchasers: Jno. Arm-
strong, Thos. Buckel, Jas. Armstrong, Jas. Williams, Thos. Rudd,
Jas. A. Williams, Robt. Gillum, Richd. M. Owens,Susannah Rudd,
Jas. Davenport, Jonth. Hollingsworth. Sold by Robt. Gillum.
Exr: Robt. Gillum and Jas. Williams.

22 June 1800. Will of WILLIAM FOWLER, planter. Wife Agnes Fowler; son John Fowler; daughter Peggy Parks and her son William Parks; sons James, William, David, Charles Fowler; (mentions land adj. Jas. and John McClintock); daughter Nancy Fowler. Exr: wife and son John Fowler. Wit: James McClintock, James Hutcheson and James Fowler.

5 Sept. 1803. Will of WM. FOWLER, dec'd proven by James Fowler and James Hutcheson.

5 Sept. 1803. Adm. of estate of JESSE ALLEN, dec'd granted to Winna Allen and David Cowan. Sec: James Mills, and James Mc-Clintock.

3 Oct. 1803. Adm. of estate of ROBERT MC CLINTOCK, dec'd granted to Marthew McClintock and James McClintock.

4 Oct. 1803. Letters testamentary granted to Moses Pinson in the estate of AARON PINSON, dec'd.

21 Aug. 1803. Sale of estate of JAMES SAXON, dec'd. Purchasers: Lewis Dotson, James Wilson, Geo. Gughan, Jos. Williams, Thos. Moore, Marey Saxon, Athey Saxon, David Bradon, Geo. Swindle, Chas. C. Allen, Chas. Collins, Manda Saxon, John Saxon, Lucy Saxon, Jos. McCanter, Henry Hazlet, Alex. Brady, Rufus Inman, Wm. Saxon, Wm. Williams, Wm. Washington, Josiah Deen, John Roberson, Jas. Jones, Robt. Saxon, John Mathis.

17 Oct. 1803. Adm. of estate of HENRY HILL, dec'd granted to wife Ellender Hill. Sec: Jacob Ducket and Thomas Hendrick.

17 Oct. 1803. Joseph Conner, minor, chose Thomas Conner as guardian. Sec: Claubourn Brown.

15 Oct. 1803. Appraisal of estate of ROBERT MC CLINTOCK, dec'd by Jas. Saxon, Robt. Hutcheson, James Hunter and James Mills.

12 Feb. 1803. Sale of estate of JAMES NEAL, dec'd. Notes and accounts: David Graham, David Speers, Geo. Roberson, Thomas Hanner, Abner Young, Robt. Scott, Saml. Laird, John Kern, John Young.

20 Oct. 1803. WILLIAM HOULDRITCH (HOLDRICH?), dec'd. James and Wm. Baley, Exr. Pr. by James Young.

18 July 1797. Estate of DANL. HORSEY, dec'd. Charles Smith, cert. Adm: Lewis Hogg, Daniel Williams and James Blakely.

16 Aug. 1803. Will of WILLIAM HOLDRITCH. Estate divided among my seven children, last five under age)-son James, daughter Lelline, William, Zachariah, Lucy, George, Polly. Money to be kept by Young & Boyce; mentions Wm. Burnside, Esq.; James Bailey; Wm. Bailey. Exr: James and William Bailey. Wit: James Bailey, James H. Dendy and James Young.

27 Oct. 1803. Appraisal of estate of AARON PINSON, dec'd by Dvaid Madden, Marmaduke Pinson and Gabriel Joel. (No date) Lists of debts owed estate by: Moses Pinson, Aaron Pinson, Isaac Pinson, John Pinson, Geo. Brock, Thos. Lewis, John Brady, Benj. Williams, Jno. Madden, Jas. Byrum, Gabl. Joel, Jacob Williams, Stephen Plant.
Exr: Moses Pinson

3 Sept. 1803. AARON PINSON, SR., dec'd. Wife Elizabeth Pinson now being deceased, his legatees chose Moses Pinson who was named Exr. in will to continue as exr. of sd will. Signed: Jno. Pinson, Jno. Horsey, Jas. Byrum, Jas. Fowler, Jos. Pinson, Jno. Pinson, Aaron Pinson, Thos. Shirley, Isaac Pinson. Wit: Moses Pinson, Jr., Aaron Pinson. Pro: Josiah Blackwell, J.P.

14 Nov. 1803. Adm. of estate of JOHN PARKER, dec'd granted to Burrel Bobo, bond by Absalom Bobo.

4 Nov. 1803. Inventory of estate of HENNERY HILL, dec'd by Abner Casey, John Powell(?) and Enoch Garret.

10 Sept. 1803. Will of FRANCES MC TEER. Daughters Elizabeth McTeer and Frances Spears; grandsons Samuel and William Vance; daughter Mary Vance; daughter Margret Olton(?). Exr: brother James Griffin and friend James Simpson. Wit: Alex. Simpson, Wm. Speare and Milley Oston(Olton?). Will proven by Wm. Speer and Milley Ostom(?) on 9 Nov. 1803.

14 Nov. 1803. Adm. of estate of JOHN PARKER, dec'd granted to Burrel Bobo. Sec: Absalom Bobo and Wm. Pasley(?)

15 Nov. 1803. Adm. of estate of JOHN ROBERSON, dec'd granted to wife Marey Roberson. Sec: Braddock Harris and Menoah Roberson.

5 Dec. 1803. Adm. of estate of ROBERT JASON, dec'd granted to wife Lana Jason. Sec: Patrick Rodgers and James Hambleton.

(No date) Appraisal of estate of WM. HOLDRITCH, dec'd by Isaac Mitchel, James Mickelford(?) and Saml. Paul. Notes on: Wm. Wilson, John Baley, Wm. Leagon, James Fuller, Elias Holcom, Wm. Baley, Zach. Baley.

18 Nov. 1803. Sale of estate of AARON PINSON, SR., dec'd. Purchasers: Moses Pinson, John Pinson, Isaac Pinson, Berry West, Benj. Williams, Wm. Henderson, Thos. Weathers, Chas. Parks, Jas. Wells, Lewis Griffin, Abel Thomas, Jno. Shirley, E. S. Rowling, Thos. Byrum, Elina Madden, Solomon Cole, Thos. Hunter, Mathew McDannel, Stephen Plant, Eliz. Hughs, G. Wharton, Jno. Horsey, Thos. Hughs, Aaron Pinson, Jr., Aaron Pinson, Sr., Andw. Henderson, Margret Pinson, Zach. Pinson, Josiah Blackwell, Thos. Davenport, Jno. Coats, Arch'd Donnel, Jr., Jeremiah Collins, David Madden, Jacob Box, Jas. Box, Wm. Hughs, Jacob Niswanger, Susannah Madden, Jno. Sims, Littleberry Sullivan, Philip Buckner, Jas. M. Caine, Thos. Shirley, Joel Hughes, Jas. Henderson. Exr: Moses Pinson.

3 Dec. 1803. Appraisal of estate of ROBERT JASON, dec'd by James and John McMahan and A. Rodgers, Jr. Anguish Campbell, J.P.

4 Oct. 1803. Application to adm. estate of ROBERT MC CRARY, dec'd by wife Marey McCrary. Sec: John Boling and Jas. Elmore.

5 Dec. 1803. Appraisal of estate of JOHN PARKER, dec'd by John and Joseph Miller, Joseph Hawler. 5 Dec. 1803. Sale of estate by Adm. Burrel Bobo. Purchasers: Burrel Bobo.

24 Dec. 1803. Sale of estate of WM. HOLDRITCH, dec'd. Purchasers: Winney Howel, Wm. Baley, Thos. Burnside, Isham Fuller, Jas. Holdritch, Jas. Baley, Solomon Fuller for Patsy and Lucy Clardy. Adm: Wm. and Jas. Baley.

2 Dec. 1803. Appraisal of estate of JOHN ROBERSON, dec'd by Aaron Moore, Thos. Goodwin and Archibald Young.

(No date) Sale of estate of HENNERY HILL, dec'd. Purchasers: Ellender Hill, Joseph Hill, Robt. Hill, Moses Whitten, Wm. Gray, Isaac Gray, Hillary Masters, Jacob Masters, Mary Kelley, Jno. Whitten, Jas. Johnston, Josha Ducket, John Ducket, B. Jackson, Jas. Flinn, J. A. Elmore, Wm. Kelley, Abner Casey, John Mason, James Janes, Wm. Bishop. Adm: Ellender Hill.

3 Jan. 1804. Application to adm. estate of THOMAS DANDEY, dec'd by Polley and Wm. Dandey. Sec: Jas. Bowes and Cornelius Dandey.

(No date) Inventory of estate of JESSE ALLEN, dec'd by Robt. Franks, John Garner and Robt. Luttrell. Sale of estate (no date) Purchasers: Winna Allen, Wm. Garrett, Richd. Millner, Arnold Millner, Jas. Parker, Isaac Nabours, Abram Cook, John Potter, Chas. Allen, Marshal Franks, Wm. Franks, Israel Hunt, David Night, Almon Grant, Nathan Henderson, Peter Goodwin, Jas. Cheek. Adm: Winna Allen and David Cowan.

(No date) Inventory of estate of ROBERT MC CRARY, dec'd by Geo. Whitmore, James Dillard and J. A. Elmore. Sale of same on 5 Jany 1804. Purchasers: Marey McCrary, Matthew McCrary, Isaac McCrary, John McCrary, Moses McCrary, Andrew McCrary, Jno. Bowling, Wm. Young, Zach. Young, Wm. Gray, Josiah Williams, Richd. Ducket, James Ducket, Wm. Hendley, Chas. Jordon, Orzel Bevis, Wm. Miles, Richd. Ferguson, Ward Ferguson, Benj. Wilson, Joshua Bishop, Wm. Liles, Thos. Young, Mikel Vickery, Jno. Anglin, Geo. Young, Jno. Greer, Joseph Adair, Wm. Lockeby, Thos. Henson, Robt. Burns, Jno. Carney, Saml Law, Jr., Jas. Dillard, Wm. Dillard, Geo. Dillard (cont'd on page 90 of Book C)

10 Dec. 1803. Israel Miller, minor, about 20 years, chose Thos. Lewis as guardian. Sec: Alexander Broady and Wm. Howell. Samuel Miller, minor, about 15 years, chose the same guardian.

(Cont'd list of purchasers of sale of ROBT. MC CRARY, dec'd) Jas. Burk, Eliphaz Riley, Benj. Lewis, Edw. Jones, Jos. Jones, Jno. Caine, Jas. Low, Wm. Liles, Holway Prater, Basil Prater, Danl. Welch, Jno. Ramage, Josiah Thetford. Adm: Mary Odle former-ly McCrary.

19 Jan. 1804. Adm. of estate of WM. MC DANNEL, dec'd granted to wife Mary McDannel. Sec: D. Rowling and Thos. Davenport.

20 Nov. 1803. Sale of estate of THOMAS BURTON, dec'd Purchasers: Lillian Burton, Silvs. Walker, Sr., Robt. Creswell, Jno. Boyd, Thos. Lewers, Thos. Word, Geo. Watts, Littleberry Sullivant, Geo. Madden, Jno. Newman, Jas. Cammack, Saml. Burton, Hennery Box, Abram Laurens, Robt. Burton. Exr: Robt. Creswell.

5 Jan. 1804. Adm. of estate of ROBERT MC CRARY, dec'd wife Mary revoked and John Bourland appointed instead. Sec: Andw. and Moses McCrary.

5 Nov. 1803. Sale of estate of ROBT. MC CLINTOCK, dec'd. Purchas-ers: Matthew McClintock, Jas. McClintock, Wm. McClintock, Alex. Mills, Jas. Mills, Robt. Fleming, Jas. Fleming, Saml. Fleming, Jno. Hunter, Jas. Hunter, Jas. Saxon, Obed. Moore, Jas. Crooks, Saml. Henderson, Wm. Word, Thos. Word, Jas. Hutcheson, Jno. Hutcheson, Jas. Howel, David Glenn, Saml. Parsons, Jas. Fowler,

Estate sale of ROBT. MC CLINTOCK, dec'd cont'd:
Jas. Parks, Nat. Nabours, Thos. Bevard(?). Adm: Jas. McClintock.

6 Jan. 1804. Additional sale of estate of AARON PINSON, dec'd.
Exr: Moses Pinson.
2 Jan. 1804. Sale of estate of ROBERT JASON, dec'd. Purchasers:
Robt. Caldwell, Sarah Jason, Thos. Rodgers. Adm: Sarah Jason
and Thos. Rodgers.

26 Jan. 1804. Will of WILLIAM BOURLAND, SR. Wife Marey Bourland;
children of dec'd daughter Rudy(?) McClure; grand-daughter Jennet
Ramage; rest of my children Mary Odle, P--bel (Isabel?) Harper,
John Bourland, James Bourland, Jennet Dooland, Sarah Grace,
Nancy Thetford, Andrew Bourland, Cassa Grace. Exr: son John
Bourland. Wit: Robt. Long, Jno. Wilson, Elizabeth Langston.
6 Feb. 1804. Above will proven by Jno. Bourland, Exr. and Robt.
Long, Wit.

6 Feb. 1804. Adm. of estate of JAMES HIGGINS, dec'd granted
to wife Tireana (Serena) Higgins.

7 Feb. 1804. Adm. of estate of GEORGE WRIGHT, dec'd granted
to Jacob Niswanger and Jno. Shirley, Sr. Sec: Robt. Freeman,
Asa Turner.

9 Feb. 1804. Appraisal of estate of JAMES HIGGINS, dec'd by
Wm. and Reuben Martin, James Mills, Lewis Crumpton.

16 Feb. 1804. Adm. of estate of CORNELIUS DANDEY, dec'd granted
to Wm. Dandey. Sec: Silvanus Walker, Jr., Robt. Word.

17 Feb. 1804. Appraisal of estate of GEORGE WRIGHT, dec'd by
Silvanus Walker, Jr., Wm. Eddins, Jonathan Forgey.

6 Mar. 1804. Adm. of estate of WM. GALLEGLY, dec'd granted to
wife Hannah Gallegly. Sec: Mathew Jones and ___ Jones.

8 Mar. 1804. Will of JOHN PAGE, dec'd. Wife Anna and son John
to execute. Wit: Wm. Fulton.
28 July 1804. Will of JOHN PAGE. Wife Anna; son-in-law Wm. Carter
and sons Wm., John, James; daughters Betsey, Frances, Jenney
and Hannah. Exr: wife and son John. Wit: Wm. Fulton and Betsey
Page.

10 Mar. 1804. Sale of estate of EDWARD JONES, dec'd. Purchasers:
Elizabeth, Betsey, Joseph, Edward, Sarah, John, and Gabriel
Jones; John and Wm. Burnside, Adi Griffin, Wiley Smith, David
Hitt, Jos. Williams, Patrk Todd, Angus Campbell, Jr., Thos.
Cummins. Adm: Elizabeth Jones and Jno. K----(?).

6 Mar. 1804. Sale of estate of JAMES HIGGINS, dec'd. Purchasers:
Tireana (Serena) Higgins, Wm. Higgins, Levi Crumpton, Jos. Al-
lison, Starling Tucker, Wm. Bramblet, Obediah Moss, Jas. Brown,
Jno. Riddle, Jas. Crumpton, Elias Cheek. Adm: Tireana(?) Higgins.

(No date) Appraisal of estate of WM. MC DANIEL, dec'd by David
Hellams, Gabriel Joel and Wm. Loyd. (No date) Sale of the estate
of above. Purchasers: Saml. Williams, Jr., Washington Manley,
Jas. McCaine, Wm. Hill, Jas. Abercrumbie, Wm. Mathis, Henry
Donal, Stephen Williams, Mary McDaniel, Robt. Allison, Geo.
Garmon, Saml. Barnet, Jacob Williams, Archd McDaniel, John Box,
John Blackwell. Adm: Mary McDaniel.

3 Nov. 1803. Sale of estate of ROBERT BURTON, dec'd. Purchasers: Sarah Burton, Danl. Wright, Wm. Kumton, Jesse Willis, John Hughs, Henery Brockman, Archable Young. Adm: Sarah Burton.

4 Feb. 1804. Inventory of estate of WM. BOURLAND, dec'd by Robt. Long, Andw. McCrary and J. A. Elmore.(No date) Sale of estate of same. Purchasers: Marey, James, William and John Bourland, Jno. Rammage, Benj. Simson, Chas. and Ward Ferguson, (others too dim to read). Exr: John Bourland.

16 Mar. 1804. Appraisal of estate of WM. GALLEGLY, dec'd as shown by widow Hannah Gallegly, Adm. by Alex. Simpson, Jas. Simpson, Jno. Simpson.

19 Mar. 1804. Adm. of estate of DAVID MC GLADERY, dec'd granted to Robert and Anna....(?) Gill. Sec: Thos. Norris, John Mitchel.

29 Feb. 1804. Inventory of estate of CORNELIUS DANDEY, dec'd by Silvanus Walker, Saml. Powell, Jas. Young. 1 Mar. 1804. Sale of same estate. Purchasers: Glanus Winn, Wm. Dandey, Jas. Young, Geo. Lawson(?), Henry Fuller, Jas. Clardy, Jno. Copeland, Geo. Roberts, Jno. Harris, Harusha(?) Walker, Wm. Huggins, Polly Dandey (widow), Mary Dendy, John Powell, Reuben Carter, Jas. H. Dandey, Saml. Powell, Sr., Sherril Tinsley, Absolum Roberts, Wm. Dandey, Wm. Wilson. Adm: Wm. Dandey.

26 Mar. 1804. James McClurkin, minor about 18 years, chose Wm. Wadkins as guardian. Sec: Ezekiel Andres (Andrews?).26 Mar. 1804. Samuel McClurkin, minor about 12 years, chose Wm. Wadkins as guardian.

23 Jan. 1804. Appraisal of estate of THOMAS DENDY, JR., dec'd by W. Burnside, Silvs. Walker and John Boyd. Debts of Jno. Bohannor. 24 Jan. 1804. Sale of estate of THOS. DENDY, dec'd. Purchasers: Polly, William, Mary, Thomas and Charles Dendy, Henry Hasel, Jno. Harris(?), Wm. Hudgens, Blackgrove(?) Glenn, Martin Vaughn, Benj. Smith, Wm. Huggins, Benj. Saxon, Dr. Hemphill, Jno. Martin, Saml. Powell. Adm.: Wm. Dendey.

2 Apr. 1804. Will of JOHN BRYSON, dec'd proven by Wit: Archibald Sayers, John Fakes, Agness Boyd. Exr: Wm. Fulton, John Simpson. 27 Mar. 1804. Will of JOHN BRYSON, planter. Wife Martha; son-in-law William Flemming; brother William Bryson's children. Exr: John Simpson, Wm. Fulton. Wit: Archd. Sayers, John Fakes and Agness Boyd.

5 Apr. 1804. Adm. of estate of WM. BERRY, dec'd by George Berry. Sec: Seth Pettypool, John Hutcheson.

7 Apr. 1804. Estate of JOHN KIRK, dec'd. Widow Elizabeth Kirk has since remarried to George Lawens(?); new adm. bond by Elizabeth and Geo. Lawens(?). Sec: Wm. Bryson and Jas. Brown replaced by David Spears, Thos. Jones and David Vance.

7 Apr. 1804. Adm. of estate of ANDREW MIDDLETON, dec'd granted to Ainsworth Middleton. Sec: John Middleton, John Roberson.

20 Apr. 1804. Appraisal bill of estate of JOHN PAGE, dec'd by Pleasant C. Sneed, Frederick Little, Stephen Tribble.

(No date) Inventory of estate of WILLIAM BERRY, dec'd by Joseph Dean, Hugh Young and John Hutcheson.

11 Apr. 1804. Sale of estate of DAVID MC GLADERY, dec'd. Purchasers: Robt. Gill, Saml. McGladery, Elizabeth and Margret McGladery. Robt. Culbertson, Clk. Annaritter Gill and Robt. Gill, Adm.

13 Apr. 1804. Appraisal of estate of JOHN BRYSON, dec'd by Washington Williams, Elijah Watson, Chas. Wilson, Jas. Nickels.

21 July 1804. Will of NATHANIEL NICKELS, dec'd proven by Wit: Jos. Hollingsworth, Jonathan Johnston. Exr: James and Charter Nickels. 22 Mar. 1804. Will of NATHANIEL NICKELS. Eldest son John; son James; daughter Elizabeth Nickels; son-in-law James McDowal; daughter Isabel Nickels; sons Nathaniel and Charter. Mentions land adj. Anguish Campbell, Jas. A. Williams; land in Newberry; sister-in-law Elizabeth Caldwell; brother Wm. Nickels; son Robert. Exrs: James and Charter Nickels. Wit: Jos. Hollingsworth, Jon. Johnson, M. Campbell.

30 June 1804. Adm. of estate of JOHN PETERSON, dec'd granted to John Watts. Sec: John Roberson, Robt. Creswell.

30 Aug. 1803. Partial sale of estate of JOHN HUGHS, dec'd. Purchasers: Wm. Lowe, Thos. Hughs, Thos. Davenport, Joel Walker. Adm: Wm. Burnside, Thos. Babb.

6 Aug. 1804. Deposition of Joseph Dean on estate of THOMAS DEAN, SR, dec'd - had heard that dec'd had made will and that will was lost and knows not the contents of same. Jos. Dean to adm. estate. Sec: Geo. Mosely, John Cunningham. THOMAS DEAN, JR., dec'd. Jos. Dean to adm. estate.

6 Aug. 1804. JOHN MC CLINTOCK, dec'd. Wife Jane to adm. est, James McClintock being dec'd. Sec: Alex. and Jas. Mills.

28 Mar. 1801. Inventory of estate of WM. MANLEY, dec'd by Jno. Cochran, Thos. Burton, David Helms.

(No date) Appraisal of estate of NATHANIEL NICKELS, dec'd by Thos. Nickels, Saml. Goodman and Jos. Hollingsworth.

5 Sept. 1804. CLABOURN BROWN, dec'd. Wife Rebecka to adm. estate. Sec: Geo. Brown, Jos. Brownlee.

3 Sept. 1804. JAMES MC CLINTOCK, dec'd. Margaret McClintock and Robert Hutcheson to adm. est. Sec: Andrw. Park and Wm. Hutcheson.

3 Sept. 1804. ASSENA HOLLAND, dec'd. Wm. Holland to adm. estate. Sec: Richard Holland, John Millar.

22 Sept. 1804. ISAAC MOSLEY, dec'd. His father Isaac Mosley to adm. estate. Sec: Burrell Mosley and Zachariah Arnal.

27 Sept. 1804. THOMAS DEAN, JR., dec'd. Inventory of estate by Geo. Mosley, Geo. Berry, John Hutcheson. 21 Sept. 1804. THOMAS DEAN, SR., dec'd. Inv. of estate by Geo. Mosley, Geo. Berry, John Hutcheson.

4 Aug. 1804. Appraisal of estate of JAMES PETERSON, dec'd by Danl Hill, Richd Hatter, James Watts, Robt. Smith.

18 Sept. 1804. Inventory of estate of CLABOURN BROWN, dec'd

Inventory of estate of CLAYBOURN BROWN cont'd:
by Silvs. Walker, Jos. Brownlee, Saml. Powel. Note on Thos.
Commer.

Oct. 1804. Adm. of estate of BENJAMIN PETERSON, dec'd by Danl
Cox. Sec: John Watson, Geo. Goddard, Allen Cox.

(No date) Appraisal of estate of ANDREW MIDDLETON, dec'd. Sale
of estate (no date). Purchasers: James Cobb, Jane and Ainsworth
Middleton.

29 Sept. 1804. Appraisal of estate of WILLIAM BERRY, dec'd by
James Dean, Hugh Young, John Hutcheson. 29 Sept. 1804. Sale
of estate. Purchasers: Elisha Cheek, John A. Elmore, Edw. Cox,
Wm. Word, Geo. Berry, Black Jane, Edw. Craddock, Lewis Stone,
Jas. Brown, Lenard Smith, Spencer Bobo, Obediah Moss, Chas.
Chas. Pucket, Saml. Fleming, Thos. Berry, Geo. Rose, Geo. Howel,
Black James, James Saxon, Vinson Brown.

18 Oct. 1804. Adm. of estate of WM. TAYLOR, dec'd to Wm. Taylor,
Jr. Sec: Jas. Hunter, Saml. Taylor.

12 Oct. 1804. Appraisal of estate of BENJ. PETERSON, dec'd by
Richd. Hatter, Danl Hill, Jas. Watts.

20 Oct. 1804. Inventory of estate of JAMES MC CLINTOCK, dec'd
by Henry Meredith, Wm. Word. Henry Langston, John Fowler.

27 Oct. 1804. Appraisal of estate of JOHN MOSLEY, dec'd by Jacob
Nisanger, John Hunter, John Watson. Shown by Isaac Mosley, Adm.
(No date) Inventory of estate of THOMAS DEAN, SR., dec'd by
Geo. Mosley, Geo. Berry, John Hudson. (No date) Inventory of
estate of THOMAS DEAN, JR., dec'd by same appr's. 29 Oct. 1804.
Sale of estate of THOMAS DEAN, SR., dec'd. Purchasers: Wm. Fow-
ler, Geo. Berry, Jos. Dean, Wm. Mosley, John McDowel, Robt.
Fleming, Jas. Hutcheson, Christopher Ross(?), Hannah Dean, Jas.
McCurley, Solomon Fowler, Littleton Persons, Solomon Waldrop,
Geo. Mosley, Saml. Parsons, Alex. Mills, Solomon Holder, Jas.
Saxon, Ebenezer Moss. Adm.: Jos. Dean. Sale of estate of THOMAS
DEAN, JR., dec'd. Purchasers: Starling Tucker, Edmond Craddock,
Jos. Dean, Jas. McCurley, Wm. Ward, Wm. Fowler, Ebenezer Moss,
John Cunningham, Hannah Dean, Widow Cunningham, Saml. Parsons,
Alex. Mills, John Fowler, Robt. Fleming, Jas. Dean, Jas. At-
taway, Henry Martin. Adm: Jos. Dean.

6 Nov. 1804. Will of JAMES JONES. Wife Lucy; sons Benjamin,
Miles; daughter Angelica Phillips; son Whitmore; daughter Jane
Duncan; son Jesse; daughter Sarah Bennet; sons Joseph and Dred.
Exr: son Joseph. Wit: Geo. Whitmore, Joel Whitten, Elizabeth
Wesson.

14 Nov. 1804. JAMES BURK, dec'd. James Dillard, Esq. applied
for wife Rebecca Burk to adm. the estate. Cert. by J. A. Elmore.

14 Sept. 1804. JAMES MEADORS, dec'd. Wife Susannah qualified
as exr. of will by applicaton of J. A. Elmore. 28 Sept. 1804.
Will of JAMES MEADORS. Wife Susannah; sons Reuben, Jason, Jehu.
Exr: wife Susannah. Wit: J. A. Elmore, Rubin Gordon, Polly Saxon.
Will proven 13 Oct. 1804.

31 Oct. 1804. Inventory of estate of ASENETH HOLLEN, dec'd by
Robt. Long, John Owens, John Cargill of Va. Adm: Wm. Hollen.

1-2 Nov. 1804. Sale of estate of ASENETH HOLLEN, dec'd.

26 Nov. 1804. Will of JOSEPH WHITMORE, dec'd proven by Whitmore Jones and Ruben Flannigan. George Whitmore qualifies as Exr. 27 May 1803. Will of JOSEPH WHITMORE. Son George Whitmore; daughter Sarah Duncan. Estate divided among all my children and the heirs of those dec'd; mentions grandson Geo. Whitmore. Exr: son George Whitmore. Wit: Whitmore Jones, Dr. Jones, Reuben Flanagan.

26 Nov. 1804. JAMES JONES, dec'd. Joseph Jones, Exr. petitions for sale. Affidavit of Geo. Whitmore, writer of dec'ds will.

(No date) Sale of estate of CLABOURN BROWN, dec'd. Purchasers: Rebeckah Brown, Glanus Winn, John Harris, Clabourn Goodman, Jos. Brownlee, Robt. Brown, James Holley, Polly Brown, George Brown, Martin Miller, Jeremiah Tribble, James Dunlap, William Roberts, Herusha Walker.

(No date) Appraisal of estate of WILLIAM TAYLOR, dec'd by John McLaughlin, James Hunter. Sale of estate of Wm. Taylor, dec'd. Purchasers: Wm. Ross, Wm. Taylor, Andrew Spears, David Spears, Nehemiah Franks, Robert Taylor, Richard Taylor, Wm. Simmons, John Ross, James Parks, Wm. Nickels, F. Nabours, Wm. Duke, Mikel Waldrop, Mary Cain, John Boyd, Wm. Franks, David McCaa, John Dandey, Gilbert McNary, Henry Strange, John Harris, Saml. Neighbors, Saml. Templeton, Saml. Taylor, Chas. Neighbors, Nancy Taylor, B. Cradock, Thos. Harris, Saml. Vance, John McDole, Wm. Rodgers, J. C. Stedman, Wm. Spears, Danl. Martin, Jos. Cason, Robt. Spears, Jos. Hall, John Nabours, John Simmons, Wm. Howl. Wm. Taylor, Adm.

1 Jan. 1805. The widow of ENOCH GARRETT, dec'd, Elizabeth Garrett, is unable to attend, asks a commission be given. James Dillard qualifies her as admx. 31 Dec. 1804 James Garrett and Miles A____(?) sec.

31 Dec. 1804. THOMAS MC CRARY, minor, chose George McCrary as guardian. Sec: Christopher McCrary and Samuel Ferguson.

10 Dec. 1804. Appraisal of estate of JAMES BURK, dec'd by James Dillard, Abner Casey, Eliphat(?) Riley. 28 Nov. 1804. Sale of est. of JAMES BURK, dec'd. Rebecca Burk, Admx.

(No date) Appraisal of estate of JAMES MEADORS, dec'd by John Hanna, Alexander George, Richard Ferguson, Thos. Beasley.

12 Nov. 1804. Sale of estate of JAMES MC CLINTOCK, dec'd. Margret McClintock and Robt. Hutchison, Adm.

7 Dec. 1804. Sale of estate of BENJAMIN PETERSON, dec'd. Purchasers: Danl. Cox, Robt. Cox, Jacob Whitworth, Thos. Hill, Danl. Day, Benj. Day, John Watts, Richd. Watts, James Watts, Richd Hatter, Benj. Chapman, James Atwood, Danl Word, John Glaze, John Bell, John Owens. Danl Cox, Adm.

Sale of estate of ALEXANDER DEALE, dec'd. Purchasers: John Deale, Polly Deale, Peter Hill, Richard Hatter, John Gates, James Cason, Drury Vaughn, Moses Wells. John Deale, Adm. 2 Apr. 1804.

9 Jan. 1805. Will of JOHN EVANS, dec'd proven by wit: James Edwards and Wm. Griffin. Josiah Evans, Exr. Griffin and Evans, Adm. Sec: Benj. Owens, David Whitford, Meshack Overby, Nimrod

Will of JOHN EVANS cont'd:
Overby and Richard Puckett.

(No date) Appraisal of estate of JOHN ORSBORN (OSBORN), dec'd.
E. S. Rowland, Adm. 27 Oct. 1804. Sale of estate of JOHN OSBORN,
dec'd.

22 Nov. 1804. Inventory of estate of JAMES JONES, dec'd. App'rs
Henry Davis, Jacob Ducket, Thos. Hendricks. (No date on sale)
Purchasers: Joseph Jones, John Jones, Dred Jones, Whitmore Jones,
Miles Jones, Joseph Duckett, Richard Duckett, Josiah Duckett,
Thomas Hendricks, Joseph Bennet, Joseph Duncan, Martha Duncan,
Wm. Dillard, Jos. Martindale(?), Moses Whitten, Wm. Caton(?),
John Jacks. Jos. Jones, Exr.

3 May 1796. Will of SILAS GARRETT, planter. Wife; sons Enoch,
Jacob, John and Silas; daughters Mary, Martha Harris, Elizabeth
Yarborough, Margaret. Son Enoch Garrett, Exr. Wit: Roger Brown,
John Garrett and Wm. Dollar. 7 Jan. 1805. Application of John
Garrett, Jr. to adm. will of SILAS GARRETT, dec'd. John Garrett,
Jr. and Wm. Dollar, Sec.

28 May 1804. Will of WILLIAM HUTCHESON. Son James and my other
children. Exr: son James Hutcheson. Wit: Wm. Hutcheson, Jr.
and James Fowler. 10 Jan. 1805. Will proven by Wm. Hutcheson,
Jr.

16 Sept. 1779. Will of JOHN EVANS of 96 Dist. Children to be
schooled; mentions land adj. John Caldwell; wife Sarah; sons
Josiah, William and John; daughters Mary Edwards, Frances Marian
and Rachel Evans. Wit: Mary Edwards, Martha Puckett and James
Puckett. Will proven 8 Feb. 1785, John Thomas, Jr., Ord. of
96 Dist.

4 Feb. 1805. Adm. of estate of SAMUEL FLEMING, dec'd by Saml.
Fleming and James Fleming, Adm. Sec: Robt. Fleming and John
Hunter.

4 Feb. 1805. Will of WILLIAM HANDCOCK, dec'd proven by Joseph
Hancock and Wm. Young. (Date not clear) Will of WM. HANDCOCK.
The surviving children of my sister Sally Rodgers (mentions
her son Wm. Rodgers) and Clement Hancock and daughter Patsey;
John Hancock and son James and other children. Exr: Wm. Burnside,
Abner Pyles. Wit: Jos. Hancock, Wm. Young and Betsy Pyles.

29 Nov. 1804. Inventory of estate of JOSEPH WHITMORE, dec'd
by Jacob Duckett, Wm. Liles, Whitmore Jones and Henry Davis.

31 Dec. 1804. Inventory of estate of ENOCH GARRETT, dec'd by
Eliphas Riley, Saml. Dillard and Alan Coffey. 16-17 Jan. 1805.
Sale of estate of ENOCH GARRETT, dec'd. Admx: Betsy Garrett.

(No date) Inventory of estate of JAMES SULLIVANT, dec'd by Chas.
Simmons, Larkin Sullivant. 5 Jan. 1805. Sale of estate. Adm:
John Boyd.

22 June 1804. John Pringle to Charles Simmons bond of $150 vs
claims of David Simmons and his portion of estate of his father
JOHN SIMMONS, dec'd and the relinquishment of guardianship of
the sd David by sd Charles. Wit: James Saxon. Pr: Lewis Graves,
J. P.

10 Jan. 1805. Appraisal of estate of SILAS GARRETT, dec'd by Wm. Prude, Eliphas Ryley and David Reeder.

(No date) Sale of estate of ISUM ELLIOTT, dec'd. Purchasers: David Greer, Saml. May, Wm. Williams, James Simmons, Jos. Williams, Wm. South, Wm. Simmons, John Wright, Thos. Elliott, Wm. Turner, Robt. Bumpass, Nathl Green, Saml Pringle, Rubin Elliott, Saml Murphy, Geo. Cunningham.

(No date) Inventory of estate of JOHN EVANS, dec'd by R. M. Owens, Meshack Overby and David Whitford. (No date) Sale of estate of Evans. Purchasers: Thos. Pinson, Wm. Griffin, Henry Hitt, John Beasley, John Long, Richd Pucket, Wm. Carter, Byrum Smith, Wm. Finney, John Shockwell, John McGowan, Nealey Pucket, John Watts, Robt. Cole, Josiah Evans, James Edwards, John Caldwell, David Wood, Thos. Smith, Danl Day, Benj Cason, Richd Griffin, Jesse Smith, Wm Hendley, Dabney Pucket, John Simpson, Elijah George, Mikel Finney, Richd M. Owings, Wm George. Josiah Evans, Wm. Griffin and James Edwards, Adm.

6 Mar. 1805. Adm. of estate of MARK HARDEN, dec'd by his father Henry Harden. Sec: John Roberson and Silvanus Adams. 23 Mar. 1805. Inventory of estate by Silvanus Adams, David Caldwell and John Roberson. 23 Mar. 1805. Sale of estate. Purchasers: John Roberson, Isaac Mosley, S. Adams, Roberson Redden, John Richey, Thos. Sims, Henry Harden, John Gaston. Henry Harden, Adm.

13 Mar. 1805. Adm. of estate of ELISHA HALCOM, dec'd granted to Marey Halcom, his wife. Sec: Thos. Goodwin and Benj. Brown.

23 July 1791. Appraisal of estate of WILLIAM BERRY, SR., dec'd by James McCurley, Jos. Parsons, John McCrary. Thomas Farrow, J. P. 21 May 1794. Additional appraisal by Jos. Parsons, Aaron Lynch and George Ross. 10 June 1794. Sale of estate (four negroes of the sd Berry). Exr: Geo. Berry.

26 Jan. 1805. Sale of estate of SILAS GARRETT, dec'd. Adm: John Garrett.

16 Mar. 1805. Adm. of estate of JESSE BARKER, dec'd granted to wife Margaret Barker. Sec: Laurens Barker and Salathiel Shockley.

(No date) Inventory of estate of ELISHA HOLCUM, dec'd by Wm. Brown, John Meador, Thos. Parks and Jos. Lyon.

(No date) Appraisal of estate of JESSE BARKER, dec'd by Robt. Ross, Rchd Millner and Robt Franks.

11 May 1805. Adm. of estate of BARTLEY BROOKS, dec'd granted to James Young. Sec: John Middleton and James Crocker.

25 May 1805. Nuncupative will of PATRICK RODGERS, dec'd proven by Andrew Rodgers, Jr. and Wm. Rodgers. Andrew qualified as exr. 25 May 1805. Verbal will of PATRICK RODGERS, dec'd. "two days before his death the 9th inst. Patrick Rodgers appointed Andrew Rodgers, Jr. his sole exr. to transact his business to the best of his knowledge for his children and to take two of them himself (Polly and John) and for Wm. Rodgers to have the other one (Pollyana). David Anderson, Ord.

16 Apr. 1805. Inventory of estate of JONATHAN REID, dec'd by David Whitford, James Nickels, James Straine and Wm. Green. 14 Apr. 1805. Wm. Reed granted adm. of estate. Sec: David Whitford and David Reed.

12 Feb. 1805. Appraisal of estate of WILLIAM HANDCOCK, dec'd by Abner Teague, Thos. Burnside and Wm. Young. Book accts on Pleasant Sneed, Benj Drake, Ephraim Anderson, John Charles, Isaiah East, John Sinclair, James Duke, John Murrow, Thos. Entrekin, Carter Erby, Stephen Vitello, Wm. Mitchell, Chas. Goodman, Wm. Farrow, Geo. Brown, Silvanus Walker, John Maddox, Judah Maddox, Chas. Clardy, Hugh O'Neal, Wm. Henderson, Wm. Young, Sr., Saml Powell, Wm. Dendey, Josiah Blackey, Sr. 19 Feb. 1805. Sale of estate. Purchasers: Robt. Gallegly, Newman Gary, James Clardy, James Cook, Jos. Vance, James A. Williams, James Hancock, John Lindley, Abner Pyles, Clement Hancock, Wm. Young, John Black, Wm. Henderson, Isabella Hancock (widow), Jos. Cason, David Speers, Jos. Williams, Saml Mathis. Exr: Wm. Burnside and Abner Pyles.

13 May 1802. Inventory of estate of WM. HUNTER, dec'd by Benj Lewis, James Underwood, John Copeland, John Miller, Elijah Teague and David Mason. Exr: Mary Hunter. (No date) Sale of estate. Purchasers: Mary Hunter, Jesse Maddox, John Saxon, John Bowland, James Entrekin, Jane Leeke, Wm. Gray, James Griffin, James Dillard, Maj. Dunlap, Mikl Dalrymple, Job Mason, Chas Griffin, Jas Wm Atwood, Wm Hudgens, Geo Miller, Jno Ward, Crawford Lewis, Thos Dendy, James Millar, Isaac Gray, Thos Cason, James Boyce, Saml Young, John Hunter, Robt Creswell, John Morrow(?). Exr: Mary Hunter.

1 May 1804. Sale of estate of GEORGE WRIGHT, dec'd. Purchasers: Edy Wright, John Shirley, Jacob Niswanger, Wm McFerson, John Roberson, Zachariah Arnold, John Creecy, Robt Shirley, Wm Williams, David Calwell, Betsy Curtis, Wm More, Saml Anderson. Adm: Jacob Niswanger.

(No date) Sale of estate of JONATHAN REED, dec'd. Purchasers: Josiah Evans, Wm. Reed, David Reed, James Reed, Jane Reed, Richd M. Owens, Jonathan Johnston, James Nichols, Howard Pinson, Wm Carter, James Edwards, Thos Pinson, Mrs. Hendricks. Wm. Reed, Adm.

(No date) Sale of estate of ELISHA HOLCOM, dec'd. Purchasers: Mary Holcom, Danl Wright, Thos Parks, Wm Brown, Joseph Holcom, Wm Arnold, Henry Feagins. Mary Holcom, Adm.

5 Jan. 1803. Will of JOHN O'NEAL, planter of Mudlick Creek. Wife Ann; sons Barney and William; daughters Margret and Jane. Exr: sons Barney and Wm. O'Neal. Wit: Chas. Wilson and Saml Ware.

2 July 1805. Adm. of estate of ISUM FULLER, dec'd granted to Sarah Fuller and Henry Fuller. Sec: Absalum and Moses Madden.

22 May 1805. Inventory of estate of BARTLEY BROOKS, dec'd by Absalom Coleman, Paul Findley and John Mosely. 9 June 1805. Sale of estate. Purchasers: John Ling(?), Thos Babb, Blackgrove Glenn, David Calwell, Isaac Mosely, Asheal(?) Mosely, Chas Goodman, Saml Goodman, Mason Moss, Ursula Brooks, James Young, Paul Findley, Abia Griffin, John Rowland, James Nickels, Wm Martin, Zach. Motts, John Fields, Silvs Adams, Richd Cowen, Silas Walker,

Sale bill cont'd:
Moses Madden, John Sims, Joseph Brownlee, Richd High. James
Young, Adm.

4 Nov. 1802. Will of ISAAC THOMAS. Wife Mary; sons William (the
youngest), Evan, John, Nehemiah, Thomas (the youngest); daughters
Sarah and Phoeby Thomas; sons Edward, Isaac, Abel; daughters
Mary Wisner and Elizabeth Cox. Exr: wife Mary and son John.
Wit: Marey Wisner, Jacob Wisner, and John Thomas.

6 July 1805. Appraisal of estate of ISAM FULLER, dec'd by James
Bailey, Andrew Rodgers, Jr. and Isaac Mitchell.

1 July 1805. Will of JOHN WESSON, dec'd proven by Benj. Wesson
and Whitmore Jones. Letters of test. granted to Henry Wesson
and Jesse Jones as exrs. 23 Jan. 1805. Will of JOHN WESSON.
Wife: Elizabeth Wesson; four children-Hicks, Sarah, Polly and
Martha Wesson. Exr: father Henry Wesson and Jesse Jones. Wit:
Absolom Harwell, Benj. Wesson and Whitmore Jones.

27 July 1805. Revocation of adm. of estate re JOHN KIRK, dec'd,
of George and Elizabeth Lawings (Owings?) by David Speer and
Thomas Jones, only sec. still in the state now consider them-
selves in danger of their securityship.

27 July 1805. Will of AQUILA RUSING, dec'd proven by Richard
M. Owen and Richd Hollingsworth. Letters test. granted to exr.
Wm. Rusing and Jos. S. Owen.

27 July 1805. Adm. of estate of JAMES BOYCE, dec'd granted to
John Rowland. Sec: Jas. Crocker and Wm. Crocker.

6 Jan. 1805. Will of AQUILA RUSING. Wife Mildred; daughters
Sarah and Keziah Rusing. Exr: Wm. Rusing, Jos. S. Owen. Wit:
R. M. Owen, Ann Owen and Richd Hollingsworth.

27 July 1805. Will of CHARLES BREADY, dec'd proven by John Cochran and Ann Wadkins. Elinor Bready and John Cochran named as
exrs, the latter renounced. 3 Oct. 1793. Will of CHARLES BRADY -
three eldest sons William, John and Alexander; mentionsss Wm.
Wadkins; wife Eleanor; two youngest sons Charles and George;
mentions my young children not yet married. Exr: wife Eleanor
Bradey and John Cochran. Wit: Ann Wadkins, Zach. Barnes, John
Cochran.

9 Apr. 1804. Adm. of estate of JOHN KIRK, dec'd granted to George
and Elizabeth Lawing (Owing?). Sec: David Speers and Thomas
Jones.

5 Aug. 1805. Will of WILLIAM BALL, dec'd proven by Stephen Garrett. Letters test. granted to exr. Lillian Ball and Reuben
Martin. 23 July 1805. Will of WILLIAM BALL. Wife Lillian Ball;
daughter Permela Ball, Mary Sadler; John, George, Elizabeth
and Stephen Hitt; William, Jeremiah, and Frances Martin; sons
Peter, James and Lewis. Exr: wife Lillian Ball and Reuben Martin. Wit: Reuben Martin and Stephen Garrett.

20 July 1805. Appraisal of estate of JOHN WESSON, dec'd by Thos.
Hendrick, Whitmore Jones, Dred Jones. Exr: Henry Wesson and
Jesse Jones.

2 Sept. 1805. WILLIAM BALL, dec'd intestate. Adm. of estate

WM. BALL, dec'd estate cont'd:
granted to Lillian Ball. Sec: James Mills and Robert Hutchison.

5 Aug. 1805. Sale of estate of JOHN O'NEAL, dec'd. Purchasers:
Marmaduke Jones, Thos Farrow, Saml Wright, Benj Hitt, Jane Buck-
hannon, John Rodgers, Wm O'Neal, Thos Scott, Washington Williams,
Alexr Huston, David Griffin, John Ligon, James McCrary, Thos
Combs. Exr: Wm. O'Neal.

6 June 1805. Inventory of estate of PATRICK RODGERS, dec'd by
James and John McMahan and Thos Burnside. (No date) Sale of
estate. Exr: Andrew Rodgers, Jr.

26 June 1805. Will of WILLIAM SIMS, dec'd proven by Lewis Graves
and John Sims. Letters of test. granted to Frederick Purtz and
Rebecca Sims named exr.

7 Aug. 1805. Inventory of estate of AQUILA RUSING, dec'd by
Laurens Hill, Clement Wells and R. M. Owen.

(No date) Sale of estate of EDMOND CRADDOCK, dec'd. Purchasers:
Ann and Polly A. Craddock. Lewis D. Yancey, Clk.

26 June 1805. Will of WILLIAM SIMS. Wife Rebecca; seven children: Nathan, Anne, Rebecca, Reuben, Simon Bluford, Rhoda Babb
and Messer Babb(?) Sims. Exr: Fredk Purtz and wife Rebecca Sims.
Wit: M. Purtz, James Sims, Jr. and Lewis Graves.

17 Sept. 1805. Sale of estate of ISUM FULLER, dec'd. Henry Fuller, Adm.

2 Oct. 1805. Adm. of estate of JOHN CARTER, dec'd granted to
wife Zebiah (Keziah?). Sec: John Richey and John Roberson.

2 Feb. 1805. Inventory of estate of WILLIAM BALL, dec'd by Reuben
Kelley, Thompson Farley, Wm. Higgins and John Garrett.

21 Oct. 1805. Adm. of estate of MICHAEL PURTZ, dec'd granted
to Frederick Purtz and Pleasant H. Wharton. Sec: Geo. and Clement
Wharton.

27 Aug. 1805. Appraisal of estate of JAMES BOYCE, dec'd by Silvs
Walker, Jr., Paul Findley and James White.

16 Oct. 1805. Appraisal of estate of JOHN CARTER, dec'd by Silvs
Adams, John Richey and John Roberson. 16 Oct. 1805. Sale of
estate. Purchasers: Charter Nichols, John Roberson, Silvanus
Adams, David Caldwell, James White, James Clemmons, Zebiath
Carter, Dr. John Creecy, Paul Findley, John Walker, Stephen
Jones, Benj Garner. (other names not clear).

8 Oct. 1805. Will of WILLIAM WHITEHEAD, dec'd proven by Jonathan
Johnson, James Strain. Letters test. to Margaret Whitehead named
exr. 22 Mar. 1805. Will of WILLIAM WHITEHEAD. Wife Mary (Mar-
garet); John and Nancy, youngest children; all my children Lusa
(Louisa?) Adkins, Benjamin Whitehead, Thomas Whitehead, Daniel
Whitehead, James A. Whitehead, Stephen Whitehead, Sarah Crain(?),
Wm. Whitehead; Exr: Charter Nickels, wife Margaret Whitehead.
Wit: Jonathan Johnson and James Strain. (N.B. Sarah Crain may
be Strain).

4 Nov. 1805. Adm. of estate of THADEUS SIMS, dec'd granted to

THADEUS SIMS estate cont'd:
George Madden and Thomas Harris. Sec: Thomas Babb and Fredk
Purtz.

(No date) Adm. of estate of WILLIAM MC HERG, dec'd granted to
John McHerg (McHarg?) and Susannah McHerg. Sec: Arch. McHerg
and Abrum Bolt.

7 Nov. 1805. Appraisal of estate of THADDEUS SIMS, dec'd by
Silvs. Adams, P. G. Wharton, and David McCaa.

19 Nov. 1805. Will of ADAM BELL, dec'd proven by Robt. Long,
Thos. East. Letters test. granted to Mary Bell named exrx. 16
Dec. 1801. Will of ADAM BELL. Wife Mary Bell; sons David, John,
Adam, Robert (if he should ever return) Bell; mentions John
Walker and Saml Ewing lands; daughters Isabela, Marey, Ester
and Elizabeth Bell. Exr: wife Mary Bell. Wit: Robt. Long, James
Bell and Thos. East.

6 Nov. 1805. Inventory of estate of WM. MC HERG, dec'd by Saml
Franks, Robt. McNess, James Cunningham and James Bumpass.

19 Nov. 1805. Adm. of estate of SAMUEL BISHOP, dec'd granted
to wife Verlinda Bishop. Sec: J. A. Elmore, Basil and Josiah
Prater. 2 Nov. 1805. Inventory of estate by Josiah Prater, John
Bowland and Jos. Rammage. (No date) Sale of estate. Purchasers:
Verlinda Bishop, John Bishop, Josiah Prater, Hollway Prater,
Basil Prater, John Philips, Chas Martin, James Batey, Lucy Whit-
ten, Jesse Jones, Enoch Garrett, Wm Gray, Wm Kelley, James Duck-
ett, James Riley, John Bourland, Chas Horton, Andw McCrary.
Adm: Verlinda Bishop.

24 Nov. 1805. Adm. of estate of BENJAMIN HODGE, dec'd granted
to Richard Hodge. Sec: John Richey and John Forgey.

25 Nov. 1805. Will of RICHARD GRIFFIN, dec'd proven by John
Cook and Chas Griffin. Letters test. to the named exr. James
Caldwell. 2 Feb. 18__(?). Will of RICHARD GRIFFIN. Wife Ellinor;
my children; land purchased of Wm. Day , Waits, Wm. Ball, Sr.,
Peter Ball, Mary Johnston. Exr: James Caldwell, Chas. Griffin.
Wit: John Cook, Geo. and Jemima Ball. 2 Feb. 1805. Agreement
between Richd Griffin and his wife Elender (Elinor?) formerly
Elinor McClain - she to relinquish dower rights to all remaining
land of his. Wit: James Calwell, Jacob R. Brown, J. P.

23 Nov. 1805. Sale of estate of THADEUS SIMS, dec'd. Purchasers:
John, Rachel and Thomas Sims; John Hodge, John Rowland. Adm:
Geo. Madden, Thos. Harris.

19 Nov. 1805. Adm. of estate of JAMES WALLIS, dec'd granted
to his widow Anne Wallis. Sec: John Simpson and James Simpson.

24 Oct. 1803(?). Adm. of estate of SAMUEL DILLARD, dec'd granted
to widow Ann Dillard and George Dillard. Sec: James and Wm.
Dillard and J. A. Elmore. 24 Oct. 1805. Inventory of estate
by David Reeder, Wm. and James Dillard.

20 Oct. 1805. Adm. of estate of ABIA GRIFFIN, dec'd granted
to Asa Griffin. Sec: A. Griffin and John Roberson.

30 Oct. 1805. Inventory of estate of WM. SIMS, dec'd by S. Adams,
David McCaa, Saml Wharton. 1 Nov. 1805. Sale of estate. Exr:

Sale of estate cont'd:
Frederick Purtz.

18 Dec. 1804. Sale of estate of JOEL BURGESS, dec'd Purchasers:
Joel Burgess, Ellen Burgess, Wm. Burgess, Jos. Brownlee, John
Madden, Larkin Sullivant, Henry Box, B. H. Myers.

6 Jan. 1806. Adm. of estate of JOSEPH BROWNLEE, dec'd granted
to Easter and Joseph Brownlee. Sec: David McCaa and Fredk Purtz.

2 Jan. 1806. William Brooks, minor, chose Blackgrove Glenn as
guardian. Sec: Silvanus and Wm. Walker.

9 Dec. 1805. Sale of estate of WM. MC HERG, dec'd. Purchasers:
Polly, Susannah, John and Elenor McHerg, James Johnston, T.
L. Duncan, J. F. Wolff. Adm: Susannah and John McHerg.

27 Dec. 1805. Appraisal of estate of ADAM BELL, dec'd by Jos.
Rammage, Patk Scott and John Dillard. (No date) Sale of estate.
Exr: Marey Bell.

27 Nov. 1805. Sale of estate of ISOM FULLER, dec'd. Widow's
dower. Adm: Sarah and Henry Fuller.

2 Nov. 1805. Inventory of estate of JAMES WALLIS, dec'd by James
Littel, Nathl Vance and David Greer. 18 Dec. 1805. Sale of the
estate. Purchasers: Ann Wallis, Wm. and Saml Boyd, John Monroe,
Thos Wilson, James McCrary, John Alton, Geo Dalrymple, , John
Dalrymple, Thos Entrekinn, Thos and West Gray. Adm: Ann Wallis.

16 Sept. 1805. ROBERT ROSS and wife MARGARET ROSS dec'd. Legatees John, David, Elizabeth, Jane and Margret Ross, sign receipt
for their shares from adm. of estate Francis Ross and Wm. Ross.
Wit: Andrw Speers and James Glenn. Also notes that Margaret
Ross, wife of Robt. Ross, each dec'd - share from the estate
of Wm. Taylor and to be equally divided among the heirs of Robt
and Margaret Ross, dec'd.

(No date) Sale of estate of JESSE BARKER, dec'd. Purchasers:
Abner Knight, Catherine Barker, Abby Barker, Lawrence Barker,
John Barker, Aggy Barker, James Barker, Enoch Chapman, Almon
Gant, James Shockley, Salathiel Shockley, John Higgins, Henry
Martin, David Peeke, Wm. Hooper, Saml Vaughn, Winnie Allen,
Willis Cheek, Wm. Franks, Robt. Moore, F. Sims, Wm. Harper,
E. Crumton, John Henderson, James Henderson, Thos. Henderson.
J. Garrett, John McHarg, James Parker, John Parker, James Gar-
rett, Stephen Garrett, E. Garrett, Hannah Shockley, John Rober-
son, Robt. Coker, Thos. Ashley, S. Duncan, Wm. Hill, Marey Hut-
son, Henry Feagans, Jos. Allison, Chas. Allen, Henderson Duke,
Francis Sims, Alex Power.

13 Nov. 1805. Sale of estate of SAMUEL DILLARD, dec'd. Adm:
George Dillard and Ann Dillard.

(No date) Sale of estate of JOSEPH WHITMORE, dec'd. Purchasers:
Geo. Whitmore, Joel Whitmore, Wm. Whitmore, John Whitmore, Paul
Abner, Benj. Jones, Jos. Jones, John Odle, Acher McCracken,
James Hughs, John Hughs, John Johnston, Wm. Bishop, Jacob Linsey,
John Ryan, James Law, Isaac Duckett, John Duckett, Jacob Duckett,
Elizabeth Allen, Thos. Watson, Wm. Ambrose, James Duckett, Wm.
Abrums, Isaac Jones, John Jones, John McCrary, Thos. Weston,
Wm. Ryley, Jos. Greer, Richd Bennett, Jos. Dunkin, James Dunkin,

Sale of estate cont'd:
John Phillips, Starling Phillips, Wm. Holland, Lucey Jones, Wm. Henley, Thos. Wesson, Julius Wesson, Thos. Hendrick, Wm. Dillard, Wm. Bourland, Jos. Duckett, Jos. Eckison, John Bell, John Abner, Wm. Dillard, Henry Davis. Exr: Geo. Whitmore.

25 Jan. 1806. Will of JAMES MOORE, dec'd proven by Joel Dendy and C. Tinsley. Exr: Cornelius Tinsley. 22 Dec. 1805. Will of JAMES MOORE. Est. equally divided among three children: Jesse, James and Jenna Moore as they come of age; wife Valley and her children. Exr: Cornelius Tinsley. Wit: James Holley, Joel Dendy.

7 Jan. 1806. Appraisal of estate of BENJAMIN HODGE, dec'd by Silvs. Walker, Jr., Jonathan Forgey, and John Richey,Sr.

24 Jan. 1806. Jesse Hughs, minor, chose Pleasant G. Sneed as guardian. Sec: Henry Johns, John Ligon.

2 Apr. 1796. Will of THOMAS CUNNINGHAM. Sons John Deen Cunningham, Thomas Cunningham, Samuel Cunningham; wife Mary. Exr: Mary Cunningham and brother Samuel Cunningham. Wit: James Dorroh, John Cunningham, Wm. Cunningham.

22 Feb. 1805. Will of CHARLES GARY. Friend Milley Coker; natural daughter Casandry Coker. Exr: Friend, Drury Coker and brother David Gary. Wit: John Coker, Wm. Gary and John Armstrong. 3 Feb. 1806. Above will proven by Wm. Gary and John Armstrong.

3 Feb. 1806. Will of THOMAS CUNNINGHAM, dec'd proven by James Dorrah and Wm. Cunningham.

3 Feb. 1806. Adm. of estate of GEORGE BERRY, dec'd by Edey Berry and John Hutchison. Sec: Hugh Young and Jos. Dean.

28 Dec. 1805. Appraisal of estate of ABIA GRIFFIN, dec'd by A. Griffin, John Armstrong and Drury F. Vaughn. 10 Jan. 1806. Sale of estate. Purchasers: James Caldwell, Brian Leeke, John Cook, Benj Goodman, Abrum Waldrop, Asa Griffin, Wm. Griffin, Saml Caldwell, James Smith, John Butler, John Armstrong, James Armstrong, Anguish Campbell, Wm. Owens, Jos. Arnolds, John Griffin, Abe Griffin, John Murrow, Mary Ann Griffin. Adm: Asa Griffin.

7 Feb. 1806. Appraisal of estate of GEORGE BERRY, dec'd by James Hutchinson, Hugh Young, Jos. Hall and Jos. Deen.

10 Feb. 1806. Adm. of estate of WILLIAM BALL, dec'd by Lillian Ball revoked upon the petition of Robt. Hutchinson and James Mills, sec.

10 Feb. 1806. Estate of WM. BERRY, dec'd. Adm. George Berry, dec'd, now replaced by Seth Pettypool. Sec: Henry Meredith, Wm. Pettypool.

11 Dec. 1805. Inventory of estate of RICHARD GRIFFIN, SR. dec'd. Notes on Ira Griffin, James Caldwell, John Jones, Jos. Griffin, John Griffin, Adina Griffin, Richd Griffin, Allen Burton, Edw Pitts, James Williams, Thos. Cunnins, Wash. Williams, E. Creswell, John Phillips, Johnston Moore, John Cummins, E. Gray, Asa Griffin, John Griffin; bad notes on Jacob Whitworth, Thos. Neel. Accts against Anguish Campbell, John Cook, W. Williams, Abner Hitt, Benj Hitt, John Smith. Doubtful accts against John

Inventory of estate cont'd:
Smith, Wm. Wheeler, James Cumins, Robt. Stewart. Wm. Pollard,
Geo. Ball, Richd. Hatter, Appr's. Sale of estate. Purchasers were
John Watts, Richd. North, John Griffin, James Griffin, Richd
Griffin, Wm. Chiles, Wm. Pollard, Benj Hatter, F. Weatherall,
Stephen Dotson, Robt. Marks, John Gray, Wm. Irby, Ad. Griffin,
John Reed, Reuben Golden, Jonathan Johnston, John Ling, John
Griffin, Ira Griffin, Stephen Watson, John Glore, John Ligon,
James Smith, John Beasley, James Edwards, James Swafford, Archey
Mason, James Caldwell, John Giles, Charles and Elinor Griffin,
Wm. Griffin, Thos. Cumins, Judah Chiles, Abner Steel, John Rob-
erson, Wm. Smith, David Owens, Robt. Stuart, Jenna Motts, Thos.
Dendy, John Pullum, Joice Jones, Saml Williams, Davis Williams,
David Nelson, Richd Owens, James Ward, Thos Reed, Benj Day,
John Beasley, Josiah Evans. Exrs: Charles Griffin, James Caldwell

3 Mar. 1806. Adm. of estate of PETER HITT, dec'd granted to
David and Thomas Hitt. Sec: Patrk Todd, Lazarus Hitt and Josiah
Evans.

3 Mar. 1806. Larkin Griffin, minor, chose Ira Griffin as guardian until age 20. Sec: Wm. Pollard and John Roberson.

4 Mar. 1806. Anthony Griffin, minor, age about 20, chose Aelius
(Alice?) and Adin(?) Griffin as guardians until age 21. Sec:
David Caldwell and James Ward.

29 Jan. 1806. Inventory of estate of JAMES MOORE, dec'd by John
and Joel Dendy, and Wm. Martin. 8 Feb. 1806. Sale of estate.
Purchasers: John Boyd, Cornelius Tinsley, John Vance, H. Walker,
Saml Powell, Jas. Saxon, James and Thomas Holley, N. Moore,
Wm. Rodgers, Geo. Lawings. Exr: Cornelius Tinsley.

(No date) Appraisal of estate of WILLIAM BERRY, dec'd.

(No date) Estate of STEPHEN MARCHBANKS, dec'd as shown by Polly
Marchbanks, appraised by Joseph Lyon, James Gilbert, Ob. Halcomb,
Thos. Goodwin. 3 Feb. 1806. Adm. of estate granted to Polly
Marchbanks. Sec: Jos. Lyon, Thos. Goodwin.

8 Feb. 1806. Sale of estate of JAMES BOYCE, dec'd. Adm: John
Rowland.

3 Mar. 1806. Nuncupative will of ELIZABETH HALL, dec'd proven
by Jos. Dean, Jos. Patterson and James Hall. 16 Oct. 1805. Verbal will of ELIZABETH HALL. Daughter Anne Hall all estate. Wit:
Jos. Dean, Jos. Patterson and James Hall.

(No date) Inventory of estate of JOSEPH BROWNLEE, dec'd by Fredk
Purtz, David McCaa and Thos. Babb.

22 Mar. 1806. Adm. of estate of THOMAS STEEL, dec'd granted
to John Cook and John Saterwhite. Sec: James Ward and John Roberson.

(No date) Sale of estate of WILLIAM SIMS, dec'd. Exr: Frederick
Purtz.

(No date) Inventory of estate of WILLIAM WHITEHEAD, dec'd by
Wm. Carter, James Strain, Wm. Green and James Nickels.

4 Apr. 1806. Will of JOHN GARRETT, dec'd proven by John Cargill.

JOHN GARRETT, dec'd cont'd:
Exr: Hannah Garrett and Joseph Garrett. 12 Aug. 1805. Will of
JOHN GARRETT. Wife Hannah Garrett; children Joseph, Sarah Prude,
Alice (Abbie?), Henry, Elisha, Rebecca, Jesse and Charles Garrett.
Exr: wife Hannah and son Joseph. Wit: Rachel and John Cargill,
of Va.(?)

15 Apr. 1806. Will of JACOB ROBERTS, dec'd proven by Danl Right
and Ezekiel Griffith. John Meador and Molly Roberts named to
exrs., the latter renouncing right. 3 Jan. 1804. Will of JACOB
ROBERTS. Wife Mary; daughters Allimon(?) Brown, Elizabeth Meadors
(or Meadows?), Sarah Gilbert; son John; daughter Mary Roberts;
sons Isaac, Joel, Thomas, Clearcy(?); Matildy and Lucindy Gilbert, children of dec'd daughter Cassey Gilbert. Exr: wife Mary
and friend John Meadows, son Isaac Roberts. Wit: Danl Wright
and Ezekiel Griffith, and John Roberts.

4 Apr. 1806. Re ISAAC MEDLEY, dec'd. Former will in possession
of James Holley destroyed by commission of the dec'd before
Wm. Burnside, Esq. Estate to be adm. by Sarah and James Medley.
Sec: Thos. Wilks and Glanus Winn. 19 Apr. 1806. Appraisal of
estate of ISAAC MEDLEY, dec'd by A. Rodgers, Jr., Wm. Coleman
and James Culbertson.

15 Apr. 1806. Adm. of estate of ABRAHAM TINSLEY, dec'd granted
to the widow Nancy Tinsley. Sec: Jesse and John Johnston.

21 Mar. 1806. Sale of estate of STEPHEN MARCHBANKS, dec'd. Adm:
Marah Marchbanks.

4 Mar. 1806. Estate sale of WILLIAM BALL, dec'd. Purchasers:
Lillian Ball, Jeremiah Ball, George Ball, Wm. Ball, Starling
Tucker, John Hunter, Nicklos Garrett, James Garrett, Saml Flem-
ming, Stephen Garrett, Garrett Sullivant, Reuben Barton, John
Hanna, Mark Goodwin, James Mills, John Garrett, Robt Criswell,
Henry Martin, John Williams. Adm: Lillian Ball.

14 Apr. 1806. Appraisal of estate of JOHN GARRETT, dec'd shown
by Hannah and Joseph Garrett. Apprs: Geo. Dillard, Geo. Young
and James Duckett.

3 Mar. 1806. Appraisal of estate of PETER HITT, dec'd by Lazarus
Hitt, Wm. Rusing and Drury Sims. 19 Mar. 1806. Sale of estate.
Purchasers: Wilson Sanders, Peter Smith, David Owen, Wm. Owen,
Richd Owen, Elijah George, Jesse Smith, Wm. Childs, Abraham
Sims, Anna Day, Michael Finney, Benj. Day, Benj. Cason, John
Pullum, Thos. Turner, James Edwards, Benj. True, Benj. Hitt,
Abner Hitt, Larkin Hitt, Mary Hitt, Thos. Hitt, David Hitt,
Lewis Ball, John Smith, Danl Welding, Mary Gray, Wm. Rusing,
Wm. Finney, Henry Hitt, James Nealy, John Rusing, James Riley,
Patrick Todd, Stephen Owen, Sarah Rooks, James Atwood, B. M.
Owen. Adm: David and Thomas Hitt.

1 May 1806. Second sale of estate of THOMAS DENDY, dec'd. Exr:
Wm. Dendy.

(No date) Appraisal of estate of ABRAHAM TINSLEY, dec'd by C.
Littel, James Bryson and Jonathan Blakely.

3 May 1806. Appraisal of estate of JACOB ROBERTS, dec'd by Wm.
Bowen, Thos. Parks, Jos. Brown and Jos. Lyon.

4 July 1806. Will of JOHN STEWART, dec'd proven by James Brown.
Charles Little named exr. 3 Jan. 1806. Will of JOHN STEWART.
Eldest son Francis; son-in-law David Studdard; youngest daughter Nelly. Exr: Chas. Little. Wit: James Brown, Jos. Vance.

(No date) Appraisal of estate of THOMAS STEEL, dec'd by John
Cummings, James Ward, and Thos. Cummings. 9 Apr. 1806. Sale
of estate. Adm: John Cook and John Satterwhite.

4 Aug. 1806. Estate of JOHN STEWART, dec'd. Exr. Charles Little
files a return on completion of exr. with receipts from each
legatee.

2 Aug. 1806. Estate sale of ABRAHAM TINSLEY, dec'd. Adm: Nancy
Tinsley.

28 Nov. 1805. Second sale of estate of BARTLEY BROOKS, dec'd.
Purchasers: John Mosley, Benj. Garner, Usley Brooks, Blackgrove
Glenn, John Roberson, Wm. Young, James Young. Adm: James Young.

4 Aug. 1806. Estate of THOMAS OWEN, dec'd to be adm. by John
Owen. Sec: Augustin Burnside and James Morse.

4 Aug. 1806. Estate of THOMAS HENDERSON, dec'd to be adm. by
Charles Henderson. Sec: Robt. Coker and Charles Allen.

28 Nov. 1805. Inventory of estate of MIKEL (MICHAEL) PURTZ,
dec'd by Silvs. Adams, A. Burnside and David McCaa. 29 Nov.
1805. Sale of estate. Adm: P. G. Wharton and Fredk Purtz.

27 Aug. 1806. In the estate of JAMES BOYCE, dec'd. John Rowland
is relieved as sec. at his own petition. Also the sd James Boyce,
dec'd replaced as sec. for Wm. Dendy in the adm. of estate of
THOS. DENDY, dec'd, adm. by Polly Dendy with sec. Israel George
and Wm. Dunlap.

28 Aug. 1806. Will of DANIEL MC GIN, dec'd proven by James Simpson and John Griffin. James Caldwell qualifies as exr. 30 Apr.
1806. Will of DANIEL MC GIN, planter. Wife Catherine McGin;
Mention of Daniel McGin, son of Wm. McGin, James McGin, Rebecca
(her father James Caldwell, also Mary Caldwell, Elizabeth Owens,
Suckey, daughter of Elisha Watson. Exr: James and Wm. Caldwell.
Wit: John Griffin, James Simpson and James Hamilton.

22 May 1806. . Will of AARON HUGHES. Wife Margaret; sons William
and Elijah Hughes. Wit: Richard Childers, John Childers and
Jesse Childers.

21 Aug. 1806. Inventory of estate of THOMAS OWEN, dec'd by James
Morse, Wm. Fowler, John Attaway and James Higgins.

12 Aug. 1806. Inventory of estate of THOMAS HENDERSON, dec'd
by Robt. Coker, John Milner, Salathiel Shockley.

(No date) Estate sale of GEORGE BERRY, dec'd. Adm: John Hutcheson.

3 Sept. 1806. Adm. of estate of JOHN SIMS, dec'd granted to
Ann Sims. Sec: Silvanus Walker, Jr. and John Sims, Jr.

19 Sept. 1806. Ann Hughs, minor, about age 15, chose William
Madden as her guardian. Sec: Moses and John Madden.

2 Oct. 1806. Will of AARON WELLS, dec'd proven by Moses and Elisha Wells. Moses qualified as exr. 30 May 1806. Will of AARON WELLS. Mother Rebecca Wells; sister Asenath Wells. Exr: sister Asenath and brother Moses Wells. Wit: Elisha and Moses Wells.

3 Nov. 1806. Will of WILLIAM MITCHELL, dec'd proven by Wm. Dendy and John Cargill. Wm. Dunlap as exr. 15 Oct. 1806. Will of WM. MITHCELL, Esq. Wife Mary; 5 children - Permelia Pyles, Sinthey Mitchell, Thomas Mitchell, Isaac Mitchell and Lewis Mitchell. Exr: ___ Blakely, Isaac Mitchell, Wm. Burnside, Wm. Dunlap. Wit: John Cargill, Va., James Cook and Wm. Dendy.

19 Aug. 1806. Estate sale of THOMAS HENDERSON, dec'd. Purchasers: Salathiel Shockley, Frankey Henderson, Jos. Goss, John Henderson, Thos. Oakley, Stephen Gow, Peter Goodwin, Chas. Allen, Wm. Coson, Wm. Gray, Wm. Fowler, Thos. Gow, James Walker, Chas. Henderson, Jacob Nabours. Adm: Chas. Henderson.

15 Nov. 1806. Adm. of estate of WM. HENDERSON, dec'd by his widow Sarah Henderson. Sec: Wm. Washington and John McGee.

18 Sept. 1806. Inventory of estate of DANIEL MC GIN, dec'd by Elijah Watson, Wm. Fulton and Danl. Williams. 24 Oct. 1806. Estate sale of same. Purchasers: James Caldwell, Mrs. McGin, Wash. Williams, Jos. Gallegly, Saml Caldwell, Saml Farrow, David Hatter. Exr: James Caldwell.

5 Oct. 1806. Estate of JOHN DILRUMPLE (DALRYMPLE), dec'd to adm. by his widow Anna. Sec: Zaddock Wood and Thos. Dalrymple. 11 Nov. 1806. Appraisal of estate by Israel Teague, Zaddock Wood, Wm. Harding.

17 Nov. 1806. Estate of JAMES DUCKETT, dec'd still to be adm. by Sarah Duckett and Levi Fowler. Sec: Geo. Young and David Reeder.

18 Nov. 1806. Will of HUGH MUNFORD, dec'd proven by James Gibson and Wm. Dillard. Geo. Whitmore as exr. 30 Oct. 1802. Will of HUGH MUNFORD. Son James; daughters Nancy Finney, Margaret Scott, Hannah Bell; son Johnstono Munford; daughter Anney Munford. Exr: Geo. Whitmore. Wit: James Gibson, Wm. Low and Wm. Dillard.

(No date) Will of AARON HARLAN, dec'd proven by Joshua Palmer and Wm. Sparks. Elizabeth and Samuel Harlan qualified exrs. 24 July 1806. Will of AARON HARLAN. Eldest son Samuel; daughter Sarah; son George; daughter Jane; sons Joshua and James; daughter Mary; sons Aaron, Joseph, and Isaiah; daughter Rebecah; wife Elizabeth Harlan. Mentions land - Robt. Swain, Samuel Harlan, James Harlan, Archibald Smith. Exr: Wife and eldest son. Wit: Joshua Palmer, Bennett Langston and Wm. Sparks.

7 Nov. 1806. Will of JOHN OWENS, dec'd proven by Menaseh Finney and Robt. Long. Daniel Owens and John Finney qualify as exrs. 11 Sept. 1806. Will of JOHN OWENS. Wife Mary; children Daniel, Mary Greer, John, Thomas, Robert, Martha, Ann, Jennett and Eliza-beth (latter children minors). Mentions land - Miles Ferguson, Abraham Holland, Alexander McQuay, Thos. Beasley, Francis Brad-dock. Exrs: son Daniel Owens and John Finney. Wit: Robt. Long, Manassah Finney, John Finney.

12 Aug. 1806. Estate sale of THOMAS OWENS, dec'd. Purchasers: John Owens, David Owens, Wm. Higgins, James Higgins, Wm. Ball,

Sale of estate cont'd:
Wm. Fowler, Starling Tucker, Benj. Brown. Adm: John Owens.

9 Sept. 1806. Appraisal of estate of JOHN SIMS, SR., dec'd by
Silvanus Walker, Jr., P. Findley and David McCaa.

28 Nov. 1806. Inventory of estate of AARON HARLAN, dec'd by
Benj. Byrd, Henry Langston and John Brown.

1 Oct. 1806. Estate sale of JOHN SIMS, SR., dec'd. Purchasers:
Ann Sims, Thos. Sims, John Sims and Rachel Sims, John Roberson,
Henry Shell, Fredk Purtz, John Creecy, David Couch, Benj. Inman,
John Rowland, Joshua Noble, Wm. Grimes, James Scott, and Henry
Fuller. Adm: Ann Sims.

5 Jan. 1807. Adm. of estate of JOHN WILLIAMS, dec'd granted
to Robt. Gaines, husband of Sarah Williams, dec'd adm. of sd
John Williams, dec'd. Sec: Thos. Gaines, and Jos. Bolton.

21 Dec. 1806. John Huggins, minor, about 20 years, chose Wm.
Huggins as guardian. Sec: Josiah Evans, Jas. Edwards.

24 Nov. 1806. Inventory of estate of AARON WELLS, dec'd by Thos.
Ligon, Thos. Cason and Robt. Hamilton. 27 Nov. 1806. Estate
sale. Exr: Moses Wells.

10 Jan. 1807. Re THOMAS DENDY, dec'd. Polly Dendy to replace
Wm. Dendey former adm.

19 Nov. 1806. Inventory of estate of JAMES DUCKETT, dec'd by
Henry Davis, David Reader and James Dillard. (No date) Estate
sale. Purchasers: Sarah, Josiah, John, Jacob and B____ Duckett;
Geo. Moss, Jas. Howerton, Jeremiah Hendrick, Mr. Bobo, Kindred
Bobo, Jas. Dillard, Wm. Alexander, Jas. Williams, John James,
Benj. Wilson, Danl Welch, John Bonds, John G. Caldwell, John
Whitten, Henry Davis, John Swinford, Jjas. Battey, Thos. McCrary,
John McCrary, Wm. McCrary, John Millar, Lewis Fowler, David
Reeder, Richd Bennett, Henry Huff, Jos. Jones, Edw. Jones, Thos.
Jones, John Garrett, Edw. Jeanes. Adm: Sarah Duckett and Levi
Fowler.

19 Nov. 1806. Inventory of estate of HUGH MUNFORD, dec'd by
(not named). (No date) Estate sale of same. Purchasers: Edw.
Jeanes, Enoch Garrett, James Gibson, Manassa Finney, James Mun-
ford, Johnston Munford, Geo. Whitmore, John Johnston, James
Dillard, Wm. Dillard, Asa Dillard, John Dillard, John Moore,
John Phillips, James Adair, Jesse Jones, John Odle, Munford
Finney, John Jeams, Jesse Jeams, Edw. Jeams (may be Jeanes),
Obediah Roberts, An Munford, John Millar, John Finney, Jesse
Wilkison, Edw. Wesson, Josiah Duckett, Wm. Johnston, Richd Ben-
nett, Miles Jones, John Jones, Isom Bradley, Wm. Kelley, Rebecca
Gray, Wm. Gray, John Bradley, Lewis Fowler.

9 Dec. 1806. Inventory of estate of JOHN OWENS, dec'd by Reuben
Meadors, Alexr. George and Benj. Adair.

(No date) Estate sale of JOHN DALRYMPLE, dec'd. Purchasers:
Anna, Thomas, James and Susanna Dalrymple, Z. Gray, Jos. Gallegly,
Geo. Raney, Wm. Neel, Zadock Wood, Steph. Williams, Thos. Gray,
Garner Gallegly. Adm: Anna Dalrymple.

3 Feb. 1807. Adm. of estate of JOSEPH JOHNSTON, dec'd to widow

Adm. of estate cont'd:
Mary Johnston. Sec: Thos. Johnston and Saml. McGladery.

13 Feb. 1807. Will of WILLIAM WHITEHEAD, dec'd proven by (not clear). Charters Nickles as exr.

4 Nov. 1806. Inventory of estate of WILLIAM MICHEL, dec'd by John Hunter, James Clardy, Wm. Dendey. Mention of Abner Pyles.

17 Feb. 1807. Peggy Harris, minor about 16 years, chose John Richey, Sr. as guardian. Sec: James Findley and Richard Hodges. 5 Nov. 1806. Estate sale of WILLIAM MITCHEL, dec'd. Exr: Wm. Dunlap.

(No date) Inventory of estate of JOSEPH JOHNSTON, dec'd by John Yeager, Thos. Johnston and Marmaduke Pinson.

11 Mar. 1807. Adm. of estate of MOSES MC CRARY, dec'd to George McCrary. Sec: Geo. Ross and John Millar.

2 Mar. 1807. Adm. of estate of ABIA GRIFFIN, dec'd to John Cook replacing Asa Griffin. Sec: Jos. Runolds(?) and Wilson Sanders.

(No date) Estate sale of FRANCIS ROSS, dec'd. Adm: John Ross.

27 Mar. 1807. Adm. of estate of WILLIAM O'NEIL, dec'd to Sarah O'Neil, widow. Sec: Wm. Fleming and Wm. Fulton.

2 Apr. 1807. Adm. of estate of ANTHONY GRIFFIN, dec'd to John Cook. Will annexed. Sec: David Caldwell and John Richey.

5 Nov. 1804. Property of JOHN BRISON, dec'd sold. Exr: Wm. Fulton.

17 Mar. 1807. Adm. of estate of ABIA GRIFFIN, dec'd (in part) by Asa Griffin; memo. returned of same by John Cook the succeeding Adm. List of items sold by Asa Griffin and purchased by Jos. Rodgers, Thos. Sadler, Wm. Owens, John G. Harris; payments to John Bulger (preaching funeral), John Cummins, Elizabeth Hollingsworth, John Harris, D. Davenport, Lydall Gordon, Jas. Golden, Jas. Ward, Dr. Mineweather, Dr. Moon, Drury Vaughn, Susanna Waldrop, Benj. Goodman, Jer. Turner, John Black, Wm. Black, John Wallace, John Saterwhite, Wm. Caldwell, Seth Fuqua, Est. of James Boyce, Dr. James Moore, Jas. Smith. List of notes due by Anguish Campbell, Sr., John Butler, Danl Toals(Tolls), James Caldwell, James Armstrong, John Cook, Jas. Smith, Mrs. Brown, Saml Farrow, Thos Farrow. Adm: John Cook.

15 Apr. 1807. Will of DAVID DUNLAP, dec'd proven by John McDavid. Wife Jane Dunlap named as exr. 21 July 1805. Will of DAVID DUNLAP. Wife Jane; sons James, Price and Mitchel; daughters Mary, Christen, and Jane; older children Robert, David, John, Martha and Elizabeth; grandsons David Bishop, Robert Green; son-in-law Caleb Earp. Exr: wife Jane Dunlap, Wm. Miller, James Dunlap, and James Powell. Wit: John McDavid, Mary Dunlap and Leanna Powell.

3 Apr. 1807. Appraisal of estate of WILLIAM O'NEIL, dec'd by Elijah Watson, Wm. Fleming, Peter Roberts and Chas. Wilson.

(No date) Appraisal of estate of WILLIAM HENDERSON, dec'd by Isaac Mosley, John McGee and Henry Hazle. 29 Nov. 1806. Estate sale. Purchasers: Wm. Washington, Jesse McGee, Sarey Henderson,

Estate sale cont'd:
Isaac Mosley, Geo. Goddard, Archd Henderson, Elizabeth Hazel,
Marey Henderson, Levi Hill, Saml Arnold, Wm. Christen, N. Saxon,
Harry Hazle, Lewis Watson, Saml Henderson, Jacob Niswanger,
Jer. Collins, Thos. Thurman, Alex. Bradey, John Locheby, John
Williams, Jos. Cole, Zebulon Savage. Adm: Sarah Henderson.

27 Feb. 1807. Inventory of estate of WM. WHITEHEAD, dec'd. Notes
on B. Y. Raney, David Stephens, Robt. Shaw, James Strain; appr'd
by Wm. Green, James Nickels, Paul Findley. 2-3 Mar. 1807. Estate
sale. Exr: Charters Nickels, succeeding Margaret Barnes(?).

1 May 1807. Estate of BARNET KERNELS, dec'd, adm. granted to
Samuel Caldwell. Sec: John Simpson, John Leonard.

19 June 1807. Will of JOHN DAVENPORT, dec'd proven by Jonth.
Johnston and Wm. Roberson. John Roberson qualifies as exr. 5
Feb. 1806. Will of JOHN DAVENPORT. Sons Ransom, Thomas, William,
Richard, David; wife Mildred. Mentions Hugh Abernathey. Exr:
JohnRoberson, Frederick Purtz. Wit: Jonathan Johnston, Wm.Rober-
son and Howard Pinson.

(No date) Estate sale of JOSEPH JOHNSTON, dec'd. Purchasers:
Thomas, Mary, Matthew and Robert Johnstonn; Robert Lowry, Saml.
McGladery, Augustin and John Yager, Washington Manley, David
Halums, Chas. Smith. Adm: Mary Johnston.

17 Mar. 1807. Inventory of estate of MOSES MC CRARY, dec'd by
Jos. James, Thos. Beasley, Jos. Williams.

3 July 1807. David Davenport, minor about 20 years, chose Fredk.
Purtz guardian.

18 Mar. 1807. Estate sale of MOSES MC CRARY, dec'd. Adm: Geo.
McCrary.

3 May 1807. Inventory of estate of BARNET KERNEL, dec'd by R.
M. Owen, Lazarus Hitt, Patrick Todd. 30 May 1807. Estate sale.
Purchasers: Gracey Kernel, Capt. John Roberson, Saml. Caldwell,
Lewis Ball, Marey Kernel, Elihu Creswell. Adm: Saml. Caldwell.

22 May 1807. Appraisal of estate of WM. DENDEY, SR., dec'd by
Danl. Cox, Thos. Turner, Wm. Smith. 22 May 1807. Estate sale.
Purchasers: Thos. Dendey, Danl. Dendey, John Dendey, F. Dendey,
Jacob Whitworth, Danl. Cox, Wm. Smith, Benj. Chapman, Emry Day,
Mary Day, Richd. Hatter, Jer. Sadler, Drury Sims, Thos. Hill,
Elihu Creswell, Wm. Chiles, Wm. Billups. Exr: John Dendey.

16 Mar. 1807. Appraisal of estate of JOHN & AMELIA BROCKMAN,
dec'd by Nathl. Power, Wm. Brown and Arch. Young. (No date).
Sale of estate. Purchasers: Henry Brockman, Thos. Parks, Joel
Deen, Saml. Vaughn, Geo. Fagans, Henry Fagans, John H. Owens,
Amelia Owens, David Madden, James Patterson, James McMurton,
Josiah Deen, John Owens, John Spurgen, Silvs. Walker, Blackgrove
(or Blackgeorge) Glenn, James Hannah, Thos. Connant, John Hughs,
Wm. Brockman, James Wilson, Minnard Harris, Henderson Whitlow,
Arch. Young, Steph. Griffin, Thos. Cook, John Maddox, Barnet
H. Algood(?), Joel Fowler, Wm. L. Allen, Almond Gant, John Arnold,
John Brown, Reuben Martin, Danl Wright, Saml Parks, John Baugh,
Wm. Higgins, Wm. Parks, Saml. Shawe, Jesse Wallis, James Warford,
Bat. Ballenger, Robt. Page, John Ashley, John Deen, Capt. Power,
Wm. Pugh, Wm. Talley. Exr: Henry Brockman.

3 July 1807. GEORGE DALRYMPLE, dec'd. Wife Ann to adm. husband's estate. Sec: Israel Teague and John McCelvey.

25 Aug. 1807. JOSEPH GALLEGLY, dec'd. Wife Sarah to adm. her husband's estate. Sec: Zaddock Wood and Robt. Gallegly.

28 July 1807. Inventory of estate of GEORGE DALRYMPLE, dec'd by David Mason, Elijah Teague, Chas. Garret.

27 Oct. 1807. ELIZABETH BRYSON, dec'd. John Hutchison to adm. estate. Sec: John Middleton.

(No date) JOSEPH GALLEGLY, dec'd. Appraisal of estate by Marmaduke Jones, James Littel, Chas. Willson.

(No date) ELIZABETH GARRETT, dec'd. Appraisal of estate by Jesse Jones, Wm. Dillard, David Reeder. 26 Sept. 1807. Adm. of estate by Jos. Garrett, Wm. Prude. Sec: Edw. Jones, Wm. Kelley.

(No date) GEORGE DALRYMPLE, dec'd. Sale of estate. Adm: Ann Dalrymple.

11 Apr. 1807. Appraisal of estate of ANTHONY GRIFFIN, dec'd by James Ward, John Cummins, Ned Jones, John Armstrong. 23 Apr. 1807. Sale of estate. Adm: John Cook. Will annexed.

(No date) Inventory of estate of JOHN DAVENPORT, dec'd by James Nickels, Benj. Malden, Wm. Green, Chas. Ligon. Notes due by Wm. Green, Lewis Ball, Wm. McCrary, Matthew Hunter, David Davenport, Richd. Davenport, Geo. Wharton, Wm. Roberson. Exr: John Roberson.

29 Apr. 1807. Estate sale of WM. O'NEALL, dec'd. Purchasers: Sarah and John O'Neall, Nancy Goodman, Thos. Farrow, John Anderson, James Tinsley, Wm. Roberson, James Golden, Thos. Rodgers, James Boyce, James Cook, Jos. Rodgers, John Baley, John Leonard, John Gates, James McMahan, John Rodgers, John Moore, David Griffin, Elijah Watson, Wm. Fleming. Adm: Sarah O'Neall.

2 Dec. 1807. Will of JAMES YOUNG, dec'd proven by James Holley and Thos. Powell. Zachariah Baley and Wm. Burnside, Exr. 21 Nov. 1807. Will of JAMES YOUNG, SR. Daughters Betsey Carter, Polly Medley(?), Lucy and Kitty Young; son John; son James; four minor children; John and Kitty to have reasonable education. Exr: Z. Bailey, Sr. and Wm. Burnside. Wit: Jas. Holley, Thos. Powell.

12 Oct. 1807. Adm. of estate of ANDREW RODGERS, JR., dec'd by wife Letty Rodgers. Sec: Zach. Baley and Robt. Pasley.

12 Dec. 1807. Adm. of estate of WM. NICKLES, dec'd by wife Catherine. Sec: John Richey and Thos. Harris.

Estate sale of JOHN WILLIAMS, dec'd. Adm: Sarah Williams now dec'd succeeded by Robt. Gaines. Return notes support of five children up to 25 Dec. 1807.

26 Dec. 1807. WM. BRYSON, dec'd. Wm. Blakely and Chas. Littel qualified as exrs. 7 Dec. 1807. Will of WM. BRYSON. Wife; 2 girls Jane and Sarah, which I fetched from Ireland; sons John, James and Robert. Exr: Wm. Blakely and Chas. Littel.

25 Dec. 1807. Adm. of estate of JEREMIAH SADLER, dec'd granted
to Nathaniel Day. Sec: John Watts and Danl Dendey.

31 Dec. 1807. Appraisal of estate of WM. BRYSON, SR., dec'd
by Saml Vance, James Brown and Jonathan Blakely.

13 Jan. 1808. Adm. of estate of JOHN HUNTER, JR., dec'd to be
by his mother, Sarah Hunter. Sec: Wm. Dunlap and John Simpson.

13 Jan. 1808. Adm. of estate of HENRY HUNTER, dec'd to his mother
Sarah Hunter. Sec: (same as above).

18 Jan. 1808. Adm. of estate of WILLIAM ROBERSON, dec'd to John
Hatter. Sec: John Roberson and John Owens.

28 Jan. 1808. Adm. of estate of FIELDING TURNER, dec'd to his
wife, Salley Turner. Sec: James Turner and Thos. Hill.

16 Dec. 1807. Inventory of estate of ANDREW RODGERS, JR., dec'd
by James Bailey, Robt. Pasley and Thos. Burnside. 5 Jan. 1808.
Sale of estate. Purchasers: David Anderson, Letty Rodgers, Thos.
Rodgers, Saml. Rodgers, Jos. Rodgers, Wm. Rodgers, Wm. Adkins,
John Davis, James Bumpass, Woodson Ligon, James Owens, Thos.
Babb, Richd Shackelford, John Wiseman, Isaac Mitchell, Abner
Pyles, John Sturgess, Thos. Strange, Thos. Burnside, James Ful-
ler, James Culberson, James Boyd, Zach. Bailey, James Shackel-
ford, Wm. Glenn, Danl Mitchell, Robt. Pasley, John Cook, Jeremiah
Glenn, Thos. Ligon, Saml Henderson, Jacob Miller, Thos. Wilks,
Francis Lester, Saml Franks, Elijah Watson. Adm: Letty Rodgers.

22 Jan. 1808. Estate sale of WILLIAM BRYSONS, SR., dec'd. No
purchasers named.

28 Dec. 1807. Appraisal of estate of JAMES YOUNG, dec'd by Glanus
Winn, Jos. Hollingsworth, James Holley and James Bailey. 30
Dec. 1807. Sale of estate. Purchasers: Wm. Milum, John Milum,
Abner Pyles, Danl Walker, James Bailey, James Medley, James
Young, Thos. Dendy, Absolum Bailey, Saml Leek, John Wilson,
Wm. Wilson, Thos. Wilks, Whitehead Wilks, Jos. Hollingsworth,
Asa Chandler, Glanus Winn, Whitehead Medley, Newman Gary, Francis
Lester, John Kellet, Andrw Wilson, James Holley, Benj. Lewis,
Wm. Kingsborough, Wm. Burnside, Zach. Bailey, Jr., John Miller,
Thos. Rodgers, Saml Gary, Joel Carter, Wm. Dendey, John McClana-
han, Chas. Dendey, Horatio Walker, James Culberson, Thos. Dendey,
Abraham Bailey, James Bailey, John Gray, Saml. Gray, Hardy Con-
nant, Chas. Harris, Wm. Roberson, John Sims, Solomon Fuller,
Zach. Bailey, Wm. Burnside.

6 Feb. 1808. Appraisal of estate of WILLIAM NICKLES, dec'd by
Silvanus Walker, Jr., Richard Hodges and Jonathan Forgey. 6
Feb. 1808. Sale of estate. Purchasers: Catherine Nickles, Israel
East, Wm. Nickles, Richd. Davenport. Adm: Catherine Nickles.

7 Mar. 1808. Adm. of estate of JACOB GILL, dec'd to Jesse Bolton.
Sec: James Gordon and Robt. Spence.

7 Mar. 1808. Adm. of estate of JOSHUA HITCH, dec'd to John Hitch.
Sec: James Hanna and Wm. Hutchison.

23 Feb. 1808. Will of WILLIAM MC MURTREY. Daughters Janney Bryson, Susanna Hall and Elizabeth McClaskey; sons William, Matthew
and Cambell (son Cambell and wife Mary, his brother's children

MC MURTREY will cont'd:
Janney and Betsy). Notes on Andrew Bradey and Cambell McMurtrey.
Exr: David Green and ____ Est. Wit: John Munroe, Matthew McMurtrey and John Teague. 9 Mar. 1808. This will proven by J. Munroe
and M. McMurtrey.

30 Dec. 1807. Inventory of estate of JEREMIAH SADLER, dec'd
by James Watts, Danl Cox and Wm. Smith. 15 Jan. 1808. Sale of
estate. Purchasers: widow Mary Sadler, Nathaniel Day, Daniel
Day, Abner Hitt, Thos. Hitt, Wm. Davis, Patrick Todd, Wm. Smith,
James Watts, James Ball, Danl. Cox. Adm: Nathaniel Day.

(No date) Appraisal of estate of WILLIAM ROBERSON, dec'd by
James Cook, John Cook and John Black. 1 Feb. 1808. Sale of the
estate. Purchasers: Richd. Hatter, John Cook, James Cook, Wm.
Young, Danl Cox, Watley Vaughn, Abner Pyles, James Griffin,
Saml Caldwell, James Boyd, Nancy Roberson, John Owens, David
Owens, Jacob Miller, John Walker, Horatio Walker, James Turner,
Richd Hatter, Sr., Wm. Hall, Zach. Mineweather, Wm. East, Sr.,
Alexr. Simpson, James Atwood, Henry Jones(?), Nathl Vance, Anth.
Griffin, widow Williams, Saml Farrow, Danl Rodgers, Robt Cox,
Thos Entracan, James Lefann, Drury Vaughn, John Leonard, Wm.
Ligon, James Hambleton, James Young, Sr., Richd North, Absalom
Simms. Adm: John Hatter.

13 Feb. 1808. Giney Ward, minor, chose Robert Ward as guardian.
Sec: Silvanus Walker, Jr. and John Roberson.

(No date) Appraisal of estate of FIELDING TURNER, dec'd by James
Walls, Danl Cox and James Turner. (No date) Sale of estate.
Purchasers: John Owens, Patrick Todd, Andrew Todd, James Watts,
Wm. Smith, Benj. Fashell, Danl Fashell, James Turner, Danl Cox,
Thos Hill, Richd Sims, Elihu Creswell, Robt Turner, Sally Turner,
James Atwood, Jos. Rennals, Danl Dendey, Wm. Pollard, Richd
Hatter. Adm: Salley Turner.

(No date) Sale of estate of JOSEPH GALLEGLY, dec'd. Purchasers:
widow, Robt. Gallegly, Geo. Gallegly, Wm. McDaniel, Joel East,
David Griffin, Hugh O'Neal.

12 Mar. 1808. Inventory of estate of JACOB GILL, dec'd by James
Gordon, James Blakely and Wm. Brown.

2 May 1808. Will of JOSHUA TEAGUE, dec'd proven by Thos. Dalrymple, Jr., Thos. Dalrymple, Sr. Abner Teague as exr. 12 May
1804. Will of JOSHUA TEAGUE. Sons Israel, Elijah, William, Abner
and James Teague; daughters Isabel Mason, Sophia Lyons, Susanna
Major and Mary McAdams. Mentions John Lewis, Wm. Caldwell, Wm.
Gray lands. Exrs: sons Elijah, Israel and Abner Teague. Wit:
Mathew Jones, Thos. Dalrymple, Jr. and Thos. Dalrymple, Sr.

15 Jan. 1808. Inventory of estate of HENRY HUNTER, dec'd by
Alexr. Glenn, Jeremiah Leek and John Copeland. 29 Jan. 1808.
Sale of estate. Purchasers: Jos. Wilson, Saml Boyd, Mrs. Sarah
Hunter, David Speer. Adm: Sarah Turner.

13 Jan. 1808. Inventory of estate of JOHN HUNTER, dec'd by Alexr
Glenn, Jeremiah Leek and John Copeland. Adm: Sarah Hunter. 21
Jan. 1808. Sale of estate. Purchasers: Wm. Barksdale, Wm. Barks-
dale,James Vance, Mrs. Sarah Hunter, James Leek, David Griffin,
Wm. Dunlap, Thos. Burnside, Chas. Harris, John Cargile, Va.,
James Cook, Elihu Creswell, Robt. Creswell, Nancy Griffin, Benj.

Estate sale cont'd:
Yancey, Wm. Fowler, Wm. Burnside, Mathew Hunter, Col. John Simpson, Abner Teague, Geo. Wolf, Wm. Scurlock, David Wason, John Leaman. Adm: Sarah Hunter.

28 May 1808. Estate of JOHN ROWLING, dec'd to be adm. by Betsey Rowling. Sec: Silvs. Walker, Jr. and John Middleton.

6 June 1808. Estate of LANEY JASON, dec'd to be adm. by Saml. Caldwell. Sec: James Hambleton and Robt. Hambleton.

6 June 1808. Estate of JOHN CARGILL, dec'd to be adm. by James Holley. Bond: Silvs. Walker, Jr. and Wm. Moore.

6 June 1808. Will of JAMES LITTEL, dec'd proven by James Simpson and David Greer. Exrs: James Nickles and Col. John Simpson.

6 June 1808. Will of RICHARD FERGUSON, dec'd proven by Nathl. Martin. Geo. McCrary and Chas. Ferguson as exrs.

9 June 1808. Will of JAMES LITTEL, planter. Wife Agnes; children Mary, Isabel, James, William, David, and Thomas. Mentions son Robert and cousin Charles Littel. Exr: friend James Nickels, Col. John Simpson. Wit: John Monroe, James Simpson and David Greer.

20 July 1807. Will of RICHARD FERGUSON, widower. Sons Ward, Miles, John, Charles and Samuel Ferguson; eldest daughter Tabitha Hartley, daughters Mary Vaughn, Frankey McCrary and Elizabeth Ferguson. Exr: Geo. McCrary, Chas. Ferguson and Saml Ferguson. Wit: J. A. Elmore, N. Martin and Turner Richardson.

10 Aug. 1808. Will of JOHN CHARLES, dec'd proven by Wm. Burnside and James Donald. Margaret Charles qualified as Exr. 14 Mar. 1808. Will of JOHN CHARLES, planter. Wife Margaret and children (not named). Exr: wife and Wm. Fulton. Wit: Wm. Burnside, Andrew Burnside and James Donald.

23 Sept. 1808. Adm. of estate of LITTLEBERRRY SULLIVANT, dec'd to wife Nanney Sullivant. Sec: Benj. Strange and Menoah Sullivant.

4 Sept. 1808. Adm. of estate of WM. MC MURTREY, dec'd to wife Mary McMurtrey. Sec: Angus Campbell, Sr. and John Rodgers, Sr.

5 Sept. 1808. Will of SAMUEL BOLLING, dec'd proven by Wm. Choice, Tully Choice. Wife Abie Bolling, Saml. Bolling and Tully Bolling qualified as exrs. 9 May 1808. Will of SAMUEL BOLLING, planter. Wife Abie; youngest sons Samuel and Thornbury Bolling; youngest daughters Lucinda and Polley Bolling; son John; all his children - Robert, Nancy Sullivant, Elizabeth Dunklin, Tulley Bolling, John Bolling, Lucinda Bolling, Saml Bolling, Polly Bolling, Thornbury Boling. Exr: Wife and sons Robt., Tully, John and Saml. Wit: Wm. Choice, Mary Choice and Tully Choice.

5 Sept. 1808. Will of JOHN MANLEY, dec'd proven by Benj. Smith and James D. Right. James Manley as exr. 3 Apr. 1806. Will of JOHN MANLEY. Wife Jane; sons James, John and William; daughters Jane and Christian. Exr: wife and son James. Wit: Benj. Smith, J. D. Right and James McDaniel.

25 Sept. 1808. Adm. of estate of JOSEPH WILLIAMS, dec'd to wife Elizabeth. Sec: Jos. Bolton and Henry Box.

10 Sept. 1808. Appraisal of estate of WM. MC MURTREY, dec'd by Jos. Blackeby, John A. Owens and James Simpson.

11 July 1808. Appraisal of estate of JAMES LITTEL, dec'd by Nathaniel Vance, David Greer and James Simpson.

28 May 1808. Inventory of estate of JOSHUA TEAGUE, dec'd by Thos. Dalrymple, Jr., Frederick Foster and Thos. Dalrymple, Sr. (No date) Sale of estate. Purchasers: Jos. Wilson, James Entrekin, Israel Teague, David Munrow, Elijah Teague, David Mason, Thos. Dalrymple, Wm. Gray, Thos. Addams. Adm: Abner Teague.

24 June 1808. Inventory of estate of RICHARD FERGUSON, dec'd by Benj. Adair, Josiah Williams and Wm. Holland.

13 Apr. 1808. Inventory of estate of JOSHUA HITCH, dec'd by Benj. Byrd, Henry Langston and John Hutchison. Adm: John Hitch. 14 Apr. 1808. Sale of estate. Purchasers: Solomon Langston, Henry Langston, Levi Crumpton, James Hunter, Wm. Hutchison, Robt. Hutchison, David Cowing. Adm: John Hitch.

(Noo date) Appraisal of estate of JOHN CHARLES, dec'd by Saml. Goodman, Robt. Hambleton, John Nickels and James Nickels.

5 July 1808. Inventory of estate of LANEY JASON, dec'd by Wm. Rodgers, James Hambleton and Stephen Owens. Adm: Saml. Caldwell.

22 June 1808. Appraisal of estate of JOHN CARGILL, dec'd by Wm. Dunlap, James Clardy, Abner Teague and Joshua Teague. 23 June 1808. Sale of estate. Adm.: James Holley.

6 Oct. 1808. Appraisal of estate of JOSEPH WILLIAMS, dec'd by DAvid Braden, John McGee and Geo. Goddard.

26 Oct. 1808. Will of REUBEN GLENN, dec'd proven by John G. Caldwell and Wm. Right. Exr: Alexr. Glenn. 26 Oct. 1808. Will of REUBEN GLENN. Wife Elizabeth. Exr: Alexr. Glenn. Wit: John G. Caldwell and Wm. Right.

(No date) Estate sale of WM. MC MURTREE, dec'd. Purchasers: Wm. McMurtree, the widow, Mathew McMurtree, John Maddox, John Blakely, Wm. Kingsborough, John Millar. Adm: Marey McMurtree.

6 July 1808. Appraisal of estate of JOHN ROWLAND, dec'd by Silvs. Walker, Jr., John Newman and Jonathan Forgey before D. Anderson. 29 July 1808. Sale of estate. Purchasers: John Newman, Elizabeth Rowland (Rowling), John Roberson, Joel Carter, Wm. Crocker, James Crocker, Silvs. Walker, Jr., Wm. Roberson, David Abrums, Harrey Hazle, David Caldwell, Jonathan Forgey, David Anderson, James Young, Geo. Joel, Joel Starns, J. S. Fuller, Joel Hughs, John Sims, Wm. Williams, Andrw Anderson, David Adams, John Hinton, John Boyce. Adm: Betsey Rowland.

29 Nov. 1808. Adm. of estate of WM. DORROUGH, dec'd by James Dorrough. Sec: Jas. Dorrough, Jr. and James Dunlap.

8 Oct. 1808. Appraisal of estate of LITTLEBERRY SULLIVANT, dec'd by Jos. Strange, Thos. Land, Larkin Sullivant. Notes on E. S. Rowling, B. C. Yancey, Robt. Creswell, Jos. Straing, Little Chas. Simmons, Henry Box and Thos. Anderson.

5 Dec. 1808. Adm. of estate of NATHANIEL ROOK, dec'd to John

Adm. of estate cont'd:
Cook. Sec: Jonathan Forgey and Ebenezer Starnes.

2 Jan. 1809. Will of NANCY REASE, dec'd proven by Danl. Wright, and Wm. Pugh as exr. 3 Feb. 1808. Will of NANCY REASE. Daughter Betsey Pugh; grandson Jonathan Allison, minor son of my daughter Polley York. Exr: James Allison and Wm. Pugh. Wit: Daniel Wright and Nancy Wright.

2 Jan. 1809. Adm. of estate of JOHN BONDS, dec'd to wife Elizabeth Bonds. Sec: David Spence and Wm. Bonds.

12 Dec. 1808. Appraisal of estate of REUBEN GLENN, dec'd by Wm. Right, Chas. Sims and Wm. Dillard.

6 Jan. 1809. Will of SAMUEL WRIGHT, dec'd by Anthony Griffin and Wm. Owen. Exr: Saml. Wright. (Jr.?). 23 Sept. 1808. Will of SAMUEL WRIGHT. Eldest son Wm. G. Wright (minor), sons James and Samuel; daughters Elizabeth, Frances, Polley and Nancey; wife Patience C. Wright. Exr: brother Wm. Wright. Wit: Washington Williams, Anthony Griffin and Wm. Owens.

3 Oct. 1808. Overton Harris, minor about 15 years, chose John Richey as guardian. Bond: David McCaa and Moses Madden.

12 Jan. 1809. Nancey C. Roberson, minor about 17 years, chose Wm. Adair as guardian. Bond: Abram Holland and Frederick Foster.

6 Jan. 1809. Rebecca Hughs, minor about 15 years, chose Geo. Wharton as guardian. Bond: Wm. Lowes and Fredk Purtz.

11 Feb. 1809. Jesse Hames, minor about 16 years, chose Robt. Mathis guardian. Bond: Aaron Pinson and Gabriel Joel.

(No date) Estate sale of JOSEPH WILLIAMS, dec'd. Purchasers: Geo. Adams, David Adams, John Yager, Wm. Smith, Wm. Willams, Elizabeth Williams, Jos. Bolton, Stephen Gains, Wm. Saxon, Gray Yager, Eliz. Waldrop, Jos. South, Saml Saxon, Danl South, Wm. Powell, Elijah Howell, Elisha Williams, James South, Mary Howell, Margaret Braden, John McGee, Mikel Marlow, John Hutson, Terrel Andrews, Mathew Bolton, Lewis Watson, David Henderson, Thos. Adkins, John Roberson, Saml Freeman, John Hazel, Wm. Williams, Martin Pugh, Henry Box. Adm: Elizabeth Williams.

(No date) Appraisal of estate of SAMUEL WRIGHT, dec'd by Danl. Williams, Elijah Watson and Charles Wilson.

12 Dec. 1808. RICHARD FERGUSON, dec'd. Inventory of estate not made, statement by Geo. McCrary, one of the exrs.

5 Jan. 1809. Appraisal of estate of JOHN BONDS, dec'd by Patrick Scott, Saml. Canady and John Dillard. 17 Jan. 1809. Sale of estate. Adm: Elizabeth Bonds.

6 Mar. 1809. Adm. of estate of WM. FRANKS, dec'd to wife Sarah. Sec: Chas. Allen and Robt. Franks.

20 Mar. 1809. Adm. of estate of ISAAC SHARP, dec'd to wife Betsey. Sec: Andrew McNight and Aaron Moore.

18 Apr. 1809. Adm. of estate of JOHN FERGUSON, dec'd to Chas. Ferguson. Sec: Geo. McCrary(?) and Geo. Ross.

18 Apr. 1809. Adm. of estate of DAVID NEEL, dec'd to wife Frances Neel. Sec: Francis Allison.

7 Apr. 1809. Inventory of estate of WM. FRANKS, dec'd by Jacob Nabours, John Rodgers and John Williams.

1 Apr. 1809. Inventory of estate of ISAAC SHARP, dec'd by Wm. Choice, Chas. Mathis, Andw McNight and John McDonald.

28 May 1809. Will of ELIZABETH JONES, dec'd proven by John Cook, Elijah George. Edward and John Jones as exrs. 6 Apr. 1809. Will of ELIZABETH JONES, widow of Edward Jones. Sons Gabriel, James and Josiah Jones; daughters Frances Ward, Marey Burnside and Nancey Burnside; other children Edward, John, Thomas, Eliza- beth, Sarah, Margret and Lucy Jones. Exrs: sons Edward and John. Wit: John Cook, Elijah George and Nancy George.

5 June 1809. Will of WILLIAM HARDIN, dec'd proven by John Cole and John McClure. Exrs: Nicholas Hardin and Geo. Hardin. 20 May 1809. Will of WILLIAM HARDING. Wife; son Abner's widow Su- sannah and his children; son Abraham; daughter Sally; son Wil- liam; daughter Elizabeth; son Nicholas; son George; son Henry. Exr: Nicholas and George Harding. Wit: Zadoc Wood, John McClure, and John Cole.

5 June 1809. Will of JEREMIAH GLENN, dec'd proven by Richard Shackelford, John Davis with Jeremiah and Wm. Glenn as exrs. 22 Dec. 1807. Will of JEREMIAH GLENN. Wife Annie; son Tiree; daughters Frances Craighead, Sarah Garland Walker, Martha New- step Moon; son Blackgrove; daughter Mary Mason; son Jeremiah; son William; daughter Elizabeth Walker. Exr: wife Annie, sons Jeremiah and William. Wit: John Dawes, Richd Shackelford and Robt. Pasley.

5(?) June 1809. Will of HAISTON(?) DIAL, dec'd by Asa Turner and _____ (not clear). Haisten and Isaac Dial exrs. 17 Apr. 1809. Will of HASTINGS DIAL. Wife Rebekah; sons Hastings and Isaac; sons-in-law Mabra Madden, Abraham Madden and John Woody; son James; grandson Hastings, son of James and wife Elizabeth. Exr: wife and sons Isaac and Hastings. Wit: John Godfrey, Asa Turner and John Cochran.

5 June 1809. Adm. of estate of BENJAMIN ALLEN, dec'd by wife Elizabeth Allen. Sec: Robt. Word and James Saxon.

5 June 1809. Adm. of estate of THOMAS HARDIN, dec'd to wife Sarah. Sec: J. Johnston and David Clopton.

7 Dec. 1808. Appraisal of estate of NATHANIEL ROOK, dec'd by James Ward, John Rusing, John Deale and Saml. Goodman. 19 Dec. 1808. Estate sale. Notes on Emanuel Rooks, Vines Dayley. Mentions John Maires. Adm: J. Cook.

2 Nov. 1808. Inventory of estate of SAMUEL BOWLING, dec'd by Solomon Hopkins, Thos. Braden and John Arnold.

(No date) Appraisal of estate of NANCY REASE, dec'd by John Pugh, John Spurgin and Edw. Pugh.

8 Dec. 1808. Inventory of estate of WM. DORROH, dec'd by L. Saxon, Jos. Downs, Wm. Arnold and John Burrow. 19 Dec. 1808. Estate sale. Purchasers: Geo. Swindle, Wm. South, Henry Strange,

Estate sale cont'd:
Robt. Barrett(Garrett?), Aaron Jones, John D. Cunningham, John
P. Cunningham. Elijah Adams, John Blakely, James Dorrah, Wm.
Downing, Wm. Roberson, Saml. McGladery, Pleasant Blackwell,
John Morrison, Saml. Wair(Ware?), Reuben Arnold, John Cunning-
ham, Sr., Wm. Ryley, Saml. Dunlap, Abraham Box, Henry Mitchell,
John Almond(Atwood?), Nathl. Roberson, Rebecca Gray, El. Gray,
Jesse Sanders, Aaron Glore, John Dial, Wm. Cole, James Parker,
Wm. Parker, Wm. Cunningham, Robt. Box, Jacob Box, Robt. Todd,
John Hollingsworth, James Hollingsworth, John Nabours, E. Casey,
Thos. Hellams, James Dorrah, John Dorrah, James McDavid, John
McDavid, N. Roberson, John Baswell, James Yager, Brice Dunlap,
Robt. Mathis, John Dorrah (son of William Dorrah), Mary Pugh,
John Roberson, Nathl. Roberson, David Ross, Saml. McClurken,
Saml. Drummond, John Gray, Robt. Gray, Robt. Lowry, Robt. Bry-
son, Benj. Nabours, N. Dorrah, John Myres, Nancy Dorrah, Mr.
Cooper, Wm. Downs, Thos. Taylor, Nathl. Nabours, Jos. Box,
John Blackstock, David Cowen, Henry Box, Alex. McHerg, Clabourn
Sims, Andw. Mathis, Wm. Millwee, James Downing, James Ware,
R. Allison. Adm: James Dorrough.

17 Aug. 1809. Will of ANGUS CAMPBELL, dec'd proven by John
Nickles, Wm. Burnside, Jonathan Johnston. Robt. Campbell as
exr.

8 Aug. 1809. Will of ANDREW PARKS, dec'd proven by Robt. Hutchison and James Hunter. Wife and James Parks qualified as exrs.
and also to adm. estate.

1 Aug. 1809. Will of ANGUS CAMPBELL, planter. Heirs of my son
Angus and his wife Milley; sons Robert and Lewellen; daughter
Patsey and husband Jesse Paine; daughter Jane and husband Jon-
athan Johnston; daughter Sarah and husband Robt. Cunningham.
Exr: Jonathan Johnston and Robt. Campbell. Wit: John Nickels,
Wm. F. Burnside and James Ward.

4 July 1809. Adm. of estate of JOHN PARKER, dec'd granted to
wife Sarah Parker. Sec: John Pitts, Theophilus Goodwin.

2 Feb. 1809. Will of ANDREW PARK. Sons James, Wm. and Andrew;
daughters Mary(?) and Isabel Fowler, Nancy, Sarah and Betsey
Park. Wife Agnes Park. Mentions land of Col. John Simpson on
James Hunter. Exr: wife Anges and son James. Wit: Robt. Hutchison, James Hunter, James Park, Sr. Codicil wit. by R. Hutcheson
and Wm. Fulton.

2 Oct. 1809. Adm. of estate of JOSEPH HALL, dec'd to wife Margaret Hall. Sec: Jos. Deen and John Fowler.

21 Aug. 1809. Adm. of estate of JOHN ROWLING, dec'd to wife
Betsey. Sec: John Walker and Silvanus Walker revoked and now
granted to Lewis Graves, sec: Jacob Niswanger and Wm. Crocker.

14 Oct.1809. Adm. of estate of JAMES SULLIVANT, dec'd to John
Osborn. Sec: Benj. Strange and Chas. Plant.

14 Oct. 1809. Adm. of estate of JESSE SMITH, dec'd to Harriet(?)
Smith and Mikel Finney. Sec: Josiah Evans and Nimrod Overby.

20 Jan. 1809. Second sale of estate of JOHN ROWLAND, dec'd.
Purchasers: Elizabeth Rowland, Geo. Joel, John Boyce. Adm:
Betsey Rowland.

2 May 1809. Inventory of estate of JOHN FERGUSON, dec'd by Thos. Lesley, Jos. Jones and David Boyce.

11 Aug. 1809. Inventory of estate of ANDREW PARK, dec'd by John Simpson, John Hunter, James Park and Robt. Hutcheson.

6 May 1809. Estate sale of WILLIAM FRANKS, dec'd. Purchasers: Sarah Franks, Wm. Hall(?). Adm: Sarah Franks.

21 Jan. 1809. Second sale of estate of JOHN MASON, dec'd. Purchasers: Philip Anderson, John Bennet, James Jones, Miles Jones, Jesse Jones, John Jones, Dred Jones, Fredk(?) Jones, Absalom Howel, Hicks Wesson, Bryson(?) Bardley. Exr: Jesse Jones.

19 May 1809. Estate sale of JOHN FERGUSON, dec'd. Adm: Charles Ferguson.

(No date) Appraisal of estate of DAVID NEEL, dec'd by Jos. Lyon, Francis Allison and Benj. Brown. 13 May 1809. Sale of estate. Adm: Frances Neel.

16 Dec. 1809. Sale of estate of LITTLE B. SULLIVAN, dec'd. Purchasers: Benj. Strange, Nancy Sullivan, Hul. Sullivan, Menoah Sullivan, Wm. Simmons, John Rodgers, Menoah Sullivan, Sr., Wm. Osborn, Sr., John Bolt, Adam Garmon, Jeremiah Glenn, Robt. Allison, John Joel, Wm. Moore, Larkin Sullivan. Adm: Nancy Sullivan. 1 July 1808. Estate sale of LANEY JASON, dec'd. Purchasers: Saml. Caldwell, Lazarus Hitt, James Caldwell, Stephen Owens, James Golden, Matthew Hunter, Robt. Hambleton, Moses Curnal, Danl. Rodgers, Phebe Williams, Wm. George, James Hambleton. Adm: Samuel Caldwell.

9 Aug. 1809. Appraisal of estate of ELIZABETH JONES, dec'd by Thos. Cummins, John Armstrong, John Gates and Elijah George.

29 July 1809. Appraisal of estate of WM. HARDING, dec'd by Joel Mason, Thos. Dalrymple, John Strong and John McClure.

29 Apr. 1809. Estate sale of ISAAC SHARP, dec'd. Purchasers: Drury Boyce, Larkin Stephens, John Deen, Jonathan Deen, Felt. Hatcher, John Crowder, Andw. Mathis, John Harris, Jos. McKinley, Betsy Sharp, Betsy Vance, David Peden, John Nash, John Howard, John House, Alex. Peden, Geo. Crowder, Thos. Mathis, John McDonnal, John Terry, Andw. McKnight, Peter Evans, Thos. House, Philip House, John Mathews, James Brown, Saml. Peden, Wm. Mathews and Wm. McMahan. Adm: Betsy Sharp.

30 Oct. 1809. Appraisal of estate of JOSEPH HALL, dec'd by James Leatherwood, Henry Meredith, James Fowler and Wm. Ward.

20 Oct. 1809. Appraisal of estate of JESSE SMITH, dec'd by John Sadler, Matthew Hunter and Meshack Overby. (No date) Sale of estate. Purchasers: wife Hariot, John and James Smith, Reuben Golden, James Strain, Nimrod and Meshack Oberby, Mikel Finney, Josiah Evans, Drummond Day.

7 July 1809. Appraisal of estate of JOHN PARKER, dec'd by David Studdard (page torn). Cert. by Lewis Cargill. (No date) Sale of estate. No purchasers named. Debts owing to James Higgens, Wm. Hill, Wm. Hellams, Jonathan Owens. Adm: Sarah Parker.

30 June 1809. Appraisal of estate of THOMAS HARDING, dec'd by

Appraisal cont'd:
Ainsworth Middleton, Jesse Johnston and John Copeland. (No date)
Sale of estate of THOS. HARDING, dec'd. Purchasers: (page torn)
Sarah Harding, John Black, Alexr. Holland, Abram Holland, John
Gambel, Geo. Gambel, James Harding, David Griffin, David Clop-
ton, John Copeland(?), Ward Ferguson, Joel Johnston, Chas. Hard-
ing, Robt. Stewart, Miles Ferguson, Jos. Young, Wm. Glazebrook.

29 July 1809. Appraisal of estate of HASTINGS DIAL, dec'd by
David Hallems, John Cochran, Wm. Hubbs(?) and Robt. Allison.

(Date not clear) Sale of estate of JACOB ROBERTS, dec'd. (N.B.
this writing is very dim). Purchasers: Mary Roberts, Wm. Gilbert,
Robt. Fleming, John Gibbs, Isaac Roberts, John Roberts, Archd.
Young, Isaiah Deen, Jos. Deen, Chas. Cox, Wm. Brown, Jacob Roberts, John Pugh, Caleb Hughs, Thos. Kevil, John Spurgin, Jacob
Cooper, John Meador, Danl. Wright, James Holcomb, Wm. Pugh (rest
not clear).

27 Apr. 1809. Appraisal of estate of JAMES SULLIVAN, dec'd by
John Boyd, Thos. Hunter, and John Madden.

(No date) Will of ROBERT PASLEY, dec'd proven over protest of
son James Pasley, and over-ruled. Wife Elizabeth Pasley qualified
as exr. Will ordered recorded.

END OF WILL BOOK C

START OF WILL BOOK D

6 Jan. 1810. Will of THOMAS LINDLEY, dec'd proven by Chas. Smith
and Colville Abercrombie. Elizabeth, James and William Lindley
qualified as exrs. D. Anderson, Ord. 18 Oct. 1809. Will of THOMAS
LINDLEY. Sons James and William; land mentioned of James Wilson,
Charles Smith, Colville Abercrombie; daughters Mary Abercrombie
and Nancy Bolt; wife Elizabeth; youngest sons Thomas, Aquilla,
John, Jonathan and Henry Lindley; daughters Elizabeth, Hanna
and Sarah. Exr: wife and sons James and Wm. Wit: Chas. Smith,
Colville Abercrombie and John Abercrombie.

16 Dec. 1809. Adm. of estate of JAMES SULLIVANT, dec'd to John
Osborn revoked by mutual consent; now granted to Randel Sullivant. Sec: Thos. Porter, Wm. Lowe, Thos. Hunter, Wm. Madden
and Chas. Madden.

(No date) Inventory of estate of ANGUISH CAMPBELL, dec'd by
Wm. Burnside, John Cook, Thos. Ligon and James Strain.

4 Jan. 1810. Inventory of estate of JAMES SULLIVANT, dec'd by
Menoah Sullivan, Benj. Adkins and John Madden.

(No date) Second appraisal of estate of ANDREW PARK, dec'd by
John Simpson, John Hunter and James Park.

27 Jan. 1810. Inventory of estate of THOMAS LINDLEY, dec'd by
Chas. Smith, Colville Abercrombie and Jesse Garrett.

24 Nov. 1809. Inventory of estate of JEREMIAH GLENN, dec'd by
Thos. Burnside, Isaac Mitchell and James Young. (date not clear)
Estate sale. Purchasers: Glanus Winn, Jeremiah Glenn, Wm. Walker,
Jeremiah Connant, John Black, Wm. Glenn, Jones Fuller, John
Harris, D. McCaa, Chas. Dendy, Stephen Wharton, Jno. Baley,

Estate sale cont'd:
Henry Fuller, John Moore, Thos. Burnside, Richd Shackelford, Tyre Glenn. Exr: Jeremiah and Wm. Glenn. 7-8 Dec. 1809. Second sale. Purchasers: Thos. Dendy, Jer. Glenn, B. Wilks, Mr. Mandley, Artis Cook, Blackgrove Glenn, Joel Carter, Geo. Roberts, D. McCaa, Benj. James, Wm. Rogers, Tyree Glenn, Wm. Moon(Moore?), John Bailey, Harmon Miller, Robt. Pasley, Danl. Mitchell, John Harris, Jacob Miller, Wm. Winn, Thos. Rodgers, Edmond Strange, Frances Medley, Danl. M. Winn, Jas. Culberson, Jones Fuller. Exr: Jer. and Wm. Glenn.

5 Feb.1810. Adm. of estate of ABRAHAM TINSLEY, dec'd to Nancy Tinsley revoked and Henry Johnson qualified as exr. and names in will produced by him. 5 Jan. 1804. Will of ABRAHAM TINSLEY. Wife Nancy; son William and daughter Sarah and Mary; debt to be paid to Jos. Cason collected from Chas. Huet (Hewett?). Exr: brother James Tinsley, father-in-law Henry Johnson and wife Nancy Tinsley. Wit: Frances Stewart, Geo. Dalrymple and Elijah Teague. 9 Feb. 1810. Appraisal of estate by Jonathan Blakely, John McCelvy and John Copeland.

17 Mar. 1810. Will of MOLLY ANDERSON, SR, dec'd proven by Mena Ann Cobb, Polly and Andw. Anderson, Jr. as exrs. 6 Sept. 1809. Will of MOLLY ANDERSON. Son Andrew and daughter Molly. Exr: Andw and Molly. Wit: Mena Ann Cobb.

17 Mar. 1810. Return of adm. of JONATHAN OWINGS, dec'd est. to wife Nancy Owings. Sec: Richard Owings and Saml. Dunlap. 31 Mar. 1810. Appraisal of estate of JONATHAN OWINGS, dec'd by Archibald Owings, Thos. Goodwin, Jas. Dunlap and Wm. Owings. 2 Apr. 1810. Sale of estate. Purchasers: Nancy, William and Archibald Owings, Richd. Owings, Adam McVickery, Thos. Childers, Elijah Whitfield, Kellet Sims, Jos. Brown, Wm. Hill, Jas. and Saml. Dunlap, Wm. Garrett, Aaron Black(?), Thos. Farrow, Jas. Moore, Geo. Walker, Jos. Holcomb, Saml. Green. Notes due on Fleming Hatcher, Stephen Fountain, Jas. Smith, Chas. Smith, Wm. Watson, Wm. Tinch. Adm: Nancy Owings.

(No date) Sale of estate of JOHN PARKER, dec'd. Adm: Sarah Parker.

3 Apr. 1810. Letters of adm. of estate of FRANCES GRIFFIN, dec'd to John Cook. Sec: John Roberson.

25 Jan. 1808. Inventory of estate of WM. JOHNSTON, dec'd by David Mason, David Greer. (No date) Sale of estate. Exr: John Monroe.

16 Jan. 1810. Second sale of estate of WILLIAM BRYSON, dec'd. Exr: Wm. Blakely and C. Little.

17 Apr. 1810. Letters of adm. of estate of ALLEN EAST, dec'd to Wm. Miller. Sec: Richard Milner(?) and John Milner.

11 Apr. 1810. Letters of adm. of estate of JOHN EAST, dec'd to same as above. Sec: the same as above.

5 Mar. 1810. John Harris, minor about 15 years, chose Jinney Harris as guardian. Sec: John Richey and Richd. Hodges.

23 Apr. 1810. Inventory of estate of JOHN EAST, dec'd by Wm. Dunlap, Alexr. Glenn and Samuel Henderson. (Same date) Inventory of estate of ALLEN EAST, dec'd by same appr's.

12 May 1810. Sale of estate of JOHN EAST, dec'd. Same date - sale of estate of ALLEN EAST, dec'd. No purchasers named in either. Adm: Wm. Millner.

2 June 1810. Letters of adm. estate of JOHN ROWLING, dec'd to Martin Shaw replacing Lewis Graves, dec'd. Sec: Wm. Crocker and John Boyce.

9 June 1810. Letters of adm. estate of LEWIS GRAVES, dec'd to Martin Graves. Sec: Wm. Moore, John Wait and Jacob Niswanger.

12 July 1810. Polly Williams, minor about 16 years, chose James Powell as guardian. Sec: Reuben Powell and Jos. Box.
18 July 1810. Letters of adm. estate of JOHN SIMMONS, dec'd to wife Catey Simmons. Sec: Elijah Walker and James Simmons.

6 Aug. 1810. Will of JOHN GRIZEL, dec'd proven by Wm. Craig, Wm. Grizel and Stephen Grizel(?). Exr: Elizabeth Grizel. 6 Mar. 1810. Will of JOHN GRIZEL. Wife Elizabeth; daughters Juda Gary and Nancy Grizel; mentions all the rest of my children. Exr: wife Elizabeth. Wit: Wm. Craig, Wm. Grizel, Stephen Gary and John McClure.

(No date) Appraisal of estate of LEWIS GRAVES, dec'd by John Wait, Jacob Niswanger and Wm. Moore.

5 July 1810. Letters of adm. estate of JAMES ALLISON, dec'd to wife Susannah Allison. Sec: Isaac Gray and Jesse Rease. 11 July 1810. Appraisal of estate. Mentions property given Jesse Reese, husband of Nancy, daughter of the dec'd. By Archibald Young, Isaac Gray and Danl. Bragg. 26 July 1810. Sale of estate. Purchasers: Susannah Allison, John Spurgen, Thos. Parks, Jas. Parks, Thos. Pope, Archd. Young, Elijah Chism, Wm. Pedden, Thos. Campbell, Nathl. Garrett, Wm. Pugh, Jos. Downey, Wm. Arnold, Henry Tompson, John Tompson,John Pew, John Riddle, Caleb Woodruff, Willis Cheake, Jas. Owings, Danl. Wright, Stepn. Garrett, Harmon Garrett, Newton Higgins, Danl. Bragg, Edw. Garrett, Saml. Woodruff, Wm. Talley, Wair Long, John Robertson, Jas. Fowler, Saml. Parks. Adm: Susannah Allison.

15 Sept. 1810. Appraisal of estate of JOHN SIMMONS, dec'd by Aaron Clore, Richd Gaines, Elijah Walker.

24 Aug. 1810. Appraisal of estate of JOHN GRIZEL, dec'd by David Temple, Sr., David Temple, Jr. and Wm. Alexander.

12 Nov. 1810. Return of adm. of estate of JOSEPH RENALETT(?), dec'd to Dugless J. Puckett. (N.B. this name may be Puckett but is not clear). Sec: Jas. Dillard and Jos. Williams.

1 Dec. 1810. Letters of adm. of estate of JUDA MADDOX, dec'd to John and James Young. Sec: Saml. Henderson and Wm. Dunlap.

9 Dec.1810. Letters of adm. of estate of SAMUEL WARD, dec'd to wife Susannah Ward. Sec: Wm. Ligon (and another Ligon not clear).

24 Dec. 1810. Will of BRITTON FULLER, dec'd proven by Zach. Bailey, Jr. and Wm. Bailey. Exr: wife Delphy Fuller. 10 Sept. 18-08. Will of BRITTON FULLER. Wife Delphy. Exr: wife. Wit: Zach. Bailey, Jr., Wm. Bailey, Sr. and Wm. Bailey, Jr.

(No date) Estate sale of JAMES SULLIVAN, dec'd. Purchasers: John Madden, Larkin Sullivan, Wm. Martin, Thos. Davenport, Benj. Strange. Adm: Randel Sullivan.

7 Jan. 1811. Letters of adm. of estate of DAVID BRADLEY, dec'd to John Meador. Sec: Thos. Parks and John Spurgen.

7 Jan. 1811. Letters of adm. of estate of MATTHEW CUNNINGHAM, dec'd to widow Susannah Cunningham. Sec: Benj. Nabours and Robt. Allen.

19 Jan. 1811. Letters of adm. of estate of JOHN WILKINSON, dec'd to Alexander Wilkinson. Sec: James Dillard and George McCrary.

(No date) Estate sale of MIKEL PURTZ, dec'd. Adm: P. G. Wharton.

(No date) Estate sale of LEWIS GRAVES, dec'd. Purchasers: Rebecah Graves, Wm. Graves, Lewis Graves, Fanney Graves, Martin Graves, Moses Madden, Geo. Madden, Jacob Niswanger, John Adams, John Willard(?), Richd. Golden, John Newman, Wm. Crocker, John Creecy, John Boyce, Martin Shaw, Jas. Sims, Martin Sims, Geo. Morgan, John Wait, Jos. Bolton, Wm. McFerson, Isaac Mosely, Larkin Gaines, Saml. Anderson, Thos. Brock, Ebenezer Harris. Adm: Martin Graves and Wm. Graves.

16 Jan. 1811. Appraisal of estate of SAMUEL WARD, dec'd by John Cook, Wm. Flemming and Elijah Watson.

(No date) Memo. of property sold of estate of JACOB GILL, dec'd. Purchasers: Jesse Belton, David Speers, Alex. Henry, Robt. Richey, Andw. Studdords(?), Jno. Gordon, Moses Hill, M. Cunningham, Mary Gill, Henry Green, Jas. Blakely, Benj. Gill.

5 Feb. 1811. Appraisal of estate of WILLIAM WILKINSON, dec'd by Geo. McGrary, Simon Reeder and David Littel. 5 Feb. 1811. Estate sale. Purchasers: Wm. Grayham, Mary Wilkinson, John Fryer, Wm. Roberson, Jos. Adair, Thos. Beasley, Alex. Wilkinson, John Pucket, Wm. Gray, Jas. Dunklin(?), Martin Burk, Jason Meador, Elisha Adair, Jas. Blakely. Adm: Alexr. Wilkinson.

(No date) Second appraisal of estate of LEWIS GRAVES, dec'd by John Wait, Jacob Niswanger and Wm. Moore.

8 Dec. 1810. Appraisal of estate of JUDAH MADDOX, dec'd by Alex. Glenn, Abner Pyles and Wm. Dunlap. 26 Dec. 1810. Estate sale. Purchasers: Robt. Gray, Saml. Hudgens, Jas. Young, Jno. Young, Hugh O'Nail, Saml. C. Henderson, Jas. Clardy, Geo. Wolff, Jno. Monroe, Jno. Maddox, Abraham Johnston, Abner Johnston, Jno. Crawford, Thos. Casey, Thos. Dalrymple, Andw. Wilson, Jno. Simpson, Andw. Winn, Israel Teague, Abner Pyles, Benj. Drake, Jos. Blakely, Wm. Farrow, Wm. McMurtrey, Wm. Wilson, David Jones, Mathew McMurtrey, Saml. Dalrymple, Thos. Wilks, Jos. Blakely, Jeremiah McCluskey, Danl. Winn. Adm: John and James Young.

1 Nov. 1810. Estate sale of JOHN SIMMONS, dec'd. Purchasers: Caty and James Simmons, Aaron Clore, Moses Myers, Jona. Gaines, Danl. Ford, Joshua Nobles, Geo. Teague, Reuben and James Powell, Jos. and Danl. South, John Young, Thos. Johnston, Jas. Jones, Norman Drummons, Harrison Daniel, Bruce Posey, Jno. South, Jno. Pringle, Edw. Ware, Jno. Cox, Reuben Carter, Steph. Gaines, Ezekiel Powell. Adm: Caty Simmons.

11 Mar. 1811. Will of JOHN JONES, dec'd proven by Thos. Hill.
Wit: Thos. and Robt. Hill . (N.B. Hill may be Hall). Joyce Jones
and Robt. Ward (Word?) qualify as exr. 7 Sept. 1804. Will of
JOHN JONES. Wife Joyce; niece Joyce J. Ward; nephews Jones and
Moses Foster. Exr: wife and friends Robt. Ward and Jones Foster.
Wit: Thos. Hall, Dennett(Bennett?) Hill, Saml. B. Shepard, Chas.
McGee. Wit. of codicil: Thos. Hill, Wm. Pollard and Jno. Owen.

12 Jan. 1811. Appraisal of estate of DAVID BRADLEY, dec'd by
Wm. Gilbert, Wm. Howard, Jno. Pugh and Jno. Spurgen. (No date)
Estate sale. Purchasers: Nancy, Elizabeth and Jane Bradley,
Jno. Meador, Andw. Edwards, Jas. Kilgore, Starling Tucker, Jno.
Pugh, Jno. and Jas. Crumpton, Jno. Alexander, Jacob Roberts,
Wm. Peden, Thos. Austin, Casander Ford, Mary (or Nancy) Glaze-
brook, Nicklus Garrett, Thos. Kevil, J. D. Mitcherson, Jas.
Vaughn, Abner Smith, Jonth Davis, Thos. Burchfield, Harriet
Richards, Henry Brockman, Jno. Roberts, Mary Glazebrook, Jacob
League. Adm: John Meador.

7 Jan. 1811. Appraisal of estate of BRITTON FULLER, dec'd by
Zach. Bailey, Jr., Geo. Roberts, and Wm. Bailey.

22 Mar. 1811. Appraisal of estate of JOHN JONES, dec'd by Jno.
Watts, Thos. Hill and Jas. Atwood.

16 Apr. 1811. Letters of adm. of estate of JOSEPH COUCH, dec'd
to wife Nancy Couch. Sec: Elijah Watson and Drury Couch.

4 June 1811. Will of DANIEL OWENS, dec'd proven by Jno. Owens
and Mary Long. Thos. Owens, Exr. 29 Mar. 1811. Will of DANIEL
OWENS. Mother Mary Owens; brothers Thomas and Robert Owens;
mentions land bought of Alex. McQuay; sisters Martha Cabaness,
Ann, Jennet and Elizabeth Owens. Exr: bro. Thos. Owens. Wit:
Jno. Owens, Mary Long and Elizabeth Owens.

(No date) Appraisal of estate of JOSEPH COUCH, dec'd by Peter
Hammond, Thos. Goodwin and Ezekiel Mathis.

July 1811. Letters of adm. of estate of FRANCES HENDERSON, dec'd
to Jesse Garrett. Sec: Reuben Martin and Ellis Cheek.

11 July 1811. Will of JOHN PINSON, dec'd proven by Robt. Carter,
Sr. and Robt. Carter, Jr. Howard and Thos. Pinson as exrs. 26
June 1811. Will of JOHN PINSON. Wife Betsey; sons John, Howard,
Thomas and Aaron; sons-in-law Wm. Strain, Richard Duty, Cornelius
Pucket, Thomas Weathers. Exr: sons Howard and Thos. Pinson.
Wit: Robt. Carter, Sr., Robt. Carter, Jr.and Richd. Pucket.

15 Sept. 1811. Letters of adm. of estate of NORMAN DRUMMON,
dec'd to wife Milley Drummon. Sec: Geo. Swindle and Aaron Clore.

16 Sept. 1811. Letters of adm. estate of CRAFFORD LEWIS, dec'd
to wife Phebey Lewis. Sec: Benj. Lewis and Stephen Spark.

(No date) Appraisal of estate of FRANCES HENDERSON, dec'd by
Chas. Smyth, John F. Wolff and Colville Abercrombie. 16 July
1811. Estate sale. Adm: Jesse Garrett.

10 Aug. 1811. Appraisal of estate of JOHN PINSON, dec'd by Jon.
Johnston, Robt. Carter, Jr., Robt. Carter, Sr. and James Nickles.

19 Feb. 1811. Appraisal of estate of MATHEW CUNNINGHAM, dec'd

Appraisal cont'd:
by B. Nabours, Robt. McNees and Robt. Allison. 14 Mar. 1811.
Estate sale of MATHEW CUNNINGHAM, dec'd. Purchasers: Mrs. Cunningham, David Cowen, Benj. Strange, Jno. Rodgers, Wm. Osborn,
Robt. Allison, Benj. Nabours, Wm. Hudgens. Adm: Susannah Cunningham.

(No date) Appraisal of estate of DANIEL OWENS, dec'd by Reuben
Meadors, Abram Holland, Thos. Martin. Exr: Thos. Owens.

12 July 1811. Estate sale of JOSEPH COUCH, dec'd. Purchasers:
Anna Couch(?), Mrs. Roady, Mrs. Nelly Couch, Jos. Couch, Jas.
Couch, Isaac Couch, Jno. Stewart, Edw. Gillespie, Wm. Nobles,
Drury Couch. Adm: Anny Couch.

28 Oct. 1811. Will of JOYCE JONES, dec'd proven by Jno. Nickless
and Robt. Ward. Danl. Jones, exr. 17 July 1811. Will of JOYCE
JONES. Daniel Jones, son of Harrison Jones. Exr: Danl. Jones
and Capt. Jno. Watts. Wit: Zach. Meriwether, Jno. Nickles and
Robt. Ward.

18 Nov. 1811. Re JOHNSTON MONFORD, dec'd. J. A. Elmore comm.
to qualify wife Easter Monford as admx. Sec: Levi Fowler and
Geo. Whitmore. 26 Oct. 1811. Appraisal of estate by J. Boyce,
J. McCoy and Wm. Dillard. 19 Nov. 1811. Petition of Easter Monford unable to attend made by her father and brother for order
of sale of estate. Granted.

18 Nov. 1811. Letters of adm. of estate of CHARLES SMITH, dec'd
to widow Lucy Smith. Sec: Chas. and Lydall Allen.

3 Oct. 1811. Appraisal of estate of CRAFORD LEWIS, dec'd by
Elijah Teague, Job Mason and Lewis Linville.

(No date) Appraisal of estate of NORMAN DRUMMOND, dec'd by Reuben
Arnold, Richd. Gaines and Robt. Gaines. (No date) Estate sale.
Purchasers: Geo. Swindle, Edw. Ware, Danl. Drummond, Moses Myers,
Robt. Delph(?), Milley Drummond, Geo. Bradey, Jas. Kenney, Robt.
Gaines, Jonathan Gaines, Jas. Hendrick, Edw. Kenney, Jas. Godfrey, Thos. Godfrey, Wm. Swindle, Geo. Teague(?), Wm. Powell,
Ezekiel Powell. Adm: Milley Drummond.

3 Dec. 1811. Letters of adm. estate of JOHN BOYCE, dec'd to
Jas. Young. Sec: Jno. Creecy and Jno. Roberson.

19 Mar. 1811. Estate sale of SAMUEL WARD, dec'd. Purchasers:
Susannah Ward, Peter Ligon, Chas. Wilson. Adm: Susannah Ward.
5 Jan. 1812. Letters of adm. estate of BENJAMIN RAMMAGE, dec'd
to wife Elender Rammage. Sec: Jas. Adair.

23 Dec. 1811. Peter, Mary Ann and Archibald Fuller, minor children of Isom Fuller, dec'd chose Jones Fuller as guardian. All
over the age of 14.

13 Jan. 1812. Tully Francis Sullivan, minor child of James Sullivan, Jr., dec'd chose Nancy Sullivan as guardian until age
of 21 years.

3 Dec. 1811. Appraisal of estate of CHARLES SMITH, dec'd by
Jonathan Downs, J. P. Wolff, Abraham Bolt and Colville Abrecrombie.

15 Oct. 1811. Estate sale of CRAFFORD LEWIS, dec'd. Purchasers: widow Lewis, Joshua Teague, Benj. Lewis, Zach. Sparks, Isaac Gray, Geo. Leeke, Jno. Bell, Mercer Entrekin, Ainsworth Middleton, David Mason, Thos. Dalrymple, Jno. Stewart, Robt. Stewart, Matthew Hunter, Matthew Simpson. Adm: Phebe Lewis.

15 Nov. 1811. Estate sale of JOHN PINSON, dec'd. Purchasers: Howard Pinson, Thos. Pinson, Jno. Pinson, Elizabeth Pinson, Aaron Pinson, Jno. Roberson, Sr., Jno. Roberson, Jr., Robt. Roberson, Wm. Roberson, Thos. Weathers, Saml. Swancy, Jas. Swancy, Richd. Puckett, Cornelius Puckett, Jas. Puckett, Cornelius Cargill, Nimrod Overby, Meshack Overby, Isaac George, Jno. Brown, Robt. Nickles, Jas. Henderson, Pleasant Wright, Jno. B. Long, Jas. Strain, Andw. Nelson, Ransom Davenport, Jones Fuller, Jas. Atwood, Jno. Creecy, Jno. Cunnningham, Saml. Wheeler, Andw. McWilliams, Jno. McWilliams, Dvaid Stephens, Jas. Caldwell, Robt. Cunningham, Joel Carter, David Brown, Thos. Sims, Jno. Richey, Joel Hughes, Moses Cole, Jno. Sims, Robt. Carter, Jr., David Whiteford, Chas. Harvey. Exr: Howard Pinson and Thos. Pinson.

15 Jan. 1812. Will of DR. JOHN CREECY. Wife Elizabeth Creecy and her children by Zachariah Sims, dec'd; Fanney Clemmons, wife of Jacob Clemmons and her son Zachariah Simpson(?); John Wait; Joel Sims; James Sims; David Anderson. Exr: friends David Anderson and Robt. Cunningham. Wit: John Wait, John Middleton and Frances Wait.

(No date) Appraisal of estate of BENJAMIN RAMMAGE, dec'd by Jno. Owens, Josiah Prater, Jno. Prater and Bazel Prater.

20 Dec. 1811. Estate sale of DANIEL OWENS, dec'd. Purchasers: Thos. Owens, Robt. Owens, Elijah Cabness, Abraham Holland, Thos. Beasley. Exr: Thos. Owens.

10 Dec. 1811. Appraisal of estate of JOYCE JONES, dec'd by Jno. Cook, Jas. Watts and Jas. Atwood.

(No date) Estate sale of JOHNSTON MUNFORD, dec'd. Purchasers: David Gamble, Jno. Gamble, Easter Munford, Jas. Munford, Jno. Finney, Josiah Duckett, Jobe Johnston. Adm: Esater Munford.

2 Feb. 1812. Letters of adm. estate of ELIZABETH HUGHS, dec'd to Cracey Calhoon and Anne Calhoon. Sec: Bailey Mahon and Wm. Downs.

9 Feb. 1812. Re JOHN CREECY, dec'd. Robt. Cunningham qualified as exr. of will.

3 Mar. 1812. Susannah Wilks, minor over 14 years, chose Daniel M. Winn as guardian. Sec: Gallanus Winn and Andw. Wilson.

3 Dec. 1811. Appraisal of estate of JOHN BOYCE, dec'd by Dr. John Creecy, Martin Shaw and Jno. Roberson. 23 Dec. 1811. Estate sale. Purchasers: David Anderson, Dr. Creecy, Wm. Richey, Martin Shaw, Wm. Crocker, Jno. Roberson, Elizabeth Boyce, Joel Starns, Ebenezer Starns, Thos. Brock, Jacob Madden, Jacob Niswanger, Jno. Sims, Jr., Jno. Sims, Sr., Israel Couch, Thos. Rodgers, Benj. Garner, Robt. Roberson, Geo. Wharton, Zach. Arnold, Chas. Brock, Joel Carter, Thos. Pinson, Thos. Davenport, Cornelius Cargill, Geo. Joel. Adm: James Young.

21 Mar. 1812. Will of WILLIAM ROBERSON, dec'd proven by Jno. and Jos. Cook. Frederick Purtz, exr. 1 Mar. 1812. Will of WM. ROBERSON. Wife (not named); sons Thomas and Isom Roberson; dec'd son Robert Roberson and his legal heirs. Exr: Fredk. Purtz and Wm. Green, Sr. Wit: Jno. Cook, David Caldwell and Jos. Cook.

21 Mar. 1812. Will of JACOB WHITWORTH, dec'd of Jackson Co., Ga. proven by David Hill(?), Chas. Venable and Jos. Davis, cert. by Saml. Henderson, Judge. Fanney Whitworth, wife, as exr.

15 Feb. 1812. Appraisal of estate of JOHN CREECY, dec'd by Jno. Wait, Jno.Middleton and Robt. Redden. 14 Mar. 1812. Estate sale. Purchasers: Elizabeth Creecy, Jos. Neely, Robt. Cunningham, Jno. Cunningham, David Anderson, Jacob Niswanger, Jonathan Johnson, Martin Shaw, Thos. Sims, Wm. Redden, Thos. Adkins, David Caldwell, Zach. Warren, Philip Wait, Jno. Sims, Jas. Sims, Joel Sims, Wm. Moore. Cert. by Robt. Cunningham. Exr: David Anderson.

6 Apr. 1812. Letters of adm. estate of JAMES GARRETT, dec'd to Stephen Garrett. Sec:; Wm. Cross and Thos. Nabours.

18 Mar. 1812. Inventory of estate of ELIZABETH HUGHS, dec'd by Wm. Cunningham, Jas. Johnston and John Cunningham.

18 Apr. 1812. Ann Williams, minor about 15 years, chose James Reagan as guardian. Sec: Robt. Gains and Chas. Reagan.

18 Apr. 1812. Will of ROBERT HAMBLETON, dec'd proven by Robt. Hollingsworth and Samuel Goodman. Qualified as exrs: Robt. Hollingsworth and Reuben Hitt. 25 Feb. 1811. Will of ROBT. HAMBLETON. Wife Elizabeth; all my children including grandson Marshall Hill (Hitt?). Exr: Robt. Hollingsworth, Reuben Hitt. Wit: Saml. Goodman, Robt. Hollingsworth and Jno. Owen.

1 June 1812. Letters of adm. estate of SAMUEL GAREY, dec'd to Drury Coker. Sec: Stephen Garret(?) and Lydall Allen.

15 Mar. 1812. Estate sale of BENJAMIN RAMMAGE, dec'd. Adm: Elender Rammage.

(No date) Appraisal of estate of ROBERT HAMBLETON, dec'd by Alex. Austin, Jno. Owen and Saml. Goodman. (No date) Estate sale. Purchasers: Jas. Watts, Robt. Hollingsworth, Jas. Strain, Alexr. Austin, Thos. Crossmore, Wm. Fleming, Lazarus Hitt, Drury Sims, Thos. Crosson, Reuben Hitt, Jos. Rodgers, Jno. Gambel(?), Jusey Hill, Jno. Lygon, Patrick Tood(?), Woodson Ligon, Jno. Yares(?), Z. Burrell, Richd. Sims, Jas. Hambleton, Benj. Hitt. Exr: Robt. Hollingsworth.

(No date) Appraisal of estate of JACOB WHITWORTH, dec'd by Jas. Watts, Thos. Chapman and Wm. Smith. Apr. 1812. Estate sale. Purchasers: Richd. Watt, Jno. Watt, Wm. Pollard. Adm: Fanney Whitworth.

4 May 1812. Appraisal of estate of JAMES GARRETT, dec'd by Reuben Martin , Henry Martin and Jno. Riddle. 9 May 1812. Estate sale. Adm: Stephen Garrett.

3 Aug. 1812. Will of RICHARD MILNER, dec'd proven by Salathiel Shockley and Drury Coker. Joshua Milner qualified as exr. Will of RICHARD MILNER. Wife and all my children. Exr: Joshua and Jas.

MILNER will cont'd:
Milner. Wit: Salathiel Shockley and Drury Coker.

1 June 1812. Letters of adm. estate of JAMES MILLS, dec'd to
Rebekah Mills, James Glenn and David Glenn. Sec: Starling Tucker
and Thos. Porter with Wm. Cowan.

1 Apr. 1812. Appraisal of estate of WILLIAM ROBERSON, dec'd
by Jas. Nickles, Jno. Carter and Cornelius Cargill. 25 Apr.
1812. Estate sale. Mention of Mr. John Cook. No other names
shown. Exr: Frederick Purtz.

(No date) Appraisal of estate of RICHARD MILNER, dec'd by Robt.
and Drury Coker and Geo. Peek (Leek?).

(No date) Appraisal of estate of SAMUEL GARY, dec'd by Robt.
and James Coker, Jno. Milner and Jno. Henderson. 17 July 1812.
Estate sale. Purchasers: Drury Coker, Jos. Coker, David Night,
Francis Coker, Mrs. Coker. Adm: Drury Coker.

8 July 1812. Appraisal of estate of JAMES MILLS, dec'd by Alexr.
Mills, Robt. Fleming, Wm. Cowan. Cert. by Jno. Hunter. 18 July(?)
1812. Estate sale. Purchasers: Jos. McClintock, Jas. Lochridge,
Wm. Fowler, Saml. Fleming, Alexr. Mills, Thos. Garrett, Maj.
N. Durkey, Robt. Fleming, Wm. B. Richards, Wm. Hambleton, Jas.
Glenn, David Glenn, Wm. Waldrop, Elias Cheek, Jos. Deen, Capt.
Jas. Parson, Wm. Rose, Jas. Ward, Jas. Leatherwood, David Hig-
gins, Wm. Ward, Jos. Kelley, Christopher Roads, Jos. Irby, Jno.
Wells, Drury Couch, Thos. Parker, Jas. Deen, Jas. Hutcheson,
Wm. Roberson, Jno. Attaway, Reuben Burton, Wm. Burton, Alex.
Pan___(?), Spencer Brown, Saml. Toms, Jas. Toms, Geo. Mosley,
Jas. Hunter, Wm. Vaughn, Capt. Parsons, J. Flemming, Jno. Todd,
Thos. Crary, Thos. Park, Dan. C. Long, Jas. McCurley, Capt.
Hunter, Moses Creecy, Wm. Cowan, Thos. Porter, Robt. Martin,
Wm. Higgins, Jno. Lee, Thos. McCurley, Reuben Martin, Reuben
Estrage(?), Wm. Irby, Jno. Wallace, Jos. Allison, Minyard Harris,
Reuben Vaughn, Edw. Garrett, Jno. Peterson, Saml. Parsons, Fran-
cis Glenn, Obediah Estrage, Thos. Garrett, Jno. Vickery, B.
Nabors, Jno. Roberson, Henry Hunter, Jos. Glenn, Isaac Miller,
Jno. Sims(?), Benj. Griffin, Saml. Neighbors, Thos. Lewers.
Adm: Rebekah Mills.

5 Oct. 1812. Letters of adm. estate of SAMUEL BARKSDALE, dec'd
to Allen Barksdale. Sec: Jno. Milner and Wm. F. Downs.

5 Oct. 1812. Will of REUBEN MARTIN, dec'd proven by Stephen
Garrett and Roberson Moore. Henry and Reuben Martin, Exrs. 5
July 1808. Will of REUBEN MARTIN. Sons Reuben, Joseph, Benjamin,
John, Samuel and Stephen Martin; mentions Wm.Vaughn; wife Joanna
Martin. Exr: sons Henry and Reuben Martin. Wit: Stephen Garrett,
Salley Garrett, Roberson Moore and Wm. Crage.

23 Oct. 1812. Letters of adm. estate of WILLIAM YOUNG, dec'd
to wife Elizabeth Young. Sec: Josiah Fowler and Benj. James.

26 Oct. 1812. Will of JOHN WATTS, dec'd proven by Martin Pollard.
Exr: Beaufort Watts and Nathl. Day. 14 Sept. 1812. Will of JOHN
WATTS. Wife Peggy; sons Richard, John Pollard, Braxton and Beau-
fort Watts; daughters Matilda, Eliza, Elvira, Louisa, Cornelia,
Narcissa and Peggy Watts. Exr: sons Beaufort, Braxton and Richard
Watts, with Nathaniel Day. Wit: Martin Pollard, James Vaughn
and Sim.(?) Deale.

17 Nov. 1812. Will of NATHAN BARKSDALE, dec'd proven by Chas. Allen and Saml. Downs. Exr: Colyar and Allen Barksdale. 8 Sept. 1812. Will of NATHAN BARKSDALE. Wife Mary; sons Allen, John, Nathaniel and Colyar Barksdale; daughters Nancy and Leanna Barksdale. Exr: sons Colyar and Allen and wife Mary. Wit: L. Saxon, Chas. Allen and Saml. Downs.

1 Nov. 1812. Will of DAVID LITTEL, dec'd proven by R. D. and C. Littel. Exr: Charles and Charity Littel. 12 Oct. 1812. Will of DAVID LITTEL, planter. Wife Charity; all my children and step-daughter Mary Farmer. Exr: Chas. Littel and Charity Littel. Wit: Robt. D. Littel, C. Littel, and Robt. Fleming.

29 Oct. 1812. Inventory of estate of REUBEN MARTIN, dec'd by Thompson Farley, John McDowell and Roberson Moore.

10 Oct. 1812. Appraisal of estate of SAMUEL BARKSDALE, dec'd by Jno. Williams, Chas. Simmons and Chas. Prim. 23 Oct. 1812. Estate sale. Purchasers: John Crisp, D. W. March, Thos. Lewers, Jas. Rodgers, Chas. Prim, John Barksdale, Susannah Barksdale, Nathl. Barksdale, Allen Barksdale, Nancy Barksdale, James Prim, Colyar Barksdale. Adm: A. Barksdale.

7 Dec. 1812. Re NATHANIEL VANCE, dec'd. Widow Mary Vance to adm. estate. Sec: John Simpson and Abraham Gary.

(No date) Appraisal of estate of JOHN WATTS, dec'd by Jno. Cook, Jas. Watts and E. Creswell.

27 Oct. 1812. Appraisal of estate of GEORGE SWINDLE, dec'd by Aaron Clore, Jno. Stephens and Robt. Gains. 29-30 Oct. 1812. Estate sale. Purchasers: Hannah Swindle, Timothy Swindle, Milly Drummond, Jas. Clardy, Jas. Gains, Benj. Tierce, Wm. Rutledge, Robt. Delph, Aaron Crump, Josiah Box, Stephen Gaines, Jona. Gaines, Wm. Moore, Zach. Neil, Micajah Sims, Thos. Atkins, Thos. Medlock, John Jones, Edmond Ware, Wm. Ware, Jno. Myers, Letty Maddox, Brothers Finch, Thos. Garner, Geo. Maxfield, Wm. Pascal, Ezekiel Pascal, Peter Barmore, Stephen Allen, Asa Franklikn, Danl. Drummond, Jas. McDavid, Jr., Jno. Stephens, Henry Wadkins, Sherman Delph, Jno. South, Marshall Lee, Robt. Gains, Wm. Saxon, Wm. Crump, Wm. Drummond. Adm: Hannah Swindle.

4 Jan. 1813. Re FRANCES HENDERSON, dec'd. Adm: Jesse Garrett. Final return.

(No date) Estate sale of REUBEN MARTIN, dec'd. Purchasers: Henry Martin, Reuben Martin, Reuben Bramblet.

12 Dec. 1812. Appraisal of estate of DAVID LITTEL, dec'd by Elisha Adair, Thos. McCrary and Richd. Holland.

4 Jan. 1813. Letters of adm. estate of BENJAMIN GILL, dec'd to Newton Higgins. Sec: Jno. Higgins and Nicholas Garrett.

4 Jan. 1813. Letters of adm. estate of WILLIAM MANLEY, dec'd to Jeremiah and Washington Manley. Sec: Jno. P. Cunningham and Jas. Johnston.

4 Jan. 1813. Letters of adm. estate of MARTIN MC HAFFEE, dec'd to widow Nancy McHaffee. Sec: Henry Morgan, Alex. McHaffee and Bailey Mahon.

4 Jan. 1813. Estate sale of JOSEPH HALL, dec'd. Adm: Margaret Hall. 4 Jan. 1813. By a complaint of Jos. Dean and Jno. Fowler, Margaret Hall's adm. is revoked (she having married Mr. McCrary who will not adm.) Jos. Dean is appointed. Sec: John and Wm. Fowler, Saml. Parsons.

14 Jan. 1813. Will of JAMES STRAIN, dec'd proven by Jas. Johnson, Jas. Nickles and David Strain. 9 Oct. 1812. Will of JAMES STRAIN. Wife Jane; son David; daughters Susannah and Jane; sons John, James and William; daughter and son-in-law Ferguson. Exr: wife Jane and son David. Wit: Jas. Nickles, Jonathan Johnston and R. Campbell.

15 Jan. 1813. Will of JOSEPH ADAIR, dec'd proven and Elisha Adair qualified as exr. 20 Jan. 1812. Will of JOSEPH ADAIR. Sons John, James, Robert and Elisha Adair; grandson Joseph, son of Elisha Adair; daughters Jane and husband Thos. Holland; Elizabeth and husband Jno. Hutson; Casey and husband Thos. McCrary; Charity and husband David Littel. Mentions land adj. John Price, Alex. Wilkerson, Thos. McCrary. Exr: Elisha Adair and John Adair. Wit: Richd. Holland, Wm. Adair and Geo. McCrary.

13 Jan. 1813. Simeon Beaufort Sims, minor about 18 years, chose Jos. Bolton as guardian.

16 Jan. 1813. Rodey Babb Sims, minor about 15 years, chose Jos. Bolton guardian. Sec: Jos. Box and Mathew Bolton.

1 Feb. 1813. Will of JAMES GAMBLE, dec'd proven by Robt. Long, Wm. Grayham. Rachel Gamble and Wm. Gamble, exrs. 20 Apr. 1799. Will of JAMES GAMBLE, farmer. Wife Rachel; sons John, Josiah, William, Isaac, Christopher, Elias, James, and George; daughters Elizabeth, Susannah Grayham and Haney Gamble. To be buried at old Presbyterian meeting house near wife and children. Exr: wife and son William. Wit: Robt. Long, Jno. Finney and Wm. Grayham.

13 Feb. 1813. Appraisal of estate of JAMES STRAIN, dec'd by Jonathan Johnston, Leonard Pinson and James Nickles.

2 Dec. 1812. Appraisal of estate of NATHANIEL VANCE, dec'd by Jno. Johnston, Abraham Gray, Thos. Gray and J. Simpson. 9 Dec. 1812. Sale of estate. Purchasers: Mary Vance, Wm. Vance, Saml. Vance, David Vance, Jas. A. Williams, Isaac Case, Alex. Winn, Reuben Griffin, John Griffin, Thos. Golden, Jno. Ligon, Jno. Johnston, Abraham Gray, Benj. Chesire, Jno. Simpson, Jno. Pitts. Adm: Mary Vance.

13 Feb. 1813. Inventory and appraisal of estate of JAMES GAMBLE, dec'd by Jesse Johnston, Thos. McCrary and Geo. McGrary.

2 Jan. 1813. Inventory of estate of BENJAMIN GILL, dec'd by Roger Brown, Wm. Brown and Jno. Higgins.

19 Jan. 1813. Appraisal of estate of JOSEPH ADAIR, dec'd by Richd. Holland, Wm. Adair and Thos. Fulton.

29 Jan. 1813. Appraisal of estate of NATHAN BARKSDALE, dec'd by Jno. Williams, Jno. Orsborn and Chas. Prim. (No date) Estate sale. Purchasers: Rodah Cannedy, Danl. Barksdale, Colyar Barksdale, Jno. Barksdale, Allen Barksdale, Nathan Barksdale, Mary Barksdale, Stephen Potter, Jas. Ward, Jas. Prim, Chas. Prim,

Estate sale cont'd:
B. Nabours, Chas. Allen, Francis Sims. Exr: Colyar Barksdale
and Allen Barksdale.

(No date) Estate sale of JOSEPH ADAIR, dec'd. Exr: E. Adair.

1 Mar. 1813. Letters of adm. estate of LARKIN SHEPPARD, dec'd
by Jno. Cole. Sec: Wm. Bonds and Nicholas Harding.

13 Jan. 1813. Appraisal of estate of MARTIN MC HAFFEE, dec'd
by Abraham Bolt, Robt. Coker, Colvin Abercrombie and Jno. Nash.
(No date) Estate sale. Purchasers: Nancy McHaffee, Alex. McHaf-
fee, John Nash, Jesse Garrett, Jos. McCullough, Hanah Homes,
Jno. Martin, Jas. Henderson, Thos. Abercrombie, Jno. Finney,
Wm. Ellison, Robt. Lowry, Jno. McNight, Jos. Mahon, Jas. Parker.
Adm: Nancy Mahaffey (N.B. this name spelled several ways).

18 Jan. 1813. Appraisal of estate of WILLIAM MANLEY, dec'd by
J. P. Cunningham, Jno. Rodgers and Robt. Allison. 15 Jan. 1813.
Estate sale. Purchasers: Jeremiah Manley, Washington Manley,
Eliza. Manley, Nancy Manley, Benj. Strainge, Harebert (Herbert)
Martin, Justus Martin, Jno. Martin, Arnold Milner, Jos. Cole,
Robt. Allison, J. Cunningham, Mathew Night, Francis Sims, Jacob
Burton, Rachel Burton, Elisha Casey, Wm. Allison, Wm. McClanahan,
Geo. Hellams, Thos. Parker, Jno. Burton, Wm. Abercrombie. Exr:
G. W. Manley and Jeremiah Manley.

(Date not clear) Estate sale of BENJAMIN GILL, dec'd. Purchasers:
Newton Higgins, Saml. Martin, Robt. Henry, Wm. Brown, Roger
Brown, Jas. Blakely, Mitchel W. Cunningham. Adm: Newton Higgins.

? Apr. 1813. Letters of adm. estate of ALLEN FRANKS, dec'd to
widow Nancy Franks. Sec: Jacob Neighbors and Saml. Franks.

3 Apr. 1813. Letters of adm. estate of JOHN ADAIR, dec'd to
Elisha Adair. Sec: Wm. Adair and Jos. Garrett.

7 Apr. 1813. Will of ALEXANDER MC WILLIAMS, dec'd proven by
Jno. Wiseman and Andrew Hunter. Exr: Saml. Leeman and Jno. Wiseman. 30 Mar. 1813. Will of ALEXANDER MC WILLIAMS. Son David;
rest of children John, Andrew, Robert, Jane and Mary McWilliams;
also Wm. Crafford, husband of daughter Esther. Exr: Saml. Leeman,
and Jno. Wiseman. Wit: J. Wiseman, Andrew Hunter and Wm. Craford.
9 Apr. 1813. Appraisal of estate by Alexr. Austin(?), Saml.
Goodman and David Reed.

13 Mar. 1811. Estate sale of SAMUEL WRIGHT, dec'd. Payments
to Eliz. Wright, to John Neely and Reuben Ligon by Exr. Wm.
Wright.

9 Apr. 1813. Appraisal of estate of ALLEN FRANKS, dec'd by Jno.
Williams, Alexr. (not clear) and Saml. (not clear).

20 Mar. 1813. Appraisal of estate of LARKIN SHEPARD, dec'd by
Nicholas Harding, Thos. Dalrymple and Wm. Bonds. (No date) Estate
sale. Adm: Jno. Cole.

18 Mar. 1813. Estate sale of CHARLES SMITH, dec'd. Adm: Lucy
Smith.

27 May 1813. Will of JOHN CARTER, dec'd proven by Thos. Pinson,
Benj. Garner and Andrew Nelson as Exrs. 3 Apr. 1813. Will of JOHN

John Carter will cont'd:
CARTER. Sons Joel and Benjamin Carter; daughters Margaret Bailey,
Ruth Brown, Elizabeth Garner and Mary Nelson; grandson Bailey
Carter. Exr: Benj. Garner, Andw. Nelson. Wit: Jno. Johnston,
Howard Pinson, Elizabeth Brown.

30 Mar. 1813. Estate sale of ALEXANDER MC WILLIAMS, dec'd. Exr:
Saml. Leeman and Jno. Wiseman.

1 May 1813. Estate sale of ALLEN FRANKS, dec'd. Purchasers:
Wm. Cashburn, Wm. Power, Saml. Franks, Eliz. Goodwin, Chas.
Williams, Joel Allen, Thos. Nabours, Alex. Brown, Joshua Franks,
Alex. Power, Alex. Mills, Nancy Franks. Adm: Nancy Franks.

2 Dec. 1812. Appraisal of estate of WILLIAM YOUNG, dec'd by
Jas. Young, Abner Pyles, Thos. Burnside and Z. Bailey. 3-4 Dec.
1812. Estate sale. Purchasers: Wm. Bryson, Wm. Childs, Ester
Culberson, Jeremiah Glenn, Benj. Cheshire, Christopher Griffin,
Saml. Gray, Danl. Mathis, Jacob Neely, Wm. Simpson, A. Rodgers,
Thos. Rodgers, Jas. Roberts, Abner Teague, Alex. Winn, Danl.
Winn, Thos. Wilks, Saml. Young, Jas. Young, Abner Fuller, Ransom
Fuller, Josiah Fowler, Eliz. Young. Adm: Eliz. Young.

(No date) Estate sale of ROBERT HAMBLETON, dec'd. Purchasers:
Robt. Hollingsworth, Jno. Sample, Reuben Hitt, Jos. Owen, Jesse
Hitt, Jno. Hitt, Jos. Rodgers, Richd. Roberts, Howard Pinson,
Geo. Roberts. Exr: Robt. Hollingsworth.

3 Aug. 1813. Will of JESSE MOATS, dec'd proven by Martin Miller
and Wm. Burnside. Isaac Moats as exr.

(No date) Letter of adm. estate of BENJAMIN BROWN, dec'd to
widow Nancy Brown. Sec: Francis Allison and Fielding Brown.

16 Apr. 1813. Appraisal of estate of JOHN ADAIR, dec'd by Geo.
McCrary, Richd. Holland and Wm. Gamble.

(No date) Appraisal of estate of JESSE MOATS, dec'd by Solomon
Fuller and David Moats.

16 Sept. 1813. Letter of adm. estate of SAMUEL DUNLAP, dec'd
to widow Elizabeth Dunlap. Sec: Thomas Goodwin and (cannot read).

6 Sept. 1813. Letter of adm. estate of DAVID CLOPTON, dec'd
to widow Priscilla Clopton. Sec: Jesse Johnston and Ainsworth
Middleton.

6 Sept. 1813. Estate sale of JOHN ADAIR, dec'd. Adm: E. Adair.

13 Sept. 1813. Estate sale of JESSE MOATS, dec'd. Purchasers:
Isaac Moats (Motes), Jesse Motes, Thos. Rodgers, Wm. Bryson,
Ransom Fuller, Posey Fuller, Chas. Goodman, Jno. Monroe. Adm:
Isaac Moates.

(No date) Appraisal of estate of SAMUEL DUNLAP, dec'd by Wm.
Owings, Gideon Thomason, David Studdard, and Wm. Hill.

(No date) Appraisal of estate of DAVID CLOPTON, dec'd by Jno.
Copeland, Henry Johnson and Wm. Dillard.

14 Aug. 1813. Appraisal of estate of BENJAMIN BROWN, dec'd by
Jno. Meador, Jos. Lyon and Wm. Parks. 20 Sept. 1813. Estate

Benj. Brown cont'd:
sale. No purchasers named. Adm: Nancy Brown.

4 Oct. 1813. Will of THOMAS JOHNSON, dec'd proven by Benjamin
Nabours. Ann Johnson as exr. 23 Mar. 1813. Will of THOMAS JOHN-
STON (JOHNSON). Wife Ann; children (not named). Exr: wife Ann
Johnson (Johnston). Wit: B. Nabours, Jas. H. Lowery and Wm.
Burton.

1 Nov. 1813. Will of CHARLES SIMS, dec'd proven by Jno. McCoy,
Benj. Saunders and Danl. Long. Sarah Sims, Claugh(?) Shelton
and Bernard Glenn named exrs. 25 Apr. 1813. Will of CHARLES
SIMS. Wife Sarah; children Claugh, George R. , James D., Judith,
Lucy Ann Sims. Exr: wife Ann Sims, Claugh Shelton, Bernard Glenn.
Wit: Jno. McCoy, Benj. Saunders, Danl. Long.

2 Nov. 1813. Letter of adm. estate of WILLIAM WASHINGTON, dec'd
to John Wait. Sec: John Wait and Rebecca Redden.

2 Dec. 1813. Will of JAMES CRAGE, dec'd proven by Danl. Long.
John Briggs as exr. 2 July 1813. Will of JAMES CRAGE. Wife Eliza-
beth; children (not named). Exr: wife; brother Wm. Craig (Crage),
Dr. Geo. Ross. Wit: Jno. Briggs, Danl. Long, Jno. Craig.

13 Oct. 1813. Appraisal of estate of SAMUEL DUNLAP, dec'd by
Wm. Owings, Gideon Thomason, David Stoddard.

5 Nov. 1813. Appraisal of estate of WILLIAM WASHINGTON, dec'd
by Michael Swindle, John McGee and Ezekiel Andrews.

5 Nov. 1813. Appraisal of estate of CHARLES SIMS, dec'd by David
Jones, Thos. Hendricks and Wm. Dillard.

20 Nov. 1811(?). Estate sale of DANIEL OWENS, dec'd. Purchasers:
Thos. Owens, Robt. Owens, Elizabeth Caberness, Abm. Holland,
Thos. Beasley. Exr: Thos. Owens.

12 Oct. 1813. Appraisal of estate of THOMAS JOHNSTON, dec'd
by L. Saxon, J. P. Cunningham and B. Nabours.

12 June 1813. Appraisal of estate of JOHN CARTER, dec'd by Thos.
Pinson, John (dim). Cert. by Cornelius Cargill.

15 Jan. 1814. Re THOMAS JOHNSTON, dec'd. Ann Johnston, exr.
petitions for release from her late husband's responsibility
as sec. for Polly Johnston and others including Robt. Lowery
now removed out of the state. Granted. Robt. Lowery with sec.
Robt. Allison and Thos. Norris, appointed.

10 Nov. 1813. Letter of adm. estate of LEWIS SAXON, dec'd to
Wm. F. Downs and Chas. Saxon. Sec: Robt. Creswell, John Simpson,
Wm. Irby, John F. Wolff, John Garlington.

3 Jan. 1814. Letter of adm. estate of ANDERSON ARNOLD, dec'd
to widow Mary Arnold. Sec: Jno. F. Wolff and Jesse Childress.

(No date) Estate sale of DAVID CLOPTON, dec'd. Purchasers: Wm.
Barksdale, Priscilla Clopton, Elizabeth Clopton, Robt. Johnston,
Robt. Stewart, Matthew Hunter, James Cole, James Brown, David
Mason, Claiborn Vaughn, Abner Young, Benj. Lewis, Josiah Williams,
Saml. Henderson, Saml. Hunter, Jno. Monroe, Robt. Johnston,
Henry Johnston, Wm. Saxon, Ainsworth Middleton, Henry Shell,

Estate sale cont'd:
Wm. Johnston, David Speer. Adm: Priscilla Clopton.

5 Feb. 1814. Letter of adm. estate eof ISAAC MOTES, dec'd to
widow Betsy Moats (Motes). Sec: Jesse Moatss and Wm. Bowlan.

7 Feb. 1814. Will of MATTHEW HUNTER, dec'd proven by Jno. Dunlap,
with Wm. Downs, James Hunter and John Hunter as exrs.

21 Dec. 1813. Estate sale of JAMES MILLS, dec'd. Purchasers:
Rebecah Mills, Mary Mills, Nancy Mills, Wm. Mills, Wm. Robeson,
Thos. McCarly, Jas. Ross, Sr., Jno. Neighbors, Jno. Hunter,
Sr., Geo. Mosely, Jno. McClintock, Wm. Ward, David Glenn, Jas.
Glenn, Thos. Fleming, Alex. Mills, David Cowan, Jno. Peterson.
Adm: Rebecah Mills.

5 Nov. 1813. Will of MATTHEW HUNTER. Mother Elizabeth; brother
James; nephew Matthew Henry and other children of my dec'd sister
Ibby Henry (i.e. Robert, Elizabeth, Sarah, James, Nancy, Jane
and Ibby Henry). Exr: Capt. John Hunter, Wm. F. Downs and brother
James Hunter. Wit: R. Creswell, J. Dunlap and ___(?) Richardson.

5 Apr. 1810. Appraisal of estate of FRANCIS GRIFFIN, dec'd by
James Word, Jno. Butler, Ned Jones and John Deale. 9 Apr. 1810.
Estate sale. No purchasers named. Adm: John Cook.

26 Nov. 1813. Estate sale of WILLIAM WASHINGTON, dec'd. Purchas-
ers: Edw. Adair, Thos. Washington, Widow Washington, Jno. Chism,
Jno. Swindle, Jas. Jones, Benj. Jones, P. Wait, Isaac Mitchell,
Thos. Garner, Jeremiah Collins, Martin Shaw, Jeremiah Warren,
Jas. Grayham, Wm. Spruel, Henry Hazel, Moses Starns, David
Green, Jacob Niswanger, Geo. Adams, Marmaduke Pinson, David
Posey, Nathl. Roseman, Wm. Anderson, Jno. Anderson, Jas. Crocker,
Jos. Bolton, Roberson Redden, Zach. Arnold, John Christian,
Lewis Christian, Wm. Andress, Jno. Andress, Jas. Hudson, Chas.
Posey, Ezekiel Powell, Wm. Powell, Wm. South, Archd. McDaniel,
Marshall Lea, Geo. Washington, Jas. Henderson, Josiah Box, Nathan
Jeffries. Adm: Philip Wait.

21 Feb. 1814. Letter of adm. estate of JOHN MILLER, dec'd to
Geo. Miller. Sec: Wm. Dunlap and Jno. Simpson.

9 Jan. 1814. Appraisal of estate of ANDERSON ARNOLD, dec'd by
Jesse Childress, Benj. Nabours, Wm. Arnold and J. F. Wolff.

5 Mar. 1814. Letter of adm. estate of NATHANIEL NICKELS, dec'd
to widow Elizabeth Nickels. Sec: Robt. Nickels and John Boyce.

5 Apr. 1814. Letter of adm. estate of JOSEPH BLAKELY, dec'd
to Jos. Blakely. Sec: Geo. Miller and Jas. Young.

2 Apr. 1814. Letter of adm. estate of JUSTINIAN MADDOX, dec'd
to John and James Young. Sec: Geo. Miller and Jos. Blakely.

(No date) Appraisal of estate of JOHN MILLER, dec'd by Chas.
Harris, Jas. Young, cert. by Wm. Dunlap.

(No date) Appraisal of estate of NATHANIEL NICKLES, dec'd by
Jno. B. Simpson, Thos. Hood, cert. by Robt. Nickles.

(No date) Appraisal of estate of ISAAC MOATS, dec'd by Jesse
Motes, Wm. Bowling, cert. by Solomon Fuller.

23 Feb. 1814. Estate sale of ISAAC MOATS, dec'd Purchasers: Dabney Palmer, Betsy Moats, Jas. Culbertson, Zach. Bailey, Wm. Glenn, Jones Fuller, Wm. Fuller, R. Fuller, A. Rodgers. Adm: Betsy Motes.

4 Apr. 1814. Will of THOMAS KEVIl, dec'd proven by Jos. Compton, Jno. Edwards and Jacob League. 18 Jan. 1813. Will of THOMAS KEVIL. Wife Agga; sister Mary Glazebrook and her heirs and bro. Benjamin Kevil. Exr: John Westmoreland and Joab(?) Teague. Wit: Jos. Compton, John Edwards, Ginney Edwards.

(No date) Appraisal of estate of LEWIS SAXON, dec'd by B. Nabors, Robt. Creswell, cert. by Wm. Dunlap.

19 Apr. 1814. Will of PHILIP ANDERSON, dec'd proven by Moses Whitten, Jos. Dunkin. Allen Anderson and Moses Whitten as exr. 27 Mar. 1814. Will of PHILIP ANDERSON. Wife Elizabeth; son Ned; daughters Lucy and Ann Davis; sons Allen and Reuben Anderson; daughter Elizabeth Anderson; son Lewis; three youngest. Exr: son Allen Anderson, friends Jos. Jones and Moses Whitten. Wit: John Bennett, Moses Whitten and Jos. Dunken.

(No date) Estate sale of NATHANIEL NICKELS, dec'd. Adm: Elizabeth Nickels.

19 Apr. 1814. Re GEORGE SWINDLE, dec'd. Wm. Arnold, Geo. Grace, Wm. Rutledge, Jas. Posey petition for release as sec. for Hannah Swindle. Granted. Jas. L. Kindred, Edw. Nix and Wm. F. Downs appointed in their place.

(No date) Appraisal of estate of THOMAS KEVIL, dec'd by Jno. Harris, Abner Smith and Jno. Meador. Cert. by Wm. Gilbert.

2 May 1814. Revocation of letters of adm. to Rebekah Mills now Hunter and her husband James Hunter in the est. of JAMES MILLS, dec'd. Her husband James Hunter appointed. Sec: John Hunter, Thos. ____, Jas. Park replacing Jas. Glenn and Mr. Cook.

5 Apr. 1814. Appraisal of estate of JUSTINIAN MADDOX, dec'd by Wm. Ligon, Geo. Miller, cert. by Jno. Black. 18 Apr. 1814. Estate sale. Purchasers: Jno. Young, B. Drake, B. Casey, Jos. Blakely, Mark Hardin, Jas. Young, Susannah Henderson. Adm: Jno. and Jas. Young.

3 June 1814. Appraisal of estate of PHILIP ANDERSON, dec'd by Jno. Jones, Jos. Dunken, cert. by Thos. Hendricks. 8 July 1814. Estate sale. Purchasers: Elizabeth Anderson, Philip Whitten, Jos. Jones, Jas. Dillard, Thos. Pinson, Henry Davis, Jas. Humphries, Wm. Humphries, Jos. Ducket, Enoch Garrett, Jno. Garrett, Jno. Casey, Thos. Porter, Wm. Bright, Jno. Scott, Jos. Hall, Joshua Davis, Jos. Scott, Allen Anderson, Watt Anderson, Lewis Jones, Wm. Parker, Marah Dunken, Jesse Porter, Moses Whitten, Henry Davis, Isaac Jacks. Exr: Moses Whitten.

8 June 1814. Re JAMES CRAGE, dec'd. Elizabeth Crage and Wm. Crage qualified as exrs.

24 Dec. 1809. Estate sale of ANGUISH CAMPBELL, dec'd. Exr: Robt. Campbell. Cert. 20 Feb. 1810.

21 Apr. 1814. Estate sale of THOMAS KEVIL, dec'd. Purchasers: Jno. House, Jno. Hughs, Jno. Mitcheson, David Cooper, Joel Diel,

KEVIL estate sale cont'd:
Jno. Spurgeon, Jacob (Joab?) League. Exr: Jno. Westmoreland.

2 May 1814. Letters of adm. estate of THOMAS YOUNG, dec'd to
Sarah and George Young. Sec: Simon Reeder and Lewis Jones.

11 June 1814. Letters of adm. estate of JOHN GOLDEN, JR., dec'd
to James Hathorn. Sec: Roberson Redden and Wm. West.

14 Apr. 1814. Re ABSALOM BOBO, dec'd. Dvaid Anderson qualified
as exr. by Charles J. Colcock, Judge of S. C. 8 July 1808. Will
of ABSALOM BOBO. Wife Amey Bobo; son-in-law Wm. Powell and his
children by my dec'd daughter viz: Betsy Gaines, Rodey Waits,
Peachy Posey, Polly Delph, Janey, Sarah, Amy, Belinda, Milly,
Virginia Powell. Exr: David Anderson and Lewis Graves. Wit:
John Golden, Sr., Andrew Anderson, James Anderson, Wm. Anderson.
30 Apr. 1813. Appraisal of estate by John Wait, Jacob Niswanger
and John Roberson. 22 May 1813. Estate sale (part). Purchasers:
David Anderson, Jeremiah Collins, Jas. Wait, Larkin Gaines,
Thos. Porter, Thos. Adkins, Wm. Pope. Adm: David Anderson.

(No date) Appraisal of estate of JOHN GOLDEN, dec'd by John
Wait, Jas. Neely, Roberson Redden.

21 Jan. 1814. Estate sale of JOHN MILLER, dec'd. Adm: Geo. Miller

18 Apr. 1814. Estate sale of JOSEPH BLACKEBY, dec'd. Adm: Jos.
Blackeby.

25 Apr.(?) 1814. Estate sale of ANDERSON ARNOLD, dec'd. Adm:
Mary Arnold.

(No date) Appraisal of estate of JAMES CRAIG, dec'd by Wm. Craig,
Alex. Filson(?). Cert. by Benj. Adair.

(No date) Re est. of JAMES MILLS, dec'd. Return of adm. Rebecca
Hunter, formerly Rebecca Mills.

(Not clear) Susannah Wilks, minor. Return of guardian David
M. Winn; payment to Alexr. Winn, her husband, for the year 1812.

3 Apr.(?) 1814. Hicks Wesson, minor about 14 years, chose Lewis
Jones as guardian. Sec: Levi Fowler, Jos. Dunken.

(No date) Appraisal of estate of THOMAS YOUNG, dec'd by David
Reeder, John Whitmore. Cert. by Danl. Reeder. Estate sale (date
not clear). No purchasers named. Adm: George Young.

2 Sept. 1814. Letters of adm. estate of ROBERT PASLEY, dec'd
to Mary H. B. Pasley, widow. Sec: Wm. Moore, Thos. Reed(?),
Wm. Moore.

5 Sept. 1814. Re ALEXANDER SIMPSON, dec'd. James and John Simp-
son qualify as exrs. 13 Apr. 1811. Will of ALEXANDER SIMPSON.
Daughters Mary Hutcheson, Margaret Glenn, Agnes Dunlap; son
John Simpson; daughters Elizabeth and Sarah Simpson; son James
Simpson. Exr: sons John and James. Wit: Jno. Speer, Jno. Blake?,
Ann Horan.

16 Sept. 1814. Will of JANE NEWPORT, dec'd proven by Archd.
Young. Rachel Feagan qualified as exr. 4 Mar. 1805. Will of
JANE NEWPORT. Daughter Rachel Feagan. Exr: Rachel Feagan. Wit:

NEWPORT will cont'd:
Archibald Young and Daniel Wright.

16 Sept. 1814. Will of HENRY FULLER, dec'd proven by Jones Fuller. Charlotte Fuller as exr. 28 Sept. 1813. Will of HENRY FULLER. Wife Charlotte; his children (not named). Exr: Charlotte Fuller and Zachariah Bailey. Wit: Jones Fuller, John Holt, Sarah Holt.

1 Oct. 1814. Estate of WILLIAM PROCTOR, dec'd. Adm. to widow Jane Proctor. Sec: Thos. Todd, Nathan Todd.

16 Oct. 1814. Letters of adm. estate of ALLEN MITCHELL, dec'd to widow Druscilla Mitchell. Sec: Wm. Arnold, (second name not clear).

18 Oct. 1814. Appraisal of estate of ALEXANDER SIMPSON, dec'd by David Greer, ___ Gray. Cert. by Jno. Leonard.

22 Oct. 1814. Letters of adm. estate of THOMAS PINSON, dec'd to widow Lucy Pinson. Sec: Dabney and Richard Puckett.

6 Nov. 1814. Will of JAMES MC DOWELL, dec'd proven by Robt. Creswell and Wm. Atkins. James McDowell as exr. 29 Apr. 1808. Will of JAMES MC DOWELL. Wife; daughter Ginny Blakely; son James. Notes due by John Manly and Andrew Burnside. Exr: son James McDowell. Wit: Robt. Creswell, Wm. Adkins, Polly Adkins.

15 Feb. 1814. Appraisal of estate of MATTHEW HUNTER, dec'd by J. Garlington, Thos. Porter and _____.

(No date) Will of JOHN CUNNINGHAM, dec'd proven by J. Cunningham and Thos. Cunningham. Wife Nancy Cunningham as exr. She renounced.8 Mar. 1814. Will of JOHN CUNNINGHAM. Wife Nancy; brothers and sisters and their heirs. Exr: wife Nancy, James and Wm. Cunningham. Wit: Jno. D. Cunningham and Thos. Cunningham, Hannah Deen.

21 Nov. 1814. Letters of adm. estate of REUBEN LIGON, dec'd to Thomas Ligon. Sec: (too dim to read).

16 Nov. 1814. Tully Francis Sullivan, minor about 17 years, chose Tully Boling as guardian. Sec: James Dunkin and Lydell Allen.

(No date) Appraisal of estate of ALLEN MITCHELL, dec'd by John South, Ira and Reuben Arnold. 12 Nov. 1814. Estate sale. Purchasers: Drusilla Mitchell, Danl. Gent, Saml. Nabours, Fleet Nabours, Jacob Nabours, Hugh Goff, Micajah Jones, Jos. McCullough, Jno. Ridgeway, Abraham Riley. Adm: D. Mitchell.

(No date) Appraisal of household and kitchen furniture of estate of WILLIAM PROCTOR, dec'd by Andrew McCaul, Jas. Watts and Jno. Gates. 5 Nov. 1814. Sale of same. Purchasers: Jno. Gates, Wm. Stuard, Jane Proctor, David Todd, Andrew Todd, Patrick Todd, E. Griffin, Wm. Smith, Saml. Hensley, A. McCaul, Jno. Porterfield, Jas. Ligon, Thos. Sims, N. Day, Moses Irby, Wm. Caldwell, Fanney Whitworth, Michael Owen, Wm. Studard, Thos. Reed, David ____. Adm: Jane Proctor.

15 Oct. 1814. Estate sale of SAMUEL DUNLAP, dec'd. Purchasers: Elizabeth Dunlap, Long Ware, Ezekiel Mathews, M. Roberson, Robt. Hand, Hannah Garrett, Jno. Simpson, Jos. Strain, David Studard,

SAML. DUNLAP est. sale cont'd:
Wm. Curry. Adm: Elizabeth Dunlap.

25 Oct. 1814. Appraisal of estate of JANE NEWPORT, dec'd by
Thos. Parks, Jonathan Wallis. Cert. by Peter Hammond.

3 Dec. 1814. Letters of adm. estate of JOHN RICHEY, JR., dec'd
to John Richey.

5 Dec. 1814. Letters of adm. estate of JONATHAN BLAKELY, dec'd
to Henry McCelvey. Sec: David Speers, Chas. Littel. D. Anderson,
Ord.

10 Dec. 1814. Will of ABSOLOM COLEMAN, dec'd proven by Wm. Baily,
Allen Walker. Sarah Coleman and Ransom Fuller, exrs. 17 Nov.
1814. Will of ABSALOM COLEMAN. Wife Sarah; her children - John
and Deborah (the youngest); sons Larkin, Alfred and Alsey Cole-
man. Mentions Mason Moss, Wm. and John Walker. Guardian of son
John to be brother Wm. Coleman, also Zach. Bailey. Exr: wife
Sarah and Ransom Fuller. Wit: Jas. Young, Wm. Bailey and Allen
Walker.

(No date) Appraisal of estate of JOHN RICHEY, JR., dec'd by
Martin Shaw, Jonathan Forgey and F. Purtz.

15 Sept. 1814. Appraisal of estate of HENRY FULLER, dec'd by
Absalom Coleman, Solomon Fuller and Jones Fuller.

7 Jan. 1815. Est. of ALEXANDER MC WILLAMS, dec'd. Return of
exrs. Saml. Leaman and Jno. Wiseman.

7 Jan. 1815. Letters of adm. estate of WILLIAM LEAKE, dec'd
to Moses and John Leake. Sec: Elisha Adair and David Speers.

26 Dec. 1810. Est. of JUDAH MADDOX, dec'd. Return of adm. James
and John Young. Payments to six legatees; mentions Saml. Henderson, John Maddox, Alexander Winn and Justinian Maddox.

7 Jan. 1815. Letters of adm. estate of SAMUEL SALISBURY, dec'd
to Mark Killingsworth. Sec: Robt. Allison and Chas. Williams.
8 Jan. 1815. Appraisal of estate by J. P. and Jas. Cunningham
and Wm. Holiday. Cert. by B. Nabours.

11 Jan. 1815. Estate sale of JOHN CUNNINGHAM, dec'd. Purchasers:
John Burton, Robt. Lowery, Edw. Salisbury, Saml. Green, Jos.
Deen. Cert. by exr. Nancy Cunningham.

17 Dec. 1814. Appraisal of estate of JONATHAN BLAKELY, dec'd
by Cornelius Tinsley, Chas. Littel, Jas. Underwood and Saml.
Vance. 21 Dec. 1814. Estate sale. Cert. by Henry McCelvey, Adm.

22 Nov. 1814. Appraisal of estate of REUBEN LIGON, dec'd by
John Black, Lemuel Allen and Wm. Holdrich. 9 Dec. 1814. Estate
sale. Adm: Thos. Ligon.

8 Jan. 1815. Letters of adm. estate of DAVID FOWLER, dec'd to
wife Sarah Fowler. Sec: Henry Meredith and James Fowler.

8 Jan. 1815. Appraisal of estate of LEONARD PINSON, dec'd by
Nimrod Overby, James Nickles and David Nelson.

28 Nov. 1814. Appraisal of estate of JAMES MC DOWELL, dec'd

MC DOWELL estate cont'd:
by Stephen Dumas, Wm. Murrow and Benj. Atkins.

21 Jan. 1815. Estate sale of SAMUEL SALISBURY, dec'd. Purchasers: Geo. Swindle, Joel Allen, David Saxon, Jas. Lowery, John B. Cunningham, Jno. Rodgers, Jno. Strain, Haisten Dial. Adm: Mark Killingsworth.

6 Feb. 1815. Letters of adm. estate of WILLIAM FOWLER, dec'd to wife Mary Fowler. Sec: John Hunter and Jas. Fowler.

6 Jan. 1815. Appraisal of estate of DAVAID FOWLER, dec'd by Thompson Farley, Ellis Cheek, Saml. Fleming and Jno. Mosley.

6 Feb. 1815. Letters of adm. estate of ZEBULON MATHES, dec'd to Geo. Miller. Sec: Wm. Burnside and Jas. Young.

26 Nov. 1814. Appraisal of estate of JOHN CUNNINGHAM, dec'd by B. Nabours, Henry Burrow(?) and Wm. McDavid.

21 Feb. 1815. Will of JOHN PUGH, dec'd proven by John Harron, Thos. Roberts, Mary Pugh and Wm. Gilbert as exr. 2 Dec. 1814(?). Will of JOHN PUGH. Wife; sister Elizabeth Gilbert; nephew Jesse Pugh. Mentions Elijah Cook; father Edward Pugh; brothers and sisters. Exr: wife and Wm. Gilbert. Wit: John Harron(?), Thos. Roberts and Jas. Garrett.

17 Feb. 1815. Ann Shanler (Chandler?), minor about 20 years, chose Nancy Box as guardian. Sec: Gabriel Joel and Thos. Brock.

15 Feb. 1815. Appraisal of estate of ZEBULON MATTHIS, dec'd by Langston East and Saml. Henderson. (No date) Estate sale. Adm: Geo. Miller.

16 Dec. 1815. Second sale of est. of JACOB WHITWORTH, dec'd with purchasers: Fanny Whitworth, Jas. Watts. Adm: Fanny Whitworth.

9 Mar. 1815. Thomas Roberson, minor, chose John Roberson as guardian. Sec: John Roberson, Sr. and Frederick Purtz.

6 Mar. 1815. Ann Shanler, minor. Return of guardian. Rec'd from Isaac Dial a negro woman. Henry Box, guardian.

9 Mar. 1815. Isom Roberson, minor about 16 years, chose John Roberson, Sr. as guardian. Sec: Jno. Middleton and Jos. Neeley.

(No date) Appraisal of estate of ROBERT PASLEY, dec'd by Jas. Young, Jeremiah Glenn and Jas. McMahan. 18-19 Nov. 1814. Estate sale. Purchasers: Zach. Bailey, Blackgrove Glenn, Jos. Babb, Thos. Babb, Jas. Culbertson, Robt. Culbertson, Baruch Duckett, Allen Coleman, Jones Fuller, Archd. Fuller, Anne Glenn, Wm. Glenn, Thos. Kelley, Wm. Kellett, Jas. McMahan, Edw. Medley, Betsy Moats, Wm. Nelson, Jno. Milum, Andw. Rodgers, Saml. Rodgers, Thos. Rodgers, David Stephens, Mary H. B. Pasley, Jno. Verrall, Jno. Baker, Ransom Fuller, Garland Walker, Wm. Walker, Michael Davenport, Robt. Pasley, Jas. Pasley, Wm. Moon(?), G. Glenn, Jas. Young, Asa Chanler, Thos. Gill. Adm: Mary H. B. Pasley.

5 Mar. 1815. Letters of adm. estate of DANIEL BRAGG, dec'd to Elizabeth Bragg and Geo. Bruton. Sec: Jno. Gilbert and Jno. Bruton. D. Anderson, Ord.

(No date) Estate sale of WILLIAM LEAKE, dec'd. Purchasers: Mathew Leake, Moses Leake, John Leake, Sarah Leake, Armistead Leake, Chas. Hewit, Jacob Miller, Jas. Templeton, Wm. Brown, Nathl. Drummond, Jas. Young, Wm. Hannah, Jas. Hannah, R. Holland, Chas. Simpson. Adm: Moses Leake.

(No date) Second appraisal of estate of WILLIAM ROBERSON, dec'd by Jas. Nickels and Charter Nickels and John Roberson.

(No date) Re JAMES MOOR, dec'd. Return of exr. Cornelius Tinsley of payments to legatees Jesse Moor, John Cooper, guardian of Jas. Moor and to Jas. Moor.

7 Apr. 1815. Letters of adm. estate of DAVID WHITFORD, dec'd to Jane and Wm. Whitford. Sec: Patrick Todd and David Hitt.

13 Feb. 1815. Appraisal of estate of WILLIAM FOWLER, dec'd by Jno. Hunter, Jr., Saml. Fleming, Jas. Fowler and Jas. Dean.

(No date) Appraisal of estate of JOHN PUGH, dec'd by Jno. Herring, Jno. Meador and Jas. Brown.

18 Apr. 1815. Letters of adm. estate of WM. PARKS, dec'd to Thos. Parks. Sec: Archd. Young and Jno. Meador.

19 Apr. 1815. Letters of adm. estate of ENOCH ALLEN, dec'd to Jno. Nabours. Sec: Jos. Tompson and Benj. Nabours. 19 Apr. 1815. Appraisal of estate by Andw. McNight and Thos. Wright.

19 Apr. 1815. Will of SOLOMON HOPKINS, dec'd proven by Jas. and Wm. McDonald. Wife and son Francis qualify as exrs. 19 July 1814. Will of SOLOMON HOPKINS. Wife; sons Francis, John and Jeremiah (mentions such as the rest have had); dec'd son James and his children. Exr: wife (not named) and son Francis. Wit: Jas. and Wm. McDonald and Jno. Smith.

(No date) Estate sale of JOHN PUGH, dec'd. Purchasers: Mary Pugh, Jeremiah Gilbert, Edw. Scruggs, Geo. Arnold, Moses Butler, Jas. Nix, Jacob Roberts, Wm. Attaway, Joshua Burton, Jonth. Phillips, Joshua Gilbert, Jas. Garrett, Jno. Mosley, Wm. Gilbert, Thos. Woodrough, Larkin Hendrix, Andw. Edwards, Thos. Garrett, Humphrey Mills, Wm. Anderson, Edw. Pugh, Wm. Jones, J. Brockman, Humphrey Wells, Jno. Spurgen, Wm. Pugh, Thos. Cannon, Thos. Roberts, Jno. Gilbert, Thos. Gilbert, Chas. Box, Jno. Harris, Wm. Cooper, Nathl. Pugh, Jas. Allen, Jacob Brown, Jno. Hughs, Francis Hunter, Dennis House, Jos. Brown. Exr: Wm. Gilbert.

(No date) Jesse Hughs, minor, guardian Pleasant C. Snead's return paid in full. Wit: Jas. Young.

(No date) Estate sale of HENRY FULLER, dec'd. Exr: Ch. Fuller.

(Date not clear) Estate sale of FRANCIS GRIFFIN, dec'd. Adm: J. Cook.

14 Sept. 1814. Est. of JOHN BOYCE, dec'd final return of adm. James Young. Paid legatees Elizabeth Boyce, Martin Shaw and Wm. Crocker their part.

11 May 1815. Est. of MATTHEW CUNNINGHAM, dec'd. Return of adm. Susannah Cunningham.

1 Mar. 1815. Appraisal of estate of DANIEL BRAGG, dec'd by Jno. Bruton, Joel Fowler and Thos. Campbell. (No date) Estate sale. Purchasers: Ann D. Jones, Nancy Arnold, Arnold Willis, Caleb Allen, Catherine Bragg, Elizabeth Bragg, Rody Bragg, Nathl. Bramlett, Zebulon Bragg, Geo. Brewton, Jno. Brewton, Thos. Campbell, Elias Cheek, Jno. Clark, Wm. Clayton, Chas. Cox, Reuben Estes, Joel Fowler, Wm. Fowler, Steph. Garrett, Jno. Gilbert, Robt. Hand, Jno. Hobby, Dennis Linsey, Moses Fountain, Jonth. Moore, Robt. Page, Thos. Parks, Asa Stone, Starling Tucker, Saml. Jones, Archd. Young, Thos. Wright. Adm: Elizabeth Bragg.

24 Apr. 1815. Appraisal of estate of SOLOMON HOPKINS, dec'd by Thos. Matthis, Thos. Graden and Drury Boyce.

(No date) Appraisal of estate of ABSALOM COLEMAN, dec'd by Jas. Young, Solomon Fuller and Jno. Walker. 25 Jan. 1815. Estate sale. Exr: Ransom Fuller.

18 Apr. 1815. Appraisal of estate of DAVID WHITFORD, dec'd by David Hitt, Clement Wells and Jno. McGowan. 24 Apr. 1815. Estate sale. Purchasers: Mrs. Whitford, Robt. Whitford, Jane Whitford, Isabella Whitford, Mrs. Jane Whitford, Jno. McGowan, Jno. Boyd, Alex. Austin, Jno. Williams. Adm: Wm. Whiteford (Whitford).

5 June 1815. Letters of adm. estate of WILLIAM GAREY, dec'd to wife Rachel. Sec: John Nix and Richd. Blackwell.

3 June 1815. Will of BENJAMIN WILSON, dec'd proven by Enos Horton, Wm. Neil. Wife Elizabeth and sons James and David S. as exrs. 22 Apr. 1815. Will of BENJAMIN WILLSON (WILSON). Wife Elizabeth; all my children; David S. Wilson (minor); Ann Scott, Elizabeth Gray, Mary Burns, Isabella McConnel, Jane Gray, Saray Boyd (wife of Wilson Boyd?), Martha and Margaret Wilson. Exr: wife, James Wilson, David S. Wilson. Wit: Wm. Neil, Enos Horton and Pheby Horton.

(No date) Estate sale of WILLIAM FOWLER, dec'd. Purchasers: Wm. Higgins, Wm. Garrett, Wm. Fowler, Rodey Dendy(?), E. Garrett, Wm. Templeton, Ob. East, Saml. Studard, R. Estes, Eliz. Waldrop, Chas. Simpson, Thos. Higgins, Jos. Martin, H. Martin, Wm. Lanford, Jno. Crow, Jas. Fleming, Drury Couch, J. Clark, M. Garrett, Wm. Garrett, Jr., Jas. Glenn, J. Hunter, G. Dean, Willis Cheek, David Glenn, Alex. Mills, Chas. Farrow, G. Mosley, Henderson Whitlow, David Cowan, Jas. Brown, Jas. Parks, S. Shockley, Aron Starns, J. Nabours, Thos. McCarley, Chas. Brooks, Jno. Stroud, Joel Allen, Jno. Garrett, Allen Adkinson, Jas. Newman, Saml. Simpson, Wm. Parks, Anthony Swann, Jno. Gilbert, Jas. Hunter, Wm. Ball, R. Stone, Jonth. Garrett, Mathew Ball, Saml. Mills, Jos. McCullough, Thos. Nabours, Alex. Powers, Jno. Mosley, Andw. Parks. Adm: Mary Fowler.

19 June 1815. Letters of adm. estate of JOHN ARMSTRONG, dec'd to Elizabeth Armstrong and Jno. Glenn. Sec: David Mason and Jno. Mason.

8 July 1815. Will of MIKEL SWINDLE, dec'd proven by Philip Wait. Aaron Clore, exr. 3 July 1809. Will of MICHAEL SWINDLE. Sons John, Daniel and George Swindle; daughters Lucy Saxon, Delila Swindle. Mentions all my children. Exr: brother Geo. Swindle and Aaron Clore (Cloar). Wit: Philip Wait, Wm. Washington and Jos. Box.

11 Nov. 1814. Estate sale of JOHN GOLDING, dec'd. Purchasers: Wm., Richard, Robert, John and James Golding, D. Anderson, Jos. Neely, Saml. Neely, James and Benj. Glover, Saml. Young, Jas. Wait. Adm: James Hathorn.

21 June 1815. Appraisal of estate of BENJAMIN WILLSON, dec'd by David Mason, Saml. McC____ and John Dillard. 22 June 1815. Estate sale. Exr: James and David S. Willson.

5 Aug. 1815. Appraisal of estate of WILLIAM GAREY, dec'd by Jas. Parker, Jas. Boyc and David Turner.

26 Aug. 1815. Est. of JOHN MADDEN, dec'd. Geo. Madden qualified as exr. Wit: Richard Pugh and Ann Madden.

7 Aug. 1815. Letters of adm. estate of JEREMIAH HOLLINGSWORTH, dec'd to Chas. Saxon. Sec: Jno. F. Wolff and Saml. Downs.

9 Aug. 1815. James L. Mitchell, minor about 18 years, chose Thomas D. Mitchell as guardian. Sec: Robt. Creswell and Wm. F. Downs.

4 Sept. 1815. Letters of adm. estate of OBEDIAH ESTES, dec'd to wife Ann Estes. Sec: Robt. Creswell and Robt. Canady.

4 Sept. 1815. Letters of adm. estate of CHRISTOPHER VICKERY, dec'd to wife Milley Vickery. Sec: Benj. Lewis and Jesse Johnston.

8 Sept. 1815. Will of MATTHEW HUNTER, SR., dec'd proven by (name not clear). James McMahan and Charter Nickels as exrs. 12 July 1815. Will of MATTHEW HUNTER. Wife Elizabeth; daughters Margaret and Nancy; son Matthew; daughters Betty, Jean and Sarah. Exr: Jams McMahan, Charter Nickels. Wit: Alex. Austin, Hugh Leaman and Saml. Leaman.

1 Sept. 1815. Appraisal of estate of JOHN MADDEN, dec'd by J. Roberson, R. Sullivan and J. Dial.

15 Sept. 1815. Appraisal of estate of MATTHEW HUNTER, dec'd by Alex. Austin, Saml. Leaman and Wm. Bryson.

2 Oct. 1815. Will of JOHN SIMPSON, dec'd proven by (name not clear). Wm. Simpson and Jno. W. Simpson as exr. 13 Feb. 1815. Will of JOHN SIMPSON. Wife Sarah; sons Wm. W. and John W. Simpson; daughters Jane and husband John Nickles; Mary and husband Anthony Griffin, Kitty and husband John R. Griffin; Nancy and husband Thos. Wright. Mentions house at Belfast; land adj owners and business associates as Jno. Boyd, Jno. Blake, Widow Glenn, Reuben Griffin, Jno. Leonard, Thos. Green, Jno. Black, Jno. Hitch, Matt. Hunter, Jno. Milam,R. Creswell, Wm. Dendy, Wm. Farrow, Robt. Gray, Jas. Simpson, brother Alex. Simpson, sister Agnes Simpson(?). Exr: sons Wm. Ww. and J. W. Simpson. Wit: Ezekiel North, Roger(?) Gray and Jno. Felts.

27 July 1815. Appraisal of estate of MICHAEL SWINDLE, dec'd by Philip Wait, R. Powell, J. Clardy and David Braden. (No date) Estate sale. Purchasers: Jas. Clardy, Thos. Atkins, Fleet Neighbors, Geo. Adams, David Green, David Braden, Wm. Powell, Robt. Bumpass, Josiah Box, Wm. South, Matt. Bolton, Saml. Freeman, Nathl. Saxon, Danl. Swindle, Jno. Chism, Wm. Redden, Jas. Powell, Geo. Turner, Philip Wait, Jas. Gains, Ezek. Powell, Ezek. And-

Estate sale cont'd:
rews, Jno. Cheek, Reuben Powell, Jas. Chism, Henry Watkins, Jno. Swindle, Alfred Martin, Wm. Christian, Jas. Hutson, Wm. South, Jas. Jones, Richard Golden, Robt. Golden, Banister Mitchell, Moses Myers, Eaton Mayberry.

(No date) Inv. and App. of estate of OBEDIAH ESTES, dec'd by Robt. Creswell, Rody Kennedy, Chas. Williams and Jno. Williams.

2 Oct. 1815. Estate of DAVID SPEER, dec'd. Robt. Creswell appointed adm. of estate at request of the widow & only brother of the dec'd.

2 Oct. 1815. Letters of adm. estate of MARK HARDING, dec'd to James Hardin (Harding). Sec: Henry Shell and Chr. Harding.

5 July 1815. Appraisal of estate of JOHN ARMSTRONG, dec'd by Jas. W. Morris, David Mason, Job Mason and Thos. Gary. 7-11 July 1815. Estate sale. Purchasers: Elizabeth Armstrong, Jno. Coles, Jno. Holland, David Mason, Job Mason, Jno. Murphy, Jno. Lester, Thos. Gary, Robt. Little, David Cole, Chas. Gary, Wm. Neal, Fredk. Foster, Danl. Cargill, Chas. Horton, Danl. McMahan, Josiah Williams, Maj. Jno. Glenn, Wm. Davis, Geo. Miller, Jno. Bryant, Ephraim Perry, Danl. Williams, Robt. Boyd, Jas. Clark, Elizabeth James, Alex. Kincaid, David Gamble, Cap. Word, Jas. Dunklin, Jas. Ryan, Vann Davis, D. Roberts, Jas. Bell, Bluford Brooks, Jno. Gary, Jonth. Davis, Benj. Adair, Elisha Hammond, Ellen Jones, Thos. Dalrymple, Nick. Hardin, Jno. Dean, Wm. Kincaid, Jno. Jamison, Jno. Tagart, Maj. Fredk. Gray, Jas. Caldwell, Isaac Gray, Jas. McMorris, Bard R. Brown, Chesley Davis, Reuben Flanagan, Jno. McMorris, Chas. Crow, Wm. Horton, Jno. Johnston, Middlebrook Seymore, Jas. Teague, Andw. Motes, Jas. Thomas, Archd. McMillan, Patk. Spence, Thos. Johnston, Wm. Bonds. Adm: Elizabeth Armstrong and Jno. Glenn.

6 Oct. 1815. Letters of adm. estate of ZACHARIAH CUNNINGHAM, dec'd to Wm. Hudgens. Sec: Wm. P. Bolt and Jas. Prim.

14 Oct. 1815. Est. of CHRISTOPHER ROWLING, dec'd Robt. Rowling qualified as exr.

18 Oct. 1815. Letters of adm. estate of THOMAS CROSSON, dec'd to wife Martha Crosson. Sec: Wm. Crosson and Jno. McGowen.

23 Oct. 1815. Letters of adm. estate of JACOB DORAN, dec'd to Robt. McNees. Bond: John Middleton.

14 Oct. 1815. Letters of adm. estate of SAMUEL WATSON, dec'd to Lewis Watson. Bond: Zebulon Savage.

30 Oct. 1815. Estate of DAVID REED, dec'd. Wife Elizabeth Reed qualified as exr. Will of DAVID REED. Wife Elizabeth; children - John Allen, Elizabeth, David and Matthew Reed. Exr: wife Elizabeth and brother Wm. Reed. Wit: Jno. W. Willams, Jno. Nickles and Jas. Nickles.

26 Oct. 1815. Appraisal of estate of SAMUEL (LEMUEL?) WATSON, dec'd by Jacob Niswanger, Zeb. Savage, Zach. Arnold and Jer. Warren.

(No date) Final return on estate of ANGUS CAMPBELL, dec'd by exr. Robt. Campbell and Jonathan Johnston. Payments to legatees

CAMPBELL return cont'd:
Robert Cunningham, Jesse Pain, Jonathan Johnston, Robert Campbell
and Angus Campbell.

6 Nov. 1815. Estate sale of JOHN MADDEN, dec'd. Purchasers:
Chas. H. Lowery, Jno. Lumpkins, Wm. Madden, Wm. Adkins, Chas.
Harry, Jno. Harry, Joel Hughs, Jno. Roberson, Chas. Madden,
David Madden, Adam Garmon, Thos. Brock, Saml. Green, Geo. Madden,
Terry Cole, Wm. McClanahan, Nathan Sims, Wm. Wilson, Jno. McCaa,
Abraham Madden, Thos. Davenport, Joel Plant, Jas. Henderson,
Thos. Hunter, Jno. Hill. Exr: Geo. Madden.

5 Oct. 1815. Appraisal of estate of CHR. VICKERY, dec'd by Jesse
Johnston, Jas. Entrekin, Jas. Simpson.

(No date) Appraisal of estate of DAVID REED, dec'd by Saml.
Leaman, Jno. Nickles, David McWilliams.

5 Sept. 1815. Estate sale of WILLIAM GAREY, dec'd. Purchasers:
Benj. Harris, Jas. Prim, Jno. Neal, Rachel Garey, Jas. Parker,
Fleet Nabours, Jno. Nevil, Jno. Blakely, Jas. Johnston, Thos.
Grimes, Thos. Garrett, R. Garey, Jno. Goggans, Wm. Plant, Joshua
Garey, Robt. Lowery, Jas. Burton. Adm: Rachel Garey.

18 Nov. 1815. Will of STEPHEN OWEN, dec'd proven by Jos. Owens,
Jonathan Johnston, Jr. and Clement Wells as exr. 1 Aug. 1815.
Will of STEPHEN OWEN. Wife; children (not named). Exr: Clement
Wells. Wit: Richard Sims, Jos. S. Owens and Jonthn. Johnston.

(No date) Estate sale of SAMUEL WATSON, dec'd. Purchasers: Jacob
Niswanger, Harry Hazel, Jno. Watson, Jas. Watson, Lewis Watson,
Willis Watson, Elijah Alberson, Jas. Mosley, Geo. Goddard, Jerm.
Warren, Jno. Adams. Adm: Lewis Watson.

7 Oct. 1815. Appraisal of estate of MARK HARDING, dec'd by Henry
Shell, Jno. Copeland and Jno. Underwood. 17 Oct. 1815. Estate
sale. Purchasers: Jno. Harding, Wm. Loveland(?). Adm: James
Harding.

(No date) Appraisal of estate of CHRISTOPHER ROWLAND, dec'd
by A. Mitchell, Wm. Strain, Jno. Hollingsworth and Saml. Leake.

6 Nov. 1815. Letters of adm. estate of ALEXANDER HENNERY, dec'd
to wife Nelley Hennery. Sec: Wm. Brown and Robt. Henery.

11 Dec. 1815. Letters of adm. estate of THOMAS HOLLAN, dec'd
to wife Jane Hollan. Sec: Elisha Adair, Thos. McCrary and Richd.
Hollan.

1 Nov. 1815. Second appraisal of estate of MICHAEL SWINDLE,
dec'd by Philip Wait, R. Powell, David Braden and Jas. Clardy.
1 Nov. 1815. Second estate sale. Purchasers: Elijah Powell,
Matthew Bolton, Wm. George, N. Saxon, Geo. Adams, Benj. Cooper,
Simeon Sims, Jno. Chism, Wm. Redden, Danl. Swindle, Robt. Dunlap,
Jas. Jones, Robt. Harris, Jno. Swindle. Exr: Aaron Clore.

1 Nov. 1815. Inv. and appraisal of estate of JACOB DORAN, dec'd
by Wm. Irby, Robt. Allison and Jno. Rodgers. Debts and book
accounts: Jas. Laughridge, Wm. Irby, Chas. Saxon, Wm. Orsborn,
Wm. Manley, Wm. Simmons, Joel Allen, Solomon Cole, Jno. Standly,
Saml. Stedman, Jos. Crooks, Jas. H. Lowery, Wm. Hudgens, Chas.
Simmons, Jas. Hannah, Benj. Griffin, Benj. Smith, Ambrose Hudgens,

Estate cont'd:
Thos. Porter, Benj. Strange, Elisha Adair, Robt. Hannah, Robt.
Creswell, Larkin Sullivan, Henry Morgan, Robt. Word (Ward?),
Edw. Gillespie, Wm. Henderson, Polly Dendy, Nehemiah Franks,
Benj. Bird, Wm. Bird, Saml. Todd, Seth Ward, Chas. Ferguson,
Jno. Williams, Robt. Nickles, Alex. Winn, Jas. Brown, Saml.
Green, Jno. Vaughn, Jas. Poole, Henry Fuller, Danl. Walker,
Jesse Cole, Wm. Downs, Jno. Wilson, Ann Johnston, Matt. Hunter,
dec'd., Levi Smith, Wm. Brown, David Glenn, Wm. Holliday, Wm.
Martin, Spencer Adkins, Robt. Holliday, Rody Cannady, Jno. Black,
Wm. Fulton, Patk. Sullivan, Jno. Mathis, Danl. Winn, B. W. Rich-
ards, Thos. Lewers, Andw. Winn, Dudley Guthrey, Martha Blakely,
Jos. Culberson, Joel Wescoat, Jno. Hill, Thos. Ward, Chas. Dendy,
Wm. Hughes, Jas. McCullough, Thos. Bain, Robt. McNees, Jno.
Sneed, Jos. Irby, Wm. Murrow, Jerm. Conant, Langston Orsborn,
Barth. Cradock, Nathl. Drummond, Jno. Spells, Joshua Smith,
Jerm. Simmons, Jno. Manly, Wm. Plant, Jos. McCullough, Thos.
Norris, Wm. Orsborn, Jas. Wright, Bartley Milam, Andw. H. Golden,
Lydall Allen, Wm. Weathers, Nathan Curry, Wm. Dennenton, Jno.
Blakely, Marshal Seay, Philip Sneed, Jas. Brison, Eliz. Simmons,
Jno. Crisp, Jas. McDowell, Jno. Henderson, Jno. P. Cunningham,
Valentine Harling, Jacob Miller, Robt. Nicolls, Nathan Ashmore,
Robt. Fleming, Wm. Hambleton, Jas. Mathis, Solomon Bobo, Eli
Sanders, Wm. Duckett, Thos. Duckett, Joel Dendy, Jno. Cunning-
ham, Wm. Clark, Richd. McNees, Jacob Niswanger, Blacksmith Allen,
David Cradock, Lydall Winn, Wheat Miller, Whitehead Wilks, Sala-
thiel Shockley, Jno. Stuart, Wm. Winn, Wm. Speer, Abraham Boyd,
Solomon Hopkins, David Nelson, Chas. Puckett, Jno. Garey, Benj.
Adair, Jno. Nickels, Thos. Floyd, Wm. Rodgers, Thos. Crage,
Wm. McClure, Harmon Waldrop, Wm. Smith, Thos. Milum, Mathew
Holliday, Chas. Burton, Wm. Burnside, Feral(?) Milum, McNees
Rodgers, Miles Ferguson, Israel Miller, Jno. Young, Jos. Piper,
Jno. Wesson, Randal Sullivan, Wm. Dunklin, Wm. Walker.

5 Oct. 1815. Appr'l of estate of DAVID SPEER, dec'd by Robt.
Ward, Benj. Byrd, Andw. Speer and Chas. Littel. Shown by Adm:
Robt. Creswell.

2 Nov. 1815. Estate sale of DAVID SPEER, dec'd. Purchasers:
Eli. Adair, Wm. Brown, Wm. Anderson, Jno. Brown, Jno. Blakely,
Jas. Blakely, Jas. Brison, Jno. Brison, Jos. Blakely, Burrel
Conant, Thos. Crosson, Wm. Clark, Jas. Clardy, Drury Couch,
Robt. Creswell, Thos. Grumbly, Robt. Cunningham, Geo. Brock,
Achd. Clardy, Barth Cradock, Jno. Cole, Jno. Davis, Thos. Davis,
Youngset(?) Dendy, Thos. Dendy, Jno. Dendy, Jas. Fleming, Saml.
Fleming, Chas. Fowler, Robt. F. Cummings, Jno. Floyd, Alex.
Fuller, Edw. Gillespie, Saml. Green, Wm. Goodwin, Thos. Glenn,
Abm. Holland, Jno. Hill, Jas. Hannah, Wm. Hannah, Wm. Holland,
Wm. Hambleton, Jas. Hunter, Jas. Hollingsworth, Wm. Hinton,
Wm. Hutcheson, Minyard Harris, Jos. Irby, Mark Killingsworth,
Rody Kennedy, Chas. Little, Jno. Leak, Moses Leak, Danl. Martin,
Jas. McDowell, Thos. McCrary, Jas. McCurley, Robt. Martin, Wm.
Nugent, Wm. Parks, Andw. Parks, Jas. Parks, Jas. Parks, Jr.,
Thos. Rodgers, Eli Sanders, Jno. Sneed, Saml. Smith, Andw. Speer,
Aaron Starns, Noah Smith, Wm. Spear, Marshal Seay, Larkin Sulli-
van, Jno. Taylor, Jane Taylor, Saml. Taylor, Zach. Tinsley,
Jos. Vance, Saml. Vance, Jas. Young, Robt. Ward, Thos. Ward,
Wm. Ward, Geo. Wolff, Jno. Wilson, Jno. Whitten, Danl. Winn,
Margret Speer, Joel Allen, Saml. Todd.

1 Jan. 1816. Letters of adm. estate of SARAH HARDING, dec'd
to Jas. Harding. Sec: Jas. Ward and Wm. Niel.

25 Nov. 1815. Appraisal of estate of ZACH. CUNNINGHAM, dec'd by Jno. Woody, Benj. Nabours and Jas. Strain.

(No date) Estate sale of CHRISTOPHER ROWLAND, dec'd. Purchasers: Alex. Winn, Abram Hall, Barth Craddock, Wm. Winn, Robt. Rowland, Jos. Brownlee, Thos. Harris, Jas. Pasley, Jno. Stanfield, Minyard Harris, Joel Burgess, Thos. Powell, Wm. Howel, Jas. Young, Wm. Fowler, Thos. Nichols, Elisha Brooks, Porter Culbertson, Richd. Carter, Danl. Rodgers, Youngset Dendy, Jno. Brown, Jas. Moore, Joel Neely, Jer. Conant, Saml. Leak, Tabitha Rowland, Danl. Mitchell, Wm. Dendy, Moses Irby, Jos. Hollingsworth, Wm. Carr, Jos. Faris, Wm. Walker, Wm. Baley, Wiley Mylum, Saml. Rodgers, Nancy Lefoy. Exr: Robt. Rowland.

20 Jan. 1816. Will of JAMES A. WILLIAMS, dec'd proven by J. W. Tinsley. John W. and Daniel Williams, exrs. 6 Jan. 1816. Will of JAMES A. WILLIAMS. Wife Mary; sons Daniel, John W. and 4 youngest children: Jas. Atwood, Franklin, Washington and Elihu Williams; daughters Sarah Cooper, Elizabeth Ann Cooper. Mentions land re Jas. Burnside, Jos. Hollingsworth, Mr. Armstrong, Thos. Golding. Exr: son-in-laws Reuben and Charles Cooper. Wit: W. Tinsley, Wm. Hudgens and R. H. Owens.

(No date) Appraisal of estate of ALEXANDER HENRY, dec'd by Rodger Brown, Jas. Fairbairn, and Wm. Brown. Notes on Jos. Piper, Jno. Higgins, Newton Higgins, Aaron Harding, Hiram Culbertson, Rodger Brown, Abner Rodgers, Luther Hitch, Jno. Adair, Tim Swan, Saml. Smith, J. Tribble, J. Tinsley, Sherard Tinsley, Wm. Harrows, Benj. Lewis, Uriah Davis, Abrhm. Boyd, Robt. Henry.

(No date) Second appraisal of estate of JOHN MADDEN, dec'd by J. Roberson, Randel Sullivan and Isaac Dial. (No date) Second sale. Exr: Geo. Madden.

(No date) Re estate of JAMES ATWOOD, dec'd. Polly Atwood and Wm. Ball qualified as exr. of will. 17 Jan. 1816. Will of JAMES ATWOOD. Wife Polly; son William Atwood and son-in-law William Ball. Exr: wife, son Wm. and son-in-law Wm. Ball. Wit: Jno. Clemons, Wm. Pollard and Tobias Cook.

30 Jan. 1816. Will of GEORGE WOLF, dec'd. Wife Nancy Wolf qualified as exr. Sec: John Sinclair and Wm. Armstrong. 7 Jan. 1806. Will of GEORGE WOLF. Daughter Mary; wife Nancy and her five children. Exr: wife Nancy, Capt. Saml. Henderson. Wit: Wm. Dunlap, Jno. Sinclair and Wm. Montgomery.

5 Feb. 1816. THOMAS DENDY, dec'd. (1799 will). Affidavit of adm. Wm. Dendy that about 15 Oct. 1810 in the presence of Saml. Powell, he paid Jas. H. Dendy and Jno. Baley his wife's legacy from the estate of her grandfather the sd Thomas Dendy, dec'd, she a daughter of Cornelius Dendy, and has lost the receipts and cannot find them. Wm. Burnside, JQM.

5 Feb. 1816. Letters of adm. estate of ATWOOD WILLIAMS, dec'd to Jno. W. and Danl. Williams.

5 Feb. 1816. Letters of adm. estate of BENJAMIN SMITH, dec'd to wife Elizabeth Smith. Sec: Robt. Creswell and Wm. F. Downs.

5 Feb. 1816. Appraisal of estate of THOMAS HOLLAND, dec'd by Thos. and Geo. McCrary, Richard Holland. 15 Feb.(?) 1816. Sale of estate. Adm: Jane Holland.(N.B. the first date not clear).

12 Feb. 1816. Second sale of estate of WILLIAM YOUNG, dec'd. Adm: Elizabeth Crocker formerly Young.

3 Feb. 1816. Letters of adm. estate of SALLY MARCHBANKS, dec'd to Jos. Lyon, Thos. Goodwin. (N.B. above entry crossed out).

22 Feb. 1816. Letters of adm. estate of BALEY CARTER, dec'd to Robt. Campbell. Sec: Jno. Middleton and Jno. Roberson.

2 Mar. 1816. Will of RICHARD M. OWENS, dec'd proven by Richard Hatter. Jos. S. Owens as exr.

4 Mar. 1816. Will of CHARLES HEWIT, dec'd proven by Wm. Dunlap and Samuel Barksdale. Jno. Hewit qualified as exr.

4 Mar. 1816. Will of PETER HAMMOND, dec'd proven by Isaac and Saml. Couch, Reuben Roberson. Peter and Isom Hammond qualified as exrs.

22 Feb. 1816. Will of CHARLES HEWIT. Wife Susanna Hewit; sons John, William and Ashley Hewit; daughters Catherine and Ruth Hewit and Susannah Neill. Exr: son John Hewit. Wit: Wm. Dunlap, Saml. Barksdale and Geo. Leek.

26 Jan. 1816. Will of PETER HAMMOND. Wife Ann; sons Isom, William and Peter Hammond; daughters Roady Roberson, Sally Garrett, Nancy McHurg, Betsy Garrett. Exr: sons. Wit: Israel Couch, Reuben Roberson, and Saml. Couch.

29 Feb. 1816. Estate sale of ZACHARIAH CUNNINGHAM, dec'd. Purchasers: Wm. Hudgens, Wm. Bolt, Susannah Clardy, Wm. P. Bolt, (N.B. Bolt not clear). Adm: Wm. Hudgens.

(No date) Estate of ALEXANDER HENRY, dec'd. Brief return. Adm: Nelly Henry. Cert. by Wm. Fulton.

(No date) Appraisal of estate of JEREMIAH HOLLINGSWORTH, dec'd by B. Nabours, Jno. Gray and Richd. Blackwell. 12 July 1812.

12 July 1812. Will of RICHARD M. OWEN. Abbeville. Wife Ann; daughter Belinda Sims; son David(?) Owen, dec'd (his five children); son Stephen Owne, dec'd (his five children); sons John, Benjamin, and Joseph S. Owen. Exr: Jos. S. Owen and Richard Sims. Wit: Thos. Childs, Richd. Hatter and Nancy Meron(?).

12 Feb. 1816. Appraisal of estate of BENJAMIN SMITH, dec'd by Wm. Irby, Robt. Creswell and Benj. Adkins. 17 Feb. 1816. Estate sale. Purchasers: Elizabeth Smith , Jno. Adkins, Jno. Hill, Wm. Irby, Turner Richardson, Wm. Smith, Noah Smith, Wm. Simmons, Jas. Ward, Edmond Wood, Rodey Canady, Chas. Vance. Exr(?): Elizabeth Smith.

9 Feb. 1816. Second appraisal of estate of ATWOOD WILLIAMS, dec'd by B. B. Cheshire, Thos. Ligon and Jno. Armstrong. (No date) Estate sale. Purchasers: Mary Williams, Wm. Crosson, B. Cooper, Allen Cox, Thos. Hill, Jno. W. Williams. Adm: Jno. W. Williams.

30 Jan. 1816. Appraisal of estate of JAMES A. WILLIAMS, dec'd by B. B. Cheshire, Thos. Ligon and Jno. Armstrong. (No date) Estate sale. Purchasers: Jas. Cook, Jno. Griffin, Anthony Griffin, Mickel Finn___, Reuben Hitt, Jno. B.(?) Williams, Drury Sims,

Estate sale cont'd:
Charles Cooper, Richd. Simpson, Marshall Pollard, David Hitt,
Alexr. Austin, John Smith, Jos. Cook, Wm. Pollard, Jno. Arm-
strong. Exr: Jno. W. Williams.

16 Mar. 1816. Letters of adm. estate of JOHN SHIRLEY, dec'd
to Robt. Shirley. Sec: Wm. McPherson.

(No date) Appraisal of estate of JAMES ATWOOD, dec'd by Wm.
Chiles, Jas. Turner and Benj. Foshee.

6 Jan. 1816. Appraisal of estate of SARAH HARDING, dec'd by
Jno. Copeland, Matthew Hunter and Geo. Leek.

15 Oct. 1815. Appraisal of estate of JOHN SIMPSON, dec'd by
Isaac Underwood, Chas. Griffin and Alex. Glenn.

1 Apr. 1816. Will of WILLIAM LEAK, dec'd proven by Wm. Dendy
and Newman Gary. Samual Leak as exr. 7 Jan. 1807. Will of WIL-
LIAM LEAKE, SR. Wife Providence; son Samuel; rest of my children (not named). Exr: Providence and son Samuel Leake. Wit:
Jas. Holley, Wm. Carter and Newman Gary.

14 Mar. 1816. Appraisal of estate of JOSEPH WILSON, dec'd by
Langston East, Alex. Glenn and Jno. Tygert. 15 Mar. 1816. Estate
sale. No purchasers. Adm: Nancy Wilson.

23 Oct. 1815. Estate sale of JOHN SIMPSON, dec'd. Purchasers:
Wm. Anderson, Saml. Austin, Jno. Armstrong, Alex. Asten, Ephraim
Anderson, Willis Brown, Jno. Bell, Richd. Brooks, Wm. Boyd,
Saml. Boyd, Henry Butler, Danl. Butler, Jno. Boyd, Jno. Burnside,
Jno. Black, Wm. Drake, Wm. Dendy, Vann Davis, Jno. Drake, Isaac
Casa, Jno. Graford(?), Elihu Creswell, Jno. S. Creswell, Thos.
Casey, Saml. Caldwell, Thos. Cummings, Benj. Cheshire, Thos.
East, Jno. Felts, Solomon Fuller, Jones Fuller, Ransom Fuller,
Fredk. Foster, Capt. Saml. Farrow, Chas. Fletcher, Wm. Farrow,
Jno. Garlington, Maj. Jno. Griffin, Capt. Chas. Griffin, Wm.
Green, Wm. Glenn, Jeremiah Glenn, Jno. Greer, Charter Griffin,
Maj. R. Griffin, Capt. Anthony Griffin, Jno. Samson, Jno. John-
ston, Abrham Jackson, Benj. Jones, Mrs. Jones, Chas. Kimble,
Jesse Moats, Jno. Monrow, Ob. Michaux, Silas Moats, Elisha Moats,
Jno. Moats, Reuben Leonard, Ezekiel North, Richd. North, Ob.
Pitts, Jesse Pitts, Jno. Pitts, Nathan Pitts, Thos. Pitts, Dr.
A. Pyle, Saml. Plant, Thos. Rodgers, Geo. Roberts, Jas. Smith,
Jas. Shackleford, Chas. Simpson, Jas. Simpson, Alex. Simpson,
Jno. W. Simpson, Wm. Simpson, Wm. Stripling, Wm. Tinsley, Isaac
Underwood, Wm. Vance, Geo. Wolff, Wm. Walker, W. P. Vaughn,
Jos. Wallis, Widow Catey Watts, Robt. Workman, Col. Jas. Wil-
liams, Maj. Thos. Wright, Thos. Wilson, Drury Vaughn, Thos.
Casey, David Vance, And. Winn, David McCaa, Jno. Milum, Wm.
Mitchell. Exr: W. W. Simpson.

7 Nov. 1815. Estate sale of JACOB DORAN, dec'd. Purchasers:
Joel Allen, Abrhm. Bolt, Jno. Baley, Wm. Barker, Wm. Boyd, James
Burns, David Craddock, Chas. Dudley, Danl. Harrison, Wm. Cunning-
ham, Nancy Doran, Thos. Davenport, Jas. Ensley, Wm. Estes, Saml.
Franks, Stephen Garrett, Thos. Gains, Edw. Gillespie, Jas. Holt,
Elisha Adair, Wm. Hopper, Jno. Harris, Jos. Irby, Jeremiah Kile,
Wm. Estes, Mark Killingsworth, Hambleton _____, Robt. McNees,
Danl. Martin, ___ McDavid, Benj. Nabours, Jacob Nabours, Duke
Pinson, Jas. Parks, And. Parks, Thos. Parks, Wm. Brown, Jacob
Roberts, Wm. Moore, Robt. Nickles, Jno. Simmons, Chas. Simmons,

DORAN estate sale cont'd:
Hiram Sims, David Studard, Philip Sneed, Edw. Winn, Jno. Wilson,
Thos. Ward, Jas. Ward, Henry Doran, Jos. Stain. Adm: Robt. McNees.

(No date) Estate sale of MATTHEW HUNTER, dec'd. Exr: James Mc-
Mahan.

5 Apr. 1816. Will of ALEXANDER MORRISON, dec'd proven by William
Black, John Leeke. Benjamin Bird as exr. 21 Mar. 1799. Will
of ALEXANDER MORRISON. Cousin Allen McDougal; nephew Alexander
Turner. Mentions Archibald Cammel, merchant of Glasgow; John
Leeke to keep possession of Millwell. Exr: Benjamin Bird and
John Simpson of Little River. Wit: Archibald Smith, Wm. Byrd
and John Leake.

27 Feb. 1816. Second estate sale of ANDERSON ARNOLD, dec'd.
Purchasers: David Cowan, Jesse Childress, Hiram Sims, Jacob
Gary, Pleasant Shaw, Andrew McNight, Chas. Parks, Henry Vaughn,
Saml. Studard, Dempsey Hellams, Nancy McHaffie, James Green,
Jas. Harris, Jno. F. Wolff, Jno. Nash, Wm. Abercrombie, Thos.
Lindley, Jas. Bolt, Jno. Armstrong, Elizabeth Lindley, Wm. Min-
ten(?), Stephen Garrett. Adm: Mary Arnold.

17 Apr. 1816. Letters of adm. estate of WILLIAM SAXON, dec'd
to John Saxon. Sec: B. H. Saxon and Jno. Barksdale.

18 May 1816. Will of GRIZLET (GRIZZLE?) HAZLETT, dec'd proven
by James Strain. Howard Pinson exr. 1 Dec. 1815. Will of GRIZLET
HAZLETT. Sons John and Robert Hazlett; daughter Nancy; nephews
William, Adam and Matthew McDaniel(?) and David Nelson. Exr:
Charles Nickles. Wit: Jas. Strain and Wm. Reed.

18 Aug(?) 1816. Amos S. Graves, minor about 17 years, chose
Joseph Neely as guardian. Sec: Geo. Madden and Jno. Watson.

(No date) Appraisal of estate of RICHARD M. OWENS, dec'd by
Drury Sims, James Ward and Thos. Ligon. 2 Apr. 1816. Estate
sale. Exr: Jos. S. Owens.

(No date) Appraisal of estate of CHARLES HEWIT, dec'd by Coleman
Carlisle, Matthew Hunter and Samuel Young.

23 May 1816. Will of THOMAS DAVENPORT, dec'd proven by Stephen
Wharton and Wm. Low. Lettice Davenport as exr./adm. 14 Sept.
1812. Will of THOMAS DAVENPORT. Present wife Lettice; son Burket;
children of first wife Salley to receivee legacy of Jno. Partlow
of Spotsylvania co., Va.; daughter Lucy Harris. Wit: Wm. Nelson,
Nathan Sims and Stephen Wharton.

23 Feb. 1816. Appraisal of estate of GEORGE WOLF, dec'd by Isaac
Underwood, James Young and Saml. Henderson. 27 Feb. 1816. Estate
sale. Purchasers: Nancy Wolf, Jas. Brown, Alex. Winn, Wm. Mc-
Murtry, Thos. Porter, Wm. Dunlap, Jno. Mason, Abner Teague,
Capt. Griffin, Shered Tinsley, Jno. Speers, Jno. Croford, Danl.
Winn, Robt. Stewart, Joshua Teague, Robt. Hunter, Ann Saxon,
Dvaid Gambrell, Saml. Boyd, Chas. Simpson, Abraham Johnston,
Jas. Boyd, Isaac Underwood, Jno. Monroe, Geo. Leek, Andw. Winn,
Jno. Copeland, Wm. Clement, Isaac Finney, Jas. Ward, H. T. Shell,
Jno. Prior, Wm. Smith, Jer. Leek, Geo. Leek, Wm. Bailey, Jas.
Harding, Jno. Wolf, Jas. Cook, Gallanus Winn, Jno. Deen, Zach.
Chisum, Jobe Mason, Ezekiel Chism, Anthony Griffin, Jas. Austin,
Jas. Harding, Jno. Sloan, Jno. Moats, Wm. Garey, Jas. Bryson,

Estate sale cont'd:
Thos. Rodgers, Wm. Underwood, Geo. Houlditch, Wm. Lofton, Isaac
Finney, Wm. W. Simpson, Benj. Cheshire, Francis Lester, Frederick
Miller, Jno. Garey, Richard Owens, Jacob Stuckman.

14 Jan. 1816. Estate sale of SARAH HARDING, dec'd. Purchasers:
John Harding, Matthew Harding, James Harding, Elizabeth Harding,
John James, Jno. Young, Abner Young, Benj. Wilson, Jesse John-
ston, Jobe Johnston, Margaret Leek, Coleman Carlisle, Anthony
Griffin. Adm: James Harding.

12 Apr. 1816. Appraisal of estate of PETER HAMMOND, dec'd by
Thos. Parks, Isaac Couch, Jeremiah Ball and Wm. Putman. (No
date) Estate sale. Purchasers: Nancy Hammond, Isom Hammond,
Peter Hammond, Wm. Garrett, Jno. Owens, Jos. Coker, Harmon Gar-
rett, Thos. Garrett, Menoah Roberson, Reuben Bramblett, Andw.
Mathis, Robt. Hand, Garlington Coker, Aaron Jones, Edsy White-
field, Isaac Couch, Reuben Estes, Jno. Sims, Jno. Stroud, Asa
Moore, Jno. Stewart, Elisha Watson, Barnett Roberson, Nicklas
Garrett, Robt. Fleming, Jacob Garey, Joshua Barrett, Lewis Car-
gill, Mitchell Putman, Nathan Garrett, Nathan Brown. Exr: Peter
Hammond.

4 Apr. 1816. Appraisal of estate of WILLIAM LEEK, dec'd by Thos.
Ball, Jerm. Conant and Jas. Bailey. 16 Apr. 1816. Estate sale.
Purchasers: Armistead Leek, Salley Leek, Joel Walker, Jas. A.
Yount, Geo. Leake, Saml. Leake, Peter Fuller, Jerm. Connant,
Wm. Harris, Whitehead Wilks, Jas. Cobb, Nathan Drummond, Jesse
Godfrey. Exr: Saml. Leak.

3 June 1816. Letters of adm. estate of WILLIAM PUTMAN, dec'd
to wife Marey Putman. Sec: Aaron Moore and Peter Hammond.

3 June 1816. Letters of adm. estate of SAMUEL WILLIAMS, dec'd
to Chas. Allen. Sec: Benj. Williams and John Davis.

3 June 1816. Letters of adm. estate of JOHN SINCLAIR, dec'd
to wife Marey Sinclair. Sec: Wm. Millner and Wm. Franks.

1 Apr. 1816. Appraisal of estate of WILLIAM SAXON, dec'd by
Wm. Underwood, Jesse Johnston and Henry Shell.

(No date) Appraisal of estate of ALEXANDER MORISON, dec'd by
Benj. Bird, Wm. Craig and Jesse Maberry. 23 Apr. 1816. Estate
sale. Purchasers: Wm. Craig, Wm. Alexander, Jesse Mabery, Jno.
Moore, Jno. Black. Maj. Dillard, Nancy Mahon, Jas. Hannah, Jno.
Farrow, Jno. Finley, Martin Burk, Jas. Vines, Jesse McClure,
Wm. Higgins, Geo. Ross, Aaron Starns, Jas. Hannah, Wm. Brown,
Jos. Terry, Geo. Dillard, Wm. Jones, Philip Staff, Bevister(?)
Couch, Rodey Brown, Wm. Glenn, J. A. Elmore. Adm. (with will
attached): Jno. Black.

6 June 1816. Letters of adm. estate of MAREY BABB, dec'd to
Jas. Culbertson. Sec: Thos. Babb and Jos. Babb.

15 June 1816. Will of JOHN SMITH, dec'd proven by Wilson Sanders,
Jno. Smith, Jr. Wife Susanna Smith as exr. 20 Nov. 1807. Will
of JOHN SMITH. Wife Susannah. Exr: wife. Wit: Wilson Sanders
and Jno. Smith, Jr.

(No date) Joshua Saxon, minor about 15 years, chose Robt. Creswell as guardian. Sec: Rody Cannady and Benj. Nabours.

12 June 1816. Appraisal of estate of WILLIAM PUTMAN, dec'd by Jno. Simpson, Danl. Putman and Wm. Putman.

17 Apr. 1815. Will of JAMES GLENN. Wife; children to be schooled; sons Francis, James and John; daughter Catherine. Exr: David Glenn and Wm. Cowan. Wit: Alex. Mills, Francis Glenn and Elizabeth Glenn.

1 June 1816. Appraisal of estate of THOMAS DAVENPORT, dec'd by Chas. Hughs, Frederick Purtz and Wm. Lowe.

(No date) Appraisal of estate of JOHN SHIRLEY, dec'd by Jacob Niswanger, James McFerson and Wm. Moore. (No date) Estate sale. Purchasers: David Anderson, Jacob Niswanger, Birey Shirley, Jas. McFerson, Saml. Freeman, Jno. Shirley, Robt. Shirley, Thos. Adkins, Wm. McFerson, Jonthn. Forgey, Jas. Watson, Geo. Elmore, Geo. Shirley, Aaron Shirley, Elizaeth Shirley, Ebenezer Starns, Martin Shaw, Ransom Fuller, Jno. Harvey, Wm. West, Wm. Redden, and Adm: Robt. Shirley.

1 July 1816. Letters of adm. estate of DAVID MOATS, dec'd to Silas Moats. Sec: John Motes and Chas. Goodman.

(No date) Estate sale of WILLIAM PARKS, dec'd. Purchasers: Nancy Parks, Thos. Campbell, Jacob Roberts, Jno. Gilbert, Saml. Parks, Jno. Stroud, Henry Brockman, Wm. Power, Nathan Parks, Jas. Long, Jos. Brown, Allen Kilgore, Willis Threlkeld, Elijah Willis, Obediah Halcom, Jos. Halcom, Jno. Wallis, Jos. Gilbert, Mrs. N. T. Rodgers, Danl. Hughs, Wm. Rice, Thos. Brown, Thos. Parks, Robt. Hand, Jr., Wm. Halbert, Jesse Wallis, Ellis Cheek, Jno. Meador, Chas. Cargill, Thos. Jones. Adm: Thos. Parks.

(No date) Appraisal of estate of JOHN SINCLEAR, dec'd by Jno. Hewit, Langston East and Saml. Barksdale.

20 June 1816. Appraisal of estate of SAMUEL WILLIAMS, dec'd by Mabra Madden, Jno. Madden, Isaac Dial and B. Nabours.

(No date) Estate sale of MATTHEW HUNTER, dec'd. Purchasers: Benj. Byrd, Allen Barksdale, Wm. Parker, Jno. Black, Wm. Blakely, Wm. Brown, Jno. P. Cunningham, Jerm. Collins, Jno. Cowen, Jno. Dunlap, Jacob Doran, Wm. F. Downs, Jas. Endlsey, Wm. Fowler, Jno. Findley, Saml. Greer, Henry Greer, Robt. Henry, Jno. Hunter, Alex. Henry, Matt. Hunter, Wm. Irby, Jno. Jowel(Joel), Thos. Jones, Chas. Littel, Jas. Laughridge, Isaac Miller, Jno. McLain, Jno. Munrow, Saml. Nabours, Jno. Orsborn, Thos. Porter, Jas. Parks, Jno. Rodgers, Wm. Kenelson, Turner Richardson, Benj. Richards, Rich. Shackleford, Wm. Simpson, Timothy Swan, David Saxon, Jno. Sneed, Abner Teague, Saml. Todd, C. Tinsley, Jas. Ward, Wm. Ward, Thos. Ward. Acting exr: Wm. F. Downs.

20 May 1816. Appraisal of estate of GRIZZELL HAZLETT, dec'd by Jonthn. Johnston, Wm. Reed, Aaron Pinson and Robt. Carter.

(No date) Estate sale of JOHN SINCLEAR, dec'd Purchasers: Marey Sinclear, Jno. Davis, Wm. Millner, Saml. Anderson, Jas. A. Lowery, Saml. Neel, Wm. Barksdale, Henry Wimbelow. Adm: Marey Sinclear.

2 Aug. 1816. Estate of MESHACK OVERBY, dec'd. Nimrod Overby and Moses Wells qualify as exrs. of will. 2 Jan. 1801. Will of MESHACK OVERBY. Wife Mary; sons Nimrod, Nicholas and Benjamin;

OVERBY will cont'd:
daughters Mary Wells, Elizabeth Green, Ann Atwood, Janah Moss
and children Elizabeth and Mason Moss. Exr: son Nimrod Overby
and Moses Wells. Wit: Jonathan Johnstono, Wm. Rucks, Jr. and
Benjamin Overby.

7 June 1816. Appraisal of estate of MAREY BABB, dec'd by James
Young, Wm. Lowe and John Mitchell. 26 June 1816. Estate sale.
Purchasers: Jos. Babb, Thos. Babb, Wm. Kellett, Jos. Brownlee,
Ransom Fuller, Eldridge Fuller, Saml. Rodgers, Jas. Culbertson,
Peter Culbertson, Elisha Chisum, Joel Burgess, Thos. Case, Robt.
Bouling, Danl. Fuller, Lewis Nelson, David McCaa, Wm. Griffin,
and Adm: James Culbertson.

July 1816. Will of HUGH SCILLION(?). Wife Jane; daughters Jane,
Amey and Patsy. Exr: wife Jane. Wit: Basil Prater and Josiah
Prater, J. D. Kern.

26 Jan. 1816. Will of JAMES ROBERTS. Wife Sarah; brother Edmond
Roberts. Exr: Jacob Niswanger and James Crocker. Wit: Jacob
Niswanger, Wm. McFerson and Jas. Crocker.

8 July 1816. Appraisal of estate of DAVID MOATS, dec'd by Chas.
Goodman, Solomon Fuller, Jr. and Jesse Motes.

16 July 1816. Estate sale of WILLIAM PUTMAN, dec'd. Purchasers:
Marey Putman, Jesse Rowland, Minnard Harris, Wm. A. Cramton,
Jno. Armstrong, Wm. Cross, Isaac Baldwin, Mitchel Putman, Almon
Grant, Reuben Putman, Wm. Simpson, Basden Guinn, Josiah Cooper,
Jacob Nabours, Wm. Barker, Henry Putman, Chas. Smith, Jas. Long,
Adam Potter, Jas. Young, Wm. Parker, Jno. Morris, Garrett Sul-
livant, Thomson Vaughn, Elisha Power, Wm. Garrett, Alex. Brown,
Jonathan Garrett, Wm. Roberson, W. Garrett. Adm: Marey Putman.

12 Aug. 1816. Will of JAMES COOK, dec'd. Mitchel and Daniel
Cook qualify as exrs with Ezekiel North.

1 Aug. 1816. Appraisal of estate of JAMES GLENN, dec'd by Alex.
Mills, Alex. Taylor and Robt. Fleming.

21 June 1816. Estate sale of SAMUEL WILLIAMS, dec'd. Purchasers:
Hillary Atkins, Saml. Boyd, Elias Brock, Jas. Clardy, J. Cole,
Isaac Dial, Jno. Fowler, Chas. Burton, Wm. Hudgens, Chas. Hobbs,
Jos. Irby, Jno. Johnston, Mabry Madden, Richd. McNees, Jno.
Madden, Thos. Morris, Benj. Nabours, Jesse Pinson, Jno. Strange,
Saml. Williams, Joel Westcoat, Benj. Norris, Geo. Wilson, widow
Marey Williams, Thos. B. Williams. Adm: Charles Allen.

14 Jan. 1815. Estate sale of JOHN RICHEY, JR., dec'd. Purchasers:
Samuel Richey, James Richey, Wm. Richey, Jno. Richey, Ginny
Harris. Adm: John Richey.

28 Feb. 1815. Will of JAMES COOK. Wife Ursula; sons Mitchell,
Daniel, Tobias and William; grandson James, son of Clayton Cook;
grandchildren Emily, Matilda, Eliza and Mary Teague; son John.
Exr: wife Ursula, sons Mitchell and Daniel. Wit: Abner Pyles,
Jno. Black and Allen Pitts. Codicil: wit: J. Black and Ezekiel
North.

31 Aug. 1816. Letters of adm. estate of JOHN VAUGHN, dec'd to
Josiah Fowler. Sec: James Crocker and John Middleton. Sale to
be on plantation of Wm. Roberson.

2 Sept. 1816. Letters of adm. estate of HIRAM GOODWIN, dec'd to wife Hannah Goodwin. Sec: Joshua Pace and Thos. DeShields.

6 Sept. 1816. Letters of adm. estate of HENRY PUTMAN, dec'd to wife Salley Putman. Sec: Stephen Garrett and Rebecca Moore.

16 Sept. 1816. Will of JOSEPH RUNNOLDS, dec'd proven by Anthony Golding and Jos. Jones. Elizabeth Runnolds and John Cook as exrs. 25 Jan. 1815. Will of JOSEPH RUNNOLDS. Wife Elizabeth; my youngest children Polley, Betsey, Anna, Lucinda, Yearby and William Runnolds. Exr: wife Elizabeth and John Cook. Wit: Reuben Golding, Anthony Golding and Jos. Jones.

(No date) Appraisal of estate of DAVID MOATS, dec'd by Chas. Goodman, Solomon Fuller and Jesse Moats. (Date not clear) Estate sale. Purchasers: Nancy Motes, Silsa Motes, Jones Fuller, Jas. Cook, Jos. Rodgers, David Greer, Wm. Perkins, Andrw. Rodgers, Peter Fuller, Abner Pyles, Jas. Culberson, Allen Coleman, Wm. Fuller, Matt. Bryson, Jonathan Motes, Porter Culberson, Robt. Monrow, Jno. Motes, Elhannon Crocker, Thos. Rodgers, Margaret Harris, Chas. Goodman, Saml. Rodgers. Adm: Silsa Motes.

20 Sept. 1816. Appraisal of estate of JOSEPH RUNNOLDS, dec'd by Jno. Deale, Saml. Goodman and Lewis Ball.

1 Sept. 1816. Appraisal of estate of HENERY PUTMAN, dec'd by Roberson Moore, Thos. Crooks and John Ashley. 28 Sept. 1816. Estate sale. Purchasers: Salley Putman, Jos. Moor, Robt. Moor, Jno. Garrett, Reuben Roberson, David, son of Jno. Garrett. Adm: Salley Putman.

18 Sept. 1816. Appraisal of estate of HIRAM GOODWIN, dec'd by Jno. Templeton, Jno. Dillard and Thos. Desheils.

7 Oct. 1816. Letters of adm. estate of JAMES BOYD, dec'd to wife Abigail Boyd. Sec: Saml Boyd and Robt. Gray.

7 Oct. 1816. Will of CHARLES SAXON, dec'd proven by Jonathan Downs, Ezekiel Mathes and Chas. Saxon, Jr. as exr. 2 June 1816. Will of CHARLES SAXON. Daughters Polly Anderson, Sally Rodgers. widow of son Lewis Saxon (Sally McNees), grandson Charles Saxon, Jr. (money due me from Ira Arnold and Allen Saxon). Exr: grandson Chas. Saxon, Jr. Wit: Jonathan Downs, Ezekiel Mathess and Rebecka Mathess.

(No date) Appraisal of estate of JOHN VAUGHN, dec'd by Wm. Rodgers, Thos. Burnside, Wm. Dukes and Elhannon Crocker. (No date) Estate sale. Purchasers: Chas. Jones, Betty Rodgers, Richd. Fowler, Josiah Fowler, Saml. Rodgers, Andrew Rodgers, Wm. Rodgers, Elhannon Crocker, Robt. Gill, Burket Duckett, Abner Pyles, Zach. Bailey, Wm. Dukes, Wm. Simpson, Danl. Mitchel, Edw. Winn, Cathy Vaughn. Adm: Josiah Fowler.

7 Oct. 1816. Will of TIMOTHY SWAN, dec'd proven by Jas. Hutchison, Jno. Simmons. Wm. F. Downs as exr. 21 July 1816. Will of TIMOTHY SWAN. Mother; wife Sarah; daughters Rebecca and Isabella; son Alexander. Money due him from ests. of Mathew Hunter and Alex. Henry. Exr: Wm. F. Downs and wife Sarah Swan. Wit: Jas. Hutchison, Jno. Simmons and David Slone.

16 Oct. 1816. Letters of adm. estate of ROBERT FRANKS, dec'd to Wm. Franks. Sec: Jno. Williams, Collar Barksdale.

4 Oct. 1816. Appraisal of estate of JAMES ROBERTS, dec'd by Wm.Moor, Jas. McFerson and Wm. McFerson. Notes on Isom(?) Pinson, Jacob Niswanger, Wm. Piper(?) and Geo. Lowery.

(No date) Estate sale of ALEXANDER HENRY, dec'd. No purchasers named. Adm: Wm. Fulton and Nelley Henry.

28 Feb. 1816. Appraisal of estate of BALEY CARTER, dec'd by Wm. Green, Thos. Davenport and Thos. W. Golding. (No date) Estate sale. Purchasers: Charles Kimble, Andrew Winn, Joel Carter. Adm: Robert Campbell.

14 Oct. 1816. Appraisal of estate of JAMES COOK, dec'd by Abner Pyles, Jos. Fowler and Wm. Dunlap. (No date) Estate sale. Exr: Mitchel Cook.

(No date) Estate sale of WILLIAM SAXON, dec'd. Purchasers: Jno. Saxon, Athey Saxon, Molly Saxon, Bethiah Saxon, Wm. Saxon, Marey Saxon, Saml. Hunter, Jas. Harding, Geo. McClure, Geo. Leek, Henry Shell. Adm: John Saxon.

2 Nov. 1816. Will of JOHN WILLARD, dec'd proven by Elizabeth Davenport. Micajah Willard as exr. 26 June 1816. Will of JOHN WILLARD. Wife Patty; s;on MIcajah; daughters Polly, Elizabeth and Sarah. Exr: son Micajah Willard. Wit: Jos. Neely, Walter Burgess and Elizabeth Davenport.

(No date) Second sale of est. of WILLIAM PUTMAN, dec'd. Purchasers: Marey Putman, Wm. Hall, Jas. Long, Saml. Studdard, Jas. Cheek, Jno. Vaughn, Wm. Meador, Mitchel Putman. Adm: Mary Putman.

16 Oct. 1816. Second sale of est. of GRIZZEL HAZLET, dec'd. Purchasers not named. Adm: Howard Pinson (will attached).

28 Dec. 1816. Will of WILLIAM POWELL, dec'd proven by David Braden and M. Norman. Jas. Powell and Philip Wait as exrs. 19 Nov. 1816. Will of WILLIAM POWELL. Wife and our two children William Wesley and Nancy Elizabeth Powell; other children by my first wife Elizabeth, Rhody, Peachy, Polly, Fanny, Sally, Amy, Belinda, Milly and Virginia Powell. Exr: brother James Powell and son-in-law Philip Wait. Wit: David Braden, Wm. Braden and Martin Norman.

15 Nov. 1816. Letters of adm. estate of AINSWORTH MIDDLETON, dec'd to John Middleton. Sec: Jos. Neeley and Jno. Roberson. 3 Jan. 1817. Appraisal of estate by Jas. Underwood, Jno. Underwood and Jno. Copelin.

(No date) Appraisal of estate of WM. POWELL, dec'd by David Braden, Zach. Arnold and Wm. Moore.

(No date) Appraisal of estate of ROBT. FRANKS, dec'd by Wm. Downs, Collyer Barksdale, Jno. Williams and Chas. Williams. 10 Dec. 1816. Estate sale. Purchasers: Nehemiah Franks, Elizabeth Franks, Wm. Franks, Wm. Parks, Jas. Ward, Saml. Arnold, Jas. Templeton, Stephen Potter, Wm. Morrow, Herbert Martin, Royale Allen, Chas. Allen, Robt. Allison, Joshua Franks, Eli Anderson, Peter Pool, Henry Simpson, Jno. Pope, Thos. Nabours, Ellis Cheek, Allen Barksdale, Chas. Prim, Stephen Garrett, Jno. Strange, Jas. Parks, Robt. Fleming, Wm. Irby, Zach. Allen, Martha Franks, Thos. Rodgers, Lydiah Williams, Alex. Mills, Nathan

Estate sale cont'd:
Barksdale, Joshua Millner, Henry Delph, Martin Glidewell, Wm.
Barker, Wm. Ransom, Wm. Franks, Jas. Millner, Wm. Henderson,
Joel Allen, Asa L. Potter, Jacob Motes, Henry Pope, Coleman
Ward. Adm: Wm. Franks.

4 Nov. 1816. OBEDIAH ESTES, dec'd. Estate sale. Purchasers:
Rody Canady, Joel Allen, Jos. Irby, Reuben Estes, Wm. Estes,
Jno. Barksdale, Allen Barksdale, Thos. Porter, Jas. Ward, Joel
Estes, Wm. Barker, Chas. Allen, Joshua Franks, Benj. Richards,
Saml. Williams, Chas. Williams, Nathl. Barksdale, David Ross.

25 Jan. 1817. ANTHONY GRIFFIN, dec'd. Current account of estate.
Paid legatees: Barnet Leak, John Butler; paid Jno. Wallis, guardian for minor child of Asa Griffin, dec'd; my own part as legatee. Adm: John Cook.
8 Jan. 1817. Return of estate of ALEXANDER DEALE, dec'd. Paid
legatees: widow's third; Jas. Cason; Thos. Hitt; Jas. Deale;
Demilion Deale; Alexander Deale; my own part. Adm: John Deale.
Cert. 10 Jan. 1817.

8 Dec. 1816. Robert Blakely, minor about 16 years, chose Wm.
Copelin as guardian. Sec: Henry McKelvy, Wm. Grayham.

12 Oct. 1816. Appraisal of estate of MESHACK OVERBY, dec'd by
David Owen, Josiah Evans and Reuben Golding. 13 Oct. 1816. Estate
sale. Purchasers: Reuben Golding, Wm. Nickols, Nimrod Overby,
Wm. Whiteford, Jno. Beasley, Elizabeth Green, Wm. Sadler, Joel
Pinson, Jas. Luker, Ransom Clear.....(?), Jno. Weathers, Mickel
Finney, Benj. R. Mitchell, Moses Wells, Geo. Neely, Jabez W.
Johnston, Eli Whiteford, Jas. Hathorn, A. Golding, H. Pinson,
Jno. Long, Wm. Nickles, Robt. Campbell, Saml. Gilbert, Jno.
Beasley, M. Finney, Jno. Weathers, Thos. Weathers. Exr: Nimrod
Overby.

19 Dec. 1816. Appraisal of estate of JAMES BOYD, dec'd by Robt.
Gray, Jno. Boyd and Saml. Boyd. (No date) Estate sale. Adm:
Abigail Boyd.

3 Feb. 1817. Letters of adm. estate of DAVID MC CLURE, dec'd
to Jeremiah Brown and Jno. McClure. Sec: Jno. Dillard and Patk.
Scott.

3 Feb. 1817. Letters of adm. estate of WILLIAM HUDGENS, dec'd
to wife Patsy Hudgens. Sec: Wm. F. Downs and Danl. Walker.

6 Jan. 1817. Second sale of estate of JAMES A. WILLIAMS, dec'd.
Purchasers: Daniel Williams, Wm. Green, Christopher Griffin,
Jno. Armstrong, Wm. Tompson, Jas. Williams. Exr: Danl. Williams.

4 Jan. 1817. Estate sale of AINSWORTH MIDDLETON, dec'd. Purchas-
ers: Jonathan Lowery, Robt. Hunter, Jas. Cobb, Jno. Mason, Jno.
Middleton, Jane Middleton, Jno. Finney, Matt. Hunter, David
Grayham, Jas. Boyd, Coleman Carswell(?), Jeremiah Leek, Jno.
Harding. Adm: John Middleton.

8 Feb. 1817. David Nelson, Jr., minor, chose David Nelson, Sr.
as guardian. Sec: Wm. McCrary, Martin Shaw.

17 Feb. 1817. Benjamin Williams, minor, chose Richard Blackwell
as guardian. Sec: Henry Gray and Abner Crenshaw.

25 Dec. 1816(?). JACOB ROBERTS, dec'd. Return of estate: pd each legatees part, debts due from Isaac Roberts and Jno. Roberts, amts pd to A. Young, Henry Threlkell, Jas. Ford, Jno. Pugh, Jno. Meadors. To Mrs. Mary Roberts, widow of Jacob (she rec'd old plantation and not entitled to further). Pd Walter Austin, husband of Matilda Gilbert; Jno. Akin husband of Lucinda Gilbert; Isaac Roberts; Josiah Deen husband of Polley; Jno. D. Mitcheson husband of Clarissa; Thos. Roberts; Jacob Roberts; Jno. Roberts; Fielder Brown, adm. of Ellender Brown, dec'd; Jno. Gilbert husband of Sarah; Mary Roberts, widow of Jacob Roberts; retained my own share as husband of Elizabeth; Exr: John Meador.

28 Feb. 1817. Return of est. of MATHEW CUNNINGHAM, dec'd. James Clardy, adm. succeeding Susannah Cunningham now his wife, mother of eight children of the sd Mathew Cunningham, dec'd. Pd Wm. Hudgens, adm. of Zach. Cunningham (one of legatees); pd Wm. Hudgens (guardian of Jane Cunningham). Money in hand as guardian of six children. Adm: Jas. Clardy.

1 July 1816. Appraisal of est. of CHARLES SAXON, dec'd by J. F. Wolff, Wm. Arnold, Wm. Milner and Wm. Henderson. 20 Jan. 1817. Estate sale. Purchasers: D. Rodgers, Wm. Milner, Geo. Brownlee, Chas. Saxon. Exr: Chas. Saxon.

7 Oct. 1816. Letters of adm. estate of JAMES MC CLURE, dec'd to Frances McClure. Sec: Nathan Langston and Solomon Smith. (No date) Appraisal of estate by Nathan Langston, Solomon Smith and Chany Bobo. Debts: Jesse James McClure; to Dr. Geo. Ross, J. D. Kern, Aaron Bobo, Wm. Grage, David Templeton and Elizabeth Ray.

10 Mar. 1817. GEORGE BALL, dec'd. Jemima Ball as exr. 28 Sept. 1807. Will of GEORGE BALL. Wife Jemima; children (not named). Exr: wife Jemima, John and Lewis Ball. Wit: Jas. Ball, Jas. Neely, Henry Hitt.

10 Mar. 1817. Letters of adm. estate of BENJAMIN SILLS, dec'd to Thos. W. Golding. Sec: Robt. Campbell and Alex. Austin.

10 Mar. 1817. Letters of adm. estate of DANIEL WOOD, dec'd to Thos. W. Golding. Sec: Robt. Campbell and Alex. Austin.

20 Jan. 1817. Estate sale of LEWIS SAXON, dec'd. Purchasers: Wm. Arnold, Ira Arnold, Jas. Atwood, Bob Allison, Lyd Allen, Joel Allen, Elias Brock, Colyer Barksdale, Lin Sims, Jas. McClerkin, Saxon Anderson, Danl. Gent, Jno. P. Cunningham, Jno. N. Nash, Joel Sims, Wm. F. Downs, Tom Floyd, Rody Kennedy, Jesse Coats, Jere. Collins, Bob Coker, Robt. Culberson, Jas. Cunningham, Jr., Thos. Brock, Jno. Rodgers, Thos. B. Williams, Capt. Jno. Neal, Gabriel Joel, Jesse Sanders, Jno. Plant, Henry Morgan, Jos. South, Jr., David Anderson, Jos. McCullough, Saml. Kinmon, Jas. Durrah, Jr., Bob Lowery, Tully Bowling, Bailey Mayhon, Henry Watkins, Saml. Nabours, Danl. Green, Isaac Mitchell, Harris Mitchell, Jno. Gray, Jas. Johnson, Jas. Tramum, Abe Ryley, Ben Strange, Jas. Durrah, Lin Lewis, Dick McNees, Berry Martin, Alex. Culbertson, Manning Killingsworth, Jas. Johnston, Negro Mat, Jno. Williams, Geo. Thomason, Elijah South, Cage Nabours, Hugh Mahaffey, Bill Johnson, Julius Martin, Jim Parker, Fleet Nabours, Abe Nixon, Capt. Jno. Boyd, Hiram Sims, Wm. Cunningham, Little Bill South, Jno. Speltz(?), Pud Shaw, Larkin Sullivan, Wm. Templeton, Saml. Williams, Sr., Jas. Pain,

Estate sale cont'd:
Jno. Strange, Gen. J. F. Wolff, Jas. Ryley, David Saxon, Chas.
A. Saxon, Chas. Saxon, Sarah Saxon (widow).

15 Mar. 1817. Letters of adm. estate of SUSANNAH SIMS, dec'd
to Jas. Smith. Sec: David Hitt and Wilson Sanders.

20 Mar. 1817. Will of WILLIAM OSBORNE, dec'd proven by Mitchell
Drake, Jno. Drake. Jno. Osborne, exr.

25 Mar. 1817. Letters of adm. estate of DANIEL WINN, dec'd
to Glanus Winn. Sec: Jas. Young and And. Winn.

25 Mar. 1817. Letters of adm. estate of WILLIAM DENDY, dec'd
to Patsey Dendy and Jas. Young. Sec: And. Winn and Glanus Winn.

24 Feb. 1817. Will of WILLIAM ORSBORNE (OSBORNE). Wife Sally;
sons John, Edward, Wm. and Elisah (Elijah?); daughters Polly,
Priscilla and Ruthey. Exr: Wife, son John, son-in-law Jesse
Orsborn. Wit: Mitchell Cook, Saml. Goggans and Jno. Drake.

1 Apr. 1817. Will of JOSIAH FOWLER, dec'd proven by Isaac Mitchell, Richd. Fowler, Thos. Fowler and Alhanan Crocker, exr.

1 Apr. 1817. Letters of adm. estate of WILLIAM WALKER, dec'd
to Elizabeth Walker. Sec: Thos. Walker and Wm. Glenn.

8 Apr. 1817. Letters of adm. estate of WILLIAM GRIFFIN, dec'd
to Elizabeth Griffin. Sec: Jno. Griffin and Richd. S. Deale.

21 Feb. 1817. Will of JOSIAH FOWLER. Wife Sarah; sons Richard,
Thomas, and Newton. Mentions adj. land of Wm. Young, dec'd;
John Black, Duke Jones, Benj. Brown. Exr: Sons Richard and
Thomas, Alhanan Crocker and Alse Fuller. Wit: Abner Pyles,
Thos. Burnside and Isaac Mitchell.

13 Feb. 1817. Appraisal of estate of DAVID MC CLURE, dec'd
by Jno. Dillard, Patk. Scott and Thos. Beasley. Estate sale: purchasers: Alexr. McClure, Jno. McClure, Jesse Johnston, Starling
Phillips, David Gambrell, Jos. Phillips, Jos. Greer, Jno. Whitmore. Adm: Jno. McClure.

(No date) Appraisal of estate of DANIEL WOOD, dec'd by Thos.
Hill, Larkin Hitt and Abner Hitt. 8 Apr. 1817. Estate sale.
Purchasers: Braxton Watts, Jas. Watts, Fanny Wood, Sally Wood,
Wm. Wood, Richd. Wood, Wm. Whiteford, Thos. Hill, Richd. Sims,
Danl. James, Danl. Jones, Benj. Hitt, Wm. Mitchell, Jas. Atwood,
Jno. Deal, Richd. Watts, M. Pollard, Jas. Mitchell, Wm. Childs,
and Adm. Thos. W. Golding.

17 Mar. 1817. Appraisal of estate of BENJAMIN SILLS, dec'd
by Thos. Salmon, Robt. Hollingsworth and Elisha Wells. 18 Mar.
1817. Estate sale. Purchasers: Thos. Salmon, Wm. Smith, Jr.,
Thos. Hill, Marshal Pollard, Jere. Sadler, Danl. Jones. Adm.:
Thos. W. Golding.

15 Apr. 1817. Estate of JOHN KIRK, dec'd. David Speer and Thos.
Jones ask release as adm. of est. and Robt. Young as sec. Replaced by Larkin Gaines with Jas. Ward as sec.

15 Apr. 1817. Will of SAMUEL HENDERSON, dec'd proven by Jas.
Jones, Alexr. Glenn and Ann Young. Jas. Young and Susannah

HENDERSON will cont'd:
Henderson qualified as exr.

(No date) Estate sale of JAMES COOK, dec'd. Exr: Mitchell Cook.

4 Mar. 1817. Will of SAMUEL HENDERSON. Wife Susannah; four children Nancy, Justinian, John and Sally. Exr: wife and Jas. Young.
Wit: Jas. Young, Ann Young and Alexr. Glenn.

(No date) Appraisal of estate of WILLIAM ORSBURN, dec'd by Jno.
Young, Jas. Young, Thos. Wilks and Jno. Drake. (No date) Estate
sale. Purchasers: Edw. Osborne, Jno. Drake, Thos. Grizzel, Alex.
Winn, Cornelius Cargill, Mitchel Cook, Vann Davis, Wm. Hewit,
Samnl Neil, Saml. Goggans, Jno. Cole, Wm. Burnside, Nathl. Dru-
mond, Jas. Young, Elhanon Crocker, Thos. Wilks, Wm. Kerr, Richd.
Davis, Lydal Winn, Stephen Williams, Jas. Sturgis, Jas. Lockerby,
Thos. Rodgers, Glanus Winn, Jona. Motes, Jno. Ridge, Isaac Finny,
A. Stowers, Mr. Monroe, Jas. Lowery, Polly Goggans, Jas. Craw-
ford, Jno. Young, Jr., Danl. Mathis, Jas. Young, Jackson Stowers,
Johnston Goggans, Langston East.

14 Apr. 1817. Letters of adm. estate of BENJAMIN GRIFFIN, dec'd
to Reuben Griffin. Sec: Anthony Griffin and Wm. W. Simpson.
3 May 1817. Will of JOHN OWEN, dec'd proven by Robt. Campbell.
Jos. Owen as exr. 2 Jan. 1817. Will of JOHN OWEN. Wife Elizabeth;
my children (not named). Exr: Jas. Watts and Nathl. Day. Wit:
Robt. Campbell, Wm. C. Ball and Rebeckah Child.

14 Apr. 1817. Appraisal of estate of GEORGE BALL, dec'd by David
Hitt, John Sadler, Jas. Neeley and Jas. Smith.

24 Apr. 1817. Appraisal of estate of JOSIAH FOWLER, dec'd by
Thos. Burnside, Benj. James, D. Mitchell and Benj. Drake. 25
Apr. 1817. Estate sale. Purchasers: Henry Johns, Thos. Harris,
Jno. Ridge, Robt. Gill, Wm. Perkinson, Sarah Fuller, Jno. Stur-
gis, Jno. Black, Thos. Casey, Chas. Goodman, Geo. Roberts, Peter
Fuller, Silas Motes, Solomon Fuller, Jas. Young, Jacob Miller,
Jno. Wilson, Jones Fuller, Barruch Duckett, Thos. Rodgers, Ransom
Fuller, Jas. Cook, Hardy Conant. Exr: Richard Fowler, Thos.
Fowler, Elhanon Crocker. Notes due to Josiah Fowler: Martin
Miller, Baruch Duckett, Saml. Rodgers, Danl. Mitchell, David
Stevens, Jas. Manley(?), Wm. Osborn, Jno. Teague, Jas. Williams,
Lewis Tinsley, J. Vaughn, Jacob Doran, Francis Medley, Jacob
Mathis, Thos. Gary, Martin Gary, Rich. Fowler, Robt. McCrakens,
Danl. Winn, Silas Motes, Thos. Dendy, Levi Fowler, Wm. Glenn,
Aner Young, Benj. James, Benj. Drummond, Danl. Williams, Bev.
Walker. Notes (desperate): Jas. Cook, Jas. McMahan, Moses Grif-
fin, Jas. Fuller, Margaret Nabours, Wm. Fuller, Jos. Shuttles-
worth, Jno. Rodgers, Wm. A. Rodgers, Nathl. Drummond, Hayman
Miller, Israel Fuller, Jno. Dendy, Jas. Culbertson, Joel Dendy,
Thos. Walker, Jere. Glenn. And. Winn, Jno. Thomas, Bev. Bet___?,
Wm. Perkinson. Exr: Richd. Fowler.

12 May 1817. Letters of adm. estate of PHILIP SNEED, dec'd to
Jno. Snead. Sec: Lydall Winn and Robt. Spence.

12 May 1817. Letters of adm. estate of ANDREW WILSON, dec'd
to Rebecah Wilson and Whitehead Wilks. Sec: Jer. Connant and
Thos. Wilks.

5 June 1817. Will of JAMES WHITE, dec'd proven by Jas. Young.
Elizabeth White as exr.

2 June 1817. Will of DAVID TEMPLETON, dec'd proven by James
Templeton, Sr. and Ezekiel Price. Wm. Crage as exr.

(No date) Appraisal of estate of ANDREW WILSON, dec'd by Benj.
James, Jas. Young and D. Mitchell. (No date) Estate sale. Purchasers: not named. Adm: Wm. Wilks and Rebecca Wilson.

(No date) Inventory of estate of SUSANNAH SIMS, dec'd by Jno.
Drake, Larkin Hitt and Wm. Ball. (No date) Estate sale. Pur-
chasers: Larkin Hitt, Danl. Day, Jas. Watts, Curtis Ker___?,
Wm. Pollard, Wm. Childs, Jno. Chapman, Jno. Smith, Avery Day,
Wm. Smith, Bluford Wells, Drury Sims, Jno. Wood, Philip Day,
Mansfield Day, Thos. Hill, Danl. Jones, Mr. Maxwell, Richd.
Lindsey, Moses Cole, Jno. Day, Lucy Smith. Adm: Jas. Smith.

19 July 1807. Will of JAMES WHITE. Wife Elizabeth; each of my
children as they come of age (not named). Exr: wife Elizabeth.
Wit: Wm. Childs, Rhoda Young and Jas. Young.

18 Apr. 1817. Appraisal of estate of SAMUEL HENDERSON, dec'd
by Jas. Young, Alex. Glenn, Jas. Riley? and Abner Teague.

23 Apr. 1817. Appraisal of estate of DANIEL WINN, dec'd by Jno.
Black, Jno. Drake and Jas. Young. __ Apr. 1817. Estate sale.
Purchasers: Glanus Winn, Danl. Cargill, Jas. Lefan, Alex. Winn,
Jno. Drake, Jas. Culbertson, Edw. Winn, Jno. Black, Danl. M.
Winn, Rebecca Winn, Patsy Dendy, And. Winn, Chas. Simpson. Adm:
Glanus Winn.

(No date) Estate sale of WM. WALKER, dec'd. Adm: Elizabeth Walker.
21 Apr. 1817. Appraisal of estate by Jere. Conant, Jno. Dendy
and Jas. Young.

9 June 1817. Letters of adm. estate of JOHN VAUGHN, dec'd to
Alhanan Crocker. Sec: Jno. Middleton and Jno. Robertson.

15 Apr. 1817. Estate of JOEL WAISTCOAT(?), dec'd. Jos. Owen
as exr. 1 May 1817. Inventory of estate by Thos. Porter, Robt.
Allen and Chas. Simmons. 1 June 1817. Inventory of book accounts.
No names listed only amounts. (N.B. this surname is not clear).

10 June 1817. Will of JOHN OWEN, dec'd. Jos. Owen qualifies
as exr.

19 Apr. 1817. Will of DAVAID TEMPLETON. Sons (and grandsons?)
David, James, John, Robert, William, Robert Hanna, David Hanna.
Exr: Dr. Geo. Ross, Wm. Craig. Wit: Wm. Craig, Jas. Templeton,
Sr. and Hezekiah Price.

17 June 1817. Will of JAMES HATHORN, dec'd proven by Jos. Neely,
Lewis Mitchell of Abbeville Dist. as exr.

(No date) Will of BRIDGET MC CLELLAN, dec'd proven by B. Allen,
John McClellan as exr.

7 July 1817. Appraisal of estate of WILLIAM DENDY, dec'd by
Saml. Powell, Thos. Powell and Saml. N. Powell. (No date) Estate
sale. Adm: Jas. Young and Patsy Dendy.

(No date) Will of BRIDGET MC CLELLAN. Daughter Janny Dendy;
son John McClellan. Exr: son John. Wit: Jno. David and B. H.
Allen.

(No date) Inventory/appraisal of estate of BENJAMIN GRIFFIN, dec'd by Jas. Bailey, Thos. Powell and Wm. Milam. 1 May 1817. Estate sale. Purchasers: Elihu Griffin, Jno. Young, H. Young, Reuben Griffin. Adm: Reuben Griffin.

6 Apr. 1817. Will of JAMES HATHORN. Wife Edney; minor children; land in Abbeville Dist. Exr: Jos. Neely of Laurens Dist., Lewis Mitchell of Abbeville Dist. Wit: Jos. Neely, Jas. Redden and Saml. J. Hopper.

28 Apr. 1817. Appraisal of estate of WM. GRIFFIN, dec'd by Thos. White, Wm. Fuller and Chartis(?) Nichols. 28 Apr. 1817. Estate sale. Purchasers: Betsey Griffin, Ransom Fuller, Aug. F. Fuller, Jno. Coleman, Thos. White, J. Carter, Jos. Babb. Adm: Elizabeth Griffin.

16 Apr. 1817. MATTHEW HUNTER, dec'd. D. Anderson, Ord. cites exr. Wm. F. Downs to pay Sarah Swan, relict of Tim. Swan legatee as her husband; did not receive it during his lifetime. 16 Apr. 1817. Wm. F. Downs ordered to sell property and pay legacy coming to the wife of Tim. Swan from Matt. Hunter and also from Alex. Henry, to satisfy debts of the sd. dec'd Swan.

26 July 1817. Will of WILLIAM POLLARD, dec'd proven by Jno. Roberson. Marshal Pollard as exr. 15 June 1817. Will of WILLIAM POLLARD. Wife Elizabeth; daughters Matilda and Elizabeth; my young children to be educated. Exr: sons Marshal Pollard, Alfred Pollard and Wm. Pollard. Wit: Jno. Roberson, Jas. Mitchel and Braxton Watts.

20 Jan. 1817. Property sale of WM. POWELL, dec'd. Purchasers: Henry Delph, Wm. Hodges, Benj. Cooper, Ezekiel Powell, Zach. Arnold, N. P. Rosmond, Zach. Taylor, Wm. West, Reuben Powell, Thos. Washington, Wm. Ware, Wm. South, Larkin Gaines, Jno. Moore, Valentine Young, Adam C. Jones, Robt. P. Delph, David P. Posey, Wm. Moore, Peter Barmore, James Powell, Sr., Moses Myers, Richd. Golding, Benj. Jones, David Bell, David Wright, Polly Powell, Wm. Henderson, David Braden, Jno. Gilbreath, Benj. Pierce, Jacob Madden, Jos. South, Jas. Jones, Henry Pope, Robt. Jones, Jas. Campbell, Jas. Kendrick, Thos. Rossmond, Saml. Freeman, Benj. Jones, Benj. Adkins, Wm. Braden, Green B. Shaw, Jas. Anderson, Jere. Collins, Wm. George, Eton Mabury, Jas. A. Stone, Jacob Reed, Henry Hazel, Jonah Boc, Jas. Moore, Jno. Watson, Wm. Cole, Teril Andrews, Jordan Williams, Wm. Spruel, Elijah Howell, Isaac Mitchel, Jos. Harris, Henry Gaines, Matt. Bolton, Jno. S. Roberson, Thos. Gaines, Wm. Crocker, Jno. Roberson, Jr., Nicholas Ware, Jas. Powell, Jr., Jesse E. Clardy, Wm. Arnold, Wm. Moor, Jr., Rev. Jno. Stone, Wm. Pope, Jas. Clardy, Jr., Robt. Posey, Jas. Cristan, Jas. Grimes, Edmond Gaines, Jno. Knight, Jas. Hutson, Benj. R. Mitchel, Elijah South, Harris Mitchell, Jno. Cristian, Zedekiah South, Nathan Jeffries, Mitchel Clardy, Wm. Grimes, Jno. Adams, Thos. Anderson, Thos. Allison, Thos. Adkins, Wm. Bolton, Benj. Rosemond, Jno. Wait, Wm. Clardy, Saml. Fifer, Wm. Jones, Benj. Miller, Wm. Redding, Mathew Wilson, Thos. Pope, Jno. Alberson, Wm. Roberson, Elijah Roberson, Philip Wait, Jacob Niswanger, Jno. Chism. Exr: Jas. Powell and Philip Wait.

4 Aug. 1817. Letters of adm. estate of JAMES FOWLER, dec'd to wife Elizabeth. Sec: Chas. Fowler.

4 Aug. 1817. Letters of adm. estate of THOMAS LEWERS, dec'd to Saml. B. Lewers. Sec: Rodey H. Canedy and Chas. Allen.

2 Aug. 1817. Will of PATRICK P. SHEA, dec'd proven by Jno. Roberson and Martin Shaw(Shea?). Elizabeth Shea as exr. 18 Oct. 1815. Will of PATRICK P. SHEA. Wife Elizabeth. Exr: wife and Robt. Creswell. Wit: Jno. Roberson and Martin Shaw.

12-13 Dec. 1815. Estate sale of ALEXANDER HENRY, dec'd. Adm: Nelly Henry.

(No date) Appraisal of estate of JOHN OWEN, dec'd by Clement Wells, Saml. Goodman and Jno. Hollingsworth.

8 May 1817. Nuncupative will of SALLEY JONES, dec'd. James Pasley and John Baley who married the sister of the dec'd objected to the probate. Hearing held by David Anderson, Ord. Deposition of Gen. Saml. Gary that Sally Dendy wished her mother to have her part of her father's estate. Will read. Ord. decreed will be recorded. 10 Apr. 1817. Nuncupative will of SALLEY JONES. Her mother, widow Polley Dendy to have her part of her father's estate. Wm. Burnside, JQ. Wit: Joel Walker and Jno. Dendy.

(No date). Estate of JOHN VAUGHN, dec'd. Adm. of estate succeeding late Josiah Fowler. Sale of estate. Purchasers not named. Present adm.: Alhanon Crocker.

(No date) Inventory of estate of JAMES WHITE, dec'd by Asa Chandler, Jno. Walker, Wm. Coleman and Paul Findley.

(No date) Inventory of estate of JAMES HATHORN, dec'd by Jno. Waits, Jno. Sims and Jno. Roberson. Book accts and debtors but not named.

(No date) Benjamin Williams, minor son of BENJAMIN WILLIAMS, dec'd, received by guardian Richd. Blackwell, his part of his grandfather Samuel Williams, now dec'd, estate pd by Chas. Allen adm. of sd estate.

1 Sept. 1817. Will of WILLIAM BRYSON, SR., dec'd proven by Wm. McMahon and Jas. Fuller. Wm. Bryson, Jr. as exr. 16 Aug. 1816. Will of WM. BRYSON, SR. Wife Jane; sons William, Hunter, Vinson, and Henry; daughters Jane and Mary; sons Matthew, James and Robert; daughter Margaret (mentions youngest two sons and two daughters). Exr: wife Jane, son William. Wit: James McMahon, Jas. Fuller and Wm. Purkeson(?).

4 Sept. 1817. Appraisal of estate of PATRICK P.(?) SHEA, dec'd by Jno. Roberson, Martin Shaw and Jno. Roberson, Jr.

14 Sept. 1817. Adm. of estate of SARAH WRIGHT, dec'd to Jacob Niswanger. Sec: Jas. Crocker and Jas. Henderson. D. Anderson, Ord. 14 Sept. 1817. Inventory/appraisal of estate by Jonathan Forgey, Jno. Shirley and Martin Shaw.

(No date) Appraisal of estate of PHILIP SNEAD, dec'd by G. F. Richeson, T. D. Boyd and Jno. Madden. (No date) Estate sale. Purchasers: Jas. Collins, Jos. Griffin, Jno. Hill, Jas. Irby, Saml. B. Lewers, Jno. Snead, Widow Snead, W. W. Simpson, Wm. Stone, Alex. Winn. Adm: Jno. Snead.

(No date) Appraisal of estate of WILLIAM POLLARD, dec'd by Robt. Pollard, Wm. Ball and Wm. Chiles. Exr: Marshal Pollard.

14 Oct. 1817. Letty Maddox, minor about 17 years and Mary Maddox,

cont'd from page 114:
minor about 14 years, chose William Maddox as guardian. Sec:
Basden Guinn, Robt. Thomson.

7 Oct. 1817. WILLIAM FOWLER, dec'd. John Hunter and James Fowler
ask release as sec. of adm. Mary Fowler. John Stewart now husband of Mary Fowler becomes adm. His sec: Thos. Porter, Wm.
Park and David Glen.

30 Sept. 1817. Appraisal of estate of JAMES FOWLER, dec'd by
Jos. Deen, Jno. Hunter, Jno. McClintock and Jas. Hutchison.

3 Nov. 1817. Adm. of estate of JOEL WESTCOAT(WAISTCOAT), dec'd.
B. Nabours revoked upon completion of his sec. Wm. Irby and
widow Cynthia Westcoat granted letters of adm. Sec: Colyer Barksdale, Chas. Pinson. (No date) Second inventory of estate by
Thos. Porter, Chas. Simmons and Robt. Allison.

3 Nov. 1817. Will of JOSEPH WOOD, dec'd proven by Jas. Cobb,
Jas. H. Harding and Elizabeth Wood as exr.

3 Nov. 1817. Letters of adm. estate of JOHN WILSON, dec'd to
widow Elizabeth Wilson. Sec: Jno. Wilson and Jno. Blackstock.

3 Nov. 1817. Will of JOSEPH HAMMOND, dec'd proven by Wm. Owings,
Jesse Childress and Thos. Goodwin as exr.

13 Mar. 1817. Will of JOSEPH WOOD. Son Zadock; wife Elizabeth.
Exr: wife and son. Wit: Jas. Cobb, Jas. H. Harden and Coleman
Carlisle.

11 Nov. 1817. Will of JOSEPH HAMMOND. Bequests already given
to sons John, Joseph and daughters Nancy Park and Elizabeth
Grizel. Son Mackey; grandson Joseph Hammond. Exr: Jesse Child-
resss and Thos. Goodwin. Wit: Thos. Childress, Wm. Owings, Jr.
and Rachel Pelse(?).

14 Oct. 1817. Appraisal of estate of WM. BRYSON, SR., dec'd
by Wm. Rodgers, Solomon Fuller, Jr., Wm. Glenn and Saml. Leaman.

3 Nov. 1817. Letters of adm. estate of JOSEPH BOX,dec'd to Josiah
Box. Sec: Elijah Pinson and Banister Mitchell.

1 Dec. 1817. Letters of adm. estate of LETTY RODGERS, dec'd
to Thos. Rodgers. Sec: Robt. Ward and Nehemiah Franks.

1 Dec. 1817. Letters of adm. estate of JOHN SPURGIN, dec'd to
wife Nancy Spurgin(Spurgeon). Sec: Jacob Roberts, Nathan Pugh
and Jos. Brown.

1 Dec. 1817. Letters of adm. estate of JOHN LESTER, dec'd to
Thos. Wilks. Sec: Mitchel Cook and Alex. Winn.

8 Dec. 1817. Will of CORNELIUS TINSLEY, dec'd proven by Saml.
Vance and Jno. Dendy. Jeremiah Tribble exr.

10 Dec. 1817. Letters of adm. estate of ANDREW WILSON, dec'd
to Whitehead Wilks revoked; to Rebecca Wilson. Her sec: Benj.
James and Jno. Black.

3 Dec. 1817. Will of CORNELIUS TINSLEY. Grandson Cornelius Tinsley Tribble but if he dies to Elizabeth or John Allen Tribble

TINSLEY will cont'd:
or eldest male child of my daughter Betsy Tribble; daughters
Betsy Tribble and Patsy Wilks. Exr: son-in-law Jeremiah Tribble
(who is to be guardian of Cornelius Tinsley Tribble.) Wit: Saml.
Vance, Jno. Dendy and J. Underwood.

26 Nov. 1817. Inventory of estate of JOHN SPURGIN, dec'd by
Jno. Meadow, Jno. Herring and Jos. Brown.

29 Dec. 1817. John Williams and James Williams, both minors,
chose Thomas Cook as guardian until their age of 21 years. Sec:
Robt. Gaines and Saml. Cook.

5 Jan. 1818. Will of CHARLES WADKINS, dec'd certified by Jno.
Dunklin(?). Ordered recorded.

5 Jan. 1818. Will of WILLIAM BROWN, SR, dec'd proven by Jno.
Meador and Thos. Jones. Jos. Brown as exr. 16 July 1811. Will
of WM. BROWN, SR. Wife Francess; eight children John Brown,
Usley Thompson, Lucy Gilbert, Mary Wood, Frances Brook, Wm.
Brown, Jr., Susannah Nix, Joseph Brown. Exr: son Joseph Brown.
Wit: Wm. Gilbert, Jno. Meador and Thos. Jones.

30 July 1810. Will of CHARLES WATKINS. Wife Elizabeth. Exr:
wife and trusty friend James Abercrombie. Wit: Mary Cochran,
Nancy Cochran and John Cochran.

27 Nov. 1817. Second appraisal of estate of JAMES FOWLER, dec'd
by Jno. Hunter, Jos. Dean, Jno. McClintock and Jas. Hutchinson.
27 Nov. 1817. Estate sale. Purchasers: Leahala(?) Fowler, Jno.
Milam, Wm. Parks, Jno. Brown, Jas. Langston, Jas. Taylor, Wm.
Hutcheson, Thos. Farrow, Francis Ross, And. Parks, Saml. Mills,
Joel Allen, Robt. McClintock, Jas. Hutcheson, Alex. Mills, Jno.
Farrow, Robt. Pool, Chas. Fowler, David Cowan, Isaac Stroud,
Wm. Word, Davis Newman, Jno. Couch, Thos. Neighbors, Geo. Mosley,
Jas. Parks, Hugh Crooks, Jas. Hunter. Shown by Isabella Fowler.

19 Dec. 1817. Appraisal of estate of JOHN LESTER, dec'd by Fredk.
Foster, Danl. Beacham and Thos. Teague. 19 Dec. 1817. Estate
sale. Purchasers: Danl. Beacham, Danl. Cargill, Jno. Hunter,
Geo. Teague, Valentine Harding, Thos. Wilks, Jno. Gamble, Wm.
Gamble, Jno. Abell, Wm. McMurtry, Fredk. Foster, Robt. Wickham,
Coleman Carlisle, Thos. Teague, Francis Lester. Adm: Thos. Wilks.

(No date) Appraisal of estate of JOSEPH WOOD, dec'd by Coleman
Carlisle, Jesse Johnston and Wm. Dillard.

(No date) Estate sale of JOEL WAISTCOAT(?), dec'd. Purchasers:
Robt. Allison, Joel Allen, Chas. Allen, Allen Barksdale, Collier
Barksdale, Wm. Bolt, Abraham Cook, Jas. Clardy, Free Caesar,
Widow Dial, Hastings Dial, Saml. Downs, Wm. Franks, Saml. Franks,
Chas. Franks, Mrs. Hudgens, Jno. Hill, Wm. Henderson, Wm. Irby,
Chas. Irby, Jas. Johnston, Mark Killingsworth, Jas. Laughridge,
Saml. B. Lewers, Jno. Lee, Herbert Martin, Jno. Milwee, Richd.
McNees, Wm. Madden, Jno. Madden, Mabra Madden, Berry Martin,
Danl. Martin, Chas. Prim, Abijah Pinson, Wm. Ranson, Ezekiel
Rowland, Jno. Rodgers, Jno. Spelts(?), Jno. Strange, Jos. Strange,
Dr. Todd, Mrs. Cynthia Waistcoat, Chas. Williams, Jno. Wilson
(Irish), Jas. Word. By adm. Cynthia Waistcoat.

17 Jan. 1818. Letters of adm. estate of SHERED TINSLEY, dec'd
to Zach. Tinsley. Sec: Jno. Dendy, Saml. Vance and Branch Ligon.

2 Feb. 1818. Will of JAMES KINMON, dec'd proven by Benj. Arnold
and Geo. Grace. Thos. Kinmon as exr. 28 Mar. 1816. Will of JAMES
KINMON. Wife Elizabeth; son Thomas; daughters Nancy Cook and
Rachel Williamson. Mentions Cornelius Cook, Thos. Williamson,
Jno. Cunningham. Exr: wife and son. Wit: Benj. Arnold, Nancy
Arnold and Geo. Grace.

19 Dec. 1817. Appraisal of estate of LETTY RODGERS, dec'd by
Thos. Burnside, Jos. Hollingsworth and Elhanon Crocker. 20 Dec.
1817. Estate sale. Purchasers: Wm. Rodgers, Thos. Rodgers, Sally
Rodgers, Polly Rodgers, Saml. Rodgers, Andw. Rodgers, Wm. Fowler,
Jos. Hollingsworth, Lettey Vaughn, Chas. Jones, Wm. Holdridge,
Zach. Holdridge, Jas.McMahan. Adm: Thos. Rodgers.

13 Feb. 1818. Will of ROBERT SMITH, dec'd proven by Saml. Hensley. Wm. Smith as exr. 29 June 1817. Will of ROBERT SMITH. Wife;
son William (his lawful heirs to inherit his portion). Mentions
Jno. Cook. Exr: son. Wit: Jno. W. Smith, Jas. H. Smith and Saml.
Hensley.

6 Apr. 1818. Letters of adm. estate of THOMAS BABB, JR, dec'd
to Wm. Babb. Sec: Thomas Babb and Jos. Babb.

(No date) Estate sale of JOHN SPURGEN, dec'd. Purchasers: Jno.
Adams, Jas. Garrett, Gabriel Wilson, Saml. Jones, Wm. Linsey,
Moses Hughs, Jos. Wood, Jno. D. Mitcheson, Jno. Westmoreland,
Jr., Jno. Roberts, Geo. Fowler, Wm. Arnold. Notes on: Jonathan
Philips, Jno. Childress, Elijah Wallis, Jesse Mills. Adm: Nancy
Spurgen.

17 Jan. 1818. Appraisal of estate of WILLIAM BROWN, dec'd by
Jno. Herring, Jno. Brown. (Thos. Jones crossed out). 23 Jan.
1818. Estate sale. Purchasers: Jos. Brown, Hartwell Lester,
Mordicah Moore, Moses Hughes, Ambrose Bramlett, Jas. Nix, Bena-
iah Canady, Wm. W. Vaughn, Edmund Scrugs, Jno. Hand, Wm. Cooper,
Reuben Eastridge, Henry Cole, Thos. Howard, Mary Wood, John
Wood, Wm. Wood, Jeremiah Massey, Jno. Meador, Wm. Gilbert, Aaron
Brown, Wm. Jones, Jas. Garrett, Zadock Ford,a Wm. Arnold, Wm.
Lyon, Mary Marchbanks, Nathaniel Austin, Abner Hendrix, Wm.
Power, Jno. Ford, Thos. Jones, Denis House, Efron Brown, Jos.
House. Exr: Jos. Brown.

24 Dec. 1817. Appraisal of estate of CORNELIUS TINSLEY, dec'd
by Saml. Vance, Saml. Powell and Jno. Dendy. 24 Dec. 1817. Estate
sale. Purchasers: Hedley Davis, J. Tribble, Wm. Ligon, B. Crad-
dock, A. Harris, W. Willis, W. Ligon, Saml. Vance, Thos. Nickles,
H. Davis, B. Connant, Jas. Todd, Jas. McCarry, Allen Walker,
Chas. Todd, Jno. Taylor, A. Starnes, Thos. Wilkes, Wm. Blakely,
Jas. Young, Joel Dendy, Elijah Teague, Jos. McCarey, B. Craddock,
Wm. Hutchison, E. Teague, C. Conant, Wm. Coleman, Mary Milum,
Saml. Vance, Thos. Harris, J. Tribble, Wm. Ligon, B. Ligon,
Wm. Chandler, Wm. Vance, J. Cole, Wm. Neill, Jno. Blakely, Jno.
Mayson, Isaac Mitchell, Burrel Conant, Jesse More, Nelley Conant,
Stealy Davis, Jno. Brown, B. Conant, B. Ligon. Exr: J. Tribble.

26 Nov. 1817. Second sale of WM. POWELL, dec'd. Purchasers:
Robt. P. Delph, Jno. Chisum, David Bell, Col. J. Roseman, Jurden
Mosley, Larkin Gaines, Wm. Graves, A. C. Jones, Wm. Braden,
Polly Powell. Exr: P. Wait and Jas. Powell.

12 Dec. 1816. Second sale of SAMUEL WRIGHT, dec'd. Exr: Wm.
Wright.

5 Feb. 1818. Appraisal of estate of JAMES KINMON, dec'd by Jas. Powell, Thos. Williams and Larkin Gaines.

1 Jan. 1815. Second sale of estate of ANDREW WILSON, dec'd. Adm: Rebecca Wilson.

9 Nov. 1817. Appraisal of estate of JOSIAH BOX, dec'd by Philip Wait, Jas. Clardy and Jas. Jones.

6 Nov. 1817. Appraisal of estate of JOHN WILSON, dec'd by Ira Arnold, Bailey Mahon and Thos. Gradon. (No date) Estate sale. Purchasers: Thos. Taylor, Abraham Nabours, Jno. Blackstock, Francis Posey, Robt. Nabours, Thos. McClure, Jno. Lindly, Richd. Ridgeway, Edmond Bolt, Jno. McDavid, Wm. Blackstock. Adm: Elizabeth Wilson.

3 Apr. 1818. Appraisal of estate of SHERED TINSLEY, dec'd by Jno. Dendy, Saml. Powell and Saml. Vance. 3 Apr. 1818. Estate sale. Adm: Zach. Tinsley.

8 Jan. 1818. Estate sale of JAMES CRAGE, dec'd. Purchasers: Elizabeth Crage, Martin Berk, Harrison Allen, Robt. Templeton, Dr. Geo. Ross, Capt. Wm. Alexander, Jno. Adair, Jno. McClure, Moses Leak, Alex. Rolland, Jas. McClure, Jno. Jones, Geo. Dillard, Wm. Crage, Robt. Crage, Exr: Wm. Crage and Elizabeth Crage.

21 Apr. 1818. Will of ROBERT PASLEY, dec'd proven by wife Elizabeth who qualified as sole exr. Son James Pasley entered protest on grounds that the dec'd was not of sound mind at the time of executing sd will. On oath of wit. dec'd was declared of sound mind and the will was ordered recorded. D. Anderson, Ord. 6 July 1816. Will of ROBERT PASLEY. Wife Elizabeth and unmarried children. Mentions daughter Martha Mitchell, all my surviving children. Exr: wife. Wit: Asa Chandler, Absalom Bailey and Wm. Bailey.

23 May 1818. Litigation on estate of JOHN KIRK, dec'd by wife Elizabeth Kirk, former adm. vs Thomas Jones and David Speers, present adm. by their attys Mr. Forter and Mr. Irby.

23 Apr. 1818. Appraisal of estate of YOUNG THOMAS BABB, dec'd by Danl. Cook, Saml Rodgers and Thos. Rodgers. Notes on Thos. Casey, Thos. Rodgers, Saml. Rodgers, Wm. Kellett, Young Jas. Culbertson. (No date) Estate sale. Purchasers: Littleton Whitton, Chas. Jones, Wm. Babb, Saml. Rodgers, Andy Rodgers, Young Jas. Culbertson, Thos. Babb, Robt. Whitton, Thos. Reid, Thos. Walker, Wm. Kellet. Adm: Wm. Babb.

(No date) Estate sale of SARAH WRIGHT, dec'd. Purchasers: Jacob Niswanger, Jno. Sims, Jas. Gaines, Thos. Adkins, Abraham Wright, Aaron Starnes, Jno. McCon___?, Jno. Roberson, Jonathan Forgey, Archd. McDaniel, Jas. Crocker, Jno. Wait, Wm. McPherson, Jeremiah Collins, Henry Wood, Henry Wilson. Adm: J. Niswanger.

1 Mar. 1818. Will of ANN JANE O'NEEL, dec'd proven by Wm. Holdrich. 21 Dec. 1808. Will of ANN JANE O'NEAL (O'NEEL). Son John Cook. Mentions dec'd husband John O'Neal. Exr: son John Cook. Wit: R. M. Owen, Miller Ligon and Wm. Holdritch. Sd John Cook qualified as exr. 5 Nov. 1818.

Sept. & Dec. 1808. Estate sale of ANGUS CAMPBELL, dec'd. Exr: Jon. Johnston, Robt. Campbell.

118

12 Mar. 1818. Second sale of estate of BENJAMIN WILSON, dec'd. Purchasers: Elizabeth Wilson. Exr: David S. Wilson.

18 Oct. 1816. Appraisal of estate of TIMOTHY SWAN, dec'd by Jas. Hutchison, Chas. Fowler and Wm. Taylor. (No date) Estate sale. Purchasers: Sarah Swan, Chas. Fowler, Jno. Crumpton, Jas. Hutcherson, Jno. Simmons, Jas. McNeely, Jas. Hunter, Harrison Allen, Nelly Henry, Jacob Nabours, Jas. Murphy. Exr: Wm. F. Downs.

1 Mar. 1819. OBEDIAH ESTES, dec'd by Adm. Ann Estes. Former sec. Robt. Creswell and Rodey Canady released. New sec: Jas. Lochridge and Geo. Grace.

5 Jan. 1819. Appraisal of estate of ROBERT PASLEY, dec'd by (not named) Next page of book appears to be missing.

END OF WILL BOOK D

START OF BOOK E

13 Apr. 1818. Letters of adm. estate of JOHN KIRK, JR., dec'd to Saml. L. Carns, 30 May 1818. Estate appraisal. Adm.: Saml. L. CArns. Mentions "his interest in estate of John Kirk,Sr., decd his father".

6 July 1818. Will of JAMES GREEN, dec'd proven by Robt. McNees. Marey Nisbett, exrx. 19 Apr. 1818. Will of JAMES GREEN. Friend Mary Nisbett. Exr: Mary Nisbet and Richd Blackwell. Wit: Robt. McNees, Sally McNees and Elizabeth Hils? Pool.

6 Apr. 1818. Letters of adm. estate of THOMAS BABB, dec'd to Wm. Babb. Thos. Babb, Jr.? and Jos. Babb. Mentions estate of Thomas Babb, Jr., dec'd (very dim).

23 May 1818. Appraisal of estate of JOHN RODGERS, dec'd (very dim, cannot read). 28 May 1818. Estate sale. (entire page dim).

14 Sept. 1818. Estate of ROBERT HUTCHESON, dec'd. Letters of adm. to John Hutcheson. Sec: Geo. Wharton and Turner Richerdson.

5 Sept. 1818. Letters test. to Honarita(?) Coley, exrx. CHARLES COLEY, dec'd. 25 July 1818. Will of CHARLES COLEY. Wife Honaretta Coley; dau. Salley Smith; sons James, John, Spencer and Jackson Coley; Joice Coley. Exr: Honaretta Coley. Wit: John Walker, Saml. Byrd and Elijah Walker. (No date) Appraisal of estate by Aaron Clore, Jno. Stephens and Jno. Walker.

2 Nov. 1818. Adm. of estate of JOHN SOUTH, dec'd to Rebecah South, widow. Sec: Elisha Williamson and Jno. Rusel.

3 Nov. 1818. Adm. of estate of WM. BAULL, dec'd to Narsisey Baull, wife/widow. Sec: Jno. and Jas. Meek.

2 Nov. 1818. Letters test. to Jos. McCanehy and Jas. McCanehy, exrs. of estate of SAMUEL MC CANEHY, dec'd proven by Jas. Bonds and Jas. Murphey. 29 Aug. 1818. Jasper Co., Georgia. Will of SAMUEL MC CONEHY of Laurens Dist., S. C. Wife: Margaret; sons Joseph and James; land purchased from Jno. Hanna and Col. Jno. A. Elmore; dau. Ruth; Anny Scott, Martha Belec(?) and Peggy Wilson. Wit: Jas. Bonds, Jas. Murphey and Peter Wm. Gautier. Codicil: Jos. and James McConehy, exrs.

5 Nov. 1818. Henery Bryson, minor, about 19 years and Hunter Bryson, about 16 years, chose Wm. Dunlap guardian. Sec: Mathew Bryson and Robt. Bryson.

(No date) Appraisal of estate of RICHARD GOLDING, dec'd by Zach. Arnold, Jeremiah Arnold, Jno. Dotson and Lewis Dotson.

13? Nov. 1818. Letters of adm. to Polley Babb, wife/widow of JOSEPH BABB, dec'd. Sec: Wm. Wilson and David Stephens.

7 Dec. 1818. Will of JONATHAN DOWNS, dec'd proven by Chas. Saxon and David P. Saxon. Wm. F. Downs, Exr. 18 Aug. 1818. Will of JONATHAN DOWNS. Children: Jane married Benj. Byrd; Milly married Lydall Allen; Frances married Wm. Kelley; Wm. F. Downs; Phebe married Jas. Bruster; Louisa(?) married Jno. Bruster; wife Sarah Downs; grandson Jonathan Allen. Exrs: wife and son Wm. Wit: Jno. F. Wolff, C. Saxon and D. P. Saxon.

7 Dec. 1818. Adm. of estate of EDWARD G. WINN, dec'd to Benj. B. Chishire(?). Bond: Hardy Conant and M. Duke Jones. Appraisal of estate 8 Dec. 1818 by Jno. Black, M. Duke Jones and Danl. Beechum.

11 Dec. 1818. Adm. of estate of JAMES STRAIN, dec'd to Elizabeth Strain. Sec: David Strain and Wm. Reed.

(No date) Appraisal of estate of JOSEPH BABB, dec'd by Wm. Lowe, Joel Burgess, Geo. Wharton and Wm. Bailey. 4 Dec. 1818. Estate sale. Purchasers: Thos. Babb, Wm. Lowe, Lewis Nelson, Polley Babb, Thos. Casey, G. Wharton, Jos. Hodge, Wm. Babb, Wm. Nelson, Bluford Wells, Chesley Connant, Dilling Wharton, Ransom Fuller, Wm. Brownlee, Eldridge Fuller, Jas. Culberson, Jas. Wills. Polley Babb, Adm.

(No date) Appraisel of estate of WM. BABB, dec'd by Wm. Chiles, Marshel Pollard and Thos. Hill. (No date) Estate sale. Purchasers: Jno. Gates, Jno. Todd, David Curington, Jas. Mitchell, Anthony Golding, Danl. Jones, Robt. Pollard, Jas. Turner, Narsissy Ball, Reason Day, Jas. Neeley, Jno. Chapman, Wm. Davis, Patk. Todd, Richd Sims, Thos. Hill, Jas. Hill, Jno. Smith, Jos. Cason, Anthony Butler, Jas. Watts, Danl. Williamson, Braxton Watts, Jas. Mitchel, Wm. Spurgin, Jno. Bolden, Mitchel Saterwhite, Josiah Cason. Narcissa Ball, Adm.

9 Dec. 1818. Appraisal of estate of JAMES STRAIN, dec'd by Jonathan Johnston, Wm. Green and Zimri Carter.

(No date) Appraisal of estate of SAMUEL MC CONAHY, dec'd by Jason Meadors, Jas. Bonds, Richd. Bonds and Jno. Dillard. Note on Robt. Stuart, Jas. Wilson and Jno. Greer.

5 Jan. 1819. Estate of MIKEL FINNEY, dec'd. Sec: Shubal Starnes and Chesley Hughs. John Cook, Adm.

4 Jan. 1819. Ruth McConahy, minor about 18 years, chose Richd. Bonds as guardian. Sec: Jos. McConahy and Jas. McConahy.

(No date) Appraisal of estate of JONATHAN DOWNS, dec'd by Jas. Cunningham, Robt. McNees, Abraham Bolt and Saml. Downs. Mostly negroes and furniture, etc.

30 Oct. 1818. Estate sale of CHARLES COLEY, dec'd. Purchasers:

Estate sale cont'd:
James Burrow, Abraham Bolt, Chas. Smith, Honaretta Coley, Wm.
Tompson, Jas. Clemmons.

14 Jan. 1819. Virginia H. Powell, minor about 16 years, chose
Reubin Powell, guardian. Sec: David P. Posey and Adam Craine
Jones.

16 Jan. 1819. Milley D. Powell, minor about 18 years, chose
Nathl. J. Roseman guardian. Sec: Larkin James and Robt. P. Delph.

1 Feb. 1819. Estate of ROBERT POOL, dec'd. Elizabeth Pool and
Elisha Adair, adm. Sec: Jas. Wilson and Abraham Hatten(?).

1 Feb. 1819. Kesiah Estes, minor about 15 years, chose Francis
Devenport as guardian. Sec: Geo. Grace and Reuben Estes.

5? Mar. 1819. Estate of JOHN TAYLOR, dec'd, Alex. Taylor and
Wm. Cowan, exr. Sec: Wm. Young and Hugh Crooks.

5? Mar. 1819. Estate of JOHN HUNTER, dec'd, Saml. Hunter, exr.
Sec: Alex. Kirkpatrick and Saml. Mills.

22 Feb. 1818. Will of JOHN TAYLOR. Wife Barbara; son Alexander;
daughter Barbara; daughter Mary; son William; step-daughter
Rebeccah. Exr: Alex. Taylor and Wm. Cowan. Wit: Jas. Hutcherson,
Wm. Young and Hugh Crooks.

6 June 1818. Will of JOHN HUNTER, SR. Wife (not named); son
William; son James and his son John B. Hunter; son John and
his son William Hunter; son Samuel Hunter; daughter Margaret
McClintock; daughter Nancy Hunter; mentions lands of Jno. Mc-
Dowell, Robt. Flemming, Riley Glenn, Caty Ross, Thos. Jones,
Jacob Nabors, Jno. Clark, Wm. Garrett, Saml. Garrett, Benj.
Bird, Jno. Fitch, Jno. Simpson. Exr: son Samuel. Wit: Alex.
Kirkpatrick and Saml. Mills.

26 Jan. 1819. Estate sale of SAMUAL MC CONAHY, dec'd. Exr: Jos.
and Jas. McConaha(McConahy).

8 Jan. 1819. Appraisal of estate of MIKEL FINNEY, dec'd by Thos.
Ligon, Damilion(?) Deal and Jas. Ward. 20 Jan. 1819. Estate
sale. Adm: Jno. Cook.

9 Feb. 1819. Appraisal of estate of ROBERT POOL, dec'd.

13 Apr. 1819. Estate of WILLIAM DENDY, dec'd. Adm. revoked Patty
Dendy and Jas. Young and Sec: Andrew Winn and Glanus Winn. Bond:
Danl. M. Winn and Andw. Winn to Pattey Dendy only.

15 Apr. 1819. Daniel Henderson, minor about 14 years, chose
Martin Shaw as guardian. Sec: Geo. Jewell(?) and Jno. Roberson.

10 Nov. 1818. Appraisal of estate of JOHN SOUTH, dec'd by Benj.
F. Tiree, Elish Williamson and Jno. Rusel.

2 Apr. 1819. Appraisal of estate of ANN JANE O'NEAL, dec'd by
Thos. Ligon, Thos. Hill and Demilion Deale.

8 May 1819. Appraisal of estate of JOSEPH MAYHONE, dec'd by
Aaron Clore, Jno. Walker, Jno. Wiseman and Jas. Simmons.

8 May 1819. Appraisal of estate of JOHN TAYLOR, dec'd. Cert. by Alexander Mills, Robt. Flemming, Jr.? and Wm. Hambleton.

5 June 1819. Inventory of estate of JOHN SOUTH, dec'd by Rebeckah South, Adm. Notes and cash. Cert. by Rachel South, adm.

5 July 1819. Estate of CORNELIUS DENDY, dec'd. Saml. N. Powell, adm. citation against Patty Dendy, admx. of Wm. Dendy, dec'd.

7 Mar.? 1819. Estate sale of ROBT. POOL, dec'd. Purchasers: Wm. Pool, Aaron Starnes, Seth? Pool, Patty Pool, John McClintock, Betsey Pool, Thos. Pool, Jno. Pool, Elisha Adair, Andrew Brown, Levie Brown, Peter Pool, Wm. Burrey, Wm. Higgens, Geo. Pool, Stephen Kelley?, J. F. Higgens, Jane Pool, Wm. Terrey, Isaac Crow, Stephen Tally, Elisha Atteway. Elisha Adair, adm. Cash rec'd from Kelley; Miss Tucker; note on John Stuart, Crumton, Thomas Pool and Timon Bobo.

1 July 1819. Samuel N. Powell, Adm. of Cornelius Dendy, dec'd vs Patty Dendy, admx. of William Dendy, dec'd, who was former adm. Citation. Return of the sd. Wm. Dendy, Esq., Exr. of Thomas Dendy, dec'd that on 1 Apr. 1809 due the estate of Cornelius Dendy, dec'd. Pd Aron Goza who intermarried with only daughter of the sd Cornelius Dendy, dec'd. Patty Dendy to pay Saml. N. Powell. D. Anderson, Ord. 17 June 1819. Saml. N. Powell, adm. Bond: Zachariah Baley, Jr. and Thos. Powell. in the estate of CORNELIUS DENDY, dec'd. Appraisement.

5 July 1819. Estate of THOMAS BLAKELY, SR., dec'd adm. to Thomas Blakely, Jr. Sec: JoHN Dandey and Charles Fowler.

5 July 1819. Will of CLABOURN VAUGHN, dec'd proven by Coleman Carlisle and Janna Lewis? Carlisle. Mary Vaughn adm. 11 June 1815. Will of CLABOURN VAUGHN. Wife Mary; son John Vaughn; my unmarried daughters (not named) and my married daughters (also not named); son and youngest daughter to receive education. Mary Vaughn, Exrx. Wit: Coleman Carlisle, Joanna Lewis Carlisle nd Elizabeth B. Carlisle. (N.B. also spelled Claiborn Vaughn).

5 July 1819. Will of JOSEPH DOWNS, dec'd proven by Chas. Saxon and J. Allen. Saml. Downs, Wm. Downs and Jonathan Downs, Exrs. 26 Dec. 1818. Wife Jane; sons Samuel and Jonathan; Mily Jennings (property concened to him); daughter Mary L. Downs; mentions Saml. Cooper; daughters Annabella Lewis, Rebeckah Alexander, Sarah Gary, Nancy Barksdale. Exrs: sons Samuel and Jonathan Downs and nephew William T. Downs. Wit: E. A. Saxon, G. F. Wolff and J. Allen.

10? July 1819. Andrew Fowler, minor about 14 years and 6 months of age, chose Charles Fowler guardian. Sec: James Park and Andrew Park.

19 July 1819. Citation against Mary Clemans formerly Mary Dendy, adm. of Thos. Dendy, Jr.?, dec'd. Charles Dendy, Samuel Garey in the rights of their wives; James Pasley in the right of his wife; the sd Mary Clemons and husband John Clemons , against legatees of sd Thos. Dendy, dec'd, Harriet Dendy, Danl. Sims, Dunlap & Underwood, Wm. Cremshaw, Dr. A. Pyles; Chas. Dendy, Saml. Garey, Jas. Pasley, Jno. Bailey; Chas. Dendy guardian of Nancey Dendy.

31 July 1819. Estate of DANIEL HENDERSON, dec'd letters of adm.

HENDERSON estate cont'd:
to Martin Shaw. Sec: Aaron Shirley and Minoah Fargey.

2 Aug. 1819. Letters of adm. estate of LEVI FOWLER, dec'd to
Nathan Fowler and Jno. Duckett. Sec: Wm. Dillard and Jno. M.
Caryth___?.

13 July 1819. Estate appraisal of THOMAS BLAKELEY, SR., dec'd
by C. Littel, Wm. Blakeley and Jas. Bryson.

6 July 1819. Appraisal of estate of CLABOURNE VAUGHN, dec'd
by Jesse Johnston, George Leek, Jno. Copeland and Jno. Underwood.

8 Apr. 1819. Appraisal of estate of JOHN HUNTER, dec'd by Wm.
Hill, Saml. Parsons, Jas. Flemming and Alexander Mills.

6 Sept. 1819. Letters of adm. estate of ISAAC UNDERWOOD, dec'd
to John Underwood. Sec: Wm. Dunlap and Thos. Fulton.

6 Sept. 1819. Letters of adm. estate of SARAH THREETT, dec'd
to John Dunlap and Robt. Dunlap, exrs. Will proven by John H.
Davis. Recorded 5 Apr. 1819. Will of SARAH THREETT. Mentions her
5 children; husabnd Reuben; son Tom; a share sufficient to buy
her husband Reuben and set him free. Exr: John and Robt. Dunlap. Wit: Jno. H. Davis, Robt. Bell and Wm. Brown. (N.B. Tom
is called both Threet and Cobb.)

5 Oct. 1819. Letters of adm. estate of HANCEL DOLLAR, dec'd
to Sarah Dollar, wife of dec'd. Sec: Charles Allen and John
Bolt.

5 Oct. 1819. Letters of adm. estate of RICHARD WHITE, dec'd
to James Simpson. Sec: Robt. Gray and James Ross.

21 Sept. 1819. Appraisal of estate of LEVI FOWLER, dec'd by
Wm. Dillard, David Boyce and John McCarey.

9 Oct. 1819. Appraisal of estate of HANSEL DOLLAR, dec'd by
Jno. Orsborn, Jno. Burny and J___? Potter.

27 Sept. 1819. Estate sale of CLABOURN VAUGHN, dec'd by Mary
Vaughn, Exr.

9 Oct. 1819. Estate sale of THOMAS BLAKELEY, dec'd by Thos.
Blakeley, Adm.

1 Nov. 1819. Letters of adm. estate of JAMES CLARDEY, dec'd
to Susanah Clardey, wife of dec'd. Sec: Arnold Millwee and Jos.
Irby.

1 Nov. 1819. Letters of adm. estate of JAMES DARD(?), dec'd
to Valentine Harlen. Sec: Robt. Allison and Robt. Dard.

8 Nov. 1819. Adm. of estate of JOHN RICHEY, dec'd to Wm. Richey.
Sec: David Caldwell, Jr.(?) and Archibald(?) Holt. Will proven.
3 July 1819. Will of JOHN RICHEY. Wife Margret; son William;
daughter Jane Harriss; son-in-law Joseph Gravess; Samuel Richey.
Exr: son William Richey and friend Martin Shaw. Wit: David Caldwell, Jr., Archibald Holte and Aron(?) Fuller.

16 Nov. 1819. Adm. of estate of ELIJAH WALKER, dec'd to Elizabeth

WALKER estate cont'd:
Walker and John Walker. Sec: James Powell, Larkin Gains and
Reuben Powell.

10 Nov. 1819. Appraisal of estate of RICHARD WHITE, dec'd by
James Glenn, Robt. Gray and Danl. Beachum. (No date) Estate
sale. Jas. Simpson, Adm.

6 Dec. 1819. Letters of adm. estate of JAMES CORLEY(?), dec'd
to Wm. Black. Sec: John Black and Thos. Powell.

6 Dec. 1819. Adm. of estate of JOHN KIRKPATRICK, dec'd to Alexander Kirkpatrick. Sec: John Hunter and Thomas Marly(?).

9 Dec. 1819. Adm. of estate of JOHN SADLER, dec'd to Plesant
Sadler and Mary Sadler, exr/exrx. Sec: Henry Hitt (will proven).
15 Sept. 1812. Will of JOHN SADLER. Wife Mary; land formerly
of James Ball; land formerly of James Pucket; mother Marey
Sadler and my sisters; son Plesant; my children (not named).
Exrs: Lewis Ball, Plesant Sadler and wife Mary Sadler. Wit:
Henry Hitt, Geo. Ball and Peter Ball.

26 Nov. 1809(?). Late bill of the goods and chattels of HANSEL
DOLLAR, dec'd. Mentions Reuben Dollar, William Barker, Har-
beriot(?) Martin, Justonion Martin, John Dollar, Saml. Irby,
Wm. Dollar, Jonathan(?) Pope. Adm: Sarah Dollar.

(No date) Appraisal of estate of JOSEPH DOWNS, dec'd by J.
Bolt, Z.(?) F. Dolff and Jas. Cunningham.

23 Dec. 1819. Estate of SOLOMON HOPKINS, dec'd. Francis Hopkins, exr. Will proven 19 Apr. 1805(?) estate to wife of sd
dec'd and wife now dec'd; order sale granted to make sd division of est. (Samuel) Solomon Hopkins, dec'd.

20 Dec. 1819. Appraisal of estate of JOHN RICHEY, SR., dec'd
by Jno. Roberson, Archibald Holt and Jonathan Fargey. Note
due dec'd on David Caldwell. Wm. Richey, exr.

9 Dec. 1819. Appraisal of estate of ELIJAH WALKER, dec'd by
Philip Wait, Larkin Gains and Jno. Wiseman.

22 Nov. 1819. Appraisal of estate of JAMES WARD, dec'd by Thos.
Porter(?), Robt. Ward and J. A.(?) Boyd. 25 Nov. 1819. Sale
bill. Purchasers: Elizabeth Ward, Saml. Vance, Jas. Barrow,
Jos. Owing, Chas. Allen, Jno. Ward, M. Franks, Wm. Adkins,
Robt. Criswell, Wm. Simmons, Wm. Hall, Jos. Vance, Jas. Temple-
ton, Ransom Fuller, Lynl_ Johnston, Robt. Holaday, Jno. Blake-
ly, Johnston Redden, Wm. Stone, Jer'y Hill, Wm. Templeton,
Wm. Irby, Wm. Coachman, Chas. Simmons, Thos. Porter, Arthur
Oneal. Valentine Harton, adm. Notes due est: John A. Craddock,
Wm. Ward, Wm. Park, David Craddock.

10 Dec. 1819. Appraisal of estate of JOHN SADLER, dec'd by
Benj. Hitt, ___ Smith and Wm. Tinsley(very dim). 13 Dec. 1819.
Sale bill. Purchasers: Aaron Pinson, John Ball, John Beasley,
John _. Williams; Benj. Hill, David Hitt, Geo. Neely, Jos.
Jones, Reuben Golding, Benj. Golding, Wm. Sadler, Wm. Tinsley,
John Deal, Jeremiah Sadler, Abner Hitt. (Very dim).

7 Jan. 1820. Inventory/appr. estate of JOHN KIRKPATRICK, dec'd
by Chas. Simmons, Jno. Davis and Wm. Goodwin. Credit due est.

KIRKPATRICK estate cont'd:
Danl. O'Harra(?) & Jones of Charleston returned dated 10 Sept.
1797.

17 Sept. 1818. Appraisal bill of ISAAC UNDERWOOD, dec'd by
John Dunlap and _____?. (Date changed to 1819). 20 Sept. 1819.
Sale bill. John Underwood, Adm.

20? Nov. 1819. Appraisal of estate of LEVI FOWLER, dec'd by
Jas. McCary(?), Wm. Dillard and _. Boyce. 10(20?) Nov. 1819.
Sale bill. No purchasers named. Cert. by Nathan Fowler and
John Duckett, Adm.

5 Jan. 1820. Return of Susanah Clardey, adm. of JAMES CLARDY,
dec'd. No goods, etc. to be found in this district. Share due
him from James Boyd, James Huggins.

3 Jan. 1820. Martha Duckett, minor about 15 years of age chose
John Duckett guardian. Sec: Nathan Fowler and Richd Fowler.

12 Nov. 1819. Wm. Croson and Jno. Green(?) sec.   THOMAS CROSON,
dec'd. Martha Croson, Adm. All appeared in Court on 20 Nov.
1819, Wm. Croson refused to adm. with sd Martha who intermarried with Thomas Guin. Martha Guin did acct for sale bill.
Thos. Guin took adm. with Thos. Burnside and Jno. Black as
sec. Former adm. revoked.

3 Jan. 1820. John Miller and wife, Thomas Yarborough and wife
against John Garrett, adm. of SILUS(?) GARRETT, dec'd with
will annexed. Sale bill of Silus Garrett, dec'd made on 25
and 26 Jan. 1805. Legatees Martha and Margret (Garrett). Margret
married to John Miller and Martha to Thomas Yarborough.

15 Jan. 1820. Adm. of estate of GREEN RICHARDS, dec'd to John
Hays. Bond: John Johnston and Isaac Gray.

8 Feb. 1820. Will of JAMES ABERCROMBIE, dec'd proven by James
Abercrombie, Jr. Gabriel Jowell (Joel?) intermarried with dau.
of sd dec'd asked will be proven, Wm. Cunningham his former
att'y. Jas. Abercrombie as exr. by his att'y Wm. Creswell.
29 Nov. 1819. Will of JAMES ABERCRUMBIE. Daughter Mary O'Danial and husband Wm. O'Danial; daughter Isabella Blackwell;
Rebecah Jowell(?) and her husband Gabriel Jowell(?); daughter
Suzanah Matthews; daughter Hannah Brook; daughter Margret Blackwell; daughter Elizabeth Andrews; grandson James Abercrumbie;
to my negro woman Jane her freedom; son James Abercrumbie;
step-son Archibald McDaniel, Jr. Exrs: son James Abercrumbie
and Elias Brook. Wit: E. L. Rowling, David Bell and John Neel.

9 Feb. 1820. Thomas Roberson, minor about 18 years, chose John
Roberson, Sr. as his guardian in place of John Roberson, Jr.,
dec'd. Bond: Martin Shaw and Wm. Richey(?).

(Date?) Robt. Creswell, adm. of DAVID SPEERS(?), dec'd with
Thos. Archibald who married the widow of intestate and Andrew
Speers the guardian appt'd by court of Equity for the minor
children of the intestate -a Wm. Fulton, Esq. has rec'd payment but not paid over to minors(?). Followed by accts of ex-
planation of what is due. Money to widow and balance for children of intestate David Speers.

5 Oct. 1819. Appraisal of estate of SARAH THREET, dec'd by

Appraisal cont'd:
Robert Young, Samuel Garey, Joseph Young and Wm. Wright. Sale
bill of SARAH THREET, dec'd. Two notes on Wm. Clark and Thos.
Cook two notes. Cert. by John and Robert Dunlap, exrs.

5 Feb. 1820. JAMES DUCKETT, died intestate. Adm. granted to
widow Sarah Duckett and Levi Fowler. Dr. George Young, Jr.(?)
intermarried with Marey Duckett first child of sd dec'd and
John Duckett, 2nd child of dec'd and Thomas Duckett, 3rd child
of dec'd and Saml. Dillard now married to Lyda Duckett 4th
child of dec'd, John Roberson married Alsey Duckett 5th child
of dec'd, all rec'd from sd Sarah Duckett and Levi Fowler adm.
their just shares of estate. Signed: George Young, John Duckett, Thomas Duckett, Samuel Dillard and John Roberson. Wit:
Thomas Ranes and Thomas Dashill(?).

14? Jan. 1820. Sale bill of SOLOMON HOPKINS, dec'd. Purchasers:
Jeremiah Hopkins, Mrs. Nancey Mahaffey, George Hopkins, F.
Hopkins, John Hopkins, Samuel Hopkins, Thornebury Bowling,
Frances Hopkins, Sollomon Hopkins, Robt. Bowling, John F. Peden,
Martin Babb, John Timmins, Plesant Shaw, Wm. Morgen, Wm. Hatch-
er, John Kellet, Thomas Caydon(?), Baley Mayhon, John Terrey.

7 Feb. 1820. Adm. of estate of GEORGE LEEK, dec'd to Abner
Young and will proven. Sec: Thomas Fuller and Mathew Hunter.
Abner Young named exr. 23 Oct. 1819. Will of GEORGE LEEK. Wife
Margaret; children: Samuel, Jenny, William, James, Margret,
Melelenda and Alzira; my Anne be supported during her mothers
widowhood. Legatees Jeremiah Leek, Samuel Young and Abner Young.
Mentions daughter Anna again to be supported during her natural
life. Exrs: Jeremiah Leek, Samuel Young and Abner Young. Wit:
_____?, Thos. Fulton and Mathew Hunter. (N.B. Millinda also is
spelled several ways as is Alzira.)

(No date) Sale bill of EDWARD G. WINN, dec'd. Purchasers: Sarah
Winn, John Handley, B. B. Black, James Cook, John Finney, John
King, Galunnus Winn, Arthur Arnold, Wm. Farrow, Jno. Black,
Thos. Gill, Jno. Findley, Marmaduke Jones, Eliza. Cook. B.
B. Cheshire, adm.

17-18 Jan. 1820. Sale bill of estate of ELIJAH WALKER, dec'd.
Purchasers: Elizabeth Walker (bulk of est.), John Walker, Jas.
Gains, Timothy Swindle, Wm. South, Jr., Wm. Ware, Thos. Moore,
Robt. P. Delph, A. C. Jones, John Sawyers, Moses Meer(?), Wm.
Reding, Larkin Gains, Geo. Tierce, F. Easter, Thos. Elison,
Ezekiel Powell, Nancy Walker, Danl. Ford, J. E. Clardy, Reuen
Powell, Geo. Glenn, Benj. Tierce, John Night, John South, Jas.
Powell, Jr., Aaron Clore, Geo. Brownlee, Wm. South, Allen Clark,
Henry Delph, James Powell, Jr., Elijah Walker, Isaac Waldrop.
Note on Wm. Yeager and Jesse Daniel. Adm: Elizabeth Walker
and John Walker.

21 Feb. 1820. Estate of REASON HOLLEN(HOLLAND), dec'd. Charles
Simpson, Adm. and sec: Mathew Hunter and Archalus Craddock
with warrant of appraisal.

27 Feb. 1820. Estate of ELISHA WILK, dec'd. Elizabeth Wilk,
exr. Will proven by oaths of Drury Sims and John Hill. (N.B.
Wilk may be WELLS, film very dim.) 1 Nov. 1813. Will of ELISHA
WELLS (WILKS? WILLS?). Wife: Elisabeth. She also exr. Wit:
John Cook, Drury Sims, Jr. and John Hitt.

25 Feb. 1820. Adm. of will of JOHN CUNNINGHAM, dec'd to Robert

Adm. cont'd:
Cunningham. Sec: George Bowen and David Anderson. Warrant of appraisal.

7 Feb. 1820. Adm. of estate of GEORGE MADDEN, dec'd to wife Phebey Madden. Sec: Turner Richardson and John Milam.

16 Dec. 1818. Sale bill of property of WILLIAM WASHINGTON, dec'd. Purchasers: Philip Wait and Aaron Pinson. Philip Wait, Adm.

6 Mar. 1820. Letters test. of estate of JAMES ABERCRUMBIE, dec'd to James Abercrumbie, Jr. as exr. order of sale.

6 Mar. 1820. Estate of DANIEL MATHIS, dec'd. Elijah Teague, adm. with John Hewit and Lewis Linull?, sec.

6 Mar. 1820. Adm. of estate of JOHN PRINGLE, dec'd to wife Drusilla Pringle. Sec: Ira Arnold and Wm. F. Downs.

6 Mar. 1820. Adm. of estate of EZEKIEL NORTH, dec'd to John Motes. Sec: Jonathan Motes and John Black.

__ Apr. 1820. Will of JOHN ROWLAND(?), dec'd proven by Robt. Rowland and John Rammage, exrs. Sec: Robt. Rammage and Edw. Deason(?) and Saml. Young. Also codicil. (N.B. see BOULAND will)

(No date) Appraisal of estate of JAMES COLEY(CORLEY), dec'd. by B. B. Cheshire, John Motes and Jonn B. Hendley(?). 22 Dec. 1820. Sale bill of estate of JAMES CORLEY, dec'd. Purchasers: Rebecah Bonhum, John Monroe, Wm. Farrow, John Black, Richd. Fowler, Lind. Colb, Jones Fuller, Peter Sadler, John Handby, John Spears, Cato (free negro), Benjamin B. Cheshir, Capt. Anthony Griffin, John Ridge, Arthur Oneal, Thomas Cob(Colb), Daniel Farrow. Wm. Black, adm.

10 Jan. 1820. Will of JAMES BOULAND (also see Rowland above). Wife: Mary; son John (not of age); son Thomas; land in Tennessee bounded by TAdlock trail, Flint and others; William (son?); son James; firm of G. L. Harrington; note to David Boyce; daughter Mary Scott; daughter Sarah; daughter Jane; daughter Charlot; son John to have English education; heirs of daughter Martha Ramage, dec'd; land belonging to Tom Charles for sons Thomas and John. Exrs: John Ramage and Robt. Bouland. Wit: Robt. Ramage, Edw. Deason and Samuel Young. Codicil: Robt. Bouland to receive his part; Sarah and Jane Bouland. Same wit.

(No date) Appraisal bill of estate of ELISHA WELLS, dec'd by Lazarus Hitt, Lewis Ball and Robt. Hollingsworth.

(No date) Appraisal of estate of JOHN CUNNINGHAM, dec'd by Geo. Borling(?), Robt. A. Cunningham and Jos. Neiley.

15 Apr. 1820. Appraisal of estate of REASON HOLLEN, dec'd by John Underwood, James Underwood and Henery Niell.

(No date) Appraisal of estate of GEORGE MADDEN, dec'd by A. Richardson (last names dim). (Date: 3 Mar. 1820?)

25 Feb. 1820. Appraisal of estate of GEORGE LEEK, dec'd by Wm. Dunlap, Jesse Johnston and Mathew Hunter.

31 Jan. 1820. Appraisal of estate of GREEN RICHARDS, dec'd by Rodey W. Roberts, John Johnston and Isaac Gray. 7 Feb. 1820. Sale bill of estate. Purchasers: John Hays, Elizabeth Richards, Andrew Whealer, James Welch, Judiah Roberts, Jas. Ecterken, Chas. Horton, Saml. Johnston, Jonathan Hays, Jno. Brown, Wm. Bonds, Jas. Enterken, Jno. Deen, Jabuz Canon, Sye Williams, Danl. Conner, Saml. Jones, Seavon Stuard, Baley Cox, Eben(?) Steart, Saml. Johnston. John Hays, Adm.

(No date) Sale bill of property of JOHN SADLER, dec'd by John Sadler, Exr. Purchasers: Plesant Sadler, Wm. Tinsley, Benjamin Hitt, John Ball, Robt.Neelie, David Hitt, John Wood, Curtis Kernel, Sarah Sadler.

(No date) Appraisal of property of JAMES ABERCRUMBIE, dec'd will to his son James Abercrumbie. Also a bill of the unwilled property. Property to James, Jr. and Rebeca Jowell. Cert. by Wm. Moor, Martin Shaw and David Bell.

13 Apr. 1820. Appraisal of estate of DANIEL MATHIS, dec'd by Thos. Dryumple(?), John Miller and Joshua Teague. 3 Mar. 1820. Bill of sale. Purchasers: Elizabeth Mathis, Elisha Teague, Joshua Teague, Isaac Case, John Deen, Jno. Blakeley, Wm. Johnston, Robt. Teague, Eliphus Jurey(?), David Mason, Jno. Johnston, Jno. Shepard, Jno. Miller, Saml. Neil, Robt. Littel, Wm. Cole, Jno. Munrow, Thomas Dylrumple, Jas. H. Lowrey, Wm. Neel, Glanus Winn, Mathew Hunter, Jas. Entrekin, Elisha Adair, Elisha Teague. Bill of the sale of estate 19 Apr. 1820. Jas. Boyd. Notes on Isaac Case, Reuben Case, Langston East, Jno. Millar, Robt. Teague, Jno. Davis, Lewis Lenvill. Elijah Teague, Adm.

28 Apr. 1820. Appraisal of property of JOHN BOULAND, dec'd by Jos. Scott, Saml. Young, D. Boyce and Edw. Deason. Notes due dec'd: George Ross, David Boyce, Jno. Ramage, Jno. Vaughn, Elisha Adair and Robt. Bouland. Robt. Bouland, Exr.

12 June 1820. Adm. of estate of THOMAS GOGGANS, dec'd to Samuel Goggans. Sec: James Goggans and John Drake.

5 Feb. 1820. Sale bill of personal estate of JOHN RICHEY, dec'd by Wm. Richey, exr. Purchasers: Jno. McCurley, David Caldwell, Wm. Richey, Martin Shaw, Jno. Roberson, Isum Roberson, Jerob Madden, Archibald Holt. Second sale on 11 Mar. 1820. Artis Cook, Jacob Fuller, Jno. Holt, Jno. Brownlee, Saml. Richey, Jno. Burgess, Benjamin Gomer(?), Jno. Richey, Jno. Roberson.

13 June 1820. Will of CHARLES WILSON, dec'd proven by Thos. Wilson and Elijah Watson. Oath of James Crawford. 4 June 1820. Will of CHARLES WILSON. Daughter Mary Wilson; mentions Wadsworth school; sons James, Charles; land bought of David McCaa; land of Robt. Cooper mentioned; to Charles Crawford; mentions six other children. Exrs: son Thomas Wilson and friend Elijah Watson. Wit: Chas. Crawford, Jas. Crawford and Chas. Wilson, Jr.

2? June 1820. Sale of property of JAMES ABERCRUMBIE, dec'd by James Abercrumbie, exr. Purchasers: Gabriel Jowell, Robt. Carter, __? Adkins, Charlittea Allen, Nathan B. Bowling, Archebal McDannel, Dr. Bell, Lucinda Allen, Jas. Wadkins, David Allen, Saml. Irby, Real Allen, Richad Blackwell, James Abercrumbie, Elias Brock, Jno. Duglass, Saml Hall, Geo. Allen,

Estate sale cont'd:
Ephrum Eldridge, Charles Brook, Wm. Hall, Robt. McNees.

(No date) Appraisal of estate of CHARLES WILSON, dec'd by Richd.
Fowler, W. G. Wright and Hezekiah Cheshire. 15? July 1820.
Sale of estate. Purchasers: Hezekiah Cheshire, B. Connant,
Arthur Oneal, Richd. Fowler, Jno. Monrow, Jno. Simpson, Wm.
Farrow, Alex. Winn, Davis Williams, Henery Johns, Saml. Austin,
Umphrey Wells, Jno. D. Griffin, Wm. Pinson, Wm. Wright, Thos.
Gill, Jno. Gates, Jas. Wilson, Anthony Griffin, Jos. Rodgers,
and notes on hand: on Hezehiah Cheshire, Duke Goodman, Jno.
Black, Wm. W. Simpson, Thos. Gill, Alexander More, Arthur Oneal,
Willard Watson, Wm. Blackerby, Jas. Simpson, Washington Wil-
liams. Elijah Watson, exr.

3 Sept. 1820. Adm. of estate of LYDAL(?) ALLEN, dec'd to Chars.
Allen. Sec: Wm. F. Downs and Jos. Neeley.

3 Sept. 1820. Will of JAMES BONDS, dec'd proven by Richard
Bonds. Wm. Criswell, atty. for David? Will. Wm. Irby, atty.
22 June 1820. Will of JAMES BONDS. Daughter Jinna Welsh; land
bought of Reughly Horton; grandson James Welsh; grand-daughter
Marey Welsh, daughter of Jinna Welsh; son Richard Bonds; daughter Nancy Murphey and her daughter Marey Murphey; son James
Bonds, son Calvin Bonds and his children: Rhode, Jesse, Richard
and John Bonds; grand-daughter Marey Bonds daughter of son
Richard Bonds. Wit: Robt. Long, James Bell and Sarah Bell.
3 Sept. 1820. Richard Bonds qualified as exr. of will. John
Bonds renounced being qualified as exr. D. Anderson, Ord. Appraisal of estate. (No date) By Jos. M. Morres, David Nabors, Jas.
Bell and Wm. Grayham.

22 Sept. 1820. Appraisal of estate of LYDAL ALLEN, dec'd by
C. Saxon, Robt. Criswell and Wm. Henderson.

2 Oct. 1820. Will of ENOS HORTON, dec'd proven by Phebey Horton.
Sec: Richard Bonds and Jas. Bell. Phebey Horton qualified as
exr. 8 Sept. 1820. Will of ENOS HORTON. Wife Phebey; niece
Mary Ann Horton, daughter of my brother Raughley Horton; nephew
John Horton. Exr: wife Pheobee Horton. Wit: Robt. Long, Richd.
Bonds and Jas. Bell.

3 Oct. 1820. Adm. of estate of ALEXANDER H. MOOR, dec'd to
Washington Williams. Sec: Jos. Wallis? and David Caldwell.

(No date) Appraisal of estate of THOMAS GOGGANS, dec'd by Alex.
Winn, John Drake and Aberham Johnston. 14 Sept. 1820. Sale
bill. Samuel Goggans, adm.

11 Sept. 1820. Appraisal of estate of ISABELLA FOWLER, dec'd
by John Black, Alexander Winn and S. Drummond.

(No date) Sale of estate of EZEKIEL NORTH, dec'd. Purchasers:
John Motes, Richd Motes, Robt. Motes, Isaac Motes, Jos. Rodgers,
North(?) Drummond, Wm. Farrow, Danl Farrow, Allen Andrews,
Elihu Motes, Mrs. John Motes, Saml. Allen. Jno. Motes, adm.

16 Oct. 1820. Estate of JOHN SAXON, dec'd. Adm. to Samuel Barksdale. Sec: John Witt(?) and Jas. H. Lowery.

20 Oct. 1820. Will of JAMES DORRAH, SR, dec'd proven by Jas.
Dorrah. Sec: (too dim to read). 23 Apr. 1810. Will of JAMES

DORRAH will cont'd:
DORRAH, SR. Wife: Anne; son James. Exr: James Dorrah, Jr. Wit:
John Taylor, D. Evans(?) and George Graves. (N.B. this whole
will is very dim and faded. Most cannot be read.)

5 May 1820. Appraisal of estate of JOHN PRINGLE, dec'd by Allen
___, John Walker and Thos. Williamson.

5 Sept. 1820. Sale of mare, estate of ROBERT PASLEY, dec'd
by exrs: Wm. Byrd and Elizabeth Byrd.

20? Mar. 1820. Sale of estate of JOHN KIRKPATRICK, dec'd. Pur-
chasers: James Kirkpatrick, Frances Posey, Wm. Wilson, Allen
Saxon, Edw. Garrett, (others too dim). Alexander Kirkpatrick,
Adm. of estate.

20 Oct. 1802(?) (1820). Appraisal of estate of ALEXANDER H.
MOOR, dec'd by David Williams, H. Chesure, Danl. Williams and
Efrum Andrews. 20 Oct. 1820. Sale of estate. Purchasers: Davis
Williams, Robt. Blakley, John Felts, John Leonard, E. Andrews,
Tobias Cook, Leonard Andrews, Alexander Austin, John Monroe,
Wm. Williams, Robt. Malone. Washington Williams, adm.

14 Nov. 1820. Will of MATTHEW JOHNSTON, dec'd proven by Robt.
McNees. James Johnston, as exr. 26 Sept. 1820. Will of MATTHEW
JOHNSTON. Grand-daughter Ethalinday Johnston; sons William
and James Johnston; daughters Elizabeth Barnett, Fanny Smith
and Mary Grant; dec'd son Thomas Johnston, his children to
inherit. Exr: William and James Johnston. Wit: Robt. McNees
and Salley McNees.

19 Oct. 1820. Appraisal of estate of JAMES DURROUGH(DORRAH),
Sr., dec'd. by Henry Durrow, _____? and John Wiseman.

6 Nov. 1820. Will of MARMADUKE PINSON, dec'd proven by Isaac
Dial Boyd and Saml. Cunningham. Pinson and Wm. Madden, exrs.
26 Apr. 1820. Will of MARMADUKE PINSON, SR. Wife: Molley; daughters Edee, Sally, Rethey and Ruth; oldest son Bijah(?) Pinson;
son Isaac; daughter Huldath Pinson; daughter Polly Strain;
son Marmaduke Pinson; land formerly of James Hollingsworth;
grandson Pinson McDaniel. Exr: Bijah Pinson and Wm. Madden.
Wit: Isaac Dial, James Boyd and S. Cunningham.

(No date) Sale of personal estate of DAVID FOWLER, dec'd by
Sarah Fowler, adm. 24 Oct. 1820. Second appraisal of estate
by Jas. Hutcheson, Jno. Hutcheson and Jno. McClintock.

5 Nov. 1820. Sale of estate of JAMES BONDS, dec'd. Purchasers:
David Mason, Jane White, Jane Welsh, Marey Bell, Richd. Bonds,
Lewis Jones, John Bonds, Jas. Welch, Reuben Meadors, Smith
Willson, John McCrarey, Jno. Murphey, Henry Murphey, Benning-
ton Stokes, Josiah Stokes, Smith Wilson, Jas. Murphey, Chas.
Forguson, Jno. Johnston, Washington Meadors, Wm. Vickery, John
Hays. Richard Bonds, Exr.

(Date?) Appraisal of estate of ENOS HORTON, dec'd by Jas. Hill,
Jno. Dillard, Wm. Grayham and Richd. Bonds. Note on Peggey
Horton.

6 Nov. 1820. Estate of BARTLET MILUM, dec'd. Adm. to Jane Milum.
Sec: Mathew Cunningham, James Horton and Efrum Hitts(?). Also
warrant of appraisal with letters of adm. D. Anderson, Ord.

2 Oct. 1820. Adm. of estate of ANDREW EDWARDS, dec'd to John Edwards. Sec: Edward Scrughs(?) and Jno. Meadors.

3 Sept. 1820. Adm. of estate of ISABELLA FOWLER, dec'd to James Parks. Sec: Chas. Fowler, Rodey Canady and Saml. Mills.

6 Nov. 1820. Adm. estate of JAMES MC CANATHEY, dec'd to Martha McCanathey. Sec: David Mason and Richd. Bonds.

13 Nov. 1820. Adm. of estate of WILLIAM MC MURTREY, dec'd to Rebecah McMurtrey. Sec: Jas. Boyd, Jno. Saxon and Jas. H. Lowery.

13 Nov. 1820. Adm. of estate of JOHN FOWLER, dec'd to John Todd. Sec: Jno. Walliss and Wm. Cowan.

13 Nov. 1820. Adm. of estate of JOHN FAIR, dec'd to Ann Fair and Geo. McCrarey. Sec: Elisha Adair and Jas. Dillard.

14 Oct. 1820. Appraisal of estate of ANDREW EDWARDS, dec'd by Geo. Sloan, Jno. Meador and Wm. Meador. (No date) Sale of estate. Purchasers: Widow Edwards, Jno. Austen, Edw. Surgess(?), Isaac Garrett, Jno. Cureton, Jas. Garrett, Jno. Childers, Jno. Meadors, B. J. Willson, Jos. Brown, Dennis House, Benj. Kilgore. Jno. Edwards, adm.

18 Nov. 1820. Adm. of estate of WILLIAM COOK, dec'd to Daniel Cook and James Wright. Sec: Tobias Cook and Wm. G. Wright.

11 Dec. 1820. Will of THOMAS HILL, dec'd proven by Marshal Pollard and Danl. Jones. Robert Malone disqualified as exr. 30 Nov. 1820. Will of THOMAS HILL. Wife Polley; land of Josiah Cason; estate of Robt. Pollard, dec'd; Mrs. Narsissy Leek(?) and Wm. Atwood, Robt. Hill, James Hill, Wm. Hill, Sarah Fanny Hill, Robt. Hill and James Hill. Exr: wife Polley Hill, friends Robt. Malone and Wm. B. Smith. Wit: Marshal Pollard, Danl. Jones and Josiah Cason.

28 Oct. 1820. Second sale of estate of JOHN RICHEY, dec'd. Purchasers: James McFerson, Wm. Richey, Jno. H. Nickles, Joel Hughs, Jno. Roberson, Catherine Nickles, David Caldwell, Saml. Richey, Rachel Anderson, Hamton Findley. Wm. Richey, Exr.

21 Nov. 1820. Second appraisal of estate of CHARLES WILSON, dec'd by E. Watson, R. Fowler, Wm. G. Wright and H. Chesure. (No date) Second sale of estate. James Burnes, Saml. Austen, Jas. Craford, Jas. Griffin, Robt. Bryson, Hez. Chesure, Jno. Monroe, A. Griffin, Henry Johns, Jno. Burnside, Jack(?) H. Chesure, S. Caldwell, Jno. Felts. Elisha Watson, exr.

7 Nov. 1820. Estate sale of JAMES GAMBLE, dec'd. Wm. Gamble, exr.

30 Nov. 1820. Appraisal of estate of WILLIAM MC MURTREY, dec'd by Thos. Dalrymple, Jno. Millar and Reuben G. Case. (No date) Estate sale. Purchasers: Rebecah McMurtrey, Anderson Goggens, Jno. Shepard, Allen Smith, Jas. Boyd, Robt. Hunter, Wm. Smith, Wm. G. Johnston, Thos. Dalrymple, Jno. Saxon, Jno. Brown, Chas. Johnston. Jas. Boyd, adm.

9 Dec. 1819. Estate sale of SAMUEL WRIGHT, dec'd. Purchasers: Saml. Beechum, Wm. Cook, Wm. G. Wright, Tobias Cook, Benj. Adair, J. Wallass, Danl. Beechum, Benj. Chesure, Wm. Lygon,

Estate sale cont'd:
Wm. Tinsley, Peter Sadler, Col. J. Williams. Wm. Wright, exr.
27 Nov. 1820. Second sale. Purchasers: Jno. Moats, Jas. Simpson, Wm. Grier, Danl. Williams, Thos. Gill, Drury Vaughn, Arnold
Bonham, Anthony Griffin, Jas. Wright, A. Bohannon, Wm. Farrow,
Robt. Campbell, A. Griffin, Benj. B. Chesure. Wm. Wright, exr.

2 Nov. 1820. Estate sale of JOHN SAXON, dec'd. Purchasers:
Wm. Saxon, Hickerson Barksdill, Jas. Copeland, Saml. Hunter,
Wm. Gammell, Jno. Underwood, Henry Hill, Ruthah(?) Saxon, Wm.
Copeland. Saml. Barksdill, adm.

12 Dec. 1820. Appraisal of estate of JAMES MC CONATHEY, dec'd
by David Mason, Henry S. Neel and Wm. Grayham. 14 Dec. 1820.
Return of sale. Note on James Williams. Martha McCannahey,
adm.

20 Dec. 1820. Estate of DAVID FOWLER, dec'd sold by consent
of Charles Fowler. (Mostly negroes). Sarah Fowler, Adm.

9 Dec. 1820. Adm. of estate of NANCY MC CRARY, dec'd to Jos.
McCrary. Sec: Thos. McCrary and Jno. Bryson.

20 Nov. 1820. Appraisal of estate of JOHN FOWLER, dec'd by
Saml. Hunter, F. Ross and Saml. Flemming. 3 Dec. 1820. Sale
bill. Purchasers: David Higgins, Roadey Fowler, Jones Fowler,
Wm. Fowler, Jno. Todd, Tompson Farley, Jane Fowler, Wm. Higgins,
Wm. Leek, Saml. Hunter, Wm. Madox, F. Ross. John Todd, adm.

18 Dec. 1817. Will of MARY FARLEY. Son: Thompson Farley. Wit:
John Wallass, Wm. Ross and Benj. Criffin.

1 Jan. 1821. Adm. of estate of CHARLES WILSON, JR., dec'd to
Jas. Wilson. Sec: Reuben Thomas and Jas. Johnston.

15 Dec. 1820. Appraisal of estate of JOHN FRIER, dec'd by Jesse
Johnston, Jno. Holland and Henry Shell.

22 Dec. 1820. Estate sale of ENOS HORTON, dec'd. Cert: 18 Nov.
1820 by Pheabey Horton, exr.

17 Nov. 1820. Appraisal of estate of MARMADUKE PINSON, dec'd,
by Isaac Dial, Jas. Boyd and Gabriel Jowell. Abigah D. Pinson
and Wm. Madden, exrs. 1 Dec. 1820. Estate sale. Purchasers:
Robt. Aleson, Richd. McDanial, Wm. Madden, Marmaduke Pinson,
Jr., S. B. Martin, John D. Boyd, Isaac Pinson, Gabriel Jowell,
David Bell.

13 Jan. 1821. Estate of THOMAS BOWLAND, dec'd. Wm. Bowland,
adm. Sec: Saml. Yonge and Edw. Desson. 13 Jan. 1821. Estate
of CHARLOTTE BOWLAND, dec'd. Same adm. and sec.

5 Feb. 1821. Will of MARY CASON, dec'd proven. Application
of Sarah Millar and David Greer. John Millar, wit. Sarah Millar,
exr. 15 Jan. 1812. Will of MARY CASON. Son William; sister
Sarah Millar; brother Thomas Cason's son, William; children
of brother Thomas Cason - Nancy, William, John, James, Samuel.
Exr: sister Sarah Millar and friend David Greer. Wit: John
Millar, Anderson Millar and Wm. Millar.

22 Nov. 1815. Will of JOHN BOX. Wife Rachel Box; grand-daughters Rachel and Luisa Box, daughters of Jemiah Box (adj. lands

132

BOX will cont'd:
of Saml. Nabors and Jane Moore; daughter Jemima Sneed; grandson Elisha Williamson; son Shadrick Box; son Robert Box; sons Abraham Box, Benjamin Box; daughters Molly South, Rachel Banks and Jemima Sneed. Exr: friend Elijah Williamson. Wit: Wm. Arnold, Robt. Nabours and Jos. McEwen. 5 Feb. 1821. Will proven by Elijah Williamson. Oaths of Wm. Arnold and Robt. Nabours.

(No date) Estate sale of ISABELLA FOWLER, dec'd. Purchasers: James Parks, Robt. Allison, Elihu Rodgers, Jos. Irby, Wm. Parks, Sr., Wm. Hutcherson, Jas. Parks, Sr., Saml. Flemming, Nancy Parks, Jno. McClintock, Jas. Higgins, Parmer Higgins, Nehemiah Franks, Saml. Atchison, Jas. Flemming, Wm. Templeton, Andw. Mills, Jr., Jos. Deen, Andw. Brown, Jno. Crumton, Hugh Crooks, Alex. Miller, Robt. Flemming, Sr., Joel Starnes, Jacob Nabours, Thos. McCurley, Jas. Gill, Nathan Hunter, Wm. Cason, Joel Allen, Mary Scean?, Saml. McCrarey, Andw. Parks, David Sloan, John Thewett, Jno. Hope, Andw. Todd, David Higgins, Wm. Hill. Jas. Parks, Adm.

20 Jan. 1821. Appraisal of estate of THOMAS BOULAND, dec'd by David Boyce, Isaac Parks? and Saml. Young. 26 Jan. 1821. Appraisal of estate of CHARLOTA BOULAND, dec'd by same. Wm. Bouland, adm.

6 Jan. 1821. Appraisal of estate of THOMAS HILL, dec'd by James Watts, Wm. Smith and Jno. Chappell. 10 Jan. 1821. Estate sale. Purchasers: Briant Leek, Henry Hill, Robt. Pollard, Jno. Chappell, Wm. Smith, Jno. McGowing, Mary Hill, Wm. Smith, Stokes Allen, Elihu Watts, Patrk. Todd, Anthony Golding, Reuben Golding, Jos.Hill, Ransom Day, Isaac Grant, Marshel Pollard, Isaac Cason, Braxton Watts, Jas. Mitchel, Jno. Hicks, Wm. Croson, Jonah Cason, Wm. B. Smith, Nathan Chapman, Wm. Philips, Jno. Malone, Danl. Jones, Jno. D. Malone, Wm. Tinsley, Danl. Foshee, David Curington, Drewry Lewis, Philip Day, Thos. B. Pollard, Abner Wells, Josiah Cason, Elihu Payne, Wm. Wright, Wm. Hill, Jr., Edw. Austin, Jno. D. Wallas, W. Beechum, D. Dial, Jno. Pasley, Anthony Butler, Beauford Watts, Danl. Dudley, Jas. Neely, Philip Chisure, Wm. Strain, Jno. Parsley, Jno. Ball, Andw. McFaul, Anthoney McFaul, Danl. Dendy, Thos. Hill, Jno. Hill, Thos. Smith, Jno. Chapman, Danl. Day, Wm. Stone, Jas. Mitchel, Drurey Vaughn. Note on Thos. Smith. Robt. Malone, Exr.

22 Jan. 1821. Inventory of goods and credits of the personal estate of JOHN FAIR(?), dec'd by Geo. McCrary and Ann Fair.

5 Feb. 1821. Estate of JAMES HOLT, dec'd. Adm. to Alsey Fullar. Sec: Jabus W. H. Johnston and Jno. Kelley.

5 Feb. 1821. Estate of JOHN ADKINS, dec'd. Adm. to John Marten. Sec: Wm. Moor and Langston Orsborn.

21 Feb. 1821. Estate of WILLIAM HALL, dec'd. Will proven by Alex. Hall, Wm. Franks and Adam Potter, exrs. Wit: Chas. Allen, John Pope? and John Dollar. 26 Jan. 1821. Will of WILLIAM HALL. Wife Alsey Hall. Exr: wife Alsey Hall and friend William Franks, and Adam Potter. Wit: Charles Allen, John Pope and John Dollar.

(No date) Sale bill of estate of LYDRAL ALLEN, dec'd. Purchasers were: Mrs. Milley Allen, Jonathan Allen, John Bolt, Robt. Creswell, Robt. Coker, Stephen Garrett, John Harriss, David Night,

Sale cont'd:
Charles Posey, David P. Saxon, Wm. Simpson, Lydral Allen, Saburt Alison, George Wolff, John Williams, Wm. Rodgers. Charles Allen, Adm.

10 Feb. 1821. Appraisal of estate of CHARLES WILSON, dec'd by Abraham Bolt, Jeremiah Mendley, Wm. Adams and James Johnston.

(No date) Appraisal bill of JOHN BOX, dec'd by Abraham Riley, A. D. Saxon and Thomas Alison. 5 Feb. 1821. Sale bill. Negro woman and child. Cert: Elisha Williamson, Exr.

5 Mar. 1821. Will of ROBERT HUNTER, dec'd proven. Mathew Hunter, Andrew Parks and James Park, Jr. exrs. Oaths of THOMAS Fulton and William Fulton, wit. 26 Jan. 1821. Will of ROBERT HUNTER. Wife: Isabela Hunter; land between Wm. Archabald and Wm. Taylor where David Brown 'lives; slaves to be emancipated if law allows and land given them. Exr: Matthew Hunter, Andrew Park and James Park, Jr. Wit: Thomas Fulton, Jr., Charlett C. Fulton, and Wm. Fulton.

5 Mar. 1821. Will of JOHN F. WOLFF, dec'd proven. Mary Wolff, Saml. Downs and George Wolff, exr. Saml. Downs, Pa____ Farrow and _____ Mathews, wit. George Wolff, exr. 3 Feb. 1820. Will of JOHN F. WOLFF. Wife Mary Wolff; son George Wolff; daughters Elizabeth Milner and Isabella Saxon; Hugh Saxon. Exr: wife Mary Wolff, Samuel Davis and George Wolff. Wit: Samuel Davis, Pattillo Farrow and Julyather Mathews.

10 Mar. 1821. Estate of JAMES HATHORN, dec'd, Joseph Neely as exr.

15? Nov. 1820. Inventory of estate of BARTLETT MILUM, dec'd by Henry Langston, James Harlon(Harton?) and Robt. Cunningham. 23-24 Nov. 1820. Sale bill of estate. Purchasers: Mathew Cunningham, Joshua Smith, Charles Irby, John Blakely, John Bosley, Ferrel Wilson, Oneall Davis, Robt. K. West, Wm. Harlon, John Milum, Jno. Higgins, Wm. Clark, Wm. Milum, Jane Milum, Jas. Parks, Ryley Milum, Saml. McKelvey, Jno. Farrow, Wm. Blakely, Benj. Milum, Z. Tinsley, Hugh Harlin, Wm. Farrow, Jno. McClintock, Jos. Hitch, Jas. Liles, Jos. Vance, Elizabeth Harlon, Valentine Harlon, Jno. Ward, Jas. Waldrop, Wm. Parks, Baron Starns, Jno. Stuart, Jas. Langston, Gaberal Styles, H. Langston, Jas. Hannah, Geo. McClintock, Andrew Todd. Jane Mylum, adm.

3 Mar. 1821. Appraisal of estate of WILLIAM HALL, dec'd by Wm. Franks, Joshua Franks, John Dollar and Stephen Potter.

22 Feb. 1821. Appraisal of estate of JAMES HOLT, dec'd by Jas. Young, Sollomon Fuller and Paul Findley. 23 Feb. 1821. Sale bill of estate. Notes on Jonathon Forgey, Robt. Miller, Charles Dotson. Alsey Fuller, adm.

6 Mar. 1821. Appraisal of estate of JOHN ADKINS, dec'd by Wm. Moor, Jno. Adkins and Wm. Marten. Sale bill (no date). John Marten, adm.

17 Mar. 1821. Appraisal of estate of MARY CASON, dec'd by Fedrick Foster, Thos. Dalrymple and Jas. Boyd.

(N.B. most of these pages are very dim. Writing is not clear.)

4 Apr. 1821. Estate of JOHN LINDLEY, dec'd. Adm. by Ruth Lindley and Jacob Niswanger. Sec: George Goddard and Lewis Watson.

4 Mar. 1821. Appraisal of estate of J. F. WOLFF, dec'd by Jesse Garrett, Sr., Chas. Allen, R. Coker and Aberham Bolt. Exr: Mary Wolff and George Wolff.

17 Apr. 1821. Estate of ELIZABETH DOLLAR, dec'd. Adm. to John Dollar. Sec: James Powell and Reuben Powell and Larkin Gains.

17 Apr. 1821. Estate of WILLIAM BABB, dec'd. Adm. to Lettey Babb. Sec: Wm. Rodgers and Thos. Babb.

2 Dec. 1820. Appraisal of estate of WILLIAM COOK, dec'd by Thos. Burnside, Thos. Wilks and Jas. Young. _ Dec. 1820. Sale bill of estate. Danl. Cook, Adm.

7 Mar. 1821. Appraisal of estate of ROBERT HUNTER, dec'd by Jas. Park, Wm. Park and Andw. Speer. 22 Mar. 1821. Sale bill of estate. Purchasers: James Park Coplin and Chas. Littel.

(No date) Sale bill of estate of CHARLOTTE BOWLDING, dec'd. Purchasers: Marey Boldon (Boland, etc.), John Greer, Geo. McCreless and Jane Boland. William Bouland, Adm. (N.B. this last name spelled various ways.)

23 Feb. 1821. Sale bill of estate of THOMAS BOULAND, dec'd. Purchasers: F. F. Carslile(also Calemies), Isaac Gray, Josiah Williams, David Mason, Wm. Bouland, John C.(?) Williams. Wm. Bouland, adm.

28 Nov. 1819(?). Property of JAMES HATHORN, dec'd sold to highest bidder. Purchasers: John Roberson, Jos. Neely, A. Adair, Jas. Glouer, J. L. Hathorn, Lewis Mitchell, Geo. Madden, Jos. Hathorn, Martin Shaw, Jas. Frankling, Capt. Shaw, E. Hathorn, Jeremiah Collins, David Bell, Benj. Mitchel, Wade Anderson, Alex. Adams, Jas. Anderson, Geo. Anderson, Wm. Grayham, Jos. Grayham, Alex. Samples, Molly Stephens, P. Wait, Marey Stephens, Wm. E. Young, Wm. Anderson, Jas. Redden, Jno. Alberson, Jr., Philip Waits, Saml. Anderson, Benj. Garner, Saml. Hopper, Jno. Wait, Wm. Crocker, Jas. Hopper, Jno. Sims, D. Wilson, L. J. Hopper, Edny Hathorn. Signed: Lewis Conner, Adm. with the will annexed of LEWIS MITCHELL, dec'd do certify.....the true sale bill of JAMES HATHORN, dec'd.

17 Apr. 1821. Alpha Walker,minor about 18 years of age, chose Saml. Phifer as guardian. Sec: Benj. Trace? and Jas. Powell.

4 May 1821. Will of JOHN TODD, dec'd proven by Wm. McClanahan, Jas. Todd and John Hobbs. 22 Jan. 1821. Will of JOHN TODD. Son-in-law Robert Bryson; son James Todd; son Charles Todd; wife Nancey Todd; sons Robert and John Todd; daughter Mary Todd. Wit: Wm. McClanahan, Jas. Todd and Jno. Hobbs.

26 Apr. 1821. Appraisal of estate of ELIZABETH DOLLAR, dec'd by Aron Clore, Jno. Parks and R. Powell.

4 June 1821. Will of JOHN MONRO, dec'd proven by Thos. Wilson. James Simpson renounces and David Grier also renounces as exrs. 1820 (no other date) Will of JOHN MONRO. Wife Sarah Monro; oldest daughter Jennet Monro; daughter Sally Monro; daughter Betsey Monro; son Robert Alexander Monro; mentions Mrs. Maddocks

Will cont'd:
land; son John Shepard Monro; son Andrew Monro; Son Larken
Monro; Son Carton Monro; daughter Nancy Monro. Exr: Col. John
Simpson, James Simpson and David Green. Wit: Thos. Fakes, Thos.
Wilson and Geo. Miller. 2 July 1821. Adm. of will (annexed) was
granted Andrew Monro. Sec: Isaac Case and Wm. East.

4 June 1821. Will of RICHARD BENNET, dec'd proven by Thos.
Hendrick and Lewis Jones. James Jones, wit. Hendrick and Jones
as exrs. 3 Dec. 1820. Will of RICHARD BENNETT. Wife Sarah;
children Anna, Miles, and Jennette. Exrs: Thos. Hendrick and
Lewis Jones. Wit: Jesse Prater, James Jones and Jno. B. Bennett.

4 June 1821. Will of HANNAH GARRETT, dec'd proven by Elisha
Garrett and Charles Garrett. Oaths of Nathan Harris and Wm.
Harris. 3 Dec. 1818. Will of HANNAH GARRETT, widow. Son Elisha
Garrett; son Charles Garrett; son Jesse Garrett. Exrs: Elisha
and Chas. Garrett. Wit: Jos. Harriss, Nathan Harriss and Wm.
Harris.

4 June 1821. Polley Owings, minor about 16 years chose John
Owings her guardian. Sec: Richd. Owings and James Owings.

(No date) Appraisal of estate of CHARLES WILLSON, dec'd by
H. Cheshire, Wm. G. Wright, R. Fowler and E. Dotson.

20 Nov. 1820. Appraisal of estate of MATTHEW JOHNSTON, dec'd
by Andrew Henderson, Mark Killingsworth and Wm. Burton. 21
Nov. 1820. Estate sale. No purchasers named. James Johnston,
Exr.

30 June 1821. Appraisal of estate of JOHN MONRO, dec'd by Fedrick Foster, Wm. ____, Jr. and John Monro.

2 July 1821. Adm. of estate of THOMAS STONE, dec'd to William
Dunlap. Sec: Jas. Lockridge and Abner Rodgers.

23 June 1821. Adm. of estate of WILLIAM BALL, dec'd to Bassell
Leek (name not clear). Sec: John Meek and Mary Hill.

9 Mar. 1821. Estate sale of WILLIAM HALL, dec'd. Purchasers:
Thos. Milner, Royal Milner, Drury Hall, Chas. Allen, Robt.
Franks, Wm. Ross, Joel Allen, John Pope, George Wolff, Philip
Gray, Alex. Powers, Elias Cheek, Wm. Henderson, Jas. Abercrumb-
ie, Nancy Studdard, Almon Grant, Hosa Blew, Titus Arnold. Adam
Potter, Adm?.

4 June 1821. Estate of JOHN SOUTH, dec'd. Elisha Williamson,
one of the former sec of Rebecah South for the adm. of est.
considers himself to be in danger, etc. Monies due estate.
Sec: John Rusel and Benj. F. Tierce.

(Papers are in the file of 1810, re note on bottom of record).
Application of Richard Owens, sec. for Nancy Owens, adm. of
the estate of JONATHON OWENS, dec'd sums due 7? July 1821,
est. not fully adm'd. Granted to Robt. Thomson, the adm. of
sd est. of dec'd this 4 June. Bond: Gideon Thomson and Thos.
Childers, his sec. 4 June 1821.

2 May 1821. Inventory of est. of WILLIAM BABB, dec'd by W.
W. Simpson, Jno. Mitchel and Joel Burgess. Notes: Jos. Babb,
Saml. Rodgers, Peter Culberson, Wm. Martin, Ransom Fuller,

Inventory cont'd:
Thos. Casey, Andw. Rodgers, Thos. Rodgers all given to Lettey
Vaughn; Wm. Abercrombie, Levi Sledge, David Martin, Thos. Babb,
Wm. Fowler, Saml. Rodgers (3rd note), Peter Stanford. 3 May
1821. Sale of estate of WM. BABB, dec'd. Purchasers: Thos.
Rodgers, Wm. D.? Simpson, E. Holcomb, Jno. Mitchell, Thos.
Babb, Wm. Rodgers. Lettey Babb, adm.

19 July 1821. Estate sale of JOHN MONRO, dec'd. Purchasers:
Widow Monro, Robt. A. Monro, David Monro, Nancy Monro, Wm.
Able, Catharine Monro, Andw. Monro, John L. Monro, Robt. H.?
Littel, Robt. Able, Robt. D. Littel, Jno. Monro, Saml. Goggins,
Abram Johnston, Jas. Littel, Fedrick Foster, David Greer, Wm.
Johnston, Sarah Monro, Wm. Allen, Elijah Teague, Thos. Griffin,
Jas. Griffin, Jno. Speer, Jno. Boyd, Wm. Blakely, Thos. Teague,
David Redden. Andw. Monro, Adm.

9 June 1821. Appraisal of estate of RICHARD BENNETT, dec'd
by Jas. Munford, Jos. Duncan and Wm. Dillard. 29 June 1821.
Estate sale. Purchasers: Jas. Low, Stephen Hill, Jno. Bennett,
Wm. Dillard, Sarah Sims, Jno. McCrary, Benj. Deason, Wade N.
Fowler, H. D. Hendrick, Sarah Bennett. Thos. Hendrick and Lewis
Jones, exrs.

6 Aug. 1821. Adm. of estate of EDWARD SMITH, dec'd to Wm. F.
Downs. Sec: Jas. Abercrombie and _____.

3 Sept. 1821. Will of ANDREW RODGERS, dec'd proven by James
Henry, Jno. Leek and Mathew Henry. 7 Dec. 1820. Will of ANDREW
RODGERS. Wife (not named); son Abner; daughter Anna Frier;
son William; children of sons Wm. and John; son Andrew; daughter
Peggey Young. Exr: son Abner Rodgers. Wit: Jas. Henery, Jno.
Leek and Mathew Henery.

3 Sept. 1821. Estate of DAVID GLENN, dec'd. Adm. to Elizabeth
Glenn. (Rest very dim). 28 Feb. 1821. Will of DAVID GLENN.
Wife Elizabeth: daughters Anna, Rebecca, Elizabeth and Jane;
son James; son George (land pur. of Jas. Dunlap); sons John
and David. Exr: wife Elizabeth and brother Francis Glenn. Wit:
J. Hitch, Jno. Stewart and Jas. Fleming.

3 Sept. 1821. Estate of JOHN COPLEN, dec'd. Adm. to Jesse Johnston. Sec: Wm. Park and Jno. Bryons.

20 Apr. 1821. Estate sale of JOHN LINDLEY, dec'd. Purchasers:
Wm. Jones, Ruth Lindley, John South, Denis? South, Ezekiel
South, John Tomson, Mathew Bolton, Moses Myres, Mikel Clardey,
Saml. Hall, Saml. Fiffer, Patric Sparen, Geo. Goddard, David
Goddard, Robt. Stephens, Jas. Gains, Thos. Styran, Wm. Halida,
Geo. Washington, Robt. Bingham, Jno. Cristen, David Boyce,
Thos. Moor, Zezekal Andrews, Jno. Walker, Harrison Daniel,
Jas. Lawless, Reuben Roberson, Archibald Norwood, Reuben Poole,
Thos. Washington, Jno. Cook, Isaac Bradon, Grace? Frier, Wm.
Puckett, Saml. Kinmon, A. C. Jones, Eliz. Clardy, Jas. Powell,
Wm. Goddard, Wm. South, Sr., Bery Frier, Danl. Goddard, Geo.
Glorur, Aaron Glure, Jas. Powell, Hudson Butler. Ruth Lindley
and Jacob Niswanger, adm.

2 Apr. 1821. Appraisal of estate of DAVID GLENN, dec'd. Mentions Elizabeth Glenn and cotton crop. Negroes. Appr'd by Jas.
Fleming, Jos. Deen, Geo. Mosley and Jno. Stuart.

137

29 Sept. 1821. Inventory of estate of ANDREW RODGERS, dec'd by Chas. Littel, John Leak and Jno. McKelvy.

13 Oct. 1821. Estate of DAVID MADDEN, dec'd. Adm. to Henery Madden. Sec: Wm. D. Simpson and Jno. Martin. (Wm. B. Smith?)

19 Oct. 1821. Estate of WILLIAM MC CLAREY, dec'd. Adm. to John Chapman. Sec: Jas. Watts and Wm. Brady(?).

7 Oct. 1821. Adm. of estate of HAMTON WALKER, dec'd to John Roberson. Sec: Wade Anderson and Jas. Wait.

4? Oct. 1821. Appraisal of estate of JOHN COPELAND, dec'd by Henry Shell, Jas. Underwood and Jas. __*__ . 4? Oct. 1821. Estate sale. Jesse Johnston, adm. Notes due dec'd: Benj. Saxon, John Abel, Chas. Blakely, Sl. Leek, Jas. Copling, Jas. Adair, Saml. Copling. (*Jas. Underwood)

13 Nov. 1821. Estate of DANIEL MATHESS, dec'd. Adm. to Elijah Teague. Sec: Jno. Hewitt and Lewis Lindvell. Adm. revoked. Lindvell granted adm. with Jno. Hewitt and Jas. Garrett, sec.

5 Nov. 1821. Estate of DANIEL PUTMON, dec'd. Adm. to Wm. Putmon. Sec: Thos. Garrett and Benj. Martin.

29 Ovt. 1821. Inventory of estate of DAVID MADDEN, dec'd by Wm. Lowe, Sr.?, Wm. Moor and Langston Orsborn. 30 Oct. 1821. Estate sale. Purchasers: Sarah Madden, Henry Madden, John Madden, Chas. Madden, Wm. D. Simpson, Langston Orsborn, Jno. Burgess, Chesley Connant, Jno. Ward, Sarah Hughs, Hirum Land?, Joab Holt.

5 Nov. 1821. Estate of THOMAS WRIGHT, dec'd. Adm. (will annexed) to Wm. Ligon. Sec: Andw. McNight and ..(blank)...

13 Nov. 1821. Will of SAMUEL LEAMON(LEEMAN), dec'd proven by Jas. McMahan, Jr., Hugh Leamon, Jas. Leamon, Jas. Hollingsworth, Jr. and Jno. Hollingsworth. 8 May 1819. Will of SAMUEL LEAMON(LEEMAN). Sons Hugh and James; daughter Elizabeth; daus. Mary Bryson, Jane Thompson, and Sarah Austin. Exr: friend Jas. McMahon and sons Hugh and James Leamon. Wit: Jas. and Jno. Hollingsworth and Jas. McMahon, Jr.

19 Nov. 1821. Appraisal of estate of THOMAS WRIGHT, dec'd by Saml. Goodman, Jonothan Johnston and Clement Wallis. (Will annexed).

(No date) Notes due estate of DAVID GLENN, dec'd. Jos. McCulah, Jno. Paterson, Jno. Hitch, Turner _____, Michel Dunlap, Pendleton Page, Robt. Teague, Geo. Grace. Elizabeth Glenn, exr.

(Next few pages too dim to read).

8 Nov. 1821. Sale bill of WILLIAM MC CLARY, dec'd. Purchasers: Jas. Watts, Wm. R. Smith, Danl. Dendy. Book acct's: Jas. Watts, Wm. R. Smith, Danl. Dendy, Jno. Chapman, Able Todd, Chas. Snow, Wm. Smith, Sr., Robt. Hunter, Nathaniel Landes?. S. Mason. Jas. Mitchel, Chas. Chapman.

19 Nov. 1821. Will of SOLOMON FULLER, dec'd proven. Exr: Solomon Fuller, Jr. 26 Feb. 1816. Will of SOLOMON FULLER. Sons Avent(?), Solomon, William, John, Ransom; wife Gilley; son

FULLER will cont'd:
Alsey Fuller; daughter Charlotte Fuller; daughter Sarah Coleman;
children of Sarah Coleman; grand-daughter Gilley A. Green; son-
in-law William Green; negro man Harry to choose who to live
with. Exrs: wife Gilley and son Solomons Fuller (Jr.). Wit:
David Stevens, Jos. Hodges and Richd. S. Drake.

7 Jan. 1822. Adm. of will of EDWARD MEDLEY, dec'd (will annexed)
to Francis Medley. Sec: Robt. Word and _____ Craddock. 6 Dec.
1821. Will of EDWARD MEDLEY. Brother James Medley's son, Edward
Newton Medley; Thomas Milton, son of Joel Walker; mother Sarah
Medley. Exr: William Coleman. Wit: Jno. H. Coleman, Alsey Fuller
and Jno. Hendley.

7 Jan. 1822. Will of WILLIAM MC CLURE, dec'd proven by Wm. Scrage
a wit. 13 May 1806. Will of WILLIAM MC CLURE. Wife Ruth; all
my children but names only William, John and James. Exrs: wife
and son William. Wit: Wm. Craig, Jno. Briggs and Wm. Briggs.

15 Apr. 1821. Estate of ROBERT HUTCHESON, dec'd. Adm. to John
Hutcheson. Turner Richardson, sec. No estate found. Adm. revoked.

29 Nov. 1821. Estate sale of THOMAS WRIGHT, dec'd. Notes on:
Wm. Wright; debt due by Thos. Ligon; Joseph Wright. Wm. Ligon,
adm.

(No date) Appraisal of estate of JOSEPH DEEN, dec'd by Jno.
Todd, Sr., Jas. Flemming, Wm. Hambleton and Jas. Hunter.

25 Nov. 1821. Estate sale of ELIZABETH WALKER, dec'd. Purchasers:
Philip Wait, Archibald Harriss, Saml. Phifer, Robt. Freeman,
Aaon Clore, Jas. Simmons, Thos. Hinson, Jas. Gains, Wm. South,
David P. Posey, Wm. South, Sr., Reuben Powell, Allen Hedley,
Harrison Daniel, Ezekiel Powell, Jas. Parker, Burket Davenport,
Geo. Washington, Adam C. Jones, Ezekiel South, Col. Wm. Ware,
Larkin Gains, Jas. Powell, Isaac Waldrop, Danl. South, Chas.
Smith, Moses Myars, Danl. Hazel, Eligah Smith, Jacob Niswanger,
Mrs. Elizabeth Myars, Adnw. Hunter. Jno. Walker, adm.

2? Jan. 1822. Estate of WILLIAM FULTON, JR, dec'd. Wm. Fulton,
Sr., adm. Sec: Anthony F. Golding and Jas. Parker.

15 Jan. 1822. Estate of ANGUISH CAMPBELL, dec'd. Robt. Campbell,
adm. Sec: Jno. Richerson (Roberson?) and Jos. Neeley.

(No date) Appraisal of estate of THOMAS STONE, dec'd by Abner
Pyles, Jas. Young and David Mc__nn. 5 Aug. 1821. Sale bill.
Sold by Wm. Dunlap, adm.

4 Feb. 1822. Will of ANN DILLARD, dec'd proven by Jno. B. Bennett.
Exr: Geo. Dillard and Jno. Dillard. 22 Dec. 1821. Will of ANN
DILLARD. Children: George Dillard, John Dillard, Polley McCrary
wife of Capton McCrary, Nancy Parks widow of William Parks,
Mildred Gurdon (Jurdon) wife of Reuben Jurdon, and Sarah Dillard;
grandson Thomas McCrary; husband Samuel Dillard, dec'd; Silas
Garrett; James Dillard (land) to Samuel Dillard; daughter Sarah
Dillard. Exrs: sons George and John Dillard. Wit: Jno. B. Ben-
nett, L. Charles Thuber(Thurber?) and Jno. Dillard?.

21 (no month) 1822. Estate of MATHEW HUNTER, dec'd, adm. to
Alexander Simpson. Sec: Richd. F. Simpson and Jno. Dunlap.

139

22 Feb. 1822. Will and Codicil of ALEXANDER TAYLOR, dec'd proven by James Taylor, exr. Wm. Cowan and Chas. Fowler, wit. 25 Dec. 1821. Wife Margaret; sons: Robert, John, James; daughters Catharine Ranson, Jane Taylor, Margaret Taylor, Hanna Taylor; grandson Alexander McCarley; grand-daughter Mary Ann Ranson. Exrs: sons Robert, James and John Taylor. Notes on: John A. Craddock, Geo. McClintock, Thos. Fulton. Wit: Wm. Cowan, Chas. Fowler and Wm. Taylor.

4 Mar. 1822. Estate of JAMES HOWARTON, dec'd, adm. to Elizabeth Howarton. Sec: Wm. Gambell and Wheate Miller.

16 Mar. 1822. Estate of JOHN SIMMONS, dec'd. James Simmons, sec. for Caty Simmons, adm. released. New sec. Geo. Tierce and Wm. Gains.

17 Mar. 1822. Estate of CHARLES JONES, dec'd, adm. to Nancy Jones. Sec: Wm. Rodgers and Wm. Lowe.

(No date) Appraisal of estate of SOLOMON FULLER, dec'd. Legateess Ransom and Alsey Fuller, Gilley A. Green, Solomon Fuller, Wm. S. Fuller, Charlota Fuller, Sarah Holt, Jno. Fuller. Cert. by Jas. Young, Martin Miller and Wm. Coleman. Solomon Fuller, exr.

29 Mar. 1822. Bluford Powell who married Mary Walker; Betsey Walker (now Otis) adm. of WM. WALKER, dec'd and her late husband; husband Jacob Otis (Oates); Anny Powell.

7? Apr. 1822. Legatees of CLABOURNE VAUGHN, dec'd against Mary Vaughn, exr. for their portion of est. Return on estate.

1 Apr. 1822. Estate of BENJAMIN SMITH, dec'd, Elizabeth Smith, adm; Charles Smith, her only son. Judgement against Chas. Simmons.

11 Mar. 1822. Appraisal of estate of ALEXANDER TAYLOR, dec'd by Chas. Fowler, Jas. Hunter, Jr. and Jas. Flemming.

11 Apr. 1822. Estate of SAMUEL MC KINTRICK, dec'd. James McKintrick, adm. Sec: David Mason and Jno. R. Griffin.

16 Apr. 1822. Estate of ROBERT HUTCHESON, dec'd. Adm. to William Hutcheson. Sec: James Park and Andrew Speare.

4 Dec. 1821. Appraisal of estate of ISAAC PATTERSON, dec'd by Wm. Ligon, Henery Johns and B. B. Chesure. Note on: Wm. G. Wright and Mrs. Harriot Walker. Sale bill of est. (No date). Pur: Branch Leek, Alsey fuller, Wm. Braxton, Alexd. Austin, Chas. D. Goodley, Sarah Hollingsworth, B. Chesure, Jno. Salmon, Jesse Roberts, Saml. Austin, Andw. Waldrop, Richd. Sims, Seamon A. Rodgers, Anthony Griffin, Alexd. Chesure, Mordica Waldrop, Bird Roberts, Jno. McGowan, Allen Gadbury, Geo. Roberts, Ob'h Chesure, Burrel Leek, Hunter Bryson, Chas. Gadbury (also Gradbury), Jas. Ligon, Sheldon Chesure, Wm. McGowan, old Missis Ligon, Peter Roberts, Jos'h Rodgers, Wm. Rodgers, Howard Pinson, O. Chesure, Alex. Deal, Robt. Gill, Robt. Campbell, Martin Collin, Wm. Caldwell, Rebeca Bowen, Andw. McWilliams, Jno. McWilliams, Brooks Smith, Jno. Craford, Aberham Tompson, Richd Cook, Wm. Baxter, Wm. McGowan. A. Gilbert, adm.

18 Feb. 1822. Sale and money due estate of WM. P. BALL, dec'd. B. Leek's part; Foryphina(?) Ball's part, Mary Hill, guardian of Foryphina Ball, daughter of dec'd. Burrell Leek, adm.

Feb. 1822. Appraisal of estate of MATTHEW HUNTER, dec'd by
Jno. Hunter, Wm. Clark and Wm. Park, Sr. Sale of estate 14-
15 Mar. 1822. A. A. Simpson, adm. Pur: Andw. Park, Easter Hunt-
er, Wm. Hutcheson, Jas. Parks, Andw. Hunter, Elizabeth Hunter,
Chas. Simpson, Jas. Parks, Sr., Jno. Taylor son of William,
Andw. Spear, Jas. E. Hutcheson, Chas. Allen, Robt. Hutcheson,
Edw. Hix, Thos. Davis, Dehditell? Dunlap, Jno. Blakely, Wm.Hola-
day, Nancy Hunter, Saml. Farrow, doctor, Jos. Prichard, Danl.
Martin, Jr., Joshua Smith, Thos. Archibald, Jas. Blakely, Sr.,
Alex. Simpson, Wm. Clark, Wm. Park, Sr., Jos. Irby, Chas. Irby,
Elihu Corley, Jno. Higgins, Jno. S. Hutcheson, Angess Hutcheson,
Robt. Flemming, Archibald Smith. Alex. Simpson, Adm. Return
of monies due est. Note on Jas. Nickels, Saml. McClintock, Andw.
Park, Jas. Park, Thos. Fulton, Wm. Nugent, Jas. Henery, Wm.
Hutcheson, Thos. Nickels, Jas. Park, Jr., Wm. Clark, Wm. Park
son of James, Wm. Park Millar, Elihu Rodgers, Robt. Hunter,
Jas. Park son of James, Jas. Waldrop, Jas. Hunter, Wm. Holaday,
Jno. A. Cradock, Andw. Park, Joshua Smith, Geo. McClintock,
Saml. McClintock, Thos. Fulton, Sr., Jas. Davis, Wm. Taylor,
Noah Smith, Jos. Richards, Danl. Martin, Capt. James Park, Capt.
Andw. Park.

16 Feb. 1822. Appraisal of estate of ANN DILLARD, dec'd by Wm.
Dillard, Wm. Harriss and Jos. Garrett. 20 Feb. 1822. Property as
sold from estate (list only). Geo. Dillard, exr.

28 Jan. 1822. Inventory of estate of WILLIAM FULTON, JR., dec'd
by Chas. Littel, Saml. Boyd and Jno. McCelvey. 29 Jan. 1822.
Estate sale. Note on Wm. G. Vance; pur: Thos. Crumbley, Jas.
Leek, Jas. Enterken, Moses Leek, Jas. Fairbarn, Jas. McClintock,
Jno. Blakely, Jesse Johnston, Jno. McCelvey, Jr., Jas. Blaakely,
Chas. Littel, Wm. Right, Jas. McCelvey, Jas. Templeton, Thos.
Fulton, David Enterken, Abner Rodgers, Agness Fulton,Marey Ful-
ton, Jas. Littel, Jas. Daniel?, Wm. Fulton. Wm. Fulton, Sr., adm.

7 May 1822. Will of MATTHEW FRANKLING, dec'd proven by Wm. F.
Downs. 30 June 1821. Will of MATTHEW FRANKLING. Friends Stephen
Garrett, Sr. and Jesse Garrett, Sr.; land bounded by Mr. Wolff,
Wm. Henderson and Stephen Potter; wife Dinah; Geo. Wolff; Mrs.
Wolff; children (not named) and their heirs (who shall always
be slaves). (Note: Matthew Frankling was manumitted according
to his will). Trustees to hold monies for children and proceeds
thereof. Wit: W. F. Downs, G. F. Wolff and Marey Wolff.

28 Jan. 1822. Sale of estate of JOSEPH DEAN, dec'd. Pur: Jno.
Dean, Jas. Hunter, Reuben Martin, Thos. Dean, H. Waldrop, Saml.
G. Williams, Wm. Park, Jno. Todd, Matthew Holaday, Robt. Spence,
Jr., Solomon Mahaffey, Jno. Cunningham, Alexander Parker, Jno.
Stuart, Jno. D. Boyd, A. Smith, Jas. Lockridge, Robt. Hutcheson,
Arthur Spence, Saml. Mills, Jos. Vance, Edw. Masfield, Joel
Allen, Wm. Higgens, Saml. Parsons, Robt. Millar, Hugh Toland,
Benj. Griffin, Jas. Ensley, Jas. Prim, Saml. Fleming, Geo. Glenn,
Rodey Canady, Elias Cheek, Jno. McClintock, Wm. Siles, Avant
Miller, Ruben Martin, Saml. Mills, E. Attoway, Jno. Dandy by
Catharine Dean, admx.

29 Mar. 1822. Appraisal of estate of CHARLES JONES, dec'd as
shown by Nancy Jones, Admx. by Wm. Burnside, Stephen Dumas and
Thos. Burnside. 2 Apr. 1822. Estate sale. Pur: Wm. Fuller, B.
Craddock, Danl. Cook, Danl. Cain, Wm. Rodgers, Wm. Glenn, Thos.
Rodgers, Matthew Bryson, Hirum Miller, Wm. Burnside, J. Hollings-
worth, Anthony Griffin, Lettey Babb, Peter Fullar, Jno. Baley,

Estate sale cont'd:
Jno. Boyd, Danl. Winn, Saml. Rodgers, Jacob Miller, Jas. Young,
Benj. Clower, Isaiah Fuller, Jos. Hollinworth. Nancey Jones,
admx.

29 Apr. 1822. Appraisal of estate of SAMUEL MC KINTRICK, dec'd.
Property left in hands of widow. Jas. McKintrick, adm. Wm. Black,
Jas. Blakely and Geo. McKitrick, apprs. 30 May 1822. Estate
sale. Pur: Robt. Spence, Moss Leek, Geo. McKintrick, Robt. Spence
Jr., Jno. Higgins, Jas. Park, David Bell, Jas. Park, Moses Leek,
Saml. Park, Wm. Mongrune, Jno. Johnston, Priscella McKintrick,
Jonathan Johnston, Wm. Mangrum, Lowthen D. Hitch, Andw. Studard,
Joel Allen, Armested Leek, Hardeman Duke, Thos. Hanah, Jas.
Parsons, Elie Baley, Asa Waldrop. Jas. McKintrick, adm.

7 May 1822. To D. Anderson, esq./ord.-will of my father CHARLES
SIMMONS, dec'd, hereby revoke the exr-ship wish adm. with will
annexed to John Garlinton. Signed: John Simons(Simmons). 7 May
1822. Application of John Garlington and request of legatees
est. of CHARLES SIMMONS, dec'd for adm. Sec: Richd F. Simpson
and Jno. Dunlap.

4 June 1822. Will of WILLIAM RUTLEDGE, dec'd proven. Jesse Grant?
and Arthur? Williams refused to adm. Will proven by Geo. Mattison
and John Night as adm. Sec: Aallen Saxon and Jas. Jones. 15
Feb. 1821. Will of WILLIAM RUTLEDGE. Exrs: Arthur Williams and
Jesse Gant(Grant?). Legatees: Arthur Williams (land of Zachariah
Neal); beloved half brother John Knight (land formerly of Aron
Crump); half sister Betsy Knight; half-sister's children and
two youngest sons of Jos. Rutledge. Wit: Benj. Mattison and Geo.
Mattison.

20 Mar. 1822. Appraisal of property of ROBERT HUTCHESON, dec'd
by Jas. Hutcheson, Jno. Hunter, Jno. Stuart and Wm. Park. Negroes
taken in possession of Wm. Hutcheson in Mar. 1818.

3? June 1822. Estate of JOSEPH MOTES, dec'd. Adm. to Richd.
F. Simpson. Sec: Washington Williams and Jno. D. Simpson.

5 June 1822. Estate of MITCHEL COOK, dec'd. Adm. to Daniel Cook.
Sec: Tobias Cook and Jas. Wright.

15 June 1822. Property of WM. RUTLEDGE, dec'd by John Wright,
adm. . Notes returned 17 June 1822. Inventory by Jno. Craford,
Geo.? Cook and R. H. __ff.

21 June 1822. Adm. of est. of WM. TAYLOR, dec'd to Samuel Taulor
at request of widow and legatees. Bond: Chas. Littel, Jas. Mc-
Daniel and Andw. Speare.

20 June 1822. Adm. of MATTHEW FRANKLIN, dec'd granted (with
will annexed) to Geo. Wolff refused by exrs. Stephen Garrett,
Esq. and Jesse Garrett, Sr. Adm. granted to Geo. Wolff. Sec:
Chas. Williams and Saml. Downs.

16 July 1822. Appraisal of estate of MITCHEL COOK, dec'd by
Jas. Young, Thos. Burnside and Thos. Wilks. Notes on: Tobias
Cook, Wm. Cook, Benj. Orliver, Henderson Irby, Edw. Orsborn.
Danl. Cook, adm.

20 July 1822. Estate sale of WM. RUTLEDGE, dec'd by Jno. Knight,
adm. Pur: Wm. Puckett, Jno. Knight, Wm. Cook, Jas. Jones.

4 July 1822. Inventory of estate of WILLIAM TAYLOR, dec'd by Wm. Templeton, Chas. Littel, Andw. Spears and Jas. McDowel. 5 July 1822. Estate sale. Notes: Robt. Stone, Capt., Wm. Goodson(Goodwin?), Martha Taylor, Wm. Templeton, Jas. Taylor, John Taylor, Wm. Park, Jas. Owens, Jas. McDowell, Wm. Speare, Jno. Bartey, Capt. Jas. Templeton, Alex. Winn, Thos. Gill, Wm. Ransum, Valuntine Harling?, Jos. Vance, Mrs. Elizabeth Word, Mathew Holaday, Royal Allen, Saml. Taylor, Thos. Archebel, N. Franks, Robt. Spence, Arthur Spence, Jane Taylor, Jas. McCullum, Berry Martin, Jas. McKintrick, Harburt Martin, Bat. Craddock, Robt. Taylor, Julas Martin, Jno. Simmons, Hardaman Duke, Jno. Davis, Jr., Robt. Hutcheson, Thos. Fulton, Chas. Madden, Joshua Smith, Jno. Dendey, Jno. McClenning, Jno. Barksdil, Wm. Blakely, Jas. E. Hutcheson, Jas. McDowel, Jno. Deen, Andw. Spence. Saml. Taylor, adm.

8 Sept. 1820. Will of JOHN CHANDLER. Wife Mary Chandler; son Wiett; land bounded by Wm. Dunlap, Abner Teague and Newman Garey; daughter Elizabeth Leek; daughters Patsey Griffin and Polley Clardey; daughter Nancey Martin; son Asa. Exrs: wife and son Asa. Wit: Wm. Dunlap, Jno. Dunlap and Thos. Stone. 2 Sept. 1822. Will proven. Wm. Dunlap, wit. Asa Chandler and Mary Chandler, exrs.

28 June 1822. Appraisal of estate of JOSEPH MOATES, dec'd by Robt. Allison, Thos. A. Brownlee and Wm. Dendy. 22 June 1822. Sale bill. Pur: Thos. Brownlee, Jno. Motes, Robt. Allison, Susan Maddon, Drury? Motes, Jonathan Moats, Wm. Madden, Jas. Prim, Mary McCormick, Jno.Madden, Wm. Moor, Jno. Milam, Phebee Madden, R. F. Simpson. R. F. Simpson, adm.

27 Mar. 1822. Inventory/appraisal of estate of JAMES HOWARTON, dec'd by Elizabeth Howarton, adm. Appr'd by Geo. McCrary, Jas. Leeks and Henery Shell. 27 Mar. 1822. Estate sale. Pur: Grasey Howarton, Westly Howarton, Jas. Leek, Moses Leek, Wm. Gambell, Benj. Adair, Elizabeth Howarton, Giney Nobles, Jas. Stewart, Saml. Farguson, David Grayham, ___ McCluskey, Sarah Gamble, John Gamble.

2 Sept. 1822. Estate of LEWIS SIBELL(?), dec'd. Adm. to Mary Sibeall(?). Sec: Wm. Lofton and Danl. Lofton.

10 Sept. 1822. Will of DAVID BRADEN, dec'd proven by Wm. Braden and Isaac Braden, exrs. Jos. Wardlaw and Benj. Tearce, wit. 11 Aug. 1822. Will of DAVID BRADEN. Sons William and Isack Braden; land in Dist. of Abbeville; son Reuben Braden; land where George Adams now lives; wife Peggey Braden; his girl's children (not named); daughters-Betsey, Margret, Sary, Peggey, Susan and Polley Ann. Exrs: sons Wm. and Isack Braden. Wit: Benj. Tearce, Jas. Wardlaw and Jesse E. Clardy.

13 Sept. 1822. Estate of DANIEL MATHISS, dec'd. Widow and bro. request adm. of David Mason. Bond: Wm. Lofton and Danl. Lofton.

13 Sept. 1822. Estate of ANDREW RODGERS, dec'd. Ann Rodgers, widow of dec'd. Personal est. to be sold to support widow. Abner Rodgers, exr. to sell estate.

8 June 1822. Deed of conveyance. Saml. Leek and Saml. Young, wit. Signed by Margret Leek, widow of George Leek, dec'd. Conveyed to children: Anne, Samuel, Jane, William, James, Peggey, Sinda and Eliza. Proven 20 July 1822 before Wm. Neill.

7 Oct. 1822. Noncupitive will of JAMES MC MAHON, dec'd presented to be proven, court is opinion that sd will not been executed to the law -words only spoken in the last sickness of dec'd. No wit. required. Will to be set aside and of no effect. D. Anderson, Ord. 7 Oct. 1822. Est. of JAMES MC MAHON, dec'd. Jas. McMahon, Jr. as adm. Bond: Baruck Duckett and Jas. Holingworth.

7 Oct. 1822. Will of WM. GILBERT, SR., dec'd proven by Isaac Beechum and Joshua Gilbert. Wm. Gilbert, Jr. as exr. 29th July 1822. Will of WILLIAM GILBERT. Wife Sarah Gilbert; daughter-in-law Catharine Gilbert or heirs of James Gilbert, her husband; Sarah Dean, wife of John Dean; other children: Elizabeth Collins, Marah Wilson, William Gilbert, Jr., John Gilbert, Nancy Austen, Jeremiah Gilbert, Rebacah Burchfield and Joshua Gilbert. Exr: son Wm. Gilbert, Jr. Wit: Hartwell Lester, Isaac Beechum and Joshua Gilbert.

7 Oct. 1822. Estate of JAMES HANNA, dec'd. Adm. to Wm. Hanna. Sec: Abner Rodgers and Jno. Underwood.

7 Oct. 1822. Estate of WASHINGTON ADAIR, dec'd. Adm. to Joseph Adair. Sec: Thos. R. Adair and Jesse Johnston.

12 Oct. 1822. Estate of JAMES CRACKER, Sr., dec'd. Proven by Ebenezer Starnes, wit. Exrs: Elizabeth, Athenion Cracker and James Cracker. 12 Jan. 1808. Wife Elizabeth; daughter Sarah (who married Meredith Brion) and is now dec'd, leaving two children; legatee Meredith Brion; land adj. Wm. Hendricks; four youngest sons James, Athanion, John and Joseph Cracker. grandchildren Henery and Whitfield Brion. Exrx: wife Elizabeth and sons Wm., James and Athanion. Wit: David Anderson, Jno. Crecy and Ebenezer Starnes.

(No date) Appraisal of estate of JOHN CHANDLER, dec'd by Wm. Dunlap, Danl. M. Winn and Elijah Teague. ___ Chandler and Mary Chandler, exrs.

9 Nov. 1822. Estate of STEPHEN DUMAS, dec'd adm. to John Dunlap. Sec: Jno. Garlington and Richd. F. Simpson.

9 Nov. 1822. Estate of JOHN ADKINSON, dec'd adm. to Elizabeth Adkinson and John Meek. Sec: Thos. Adkinson and Jno. Bladon.

19 Nov. 1822. Estate of FELT HATCHER, dec'd, adm. to Margaret Hatcher. Sec: Wm. Mahan and Posel Halcomb. (N.B. Felt may be Fell.)

23 Nov. 1822. Estate of COLEMAN BAILEY, dec'd adm. to Zachariah Bailey. Sec: Zachariah Bailey, Sr. and Absalum Bailey.

2 Dec. 1822. Estate of WILLIAM PETTY POOL, dec'd, adm. to Elizabeth Pool. Sec: John Hutcheson and Jno. Stuartt.

2 Dec. 1822. Will of WILLIAM CUNNINGHAM, dec'd proven by Henery Morgen and S. Cunningham. John Cunningham, exr. 4 Sept. 1822. Will of WM. CUNNINGHAM. Son John; son William. Exr: Martha Cunningham and John Cunningham. Wit: Henry Morgen, Wm. Pitts and L. (S.?) Cunningham.

25 Oct. 1822. Appraisal of est. of JAMES HANNAH, dec'd by Jas. Fareborn, Moses Leak and Robt. Cunningham. (No date) Estate

Sale cont'd:
Pur: Jas. Ensley, Wm. Hannah, Robt. Cunningham, Jno. Blakely,
Jno. Puckett, Wm. Hannah, Jr., Mathew Henery, Jas. Fareborn,
Jas. Hannah, Ephrum Potts, Saml. Flemming, Jno. Holland, Thos.
Crage, David Hannah, Jos. Hannah, Jas. Daniel, Robt. Hannah,
Jas. Burk, Norward Thompkins, Jno. Bailey. Wm. Hannah, adm.

24 Mar. 1822. Inventory/appraisal of estate of CHARLES SIMMONS,
dec'd. Signed: 24 May 1822. Jno. Dunlap, Wm. Dandey and H.
Cleaveland.

19 Nov. 1822. Appraisal of estate of JAMES CROCKER(CRACKER),
dec'd. Notes on: Elhanion Crocker, A.(?) Pinson, Wm. Crocker.
By Hardey Connant, Jno. Wait and Jno. Roberson.

24 Nov. 1822. Sale of estate of CHARLES SIMMONS, dec'd. Pur:
Jno. Garlington, Sarah Madden(?), Danl. Walker, Jno. Adkins,
Zachariah Tinsley, Jas. Hunter, Valuntine Harlingone, Jno.
Simmons, Chas. Simmons, Wm. Simmons, Robt. Spence, Sr., Richd.
F. Simpson, Robt. Spence, Jr., Henry Cleveland, Jas. Lockridge,
Thos. Ward, Whitfield R. Prim, Julas Martin, Thos. Gill, Robt.
Criswell, Jno. Dunlap, Doct. Saml. Farrow, Capt. James Temple-
ton, Jno. Templeton, Jos. Vance, Arthur Spence(?), Danl. Cook,
Jas. Regen, Chas. Killingsworth, Jno. McDowell, Robt. Hollady,
Jno. Taylor, Elizabeth Smith, Nancy Franks, Jos. Smith, Nehemiah
Franks, Jno. G. Klink(?), Robt. Soone. Jno. Garlington, adm.

(No date) Second sale of est. of WILLIAM TAYLOR, dec'd. Pur:
Ransom Fuller, Jas. Taylor, Chas. Little, Wm. Speer, Martha(?)
Taylor, widow, Jno. Milan, Jas. Parks, Sr., Robt. Sloan (carpen-
ter), Robt. Sloan (son-in-law to Robt. Taylor), Jno. Taylor,
Wm. Goodwyn, Nehemiah Franks, Jas. Owens, Arther Spense, Jas.
Irby, Robt. Spense, Jr., Harley(?) Madden, Saml. Taylor, Jr.,
Thos. Gill, Danl. Martin, Bartholomew Craddock, Mitchel Dun_gh,
Jno. Blakely, son of James, John Templeton, Wm. Taylor son
of Robt., Velentine Harldan, Elias Cheek, Hugh Workman, Jas.
Bryson.

25 Oct. 1822. Return of estate of WASHINGTON ADAIR, dec'd by
Jos. Adair, adm. Cert. by Chas. Forguson, Jas. Underwood and
Jno. Young. 26 Oct. 1822. Amt. of sale bill of estate. Signed:
Joseph Adair.

18 Sept. 1822. Appraisal of estate of DAVID BRADEN, dec'd by
Jas. Clardy, Zachariah Arnold and Benj. F. Tearce. Estate sale.
(No date) Pur: Wm. Golding, Wm. Roberson, Wm. Braden, Jno.
Cook, Jno. Sawyers, Isaac Braden, Elijah Chism, Ellis Chardy,
Jno. Lockhat, Geo. Washington, Jos. Wardlaw, Ellis Clardy,
Jno. Lockhart, Martin Norman, Wm. South, Reuben Braden, Max-
field Owens. Desperate notes and acct's: Jno. Chism, Jno. Saxon,
Frances Sharp, Nath. Robertson, Josiah Box, Geo. Adams, Jos.
Joel, Larkin Gaines, Thos. Anderson, Ezekiel Powell. 31 Oct.
1822. Wm. Braden and Jno. Braden, exrs.

11 Nov. 1822. Appraisal of estate of WILLIAM GILBERT, dec'd
by Larkin Stepp, Thos. Goodwin and Wm. Halburt.

(No date) Appraisal of estate of WILLIAM CUNNINGHAM, dec'd
by Chas. Williams, Jno. Pitts and Aaron Clore. 5 Dec. 1822.

6 Dec. 1822. Estate of JOHN MC CLAHAN, dec'd adm. to Saml.
McClahan. Sec: Jas. Packerd and Allen D. Saxon. (N.B. this

is actually McClanahan). 14 Dec. 1822. Appraisal of estate of JOHN MC CLANAHAN, dec.d by L. Cunningham, Wm. Arnold and Henery Burrow. Sale bill of estate (no date). Pur: Nancy Mc-Clanahan, Jane McClanahan, Mary McClanahan, Saml. McClanahan, Allen Saxon, Danl. Johnston, Stephen Garrett, Timothy Swindle, Jno. Satewhite, Jones McClanahan, Jno. Pitts, notes on Jno. B. Simpson, Wm. Wallis. Saml. McClanahan, adm.

28 Dec. 1822. Estate of THOMAS KINMON, dec'd adm. to Winneford Kinmon and Benjamin Arnold. Sec: Thos. Gradon and Bailey Mahon.

5 Jan. 1823. Will of WILLIAM RUTLEDGE, dec'd proven by John Knight and Larkin Gains. 11 Dec. 1816. Will of WILLIAM RUTLEDGE. Exr: Cornelius Cook, Sr. and Jos. Rutledge. Land purchased of Wm. Daniel where I now live; land purchased of Zachariah Neal, Wm. Maddox and Aaron Crump; brother Jno. Knight; uncle Joseph Rutledge (his exr.); gift to the church at Turkey Creek; Cornelius Cook, Jr.; Nelly Thompson; sister Polly and their(?) heirs: Fanny, Betsey, Amey and Delila; sister Nancy Night. Wit: Larkin Gains, Betsey Gains and Robt. T. Delfh.

5 Dec. 1822. Sale of estate of ANDREW RODGERS, SR, dec'd. Abner Rodgers, exr.

28 Oct. 1822. Second appraisal of estate of SAMUEL MC KINTRICK, dec'd. by Wm. Clark, Geo. McKintrick and Jas. Blakely. 28 Oct. 1822. Pur: Prisilla McKintrick-widow, Robt. Spence, Jr., Wm. Clark, Geo. McKintrick, Jno. Bird, David Brown, Jas. Devaul, Geo. Wallass(Wallace), Robt. Blakely, Wm. Mangrum, Danl. Martin, Jas. Park, Sr.

11 Dec. 1822. Appraisal of estate of COLEMAN BAILEY, dec'd by Zachariah Bailey, Jr., Jas. Bailey, and Abraham Bailey.

30 Oct. 1822. Appraisal of estate of LEWIS LINVELL(?), dec'd by Wm. Lofton, Danl. Lofton and Thos. Davis. 28 Nov. 1822. Inventory of the sale. Pur: Mary Linvell, Jno. Linvell, Ephrum Jones, Jeremiah Stokes, Prudence Williams, Wm. Lofton, Jain Linvell, Saml. Jones, Jno. Johnston, Wm. Reeder, Jno. Brown, Aaron Johnston, Jno. Fowler, Jas. Murphey, Elizabeth Richards, Jno. Dalrymple, Jas. Bonds, Thos. Davis, Jno. Walsey, Nicklus Rhodes, Margret Horton, Menassa Linvell, Jas. Boyd, Joel Cannon, Ephrum Perry, Jas. Boyce, Jno. Entrekin, Geo. Abernatha, Delila Roberts, Jas. Entreken, Thos. Dalrymple.

3 Dec. 1822. Appraisal of estate of WILLIAM P'POOL, dec'd by John Hutcheson, John Deen and Geo. Mosley. 18 Dec. 1822. Estate sale. Pur: Elizabeth Pool, Nancy Pool, Seth Pool, Aaron Starnes, Peter Pool, Seth Telly, Stephen Terry, Cristopher Rhoades, Wm. Ferry,Sr., Berry Pool, Jno. Crow, Wm. Ateway,a Wm. Terry, Sr., Jno. Pool, Rebacha Pool, Thos. Farrow, Madten Pool, Chas. Fowler, Anderson Brown, David Higgins. Elizabeth Pool, adm.

3 Feb. 1823. Fanney Johnston, about 19 years and Annouta Johnston, about twn years, chose Henery Morgan as guardian. Sec: John R. Simpson and Robert Nickles.

3 Feb. 1823. Estate of JAMES CRISWELL, dec'd will proven , all exrs. deceased, Robt. Criswell taken oath as adm. (will annexed). Sec: Alexander Kirkpatrick and William F. Downs.

3 Feb. 1823. Adm. of estate of WILLIAM KIRKPATRICK, dec'd to

WILLIAM KIRKPATRICK, cont'd:
James Kirkpatrick. Sur.: Alexander Kirkpatrick and Alfred Barrett.

3? Feb. 1823. Will of MATHEW HUNTER, dec'd proven by David Mason
and John Underwood. Charles F. Gary and Coleman Carelisle (Car-
lisle), wit. David Mason, exr. 8 Aug. 1822. Will of MATHEW HUN-
TER. Wife Peggey; daughters Salley and Polley Hunter, Nancy
Davis, Jane Waldrop, Betsey Johnston, Peggey Johnston. David
Mason and Jno. Underwood, exr. Wit: Martin J. Garey, Charles
F. Gary and Coleman Carlisle.

26 Nov. 1822. Appraisal of estate of FELT HATCHER, dec'd. Nathan
Massy, Richard Childers and John Killet, appr's. Margaret Hatch-
er, adm. (No date). Sale of estate. Pur.: Margaret Hatcher,
James Peden, Alex. Crumlee, John Howard, Beneah Cennady, James
Kellett, Polley Connell, Thos. Babb, Wm. Hatcher, Robt. Wood,
Andrew Matthis, James Sims, Wm. Mahan. Margaret Hatcher, adm.

20 Feb. 1823. Estate of MATHEW HUNTER, dec'd. John Dunlap and
Richard F. Simpson, surety for Alexander Simpson, adm. Adm.
revoked and adm. granted to Richard F. Simpson with John D.
Simpson and John Garlington, sur. 15 Mar. 1822, personal estate
sold by order of David Anderson, Ord.

3 Mar. 1823. Adm. of estate of WILLIAM MC MAHON, dec'd to John
Blakely. John Adkins and James Todd, sur.

3 Mar. 1823. SAMUEL LUKE, dec'd. Will not found by John Stuart,
who says on oath there was one made. Luke's wife called on him
to take adm. John Stuart took oath as adm. with John Ross and
Ephraim Pitts, sur.

3 Mar. 1823. Estate of ANNA GARRETT, dec'd. Stephen Garrett,
adm. granted. Jesse Garrett and John _.? Harris, sur.

28 Feb. 1823. Inventory/appraisal of property of MATHEW HUNTER,
dec'd by Jerry Leek, Saml. Young and John Hewit. Note s on Jas.
Griffin and Avery Starnes (wit: James Boyd) and Job Dalrymple.
Signed: David Mason.

3 Mar. 1823. Adm. of estate of BARTLET MAYBUM(?), dec'd to Ferrel
Maybum. Wm. Maybum and John Maybum, sur.

11 Jan. 1823. Estate of THOMAS KINMON, dec'd appraised by Ira
Arnold, Wm. Maddox and Joel Ellison. Shown by Winiford Kinmon
and Benjamin Arnold, adm. 15 Jan. 1823. Inventory of sale. Pur:
Winiford Kinmon, John Myhon, James Kinmon, Benj. Arnold, John
Sullivan, Geo. Mathison, H. G. Johnston, Thos. Mayhon, Allen
Saxon, Varnel Mehaffey, Alex. Mehaffie, James Ryley, Zachariah
Nickles, Daniel Gent, Joseph McCullah, John Thomas, John Nabours,
Thos. Taylor, Abner Gains, Ann Nixon, Baley Mahon, John Crook,
James Cook, Frances Posey, Abner Nixon, George Grace, Charles
Key, Benjamin Maddox, Wm. Pyles, Burkely Ragwell, Saml. Nabours,
Wm. Morton, Saml. Maddox, Elias Howell, Saml. Kinmon, Martin
Davis, John Joiner, Noah Rivers, Allen Nabours, Wm. Houghs,
John Young. Notes and dates due: Thos. Medlock (1817), Austin
Arnold (1822), Wm. McDavid (1818), James Mares? (1819), John
Chisum (1820), James and Wm. Wair? (1822), Joseph Camp (1820),
John Walker (1823), S. Flowers? (1822), L. Gains (1823). Wini-
ford Kinmon, adm.

24 Feb. 1823. Inventory/appraisal goods and chattels of MARY
CRISWELL, dec'd who had a life estate under the will of her

CRISWELL cont'd:
dec'd husband JAMES CRISWELL, shown to us by Robt. Criswell,
adm., with will annexed, on the estate of sd James Criswell,
dec'd. Appr's: James Watts, William Smith and William Payne.
24 Feb. 1823. Sale of estate. Pur.: E. Criswell (mostly religious
and sermon books) and slaves, Nathaniel Sanders.

3 Mar. 1823. Creditors of RICHARD WHITE, dec'd against James
A. Simpson, adm. Simpson failed to appear.

3 Mar. 1823. Estate of WILLIAM COOK, dec'd. Daniel Cook and
James Wright, adm. Tobias Cook, one of the sur. "considers himself in danger". Sale of estate was 20 Dec. 1820. Daniel Cook
refused to give new surety and adm. revoked. Adm. cont'd for
Wright. Bond made by Ezekiah Chesure and Danl. S. Chesure.

9 Feb. 1822. Appraisal of estate of ANGUISH CAMPBELL, JR., dec'd
by Anthony Griffin, John Cook and H. B. Hall. Robt. Campbell,
adm. 2 Mar. 1822. Sale Bill. (N. B. also spelled Angus)

9? Feb. 1821. Accounting by citation on est. of LEWIS SXON,
dec'd by Charles Saxon and Wm. F. Downs, adm. Widow's third
paid; pd to children of sd dec'd: William F. Downs, Charles
Saxon, David Saxon and Mary Saxon; mentions Ira Arnold (shows
how accounts paid). Includes several pages.

20 Feb. 1823. Appraisal of est. of WILLIAM KIRKPATRICK, dec'd
by Thos. Gradon, Plesant Shaw and James McNight. Shown by James
Kirkpatrick. (No date). Sale of estate. Pur.: William Spruell,
A. Kirkpatrick, James McNight, Saml. McClelland, Benj. G. Rus-
sell, Thos. Gradon, Richard Ridgeway, John Thomas, Robt. Duff,
Jno. Kirkpatrick, William Taylor, William McDavid, Isaac Thomas,
Doctor S. Taylor, Thomas Kirkpatrick, Simmion Spruell, Jas.
Kirkpatrick, James Nobles, James Pool, George Bronlee, B. G.
Ross, James Nabours, Percey G. Russell. List of debts due late
Wm. Kirkpatrick, dec'd: Saml. Boland, Baley Mayhon, Miss? Bou-
ling, Plesant Shaw, John Cowin, David Garrett, Thos. Garrett,
James Cowin, Jesse Garrett, Saml. Kinmon, Andrew McNight, Polley
Nixon, Alison Nixon, John Kenedy, John Mayhon, Thomas Hay, Mathew
Gradon, John Saterwhite, "Negro Cupit", Benjamin Arnold, Aberham
Smith, John Nabours, Arnold Tom, Edmon Ragsdell, James and John
Kirkpatrick.

9 Apr. 1823. Adm. of estate of WILLIAM DANDY, dec'd to John
S.? James. Sur: Benjamin James and James Watts, Jr.

21 Mar. 1823. Inventory of estate of BARTLET MILAM, SR., dec'd
by Sam. N. Powell, Nat. Day and Thos. Nickles. Shown by Ferrel
Milam, adm. 22 (Sat.) Mar. 1823. Sale of personal estate. Pur:
Elizabeth Milam, Judah Milam, John Milam, Hedley Davis, Ferrel
Milam, John Gray, Nancey Milam, Hettey Milam, Riley Milam. 7
Apr. 1823. Certified by Ferrel Milam, adm.

8 Mar. 1823. Inventory of estate of ANNA GARRETT, dec'd by Wm.
Putman, Jonathan Jones and Dillis(Willis?) Cheek. 21 Mar. 1823.
Sale Bill. Pur.: John Ashley, Jr., John Garrett, William Garrett,
Nancy Garrett, Ed. Garrett, Robert Moor, Rodey(Roda) Hughs,
William Ashley, John Ashley, Sr., Garrett Sullivan, Jessey Gar-
rett, Stephen Garrett, Nickles Garrett. Stephen Garrett, adm.

14 Apr. 1823. Adm. of estate of WILLIAM GLENN, dec'd to John
Cook. Sur: Anthony Griffin.

24 Mar. 1823. Inventory and appraisal of certain negroes belonging to estate of CHARLES SIMMONS, dec'd by John Dunlap, Samuel Farrow and Henry C. Young. (Same date). Sale Bill. Pur.: Dublin Hunter, a free man of color, Charles Smith, John S. Jones and John Garlington. 25 Mar. 1823. John Garlington, adm. Will annexed.

15 Apr. 1823. Will of JAMES BROWN, dec'd proven by William Brown, exr. Wit: William Wright and James Wright. Robert Creswell renounced executorship. 17 Feb. 1822. Will of JAMES BROWN. Daughters: Jane, Peggy and Mary; beloved wife (not named); mentions line of Robert Young; son William Brown and his heirs; daughters Rachel and Elizabeth. Son William and friend Robert Creswell, exrs. Wit: R. Creswell, William Wright and James F. Wright.

26 Apr. 1823. Will of JOHN LEONARD, dec'd proven by Marey Cole, wit. John R. Griffin, exr. and Allen Andrews. 25 May 1819. Will of JOHN LEONARD. Names: Jacob Croswhite and heirs; mother Mary Cole; Nancy Leonard the widow of Golding Leonard, dec'd; Franky Torrance late widow of Richard Leonard, dec'd; John Person and Nancy Person, his wife; brother-in-law Ephraim Andrews; children of Golding Leonard, dec'd: Henry Garland, John Golden and Frances Elijah Leonard; children of Reuben Leonard, dec'd: Nancy Foster, Betsey and John Leonard; children of sister Nancy Person; friend John K.(R.?) Griffin and loving nephew Allen Andrews, exrs. Wit: Charles Griffin, Mary Cole and Leonard Andrews.

13 Jan. 1823. Sale of negro man Brister, the estate of WILLIAM POLLARD, dec'd by William Pollard, Jr., exr.

(No date) Sale bill of estate of WILLIAM CUNNINGHAM, dec'd. Pur.: Martha Cunningham, William Burton, John Cunningham, William Morgen, James Durough, John Durrow, Henry Morgan, Samuel Irby, William Holay, Thomas Elison, William Pitts. Jno. Cunningham, exr.

23 Apr. 1823. Estate of WILLIAM DANDY, dec'd. Pattey Dandy, adm. Andrew Winn, sur. Pleads for an accounting. Adm. revoked and granted to Joshua Teague with Abner Teague and Thomas Teague, sur. Pattey Dandy to pay over to new adm. all remaining sums.

20 Mar. 1823. Appraisal of estate of SAMUEL LUKE, dec'd. by Benjamin Byrd, David Templeton and Robert Cunningham. John Stuart as adm. 21 Mar. 1823. Sale Bill. Pur.: Benj. Byrd, Benj. Pucket, Henry Pitts, B. H. Allen, Martha Luke, Alex. Luke, Charles Fargason, Joseph Harlon, John Luke, Benj. Ducket, Wm. Glenn, Geo. Ross, Saml. Gilland, Aaron Starnes, Wm. B. Sheldon, James Luke, Saml. Forgason, Allen Ducket, Martha Luke, Robt. Cunningham, Isaac Bagnel, Wm. Jones, James Cambell, Saml. Devaul, Thos. Crage, James Blakely, John Blakely, Robt. Gilland, Isaac Luke, John Stuart.

27 Nov. 1822. Appraisal of estate of STEPHEN DUMAS, dec'd. John Dunlap, adm. Appraised by W. W. Simpson, Wm. Rodgers and Wm. Moore. 29 & 30 Oct. 1822 and 29 Jan. 1823. Sale Bill. Pur.: Geo. Bowing, Letty Babb, Bailey and James Brown, A. Chandler, Fanney Dumas, John Davis, H. Davis, John Dunlap, Mary Dumas, G. Fullar, A. Fullar, James Fullar, Wm. Fullar, H. Fullar, R. Golding, E. Hix, Mathew Henry, Israel Holt, Wm. Hays, N. James, R. James, C. Irby, John Kelley, Jacob Miller, Jacob Oates, A. Oneil, John Nickles, H. Pasley, F. Powell, Wm. A. Rodgers, Andey Rodgers, Thos. Rodgers, Jos. Rodgers, Saml. Rodgers, W. W. Simpson, J. Teague, S. Lines, E. Watson, Lyl Walker, W. Wilks,

DUMAS, cont'd:
John Young, B. Gllover (Glover?).

6 Jan. 1823. Will of GEORGE LEEK, dec'd, Abner Young, exr.;
widow 1/3 part; inventory and appraisal by Robt. Criswell, Fedrick Foster and Wm. Dunlap. Plat where widow lives annexed and
made by Wm. Dunlap as No. 2. Inventory follows, very long. 9
& 10 Jan. 1823. Sale of property. Pur.: Saml. Young, Robt. Criswell, James Bardoe, Fedrick Foster, Margret Leeke, James Hiffs,
Margret Hooker, Wm. Copeland, Charles Littel, James Luke, Jr.,
Joseph Young, Jr., Armisted Leek, Wm. Brown, John Davis, E.
Teague, Joseph Young, Sr., Samuel Leek. Balance sold 2 May 1823
to Margret Hooker.

22 May 1823. Adm. of estate of JOHN JONES, dec'd to William
G. Pitts, adm. Daniel Mangum and Killis Anderson, sur. 4 June
1823. Appraisal of estate by David Mangum, James Garner and
James McKintrick. Notes on Janes Garey, Wm. Linvill and Wm.
Abernathy. 5 June 1823. Sale Bill. Pur.: Margret Jones (widow),
Thomas Dalrymple, Wm. Anderson, Wm. Gallaga, James McKitrick,
James Garner, Martin Gary, Killiss Anderson, Allen Vance, David
Dalrymple, Jesse Garey, Wm. Johnson, Alexander Chambers, Chesley
Butler, David Greer.

7 July 1823. Will of HUGH GOFF, dec'd proven by Ira Arnold,
exr. John L. Maddox, wit. 22 Jan. 1823. Will of HUGH GOFF. Wife
Rebecah land on Pylis? Branch bounded by Ira Arnold, Joel Alison, Allen Saxon and Wm. Arnold; land to go to Ira Arnold later;
son Thomas; daughter Cristan Mears. Wife Rebeckah Goff and Ira
Arnold, exrs. Wit: J. L. Maddox, Wm. Arnold and Joel Allison.

28 May 1823 Inventory and appraisal of WILLIAM DANDY, Esq.,
dec'd by Benjamin James, Thomas Powell and Whited Wilks. 29
May 1823. Sale Bill. Pur.: Silvanus Walker, Capt. Alex. Winn,
John Blakely, Hardy Davis, John Davis, Newman Gary, Joel W.
Johnston, Marcus Motes, Andrew Winn, Benj. Janes, Glanus Winn,
Thos. Powell, Abner Teague, Lydral Winn, Capt. R. Janes, Mathew
Henry, John Young, David Martin. Joshua Teague, adm.

12 Mar. 1823. Appraisal of property of WILLIAM MC CLAHAN (MC
CLANNAHAN), dec'd. by Wm. Moor, James Todd and A. Kirkpatrick.
24 Mar. 1823. Sale Bill. Pur.: Catharine McClahan, Samuel Irby,
John Campbell, Elizabeth Word, James Todd, Jr., James Todd,
Sr., Arthur Spence, Charles Madden, Sr. John Blakely, adm.

5 June 1823. Appraisal and inventory of estate of JAMES BROWN,
dec'd as shown by Wm. Brown, exr. Appr'd by Wm. Wright, John
Young and Joseph Young.

6 Jan. 1823. Appraisal of estate of JOHN ADKISSON (ADKISON),
dec'd by Burwell Leek, James Watts, Sr. and Barnet Leek. 8 June
1823. Sale of estate. Pur.: John Chapman, David Cureton, Charles
Snow, Anthony Golding, Allen Cox, Wm. Smith, John Ball, Elihu
Watson, Saml. Todd, Drury F. Vaughn, Archibald Todd, Charles
Ingram, Charles Chapman, John Rudd, Thomas Rudd, Wm. R. Smith,
Wm. Wadkins, Jno. Smith, Tandy Walker, Elizabeth Adkisson, Rich-
ard Sims, Saml. Jones, Thos. Adkisson, John McWilliams, Braxton
Watts, John Chappell, John Smith, Lewis Ball, John Armstrong,
George Neely, David Cureton, Andrew McCall, Richard Watts,
Thomas Hill, John Bolden, Ransom Day, Elihu Dotson, Henry R.
Hall, John Meek, Thos. Adkison, E. Adkison. John Meek, adm.

26 Apr. 1823. Inventory of estate of WILLIAM DANDY, dec'd, Mer-

WM. DANDY cont'd:
chant by John Garlington, Samuel Farrow and James Watts. 26
Apr. 1823. Inveventory of notes on hand: Henry Johns, B. A. Walk-
er, John D. Mitchison, William Bird, R. A. Simpson, Wm.? S.
Farrow, John Dandy, James Lee, James Parks, R. W. Sanders, Jones
Fuller son of Jones, Elizabeth Word, Mody Kenedy, Wm. Irby,
Sr., John Threat, Capt. James Hunter, Wm. Rowland, _____ McKees,
S. Rowland, Chesley Conant, Wm. G. Wright, Robt. Whitten, Jno.
B. Griffin, Jos. Irby, Valentine Boling, Wm. Lockhart, Jno.
Dendy, Thos. Rodgers, Negro Jim, Hannah Smith, Joel Allen, Geo.
Gruld?, Joel Dandy, Jno. Garlington, Allen Kelley, Edw. Hix,
(Judgements) Dandey & Reed vs Wm. Burnside, Saml. Boyd, David
Bell, Wm. Morten, James Ross, Robt. Hutcheson, James Medley,
Robt. Jones, Jonathan Reed, Thos. Rodgers, Wm. Baily, Jos. Dial,
Jno. Young, Jno. Pope, James Todd, Saml. Rodgers, Burrel Connent,
Jno. Duglass, Malium? Walker, Robt. Carter, Jonas Fulor son
of Jonas, Mitchell Smith, Jas. A. Barron, Rulum? Powell, Ruben
Brownlee, Isaac Mitchel, Edmon Cradock, Morrice Motes, Chas.?
King, Jno. N. Nash, Robt. Bryson, Geo. Pool, Jas. Rowland, Wm.
F. Rodgers, Wm. Smith, Sr., Palmer Higgins, Adm. of Wm. Fulton,
Jr., Jno. A. Cradock, Wm. Lee, Jr., Jno. Word, Allen Connant,
Est. of Chas. Jones, dec'd., Jas. Wright, Martha Dandy, Thos.
Dandy, David West (Spartanburgh), Wm. H. Farrow, Hiriam Sims,
Wm. Jones, Thos. Casey, Wm. Simmons, Isaac Mitchel, Jas. Paisley
& Danl. Cook, Wm. Park, Edmond Winn, Andrew Winn, Danl. & Thos.
Walker, Saml. Bowin, Robt. Fleming, David Craddock, Jno. Patter-
son, Hugh Crooks, James Hunter (Miller), Geo. Moor, Jas. Dial,
Jr., Jas. Young, Esq.; Notes for collection: Wm. Bell, Ransum
Fuller, Saml. Morten, Jesse Moor, Geo. Wharton, Wm. Morrow,
Dillard Watson, Arthur McNeel, Alex. Park, Jos. Owens, Thos.
Ware, Jos. Vance, Elisha Adair, Joel Allen, Harrey Brown, Abso-
lum Baily, Wm. Ball, Allen Burns, Aaron Burns, David Burns,
Nehemiah Franks, Jas. Fullor & Wm. Dandy, Jno. McKelvey, Jr.,
Wm. Nelson, Jr., Andw. Rodgers, Jno. Roberson, Elisha Rodgers,
Drury Shell, Jos. Irby, Wm. Thompson, Lydral Winn, Jas. Parks,
Sr., Frances Ross, Saml. Parsons, Jos. Burns, Willis Hogg, Est.
of Mathew Hunter, Byrd Barrett, Merrion Franks, Jno. Calhoun,
D. P. Saxon, Jno. Blakely, Mrs. Martha Sanders, Zachariah Baley,
Jr., Jno. Henderson, Saml. Vance, Isaac Otteway, Mitchel Smith,
Jno. Brown son of David, Bartlet Mylum, Sr., Harvest? Miller,
Ann Johnston, Geo. Leek, Jonathan Allen, Jas. Templeton, Jas.
Smith (wagon maker), Wm. Killett, Wm. Ducker, Jno. Garlington,
Thos. Blakely son of Thomas, Jno. Neel, Benj. Chesher, Saml.
Templeton, Jno. Word, Joshua Smith, Wm. Blackstock, Chas. Saxon,
Est. of Jos. Deen, Marmaduke Pinson, Wm. Coleman, Mathew E.
Cunningham, Henry Gray, Jno. Dandy, Rody Cennady, Bartlet Mylum,
Jr., Nath'l Day, Jno. Paterson, Wiley Milum, Jno. Pope, D. P.
Saxon, Israel Mitchel, Jno. McClahan, Stephen Potter, Moses
Pinson, Robt. Stone, Wm. Benson, Israel Fowler, James Ross,
James Blakely son of James, Danl. Martin, James Barron, Elihue
Rodgers, Saml. Franks, D. A. Pinson, Chas. Smith, Harburt Morten,
Wm. Cunningham (dec'd), Harely Davis, Jones Fuller son of Jones,
Jonathan Reeder, Wm. Pope, Currey Martin, Mrs. Susan Henderson,
Nathl Barksdill, Isaac Meed, Thos. Casey, Mrs. Matilda Garner,
Wm. Winn, Bradock Massey, Jno. Mosely, Mrs. Mary Barksdill,
Wm. Hamilton, Wm. Baily, Jr., Hancock Smith (Union), Andw. Hunt-
er, Wm. Glenn, Mrs. Jane Cunningham, Wm. Wilson (dec'd), Danl.
Orsborn, Burrel Thompson, Wm. Templeton, David Knight, Elizabeth
Smith, Jonathan Delorey, Black G___ Glenn, Geo. Grayham, David
McWinn, Braxton Watts, James L. Miller, Jeremiah Manley, Jno.
G. Burgess, Alex. Cockham, Frances Glenn, James Fulton, Sr.,
David & Saml. Studard, Richd Farrow, Baley Mahon, Nancy Wolff,

cont'd:
Sarah Fuller, Thos. Fulton, Jr., Geo. Wolff, Chas. Edwards,
Richd F. Simpson, James Roberson, Saml. Nugent, Jno. Parsons,
Wm. Babb, Elizabeth Milner, Capt. James Templeton, Chas. Irby,
Wm. Leary?, Zachariah Pendleton, Abraham Yarborough, Allen Kelly,
Danl. Dandy, John Todd son of Robert, Watts & Williams, Chas.
Todd, Arthur Spence, Davis S. Harry?, Philip Gray, Eph. Rober-
son, Jno. Stoops, Jno. H. Armstrong, Mary Williams, Thos. Cun-
ningham's widow, Chas. Simmons (teacher). Accounts due to Wm.
Dandy alone: Wm. Purkins, Robt. Simpson, Wm. Irby, Sr., Jno.
Walker, Jesse Piper, Elisha Adair, Andw. Park son of James,
Jno. Burgess, Jno. A. Craddock, James Todd, Jr., Thos. C. Dandy,
Abner Night, James Simpson, Leamanus Deal, Burrel Connant, Thos.
Janes (Jones?) (Abbeville), Chas. King, Wm. Black, Thos. Mc-
Crary, Wm. Glenn, Robt. D. Sanders, Allen Kelley, Jno. Dandy,
Elias McClenning, Robt. Park, Wm. Alexander, Esq., Wm. Pitts,
Jos. Prichard, Capt. Abner Rodgers, W. J. Walker, Rody Cannady,
Col. Robt. Word, Benj. H. Allen, Robt. Spence, Jr., James H.
Irby, Esq., Peter Farrow, Jeremiah Cole, Wheate Miller, James
Blakely son of Thomas, Coleman Garrett, Saml. Miller, Chas.
Connant, Marthey Dandy, Wm. Taylor (Dunkins Creek), David Crad-
dock, Joel Dandy, David P. Saxon, Robt. Ross, James Lyles, Pamud
Taylor, Jno. A. Mitcheson (gone), Jno. Adkins, Saml. Boyd, Edw.
Hix, James Henderson, Nathl. Day, Polley Coil, Wm. McClahan,
Danl. C. Johnston, James Porsley (Paisley?), Henery Davis, Zach-
ariah Tinsley, Jepah Tribble, Richd. Jnoiss(?), Thos. Lyles,
Clark Paily, Hezekiah Chesure, Nancy Cooper, James Watts, Robt.
Blakely son of James, Cesar Elphant, James Parks, Sr., Martin
Glidewell, Isaac Dial, Jr., Wm. Henderson, Aaron Word, Geo.
McKitrick, Mitchel Smith, Thos. Porter, James Watts, Jr., Perti-
lah Farrow, Wm. Patton, Reubin Powell, Miss Elizabeth Dial,
Martha Sanders, Jno. L. James. 28 Apr. 1823. Sale Bill of estate
of Wm. Dandy, dec'd, Merchant. (N. B. three (3) full pages of
goods purchased by the same people as above.) John S. James,
adm.

23 Apr. 1823. Appraisal of estate of WILLIAM GLENN, dec'd by
Thos. Ligon, Sr., Joseph L. Owen, Anthony Griffin and James
Ward. 8 May 1823. Sale Bill. Jno. Cook, adm. (No purchasers
named.)

16 Aug. 1823. Adm. of estate of LAZARUS HITT, dec'd to John
Hitt. Sur.: Henry Hitt and Lewis Ball.

16 Aug. 1823. Settling of accounts of DANIEL MATHIS, dec'd,
consent of Mary Linvell, admx. Lewis Linvell (now dec'd) and
David Mason now the adm. 13 Mar. 1820. Sale Bill of dec'd with
Elisha Teague, adm. (now revoked).

27 Aug. 1823. Appraisal of estate of LAZARUS HITT, dec'd by
James Ligon, Wm. Rodgers and Wm. Furguson. 2 Oct. 1823. Sale
Bill. Notes on James Ligon and John Hitt.

(No date) Appraisal of estate of HUGH GOFF, dec'd by S. L. (L.
L.?) Maddox, Joel Elison and Wm. Maddox. Negro girl to remain
in possession of Rebecah Goff, at her death to Ira Arnold.

7 Oct. 1823. Will of ELIZABETH SIMMONS, dec'd proven by John
Garlington, exr. John Dunlap, wit. 27 Mar. 1822. Will of ELIZA-
BETH SIMMONS. Daus.: Salley Madden, Elizabeth Smith, Jane Franks;
mention of Jno. Garlington, Jno. Clark, Sheriff of Laurens Dist.,
James Templeton's son Taylor, Nehemiah Franks; sons: William
Simmons, John Simmons and his children by his last wife, Charles

SIMMONS will cont'd:
Simmons; her dec'd husband Charles Simmons; land est. of James
Word, dec'd and Alexander Kirkpatrick. Jno. Garlington, exr.
Wit: Jno. Dunlap, Henry C. Young and R. F. Simpson.

27 Sept. 1823. Adm. of estate of CORNELIUS CARTER, dec'd to
Thomas Carter. Sur.: Zimri Carter and Robert Carter.

9 Oct. 1823. Adm. of estate of WILLIAM HAMBLETON, dec'd to Jane
Hambleton. Sur.: James Hunter, Charles Fowler and Samuel Hunter.

6 Oct. 1823. Adm. of estate of RICHARD FOWLER, dec'd to Joshua
Teague. Sur.: Abner Teague and Jno. McClellan.

6 Oct. 1823. Adm. of estate of MARY VAUGHN, dec'd to John Simpson. Sur.: Jesse Johnston and Henry Shell.

6 Oct. 1823. Adm. of estate of ELIZABETH MILUM, dec'd to Ferrel
Milum. Sur.: Wm. Milum and Jno. Milum.

13 Oct. 1823. Application of Elizabeth Runnalds to have will
of THOMAS TURNER, dec'd proven. Joseph Hill, wit. Will not proven
but adm. to Elizabeth Runnalds with Wm. Ligon and Jno. McGown,
surety.

22 Oct. 1823. Appraisal of estate of MRS. ELIZABETH MILUM, dec'd
by Nathl. Day, Saml. Taylor and Saml. Powell. Ferrel Milum,
adm. 27? Oct. 1823. Sale Bill. Pur.: Wm. Milum, Jno. S. James,
Judah Milum, Kittey Milum, Wm. Blakely, Joshua Milum, Jno. Gray,
Mary Milum. Certified 3 Nov. 1823 by Ferrel Milum, adm.

3 Nov. 1823. Adm. of estate of BENJAMIN ADAIR, dec'd to John
Adair. Sur.: Jason Meadors and Abner Rodgers.

3 Nov. 1823. Adm. of estate of JOSEPH MARTIN, dec'd to Nancy
Martin. Sur.: Nicklus Garrett and Thomas Garrett.

1818 - Return of William Hutcheson, adm. of ROBERT HUTCHESON,
dec'd. Received in East Florida when intestate deceased. Purchased from Elenor Hutcheson, widow and others residing in the
Province of Florida (list of negroes). Negroes brought into
the limits of the United States contrary to an act of Congress
passed in 1808, sold them in the states of Georgia and So. Carolina according to law. Sale bill of property was in S. C. at
the time, 23 Sept. 1822. Pur. of other goods: James Hutcheson,
Jno. McCay, Elenor Hutcheson, James E. Hutcheson. 1819 - amounts
paid out by John Hutcheson before administration: Hugh Crooks,
Robert Criswell, I. H. Irby, F. Richardson, James E. Hutcheson,
James Hutcheson, Elenor Hutcheson. Signed: Wm. Hutcheson.

21 Oct. 1823. Adm. of estate of JOHN SIMPSON, dec'd to Hose
Holcomb. Sur.: Archebel Young and Thomas Wright.

15 Nov. 1823. Adm. of estate of JOHN PUCKET, dec'd to James
Pucket. Sur.: Jason Meadors.

18 Nov. 1823. Adm. of estate of JOHN WILLIAMS, dec'd to Charles
Williams and Samuel Williams. Sur.: Allen Barksdill, Rodey Kannady and Coller? Barksdill.

29 Oct. 1823. Appraisal of estate of CORNELIUS CARTER, dec'd
by Wm. Ligon, David Adair and Saml. Goodman. 15 Nov. 1823. Sale

CORNELIUS CARTER sale cont'd:
bill. Pur.: Zimri Carter, Thomas Carter, James Carter, Joseph
Rodgers and Samuel Jones.

18 Nov. 1823. Adm. of estate of JESSE PRATER, dec'd to James
Word(?). Sur.: John Clerkerson(?) and Joseph Dunkin.

17 Nov. 1823. Adm. of estate of JAMES MURPHY, dec'd to John
Murphy. Sur.: William Grayham and Jason Meadors.

18 Nov. 1823. Adm. of estate of MARGRET MC CANNAHA, dec'd to
Joseph McCannaha. Sur.: Henry S. Neel and Wm. Grayham.

18 Nov. 1823. Adm. of estate and will proven of SIMON READER,
dec'd by Jason Meadors. Sur.: Geo. Young, Jr. and Elijah Cabness.
(Will annexed). Proven by witnesses of will. 9 Nov. 1818. Will
of SIMON READER. Sons: William and Thomas Reader; daughters:
Sarah, Polly and Charlotte Reader (N. B. girls also called Patsy
and Charlota); wife (not named). Wit: Robt. Long, Robt. Owens
and Thos. Owens.

18 Nov. 1823. Adm. of estate and will proven of JOSIAH PRATER,
dec'd by Joseph Dunken. Sur.: John Atcheson. 6 Apr. 1822. Will
of JOSIAH PRATER. Wife Ann Prater; son Israel Prater. At death
of wife and son, property on south side of Little Creek to go
to negroes Sam, Stephen, Clarkey and Betty along with cows,
farm tools, etc.; sons Jesse and Thomas Prater; Joseph Duncan
receives a negro man; daughter Judith Prater; son Amos Prater;
daughters Polly Prater, Tabitha Janes, Delilah Thomas and Rachel
Ensley. Joseph Duncan, Thomas Prater and Jesse Prater, exrs.
Wit: John Atcheson and Joseph Atcheson.

18 Nov. 1823. Will proven and executorship of estate of JAMES
UNDERWOOD, dec'd by James Underwood and John Blakely. Wit: Robt.
Creswill.

18 Nov. 1823. Will of AMEY CABNESS, dec'd proven by Elijah Cab-
ness, exr. Wit: L. D. Kern. 4 Oct. 1823. Will of AIMY CABNESS.
Nephew: Elijah Cabness, also named exr. Wit: John F. Vivrn?,
Jr., L. D. Dern and John Davis. Signed: Aimy Cabaness.

4 Oct. 1823. Will of ELIZABETH CABANISS. Son: Elijah Cabaniss,
also exr. Wit: John F. Vrevn?, Jr., John Henderson and John
Davis.

29 June 1822. Will of JAMES UNDERWOOD. Sons: William, Robert,
John, James and Matthew M.; daughters: Jane and Mary; step-
daughter: Nancy Copeland, dec'd son Isaac Underwood; beloved
wife (not named). Son James Underwood and son-in-law John Blakely, exrs. Wit: Robt. Creswill, Jno. H. Davis and Watts Deere.

17 Nov. 1823. Adm. of estate of PHILEAH? DAY, dec'd to Nathaniel
Day. Sur: Jno. Garlington and Jno. Dunlap.

10 Nov. 1823. Appraisal of goods (1 fur hat and wearing apparel)
of THOMAS TURNER, dec'd by John Cook, John McGown and James
Word. Elizabeth Runnalds, admx. __ Nov. 1823. Sale Bill. Includes
notes (not listed).

19 Dec. 1822. Appraisal of estate of JAMES MC MAHEN (MC MAHON),
dec'd by James Hollingsworth, Barruch Ducket and Joseph Hollingsworth. (No date) Sale Bill. Pur.: Miss Nancy McMahon, John Mc-
Mahon, John Craford, Wm. McMahon, Barruch Ducket, Jacob Ottis?,

MC MAHON appraisal cont'd:
Thomas Motes, John Philups, Benjamin Glover, Peter Fullar, James
Hollingsworth, William Hannah.

30 Oct. 1823. Appraisal of estate of WILLIAM HAMBLETON, dec'd
by James Hunter, Jesse Deas? and John Hunter. Jane Hambleton,
admx. Test: James Tayler.

10/15 Oct. 1823. Appraisal of estate of MARY VAUGHN, dec'd by
John Underwood, Jesse Johnston and Henry Shell. John Simpson,
adm.

1 Dec. 1823. Susanah Estes, about 19 years, and Nancy Estes,
about 13 years, chose Joel Estes their guardian. Sur.: Robert
Scott and David Chandler.

27 May 1823. Estate of CHARLES SIMMONS, dec'd with __ Garlington
as adm. with will annexed; account current. 1st sale bill 27
May 1823, amount returned as due by Charles Simmons (mostly
hire of negroes); estate of Mrs. ELIZABETH SIMMONS, dec'd; William Irby; 2d sale bill due 25 Mar. 1824; Nehemiah Franks and
his wife Jane (Simmons) Franks; John Hitch (taxes), John McManis
(surveyor); Samuel Farrow, Allen Kelley, Thomas F. Jones, Dub-
ling Hunter, John Garlington, adm. Final settlement 25 Sept.
1823. Wm. Simmons, his share 8 Oct. 1823. John Simmons his share
7 Oct. 1823. Miss Elizabeth Smith her share 7 Oct. 1823. Sarah
Madden her share 13 Oct. 1823. Charles Simmons his share 15
Nov. 1823. David McCaa and Polley McCaa their share 18 Nov.
1823. Nehemiah Franks and Jane his wife, sale of negroes for
Jane, 6 Oct. 1823. Attested to by legatees of Chas. Simmons,
dec'd and Mrs. Elizabeth Simmons, the widow and relict: John
Simmons, David Anderson for D. McCaa and wife, Charles Simmons,
Wm. Simmons, N. Franks, Elizabeth Smith and Salley Madden.

7 Jan. 1824. Will of EDWIN GARLINGTON, dec'd proven by John
Cook. John Garlington, exr. 1 Oct. 1823. Will of EDWIN GARLING-
TON. Wife, Eleanor; mentions marriage contract; son John Gar-
lington, exr. Wit: John Cook and Wm. Ball.

5 Jan. 1824. Adm. of estate of WILLIAM HILL, dec'd to Turner
Richardson. Sur.: John Madden and John D. Boyd.

13 Nov. 1823. Sale Bill of estate of WILLIAM HAMBLETON, dec'd.
Pur.: John McClintock, Starling Tucker, Robertson Hamilton,
James Hunter, James Taylor, John Hamilton, Samuel Boyd, Henry
Langston, Robert Fleming, James Hamilton, Peggy McClintock,
Saml. Mills, Thos. McCoreley, Edw. Garrett, Jno. Cowan, Wm.
Cook, Chas. Lawler, Jno. Boyd, Wm. McCrea, Jno. Byrd, Saml.
Hunter, Jno. Dunlap, Hugh Toland, Wm. Clark, Alex. Mills, James
Taylor, Wm. Cowan, Geo. Glenn, Jno. Taylor, James Simpson, Jno.
Hamilton, Jno. Todd, Wm. Fleming, Jacob Nabers, Tucker Higgins,
Wm. Park, Alex. Powers, James Simpson. Signed: Jane Hamilton.

29 & 30 Oct. 1823. Sale Bill of estate of MARY VAUGHN, dec'd.
Jno. Simpson, adm. No purchasers named.

22 Dec. 1823. Sale Bill of estate of WILLIAM GLENN, dec'd. Jno.
Cook, adm. Some sold on 8 May 1823. Signed: Jno. Cook, 8 Jan.
1824.

8 Nov. 1823. Appraisal of estate of JOHN SIMPSON, dec'd by Steph.
Garrett, Jno. Ashley and Wm. Holbert. Peter Hammond, J. P. 25

SIMPSON cont'd:
& 26 Nov. 1823. Sale Bill. Pur.: Jno. Coleman, James Putman, Hosea Garrett, James D. Smith, Harmon Garrett, Nimrod Putman, Jno. Cowen, Jesse Garrett, Stephen Garrett, Wm. Powers, Jno. Millender, Wm. Cross, Peter Hammond, Wm. Knight, Henry Vaughn, Wm. Brook, Jno. Ashley, Jr., Austin Moore, Wm. Fowler, Wm. Holbert, Jeremiah Ball, James Vaughn, Wm. Ashley, Martin Ball, Jno. Garrett, Wm. Putman, Danl. P. Meekey, Wm. Brown, Reuben Robertson, Zachariah Davis, James Coker, David Higgins, Salathiel Shockley, Jr., Hartwell Lester, Zachariah Davis, Reuben Thomas, Saml. Stroud, Joseph Long, Hosea Simpson, Wm. Barker, Jesse Davis, Jno. Vaughn, Garrett Sullivan, Wm. Parker, Geo. Crowthers, Elizabeth Ashley, Molly Holcomb, Jonathan James, Hezekiah Gray, Lewis Cargle, Thos. Knight, Presley? Owens, Tolliver Robertson, and Notes: Jno. Balden, Jos. Coker, Jos. Parker, Henry Vaughn, Richd. Owens, James G. Crocker, James Hammond, Jno. G. Smith, Saml. Simpson, Pursley? Owens, Thos. Porter, Jonathan Delong, David Knight, David Sims, Jonathan Vaughn, Saml. Gray, Francis and Silas Coker, Frankey Brooks. Signed: Hosea Holcombs.

5 Jan. 1824. Adm. of estate of JOHN PRATER, dec'd to Jason Meadors. Sur.: John Murphey and John Simpson.

5 Jan. 1824. Adm. of estate of DANIEL JONES, dec'd to Turner Richardson per request of widow of dec'd. Sur.:; Jno. Madden and John ____.

23 Dec. 1823. App. of estate of AIME CABNESS, dec'd and estate of ELIZABETH CABNESS, dec'd by Jason Meadors, Thomas Owens and John Boyse.

24 Nov. 1823. Appraisal of estate of SIMON READER, dec'd by Geo. McCrary, Thomas and Robert Owens. Notes on Benj. Adair, Elenor Bommay?, John Duckett, Samuel Stroud, Alexander Luke and Richard Duckett.

28 Nov. 1823. Appraisal of estate of JAMES MURPHEY, dec'd by Abraham Gray, Daniel Lofton and Jno. Jonas. 2 Dec. 1823. Sale Bill. (No purchasers named). Jno. Murphey, adm.

5 Jan. 1824. Adm. of estate of WILLIAM GILLAND, SR., dec'd to William Gilland, Jr. Sur.: Thomas Craige, Henry Pitts.

4 Dec. 1823. Appraisal of estate of JESSE PRATER, Esq., dec'd by Joseph Duncan?, William Dillard and Thomas Prater. (3 pages). 7 Dec. 1823. Sale Bill. Pur.: Elizabeth Prater, Wm. Dillard, Wm. Duckett, Joshua Duncan, James Law, Joseph Duncan, Thomas Prater, James Nabours, James Prater, Josiah Dunkin, Joseph Garrett, Isaac Mathews, Claxton Day, Jno. Odell, Thorington Holoman.

13 Jan. 1824. Appraisal of estate of JOHN PRATER, dec'd by Elijah Cabaness, George Dillard and George Young, Jr. (Includes wearing apparel of both dec'd and his dec'd wife). 22 & 23 Jan. 1824. Sale Bill. (No purchasers named). 1 acct. on Joseph Greer and 1 acct. on James Prater. Jason Meadors, adm.

17 Dec. 1823. Appraisal of estate of JOHN H. PUCKETT, dec'd by Geo. McCrary, Thos. Craig and Moses Leek. Bad debts due est: Wm. Glenn, Enoch Ducker, Jno. Deshields, Jno. Dillard. 18 Dec. 1823. Sale Bill. James Puckett, adm.

22 Nov. 1823. Appraisal of estate of BENJAMIN ADAIR, dec'd by

ADAIR estate cont'd:
John Luke, Geo. McCrary and Robt. Craig. Notes on Geo. McCrary,
Alexander Luke, Samuel Rose, Samuel Forgeson, Geo. McKintrick,
A. Studdards, W. Vickery, H. Puckett, James Gamble, Elias Gamble,
Uriah Davis, Wheate Miller, John Luke. 25 & 26 Nov. 1823. Sale
Bill. John Adair, adm. (No purchasers named).

2 Feb. 1824. Will of JOSEPH PATTERSON, dec'd proven by William
Rose, wit. 21 May 1820. Will of JOSEPH PATTERSON. Sons: Robert
and Joseph; wife: Rebeca. Wit: Elizabeth Workman, Samuel Workman and William Rose.

21 Jan. 1824. 2nd Sale Bill of estate of MATHEW HUNTER, dec'd
by Charles C. Nickles, exr. Widow: Elizabeth Hunter.

2 Feb. 1824. Adm. of estate of JOHN ENTERKIN, dec'd to Samuel
Barksdill. Sur.: John Barksdill and Wm. F. Davis.

24 Nov. 1823. Appraisal of estate of JAMES UNDERWOOD, dec'd
by Jesse Johnston, Henry Shell and Wm. Blakely. 18 Dec. 1823.
Sale Bill. James Underwood (Jr.) and John Blakely, exrs.

19 Feb. 1824. Will of GEORGE MOSLEY, Sr., dec'd proven by Flem-
ming Mosley and Roberson Mosley. For a sale on property not
willed. 10 Nov. 1823. Will of GEORGE MOSLEY, SR. Children: George
Mosley, (Jr.), Betsey Moore, Roberson Mosley, Flemming Mosley,
Nancy Mosley, Tully E. Mosley, Sophia Mosley, Thomas A. Mosley,
Eliza A. Mosley and Austin C. Mosley (none of age); wife Polley
Mosley; sons: Fountain Mosley and John Mosley; daughters Frances
Belcher and Polly Young. Roberson and Flemming Mosley, exrs.
Wit: John Wallis, Sr., William Rose, James Hunter and Samuel
Mills. Codicil attached.

26 Nov. 1823. Appraisal of estate of RICHARD FOWLAR, dec'd by
Elisha Watson, Danl. S. Beachum and H. Cheser. Joshua Teague,
adm. List of book acct's, good and desperate: Jno. Black, James
Bain, Danl. Beechum, Henry Beechum, Wm. Crosson, Ezekiah Chesure,
Robt. Coleman, Barruch Duckett, Sarah Fowlar, Jno. Verell, Mrs.
Allen, Reuben Griffin, Henry Johns, Mamon Mills, Jno. Moses,
Isaac Motes, Benj. G. Olliver, Wm. Purkerson, Peter Roberts,
Elijah Teague, Thos. Teague, Aberham Tompson, Joseph Rodgers,
Siminion Teague, Doctor Elihue Watson, Elihu Watson, Willard
Watson, Danl. Williams, Duke Jones, Thos. Gill, Thos. Fowlar,
Joseph Butler, James Cook, Jesse George, Anthony Griffin, Nath'l.
Drummond, Nancy Roberts, Wm. Wright. Sale Bill (No date). Pur.:
Alexander Austin, Jno. Black, Danl. Cargile, Ezekiah Chesure,
Coleman Roberts, Peter Fullar, Jones Fullar, James Goodman,
James Holden, Thos. Fowlar, Robt. Monroe, Jno. McClanna, Robt.
Duckett, Jno. Millar, Wm. Farrow, Richd. North, Jno. Phillips,
Thos. Rodgers, Thos. Teague, Polley Fowlar, Alex. Winn (Capt.),
Elisha Watson (Doctor), Silvanus Walker, Elihu Watson, James
Wright, Glanus Winn, Bartlet Saterwhite?, Robt. Gill. Notes
belonging to est.: Martin Millar, James Right, James Young,
Zachariah Chesure, Hezekiah Chesure, Hanner Millar, Wm. Fowlar,
Jno. Leonard, Wm. Allen, Abner Teague, Danl. Beechum, Jno. Motes,
W. D. Simpson, Jno. Phillips, Joshua Teague, Joseph Smart, Denia-
lion Deale; Sheriff's books-Thomas Rodgers, Charles Jones and
Burrell Cannon.

10 Jan. 1824. Est. of WADE ANDERSON, dec'd. Jno. Garlington,
exr. Jno. S. James, adm.

28 Feb. 1824. Appraisal of estate of ROBERT GILLAND, dec'd held

157

GILLAND cont'd:
by Benjamin Byrd, David Templeton and James R. Couch. 27 & 28
Jan.1824. Sale of goods by Robt. Gilland, adm.

1 Mar. 1824. Adm. of estate of JOHN JONES, dec'd to Robert Houston. Sur.: William Clark and Jason Meadors.

(No date) Appraisal of estate of MARGRET MC CONNATHY, dec'd
by Henry S. Neely, Wm. Grayham and Jno. Dillard. Sale Bill.
(No date) No purchasers named. Signed: Joseph McConthay.

27 Jan. 1824. Sale bill of estate of JOSIAH PRATER, dec'd by
Thomas Prater and Joseph Duncan, exrs. Pur.: Wm. Aberham(Aberams),
Richard Bonds, James Beaty, Nancy Prater, James Low, Jno. Watson,
Thos. Odell, Danl. Reeder, Benj. Wesson, Wm. McKee, Thos. Hen-
derson, Jos. Duncan, Wm. Reeder, Nancy Owens, Thos. Duckett,
Thorton Holdman, Amos Prater. Joseph Duncan, exr.

8 Mar. 1824. Adm. of estate of JAMES TEMPLETON, SR., dec'd to
William Templeton and James Templeton, Jr. Sur.: Hugh Workman
and William Speare.

1 Mar. 1824. Adm. of estate of ARCHABEL CRADDOCK, dec'd to Wm.
Clark. Sur.: Robt. Houston and Jason Meadors.

1 Mar. 1824. Adm. of estate of JOHN DILLARD, dec'd to Elizabeth
Dillard. Sur.: Isaac Jacks and Geo. Dillard.

10 Feb. 1824. Adm. of estate of MARY HILL, dec'd to Turner Richardson. Sur.: Wm. Clark and John Hunter.

5 Jan. 1824. Adm. of estate of WADE ANDERSON, dec'd to John
S.(L.?) James. Sur.: Benj. James and James H. Irby.

15 Dec. 1823. Appraisal of estate of PHILIP DAY, SR., dec'd
by James Watts, Wm. B. Smith, John Chapman and William Smith.
Nathanial Day, adm.

25 Feb. 1824. Appraisal of estate of Doctor WADE ANDERSON, dec'd.
"Doctor's medicine and instruments - we do not consider our-
selves competent judges - recommend the amount of them should
be the sum sold for." Jno. Findley, Aquillar McJunkens and Geo.
Funk. 25 Feb. 1824. Sale Bill (medical materials). Pur.: Dr.
Ludy Pyles, Dr. Jno. H. Davis, ___ Farrow, Isaac Teague, Thomas
Teague, Maj.? Anderson, Geo. Anderson, Esq., Zach. Arnold, B.
P. Delph, R. B. James, Maria L. Anderson, Capt. R. Cunningham,
Perry West, Jeremiah Warren, Jno. L.? James, Jony Fullor.

19 Mar. 1824. Estate of THOMAS HILL, dec'd. Polley Hill, wife
of dec'd and her children Robert and James Hill, she as guardian; Turner Richardson, guardian for William Hill, Sally Hill
and Fanny Hill, minors; accounting by Robert Malone, acting
exr. 10 Mar. 1824.

21 Jan. 1824. Appraisal of estate of DANIEL JONES, dec'd by
Jno. Chappel, James Watts and Josiah Cason. 22 Jan. 1824. Sale
Bill. Pur.: Sarah L.? Jones, Poston? Jones, James Mitchel, Wm.
B. Smith, Wm. Alwood?, Thos. Smith, Wm. McGowan, James Watts,
Jr., Wm. Smith, Geo. Neely, Anthony Griffin, Anthony Golding.
24 Jan. 1824. Rec'd of S. S.(?) Jones - cash. 9 Mar. 1824. Signed
by F. Richardson.

(N. B. F. Richardson should be T. Richardson.)

9 Mar. 1824. Appraisal of clothing of WILLIAM HILL, dec'd by
R. A. Malone, John Ball and Wm. B. Smith. Turner Richardson,
adm. 9 Mar. 1824. Sale Bill. William Smith purchased all. Turner
Richardson, guardian for S. S. Hill and Fanney Hill. F. Richardson, adm.

8 Mar. 1824. Appraisal of estate of GEORGE MOSELEY, dec'd by
John Wallis, Sr., William Rose, James Hunter, Jr., Samuel Mills
and John Deen.

18 & 19 Dec. 1823. Sale Bill estate of JOHN WILLIAMS, dec'd.
Pur.: Chas. Allen, Esq., Monima Williams, Matilda Williams,
Lydall Williams, Jno. Garlington, Rody Kenady, Joel Allen, James
Brown, Ellis Cheek, Roberson Moselly, Chas. Williams, James
Parks, Jr., James Parks, Nehemiah Franks, Jr., Solomon Goodwin,
Adam Potter, James Watt, Robt. Fleming Little, Saml. Mills,
B. L. Posey, Wm. Powers, Jr., Wm. Parks, Sr., James Deal, Sr.,
Coleman Hunter, Wm. Hill, Chas. Irby, Chas. Smith, Jacob Nabers,
Andw. Speers, Allen Barksdale, Walton Wallis, James E. Hutcher-
son?, Robt. Holleday, Wm. Putman, Chas. Little, Jno. Nabers,
Henry C. Young, James Farrow, Chas. Fowler, Richd. F. Simpson,
Robt. Franks, Edw. Hix, Ambrose Hodgins, Capt. James Templeton,
Jno. Byrd, Jno. Taylor, Fleming Mosley, Jno. Dunlap, Jno. Cowen,
Wm. Speers, Kitt Hardy, Wm. F. Downs, Jno. Ransom, David P.
Saxon, James H. Irby, Jno. R. Crisp, Capt. Andw. Parks, Nathl.
Barksdale, Saml. Fleming, Jr. Chas. Williams and Dr. G. Williams,
adm. 12 Dec. 1823. Appraisal of estate of JOHN WILLIAMS, dec'd
by Chas. Allen, A. Barksdale and Collyer Barksdale. Chas. Wil-
liams and Lem.? E. Williams, adm.

24-25 Mar. 1824. Appraisal of estate of JAMES TEMPLETON, SR.,
dec'd by James Taylor, Wm. Speers and Nathl. Day. William and
James Templeton, adm. Signed: 27 Mar. 1824. 25 & 26 Mar. 1824.
Sale Bill. Pur.: James Templeton, Jr., Polley Templeton, Mrs.
Jane Templeton, Jno. Templeton, David C. Templeton, Jno. McDowl,
Andw. Park, Wm. Park, Jno. Taylor son of William, Wm. Taylor,
Sr., Saml. Taylor, Sr., Robt. Spence, Jr., Saml. Taylor, Jr.,
James Parks, Sr., David Martin, Wm. A. Milam, Ferrel Milam,
Nathl. Day, Mrs. Jennett Taylor, Benj. Milam, James Collins,
James Parks son of James, Jno. Blakely son of William, Joshua
Milam, Thos. McDonal, Wm. Speers, Mrs. Mathew Taylor. 13 Apr.
1824 signed Wm. Templeton and James Templeton.

6 Mar. 1824. Appraisal of estate of JOHN DILLARD, dec'd by Jos.
Jones, Jno. Dillard and Geo. Dillard. 7 Mar. 1824. Sale Bill
by Elizabeth Dillard. Pur.: Elizabeth Dillard, Ann Dillard,
Wm. Person, Siminion Dillard, Jeremiah Burns, David Boyce, Jos.
Janes, Jno. Dillard, David J. Wilson, Jno. Roberson, Wm. C.
Person, Menasseh Williams, Geo. Dillard, Thos. Prater, C. Suli-
van, Johnston Deason, Claxton Ray, Hicks Deson, Geo. Young,
Jos. Garrett.

15 Feb. 1818. Appraisal of estate of MARY HILL, dec'd by Turner
Richardson, adm. He can find no property, etc. to appraise.
(N. B. This date apparently incorrect. See page 158)

23 Dec. 1823. Appraisal of estate of Capt. JOHN LEONARD, dec'd
by Saml. Williams, Jno. Felts, Reuben Griffin and Saml. Caldwell.
Jno. B. Griffin and Allen Andrews, exrs. Signed and certified
15 Feb. 1824. 26 & 27 Dec. 1823. Sale Bill. Pur.: Cristopher
Griffin, Thos. Wright, Richd. F. Simpson, Peter Sadler, Wm.
Butler, Danl. Williams, Jno. Felts, Robt. Flowed, Duke Goodman,

JOHN LEONARD, cont'd:
Ann Horner (widow), Dr. Elijah Watson, Jno. Feneson, Reuben
Griffin, David Williams, Robt. Monroe, Thos. Todd, Caleb Pitts,
Allen Andrews, Toleson Jones, Francis Andrews, Ludy Pyles, Wade
Griffin, Robt. Golding, James Wright, Johnston Jones, Jno. Simp-
son, Ezekiah Chesure, Jno. Jameson, Wm. Allen, David Vance,
Wm. Magowen, Richd. Reeder, Danl. Williams, Danl. Farrow, Jno.
R. Griffin, Wm. Green, Elisha Golding, Reuben Golding, James
Blackburn, Wm. Day, Wm. Watts, Wm. Hays, Mrs. Mary Fowler, Tobiah
Jones, Wm. Richey, Anthony Griffin, Danl. Pitts, Joseph Wallis,
Wm. Davis, Wm. Andrews. 16 Apr. 1823. Notes & Accts: Allen An-
drews, Wm. Andrews, Nancy Leonard, Jno. Simpson, David Williams,
Wm. D. Simpson, Jno. R. Griffin, Jesse Motes, Dr. Ludy Pyles,
Wm. Plant, Danl. Williams, Wm. Croson, Jno. Nickles, Francis
Andrews, Robt. Bryson, Jno. Philips, Geo. Grant, Lewis Wilson,
Tobias Cook, Henry Hitt, Wm. Fergerson, Jno. Goggins, Jesse
Blakely, Burrel Connant, Peter Roberts, Joseph Owens, James
Medley, James Nickles, James Standly, James Williams, Danl.
Fuller, Jno. Burnside, Wm. Allen. 18 Apr. 1823. Jno. R. Griffin
and Allen Andrews, exrs.

3 May 1824. Adm. of estate of HENRY MORGEN, dec'd to Wm. Morgen.
Sur.: Mary Morgen, Mark Killingsworth, Jno. Hopkins and Jeremiah
Hopkins.

3 May 1824. Adm. of estate of DANIEL CRADDOCK, dec'd to Sarah
Craddock. Sur.: Jno. Garlington and Thomas Crumby.

6 Feb. 1824. Appraisal of estate of JOHN ENTERKIN, dec'd by
Fedrick Foster, J. Johnston and Jno. Brown. 16 Feb. 1824. Sale
Bill. Pur.: James Boyd, Elijah Griffin, Polly Enterkin, Saml.
Barksdill, Jno. Barksdill, Henry Dean, Jno. Lord, James Enterkin,
Wm. Lord, Milley Vance, Thos. Enterkin, Saml. Neel; due from
Jno. Barksdill-settlement; note on Saml. Mathews (bad debt).
Saml. Barksdill, adm.

25 Jan. 1824. Appraisal of negroes belonging to estate of EDWIN
GARLINGTON, dec'd by Robt. Malone, James Neely, Sr. and Nathl.
Day. Also appraisal of residue of estate accumulated since his
marriage. Jno. Garlington, exr. 12 Jan. 1824. 26 Jan. 1824.
Sale Bill. Pur.: Wm. D. Simpson, Jno. Garlington, Mrs. Eleanor
Garlington (negroes and seperate est. by marriage contract to
be sold and divided amongst his children). Pur. of residue of
estate: James Neely, Jno. Chappell, Robt. Malone, Wm. Hill,
Mrs. Jane Watts, Jno. Moore, Jno. Garlington, Mrs. Eleanor Gar-
lington, Jno. Beasley, Jno. Ball, Wm. Smith, James Watts, Jno.
Meek, Alex. McWilliams, Burrel Leek, David Curenton, Wm. Tinsley,
Geo. Neely, Joseph Cason, Esq., Capt. Anthony Griffin, Wm. At-
wood, Thos. Todd, Lewis Smith, Andw. McCall, Wm. Pollard, Rhoda
Catinline, Wm. D. Simpson, Elihu Smith. Note ret'd on Joseph
Garlington.

5 Mar. 1824. Appraisal of estate of JOHN JONES, dec'd by Benj.
Bird, James Templeton and David Templeton. 5 Mar. 1824. Sale
Bill. Pur.: Betsy Jones, widow; Jno. Craig, Wm. Craig, Wm. B.
Sheldon, Aaron Starnes, James Dillard, Phillip Campbell, Thos.
Rains, Wm. Inlow, West Miller, Geo. McCrary, Geo. W. Dillard,
Dan Jones, Isaac Bragnel, Thos. Deshedds, Saml. Farrow, Robt.
Houston (adm.).

15 Mar. 1824. Appraisal of estate of ARCHELUS CRADDOCK, dec'd
by Robt. Houston, Jesse Teague and Solomon Smith. Wm. Clark,
adm. 19 Mar. 1824. Sale Bill. Pur.: Mary Craddock, widow; Solomon

ARCHELUS CRADDOCK cont'd:
Smith, Robt. Houston, Aaron Starnes, James Liles, Benj. Byrd,
Jesse Teague, Wm. Clark, Jno. H. Byrd, James Couch, James Ensley,
James Duckett, Nathan Bishop, James Harlon, James Blakely, Alex.
Simpson, Jno. R. Clark. Note on Jno. J. Miller.

16 Dec. 1823. Sale Bill personal estate of PHILUP DAY, dec'd.
Pur.: Jno. Chapman, Danl. Dandy, Burrel Leek, Isaac Grnt, James
Watts, David Cureton, Drury Vaughn, Jemima Day, Nathl. Sadler,
Mrs. Jennata Watts, Wm. Smith, Sr., Anthony Golding, Danl. Fushee,
Josha Cason, Saml. Todd, Wm. Caldwell, Thos. Anderson, Wm. Poll-
ard, Jno. L. Chapman, Saml. Waldrop, Elihu Watts, Wm. Alwood,
Thos. Solomon, Jno. Hazel, Walter P. Vaughn, Chas. Snow, Wm.
Tompson, Roda Valentine, Wesley Smith, Jno. Cox, Larkin Griffin,
Elihu Payn. Nathl. Day, adm.

24 May 1824. Appraisal of estate of HENRY MORGEN, dec'd by Jesse
Pitts, James Cunningham, Jr.? and Aberham Bath?. Wm.Morgen,
adm.

24 May 1824. Appraisal of estate of DANIEL CRADDOCK, dec'd by
Nat. Day, Saml. N. Powell and Thos. Nickles. 24 May 1824. Sale
Bill. Sarah Craddock, admx. Pur.: Jno. Garlington (also wit.).

22 June 1824. Sale of negro by George White at the suit of Jno.
Dunlap as property of Patsey Dandy before inventory of estate
of WM. DANDY, Esq., dec'd. Joshua Teague, adm.

9 Mar. 1821. Appraisal of estate of ROBERT HUNTER, dec'd by
James Park, Jr., Wm. Park, Sr. and Andw. Speer. 24? Mar. 1821.
Sale Bill. Pymts due 1822 and 1823. James Park, Jr. and Andw.
Park, exrs.

31 July 1824. Adm. of estate of EDMOND P. GAINES, dec'd to Julian
Gaines (also spelled Justian Ganes), and James Gaines. Sur.:;
Jno. Craford and Randolf S. Murff.

14 Aug. 1824. Adm. of estate of ELHANION CROCKER, dec'd to Jas.
Crocker. Sur.: Jacob Niswanger and Jno. Sims.

14 Aug. 1824. Will of BENJAMIN FOSHEE, dec'd proven. Susanah
Foshee renounces adm. Proven by oaths of Ephrum Knight, wit.
Benj. Foshee, Jr. qualified as exr. 25 Nov. 1807. Will of BEN-
JAMIN FOSHEE. Wife Susanah Foshee; six children: Nancy Foshee,
Sally Turner, Abbey Turner, Jenney Turner, Benjamin Foshee (Jr.)
and Daniel Foshee. Susanah Foshee and Benj. Foshee, exr. Wit:
H. Walker, Ephram Knight and Danl. Foshee.

10 Mar. 1824. Sale Bill of estate of GEORGE MOSLEY, dec'd. Pur:
Josiah Pinson, Fleming Mosley, Robert Mosley, Polley Mosley,
Isaac Pinson, Roberson Mosley, Wm. Rose, Jno. P-Pool, Anderson
Brown, James Moor, Susanah Brown, James Mosley, Nancy Mosley,
Thos. Garrett, Martin Ball, Henry Meredith, Wm. Langsford, Dan'l
Turner, Mrs. Mosley, Caleb Woodruff, Saml. Mills, Josiah Parsons,
James Riddle, Allen P'Pool, Joseph C. Parsons, Jacob Nabours,
Jno. Cowen, Jno. Millar, Stephen Folley, James Hunter, Even
Bell, Saml. Garrett, Jno. Owens, Andw. Mathews, Jno. Todd, Elias
Cheek, Jno. Ateway, Robt. Holaday, Wm. Owen, Wm. Terry, Moses
Glaspee, Jno. McClintock, Benj. Griffin, David Kie, Edmond Gar-
rett, Saml. Fleming, Jno. Farrow, Jno. Mills, James Park, Moses
Griffin, Thos. Garrett, Salley Brown, Saml. Stuart. Fleming
and Andw. Mosley, exr.

5 Sept. 1824. Will of JAMES BELL, dec'd proven. Jno. Dillard and Robt. Long, wit. Sarah Bell, ex. 27 Mar. 1824. Will of JAMES BELL. Beloved wife Sarah; sons John and Robert; my other children: Elizabeth Milum, Adam Bell, Susana Bell and James Bell, Jr. Sarah Bell, ex. Wit: Jno. Dillard, James Fisher and Robt. Long.

6 Sept. 1824. Adm. of estate of LEVI GARRETT, dec'd to Moses Garrett. Sur: Jesse Garrett and Charles Garrett.

6 Sept. 1824. Adm. of estate of JOHN MEADOR, dec'd to William Meador and Nathaniel Parks. Sur.: Thos. Crymes, Wm. Johnston and Thos. Parks.

16 Sept. 1824. Adm. of estate of PARLEY GROSVENOR, dec'd to William Irby. Sur.: Joseph Irby and Thos. Lockhart.

17 Aug. 1824. Appraisal of estate of BENJAMIN FOSHEE, SR., dec'd by James Watts, David Cureton and Robt. Malone. Benj. Foshee, Jr., exr.

18 Aug. 1824. Appraisal of estate of EDMOND P. GAINS, dec'd by R. L. Murff, Jno. Craford, Geo. Tiree, and Henry P. Gains. 18 Aug. 1824. Sale Bill. Pur.: Thorton Davis, Jno. Gains, Jno. Davis, Wm. F. Jones, Chas. Jones, Zachariah Taylor, H. P. Gains, Robt. Posey, Wm. Gains, Jonadal Gains, Geo. Tiree, Jno. Hall, James Medlock, Thos. Begley, Zachariah Downs, Peter Bemare, Hirum Davis, Isaac Waldrop, James Clardy, Jno. Jones, Jno. Night, A. N. Ware, James Hayden, James Arling, Reuben Powell, James Simmons, James Grimes, Sr., Benj. Tiree, Wm. Tiree. Julian and James Gains, adm.

4 Oct. 1824. Will of SAMUEL POWELL, dec'd proven by Benj. James and Silus Merur Bailey. Thos. Powell, Saml. N. Powell and Zachariah Bailey, exrs. (No day) June 1820. Will of SAMUEL POWELL. Names two grandchildren: Oliver Powell and (blank) Powell; my three children: Thomas Powell, Samuel Powell and Elizabeth Bailey with Thos. and Saml. Powell and Zachariah Bailey (husband of daughter) as exrs. Wit.: James Bailey, Benj. James and Silus Merur Bailey.

4 Oct. 1824. Adm. of estate of JOHN WALLIS, dec'd to Walton W. Wallis. Sur.: Sterling Tucker and Turner Richardson.

21 Aug. 1824. Appraisal of estate of ELHANION CROCKER, dec'd by Geo. Anderson, Geo. Funk and Hardey C. Connant. Notes: Judy Mitchel, Wm. Byrd, Jno. Crocker, James Young, Joel Walker. Book Acct's: Posey Fullar, Jno. Crocker, Fienus Medley, Martha Mitchel, Wm. Crocker.

16 Oct. 1824. Adm. of estate of DAVID ROSS, dec'd to James Durrow. Sur.: Jno. Cunningham Sadler and Robt. Nickles.

16 Oct. 1824. Adm. of estate of JOHN RYLEY, dec'd to Richd. Carter. Sur.: Robt. Carter and Joel W. Pinson.

16 Oct. 1824. Adm. of estate of REUBEN CASE, dec'd to Isral Chandler. Sur.: Isaac Case and John Abernathy.

5 Oct. 1824. Appraisal of estate of PARLEY GROSVENOR, dec'd by Jno. Garlington, James Watts, Jr. and A. Granshaw?. Sale Bill (no date). Wm. Irby, adm. Pur.: Robt. Fleming, Chas. Littel,

PARLEY GROSVENOR cont'd:
Saml. Morgen, Wm. Irby, Robt. Halladay, Mathew Holaday, Robt.
Word, A. Rodgers, Jno. Cowen, James Parks, Wm. Teague, Jesse
Fullar, Rundle Cheek, Danl. Farrow, Saml. Irby.

(No date) Appraisal of estate of JAMES BELL, dec'd by Richd.
Bonds, Jno. Dillard and Thos. Y. Zeasley(Beasley?).

17 Sept. 1824. Inventory of personal estate of JOHN MEADORS,
dec'd by Joseph Brown, Benj. Griffith and D. F. Algood.

27 Nov. 1824. Appraisal of estate of SAMUEL POWELL, dec'd by
Benj. James, Wm. Caldwell and Zachariah Bailey.

1 Nov. 1824. Will of SAMUEL NISBET, dec'd proven. Adm. to Wil-
liam Nisbet. Sur.: Drury Boyce and Jno. Nash. 4 Aug. 1824. Will
of SAMUEL NISBET. Beloved wife Mary; land purchased from Francis
Hopkins; daughter Nancy; sons and daughters: James, William,
Nathaniel, Demsey, Polley, Samuel, Thomas and Elizabeth. Son
William as exr. Wit.: Drury Boyce, Jno. Nash and Michel Dickson.

29 Oct. 1824. Will of THOMAS HUNTER, dec'd proven. Maryum Hunter
and Jno. Hunter, exr. 24 Feb. 1824. Will of THOMAS HUNTER. Wife
Maryum Hunter; children under lawful age (not named); son John
Hunter. Maryum and John Hunter, exrs. Wit.: F. Richardson, Wm.
Nelson and Chas. W. King.

22 Oct. 1824. Sale Bill of estate of HENRY MORGEN, dec'd. Pur.:
Polley Morgen, Thomas Morgen, James Morgen, Chas. Irby, Jno.
Hopkins, Frances Pasley, Wm. Yeargin, Wm. Ridgway, Wiley Yeargin,
Danl. South, Francis Posey, James Daniel, Aberham Bolt, Wm.
Dickeson, Joseph Dial, Danl. Garrett, Jeremiah Hopkins, Wm.
Mehaffey, Robt. Ellison, Jos. Morgen, Wesley Yeargin, Blance
Posey, Lewis Mehaffe, Stephen Garrett, Mathew Johnston, Jno.
Babb, Curtis Connant. Wm. Morgen, adm.

1 Nov. 1824. Adm. of estate of THOMAS DALRYMPLE, dec'd to Lewis
Dalrymple. Sur.: James Boyd and Isaac Tinsley.

16 Oct. 1824. Will of JAMES YOUNG, dec'd proven. Wm. Agustin
Young and Turner Richardson, exrs. 25 June 1824. Will of JAMES
YOUNG. Beloved wife Mary Ann Young; land where Jonathan Motes
now lives; mentions estate of wife's mother; his Abbeville plantation; his Laurens lands; his children underage (not named).
Sons Gallatin Young, Wm. Agustin Young and friend Turner Richardson, exrs. Wit.: Benj. Young, Wm. Moore and Hugh Saxon.

11 & 15 Nov. 1824. Appraisal of estate of THOMAS HUNTER, dec'd
by David Madden, A. Madden and Wm. Madden.

1 & 5 Nov. 1824. Appraisal of estate of DAVID ROSS, dec'd by
Jehue Pitts, Jas. Smith, Danl. Johnston and Robt. Nickles. (No
date) Sale Bill. Pur.: Jane Blake, David Boyd, Jno. B. Simpson,
James Durroh, Robt. Garrey, A. W. Saxon, Capt. Powell, Wm. Mor-
gen, Jno. Smith, Allen Akins, G. W. Brownlee, Jno. Cunningham,
D. McCullough, Reuben Clements, Jane Black, Jeremiah Mandley,
Robt. Boyd, Wm. Yeager, Jno. Pitts, Geo. W. Swindle, Danl. John-
ston, Reuben Pitts, Wm. Adams, James Culberson. Notes: J. B.
Simpson, Robt. Boyd, Jehue Pitts, Wm. Wallis, David McCullough.

16 Nov. 1824. Will of JOSIAH EAST, dec'd proven. Langston East,
exr. and Wm. Neel, wit. 27 Aug. 1818. Will of JOSIAH EAST. Son:

JOSIAH EAST, cont'd:
Langsdon East and his daughter Rebecah; emancipate negro woman
Nance; my three children: Langsdon East, Sarah Drake and Nancy
East. Son Langsdon East and Sarah Drake, exrs. Wit: Wm. Neill,
Richd. Davis and Senthey Saxon.

21 Sept. 1824. Inventory of estate of LEVI GARRETT, dec'd by
Nathen Harris, Geo. Dillard and David Reeder. 23 Sept. 1824.
Sale Bill. Pur.: Mary Garrett, Jno. Garrett, Jesse Garrett,
Wm. Dillard, Jos. Harris, Siminion Murphey, Geo. Dillard, James
Dillard, Jesse Brighs, Isaac Bragnel, Jno. Johnston, Jno. Dil-
lard, G. W. Dillard, Mary Dillard, Wm. Harris, Nathen Harris,
Isaac Mill, Jos. Garrett, Geo. Boyce, Jno. Troutman, Spencer
Bobo, Jno. Norman, Wm. Bobo, Saml. Dillard, Chas. Forguson,
Thos. Young, Saml. Boyce, Wm. Hill, Isaac Hill. Moses Garrett,
adm.

15 Nov. 1824. Adm. of estate of WILLIAM GRAIG, dec'd to Saml.
Craig. Sur.: Jno. Dunlap and Wm. Graham.

27 Nov. 1824. Will of MARY SATTERWHITE, dec'd proven. James
Mitchel, exr. 2 Mar. 1820. Will of MARY SATTERWHITE. Daughters:
Martha Hill and Sarah Whitlow; grand-daughter Mary Hill; sons
James and John Mitchel. Sons John and James named exrs. Wit:
Elihu Criswell and Benj. Hatter.

28 Oct. 1823. Appraisal of estate of ANN GLENN, dec'd by Wm.
Byrd, Jos. Hollingsworth and Wm. Rodgers. Shown by Jeremiah
Glenn, exr. of JEREMIAH GLENN, dec'd. 4 Dec. 1823. Sale Bill
of estate of JEREMIAH GLENN, dec'd by Jeremiah Glenn, exr.

7 Dec. 1824. Will of WILLIAM GREEN, dec'd; William Boland pro-
tested will being proven; William Green, Jr. named exr. with
witnesses and Jonathan Johnston, Sr. writer of sd will; sd will
to be recorded, etc. D. Anderson, Ord. 8 Oct. 1823. Will of
WILLIAM GREEN. Beloved wife Agnes Green; daughter Sarah Rodgers;
mentions land of Howard Pinson; Jonathan Johnston; son William
Green; daughters Martha Bouland and Elizabeth Motes ($2.00 ea.).
Son Wm. Green, exr. Wit: Wm. Reed, Wm. H. Motes and Jane Rodgers.

6 Dec. 1824. Will of COLEMAN CARSLILE (CARLISLE), dec'd proven.
Thos. A. Carlisle, exr. 11 Jan. 1824. Will of COLEMAN CARSLILE.
Beloved wife Sarah Carlisle; beloved children: Elizabeth B.
Abel, James G. Carlisle, Thos. A. Carlisle, Gideon N. Carlisle,
Sarah H. Carlisle, Eliza L. Carlisle, Jonna L. Carlisle, Wm.
H. Carlisle. Sarah Carlisle, Jno. Abel and Thos. A. Carlisle,
exrs. Wit: Wm. Right, James Leake, Sr. and Jno. Able.

6 Dec. 1824. Adm. of estate of JASON MEADORS, dec'd to Washington Meadors. Sur.: Geo. McCrary and Chas. Forgeson. (No date
but please notice one later in the following material). Pur.:
Jonathan Motes, Jno. Meador, Thos. Park, Saml. Park, Jno. Meador,
Wm. Johnston, Nathan Pugh, Lucey Meador, Geo. Stone, Isaac Wall-
is, Brenchley Clifton, James Nix, Wm. Linsey, Geo. Glenn, Hiram
Jones, Amos Cooper, Wm. Anar, Jno. Atwood, Wm. Young Salsbury,
Wm. Couch, Andw. Peden, Paul Salsbury, Religh Stone, Benj. Grif-
fith, Chas. Cox, Jno. Garrett, Hartwell Lester, Jno. B. Hendrix,
Archebel Young, Wm. Bryson, James Park, Thos. Right, Wm. Gilbert,
Thos. Howard, Blackmon Ligon, Joel Teague, Wm. Arnold, Wm. Mc-
Neely, Jno. Meador, Jacob Meador, Thos. Meador, Wm. Johnston,
Jas. Garrett, Henry Dean, Saml. Park, Thos. Westmoreland(also
Whitmoreland), Robt. Hand, D. F. Algood, Siminion Lavender,

JASON MEADORS cont'd:
Jeremiah Howard, Geo. Glenn; <u>24 Sept. 1824</u>. Thos. Woodruff,
Jno. Hughs, Warren Drummond, Jacob Roberts, Saml. Miller, Jno.
Bradley, Zachariah Gray, Chas. Cox, Jesse Davis, David Holcomb,
Jesse Wallis, Joshua Gilbert, B. Cennady, Thos. Crymes, Robt.
Taylor, Saml. Miller, Esau Hughs, Jno. W. McCrary, Isaac Wafford,
Jno. Edwards, Jos. Brown, Henry Martin, Nathl. Holcomb, Benches?
Cennada, Jno. House, Beneniah Canady, D. F. Algood, Edw. Scrughs,
Thos. Helton, Jno. Mamanuel Lygon, Edw. Surges, Hosea Holcomb.
Nathl. Parks and Wm. Medow(Meador), adm.

10 Dec. 1824. Will of ROBERT YOUNG, dec'd proven. Jno. & Jos.
Young, exrs. 27 Oct. 1824. Will of ROBERT YOUNG, farmer. Wife
Sarah; son Joseph; son Reason; son Jeremiah Madison Young; son
Elihu; son Newton Sprous Young; daughters Mary and Rachel Young,
Elizabeth Low Holland. Jno. & Jos. Young, exrs. Wit: Martin
Gary, Wm. Wright and Robt. Rowland.

10 DEc. 1824. Adm. of estate of WILLIAM CRISTIAN, dec'd to Jno.
Cristian. Sur.: Wm. Moore and Wm. Gafford.

10 Dec. 1824. Adm. of estate of HAMON MILLER, dec'd to Jacob
Miller, Jr. Sur.: Jacob Miller, Sr. and Jones Fuller.

11 Dec. 1824. Appraisal of estate of COLEMAN CARSLILE, dec'd
by Saml. Young, Jno. Young and Jos. Young.

5 Dec. 1824. Appraisal of estate of JOHN RYLEY, dec'd by Bleu-
ford Wells, Wm. Reed and Josiah Hollingsworth. (No date) Sale
Bill. Pur.: Mrs. Ryley, Jno. W. Johnston, Howard Pinson, David
Hill, Labon Sturges, Lucy Pinson, Wm. McGowen, Jonathan John-
ston, Sr., Wm. Reed, Abrum Sturges, Wm. Ligon, Aron Pinson,
Robt. Whitford, Joel Pinson, Cornelius Riley, Allen Smith, Elihue
Riley. Richd. Carter, adm.

25 Nov. 1824. SAMUEL BISHOP died intestate (1805). Adm. granted
to Verlinda Bishop, widow. Sur: Bazel Prater and Josiah Prater.
Legatees following below do release Bazel Prater and the Est.
of Josiah Prater from all accounting, etc. - Wm. Bishop, Jno.
Adair, Josiah Bishop and Joshua Bishop. Wit: Jno. F. Young and
Wm. Gillum.

21 Dec. 1824. Adm. of estate of CASEY GREEN, dec'd to Wm. Green.
Sur.: Joel Pinson and Isaiah Hollingsworth.

27 Dec. 1824. Release for David Strain, surety for Elizabeth
Strain. New adm. bond with Jno. Hitt and Wm. Reed.

3 Nov. 1824. Appraisal of estate of JAMES YOUNG, dec'd by Alsey
Fullar, Z. Bailey and Jno. McClan. (Laurens Dist.) Schedule
of appraisal of est. in Abbeville Dist. 10 Nov. 1824. Alsey
Fullar, Z. Bailey and Jno. McMakin.

3 Jan. 1825. Estate of WILLIAM CRAIG, dec'd. Jno. and James
Craig and Rev. Wm. Alexander, exr. Will proven by Jno. Temple-
ton and Levi Burk. 10 Oct. 1824. Will of WM. CRAIG of Enoree.
(Laurens Dist.). Sons John, William, Thomas, Robert and James;
daughter Eleanor; grandson Wm. C. Harlen; grand-daughter Cinthia
E. Harlen. Jno. & James Craig, Rev. Wm. Alexander, exrs. Wit:
James Craig, Jno. Templeton, Jno. Craig and Levi Burke.

9 Dec. 1824. Appraisal of estate of JOSIAH EAST, dec'd by James
Young, James Boyd and Alexander Glenn. 9 Dec. 1824. Sale Bill.

Sale Bill cont'd: Pur.: Jno. Smith, James Boyd, Robt. Smith, Langston East.

13 Dec. 1824. Appraisal of estate of WILLIAM CRAIG, dec'd by Wm. Grayham, Geo. McCrary and Wm. Gambell. 15 Dec. 1824. Sale Bill. (No purchasers named). Saml. Craig, adm.

22 Oct. 1824. Appraisal of estate of JOHN WALLIS, dec'd by Thompson Farley, Elis Cheek and James Flemming. 22 Oct. 1824. Sale Bill. Pur.: Elizabeth Wallis, Sterling Tucker, Martin Ball, Benj. Griffin, Wm. Hill, Westley Wallis, Jno. Todd, Sr., Jno. Todd, Marton Hall, Wm. Sims, Wesley Wallis, Saml. Workman. W. W. Wallis, adm.

3 Jan. 1825. Appraisal of estate of ANDREW FOWLER, dec'd in hands of his guardian, Charles Fowler. Real estate, by guardian vs Jno. Stuart; a legacy from the estate of Andrew Park, dec'd, in hands of James Park. Appraised by James Hunter, Jr., Wm. Hill, Wm. Hutcheson and James Femming(Flemming?). 3 Jan. 1825. Adm. of estate of ANDREW FOWLER, dec'd to Jno. Stuart and Mary Stuart. Sur.: James Hunter and Wm. Hutcheson.

12 Nov. 1824. Appraisal of estate of SAMUEL NISBETT, dec'd by Willis Buchane, Thos. Gradon and Drury Boyce. Wm. Nisbett, exr. Sale Bill. Pur.: Ames Riley, David Peden, Geo. Gundiff, Drury Gordon, Sims F. Arnold, Simon P. Adams, Thos. Goldsmith, Jonathan Allen, Hirum Tompson, Wm. Kellett, Liza Barker, Wm. Babb, Nathen Gradon, Geo. Tanksley, Wm. West, Jno. Nash, Jas. Alexander, Moses W. Peden, Francis Davenport, Jno. Terrey, Jno. Kellet, James Babb, Thos. D. Peden, Wm. Nisbett, Polley Nisbett, Sr., James Nesbitt, Nathan Nesbitt, Dempsey Nisbett, Polly Nesbitt, Jr., Saml. Nisbett, Solomon Mehaffe, Danl. Parks, Wm. Benham, Wm. Wood, Jno. Craford, Wm. Green, Henry F. Boling, Martin Babb, Wm. Mehaffey, James Morten. Wm. Nisbett, exr. (N. B. Nesbitt, Nisbett, Nisbitt, various spellings).

(No date) Sale of estate of THOMAS HUNTER, dec'd by Jno. Hunter, exr. Pur.: Wm. Madden, David Madden, Joel Burgess, Wm. Stone, Wm. Madden, Jr.

9 Nov. 1824. Appraisal of estate of THOMAS DALRYMPLE, dec'd by David Mason, Wm. East, Sr. and Isaac Tinsley. Lewis Dalrymple, adm. 25 & 26 Nov. 1824. Sale Bill. Pur.: Job Dalrymple, Mitchel Dalrymple, David Dalrymple, Isaac Tinsley, Robt. Hunter, David Mason, Aberham Johnston, Jno. Jones, Mikel Vickery, Alexander Glenn, James Boyd, James Enterkin, Wm. East, Sarah Dalrymple, Ephrum Williams, B. G. Oliver, Isaac Case, Jobe Couch, Lewis Dalrymple, Jno. Hunter, Jno. Linvell, Thos. Enterkin, Chesley Butler, Iven Linvell, Jno. Murphey, Wm. Hunter, Saml. Jones, Saml. Abernathy, Jno. Deen, Nathan Vance, Geo. Johnston, Alexander Winn. Lewis Dalrymple, adm.

9 Jan. 1825. Adm. of estate of JOHN MC CRARY, dec'd to Mathew McCrary. Sur.: Geo. McCrary and Jos. Greer.

19 Oct. 1824. Inventory of personal estate of REUBEN CASE, dec'd by Saml. Abernathy, Jno. Abernathy and Wm. East, Sr. Shown by Israel Chandler. Notes: Thos. Ware, Wm. Prater, Wm. Cole, Saml. Hulsey, Thos. Garey, Wm. Bonds, Wm. Johnston (all doubtful); notes on David Brooks. 4 Nov. 1824. Sale Bill. Pur.: Isaac Case, Anne Case, Anora Case, Danl. Mangrum, Peter Sadler, Wm. Levil (Linvell?), David Vance, Aberham Johnston, Jehue Johnston, Israel

Sale cont'd:
Chandler, Jno. Saxon, Saml. Abernathy, Jno. Abernathy, Wm. Neel,
Esq., Wm. Enlow, Jno. Davis, Cornelius Flowed(Floyd), Mikel
Dalrymple, Jno. Miller, Jacob Lewiston, Jno. Watts, James Littel,
Geo. Johnston, Josiah Williams, Wm. Davis, Jno. Boseman, Nathl.
Vance. Israel Chandler, adm.

20 Jan. 1825. Adm. of estate of JOHN FULLER, dec'd to Isaac
G. Teague. Sur.: Geo. Bowing and Geo. Anderson.

11 Dec. 1824. Inventory of estate of MARY SATTERWHITE, dec'd
by W. W. Simpson, Danl. Cook, Wm. Low and Henry Fuller. James
Mitchel, exr. 12 Dec. 1824. Sale Bill. Pur.: Zachariah Bailey,
Henry Fuller, Nancy Cooper, Jones Fuller, Isaac Mitchel, Geo.
Roberts, Danl. Cook, Wm. W. Simpson, Rowland Burgess, Peter
Fuller, Isaac Mitchel, Wiley Hill, Alsey Fuller. Notes due:
Sarah Parks, Robt. Blanks, Willis Hog (good).

4 Jan. 1825. Appraisal of estate of WILLIAM CRISTIAN, dec'd
by Saml. McClurkin, Thos. Washington and Mathew Ballon. Jno.
Cristian, adm. 4 Jan. 1825. Sale Bill. Pur.: Abner McDonald,
Jno. Cristian, Jane Cristian, Thos. Washington, Wm. Moor, Benj.
Tompson. Note on Benj. Thomas.

27 Dec. 1824. Appraisal of estate of JASON MEADORS, dec'd by
Geo. McCrary, Reuben Meadors and Richd. Bonds. Note on John
Meadors of Virginia; note on Reuben Meadors. 30 Dec. 1824. A Sale
Bill on est. Washington Meadors, adm. No purchasers named. The
negroes, household, military equipage. Note on Jno. Meadors
of Va. and one on Reuben Meadors.

23 Dec. 1824. Appraisal of estate of HAYMON (HAYMUN) MILLER,
dec'd by Peter Fuller, Jones Fuller and Wm. Fuller. 30 Dec.
1824. Sale Bill. Jacob Miller, Jr., adm. Pur.: Henry Fuller,
Martha Miller, Jones Fuller, Peter Fuller, Hagin Motes, Israel
Fuller, Robt. Hollingsworth, James Roberts, Wm. McWilliams,
Wm. A. Young, Saml. Rodgers, Jno. Black, Elijah Watson, Wm.
Rodgers, Jacob Miller, Sr., Jesse Robertson, Robt. Coleman,
Burd Roberts, Ase Chandler, James Ligon, Wm. Fuller.

7 Feb. 1825. Adm. of estate of ELIZABETH GLENN, dec'd to Geo.
W. Glenn. Sur.: James Hunter and Fleming Mosley.

(No date) Appraisal of estate of CASEY GREEN, dec'd by Jonathan
Johnston, Wm. Reed and Jno. Hitt. 8 Jan. 1825. Sale Bill. Pur.:
Agnes Green. Wm. Green, adm.

21 Dec. 1824. Cane Creek. Appraisal of estate of WILLIAM GREEN,
dec'd by Jonathan Johnston, Wm. Reed and Jno. Hill.

30 Dec. 1824. Sale Bill estate of COLEMAN CARSLILE, dec'd. Pur:
John L. Abell, Gidion N. Carslile, Aberham Johnston, Saml. Neil,
Francis Hatton, Jno. Gamble, Wm. Fulton, Jno. Young, Jno. Leek,
Martha Leek, Jane Midleton, Jno. Underwood, Wm. Lord, Wm. Stuart,
Beveley Walker, Wm. Hewit, Wade H. Griffin, Lydral Winn, Wm.
Tinsley, Henry Johnston, James Leek, Thos. Enterkin, Jno. Holland,
Silvanus Walker, Hardy David, Saml. Young, Josiah Williams,
Thos. A. Carslile, Henry Stroud, Henry Shell, Jno. Copling,
Moses Ross, Josiah Mylam, Elijah Shepard, Jno. Brown, Jno. Mc-
Kelvey, Saml. Hunter, D. H. Griffin, Wm. Tinsley, Jno. Barks-
dill, Adam Bond, Mitchel Vickery, Jno. Johnston, James Leek,
Jr., Adam Boland, Sarah H. Carslile, David Enterkin, Jno. Clop-

Sale cont'd:
ton, Jacob Boland, James Brady, Robt. Wickham, Jr., David Gamble,
Geo. McKitrick, James Cob, Hikeson Barksdill, Saml. Hunter,
Midleton Cob, Thos. A. Carslile, Allen Midleton, Jno. Simpson,
Wm. Gambell, James Harden.

25 Jan. 1825. Appraisal of estate of WILLIAM CRAIG of Enoree,
dec'd by Jno. Boyce, Benj. Byrd and Geo. Gordon. Legacies: Thos.
Craig, Robt. Craig, Wm. C. Harlings, Jane Harlings, Jno. Craig,
James Craig, Elenor Copland, Wm. L. Craig; judgements and notes.

5 Feb. 1825. Sale of estate of WILLIAM CRAIG, dec'd. James and
Jno. Craig, exr. (No purchasers named).

28 Dec. 1824. Appraisal of estate of ROBERT YOUNG, dec'd by
Wm. Brown, James Underwood and Jno. Hunter. (Long list). Sale
Bill. (No date) Pur.: Sarah Young, Beveley A. Walker, Jno. Hunt-
er, Mathew H. Henry, James Leek, Thos. Fulton, Jr., Robt. Bell,
Jesse Johnston, James Bryson, Chas. Littel, Jeremiah Trible?,
Chas. Simpson, Nathen Blakely, Wheat Miller, Hardy Davis, Wm.
Brown, Henry Duckett, Shelton Rodgers, Jeremiah Holland, Joseph
Young son of Robert.

27 Jan. 1825. Appraisal of estate of JOHN MC CRARY, dec'd by
Perry Jones, Geo. Young, Jr. and Joseph Greer. Accounts: M.
Willson, Wm. McGumery, Geo. B. Armstrong, Estate of Jno. Bouland,
Jno. Greer, James Johnston, Francis Burns. 1 Feb. 1825. Sale
Bill. Mathew McCrary, adm. (No purchasers named).

23 Feb. 1825. Citation, Thomas Powell against John Dunlap, adm.
of STEPHEN DUMAS, dec'd; presenting accounts; Sale Bill of dec'd
29 & 30 Nov. 1822; 2nd sale 29 Jan. 1823; widow and her now
husband; nine children of the dec'd; Stephen Lines who married
Sarah Dumas, dau. of dec'd; John Kelley who married Betsy Dumas,
dau. of dec'd; Brooker Smith who married Polley Dumas, dau.
of dec'd; Thomas Powell who married Lucy Dumas, dau. of dec'd;
adm. to retain inheritance for minor children of dec'd - their
guardian: Nathaniel, David, Tilda, Nancy and Eleline Dumas.

5 Feb. 1825. Martha Vaughn, minor about 17 years chose James
Hips? her guardian until age 21. Sur.: Saml. Neel and Wm. Fulton.

3 Feb. 1825. Adm. of estate of JOSEPH LYNCH, dec'd to William
E. Lynch. Sur.: Henry C. Young and Wm. F. Downs.

7 Mar. 1825. Adm. of estate of MARY PUGH, dec'd to Jacob Roberts.
Sur.: Hosa Holcomb and Nathan Holcomb.

7 Mar. 1825. Adm. (will annexed) of estate of JOHN PRATER, dec'd
to Joseph Dollar. Sur.: Joseph Greer and Charles Farguson.

7 Mar. 1825. Adm. (will annexed) of estate of DAVID GLENN, dec'd
to George M. Glenn. Sur.: James Hunter and Fleming Mosley.

7 Mar. 1825. Adm. (will annexed) of estate of JOHN BALL, dec'd
to Martin Ball. Will proven. Sur.: Jeremiah Ball and Benjamin
Martin. 20 Dec. 1824. Will of JOHN BALL. Bro.: Martin Ball;
bros & sisters: Reuben Ball, James Ball and Katherine Martin.
Mentions father (not by name); bro.: Peter Ball. Carpenters
and mechanical tools. Wit: Thos. Garrett, Benj. Martin and Reuben
Martin.

12 Dec. 1822. Sale of estate of COLEMAN BALEY (BAILEY), dec'd.
Pur.: J. Hollingsworth, James Bailey, Benj. Oliver, Whit Chandler, Saml. Bailey, Zachariah Bailey, James Bailey, Moses Hollingsworth, A. Bailey, Jos. Bailey, Joel Carter, A. Chandler, Jos. Rodgers, Peter Fuller, Thos. Walker, Fanny Bailey, Zachariah Bailey, Jr. Z. Bailey, adm.

19 Mar. 1825. Adm. of estate of SARAH FOWLER, dec'd to John Odle. Sur.: Elijah Watson and Ezekiah Chesure.

28 Mar. 1825. Adm. of estate of HARDY CONNANT, dec'd to Elizabeth Connant. Sur.: Geo. Bowing and Alsey Fuller.

21 Mar. 1825. Appraisal of estate of ELIZABETH GLENN, dec'd by James Fleming, Fleming Mosley and Jno. Deen. 23 Mar. 1825. Sale Bill. Pur.: Elizaeth Glenn, Alexander Glenn, Isaac Attoway, Jno. Taylor, Chas. Williams, Wm. Cowen, Harling Brown, Robt. Fleming, Fleming Mosley, Josiah Parsons, James Glenn. Geo. M. Glenn, adm.

15 Dec. 1824. Sale of estate of ELHANION CROCKER, dec'd. Pur.: Malinda Crocker, Larken Gains, Jno. H. Byrd, Hanie Hendrick, Shubal Starns, Joseph Crocker, James Fuller, Sr., Alsey Fuller, Jacob Niswanger, Thos. B. Williams, Wm. Smith, James Middleton and family, Geo. Anderson, Nathan Sims, Aquillar McJunkin, Jno. R. Crocker, Joseph Prichards, Wm. Byrd, Riley Shirley, Posey Fuller, Martin Groves, Robt. Nickles, Jno. Starnes, Peter Fuller, Judy Mitchel, Robt. Cunningham, Thos. Fowler, Jno. Odle; Notes not formerly ret'd: Wm. Crocker and Obediah Misher.

21 Mar. 1825. Appraisal of estate of DAVID GLENN, dec'd by James Fleming, Fleming Mosley and Jno. Deen. 25 Mar. 1825. Sale Bill. Pur.: Elizabeth Glenn, Alexander Glenn, Francis Glenn, Saml. Fleming, James Glenn, Chas. Williams, Mitchel Dunlap, Jesse Atteway, James Fleming, Isaac Atteway, Peter Hamons, Fleming Mosley, D. J.? Glenn, Wm. Cowan, Jno. Todd. Geo. M. Glenn, adm.

27 Apr. 1825. Inventory of estate of MARY PUGH, dec'd by James Parks, Saml. Parks and Joel Person. 28 Apr. 1825. Sale Bill. Pur.: Joseph Moor, Thos. Jones, Jos. Terry, Jno. House, Chas. Case, Eli Cooper, Isaac Cooper, Chas. Cox, Nancy Spurgeon, Wm. Gilbert, James Gray, Wm. Compton, Drury Spurgeon, Wm. Couch, Thos. Roberts, Wm. Arnold.

16 Apr. 1825. Inventory of estate of JOHN BALL, dec'd by Nicholas Garrett, Reubin Burditt and John Burditt. Note on Martin Ball, Hampton G. Person acc't, David Higgins, acc't, Benjamin Martin, acc't.

22 Dec. 1824. Sale Bill estate of DR. WADE ANDERSON, dec'd. Pur.: Maria S. Anderson, Geo. Anderson, Jo. H. Prichard, B. L. Posey, Geo. Franks, Asa Chandler, Andw. Rodgers, Gamble Thomas. Signed: 1 Jan. 1825 by Jno. S. James, adm.

24 Mar. 1825. Appraisal of estate of JOSEPH LYNCH, dec'd by Jno. Dunlap, Capt. Wm. Irby and Harvy Cle____. Acct's due: Jos. Langston, Edmund Craddock, Thos. Lynch, David Higgins, Archibald Lynch, Jno. N. Nash, Sarah Lynch, Harmon Waldrop, Philip Campbell, Eppy Smith, Molly Farrow, Jno. Couch, Thos. Liles, Nathan Bishop, Landy Waters?, Henry Langston, Jos. Miller, Nathan Couch, Bazzle Wheat?, Francis Glenn, Benj. Stone, Chaney Stone. 24 Mar. 1825. Sale Bill. Pur.: Thos. Westbrook, Wm. Ran-

Sale Bill cont'd:
som, Jno. D. Boyd, Mrs. Lynch, Jos. Lynch, Chaney Stone, Jno.
McClellan, Andw. Starns, Aaron Lynch, Wm. Farrow. Wm. E. Lynch,
adm.

(No date) Appraisal of estate of JOHN FULLER, dec'd by Whilee
Wilks, Stephen Lynes and David Martin. Sale Bill. (No date).
Pur.: Alsey Fuller, Beaufort Powel, Annes Roberts, Danl. M.
Winn, James Young, Stephen Lines, Jno. Young, Sylus Fuller,
David Martin, Saml. Brooks.

6 Apr. 1825. Appraisal of estate of HARDY CONANT, dec'd by Alsey
Fuller, Howel Mosley and Chas. Nickles. 30 Apr. 1825. Sale Bill.

18 Apr. 1825. Adm. of estate and will proven of JOHN FINNEY,
dec'd. Wm. Gambell, adm. Sur,: Jno. Boyce and Washington Meadors.
24 Jan. 1820. Will of JOHN FINNEY. Son John Finney; wife Nancy
Finney; daughters Elizabeth, Ann, Polley, Sarah, Peggy and Martha
Finney. Wit: Jason Meadors, Wm. Copeland and Polly Meadors. 5 May
1825. Inventory of est. with will annexed, by Wm. Graham, Geo.
McCrary and J. W. Bell?.

6 June 1825. Decree in the case of JOHN JONES, dec'd vs Wm.
C. Pitts, adm. by Margaret Jones, widow of dec'd for an account-
ing. Sale 5 June 1823?. Debts paid: Saml. Vance, Page & Level,
Jacob Gary, Oneall & Johnson-Atty's, Noah Level and Martin Gary.

20 June 1825. Estate of WILLIAM HUTCHINSON, dec'd. James Hutchinson, Jr., adm. Sur.: Joel Allen and Richd. F. Simpson.

2 May 1825. Writ of summons for partition in the case of Shubal
Starns vs Jno. Shurley (Shirley) and others. To: John Shurley,
Aaron Shurley, Bunley? Shurley, Lydia Shurley, Jane Shurley,
Elizabeth Shurley, Easter Shurley, Polly married to Graham Elmore, Sarah married to Wm. McPhearson, Huldy married to George
Elmore, Rebecca married to Elijah Elmore, Edy Wright a widow,
legal heirs of REBECCA SHURLEY, who died intestate. To appear
at court 6 June 1825 in Laurens Dist. - settlement of est. Land
granted to Richard Shurley bounded by Jacob Niswanger, Bunley
Shurley and Shubal Starns. Signed: 9 May 1825. All appeared
in court 6 June 1825. Mention of Wm. Moore and Jonathan Forgey,
respectable free holders; land to be sold by Sheriff on 1st
Monday of July next.

6 June 1825. Estate partition/settlement of JOHN JONES, died
intestate, for Margaret Jones (widow), Nancy Jones, Joseph Jones,
Thos. D. Jones and Mary Jones, his legal heirs vs Wm. C. Pitts,
adm. Land originally granted to Wm. McTeer, dec'd, bounded by
Alex. Simpson, Jr., James Waller?, Nathaniel Vance, Samuel Abernathy and A___ H___. Margaret Jones guardian of sd minors. Summons of partition acknowledged. Wit: W. E. Lynch. 20 June 1825.
James Joiner, free holder; land to be sold by Sheriff.

4 July 1825. Adm. of estate of ANDREW MC NIGHT, dec'd to Elizabeth McNight. Sur.: A. McNight and W. F. Downs.

2 Oct. 1824. Deed of ANDREW MC NIGHT. Property should not be
sold, etc. names Hiram and Andrew, sons; wife not to forget
Nelly (no last name). Test.: Wm. Helms and Andw. Helms. 30 Apr.
1825. Wm. Helms swore to above deed; Jno. Cunningham, J.P. 4
July 1825. Will (deed) proven.

28 June 1825. Appraisal of estate of SARAH FOWLER, dec'd by

FOWLER est. cont'd:
Thos. Burnsides, Danl. __. Beacham and _____. Notes on Jos.
Crocker, Thos. Gill, Jno. Odle, Peter Fuller, Thos. Reeder,
Danl. Cook, Thos. S. Wilks, Wat Drummond, Barruch Ducket, Francis
Medley, Thos. Harris, James Wright, Jesse Motes, Allen Fuller,
Joshua Teague, adm. of Richard Fowler, dec'd., Thos. Teague,
Danl. Walker, Robt. Word, Est. of James McMahon (desperate),
James Young, Agnes Young, Wm. Young; estate of Sarah Fowler
is entitled to a legacy under the will of THOMAS DUCKET, dec'd
her father. Sale Bill. Pur.: H. Chesher, Barruch Ducket, Danl.
Jones, Danl. Cane, Jos. Rodgers, Wm. Rodgers, James Malding,
James Hollingsworth, Jones Fuller, Thos. Wilks, Wm. Brison,
Peter Fuller, James Fuller, Joseph Legin, Marthey Fowler, Jacob
Miller, Duke Jones.

4 July 1825. Writ of summons in case Ex Parte Joseph Babb and
Mary his wife. To Mary Colb (Babb?), widow of WILLIAM GLENN,
dec'd (who died intestate) and John, Catharine, Jeremiah and
Anna Glenn, minors and legal heirs of sd dec'd.; 3d Monday of
July 1825 for property settlement. Land bounded by Wm. Thomp-
son, Martin Walles?, Solomon Fuller, James Furgason and Mrs.
Gowen?, originally granted to Joseph Babb. Alsey Fuller, guard-
ian of minor children of dec'd.

2 July 1825. Appraisal of estate of WILLIAM HUTCHINSON, dec'd
by Jno. Hutchinson, J. Hitch and James Park, Sr.

20 June 1825. Will of SAMUEL TODD, dec'd proven. Ex. Saml. B.
Lewers. Pattillo Farrow, atty for heirs. 29 Dec. 1824. Will
of SAMUEL TODD. $3000 to Gospel Ministry in village of Laurens;
friends Jno. Todd, James Williamson and Wm. Blakely, trustees
of same; $2000 for building a church; Thos. Pool, Esq., of Spar-
tanburgh; James Brannon of Spartanburgh - money for Miss Mary
Ann Hall; sister Jane Hamilton and her son Samuel; nephew John
Hamilton; niece Martha Hamilton; nephew Samuel Todd son of bro.
John Todd; nephew Samuel R. Todd son of bro. Andrew Todd; niece
Eliza Todd, dau. of bro. Andrew; niece Jane Todd, dau. of Andw.
(property in Charleston); bro. Andrew Todd and his three daus.
Mary, Lititia and Margaret. Saml. B. Lewers, exr. Wit: Henry
C. Young, A. Barksdale and R. F. Simpson.

16 July 1825. Appraisal of estate of ANDREW MC KNIGHT, dec'd
by James Durrah, Abraham Bolt and Bailey Mahon.

4 July 1825. Partition/Ex Parte Joseph Babb and Mary his wife.
Martin Miller and Solomon Fuller, free holders, on est. of WM.
GLENN, dec'd. Land to be sold by Sheriff 1st Mon. Dec. next.

18 July 1825. Protest by heirs of REBECCA DIAL, dec'd, Isaac
Dial and Robt. McKees, exrs. for probate. Robt. McKees renounces
ex'ship. 16 Apr. 1825. Will of REBECAH DIAL. Son James Dial;
sons-in-law: Mabury Madden, Abraham Madden, John Moodie, James
Johnson and his issue by Rebecca (Dial) Johnson; grand-daughter
Rebecca Johnson; son Isaac Dial. Wit: Saml. H. Lockhart and
David Helms.

5 Sept. 1825. Will of SOLOMON LANGSTON, dec'd proven. Will of
SOLOMON LANGSTON. 25 Feb. 1810. Sons Henry Langston, Solomon
Langston, Jr. (land in Greenville Dist.), Bennett Langston (land
pur. from Wm. Cooper, Jr.); wife Sarah Langston; daughters Amy
Christopher, Leodocia Springfield; Patty Jones; Mary Holder;
daughters Sarah Miller and Selah Styles. Sons Henry and Solomon

SOLOMON LANGSTON will cont'd:
exrs. Wit: John Hitch, John Styles and Bazil Wheat. 1 Sept.
1825. Appraisal of estate of SOLOMON LANGSTON, dec'd by Solomon
Smith, Robt. Cunningham and James Harlan.

2 July 1825. Sale Bill of negroes left by HASTING DIAL, dec'd
to his wife Rebecca Dial. Isaac Dial, exr.

(No date) Appraisal of estate of REBECCA DIAL, dec'd by Chas.
Irby, Wm. Strain and David Helms. Sale Bill. Pur.: Elizabeth
McKnight, A. Nixon, J. Armstrong, Wm. Thomas, James McKnight,
Andw. McKnight.

17 Oct. 1825. Adm. of estate of ISABELLA HUNTER, dec'd to Andw.
Park and James Park, Jr. Sur.: Richd. F. Simpson and Wm. Winder
Hitch. 22 Oct. 1825. Appraisal by Andw. Spears, Wm. H. Fulton,
Joel Allen and Chas. Williams.

15 Aug. 1825. Adm. of estate of TIMOTHY COCKRAN, dec'd to Thos.
F. Jones. Sur.: Jno. Dunlap and Abner Crenshaw. 30 Sept. 1825.
Appraisal of est. by Wm. Irby (other two names not clear). 3
Oct. 1825. Sale Bill. Pur.: Harvey Cleavland, Jno. Lockhart,
Jno. L. Harris, Lane Posey, Jno. Coats, James Williamson, Joel
Tucker, Foster? Golding, James Watkins, Jno. McCarty, Saml.
Mason, James Brown.

17 Oct. 1825. Adm. of estate of JOHN W. MOTES, dec'd to Jesse
Motes. Sur.: Wm. Coleman and Jno. Kelly.

7 Nov. 1825. Adm. of estate of JACOB NEIGHBOURS, dec'd to John
Neighbours. Sur.: Solomon Gooden and Presley Owens. 10 Nov.
1825. Appraisal of estate by Joel Allen, Chas. Williams, Wm.
Franks and Solomon Gooden.

(No date) Sale Bill of estate of SOLOMON LANGSTON, dec'd. Pur.:
Henry Langston, Ephraim Christopher, Richard Starns, Hugh Toland,
Moses Leek, Wm. H. Fulton, Wm. Murphy, Saml. Langston, Harvest
Miller, Wheet Miller, Sarah Miller, Thos. Springfield, Saml.
Stiles, James Couch, Basil Wheat, John Stewart, Gabriel B. Styles,
Thos. Craig, Thos. Strain, James Campbell, Harvy Miller, Aaron
Starnes, Geo. Ross, Wm. Murphy, Joshua Smith, Dr. George Ross,
James Harlon, Sarah Word, Saml. Dillard, Archibald Sloan, James
Langston, Richd. Farrow. Henry Langston, exr.

14 Nov. 1825. Adm. of estate of WILLIAM COLLINS, dec'd to Moses
Hughs and Isaac Hughs. Sur.: Moses Holcomb and Wm. Meador.

5 Dec. 1825. Adm. of estate of GEORGE ROSS, dec'd to Abner Crenshaw. Sur.: Robt. Creswell and Wm. D. Downs.

23 Nov. 1825. Will of JAMES PARK, SR., dec'd proven. 11 Nov.
1825. Will of JAMES PARK, SR. Wife Rachael; land granted to
dec'd by Andrew Park; wife now pregnant; sons: Robt. Hunter,
Mathew Brown and Thomas Porter; land bought of Saml. Taylor;
land bought of David Spears; W. Simpson; son John Park; land
of John Blakely, Jno. Bealy; son William Park; son Andrew Park;
son-in-law Andrew Park; my children: James, William and Andrew
Park; son-in-law Andw. Park and wife Isabel, Robt. Hunter, Mathw.
Brown, and Jane Elizabeth Park; Mr. Farrow. Wife and son James,
and son-in-law Andw. Park, exr. Wit: Andw. Kennedy, Jas. Park,
Jr., Wm. Fulton, Jane Brown and Andw. Speary.
(N. B. both son and son-in-law named Andrew Park.)

5 Dec. 1825. Adm. of estate of MAREY LINVILLE, dec'd to Even Linville. Sur.: Jno. Brown and Jno. Jones.

23 Oct. 1825. Adm. of estate of WILLIAM BOULAND, dec'd to Geo. Bowen. Sur.: J. Finley and Jno. Look.

4 July 1825. Adm. of estate of JOSIAH PRATER, dec'd to Mathew McCrary. Sur.: Henry C. Burns and Perry ____. 28 July 1825. Sale Bill. 27 July 1825. Appraisal of estate. Note on Jno. Mc-Crary, dec'd; Abram Holland; acct against Francina Prater. Henry C. Burns, Geo. Young, Jr. and King Prater, Sr., apprs.

19 Dec. 1825. Adm. of estate of JOSEPH REMAGE, dec'd to Jno. Remage. Sur.: Wm. Scott and Geo. Dill.

5 Dec. 1825. Adm. of estate of BENJAMIN JAMES, dec'd to Jno. S. James. Sur.: Jno. Garlington and Jno. Dunlap.

19 Dec. 1825. Adm. of estate of PATRICK J.? NOLEND, dec'd to Wm. Abrams. Sur.: Thos. Abrams, Jos. Abrams and Benijah Neel.

14 Nov. 1825. Adm. of estate of WILLIAM COLLINS, dec'd to Moses Hughs and Isaac Hughs. Sur.: Moses Holcomb and Wm. Meador. 19 Nov. 1825. Appraisal of estate by Hartwell Lester, Nathl. Parks and Hosa Holcomb. 28 Dec. 1825. Sale Bill.

27 Aug. 1825. Adm. of estate of BERRY WEST, dec'd to Jno. West. Sur.: Zachariah Arnold and Elihu Watson. 8 & 9 Sept. 1825. App. remaining property. (widow's beds and furniture included) by Lewis and Jno. Watson and Wm. Moore. Sale Bill. Pur.: Jno. Adams, Jno. Graham, Geo. Cowen, Wm. Norman, Jacob Huse, Wm. Crocker, Wm. Flen, Wm. P. Gains, Zach. Arnold, Judy West, Elihu Watson, Lewis Watson, Jacob Nabours, Wm. Moore, Riley Milum, Geo. Warren, L. D. Macpharlon, R. Powel, Wm. West, Wm. Reddon, Jno. Gethard, Zach. Taylor; 16 Sept. 1825. Sale cont'd: Notes: Jno. Addams, Wm. West, Hutson Butler, Wm. Flen, James McFerson, Benj. GArner. 11 Nov. 1825. Sale cont'd: Pur.: Jno. Smith, Zachariah Arnold.

17 Oct. 1825. Adm. of estate of JOHN W. MOTES, dec'd to Jesse Motes. Sur.: Wm. Coleman and Jno. Snelley. 1 Nov. 1825. Appraisal of estate by Wm. Coleman, Richd. Golding and Solomon Fuller. 1 Nov. 1825. Sale Bill. Pur.: Wm. Motes, Silas Motes; Notes due: Asa Chandler, Francis F. Dendy, Peter Fuller, Jones Fuller, Joshua Skerlock, Jno. Bailey, Ranson Davenport, Dendy Motes.

12 Dec. 1825. Adm. of estate of WILLIAM WHITEHEAD, dec'd to Martin Shaw. Sur.: Geo. Bowen and Jos. Neely.

3 Oct. 1825. Return of Hasting D. Johnson, guardian of Rebecca Johnson, minor. Rec'd of Isaac Dial, exr. of Rebecca Dial, dec'd. 14 Nov. 1825. Part of est. to be sold.

24 Nov. 1825. Sale Bill of estate of JACOB NABORS, dec'd. Pur.: Jno. Garret, Reuben Putnam, Presley Owens, Jno. Franks, Stephen Garrett, Chas. Allen, B. L. Posey, Jno. Cowan, Nathl. Barksdale, Wm. Bowen, Ellis Cheek, Jno. Harris, Chas. Baty, Lydall Williams, Robt. Spence, Gideon Owens, Levi Shockley, Salathiel Shockley, Jno. S. Cox, Starling Goodman, Nancy Powers, Robt. Fleming, Robt. Franks, Alex. Powers, Jno. S. Hutchinson, Jno. McClintock, Reuben Martin, Peter Pool, Wm. Hunter, Wm. McCrary, Thos. Crooks, Jno. Powers, Wm. Nabors, Abner Knight, Joseph

NABORS cont'd:
Person, Roberson Mosley, Wm. Parks, Elizabeth Nabors, Rebecca
Nabors, Wm. Powers, Joel Allen.

(No date) Sale Bill of estate of SARAH FOWLER, dec'd. Pur.:
Peter Fuller, Danl. Winn, Jno. Davis, James Goodman, Stephen
Lines, Alsey Fuller, Alex. Austin, B. Lane Posey, James Fuller,
Thos. C. Reeder, Dr. Watson, Joshua Teague, H. Chesher, Bleu-
ford F. Griffin, Wm. Smith, Robt. Coleman, Hutchison Whitter,
Alsey Fuller, Jr., Robt. Milam, Barach Ducket, Jno. Black, An-
thony Leak, Jno. Williams, Wm. Cauder, James Austin, Jno. Odell,
Jacob Miller, Wm. Wright, Jno. H. Davis, Wm. Parkson, Thos.
Rodgers, Thos. Fowler Lively, Thos. Ducket, Jno. Armstrong,
Joel Tucker, Dr. Robt. Monroe, Franklin Williams, Henry Pasley
Beck, Ac. Duke Jones, Isham Fuller, Saml. Rodgers, Jno. Drake,
James Wright, Richd. Owens, Nancy Jones.

2 Jan. 1825. Adm. estate of MICHAEL DUNLAP, dec'd to William
Park. 10 Jan. 1825. Appraisal of estate by James Park, Jr.,
W. W. Hitch and J. E. Hutchinson.

8 ___ 1825. Appraisal of estate of SAMUEL HENDERSON, dec'd by
Joshua Teague, Robt. S. Abell and Elijah Teague. 8 ___ 1825.
Sale Bill. Pur.: Wm. Henderson, Thos. Ligon, Martin Miller,
Stephen Potter, Saml. Farrow, Joshua Franks, Jno. Millner, Jas.
Henderson, Joshua Teague. James Young, exr.

25 Oct. 1825. Appraisal of estate of WILLIAM BOWLAN, dec'd by
(page very faded). 11 Nov. 1825. Sale Bill. Pur.: Mrs. Bowlan,
Geo. Funk, Alsey Fuller, Geo. Anderson, David Anderson, Richd.
Golding, Bartlett Brooks, Jr.?, Wm. Moats, Wade Pucket, Jr.,
Hanna Hendrick, Geo. Bowen, Silas Moats. Geo. Bowen, adm.

5 Jan. 1826. Sale Bill estate of ISABELLA HUNTER, dec'd. Pur.:
A. Simpson, H. Crook, Capt. A. Park, B. Milam, Capt. J. Park,
W. Park, Jr., J. Park, R. Spence, M. H. Henry, N. Park, W. W.
Watts, J. Templeton, J. Blakely, W. Blakely, W. Speers, B. L.
Posey, W. Taylor, J. Smith, G. McKitrick, W. Templeton, D. Mar-
tin, M. H. Fulton, W. Brown, T. Blakely, R. Taylor, J. S. Hutch-
ison, S. Nugant, R. Cunningham, C. Smith, Thos. Davis, R. Slone,
T. Slone, L. Williams, J. E. Hutchinson, James Park, Jr. and
Capt. Andw. Park, adm.

5 Dec. 1825. Adm. of estate of MRS. MARY LINVILLE, dec'd to
Evan Linville. Sur.: Jno. Brown and Jno. Jones. 26 Dec. 1825.
Appraisal of estate by Wm. Lofton, Jno. Jones and Danl. Lofton.
Sale Bill. Pur.: Wm. Linville, Jno. Smith, Jno. Brown, Evan
Linville, Silvey Linville, Jno. Linville, Jno. Barksdale, David
Mason, Abner Young, Jeremiah Stark, Jno. Murphey, Ezekiel John-
son, Jno. Dean, Leven? Stewart, Wm. Abernathy, Humphrey Lindsey,
Jno. Johnson. Notes on: Jno. Linville, James Boyd, James Cannon,
James Murphey, James Entrakin, Providence Williams, Evan Lin-
ville.

2 Jan. 1826. Adm. of estate of JOSEPH JONES, dec'd to ---- Whitmore. 10 Jan. 1826. Appraisal of estate by King Prater, Jos.
Dines? and Wm. Dillard. (N. B. also dated 10 Feb. 1826.) An
acc't on Jno. Green. 18-19 Jan. 1826. Sale Bill. No pur. named.

20 Jan. 1826. Sale Bill estate of MICHAEL DUNLAP, dec'd. Pur.:
Jno. Byrd, Jno. Templeton, Jos. Templeton, Capt. A. Park, Rebecca
Dunlap, James Glenn, C. Williams, Elizabeth Glenn, W. W. Watts,

174

DUNLAP cont'd:
Hugh Crook, James Park, Jr. William Park, adm. Note on Andrew Park.

(---) Receipts given Francina Prater for money paid by her for land, assigned her belonging to the estate of JOSIAH PRATER, dec'd. 14 Mar. 1828, signed Joseph Garrett; 2 Feb. 1829, signed W. E. Lynch; 4 Feb. 1828, signed W. E. Lynch; 14 Mar. 1828 signed Jno. Boyce; 10 Oct. 1828 signed Matthew McCrary, Luke and Sarah Wesson; 17 Feb. 1829 signed Matthew McCrary, Margaret and Wm. King, Jr.; 17 Mar. 1828 signed W. E. Lynch; 18 Dec. 1829 signed Henry S. Neel, Martha Prater and King Prater, Jr. For Mrs. Sinah Prater and her daughter Ruth Prater, dec'd. 6 Mar. 1830. Alfred Kern (Jno. F. Kern, Jr. & Co.). Jno. Whitmire, J.P.

16 Aug. 1828. Estate of MISS RUTHY PRATER, dec'd to Thos. Young.

END OF BOOK

VOLUME F

2 Jan. 1826. John Bouland, minor about 19 years, chose Samuel Dillard guardian. Wm. Scott and Isaac Jacks, sur.

2 Jan. 1826. Adm. of estate of JOSEPH JONES, dec'd to John Whitmore. Joseph Dunkin and Nathan Fowler, sur.

2 Jan. 1826. Adm. of estate of MITCHEL DUNLAP, dec'd to Wm. Park. James Park and Geo. M. Glenn, sur.

2 Jan. 1826. Adm. of estate of CATHARINE DEEN, dec'd to John Deen. Chas. Fowler and Jno. McClintock, sur.

2 Jan. 1826. Will of ARCHIBALD MC DANIEL, dec'd proven by Turner Richardson and Joel Weathers. Elias Brooks and Jno. Burton renounce being exrs. James Boyd qualified as exr. 5 Oct. 1825. Will of ARCHIBALD MC DANIEL. Beloved wife Margrett Wade McDaniel; son Thomas McDaniel; son Mathew McDaniel; son Joel McDaniel; dau. Elizabeth Moor. Elias Brook, Jno. Burton and James Boyd, exr. Wit: Turner Richardson, Joel Weathers, Polley Strain and James Boyd.

9 Jan. 1826. Adm. of estate of HENRY PITTS, dec'd to John Pitts. Reuben Pitts and John Millam, sur.

4 Feb. 1826. Will of ROBERT CARTER, dec'd proven. 6 Dec. 1825. Will of ROBERT CARTER. Beloved wife Elizabeth "Betsey" Carter; son Robert Carter (Jr.); mentions Joel Pinson's line, Sarah "Salley" Riley's spring, J. W. H. Johnston where he formerly lived, Capt. Cunningham's mill seat; son Richard Carter; dau. Patsey Orsborn, dau. Polley Pickens, son Zimry Carter, son James Carter, dau. Elizabeth Bayley. Zimry, Richard and Robt. Carter, exrs. Wit: Nancy Carter, Margret Pinson and Jonathan Johnston.

6 Feb. 1826. Adm. of estate of ROBERT FLEMING, dec'd to Saml. Fleming. James Hunter and James Fleming, sur.

11 Feb. 1826. Will of JOHN MC CURLEY, dec'd proven. 6 Mar. 1825. Will of JOHN MC CURLEY, planter. Wife Polley McCurley; son George and daus. Nancy Davis and Peggey Shirley; four single daughters (not named); son-in-law ____ Shirley (not otherwise named). Polley McCurley and son George McCurley, exrs. Wit: Lemarus

MC CURLEY cont'd:
Deale, Nathan Sims and Martin Groves.

20 Feb. 1826. Adm. of estate of JOHN ATTOWAY, SR., dec'd to John Attoway, Jr. (Also spelled Attaway). Wm. F. Downs and Joel Allen, sur.

20 Feb. 1826. Adm. of estate of JOHN YOUNG, dec'd to Sarah Young. John Black and Robt. Criswell, sur.

20 Feb. 1826. Adm. of estate of LUDEY PYLES, dec'd to Agatha Pyles. John Black and Robt. Criswell, sur.

20 Feb. 1826. Adm. of estate of EASTER HUNTER, dec'd to Wm. Boyd. Robt. Criswell and David Mason, sur.

20 Feb. 1826. Adm. of estate of THOMAS GREEN, dec'd to William Lord. David Mason and James ____, sur.

20 Feb. 1826. Will & Codicil of DANIEL OSBORNE, dec'd proven. Langston Osborne (also Orsborne), exr. 1 Nov. 1822. Will of DANIEL OSBORNE(ORSBORN), SR. Son Langston; dau. Pheaba Adkins; dau. Polley, wife of John Martin; dau. Edatha, wife of Duke Pinson; land adj. Wm. W. Simpson, Ross Orsborn, Wm. Stone and John Martin; grandson John Pinson; sons Daniel, Ross and William Osborne; dau. Anne, wife of Wm. Martin; dau. Elizabeth; with Langston Osborne, exr. Wit: A. Cranshaw, Franklin Cleveland and John Garlington. 25 Apr. 1823. Codicil. Dau. Willey, wife of Thos. Case. Wit: Jno. Dunlap, Saml. Farrow, Jr. and Addison Pyles.

15 Feb. 1826. Appraisal of estate of JOHN MC CURLEY, dec'd by Lemarus Deale, Jonathan Forgey and Martin Graves(Groves).

12 Jan. 1826. Appraisal of personal estate of HENRY PITTS, dec'd by John Parks, John Pitts and Jones Smith. Shown on 12 Jan. 1826. 24 & 25 Jan. 1826. Sale Bill of goods and chattels, John Pitts, adm. Pur: Frances Beck, James Culberson, Jesse Clardy, John Pitts, Seybourn Jones, Reuben Stephens, James Powell, John Craford, Wm. Clardy, Thos. West, Jno. Smith, Miecas? Brooks, Joshua Pitts, James Smith, Danl. South, Zachariah Taylor, John Cristian, Joseph Wardlaw, Thos. Washington, B. Lane Posey, Robt. Stephens, Thos. Ware, David Simmons, Wm. Cooper, Mrs. Hannah Pitts, A. C. Jones, Dr. Danl. Owens, Isaac Waldrop, Jno. Goggens, Wm. Neel, Reuben Pitts, Nelson Norris, Stephen Devenport, Joshua Garey, Peeler Galahar, Saml. Phifer, Jos. Daniel, Willey Yager, Reuben Powell, Jno. Satewhite, Mrs. Mansfield Owens, Jno. Culberson, Wm. Cunningham, Mrs. Catherine Pinson, David Boyd, Wm. Bradon, Jno. South, Garey Pitts, Geo. Brownlee, Thos. Pitts, Isaac Teague, Richd. Tiere, Henry Pitts, James Simmons, Philip Wate, Jesse Daniel, Reuben Clement, Wm. South, Belton Pitts.

20 Mar. 1826. Adm. of estate of MATHEW CUNNINGHAM, dec'd to James F. Blakely. Thos. Blakely and Robt. Cunningham, sur.

20 Mar. 1826. Adm. of estate of FRANCES GLENN, dec'd to Alexander Glenn and Margret Glenn. James Hutchison and Saml. Hunter, sur.

20 Mar. 1826. Adm. of estate of ELIZABETH WASHINGTON, dec'd to Thomas Washington. Levi Hill and Harey Haisel, sur.

20 Mar. 1826. Probate of will of ROGER BROWN, dec'd. Codicil and will proven. Brexey Brown, exr. 8 Dec. 1818. Will of ROGER BROWN on Dunkins Creek, Laurens Dist. Mention of married children; dau. Elizabeth Gill; daus. Lyda, Anney, Judy, Rebaca, Mary, Feby (Pheby), Matty; sons Jesse, William and Roger; daus. Bexey, Ginney, Peggey, Rachel, Fanney; wife Bexey (also Brexey, who is exr.) Wit: Wm. Adair, Luther Hitch, Sr. and Joseph Hitch. Addendum signed 21 Aug. 1823. Codicil mentions son Jesse and dau. Geney, son Roger. Dated 10 Sept. 1824. Wit: Jos. N. Hitch, Sarah Hitch and Rosannah Hitch.

23 Mar. 1826. Will of WILLIAM BURNSIDE, dec'd proven. 14 Nov. 1803/5? Will written. Mentins: brother Thomas Burnside; father's estate; four youngest sisters: Elizabeth, Martha, Ann Jane and Hannah Burnside. Thos. Burnside and Jno. B. Kennada, exrs. Wit: Wm. Black, James More and James Cook.

10 Mar. 1826. Sale Bill of estate of JOHN MC CURLEY, dec'd by Polley McCurley, adm. Pur.: Andw. Burnside, Jno. Fowler, Asa Forgey, Lamurus Deale, Rachel Milum, Joel Hughs, Chas. Brook, Da___ McFerson, Geo. Shirley, Aron Murphey, Jno. McCan.

2 Mar. 1826. Appraisal of estate of DANIEL OSBORN, SR., dec'd y Thos. Babb, Wm. Stone and Wm. W. Simpson.

(No date) Appraisal of estate of ROBERT CARTER, dec'd by Jonathan Johnston, Wm. Reed and Jno. White. Shown by Richd. and Zimry Carter, exrs.

5 Apr. 1826. Will of JOHN WILSON, dec'd proven. 11 Aug. 1825. Will. Wife Jean Wilson; all my children (not named). Turner Richardson and Robt. Allison, Sr., exrs. Wit: Chaney Stone, James Tood (Todd?) and Jos. A. Lynch.

5? Apr. 1826. Will of ANN G. GORDON, dec'd dated 9 May 1823 proven by Wm. Dunlap, appointed exr. Geo. Gordon, husband of dec'd entered cavit against probate, he had lived seperate and apart from wife Ann; Ann had brought suit in Court of Equity, Laurens Dist. for support and maintanence of herself and children; court so decreed; Wm. Dunlap as trustee. Will of ANN J. GORDON. Daus: Catharine Alexander, Jain Gordon; Charlotte Fulton. Wm. Dunlap, exr. Wit: Joseph Griffin, Wm. Milligan and Sarah E. Saxon.

(No date) Inventory of estate of EASTER HUNTER, dec'd by Wm. Boyd, adm. Notes on: Chas. Simpson and John Felts.

24 Feb. 1826. Appraisal of estate of ROBERT FLEMMING, dec'd by James Flemming, James Hunter, Jno. Hunter and James Taylor. 28 Feb. 1826. Sale Bill. Pur.: Wm. Roberson, Thos. Millender, Elizabeth Fleming. Saml. Fleming, adm.

18 Apr. 1826. Adm. of estate of JAMES PALMORE (PALMER?), dec'd to Henry McCelvey. David Gambell and Wm. Copland, sur.

24 Mar. 1826. Appraisal of estate of RODGER BROWN, dec'd of Laurens Dist. by Thos. Craig, James Farebourn and Moses Leek.

11 Apr. 1826. Appraisal of estate of WILLIAM BURNSIDE, dec'd by Jos. Hollingsworth, Wm. Bryson and James Hollingsworth. Thos. Burnside, exr.

7 Mar. 1826. Appraisal of estate of JOHN ATTAWAY, SR., dec'd by James Hunter, Jr., Chas. Williams, Roberson Mosley and John Deen. John Attaway, Jr., exr.

24 Jan. 1826. Appraisal of estate of CATHARINE DEAN, dec'd by John Hutcheson, Jno. McClintock and James Taylor. 25 Jan. 1826. Sale Bill. Pur.: Jno. S. Hutcheson, Jno. Hutcheson, Jno. Dean, Chas. Fowlar, Mathew Holaday, Jno. Higgens, Elias Cheek, Tucker Higgens, Lydrell Williams, Archebald Stone(Slone?), Jno. Mc-Clintock, Thos. F. Jones, Anna Dean, Thos. Dean, Dr. S. Farrow, Fleming Mosley, Nancy Hutcheson, Nathl. Barksdill, Wm. Cowen, Polley Dean, James Taylor, Wm. Park, Wm. Brown. John Dean, adm.

18 Apr. 1826. Will of ELIJAH TEAGUE, SR., dec'd proven. Will dated 2 Oct. 1824. Division of his land adj. James Boyd, Danl. Mathes, dec'd; four daus: Elizabeth Hipps, Sarah McAdams, Marey Wilson and Catharine McAdams; dau. Rachel Teague; heirs of son Joshua Teague, dec'd; son Robert Teague; son Abner Teague; son -in-law Joseph Hipps. Abner Teague and Jos. Hipps, exrs. Wit: Jno. Millar, Elijah Teague and Chas. McCluskey.

16 Feb. 1826. Appraisal of estate of DR. LUDY PYLES, dec'd by Jno. Black, Abner Pyles and Jno. H. Davis. 9 Mar. 1826. Sale Bill. Pur.: Jno. Black, Jno. H. Davis, David Johnston, Patrick McDarrall(McDowell?), Abner Pyles, Addison Pyles, Thos. Teague, Washington Williams. Agatha Pyles, adm.

5 May 1826. Will of JOHN MATHES, dec'd proven. Will dated 27 Jan. 1826. Wife Hettey; land adj. David Garry, Jesse Garrett and Arnold Milener; dau. Polley Mathes; dau. Salley Garrett. Hetty Mathes and Jesse Garrett, Jr., exrs. Wit: Jno. Bolt, A. Milener, James Parker and Asa Garrett.

7 Apr. 1826. Appraisal of estate of ARCHEBALD MC DANIEL, dec'd by Gabriel Thomas, Jno. Burton and Benj. Williams.

3 Mar. 1826. Appraisal of estate of ELIZABETH WASHINGTON, dec'd by Levi Hill, Geo. Gowell and Henry Hazlet. Thos. Washington, adm. 4 Apr. 1826. Sale Bill. Pur.: Jos. South, Jos. Daniel, Geo. Washington, Wm. Savage, Jno. Cristian, Jas. McClurken, Thos. Washington, David M'Collough, Hirum Clark, Jesse Clardy, Philip Wait, Mrs. Elizabeth Wadkins, Elias Brook, Benj. F. Tiree, Zimry Madden, Saml. Hall, Wm. Cooper, Jno. Smith, Wm. More, Wm. Henderson. Notes on: Robt. and Timothy Stevens, Jno. Pope.

10 Apr. 1826. Appraisal of estate of MATHEW CUNNINGHAM, dec'd by Robt. Cunningham, Robt. and Thos. Blakely. 12 Apr. 1826. Sale Bill. Pur.: Thos. Blakely, Polley Cunningham, James Burk, James Blakely, Wm. Fulton, Robt. Blakely, James Devaul, Jno. Blakely, Robt. Cunningham, Jno. Young, Robt. Hutcheson, Thos. Fulton, Andw. Park, Mathew Blakely, Robt. H. Littel, Wm. Taylor, Archebald Smith, James Parks. Book acct's on: Jno. Higens, Joshua Smith, Jno. Craig, Elizabeth Holcomb, Hugh Fowler, Jno. Lean?, Geo. P'Pool, James Langston, Jno. H. Horling, Edmond Cradock, Persila Martin, Robt. Hannah. James F. Blakely, adm.

5 May 1826. Appraisal of estate of ANN G. GORDON, dec'd by Benj. Byrd, David Templeton and Walter Stuart. Wm. Dunlap, exr. Note on Thos. Fulton.

10 May 1826. Appraisal of estate of JOHN MATHES (MATHIS), dec'd by Saml. Downs, Jno. Babb, Jr., James Garrett, Sr. and Thos.

MATHES cont'd: Packer.

4 Apr. 1826. Appraisal of estate of FRANCES GLENN, dec'd by
James Hutcheson, Chas. Smith and Jno. McClintock. 6 Apr. 1826.
Sale Bill. Pur. not named. Alexander and Margret Glenn, adm.

15 May 1826. Adm. of estate of JOHN MC DOWALL, dec'd to Wm.
Templeton. John and James Templeton, sur.

5 June 1826. Will of ALEXANDER GLENN, dec'd proven. Will dated
5 Jan. 1826. Dau. Nancy L.? Rice and her children. Dr. Hezekiah
Rice, James Young and Richd. F. Simpson, exrs. Wit: Langsdon
East, James Craford and James Young.

21 May 1826. Adm. of estate of BURGUET (BURKET) DEVENPORT, dec'd
to Peggey Devenport. Thos. Lockhart and Jonathan Forgay, sur.

28 Apr. 1826. Appraisal of estate of ELIJAH TEAGUE, dec'd by
Jno. Millar, Jno. Hewit and Elijah Teague. 19 May 1826. Sale
Bill. Abner Teague, exr.

19 June 1826. Will of WILLIAM MC CRADY, dec'd proven. Will dated
3 May 1826. Son James McCrady; Jane McCrady, Morgan McCrady
and Caroline McCrady children of my son John McCrady; beloved
wife Mary; son Robt. Carter McCrady. Wife and son Robt. C. Mc-
Crady, exrs. Wit: Wm. Fullar, Alsey Fullar and Geo. Nickle.

22 June 1826. Adm. of estate of PATSEY MENG, dec'd to Clough
S. Meng. Edw. Hix and Jno. Dunlap, sur.

22 June 1826. Adm. of estate of THOMAS JONES, dec'd to Jonathan
Jones. Thos. Garrett and Jno. Garrett, sur.

8 Apr. 1826. Appraisal of estate of JAMES PALMER, dec'd by Wm.
Gambell, Reuben Meaders and James Adair. 15 May 1826. Sale Bill.

2 Mar. 1826. Appraisal of estate of THOMAS GREEN, dec'd by James
Boyd, Jno. Barksdill, Jno. Brown and Abel Johnston. 4 Mar. 1826.
Sale Bill. Wm. Lord, adm.

(No date) Sale Bill estate of JOHN MATHES, dec'd. Pur.: Jno.
Belt, Jr., Saml. Downs, Jesse Garrett, Edw. H. Garrett, Asa
Garrett, Ambrose Hugins, Ambrose Hugins, Jr., David Martin,
Betsey Rowling. Betsey F. Mathes and Jesse Garrett, adm.

15 Mar. 1826. Appraisal of estate of JOHN YOUNG, dec'd by Jno.
Black, James Young and Abner Pylkes. App. of property given
to his son-in-law Martin Garey, married to dau. Eliza. 29 Apr.
1826. App. of est. given to his son Washington Young. 16 Mar.
1826. Sale Bill (no date and no pur. named). Notes due on Jno.
and Wm. Black, Jos. Blakely, Jonathan Goggins, Capt. Wm. Perkins,
Jno. Simpson, Jno. Godfrey, Elijah Teague, Wm. Abernathy, Geo.
Johnston, Wm. Green, Abner Teague, Robt. Monroe, Jno. Millar,
Langston East, Andw Monroe, Jno. Davis, Robt. Case, Joshua Teague,
Wm. G. Wright, James H. Lowery, Lewis Dalrymple, Jno. B. Stan-
ley, Jno. Saxon, David Jones, Robt. Stuart, Wm. Winn, Wm. Mixson,
Thos. Enterkin, Wm. Neel, Jno. Moreh, Robt. Monroe, Saml. Neel,
Geo. Teague, Ludy Pyles, Milsford Wilson, Jno. Drake, Joshua
Wilson, Nathl. McCay, Sr., Jane Tygart, Jno. Tygart, Geo. John-
ston, Jno. Clopton, Sylvanus Wallis. Sarah Young, adm.

9 Mar. 1826. Sale Bill of estate of JOHN ATTAWAY, dec'd (also

ATTAWAY cont'd:
spelled Allaway in the records), John Attaway, Jr., adm. Pur.:
Mrs. Attaway, Jno. Attaway, Chesley Attaway, Robt. Franks, Isaac
Attaway, Solomon Goodwin, Clopton Roads, Roberson Mosley, Jno.
Tood (Todd?), Jno. Deen, Wm. Right, Jno. Todd, Jr., Jno. Mc-
Clintock, Jno. Brown, Elias Cheek, Jno. Taylor, Jno. Millar,
Danl. Roberson, Robt. Cooper, Joel Allen, James Taylor, James
Park, Jesse Attaway, Saml. Mills, Bryant Parsons, Wm. Terry,
Jno. Terry, Robt. Crocker, Saml. Hunter, Burns Crow?, Hamton
Parsons.

3 July 1826. Adm. of estate of PERIDON DANIEL KERN, dec'd to
Jno. F. Kern. John ??? Kern and Jno. Dunlap, sur.

13 June 1826. Appraisal of estate of JOHN WILLSON, dec'd by
Robt. Holiday, James Brown and James Blakely. Turner Richardson and Robt. Alison, exrs.

24 July 1826. Appraisal of estate of WILLIAM MC CRADA, dec'd
by Alsey Fuller, Geo. Nickle and James Nickle. (also McCrady).

7 July 1826. Appraisal of estate of ALEXANDER GLENN, dec'd by
James Young, Wm. Dunlap and James Craford. Dr. Hezekiah Rice
(also Rise), exr.

29 May 1826. Appraisal of estate of BURKET DEVENPORT, dec'd
by Jonathan Forgey, Martin Groves(Graves?) and Nathan Sims.
Peggey Devenport, adm. 15 June 1826. Sale of part of the estate
of Burguet Devenport, dec'd. Pur.: David Anderson, Chas. Brook,
Chas. Devenport, Hosten Madden, Jr., Nathan Sims, Peggey Devenport, James Scott, Wm. Brire, Hoisten Madden.

5 July 1826. Appraisal of estate of THOMAS JONES, dec'd by Hosa
Holcomb, Benj. Griffith and D. F. Allgood.

22 July 1826. Adm. of estate of JAMES JONES, dec'd to James
Crocker. John Watson and Benj. Watson, sur.

7 Aug. 1826. Will of SUSANAH MEADORS, dec'd proven. Will dated
18 July 1823. Son Reuben; grand-dau. Anne Meadors, dau. of son
Reuben; sons Jason and John Meadors; dau. Ann Saxon, wife of
James Saxon, Esq. Reuben Meadors, exr. Wit: Washington Meadors,
James Bryson and Wm. Fulton.

7 July 1826. Adm. of estate of ARCHE FARLEY, dec'd to Wm. R.
Farley. James Irby, David P. Saxon and Jno. Dunlap, sur.

(No date) Appraisal of estate of JOHN MC DOWELL, dec'd by James
McDowell, James Williamson and Wolf Benjamin. 2 June 1826. Sale
Bill. Wm. Templeton, adm.

7 Aug. 1826. Polley Prater, about 18 years, Nelley Prater, about
13 years and Price Prater, about 16 years, chose James Adair,
guardian. David Mason and John Leek, sur.

19 Aug. 1826. Will of CHARLES NICKLE (NICHEL), dec'd proven.
Will dated 12 Sept. 1818. Beloved wife Anney Nickles (8 youngest
children to live with their mother); 4 sons-Geo. William, Turner
and Thomas; 4 daus.-Ginna, Betsey, Neomiah and Salley; son John;
dau. Margrett; son Robert; dau. Catharine; son James; and dau.
Polley. James McMahon and Jos. Hollingsworth, exrs. Wit: James,
Joseph & Wm. Hollingsworth.

180

21 Aug. 1826. Adm. of estate of JOHN O. RODGERS, dec'd to Thomas Duckett, Sr. John Odle and Thomas Duckett, Jr., sur.

21 Aug. 1826. Adm. of estate of WHEATE MILLER, dec'd to Jno. Leek. Armstead Leek and Wm. Neill, sur.

27 July 1826. Appraisal of estate of PERIDON DANIEL KIERN(KERN), dec'd by Jno. Boyce, Benj. Bird and Robt. Owens. Jno. F. Kern, Jr., adm.

7 Aug. 1826. Adm. of estate (will annexed) of JAMES MEADORS, dec'd to Reuben Meadors. Washington Meadors and John Meadors, sur.

9 Sept. 1826. Appraisal of estate of CHARLES NICKLE, dec'd by Alsey Fuller, Geo. Funk and Geo. Holdridge.

7 Sept. 1826. Will of JOSEPH JONES, dec'd proven. Will dated 21 July 1826. Names Nancey and John Watson; son Joseph (Jr.); grandson Leander Dunkin; son John Jones (sum of $1.00 only); John Watson's children. Joseph Jones and Jno. Watson, exrs. Wit: Benj. Duckett, Wm. Duckett and Geo. Smith.

16 Sept. 1826. Inv. of personal estate of WILLIAM WHITEHEAD, dec'd by Martin Shaw, adm....virtue of sd adm. of Chas. Nickle, exr. of Wm. Whitehead, Sr., dec'd the sum of $35.03½...do not know of any other property.

18 Sept. 1826. Adm. of estate of GREEN LEE B. CAMPBELL, dec'd to Benj. Griffith. Henry C. Young and Joel Allen, sur.

7 Aug. 1826. Adm. of estate of DAVID COWEN, dec'd to Leila Cowen. Wm. Garrett and Saml. Parsons, sur.

6 Sept. 1826. Appraisal of estate of JAMES JONES, dec'd by James Anderson, Zebalon Savage and Jno. Watson.

4 Sept. 1826. Adm. of estate of MARTHA LUKE, dec'd to John Luke. Saml. Craig and Thos. Craig, sur.

2 Oct. 1826. Will of ENOCH BREAZEAL, dec'd proven. Will dated 10 Apr. 1826. Beloved wife Rutha; beloved dau. Haruntal/Hamulal? Hill; beloved dau. Hulda Johnston; beloved dau. Caroline Brea- zeale; real est in Edgefield and Abbeville Dist; son-in-law Willey Hill; son-in-law Geo. W. Johnston. (Last two exrs.). Wit: Zachariah Bailey, Jr., Tobias Cook and Robt. Campbell.

4? Oct. 1826. Adm. of estate of THOMAS LIGON, dec'd to Wm. Ligon. Saml. Allen, Jno. McGowen and Wm. McGowen, sur.

6 July 1826. 2nd sale bill of estate of JOSIAH EAST, dec'd. Langston East, exr. Sold 1 negro.

14 Oct. 1826. Adm./will annexed, est. of JUDITH MITCHEL, dec'd. Will proven. Mansell Owings with Thos. Washington and Moses Myers, sur. Will dated 31 Mar. 1826. Sons: Thomas Cobb, Charles Cobb, John Cobb; dau. Sucky Wilson; son James Cobb; dau. Susanah Owings. Wit: Jos. Cooper, Richd. Gains and Temple M.? Cooper.

16 Oct. 1826. Will of THOMAS BURNSIDE, dec'd proven. Will dated 7 May 1826. Four youngest sisters - Elizabeth, Martha, Ann Jane and Hannah Burnside; nephew Thomas Burnside, son of Andrew Burn-

side. James Hollingsworth and nephew Thomas Burnside (son of Andrew), exrs. Wit: James Young, Marey Burnside & Andw. Rodgers.

16 Oct. 1826. Adm. of estate of JAMES IRBY, dec'd to Charles Irby. Jno. Dunlap and Wm. Irby, Jr., sur.

14 Oct. 1826. Will of EPHRAIM KNIGHT, dec'd proven. Wm. Knight, exr. Will dated 27 Jan. 1826. Sons William and Ephraim Knight; Lucinda Knight; wife; daus. Polly Joel and Lucinda Knight. Wit: James Hill, Levi Hill and Joseph Pollerd.

16 Oct. 1826. Will of JOHN COPLAND, dec'd. Not enough witnesses signed and could not be admitted to be proven. James Copland took oath as adm. Saml. Copland and Jno. Copland, sur.

8 Aug. 1826. Inv. of property of JAMES MEADORS, dec'd by Wm. Blakely, Wm. Blakely, Sr. and Saml. Vance. 25 Aug. 1826. Sale Bill. Reuben Meadors, adm.

8 Aug. 1826. Inv. of property of SUSANAH MEADORS, dec'd by same as above. 25 Aug. 1826. Sale Bill. Same exrs./adm. as above.

6 Nov. Adm. of estate of DAVID COWEN, dec'd to James Cowen. Drury Boyce and Joel Allen, sur.

1 Nov. 1826. Adm. of estate of ROBERT HOLLINGSWORTH, dec'd to Wm. Ligon. Burell Leak and Jno. McWilliams, sur.

14 Oct. 1826. Adm. of estate of JONES FULLAR, dec'd to Morton Millar. Wm. Purkison and Israel Fullar, sur.

2 Nov. 1826. Adm. of estate of JOHN BELL, dec'd to Zachariah Sparks. Jos. McConathy and Washington Meadors, sur.

6 Nov. 1826. Adm. of estate of GEORGE DILLARD, dec'd to Saml. Dillard. Nathan Harris and James Burk, sur.

14 Oct. 1826. William A. Fullar, minor about 15 years, chose Martin Millar guardian. Wm. Purkison and Israel Fullar, sur.

23 Sept. 1826. Appraisal of estate of MARTHA LUKE, dec'd by John Adair, Thos. Craig and B. Burket. Jno. Luke, adm.

16 Sept. 1826. Appraisal of estate of JOSEPH JONES, dec'd by Berrey Jeanes, Geo. Young, Jr. and Joseph Dunkin. (N. B. Jones is also spelled Jeanes). 22 Sept. 1826. Sale Bill. Jos. Jeanes and Jno. Watson, exrs. Wit: Wm. E. Lynch.

14 Oct. 1826. Estate of JAMES BAILEY, dec'd. Silus Bailey, James M. Bailey and Benj. Brown named exrs. of will. Brown renounces; will proven. Will dated 19 Jan. 1826. Beloved wife; children: William Bailey, Zachariah Bailey, Polley Brown, Salley Dunkin, James Bailey, Silus M. Bailey, Winneford Bailey, Betsy Bailey and Leviney Bailey; son William's children - Beath?, Maddison, Susana and James Bailey. Benj. Brown, James Bailey and Silus M. Bailey, exrs. Wit: Jno. Sneed, James Nickels, Jr. and Wm. Bailey.

14 Nov. 1826. Will of CATHARINE ROSS, dec'd proven. Will dated 11 Oct. 1826. Daus. Jane, Elizabeth and Sarah; sons John, James, Francis. Son-in-law Wm. Cowan and Francis Ross, exrs. Wit: Alex-

ROSS cont'd:
ander Mills, Sr., Samuel Fleming and James Mills.

14 Nov. 1826. Will of WILLIAM HOLIDAY, dec'd proven. Will dated
12 Jan. 1822. Beloved wife Jenney; sons William, Robert and
Mathew; daus. Nancy Russel and Margret Holiday; Polley Mulanahon
wife of James Mulenahan (also spelled Mehanahan - McClanahan?).
Wife and son Robt., exrs. Wit: Philip Weit?, Thos. Hood and
Redah Weit.

14 Nov. 1826. Will of WILLIAM YOUNG, dec'd proven. Will dated
21 Feb. 1826. Wife Rachel; sons John and James Young and their
children; grandson John Coinne and his mother, my daughter,
Agnes Conine; grandchildren John and James Young, sons of my
son John Young and their older bro. Washington Young; Nancy
Vaughan (an inmatee of my family). James Young, exr. Wit: Jno.
Black, Sarah Young and James Crawford.

14 Nov. 1826. Will of MANOAH ROBERTSON, dec'd proven. Will dated
31 July 1826. Wife Milly; sons Vinson and Reuben; dau. Peggey;
dau. Milley; older children: Jane Moore, John Robertson, Ludy
Gantt. Wife and son Reuben, exrs. Wit: Wm. Owings, J. Moore
and Folver(Fowler?) Robertson.

19 Sept. 1826. 2nd appraisal of estate of PERIDON D. KERN, dec'd
by Jno. Boyce, Robt. Owens and Benj. Byrd. 19 Sept. 1826. Sale
Bill. Pur.: Thos. Fulton, Jr., Andw. Starns, Robt. Owens, Benj.
Byrd, Jno. Davis, Robt. Pitts, Saml and Thos. Craig, Richd.
Turner, Ephraim Pitts, Wm. Pucket, Simpson Alexander, Lewis
Craig, Richd. Farrow, Robt. Pucket, Davis Fowlar, Jno. Adair,
Robt. Gilland, Jas. Blakely, Jno. Mehan, James Dillard, Jno.
L. Kerm, Sr., Jno. Blakely, Wm. Dillard, Jno. F. Kern, Sr.,
Wm. Alexander, Danl. Hirum Craig, Danl. Starns, Sarah Kern,
Jno. Cargill, Andw. Starns, Jesse Alexander, Jno. Boyce, Wm.
Smith, James Fulton, Thos. Gor, Enoch Pyles, Joshua Saxon, Wm.
Fulton, Jno. F. Kern, James Rains, Jos. Garrett, Thos. Fulton,
Martin Lambling, Henry Millar, Wm. Braston Lambling, Samson
Alexander, Robt. Cunningham, Jno. Lester, Saml. Horsting, Salla-
mon Duke, Jno. Templeton, Sarah P. Kern. J. F. Kern, adm.

11 Nov. 1826. Appraisal of estate of JOHN O. RODGERS, dec'd
by Jos. Duckett, Branch Odell and Jno. Watson. Appr'd on 8 Sept.
1826. Sale Bill. 8 Sept. 1826. Pur.: Margret Duncan, Branch
Odle, March Oddle, Geo. Duckett, Joshua Davis, Joseph Duckett,
Jesse Jones Weson (Weason), Thos. Duckett, Jos. Duncan, James
D. Sims, Rignal Williams, James Duckett, Wm. Odle, Wm. Dunken,
Josah Dunken, Jno. Snelgrove, Wm. Dillard, Benj. Duckett, Jacob
Duckett, Jeremiah Philips, Joshua Hendrick, March Dunken, Wm.
Whitmore, Jos. Shelton, Jno. A. Casey, Jno. Helthan, Henry Boozer
and Thos. Hendrick. Thos. Duckett, adm.

14 Nov. 1826. Adm. of estate of WILLIAM HUTCHISON, dec'd to
James Templeton and Wm. Hutchison. Jno. McClintock and Chas.
Smith, sur.

12 Oct. 1826. Appraisal of estate of GREENLEE B. CAMPBELL, dec'd
by Thos. Crymes, D. F. Allgood and Hosa Holcomb. 12 Oct. 1826.
Sale Bill. Pur.:; Pheabah Campbell, Thos. Campbell, Saml. Woodroff, Jesse Wallis, Andw. Johnston, Nancy Spurgen, Rebecah Campbell, Chas. Cox, Drury Spurgen, Jno. Mosley, Hezekiah Gray,
Benj. Griffith, Jos. Brown, Milla(Milia) Griffith, Isaac Cooper,
Lesley Gray(Garey), Jno. House, James Campbell, Robt. Westmore-

CAMPBELL cont'd:
land, Allen Woodroff, Merit L. Cruggs, Jno. Chappell, Robt.
Campbell, Jno. Clark. Notes on: Wm. Hill, Jno. Cooper, Jesse
Lendore, James Parks, Thos. Campbell, Henry Brackman, Jos. Campbell. Benj. Griffith, adm.

28 Nov. 1826. Will of ALEXANDER AUSTIN, SR., proven. Will dated
18 Sept. 1826. Beloved wife Agnes; children - Alexander, Samuel,
Robert, John, Janet H. and Sarah Austin; dau. Hareata (Harriet?)
Austin; son James; son William; mentions land adj. Elizabeth
Nickles, Crawford's tract; William Whiteford; grandchildren
- David and Agnes Whiteford. James, Alexander and Saml. Austin,
exrs. Wit: Alsey Fuller, John Cook and Franklin Cook.

8 Nov. 1826. Inventory of property of EPHRAIM KNIGHT, dec'd
by Levi Hill and Jno. Watson.

25 Nov. 1826. Adm. of estate of LEWIS DAY, dec'd to John Chappell. John Ball and John R. Watts, sur.

4 Dec. 1826. Adm. of estate of BURGESS MC FERSON, dec'd to Drury
Boyce. Bailey Mahon and James M. Arnold, sur.

22 Nov. 1826. Appraisal of estate of GEORGE DILLARD, dec'd by
Jno. C.? Murrell, Thos. Duckett and Jos. Garrett. 23 Nov. 1826.
Sale Bill. Pur.: Elizabeth Dillard, Thos. Duckett, J. F. Dillard,
D. Felder, F. Foster, J. Kern, J. Dillard, J. Martendill, Wm.
Parson, Jno. Garrett, A. Kay, J. Puckett, J. Boyce, S. Hunt,
J. Burke.

4 Dec. 1826. Adm. of estate of MARY DODD, dec'd to Daniel Felder. Jesse Alexander and Saml. Dillard, sur.

20 Oct. 1826. Appraisal of estate of JAMES IRBY, dec'd by Hugh
Saxon, H. Cleaveland and Wm. Horton.

24 Nov. 1826. Appraisal of estate of MANOAH ROBERTSON, dec'd
by John Atwood, Mark Noble and Isaac D. Garnet.

4 Nov. 1826. BENJAMIN FOSHEE, SR., dec'd. Benj. Foshee, Jr.,
exr. Life estate to SUSANNAH FOSHEE, wife, now dec'd. Est to
be sold.

4 Dec. 1826. Adm. of estate of JAMES CRAIG, dec'd to Thomas
Craig. Moses Leek and Wm. F. Downs, sur.

6 Nov. 1826. Estate of PERIDON D. KERN, dec'd. Jno. F. Kern,
Jr., adm. Notes due est. Abraham Holland, Jno. F. Kern, Sr.
(as J. F. Kern & Sons).

8 Nov. 1826. Estate of DAVID LITTEL, dec'd. Chas. Littel, exr.
Wife CHARITY LITTEL, life estate, dec'd. Est. to be sold.

2 Oct. 1826. Estate of JAMES BROWN, dec'd. Wm. Brown, exr. Life
est. to wife (now dec'd). Est. to be sold.

17 Nov. 1826. Adm. of estate of JONATHAN FORGEY, dec'd to Manoah
Forgey. Asa Forgey and James McFerson, sur.

7 Dec. 1826. Est. of HANNAH ADAIR, dec'd. James Adair, exr.
Wm. L. Beavens and others entered protest of sd will by P. Farrow, his attorney, Wm. F. Downs, Esq. in support of will; adm.

ADAIR cont'd:
granted to James Adair; estate to be sold.

23 Nov. 1826. Appraisal of estate of THOMAS LIGON, dec'd by
Jno. Cook, Joseph Ligon and Jno. McGowan.

13 Oct. 1826. Appraisal of estate of ENOCH BREAZEAL, dec'd by
Danl. Cook, Zachariah Bailey, Jr., and Henry W. Parsley. Willey
Hill and Geo. W. Johnston, exrs.

25 Oct. 1826. Will of HANNAH ADAIR. Grand children: Patsey Gamble
and Jinny Beavers; living children - Elenor Ramage, James Adair,
Hannah Meadors, Susannah Castels, Nancy Langston; Wm. Castels.
James Adair, exr. Wit: Thos. L. Leek, Isham Milam and Susanah
Prater.

13 Dec. 1826. Will of JOHN CRAWFORD, dec'd proven. Jno. Black,
exr. Will dated 4 Aug. 1824. "Considerable afflicted in body"
- sons John and James Crawford. Neighbors and friends Jno. Young
and Jno. Black, exrs. Wit: Geo. Teague, G. W. Young and Danl.
Cargill.

7 Dec. 1826. Appraisal of estate of ROBERT HOLLINGSWORTH, dec'd
by John McGowing, Lewis Ball and Jno. Boyd. Wm. Ligon, adm.

7 Nov. 1826. Sale Bill estate of JAMES BROWN, dec'd. Wm. Brown,
exr. Note due the estate.

21 Nov. 1826. Sale Bill estate of THOMAS LIGON, dec'd. Pur.:
James Austin, Saml. Allen, Jno. Armstrong, Thos. Austin, Henry
Beechum, Danl. Beechum, Geo. Brown, Jno. Collier, Asa Chandler,
Jno. Cook, Thos. Carter, Wm. A. Ligon, Anthony Leek, Wm. Ligon,
Sr. (for Virgil Ligon), F. Woodson Ligon, Susanah Ligon, Jno.
Floyed, Jones Fuller, Thos. Fowler, Isaac Grant, Saml. Goodman,
Anthony Golding, Jno. Gates, Jno. Hitt, Honee Hendrick, Jno.
Jones, Edw. Jones, Jos. Ligon, Thos. Ligon, Burrel Leek, Susan
Ligon, Robt. Malone, Wm. McGowan, Obediah Meshure, Jno. McWil-
liams, Robt. A. Malone, Benj. Malden, Saml. McWilliams, Jos.
S. Owens, Wm. Purkinson, Jno. Philips, Thos. Budd, Geo. Roberts,
Thos. Reeder, Thos. Rodgers, Wm. R. Smith, Richd. Sims, Wm.
Smith, Sr., Wm. Todd, Wm. Tompson, Abraham Tompson, Jno. D.
Williams, Wm. Wright, Alexander Winn, James Wright, Braxton
Watts, Geo. Wright, Elijah Watson, Franklin Williams, Alexander
Austin, Washington Williams, Richd. Golding, Brefort Wells,
Jno. Moor, Jr., Wm. Atwood, Susan Ward, James Long, James A.
Williams. Wm. Ligon, adm.

18 Dec. 1826. Adm. of estate of JANE KELLET, dec'd to Martin
Kellet. Robt. Coker? and Jno. F. Hallams, sur.

7 Dec. 1826. Return of JAMES ADAIR, guardian of minor children
Polley Prater, Rice Prater and Elender Prater. Money rec'd from
Joseph Dollar.

13 Oct. 1826. Appraisal of estate of DAVID COWAN, dec'd by Thos.
Gradon, Jno. Cowan and Plesant Shaw. Also a note on Jno. Simpson.

8 Dec. 1826. Adm. of estate of JOHN DRAKE, dec'd to Wm. Black.
Jno. Black and James Young, sur.

18 Dec. 1826. Adm. of estate of EDMOND CRADOCK, dec'd to Samuel
Farrow. P. Farrow and W. F. Downs, sur.

30 Nov. 1826. Appraisal of estate of THOMAS BURNSIDE, dec'd by Jonathan Hollingsworth, James Young, Saml. Rodgers and Benj. Brown.

22 Dec. 1826. Adm. of estate of FRANCES J. KENION, dec'd to Peter Gallaher. Wm. Bradon and James Simmons, sur.

7 Sept. 1826. Sale Bill estate of JAMES JONES, dec'd. Pur.: James Glover, Geo. Washington, James Watson, Lewis Jones, Wm. Gaines, Thos. Washington, James Grayham, G. D. Madden, Wm. Mc-Clure, Wm. West, Nancy Jones, Cooper Ware, Mary Norman, Jno. Golding, Jno. Adams, Zachariah Taylor, Reuben Powell, James E. Bunton, Levi Hill, James Anderson, Andy Anderson, Elie Jones, Jno. Grimes, Thos. Redden. James Crocker, adm.

12 Dec. 1826. Appraisal of estate of JAMES BAILEY, dec'd by James Hollingsworth, Jno. Young and Wm. Hollingsworth.

29 Dec. 1826. Appraisal of estate of JUDITH MITCHELL, dec'd by R. Powell, Tirel Andress and Mitchel Clardy. 5? Jan. 1827. Sale Bill. Pur.: Thos. Washington, James Franklin, Honey Hazel, Wm. Holaday, James Glover, James E. Glenn. Notes due est.: Martin Wilson, James Wilson, Wiley Dotson, Joseph Neely, Wm. Braden, Thomson S. Glenn. Mensil Owens, exr.

18 Dec. 1826. Inv. estate of DAVID COWAN, dec'd by Thos. Graydon, Plesant Shaw and Stephen Morten.

18 Dec. 1826. Appraisal of estate of MARY DODD, dec'd by Wm. Harris, Thos. Duckett and Jno. F. Kern. 19 Dec. 1826. Sale Bill. Pur.: Widow Betsy Dillard, Saml. Beavours, Danl. Felder, Saml. Hunt, Saml. F. Hunt, Elie Veneburner, Jesse Alexander, Jno. Cargill, Isaac Bagnell, Saml. Dillard, Mrs. Jones, Jno. Dillard, Jno. F. Kern, Burrum Bobo, Cilus Felder. Danl. Felder, adm.

20 Nov. 1826. Appraisal of estate of JOHN BELL, JR., dec'd by Henry S. Neel, Richd. Bonds and Jno. Dillard. 22 Nov. 1826. Sale. Zachariah Sparks, adm.

11 Nov. 1826. Inv. of estate of JOHN COPELAND, dec'd by Wm. Gambell, Henry Hill and John Lyon. James Copeland, adm. 10 Nov. 1826. Sale Bill. Pur.: Margret Copeland, Jesse Johnston, James Littel, Jno. Copeland.

5 Dec. 1826. Appraisal of estate of WILLIAM HOLADAY, dec'd by Thos. Hood, Jno. D. Cunningham and Richd. Blackwell. 14 Nov. 1826. Janney Holaday, exr. gives up property willed to her by dec'd husband, William, it to be sold together with property he died intestate, proceeds divided between herself and children. Wit: Jno. Russel.

22 Nov. 1826. Appraisal of estate of CATHARINE ROSS, dec'd by James Taylor, Stephen Garrett and James Hunter.

(No date) Sale Bill estate of THOMAS JONES, dec'd. Pur.: Edw. Surges (Sturges?), Zach. Westmoreland, Thos. Crymes, Henry Jones, Wm. Jones, Jno. Austin, Saml. Woodruff, Thos. Garrett, Joel Person, Milley Jones, Chas. Cox, Wm. Thaxton, Isaac Wofford, Wm. Johnston, Jno. House, Wm. Wood, Elisha McHue, Jeremiah Howard, Mary Jones, Nathan Pugh, Thos. Parks, James Garrett, Garnet Bramblet, Hosa Holcomb, James Nix, Jno. Westmoreland, Wm. Lyon, Abel Jones, Jno. McNeely, Joseph Brown, Jno. McNeel, Frances

JONES cont'd:
Jones, Abby Brown, legacies rec'd of Josiah Turner, rec'd of
Wm. Haistings. Jonathan Jones, adm.

(No date) Sale Bill estate of JAMES IRBY, dec'd. Pur.: Joshua
Saxon, James Wilson, Robt. Alison, Wm. Taylor, Valentine Harling,
Benj. Tousand, Saml. Irby, Robt. Alison, Jr., Wm. Irby, Wm.
Wilson, James Bowling, Sid Winn, Robt. Holaday, David Saxon,
Drury Martin, Thos. Jones, Chas. Irby, Sam. Bowling, Frances
Irby, Marthan Tousand, Nancy (Nanie) Hughs, Zach. Walton, Ambrose
Huggens, Wm. South, Thos. McCurley, Peter Wilson, Sam Taylor,
Frances Thorneton, Zebulon West, B. L. Posey, Edmond Howard,
Peter Wasin, Wm. South, Jeremiah Hopkins. Charles Irby, adm.

29 Nov. 1826. Appraisal of estate of JONATHAN FORGEY, dec'd
by A. Starnes, Wm. Moore and Lemarius Deale. Due estate from
Cotten Misheen and son Manoah Misheen. Menoah Forgey, adm.

5 Jan. 1827. Adm. of estate of WINNEY ALLEN, dec'd to Hastings
Dial. Joel Allen and Sim Wood, sur.

20 Dec. 1826. Appraisal of estate of ALEXANDER AUSTIN, dec'd
by Saml. Goodman, Joseph S. Owens and Wm. Ligon. Includes pro-
erty willed to Mrs. Agnes Austin by her husband Elex. Austin.
Alex. Austin, exr. Negroes willed to: Alexander Austin, Caroline
and Henretta Austin. Certified 4 Jan. 1827. 20 Dec. 1826. Sale
Bill. Pur.: Sollomon Fuller, Saml. Austin, Saml. Todd, Agnes
Austin, Robt. A. Monroe, Capt. A. Griffin, Capt. Jno. Boyd,
Danl. Beecham, Robt. Coleman, Wm. Atwood, Wade Puckett, Robt.
Austin, Wm. Austin, Jno. Moor, Sr., James Austin, Jane Austin,
Alfred Smith, Jno. Austin, Elijah Watson, Duke Goodman, Wm.
Whiteford, Edw. Jones, Jno. Collier. Notes and acct's due Alex.
Austin, dec'd. - Wm. Smith, Wm. Thompson, Wm. Wright, Elizabeth
Watson, Braxton Watts, Wm. Wood, Geo. Wright, Gillum Goodman,
Robt. A. Monroe, Elijah Watson, H. Chesure, Andw. McCaull, Ran-
som Devenport, Jno.Monroe, James Nickles, James Braxton, Wm.
Crosen, Wm. McGowan, Richd. Vims, Jno. Boyd, Wm. Smith, Wm.
Cook, Labon Sturgess, Alex. Deale, James Word, Virgil Owens,
Jno. Chappel, Saml. Goodman, James Austin, Demilion Deale, Wm.
Bryson, Bob Bryson, Archey Todd, Abraham Tompson, Henry Hitt,
Jno. Paterson, Jeses Hitt, Edw. Spearman, David Goodman, Elihu
Watson, Robt. Hollingsworth, Robt. Coleman, Wm. Braxter, Jno.
Nickles, Jno. Gates, Hugh Leeman, Thos. Ligon, Jr., James Leeman.

(No date) Sale Bill estate of DAVID COWAN, dec'd. Pur.: James
Cowan, Ann Cowan, Joseph McCullars, Rebecah Cowan, Frances Cowan,
Jno. Wasson, David Studdard, Jno. Cowan, Geo. Glenn, Absalum
Nixon, Joseph Gaines, Plesant Shaw, Willis Binnion, Abner Nixon,
Alfred Sims, Allen Saxon, Jno. Tompson, Thos. Posey, David Mc-
Cullar, Jno. Tirey, Henry Arnold.

6 Dec. 1826. Appraisal of estate of WILLIAM HUTCHISON, SR.,
dec'd by J. Hitch, Chas. Smith and Jno. McClintock. 7 Dec. 1826.
Sale Bill. Pur.: Jane Hutchison, Chas. Fowler, Wm. Hutchison,
James Templeton, Robt. Hutchison, Mary Ann Hutchison, Nancy
Hutchison, Abner Hutchison, James Parks, Jr., Wm. H. Farrow,
James Hutchison, Sr., Catharine Hutchison, Danl. Harmon, Wm.
Templeton, Jno. Blakely, Saml. Templeton, Wm. D. Hitch, Wm.
Park, James E. Hutchison, Jno. Hitch, Jno. H. Byrd, Joseph Piper,
James Glenn. Judgement against Saml. Nugent in favor of Wm.
Hutchison, dec'd.

19 Dec. 1826. Appraisal of estate of HANNAH ADAIR, dec'd by

ADAIR cont'd:
Wm. Copland, Geo. McCrary and _____. 20 Dec. 1826. Sale Bill.
Note on Wm. Graham. James Adair, exr.

17 Oct. 1826. Sale Bill estate of DAVID COWAN, dec'd. Pur.:
Jno. Cowan, Isaac Tompson, Frances Cowan, Wm. Williams, Jno.
Blackstock, Stephen Martin, Allen Saxon, Absolum Nixon, Jesse
Garrett, Anna Cowan, Drury Gradon, Joel Avery, Jno. Armstrong,
James Mc. Arnold, Silus Arnold, Wm. Saxon. Leila Cowan, adm.

5 Jan. 1827. Hollen Littel, minor about 15 years of age, chose
Charles Littel guardian. N. Day and Jno. Dunlap, sur.

26 Oct. 1826. Estate of JONES FULLAR, dec'd appraised by Wm.
Lowe, Zach. Bailey, Jr. and Wiley Hill. Notes: Jno. Millar,
James M. Norell, Geo. Wharton, Wm. Spence, Braxton Watts, Paul
Findley, Arch Fullar. Morten Miller, adm.23 Nov. 1826. Sale
Bill. Pur.: Nathaniel Day, Sarah Fullar, James Brownlee, Asa
Chandler, Henry Fullar, Archey Fullar, Geo. Johnston, Hamon
Fullar, Jno. McClehan, Robt. Miller, Wm. Stone, Thos. Babb,
Peter Fullar, Jones Fuller, Wm. Winn, David Martin, Richd. Har-
ris, Zach. Bailey, Joel Hall, James Todd, Wm. Lowe.

27 Dec. 1826. Appraisal of estate of JANE KELLETT, dec'd by
Jno. Hellams, Wm. Choice and James Babb. 30 Dec. 1826. Sale
Bill. Pur.: Martin Kellett, James Kellett, Richard Owen, Samson
Babb, Archebal Owens, James Babb, John L. Harris, Elizabeth
Kellett, Wm. Babb, Nathan Nisbett, Jeremiah Hopkins, John Wil-
liams, John Hatcher. Martin Kellett, adm.

5 Feb. 1827. Will of JOHN MC KELVEY, dec'd proven. Mary McKelvey,
exr. James Leak?, Jr. and William Fulton, wit.

29 Dec. 1826. Appraisal of estate of DR. JAMES CRAIG, dec'd
by John Boyce, James Farebarn and Geo. McCrary. 2 Jan. 1827.
Sale Bill. Thomas Craig, adm. Notes and acct's due James Craig,
dec'd. Thos. Duckett, John W. Cargill, John Craige, James Puckett, Wm. Alexander, Robert Hustons, Anthony Foster, Robt. Harting, James Foster, John Luke, Thomas Jones, Wm. Musgrove, James
Martindill, Thos. Young, Jno. Templeton, Jno. Ross, A. Hollands
(all good); Jno. Dillard, Jos. Cooper, Jas. Campbell, Solomon
Bobo, James Berry, Stephen Hughs, Gillum L. _ckey, Wm. Hucka-
bey, Robt. Hannah, Jno. F. Harmings, Geo. Golding, Jas. Phillip,
Wm. Jones, James Puckett adm. of Jno. Puckett, dec'd, Thos.
Prator, Wm. Sparks, Robt. Templeton (all desperate); Thos. Young,
James Martindill; Judgements - James Craig; exrs. of Wm. Craig
vs. Abraham Holland (doubtful); James Craig part of his father
Wm. Craig, dec'd, Thos. Craig, adm. ; notes - Robt. Gilland,
Geo. Dillard, Robt. Haistings, Jno. Templeton, Sr., James Camp-
bell, Thos. Duckett, Thos. W. Waters, Jno. Luke, Philamon M.
Waters, Linsday Whitten, A. F. Holland, Saml. Bevours, Green
B. Draper, Noah Garrett, Richd. Farrow, Jno. Harming, Hardiman
Duke, James Basley, Robt. L. Jones, Jesse I. Weson; Gimima Lee,
James Campbell, Philup Campbell, Isaac Bagnell, Robt. Puckett,
Moses Hill, Benj. Adair. Notes are also in name of Ross & Craig,
a co-partnership. Glenn Alexander, Wm. Musgrove, Alexander Wil-
son, Henry Langston, James Devaul, Elizabeth Owens, Vid. S.
Sims, Stuart Walton, John Fowlar, W. M. Waters, James Dillard,
Jos. Harland, Jos. Garrett, Sarah Lynch, John Hitch, Moses Casey,
Rodger Brown, Jesse Normand, Aron Casey, Nancy Gilland, Hugh
L. H. Luskey; Milanda Lynch, M. Waters, dec'd, Saml. Hunter,

ROSS & CRAIG acct's cont'd:
Henry Jones, Miss Nancy Lynch, Hugh Tolen, Curtis Hughs, Bassill Wheate, Reuben Newman, Mary Martindale, Naomi Lynch, dec'd, Crow Johnston, Avary Newman, James Alexander, Alexander Simpson, Newman Simpson, Isaac Hill, John Gilland, Martin Hamond, Barey Jones, Casey Aron, Jr. (see above Aron Casey), Wheate Millar, dec'd, Richd. Stone, Lynsey Waters, Wm. Robt. Hannah, Robt. Stone, John Henley, Syntha Casey, Jesse Casey, Jos. Green, John Minar, Elisha Campbell, Wm. Allen, Robt. Powell, Wm. Glenn, Wm. Dillard, Thos. Lynch, Robt. Brown, Wm. Pennington, Alexander Luke, Wm. Cradock, James Littel Hannah, Widow Sarah Ward, Geo. Rese, Robt. Templeton, Jas. Langston, Richd. Davis, Jno. Dillard, Jno. Watts. Thos. Craig, adm.
Inv. of the notes and book acct's of Craig & Martindale the year 1826: Jno. Templeton, Joshua Brown, Reuben Meadors, Jos. Dollar, Richd. Farrow, Henry Fowler, Andw. Studards, Hugh Toland, Wm. Alexander, Thos. Leek, P. D. Kern, Jno. Craig, Sidney Craddock, Samson Alexander, James L. Craig, Robt. Gilland, Deliliah Couch, Wm. Jones, Reuben Meadors, Jno. Henderson, Jesse Dodd, Jno. Martindill, Richd. Farrow, Wm. Musgrove, Robt. L. Jones, James Craig, Philip Waters, Joel Foster, Danl. Felder, Sophiah Ross, Henry Strand, Elizabeth Farrow, Henry S. Neil, Jos. Abrahams, Willis Arnold, James Fareborns, A. A. Fareborns, Thos. Blakely, Jacob Langston, Felding Foster, James Burk, Jos. McConatha, Henry Pitts, Jr., Walter Stuart, Perry Jones, Ephriam Pitts, Henry Langston, Wm. Aberhams, Saml. Langston, Elenor Henry, Thos. Deshield, Henry Duke, Parmer Higgens, Jesse Ramage, Isaac Bagnell. Acct's due Craig & Young - Thos. Hendrick, Geo. Young, Geo. Young, Jr., Henry Langston, Thos. Leek, (basically the same names as above accounts). Thos. Craig, adm.

29 Sept. 1824. Will of JOHN MC KELVEY, planter. Sons James and George; Peggy Laird, wife of Archebald Laird; William McKelvey; son John; Nancy Dalrymple, wife of John Dalrymple; son Samuel; son Jabez; son Hugh; beloved wife Mary; also children who are - Thomas, Rachel, Alexander, Anna, Nelly, Polley and Isaac McKelvey. Wife exr. Wit: James Leak, Jr., Jabez McKelvey and Wm. Fulton. Proven 5 Feb. 1827.

21 Dec. 1826. Appraisal of estate of WILLIAM YOUNG, dec'd by Jno. Black, James Crawford and Langsdon East. 8 Dec. 1826. Sale Bill. Pur.: Judith Young, James Young, Jno. Black, Jno. Godfree, Isaac Case, Thos. Rodgers, Robt. Monroe, Jno. Hunter, Jas. Henderson. James Young, exr.

27 Nov. 1826. Appraisal of estate of DAVID LITTEL, dec'd by Geo. McCrary, Wm. Blakely and J. Fareborne. 28 & 29 Nov. 1826. Sale Bill. Pur.: James Copland, Jas. Littel, Jno. Littel, Parshel Middors, Doct. Garey Mercey, Andw. Park, Chas. Forguson, Saml. Mylum, Jas. Ansley, Thos. Fulton, Saml. Copland, A. Hutcheson, Chas. Littel, Alexander Fareborn, Nancy Littel, Aberham Holland, David Bailey, B. Puckett, Jno. Taylor. Chas. Littel, exr.

5 Feb. 1827. Thomas Littel, minor about 18 years, chose Saml. Copland, guardian. Wm. Gamble and Thos. Craig, sur.

10 Feb. 1827. Adm. of estate of LEWIS WATSON, dec'd to Rutha Watson. Willis Watson and Bary Watson, sur.

26 Feb. 1827. Adm. of estate of JAMES STARLING, dec'd to James Smith. Jehu Pitts and John Pitts, sur. Order of appraisement and sale, etc.

26 Feb. 1827. Adm. of estate of EDMOND SPEARMAN, dec'd to Robt. Floyd. Chas. Floyd and Patrick Todd, sur.

20 Dec. 1826. 2d appraisal of estate which was a life estate given by dec'd to his wife Susanah Foshee, widow of BENJAMIN FOSHEE, dec'd. Appraised by David Curiton, Robt. Malone and Elihu Watts. 21 Dec. 1826. Sale Bill of estate. Pur.: Daniel Foshee, Jos. Cason, Chas. Egerton, Sarah Turner, Benj. Foshee, Mary Hill, David Curiton, Hickerson Whitworth, Elihu Watts, James Watts, Alfred Owens, Elizabeth Pollard, Henry Hill, Jos. Creson, Abner Wells, Thos. Hill, Polley Turner, Sally Turner, Hickeson Whitten, Wm. Atwood, Edw. Jones, Philip Day, Alexander Deale, James Watts, Mary Dial, Cason Hill, Robt. Puckett. Benj. Foshee, exr.

5 Mar. 1827. Adm. of estate of SARAH S. GRIGSBY, dec'd to Benj. Grigsby. Turner Richardson and James Bruton?, sur. 5 Mar. 1827. Return of Benj. Grigsby - there is no property of S. S. HILL now SARAH S. GRIGSBY, dec'd. F. Richardson was her guardian.

5 Mar. 1827. Adm. of estate of JOHN HAREY?, dec'd to Turner Richardson. John Hunter, sur.

3 Mar. 1827. Appraisal of estate of MRS. JENANA MARTEN, dec'd as shown by Henry Marten, adm. (also shown as JENNA MARTIN). Appr'd by Archebal Young, Jonathan Wallis and Robt. Hand, Sr.

30 Dec. 1826. Appraisal of estate of EDMOND CRADDOCK, dec'd by Joshua Saxon, Hugh Saxon and Henry Cleveland. 2 January 1827. Sale Bill. Pur.: James Dunlap, Robt. Allison, B. L. Posey. S. Farrow, adm.

(No date) Notes due JAMES PARKS, SR., dec'd: Thos. Adair, James Park, Wm. Hutchison, Wm. Park, Saml. B. Levears, W. W. Wallis, Robt. Park, Wm. Threate, J. Craddock, Jno. & Robt. Sloan, Jno. & David Sloan, Thos. Porter, Wm. Fullen, Thos. Vito, Thos. Becknel, Thos. Crumton, Faney Cockrim, Jno. Berrey, Jno. Hill, Jno. Hewart, Jos. Dollar, Frances Ross, Sr., Jeremiah Vitto, N. Duke, Chas. Park, Jno. A. Craddock, Mitchel Smith, Chas. Simmons; book acct's due: Andw. Park, James E. Hutchison, Capt. James Park, Wm. Hutchison, Geo. McClintock, James Templeton, Easter Hunter, Jno. Crumton, Robt. Hunter, Isabela Hunter, Mitchel Dunlap; desperate acct's: Jno. A. Craddock, James Jones, Mathew Hunter, dec'd, James Hunter Millar, Danl. Martin, Robt. Sloan, James Smith, Wm. Hutchison, Margret Crooks, James Hunter. Andw. Park (Capt) and James Park, Jr., exrs.

(No date) Notes/acct's due ISABELA HUNTER, dec'd. Samuel Flemming. James Park, Jr. and Andw. Park, adm.

15 Mar. 1827. Appraisal of estate of LEWIS WATSON, dec'd by Zachariah Arnold, Saml. Freeman and Jno. Watson.

7 Mar. 1827. Appraisal of estate of EDMOND SPEARMAN, dec'd by Jno. Cook, Chas. Egerton and Jno. Armstrong. Robt. Floyd, adm. 15 Mar. 1827. Sale Bill. Pur.: Susanah Spearman, Patrick Todd, Jno. Harmon, Wm. Smith, Alex'r Deale, Walter P. Vaughn, Anthony Griffin, Robt. Floyd, David Curiton, Frances Hill, Jos. Owen, James Criswell, Janetta Watts, James Wells, Edmond Cason, Travis Hill, Thos. Spearman, Wm. Wadkins, Jno. Rudd, Wm. Williams, Wm. Atwood, Drury Vaughn, Abner Wells, Wm. B. Smith, Jos. Devenport, Lazarus Hitt, Jos. Cason, Saml. Todd, Jno. Day, Thos.

SPEARMAN cont'd:
Harmon, Thos. Adkerson, Johnston Devenport, Chas. Curiton, Thos.
Devenport, Jno. Armstrong, Jno. Gay, Jno. Budd, Faris Hill,
Jos. Gates, Ingrum Nun, (16 Mar. 1827) Mark Higgens, Andw. Mc-
Caul, Francis Devenport, Wm. Wood, James Goodman. Robt. Floyd,
adm. 5 Mar. 1827. Notes due estate: Joshua Hollis, Joshua Hays,
James Clark, Wm. Harmon, Thos. Todd, Robt. Malone, Jno. Adker-
son, Wm. Atwood, Larkin Hill, James Burton, Jos. Williams, Wade
Linsey, Alexander Gates, Wm. Abney, Jos. Devenport, Saml. Todd,
Anthony Griffin, Anthony Leek, Howard Pinson, Mary Hill, Obriant
Leek.

18 Apr. 1827. Martha Guinn, former wife of ___ Croson, dec'd
and her minor children Julian Croson, Hana M. Croson, Permela
A. Croson and Thos. B. Croson all under 16 years of age, chose
John Black as guardian. Robt. Criswell, sur.

17 Apr. 1827. Adm. of estate of WILLIAM PARSONS, dec'd to Saml.
Parsons, Jr. and Archebald B. Parsons. Saml. Parsons, Sr. and
Isaiah Parsons, sur.

12 Mar. 1827. Appraisal of estate of JAMES STARLING, dec'd by
Isaac Teague, Elias Teague and Archabald Norris. 15 Mar. 1827.
Sale Bill. Pur.: James Jones, Archebald Norwood, Robt. Stephens,
Chas. Smith, Elias Teague, Henry Starling, Jno. Stephens, James
Grimes, Zachery Taylor, Jno. South, Reuben Powell, Jno. Pitts,
Peter Gallehair, James Clardy, Wm. Williamson, Jno. Crafford,
Elizabeth Starling (also Sterling). James Smith, adm.

12 Dec. 1826. Appraisal of estate of LEWIS DAY, dec'd by James
Gillum, Jno. Ball and Wm. P. Hill. 12 Dec. 1826. Sale Bill.:
Pur.: Reuben Golding, Daniel Day, Jno. Chappell, Wm. Carter.
Jno. Chappell, adm.

21 Apr. 1827. Will of SAMUEL AUSTIN, dec'd proven. Will dated
10 Nov. 1826. Son James Austin; dau. Elizabeth Munroe; daua.
Nancy Cardes?; land bought of Margret Hunter; land adj. Wm.
Thompson; dau. Nelley Straight; dau. Margret Caldwell; son Thomas
Austin; land bought of James Nickle; son John Alexander Austin;
mention of Widow Hunter; beloved wife; son William Henry Austin;
(N. B. wife may be named Nelley also). Maj. James Austin and
John Monroe, Sr. with son Thomas Austin, exrs. Wit: John Moore,
James Austin, Danl. Drummond. (N. B. also spelled Austen).

21 Apr. 1827. Adm. of estate of PATRICK J. NOLAND, dec'd to
Peter Gallahair. Rody Kenady and James Simmons, sur.

16 Apr. 1827. Adm. of estate of WILLIAM ABERHAMS, dec'd to Henry
S. Neel. Chas. Ferguson and Zachariah P. Parks?, sur.

(No date) Sale Bill of estate of WINNEY ALLEN, dec'd. Haistings
Dial, adm. Pur.: Syntha Aberham, Lusida Allen, Haistings Deal,
Sr., Even Bell, Lydral Allen. (N. B. Diel/Dial/Deal).

25 Apr. 1827. Appraisal of estate of SAMUEL AUSTEN, dec'd by
Wm. Austen, Jno. Moore, Wm. Thompson and Jno. Nickles.

5 Jan. 1827. Return of Alsey Fullar, guardian of minor children
of WILLIAM GLENN, dec'd. Board with A. Fullar; tuition with
Presley & Bailey & Alexander Deale; notes belonging to Catharine
Glenn; notes belonging to Jeremiah Glenn and Anne Glenn.

16 Dec. 1826. Appraisal of estate of BURGESS MC FERSON, dec'd

MC FERSON cont'd:
by Drury Boyce, William Boyce, John Pedon and William Chayce.
16 Dec. 1826. Sale Bill. Pur.: John S. Peadon, John Nesbet,
Dempsey Nesbet, William Boyce. Drury Boyce, adm.

17 Mar. 1827. Sale Bill estate of LEWIS WATSON, dec'd. Pur.:
John West, Ruth Watson, Geo. Shirley, Z. Arnold, John Adams,
B. Watson, Ellender Watson, Pheby Watson, Berrey Watson, Willis
Watson, Bevely Watson, Capt. John Watson, Phillip Watson, Reuben
Powell, James Crocker, E. Shirley, Eli Shirley, Elihu Watson,
Jonathan Shirley, James McFerson, Shubet Starnes, Wiley Watson,
Wm. Moor, Sr., Pendleton Zains, Wm. Phlinn, Artis Cook.

26 May 1827. Adm. of estate of DANIEL ORSBORN, dec'd to Langston
Orsborn. William Mear and Owen Summer, sur.

20 Feb. 1827. 2nd Appraisal of estate of PETER GROVENER, dec'd
by Wm. Ransom, Mathew White and W. G. Davis. (No date) 2nd Sale
Bill. Pur.: Jno. Dunlap, James Piddle, James Bell, Thos. Adkins,
Edw. Hicks, Wm. Irby, Thos. Dean, Saml. Hudgins, J. E. Hutchison. Wm. Irby, adm.

(No date) Appraisal of estate of WILLIAM PARSONS, dec'd by Saml.
Parsons, Saml. Flemming, John Taylor and Isaiah Parsons. Saml.
Parsons and H. B. Parsons, adm. (No date) Sale Bill. Pur.: Mary
Parsons, Alsey Parsons, Milley Parsons, Joseph E. Parsons, John
Taylor, William Parsons, Starling Tucker, John Garrett, Saml.
Flemming, John Philups, Wm. Cowen, Esq., Susan Meadors, Barnet
Parsons, Flemmen Mosley, Martha Holladay, Mary Smith, Isaiah
Parsons, Chas. Williams. Saml. Parsons, Jr. and Archebald B.
Parsons, adm.

4 June 1827. Will of ABNER JOHNSTON, dec'd proven. Will dated
2 Oct. 1826. Dist. of Newbury, S. C. Wife Rebecah Johnston;
son Jabuz; dau. Permely Neighbours; son Jeremiah; dau. Mehalaha;
son Joseph; dau. Elizabeth; son Benjamin; son George Washington
Johnston. Wife Rebecah Johnston and friend Frank Beck?, exrs.
Wit: Richd. L. Cannon, Thomas Butlar and James Neal.

4 June 1827. Will of JANE MIDLETON, dec'd proven. Jane Midleton,
Jr., exr. Will dated 8 Jan. 1823. Dau. Jane Midleton; her share
in dec'd husband's est.; his sons Andrew and Ainsworth Midleton;
(both of whom departed this life intestate and without issue);
dec'd husband's will, etc. Jane Midleton, exr. Wit: R. Criswell,
Colemon Carlisle and Gideon Carlisle.

2 Nov. 1826. Appraisal of estate of WHEATE MILLAR, dec'd by
John Holland, David Enterkin and Armested Leek. Return from
the sale of estate. John Leake, adm.

10 May 1827. Appraisal of estate of WILLIAM ABERHAMS, dec'd
by John Dillard, Thomas Holly and Richd. Bonds. Note on James
Prater, William May, Joseph Ramage. 11 May 1827. Sale Bill.
Henry L. Neel, adm.

17 Feb. 1827. Inventory of estate of JOHN MC KELVEY, late of
Laurens Dist., planter, dec'd by James Leak, David Enterkin
and Chas. Little.

23 Mar. 1827. Appraisal of estate of JOHN HARREY, dec'd by Benj.
Williams, John Fowlar and Gabriel Thomas. (Also dated 26 Mar.)
26 Mar. 1827. Sale Bill. Turner Richardson, adm. Pur.: Mrs.

HARREY cont'd:
Jane Harrey, James Huggens, Isaac Pinson, John Fowlar, James
Alexander, Elihu Madden, Lewis Smith, Wm. Henderson, James Mc-
Dowall, Elijah Smith, Jno. M'Clan, John Todd, Robt. Wilson,
Lewis Wadkins, Lewis Smith, Jno. McClahan, James Morgin, Marma-
duke Pinson, Jno. Pitts, Pheby Madden, Robt. Allison, Mabra?
Hunter, Thos. Brownlee, Jno. L. Madden, John Burton, John Madden,
Haiston Madden, Turner Richardson, Wm. Madden. Certified 15
Apr. 1827.

8 June 1827. 2nd Appraisal of estate of DANIEL ORSBORN, dec'd
by Wm. Moor, Joel Burgess and Owen Summer___? 8 June 1827. Sale
Bill of residue of est. Pur: Elizabeth Orsborn. Langston Orsborn, adm.

6 July 1827. Will of JOHN STONE, dec'd proven. Will dated 10
Aug. 1826. Four children: John, George, Anney (Stone) and Polley
Henry; Reuben Arnold his part; two youngest daus. Faney and
Polley Kenedy. Rev. Zachariah Arnold of Laurens Dist., S. C.
and Doctor F. Connor of same dist., exrs. Wit: Geo. Connor,
Jr., Jno. W. Connor and Gab'l E. Trentten?.

23 June 1827. Adm. of estate of JOHN MIDLETON, dec'd to James
Crocker. Jacob Niswanger and William Moor, sur.

28 June 1827. Adm. of estate of WILLIAM MC CRAY, dec'd to John
Hutchison. Mathew Holladay and James Flemming, sur.

22 July 1827. By consent of Turner Richardson, adm. of DANIEL
JONES, dec'd and Weldon Jones, att'y for Harrison Jones, the
only heir with the sd widow of the dec'd and John McClanahan
who married the widow, settlement of overpayment.

7 July 1827. Appraisal of estate of ABNER JOHNSTON, dec'd by
Joel Elling, Wm. Arnold and Jno. Rusel.

6 Aug. 1827. Life est. left by PETER HAMMOND, dec'd to his wife
Nancy Hammond, now dec'd, to be sold and a division made. 6
July 1827. 2nd appraisal of estate by Lewis Cargill, Mark Noble
and John Atwood. Peter Hammond and Isum Hammond, exrs.

21 Dec. 1826. Appraisal of estate of JOHN DRAKE, dec'd by Jno.
Black, A. B. Johnston and David Vance. Wm. Black, adm. 22 Dec.
1826. Sale Bill. Pur.: Sarah Drake, Lewis Dalrymple, John Godfrey, Wm. Hays, David Brooks, David Vance, Jno. B. Standley,
Artha Oneal, Wm. Farrow, Abraham B. Johnston, Jno. Black.

17 Jan. 1827. Appraisal of estate of JOHN CRAFORD, dec'd by
Langsdon East, Abner B. Johnston, James Young and Abraham Johnston. (N. B. also spelled Crawford). John Black, exr.

16 Aug. 1827. Appraisal of estate of JOHN MIDLETON, dec'd by
G. Anderson, Geo. Funk and Joseph Irby.

31 July 1827. Inventory estate of JOHN STONE, dec'd by John
Watson, Wm. Moor and Elihu Watson. 2 Aug. 1827. Sale Bill. Pur:
John West, Wm. Stone, Reuben Arnold, John Stone, Larkin Gains,
David Black, Elias Huskeson, Wm. McClure, Wm. Knight. Zachariah
Arnold, exr.

4 Aug. 1827. Adm. of estate of CATHARINE TINSLEY, dec'd to Jesse
Johnston. John Blakely and Langsdon East, sur.

6 Aug. 1827. Adm. of estate of NANCY HAMMOND, dec'd to Peter Hammond. William Halbert and Jonathan Abbercrumbie, sur.

18 Jan. 1827. Sale Bill estate of JOHN CRAFORD, dec'd. Pur: James Craford, Abraham Johnston, James Neel, James Hinsley, James Boyd, Wm. Milligen, James Young, Geo. Johnston, Joshua Teague, Jno. Black, Saml. Neel, Robt. A. Monroe, Thomas Toushend (Townsend?), Mrs. Caldwell, Benj. Blakely, Saml. Young, Langsdon East, Alexander Winn.

12 May 1827. Sale Bill estate of SAMUEL AUSTIN, dec'd. Pur: Elizabeth Reed, Wm. Braxten, James Austin, Braxton Watts, Wm. Right, Alexander Austin, Thomas Austin, Robt. Monroe, Widow Austin, Geo. Wright, Wm. H. Ligon, Wm. Tompson, Elender Robertson, Wm. Bryson, Jr., John Nickel, Robt. Austin, Hugh Leamen, Jos. McGown, Jos. Ligon, Wm. Gordon. James Austin, exr.

25 Aug. 1827. Will of JESSE MOTES, dec'd proven. Will dated 1 Aug. 1827. Sons Macklin Motes and Jesse Milford Motes; beloved wife Sarah Motes. Friend Alsey Fuller and sons Dandy and Hagen Motes, exrs. Wit: Robt. Campbell, Joseph Willcutt and Solomon Fuller.

3 Sept. 1827. Will of THORNBERRY BOLLING, dec'd proven. Will dated 13 June 1822. Mother Abigail Bowlling; Thornberry Bowling, son of Samuel Bowling; my share and interest in the Fork Shoal Library Society; Samuel Parrett, son of Alford Parrett; Samuel Bolling, son of John Bowlling; land in Alabama where John Bowling lives; four brothers - Robert Boling, Tully Bowling, John Bowling and Samuel Bowling; three sisters - Nancy Stronge, Lucinda Johnston and Polley Parrett; heirs of my sister Elizabeth Dunkling; Henderson Sullivan and Joseph N. Johnston. Tully Bowling, Henderson Sullivan and Joseph N. Johnston, exrs. Wit: Micajah Berry, Tully Bowlling and Sophia Choice. (N. B. the surname Bowling is spelled various ways throughout this document).

21 July 1827. Appraisal of estate of JANE MIDLETON, dec'd by Wm. Dunlap, Robt. Bell and Abner Young. Jane Midleton, exr.

17 Sept. 1827. Adm. of estate of WILLIAM PUTMAN, dec'd to Stephen Garrett and Nimrod Putman. F. Cleveland and Robertson Moore, sur.

25 Sept. 1827. Adm. of estate of JAMES CALDWELL, dec'd to Geo. Forrest Caldwell. Will proven. Will dated 24 Apr. 1827. Land purchased of Danl. Farrow to be sold and ten negroes, etc.; bro. David Robert Caldwell (under 21 yrs.); land adj. John W. Simpson, David Vance and John Black. Bro. George Forrest Caldwell and friend Dr. John W. Simpson, exrs. Wit: Drayton Vance, P. C. Caldwell and O. B. Higgins.

17 Sept. 1827. Will of NATHEN FOWLER, dec'd proven. Will dated 8 Apr. 1827. Loving wife Martha Fowler; loving dau. Sarah Ann Fowler; heirs of Levi Fowler, dec'd. Worthy friends Thomas Owens and Geo. Young, Jr., exrs. Wit: Thos. Young, Jno. Whitmore and Jno. Addington.

24 Sept. 1827. Adm. of estate of JENNET MC CLAHAN, dec'd to Samuel McClahan. James Parker and Andw. McKnight, sur.

13 Sept.? 1827. Appraisal of estate of CATHARINE TINSLEY, dec'd

TINSLEY cont'd:
by John Hunter, Saml. Young and Jno. Huett. 14 Sept. 1827. Sale
Bill. Pur: Wm. W. Watts, James Boyd, James Watts. Jesse Johnston, adm.

6 Oct. 1827. Adm. of estate of WILLIAM BALL, dec'd to Marta
(Martha) Ball. Moses Wills and Washington Wells, sur.

20 Oct. 1827. Adm. of estate of JAMES GLOVER, dec'd to George
Anderson. Marstin Shaw and Abraham Madden, sur.

___ Oct. 1827. Appraisal of estate of WILLIAM PUTMAN, dec'd by
Robertson Moor, Willis Cheek and Thomas Crook.

23 Oct.? 1827. Appraisal of estate of WILLIAM BALL, dec'd by
Nimrod Neely?, Wm. Tinsley and Lewis Ball. 23 Oct. 1827. Sale
Bill. Pur.: John Ball, Jno. Chappell, Jinney Ball, Anthony Gold-
en, Roberson Redden, Jos. Cason, Geo. Redden, Robt. Valentine,
Jno. Watts, Mathew Ball, R. L. Puckett, Washington Wells, Jno.
Sadler, Geo. Neely, Jno. Chapman, Martha Ball, Wm. Atwood, Lar-
kin Tinsley, Wm. Tinsley, Jno. Wood, Wheate Williams, Wm. Hitt,
Chas. Egerton, Roberson Puckett, Jemimah Ball, Anthony Leek.
Martha Ball, adm.

Jan.-Sept. 1827. Money rec'd due estate of JAMES IRBY, dec'd.
Chas. Irby, adm.

11 Nov. 1827. Appraisal of estate of NATHEN FOWLER, dec'd by
Geo. Young, Jr., Geo. Dillard and Joseph Jones. Notes on: David
Boyce, Ezekiel Rice, Wm. Dillard, Thos. Owens, Moses Garrett,
Chas. King, Benj. Gains, Joseph Jones, Menasa Williams, Sarah
Duckett, Jno. Garrett. Taken on 9 Nov. 1827. 7 Nov. 1827. Sale
Bill. Thos. Owens, exr.

1 Sept. 1827. Appraisal of estate of JESSE MOTES, dec'd by Jos.
Wilcutt, Wm. Hollingsworth and Jos. Hollingsworth. (Jesse Motes,
Sr., dec'd). Includes notes due. Certified 20 Oct. 1827 by Alsey
Fuller, acting exr. 22 Sept. 1827. Sale of cotton belonging
to estate.

(No date) Appraisal of estate of CHARLES NICKLES, dec'd by Jos.
Hollingsworth, Geo. Funk, Geo. Holdridge and James Nickles.

8 Nov. 1827. Appraisal of estate of JAMES GLOVER, dec'd by Wm.
Graves, Jno. Wait, Jno. Sims and Wm. Anderson.

(No date) Sale Bill estate of ABNER JOHNSTON, dec'd. Rebecah
Johnston, exr. Pur.: John Gains, Rebecah Johnston, Allen Saxon,
James Rily, John Loveless, Lewis Arnold, John Bagnell, Sr.,
Frank Beck, Reuben? Medlock, Vinsen Shaw, Jno. Mayhon, Frank
Banks.

3 Dec. 1827. Adm. of estate of WILLIAM TAYLOR, dec'd to Thomas
Blakely. Chas. Blakely and Robt. Blakely, sur.

3 Dec. 1827. Adm. of estate of HARRIS GOODWIN, dec'd to Cealey
Goodwin. Larkin Stepp and Wm. Halbert, sur.

3 Dec. 1827. Adm. of estate of JOSEPH N. HITCH, dec'd to Luther
D. Hitch and Wm. W.? Hitch. James Devall and Jno. Byrd, sur.

3 Nov. 1827. Adm. of estate of ELENDER GARLETON, dec'd to Andrew

GARLETON cont'd:
McCall. Patrick Todd and John Chappell, sur.

12 Nov. 1827. Adm. of estate of ADAM POTTER, dec'd to Elizabeth
Potter. Stephen Potter and ____ Barksdill, sur.

3 ___ 1827. Will of MAREY MEADORS, dec'd proven. Will dated
18 Oct. 1827. Daus. Susan and Polley; husband's and son William's
wearing apparel; sons Washington, Warner, Morris, John and Henry;
dau. Elizabeth. Son Warren W. Meadors, exr. Wit: Henry S. Neel,
Elizabeth Neel and Thos. Young.

22 Dec. 1827. Will of WILLIAM THOMPSON, dec'd proven. Will dated
11 Nov. 26. (Name also spelled Tompson). Beloved wife Nancy;
loving dau. Molly Tompson; beloved dau. Elizabeth Leeman; beloved dau. Williemson (N. B. this is not full name evidently);
beloved son Abraham Thompson; beloved son William; grand son
William Tompson, son of Abraham. Friend Anthony F. Golding,
exr. Wit: Sally M. Hall, Cyntha Armstrong and Martha S. Chappell.

14 Nov. 1827. Adm. of estate of MATHEW BLAKELY, dec'd to John
Blakely. Wm. Hutchison and Robt. Slone, sur.

25 Aug. 1827. True sale bill of property of PETER HAMMOND, dec'd
not willed to his wife NANCY HAMMOND, dec'd. Pur.: Wm. Cowen,
Wm. R. Davis, Jno. Cowen, Jno. Hammond, Jno. McMahen, Jno. Glenn,
P. Hammond, James Noble, G. Puckett, Wm. Canada, Jesse Garrett,
Wm. Quatz, Thos. Step, Wm. Bramblet, Jno. Grant, Chas. Cargill,
Abner Knight. Peter Hammond, exr est. of Peter Hammond, Sr.,
dec'd.

2 Dec. 1827. Return of sale bill property of NANCY HAMMOND,
dec'd by Peter Hammond, adm. Pur.: Jno. Cowen, Wm. Quals, Jno.
Simpson, Jno. Garrett, James Hammond, Lewis Cargill, Reuben
Estes, John Hammond, Jno. Grant, Solomon Grigsby, Wm. Bramblet,
Danl. Long, Sarah Armstrong, Danl. Loving, Jno. Waters, Isam
Hammond, Silas Arnold, Harmon Garrett, Mark Noble, Reuben Rober-
son, Thos. Waters, Thos. Noble, Robt. Hand, James Moor, Wm.
Halbert, Thos. Step, Pusila Tinsley, Jesse Davis.

26 Sept. 1827. Sale Bill estate of JOHN MIDLETON, dec'd. Pur.:
Margret Midleton, John Midleton, Andrew Midleton, James Midleton,
Polly Stuard, Joseph Irby, Shubal Starnes, Geo. Madden, Stanford
Glover, Wm. Anderson, James Anderson, James Richards, Andrew
Anderson, John Smith, Jno. R. Crocker. James Crocker, adm.

5 Dec. 1827. Inventory of estate of ELENDER GARLINGTON, dec'd
by James Watts, Jno. Chappell and Saml. Todd. 12 Dec. 1827.
Sale Bill. Pur.: Jno. Williams, Jenet McGowan, James Watts,
Geo. Ball, Elihu Watts, Edw. Jones, Richd. Sims, Patrick Todd,
Jno. Malone, Wm. Atwood, Andw. Rodgers, Wm. R. Smith, Anthony
Griffin, Saml. Todd, Jno. Ball, Jane Procter, John Jones, John
Wells, Chas. Egerton, Thos. Hill, Abraham Gullet, Walter P.
Vaughn, Patrick Symmes. A. McCall, adm.

17 Nov. 1827. Appraisal of estate of ADAM POTTER, dec'd by Chas.
G. Franks, Stephen Potter and Joshua Franks. 5 Dec. 1827. Sale
Bill. Pur: Cally Barksdill, Reuben Dollar, Wm. Davis, John Dol-
lar, Sarah Dollar, Ira L. Potter, Stephen Potter, A. Deen, Nathl.
Barksdill, Mary Franks, Joshua Franks, Martin Gladwell, Harvy
Cleveland, Wm. F. Downs, Chas. Simmons, Braddock Mosley, John
King, John Orsborn. Elizabeth Potter, adm.

24 Nov. 1827. Appraisal of estate of JOSEPH N. HITCH, dec'd by Robt. Cunningham, James Devaull and Walter Stuart. 28 Nov. 1827. Sale Bill. W. D. Hitch, adm.

7 Jan. 1828. Adm. of estate of JANE AUSTIN, dec'd to William Austin. Alexander Austin and Samuel Austin, sur.

7 Jan. 1828. Adm. of estate of MARY ANN CALDWELL, dec'd to William Caldwell. John Davis and Thomas F. Owen?, sur.

7 Jan. 1828. Adm. of estate of JAMES HENDERSON, dec'd to William Henderson. Joshua Franks and Ira Potter, sur.

7 Jan. 1828. Est. of JAMES MC MAHAN, SR., dec'd. James McMahan, Jr., adm. Records amounts paid to date. Sur. refuse to continue. Adm. revoked and given to James Hollingsworth.

3 Dec. 1827. Appraisal of estate of MATHEW BLAKELY, dec'd by Thos. S. Wilks, Thos. Blakely and Wm. Blakely. Sale Bill of dec'd. Notes. John Blakely, adm.

8 Oct. 1827. Sale Bill estate of WILLIAM PUTMAN, dec'd. Pur.: Dubybella Putman, Reuben Estes, Edw. Garrett, Edmond Garrett, Martin Ball, Hosa Garrett, Isaac Garrett, Zachariah Davis, Jesse Garrett, James Hughs, Asley Garrett, Reuben Putman, Dubeybella Pringle, Robt. Hand, Bosden Guinn, Danl. Robertson, John Garrett, Mark Owen, James Cook, Nimrod Putman, Abner Putman, John Cowen, Nehemiah Franks, Thos. Crooks, Tollever Roberson, Solomon Glasby, Abner Knight, James Noble, Norman Garrett, Reuben Dollar, Stephen Garrett, Wm. Cheek, John C. Putman, Wm. Bramblett. (also spelled Duleybella Putman). Stephen Garrett and Nimrod Putman, adms.

12 Jan. 1828. Robert Hollingsworth, about 20 yrs., Susana Hollingsworth, about 18 yrs., and Unisa Holingsworth, about 15 yrs., chose William Ligon guardian. John McGowan and Alexander Austin, sur.

17 Dec. 1827. Appraisal estate of MARY MEADORS, dec'd by Ishum Milum, James Bradocks and Richd. Bonds. 18 Dec. 1827. Sale Bill. W. Meadors, exr.

13 Dec. 1827. Appraisal estate of WILLIAM TAYLOR, dec'd by Robt. Cunningham, Wm. Goodwin and Andw. Parks, Sr.

4 Feb. 1828. Adm. estate of JAMES SMITH, SR., dec'd to James Smith, Jr. Israel Teague and Aron Clore, sur.

15 Jan. 1828. John Black and Thos. Burnside vs Thos. & Martha Quin?. Court of Equity re minor children of THOMAS CROSON, dec'd i. e.: Julian, Melidon, Permila and Thomas. Maj. John Black, guardian.

18 Jan. 1828. Appraisal of estate of JAMES HENDERSON, dec'd by Joshua Franks, Ira L. Potter, Wm. F. Downs and Stephen Potter.

22 Dec. 1827. Appraisal of estate of HARRIS GOODWIN, dec'd by Hosa Holcomb, Nathan Holcomb and Thos. M. YOung. Cealia Goodwin, adm. 6 Feb. 1828. Return of good notes and book acct's belonging to estate. Celey Goodwin, adm. Notes on Jno. Guin, Larkin Bramblett, Danl. Wallis, Wm. Couth, Danl. Long, etc.

6 Dec. 1827. Inventory of crop of WILLIAM ABERHAMS, dec'd by Jno. Dillard, Z. Sparks and Mathew McCrary. 6 Dec. 1827. Inv. of the general or last property. Henry S. Neel, adm.

6 Feb. 1828. Adm. of estate of JAMES WILLSON, dec'd to Sarah Willson. Henry R. Bowling and Edw. Weasson, sur.

15 Feb. 1828. Will of SUSANAH LIGON, dec'd proven. Will dated 28 Aug. 1827. Estate to be sold and divided between all my sur- viving children; dau. Polly Holmans; dau. Susannah Grier. Sons William Ligon and Joseph Ligon, exrs. Wit: Anthony G. Golding, Eliza Ligon and Reuben Hill.

19 Feb. 1828. Adm. of estate of CHARLES FURGESON, dec'd to John F. Kern. John J. P. Kern and John Boyce, sur.

9 Nov. 1827. Estate sale of JAMES GLOVER, dec'd. Pur.: Elizabeth Glover, Zebulon West, Alexander Winn, Wm. Savage, Lewis Smith, Joseph Neely, Geo. Madden, Jno. Sims, Standford Glover, Jonathan Shirley, David Anderson, Robt. Flemming, Alexander Austin, Robt. Cunningham. Notes and accounts belonging to estate. 13 Dec. 1827. 2nd sale of estate. Geo. Anderson, adm.

(No date) Appraisal of property of JAMES CALDWELL, dec'd by Anthony F. Golding, Wm. Vance, David Vance and Allen Andrews. Appraise bill of property to be disposed of at publick auction. (No date on either). Geo. F. Caldwell, acting exr. 26 Dec. 1827. Sale bill. Pur: Saml. Caldwell, A. F. Golding, Allen Andrews, Jno. W. Williams, Saml. Waldrop, Peter SAdler, Henry Craddock, Hosa Johnston, Littel B. Turner, David Vance, Wm. Jones, Saml. Abernathy, Robt. Black, Jno. M. Simpson. Notes due.

3 Mar. 1828. Estate of BARTLET MILUM, JR., dec'd. Jane Milum, adm. An accounting on estate, etc. paid legacies to Aron Milum, Polly Milum, Sally Milum. Allen, Emely, Elizabeth, July Ann, Polley and Rebeca Milum. Adm. revoked and granted to Wm. Fuller husband of the former adm. Jones Fuller and Jacob Millar, his sur.

30 Dec. 1827. Return of James Scott, guardian of Martha, Sarah, Ann, Patrick, Thomas, Margret and Elizabeth Watts?, minors. Rec'd from Joseph McConatha, adm. of Saml. McConatha. (N. B. children may be named Scott, not clear).

19 Feb. 1828. Appraisal of estate of JAMES SMITH, dec'd by John B. Simpson, James Durroh and Jehu Pitts. 20 Feb. 1828. Sale Bill. Pur.: John Smith, Isaac Teague, Danl. Johnston, Richd Waldrop, James Smith, Henry Pitts, James Crocker, Plesant Shaw,. Adm. of James Smith, Sr., dec'd, James Smith, Jr., adm.
14 Jan. 1828. Appraisal of estate of WILLIAM THOMPSON, SR., dec'd by Thos. Ligon, Richd. Golding and Saml. Allen. (Property which is to be sold). Appraisal of property which is not to be sold, 14 Jan. 1828. Sale Bill 15 Jan. 1828. Pur: Hugh Leeman, Anthony F. Golding, James Wright, James Leeman, Hunter Brison, Wm. H. Ligon, Abraham Thompson, Wm. Thompson, Jno. Moore, Wm. Bryson, Obediah Mishure, Wm. Austin, Wilson Sanders (rest very difficult to read; print is faint).

7 Apr. 1828. Will of MARTIN MILLER, dec'd proven. Will dated 6 Oct. 1827. William Arthur Fuller; beloved wife Martha; child- ren not named. Sons Franklin Miller and Albert Miller, exrs. As they are minors, I appoint friend Jones Fuller, N. C. to

MILLER cont'd:
manage my estates until they are of lawful age. Wit: Solomon
Fuller, Robt. Bryson and Wm. Bryson.

7 Apr. 1828. Will of JOHN RODGERS, dec'd proven. Will dated
20 July 1827. Wife Salley Rodgers; son James L. Rodgers; daus.
Lucinda Brownlee, Tabitha Martin married to Berry Martin, and
Jane Rodgers. Exrs: son James S. Rodgers, son-in-law Thomas
Brownlee and friend Charles Allen. Wit: Henry S. Beadel, Wm.
Pitts, Jr. and Marey Reynolds.

23 Mar. 1828. Adm. of estate of JAMES GRIFFEN, dec'd to Wade
H. Griffen. Thos. Teague and Wm. Lereel?, sur.

(No date) Sale of property of SUSANAH LIGON, dec'd. Pur.: Saml.
Allen, Jno. Philips, Wm. H. Ligon, David Greer, Wm. Harris,Saml.
Rodgers.

15 Apr. 1828. Will of MARY WILLIAMS, dec'd proven. Will dated
12 Aug. 1826. To Mary Amanda Cooper, dau. of Elizabeth Cooper,
wife of Reuben Cooper; Elizabeth Cooper my dau.; sons-Elihu
Duke Williams, Franklin Williams and Washington Williams; all
my children whose names shall not be found herein. Sons named
here are her exrs. Wit: Anthony F. Golding, Samuel Goodman and
I___ W. Williams.

14 Apr. 1828. Appraisal of estate of MARTIN MILLER, dec'd by
Solomon Fuller, Jesse Motes and Henry Fuller.

20? Feb. 1828. Appraisal of estate of JAMES WILLSON, dec'd by
W. B. Rowland, Edmond Wesson and Lewis Jones. 21 & 22 Feb. 1828.
Sale Bill. Pur.: Ephraim Jones, Thos. Prather, Saml. Jones,
James Blackburn, Wade Johnston, Washington Medors, Warner Mead-
ors, Gideon Conner, Wm. Page, Wm. Burge, Saml. Young, Jno. John-
ston, Abner Teague, Jno. Dillard, Jno. Fergeson, Wm. Lord, Thos.
McCracken, Mary Meadors, Wm. McHue, Richd. Fergeson, Sarah Will-
son, James Adair.

5 Mar. 1828. Appraisal of estate of CHARLES FERGUSON, dec'd
by John Boyce, Jno. Luke, Sr., and Geo. McCrary. 10 Mar. 1828.
Sale Bill. Signed: John F. Kern, Jr.

28 Nov. 1827. Appraisal of estate of Dr. GEORGE ROSS, dec'd
by Benj. Boyd, Jno. Boyce and Thos. Cargill.

4 May 1828. William A. Fuller, minor of 15 years, chose Jones
Fuller of N. Carolina his guardian. Jacob Miller and Henry Fuller
his sur.

5 Apr. 1828. Appraisal of estate of JAMES GRIFFIN, dec'd by
Wm. Leavell, Wm. D. Vance and J. Johnston. Wade H. Griffen,
adm., and son of James Griffen. 14 Apr. 1828. Sale Bill of personal estate.

8 May 1828. Sale Bill of estate of MARTIN MILLER, dec'd. Pur:
Jacob Miller, Jno. McClanning, Israel Fuller, Martha Miller,
Garlington Young, Wm. Ligon, Henry Fuller. Jones Fuller of N.
C., exr.

23 May 1828. Adm. of estate of HENRY JOHNSTON, dec'd to Jesse
Johnston. John Abel and Saml. Copeland, sur.

2 June 1828. Adm. of estate of WILLIAM VAUGHN, dec'd to James

VAUGHN cont'd:
Henderson. Robt. Coker and Jno. Henderson, sur.

17 May 1828. Appraisal of estate of JOHN RODGERS, dec'd by C.
Barksdill, Jno. Woody and Wm. Pitts, Sr.

6 Dec. 1828. Appraisal of estate of HENRY JOHNSTON, dec'd by
Jno. Simpson, James Copeland and Heney Johnston.

7 June 1828. Appraisal of estate of WILLIAM VAUGHN, dec'd by
R. Coker, Jno. Henderson and Harper Coker. 18 June 1828. Sale
Bill. Pur: Wm. Simpson, Jno. Henderson, Jno. Simpson, Chas.
Saxon. James Henderson, adm.

4 Aug. 1828. Will of MARTIN BALL, dec'd proven. Will dated 4
Sept. 1827. Wife Hannah. Thos. Garrett, Esq., exr. Wit: Jeremiah
Ball, Benjamin Martin and Reuben Ball.

19 May 1826. Sale bill of real estate of ELIJAH TEAGUE, dec'd
with Abner Teague, exr.

(No date) Statement of notes and open accounts due the estate
of CHARLES FERGUSON, dec'd. Jno. F. Kern, adm.

5 Sept. 1828. Will of JAMES DUNKEN, dec'd proven by Bordewine
Roberts and Benj. Duckett. First proven by oath of Margret Flanagan, one of the wit. and qualified Bordewine Roberts, exr.
Will dated 20 May 1820. Dau. Mary Dunken; son Joseph Dunken;
son Jonathan Dunken; dau. Elizabeth Jones, wife of Whitman Jones;
dau. Margret Jeanes, wife of John Jeanes; children of my dec'd
son David Dunken; dau. Sarah Jones, wife of Frederick Jones.
Exrs: Bordewine Roberts and Benjamin Duckett. Wit: Margret Flanagan, Reuben Flanagan and James Flanagan.

7 June 1828. Sale Bill property of HENRY JOHNSTON, dec'd. Pur.:
Wm. Johnston, John Gambell, John Horton, Job Johnston, John
Johnston, Nancy Yeget, Thos. Enterkin, Saml. Young, Thos. Mar-
shall, Robt. Johnston, Jesse Johnston, Saml. Furgeson, Philip
Martin, Rich Godfree, Chas. Littel, James McHarden, Elizabeth
Copeland, Wm. Boyd, Saxon McCoy, Catharine Boland, Robt. M.
Littel, John Simpson, Wm. Laird. Notes on James Copeland, Nancy
Tygert, James Simpson, Thos. Enterkin, Wm. Johnston, Thos. Enter-
kin, Obediah Roberts, Jno. Barksdill. Jesse Johnston, adm.

6 Sept. 1828. Adm. of estate of DANIEL SMITH, dec'd to Henry
D. Kelsey. Asa Forgey and Geo. Moore, sur.

14 Sept. 1828. Citation against William Fuller, adm. of BARTLET
MILUM, dec'd. Joseph Harten, guardian of Almon Milum, Emity
(Emily?) Milum, Elizabeth Milum and Judy Milum; Elizabeth Milum
has since married; Wm. Fuller's attorney, W. James Irby and
Mr. P. Farrow for sd Jos. Harton.

25 Sept. 1828. Adm. of estate of WILLIAM COLEMAN, dec'd to John
H. Coleman. John Wood and John Findley, sur.

18 Sept. 1828. Return taken out by Thomas Hilton and Rebeca
his wife against Wm. Park, adm. of MITCHEL DUNLAP, dec'd. to
pay over accounts.

15 Sept. 1828. Appraisal of est. of JAMES DUNCAN, dec'd by Steph.
Hill, Ryland Roberts and Edw. Jones. 27 Sept. 1828. Sale Bill.

DUNCAN cont'd:
Pur: Thos. Garrett, Joseph Duncan. Brady W. Roberts, exr.

9 Aug. 1828. Inventory of est. of MARTIN BALL, dec'd by Henry
Martin, Benjam Horten and Reuben Ball. 29 Aug. 1828. Sale Bill.
Pur: Saml. Parson, Reuben Ball, Ambrose Garrett, Wm. Stephens,
John Garrett, Jeremiah Ball, Ransom Fuller, Jesse Garrett, Steph.
Garrett, Fleming Mosley, Thompson G. Parsons, Wm. Powers, Sr.,
Saml. Fleming, Edmond Garrett, Wm. Simpson, Thos. Garrett, Star-
ling Tucker, Towlar Roberson, Robt. Hand, Wm. Powers, Jr., Saml.
Hunter, David Higgins, Stephen Garrett, Jr., Harmon Garrett,
Isaac Garrett, Henry Martin, Homer Garrett, Isaac Brown, Jacob
Bowen, James B. Higgen, Wm. Bowing, James Higgins, Jr., Lewis
Cargill, Reuben Thomas, Lewis Cooper, Wm. Ashley, Saml. Franks,
James Bell.

20 Oct. 1828. Will of WILLIAM IRBY, dec'd proven. Will dated
17 Sept. 1828. Dau. Nancy Dill (grocery store in village of
Laurens) dec'd being a partner of her husband, John Dill; son
William Irby; dau. Frances Cheek; son Joseph Irby; dau. Eliza-
beth Benham; son James H. Irby (lot in village); dau. Henretta
Cook; son Samuel Irby; dau. Sarah Klink; grandson Irby James
Dunkling; disposal of town lots, grave yard, village property,
etc. (N. B. grandson also named Dunken/Duncan); other children
-names vary in spelling, i. e. Clink, Dice. Wit: Thos. F. Jones,
P. Farrow and Wm. G. Davis.

23 Oct. 1828. Est. of JOHN CHANDLER, dec'd. Asa Chandler, exr.
and his mother, Mary Chandler Ware, exr. Dec'd willed wife a
life estate in his proven will; Mary has departed this life
and and estate should be sold according to will and divided.
Appraisal granted.

20 Oct. 1828. Adm. of estate of ABNER TEAGUE, dec'd to Frederick
Foster. Abner Cranshaw and John S. James, sur.

7 Oct. 1828. Adm. of est. of MOSES COLE, dec'd to Marshal Starnes
with John White and Geo. Anderson his sur.

20 Oct. 1828. Adm. of estate of JOHN BOYD, dec'd to John D.
Boyd. Wm. G. David and Nathl. Day., sur.

(No date) Sale Bill estate of JENNET MC CLANAHAN, dec'd. Saml.
McClanahan, adm. Pur: Jno. Goggins, A. M. Saxon, James Conner,
Mansfield Nixon, E. Ridgway, Danl. Johnston, James Poole, Jeremiah Manley, Wm. Manley, Henry Burrow, Howey Nabours, Jno. Cunningham, Catharine Pinson, Danl. South, Andw. McKnight.

(No date) Appraisal of estate of MARY WILLIAMS, dec'd by J.
L. Watts, Jno. D. Williams and Jos. Ligon. Notes on: John D.
Williams, exr. of Jos. Williams; Reuben Cooper. Franklin Wil-
liams, exr.

3 Nov. 1828. Adm. of estate of WILLIAM THOMAS, dec'd to Gambrel
Thomas. Reuben Thomas and James Wilson, sur.

3 Nov. 1828. Will of SARAH MILLER, dec'd proven. Will dated
19 Sept. 1828. Step son John Miller; cousin Jeremiah Cason;
step-dau. Mary Smith; Nancy Cason, dau. of Wm. Cason; Sally
Parks, dau. of Sally Parks now living on David Mason's place;
step-dau. Rebecah Cason; William Miller; bro. William Cason
and bro. Thomas Cason's children: Elizabeth Burkhalter and Thos.

MILLER cont'd:
Cason also bro. Thomas Cason's sons William Cason, John Cason
and Samuel Cason. Step son John Miller and Joshua Smith, exrs.
Wit: Frederick Foster, Henry Garling, Jr. and Alfred Nance.

3 Nov. 1828. Citation by John Miller to show cause if any ab-
jection for the sd Miller to adm. est. of MARY CASON, dec'd
he being the exr. of Sarah Miller, exr. of sd Mary Cason, dec'd.
He was qualified as exr.

5 Nov. 1828. Will of WALTER P. VAUGHN, dec'd proven. Will dated
18 July 1827. Niece Elizabeth Chappell Vaughn, dau. of my bro.
Drury Vaughn, she under 18 yrs of age. Sd niece and friend Chas.
Eggerton and bro. Drury Vaughn, exrs. Wit: A. B. Cook, Chas.
Egerton and Archebald Todd.

21 Nov. 1828. Petition of Zimrie Carter and Richd. Carter, exrs.
of ROBERT CARTER, dec'd noting the life est. given to ELIZABETH
CARTER, now dec'd, est. should be sold. App. granted.

18 Nov. 1828. Will of ANN JANE BURNSIDE, dec'd proven. Will
dated 29 Jan. 1827. Her share of her father and bro's William
and Thomas Burnside's estate to her three sisters: Elizabeth
Burnside, Martha Burnside and Hannah Burnside. William Burnside
and George Burnside, sons of Andrew Burnside as exrs. Wit: James
Hollingsworth, Danl. Jones and Nancy Jones.

18 Nov. 1828. Will of MARTHA BURNSIDE, dec'd proven. Will dated
29 Jan. 1827. All her share of father and bro's William and
Thomas Burnside's estate to her three sisters: Elizabeth Burnside, Ann Jane Burnside and Hannah Burnside. William Burnside,
son of Andrew Burnside and George A. Burnside, exrs. Wit: James
Hollingsworth, Daniel Jones and Nancy Jones.

18 Nov. 1828. Adm. of estate of ELLIS MOTES, dec'd to Jones
Fuller. Geo. Roberts and Wm. Fuller, sur.

17 Nov. 1828. Adm. of estate of EPHRAIM JONES, dec'd to Lewis
Jones. Saml. Jones and Woolf Benjamin, sur.

17 Nov. 1828. Adm. of estate of NATHAN PUGH, dec'd to William
Crumton. Hosa Holcumb and Wm. Halbert, sur.

21 Nov. 1828. Appraisal of estate of WILLIAM THOMAS, dec'd by
J. Moore, James Smith and Geo. Cook. 22 Nov. 1828. Sale Bill.
Pur: James Wilson, Geo. Cook, Jno. Vaughn, Jr., Reuben Thomas,
David Knight, Jno. Vaughn, Sr., George Vaughn. 1 Dec. 1828.
Notes and cash on hand. David Knight, Gambrel Thomas, Wm. Bow-
land, Jno. Vaughn, Abner Knight, Thos. Garrett. Gambriel Thomas,
adm.

6 Dec. 1828. Adm. of estate of ELIZABETH ADKISON, dec'd to Saml.
Todd. John Chappell and Saml. J. Adkison, sur.

6 Dec. 1828. Adm. of estate of JOHN M. ADKISON, dec'd to Saml.
J. Adkison. John Chappell and Saml. Todd, sur.

27 Oct. 1828. Appraisal of estate of MOSES COLE, dec'd by R.
Puckett, J. White and Wm. Braxton. Marshal Starnes, adm. 27
Oct. 1828. Sale Bill. Pur.: James Pinson, Joel Weathers, Richd.
Weathers, Wade Puckett, Seth Miller, Aron Pinson, Elihu Rigby,
Bowfort Tinsley, Jno. Busbey, Elihu Ryley.

25 Nov. 1828. Appraisal of estate of HUNTER BRYSON, dec'd by Wm. Bryson, Mathew Bryson, Abraham Tompson and Robt. Bryson.

8 Oct. 1828. Appraisal of estate of DANIEL SMITH, dec'd by James Cook, S. R.? Cook and H. P. Gains. 8 Oct. 1828. Sale Bill. Pur: Prior Morrison, James Mattocks, Henry P. Gains, Aaron Clore, Silus P. Gains, Thos. Cook, Henry B. Kelsey, Wm. Pucket, Mansfield Nixon. Henry B. Kelsey, adm.

11 & 12 Nov. 1828. Sale Bill property of WILLIAM COLEMAN, dec'd. Pur.: Geo. W. Johnston, Joseph Wilcutt, Philip S. King, Israel Holt, Wm. G. Coleman, Wm. H. Motes, Andrew Winn, Larkin Coleman, Danl. Carter, Jno. W. Coleman, Robt. Nickel, Polly Coleman, Jacob Miller, Wm. Golding, Allen Walker, James Long, Alsey Fuller, Danl. Winn, Harmon Fuller, JOhn Kelley, Madison Motes, Jones Fuller, Wm. Fuller, Betsey Carter, Wm. A. Young.

9 Dec. 1828. Appraisal of estate of ABNER HILL, dec'd by Robt. Malone, Francis Hill and Daniel Foshee. 11 Dec. 1828. Sale Bill. (N. B. name now shown as Hitt). Pur.: Wm. R. Smith, John Chappell, John Hazlet, Wm. Smith, Jno. D. Williams, Abraham Hollingsworth, Saml. Pool, Benj. Malden, Lewis Ball, Danl. Dendy, Jesse Hitt, J. P. Watts, James Watts, Elizabeth Hitt, Travis Hill, Wm. Sanders, Jno. P. Watts, Thos. Salmon, Saml. Adkison, Ricd. Owen, Jr., Richard Sims, Nancy Clark, Patrick Todd, Wm. Cook, Danl. Adkison, Jesse Hitt, Anthony Golding, Wm. Butler, Peter Hitt, John Hitt, Jr., John Gates, Elihu C. Watts. John Hill, adm.

31 July 1828. Appraisal of estate of DAVID GLENN, dec'd by John Owens, Chas. Gill and Richd. Owens. Bible, clock and 1 negro girl. Sale Bill same day. No purchasers named.

24 Nov. 1828. Appraisal of goods of WALTER P. VAUGHN, dec'd by A. Griffin, Wm. Smith and David Curiton. Drury Vaughn, exr. 25 Nov. 1828. Sale Bill. Pur.: James C. Vaughn, William B. Smith, Casen Hill, Patrick Smith, Duke Goodman, Samuel Todd, James Criswell, David Curiton, Wm. Smith, Thos. Chappell, James Watts, Chas. Snow, James Goodman, Robt. Stewart, Capt. A. Griffin, Philace Bryson, Saml. Aderson, Henry Hitt, Danl. Dumas, James Miller.

11 Nov. 1828. Appraisal of estate of ABNER TEAGUE, dec'd by Wm. Neill, Jr., Elijah Teague and M. D. Watts. Sale Bill (no date). Pur: Mrs. Susanah Teague, W. D. Watts, David Brooks, John Miller, William Neill, Elihu Griffin, Saml. Young, Wm. Brown, Thos. Wilson, Elijah Teague, Saxon McClay, James W. Merton, Thos. Dalrymple, Wm. Davis, Thos. Teague, Saml. Neel, Saml. Enterkin, Joseph Hips, Jr., Aberham Johnston, Saml. Hunter, Elijah Griffin, Jobe Johnston, Thos. Enterkin, Jr., James Stewart, James Boyd, Thos. Enterkin, Sr.

31 Dec. 1828. Appraisal of est. of THOMAS OWENS, Esq., dec'd also of the property in copartnership by sd Thos. Owens, Esq. and by Robt. Owens, adm. Appraised by John Luke, Sr., Geo. Dillard and John Dillard. Sale Bill not dated.

9 Dec. 1828. Appraisal of estate of EPHRAIM JONES, dec'd by Abraham Gray, Thos. Dalrymple and Ephraim Dalrymple. Lewis Jones, adm. 10 Dec. 1828. Sale Bill. (First page too dim to read). 2nd page: John Jones, Lewis Jones, Saxon McCay, Jno. Dalrymple, David Dalrymple, Jno. Brown, James McCartey, Jno. Saxon, James

JONES cont'd:
Linsey, Robert Littel, Wm. Adams, Thos. Dalrymple, Ephraim Dalrymple, David Mason, Hyrum David, Michael Dalrymple, Jobe Dalrymple, Humphrey Linsey, John Shepheard, Saml. Neil, Elijah Teague, Thos. Teague, Jno. Miller, Geo. Johnston. Lewis Jones, adm. of E. Jones, dec'd.

17 Nov. 1828. Upon the death of ABNER TEAGUE, one of the exrs. of ELIJAH TEAGUE, dec'd, Joseph Hipps also being appointed exr. too oath of test. and appraisement was granted him in the estate of sd ELIJAH TEAGUE, dec'd. 21 Nov. 1828. Appraisal of estate by James Boyd, Joseph Hipps and John Miller. Note on Thos. Wilson and Joseph Hipps.

15 Dec. 1828. Polley Young and William Young, minors the age of 15 years, and chose Joseph Young their father their guardian. Robt. Rowland and John Young, sur.

4 Dec. 1828. Appraisal of estate of ELLIS MOTES, dec'd by Jesse Motes, Henry Fuller and Solomon Fuller. 5 Dec. 1828. Sale Bill. Jones Fuller, N. C., adm.

(No date) Sale Bill of estate of MARY CASON, dec'd. Pur: Abner Young, Abner Teague, Thos. Teague. John Miller, exr.

(No date) Appraisal of estate of SARAH MILLER, dec'd by Wm. Neill, Frederick Foster and Saml. Neill. John Miller, exr. 1st Sale Bill not dated. 2nd Sale Bill dated 25 Apr. 1829. Pur. at 1st sale: John Miller, Frederick Foster, James Boyd, Hedly Davis, Sarah Brooks, Michael Dalrymple, David Boyd, Wm. Brown, Thos. Williams, Saml. Enterkin, G. Marshall, Wm. Boyd, Abraham Johnston, Jesse Enterkin, Gideon Cannon, Thos. Teague, Wm. Moore, Thos. Dalrymple, Henry Shell, Jr., Saml. Neill, E. Dalrymple, Abner Young, Allen Midleton, Wm. Lord, Thos. Enterkin, Joshua Smith, Geo. Johnston, John Dalrymple, Saxon McCay.

(No date) Appraisal of property of MARY CASON, dec'd by Wm. Neill, Frederick Foster and Saml. Neill. (See above for Sale Bill). Estate comprised of 6 negroes.

5 Jan. 1829. Will of JOSEPH YOUNG, dec'd proven. Will dated 28 May 1823. Son Robert; son Joseph land adj. Robt. Criswell and Susannah Leek, surveyed by Wm. Dunlap 25 Feb. 1823; dau. Elizabeth Rowland; son John land adj. Martha McClintock, Robt. Young, James Brown and my son Joseph Young. James Young, son of Wm. Young, sole exr. Wit: Wm. Dunlap, J. Craddock and J. Dunlap.

6 Jan. 1829. Adm. of estate of BA'T. CRADDOCK, dec'd to John Garlington. Saml. McClanahan and Chas. Littel, sur.

5 Jan. 1829. Estate of LUCY SMITH, dec'd. Will proven. Legatees entered a protest against probate of sd will by James Irby, their att'y. Wm. Young appeared in behalf of sd will. Will to be recorded this 5th day Jan. 1829. Letters test. to P. Charles Allen as exr.

25 Jan. 1829. Adm. of estate of JOHN W. MOTES, dec'd to Moses Griffin. Jno. Findley and Israel Holt?, sur.

4 Feb. 1829. Will of ELIZABETH BURNSIDE, dec'd proven. Will dated 7 Nov. 1828. All est. and her part of father's est. and

BURNSIDE cont'd:
my interest in my two sisters Martha, Ann Jane and Hannah Burnside. Wm. and George Burnside, sons of Andw. Burnside, exrs.
Wit: James and Anna Young, and Mary Burnside.

30? Dec. 1828. Appraisal of estate of JOHN ADKESON, JR., dec'd
by James Watts, David Curiton and Francis Hill. 30 Dec. 1828.
Sale Bill. Joseph Owen, Drury Vaughn, James Cook, Patrick Lynnet, Chas. Snow, Saml. Pool. Saml. Adkeson, adm.

2 Feb. 1829. Adm. of estate of ABRAHAM GRAY, dec'd to Leslie.
John Deen and John Taylor, sur.

29 Dec. 1828. Inventory of estate of ELIZABETH ADKISON, dec'd
by James Watts, David Curiton and Francis Hill. 30 Dec. 1828.
Sale Bill. Pur: Samuel Adkison, Anthony McFall, James Miller,
Anthony Golden, Richd. Watts, Richd. Golden, Lewis Ball, Wm.
Wood, Francis Hill, Jno. Hazel, Wm. Cook, Nathan Proctor, Wm.
Austin, Wm. Todd, Rody Valentine. Saml. Todd, adm.

23 Dec. 1828. Appraisal of estate of ANN JANE BURNSIDE, dec'd
by Saml. Rodgers, James Hollingsworth and Benj. Brown.

23 Dec. 1828. Appraisal of estate of MARTHA BURNSIDE, dec'd
by same as above.

13 Feb. 1829. Appraisal of estate of ELIZABETH BURNSIDE, dec'd
by James Young, Benj. Brown, Saml. Rodgers and J. Hollingsworth.
William Burnside, exr.

1 Jan. 1829. 2nd Sale Bill of estate of SUSANAH LIGON, dec'd.
Pur.: John Owen and Thos. Ligon.

9 Nov. 1828. Richard Carter, Robert Carter, John R. Carter and
Henry N. Carter, all minors, chose Zimry Carter, guardian. Sur.
not clear.

26 Nov. 1828. Appraisal of estate of JOHN CHANDLER, the Second,
dec'd by Alsey Fuller, Richd. Golden and Wm. Dunlap. Sale Bill.
(Date dim). Pur.: Elihu Griffin, Wait Chandler, Thos. Blakely,
Elijah Teague, John Davis, Danl. Martin, Silus Dendy, West Chand-
ler, Robt. Milum, Wm. Dunlap, Robt. Milum, Saml. Barksdill,
Clardy Davis, Jno. Blakely, Joel Dendy, Jeremiah Leek, Orsborn
Reder, Asa Chandler.

15 Mar. 1829. Adm. of estate of ALLEN SAXON, dec'd to Hugh Saxon.
Charles Williams and Allen Barksdill, sur.

7 Feb. 1829. Inventory of estate of ABRAHAM GRAY, dec'd by Elias
Cheek, R. Cottrell and Thompson Farley. 25-26-27 Feb. 1829.
Sale Bill. First notes due 25 Dec. 1830. Notes on: Jesse Gray,
James Park, Richard Cottrell, Harmon Garrett, Chas. Farrow,
David Higgen, Thos. F. Farrow, Robt. Hand, Zana Gray, Edw. Gar-
rett, Forrest Farley, Jno. Taylor, Saml. Meredith, Eliza Gray,
Foley Brown, Tolletson Gray, Benj. Griffin, Andw. Martin, Abra-
ham Gray, James Kenedy, Saml. Gentry, John Dean, Wm. Fowler,
John Harris, Anderson Moore, Elias Cheek, Gabriel B. Styles,
Flemming Mosley, Nelson Meredith, Wm. Holbert, Jno. Atteway,
Jno. Hannah, Jno. Todd, Zachariah Gray, Lowery Sanford, Saml.
Flemming, Alex. McCurley, Wm. Stone, Jno. Sandford, Ira Waldrop,
Wm. Sandford, Thos. Campbell, Frances Ross, Walton Wallis, Wm.
Powers. Leslie Gray, adm.

24 Mar. 1829. Will of ZACHARIAH ARNOLD, dec'd proven. Will dated
15 Nov. 1828. Beloved wife Mary Arnold; son Lewis I.? *Arnold;
son William A.* Arnold; dau. Sarah Arnold; dau. Nancy E. E. Arnold; grandson George Berry West mothers share; Mary West; Jesse
Brown Mosley if he will stay and work on my plantation with
my family until he is of age; dau. Rebecah Flinn; (son's middle
initial appears to be a "J" in later part of will and son's
middle name is Anthony*). Wife and John West, exrs. Wit: Reuben
Powell, Reuben Arnold and Mark Mosley. Follows a memo. of property given to his children naming Mary West, Judy West, mother
of George B. West, Rebeca Flinn.

6 Feb. 1829. Appraisal of estate of JOSEPH YOUNG, dec'd by Wm.
Dunlap, Saml. Young, Jno. Holland and W. D. Watts. James Young,
exr. 7 Feb. 1829. Sale Bill. Pur.: Robt. Holland, Joseph Young,
James Young, Robert Bell, James Young, Jr., Robert Rowland,
Joshua Teague.

6 Apr. 1829. Will of ESTHER BROWNLEE, dec'd proven. Will dated
19 Nov. 1828. James Brownlee in trust for my dau. Alsey Babb.
James Brownlee, exr. Wit: F. Richardson, Jno. Martin and Mary
L. Richardson.

6 Apr. 1829. Application of July Ann Gains, widow and mother
of Gracy Adline Gains, minor, for James Clardy be appointed
her guardian. James Crocker and Mensill Owens, sur.

26 Jan. 1829. Appraisal of estate of BATHOLUME CRADDOCK, dec'd
by R. W. Simpson, Abner Pyles and David Martin. 26 Jan. 1829.
Sale Bill of estate of BARTHALOMEW CRADDOCK, dec'd. Cash rec'd
of William W. Simpson for cotton sold in Columbia, 30 Mar. 1829.
Signed: John Garlington.

(No date) Appraisal of estate of JOHN BOYD, SR., dec'd by Feril
Milum, Hardy Davis and John Dandy. (Long list of slaves, and
notes due estate). 1 Jan. 1829. Sale Bill of estate. Pur: J.
S. James, Ransom Fuller, Andrew Floyd, Wm. Low, Sr., Joel Allen,
Nathl. Vance, John Bird, Walter Deen, Saml. Fleming, John Floyd,
J. H. Bird, Johnston Floyd, Francis Ross, Chas. Allen, P. Bobo.

6 Apr. 1829. Adm. of estate of JOHN BROWN, dec'd to James Brown.
James Crocker and Robert Ward, sur.

11 Apr. 1829. Will of PEGGEY FORGEY, dec'd was proven. Will
dated 9 June 1828. Dau. Rachel McFerson; James McFerson; sons
Menoah and Asa Forgey; Robert Cunningham; negro to be valaued
by Martin Shaw, James Henderson and George Anderson. Friend
Geo. Anderson, Merchant, my exr. Wit: Elijah Elmore, Rachel
Anderson and D. Anderson.

18 May 1829. Adm. of estate of JOHN MC MICKEN, dec'd to Esther
McMicken. Hosa Holcomb and Larken Stepp?, sur.

11 Apr. 1829. Appraisal of estate of ESTHER BROWNLEE, dec'd
by Lewis Smith, Thos. Babb and Henry Fuller.

8 Dec. 1828. Appraise bill of ROBERT CARTER, dec'd the 2nd by
Wm. Green, David Straine and Wm. Reed. 9 Dec. 1828. Sale Bill.
Pur.: Martin Shaw, Wm. Green, Jones Fuller, Wm. Barten, Robt.
Whiteford, Wm. Braxton, Isom Fuller, James Pinson, Geo. Redden,
Asey Fuller, Wm. Beasley, Mrs. Green, Wm. Nickle, D. Anderson,
Bluford Wallis, James Caldwell, John Fendley, Jno. Hill, Andw.

CARTER cont'd:
Anders, R. Puckett, Richd. Carter, James Carter, Elihu Riley,
Martin Strains, Alsey Fuller, Jno. McWilliams, Jno. Beasley,
Andw. Andrews, Haney Hendrick, Polly Riley, James Pinson, Joel
Pinson, W. W. Puckett, Jno. McGowan, Benj. Malding, Seth Welborn,
J. H. Coleman, Betsy Orsborn, Wm. Barton, Pattey Orsborn, Wm.
Green, Salley Riley, Alford Smith, F. R. Puckett. Zimrie Carter,
exr.

4 Apr. 1829. Appraisal of estate of ZACHARIAH ARNOLD, dec'd
by Saml. Freeman, Elihu Watson, Jno. Watson and Zebulon Savage.
25 Apr. 1829. Sale Bill of part of est. Pur: Geo. Moore, Wm.
Flinn, Berry Watson, Geo. Shirley, Patrick O'Hare, Wm. Flinn,
Jr., Jno. Watson, Sr., J. J. Richardson, Cornelius Cook, James
Book, Jno. Smith, Mrs. E. Glover, Henry Pope, Thos. Adkins,
Shubal Starne, James N. Golding, David P. Posey, Buckner Mosley,
Elihu Shirley. John West, exr.

1 Apr. 1829. Appraisal of estate of ALLEN SAXON, dec'd by S.
L. Madden, Saml. B. Craford and Wm. Arnold. Hugh Saxon, adm.
2 Jan. 1829 and 2 Apr. 1829. Sale Bill. Pur.: Ira Arnold, Jeffer-
son Arnold, Wm. Arnold, Saml. Craford, John Arnold, Wm. Arnold,
Geo. Brownlee, Wm. Cook, Geo. French, Silus Gains, Elias Fowler,
James Benjaman, Latimus Flemming, Andw. McKnight, Saml. Madden,
Jno. Mayhorn, Absolum Nixon, B. Lain Posey, Frank Posey, Wm.
Puckett, Hugh Saxon, Pleasant Shaw, John Smith, Persilla Saxon,
Jno. Williams, Lydral Williams, Nathan Puckett, Chas. Posey,
James Rogers, Jno. Simons, Jno. Walker, Larken Lowery.

5 May 1829. List of acct's found open on the books of ALLEN
SAXON, dec'd for the year 1822-1829.

20 Apr. 1829. Appraisal of estate of PEGGEY FORGEY, dec'd by
J. Findley, Lemarius Deale and Jno. H. Lockhart. Also dated
21 Apr. 1829. Sale Bill 21 Apr. 1829. Pur.: Menoah Forgey, Asa
Forgey, James McFerson, Joseph Irby, Geo. Moore, Wm. McFerson,
Martin Shaw, Jno. Adams, Sarah Fuller, Joel L. Anderson, Jno.
Boyd, Abraham Madden, Joseph Neely, Elias Brock, Seth Moore.
Notes due: Wm. McFerson, Jones Fuller, Lorenzadow McFerson,
Meryam Hunter, Jno. McCan, Joseph Irby, Saml. Richey, Robt.
Miller, (runaway) Foster Golding, Jacob Fuller, Seth Moore,
(runaway) Martin Graves, Wm. Winn, Joseph Prichard, Elizabeth
Shirley, Thomas Gray, Dilling Whorten, Jno. Arnold, Geo. Moore,
Alexander Winn, A. G. Buller, Martin Shaw. Geo. Anderson, exr.

13 May 1829. Citation against Peggey Devenport, adm. of BURQUET
DEVENPORT, dec'd taken out by Thomas Lockhart and Menoah Forgey,
adms. of JONATHAN FORGEY, dec'd. Lockhart was sur. for Peggey
Devenport, sur. revoked. It is said Peggey is married to a person
who has another wife living, etc. - parties made choice of Asa
Forgey as adm. of est. of BURKET DEVENPORT, dec'd. Thos. Lockhart and Menoah Forgey, sur.

12 Dec. 1828. Sale Bill of personal property of MARY WILLIAMS,
dec'd. Pur.: G. H. Crawford, C. D. Williams, Henderson Pittis,
Anthony Griffin, Henry Williams, Wm. Shepard, E. D. Williams,
Jno. D. Williams, Washington Williams. Note on Washington Williams given 22 Apr. 1829. Frankling Williams, exr.

7 Jan. 1829. 2nd Bill of personal estate of JAMES GRIFFIN, dec'd.
Huzen Johnston, Wm. Vance and Wm. Leavell. 7 Jan. 1829. 2nd
Sale Bill. Pur.: Wade Griffin, Richd. S. Griffin, Wm. M. Vance,

GRIFFIN cont'd:
Hedley Davis, Mrs. A. Horan, Danl. Shell, David Vance, D. F.
Sague?, Cranshaw Floyd, Harrison Jones. Wade H. Griffin, adm.

15 Jan. 1829. Appraisal of estate of WILLIAM IRBY, dec'd by
Thos. F. Jones, D. P. Saxon and Henry Cleveland. Jno. G. Klinck,
Justice. 7 Jan'y 1828. Sale Bill. Pur.: J. H. Irby, Wm. Irby,
Robt. McNees, James Cheek, Frances Cheek, J. G. Klink, Saml.
Irby, W. W. Vance, Jno. Davis, Noah Henderson, R. F. Simpson,
Jno. Simmons, F. A. Sharp, Wm. Park, William Perry.

9 July 1829. Will of JOHN MAYORS, dec'd proven. Will dated 14
May 1829. (also spelled Mayers/Meyors). To my "virtuous innocent
cuzen" Rachel Brown ..... if she marry some sober, sturdy, in-
dustrious young man....should she marry a gambler, drunkard
or a debauchee legacy shall not go to him or her.....as I have
been some trouble to the family of Bexey Brown during my sickness...their estate endebted to Dr. Young...also money lent
Mrs. Brown by Mr. Flanagan; to my cousin William Brown my tools
which are at Squire McClellans; to my friend, fellow traveler
and cousin Edward Flanagan and if he can find out the grave
of my mother in Columbia to place a headstone there, etc. Edw.
Flanagan, Moses Leake and Thos. Craig, exrs. Wit: Matthew E.
Cunningham, Sarah Carlisle, Davis? Leek and Nancy Cunningham.

4 Aug. 1829. Return of Samuel Copeland, guardian for Thomas
Littel, minor, his ward, of Charles Littel, exr. of DAVID LITTEL,
dec'd.

(No date) 2nd appraisal estate of BURQUET DEVENPORT, dec'd by
Thos. Lockhart, Jno. Finley and Lemareus Deale.

9 July 1829. Samuel Bell, minor, chose William Gambell, guardian.
Henry Shell and Saml. Copeland, sur.

15 Apr. 1829. Appraisal of estate of JOHN BROWN, dec'd by J.
Taylor, R. Mosley and W. Ross. 26 Apr. 1829. Sale Bill. Pur.:
Anne Brown, Harling Brown, Nicklus Brown, James Brown, Susan
Brown, Anderson Brown, Salley Brown, Nancey Brown, Starling
Tucker, Wm. Hunter, Chas. Farrow, Jno. Taylor, Nathan Bramblett,
Stephen Tulley, Gabriel Stiles, Even Read, Wm. Elliott, Fleming
Mosley, Chas. Fowler, Jno. Todd, Sr., Eycel Farley, Berrey Pool,
Jno. Attaway, Peter Hammond, Peter Pool, Even Real, Caleb Wood-
ruff, Martin Pool, Joel Allen.

7 July 1829. Appraisal of estate of JOHN MEYRES, dec'd by M.
E. Cunningham, James Fareborn and M. B. Sheldon. Notes on Jno.
McClintock, Moses Leak, Abner Teague and David Martin.

7 Sept. 1829. Adm. of estate of WILLIAM DILLARD, dec'd to Henry
Gray. Jno. Cunningham and Chas. Williams, sur.

7 Sept. 1829. William Neel and Langsdon East named exrs. of
will of ABRAHAM JOHNSTON, dec'd, the sd. Langsdon East is dec'd.
Will proven by John Hewit, wit. Anna Johnston, widow of sd.
dec'd granted adm. (will annexed). Will dated 19 July 1829.
Beloved wife Anna; four single children: Adey Johnston, Abraham
Johnston, Margret Johnston and Jesse Johnston; dau. Sarah Monrow; sons William and George; (N. B. Adey above is later named
Andrew); John Johnston and Andrew Monro. William Neel and Langsdon East, exrs. Wit: Jno. Hewit, Anderson Cobb and Wm. Horan.

2 Nov. 1829. Will of ELLENDER HILL, dec'd proven. Sale ordered

HILL cont'd:
of estate. John F. Kern, wit. Benjamin Hill, adm. Sale on the plantation for division of income to legatees. Will dated 30 Aug. 1828. Son William Hendrick Hill; son David Hill; son Stephen Hill; dau. Mary Burns; dau. Catharine Flinn; grand dau. Mary Turner, child of my son David; grand son Jacob William and grand dau. Elizabeth Emeline, children of my son Benjamin Hill; grand dau. Anne child of my son Isaac Hill; Mary Hill, wife of my son David; Susey Hill, wife of my son Benjamin Hill. Benjamin Hill, exr. Wit: John F. Kern, Jr., Jh. L. Kennedy and Alfred A. Kern.

20 Oct. 1829. Adm. of estate of DANIEL MARTIN, dec'd to James S. Rodgers. Harrey Young and Ledwill G. Williams, sur.

19 Oct. 1829. Adm. of estate of LANGSDON EAST, dec'd to William East. Wm. M. Vance and John R. Griffin, sur.

19 Oct. 1829. Adm. of estate of JOHN C. MURREL, dec'd to Thomas J. Dillard. Saml. Dillard and James Burk, sur.

20 Oct. 1829. Will of DAVID MASON, dec'd proven. Will dated 8 May 1820. Beloved wife Isbel Mason; son John; son James; John Young; dau. Mary; Hedley Davis; Abner Young; Samuel Young; dau. Elener's children; daus. Dorritha and Mary; Mary Ann Gray. Sons John and James Mason, exrs. Wit: Joshua Teague, Chesley Davis and Elijah Teague.

15 Aug. 1829. Will of REUBEN MEADORS, dec'd proven. Will dated 9 July 1829. Beloved wife Hannah; children - Susannah Prather, Preskal Meadors, Oney Meadors, Polley Parson, Martha Meadors, Reuben Meadors and James A. Meadors. Wife and son Preskal Meadors my exrs. Wit: H. S. Neel, Isham Milum and Robt. Adair.

20 Oct. 1829. Adm. of estate of JOHNSTON WEASON, dec'd to James Blackburn. Bleuford Griffin, Saml. Vance and Stephen Blackburn, sur.

19 Oct. 1829. Adm. of estate not disposed of by will of DAVID MASON, dec'd, to John Mason. Bond with Saml. Young, Hedley Davis and Jno. Young.

16 Oct. 1829. Inventory of estate of REUBEN MEADORS, dec'd by James Adair, Isham Milum and Warner W. Meadors. Notes due est: James Littel, Saml. Copeland, Archebald Prater and Sarah E. Saxon.

20 Nov. 1829. Will of DANIEL DANDY, dec'd proven. Will dated 9 Sept. 1829. Jenne, my dau.; youngest child comes of age (not named). Marcus Dandy and William Dandy, exrs. Wit: Jno. Chapman, Jno. W. Smith and Jat.? S. Godfrey.

15 Nov. 1829. Citation by Jacob Miller, Jr. to have the will of JACOB MILLER, SR., proven and recorded, Jones Fuller against probate and other legatees of sd. dec'd, their att'y Henry H. Young, Esq. against recording will and James H. Irby, Esq. for recording sd will, with due consideration, court is of the opinion that sd will was gained by undue influence and fraud was practiced on sd Jacob Miller, Sr., dec'd. Will not to be recorded. D. Anderson, Ord.

29 Oct. 1829. Inventory of Rights and Credits of the estate

cont'd:
of JOHNSTON WEASON, dec'd by F. F. Collins, Thos. Prater and
Edw. Weason. Note on Gideon Cannon, Edw. Weason, Danl. Owens,
James Gains, John E. Williams, Mrs. Sarah Ann Bennet, Saml.
Dillard, B. B. Gains, Fredrick Weason, Joseph Ramage, Wm. Par-
son, Briton Wiggans, Archabald Prather, David Cato, Saml. Mathews
with James Blackburn, adm. 6 Nov. 1829. Sale Bill. Pur.: Mrs.
E. Weason, Joseph Jeans, Edw. Weason, Jehue Weason, Thos. Ful-
ton, Mrs. E. Prather, Thos. Abrahams, Wm. Mountgomery, Wm. Fel-
der, Jesheph? Abrahams, Jno. Adair, Moses Betey, Lewis Parsley,
F. F. Calmos, Geo. Abrahams, James Adair, Delia Bennet, Wm.
H. Fulton, B. Mathews, F. J. Dillard, Saml. Mathews.

7 Dec. 1829. Sale Bill of personal est. of THOMAS HUNTER, dec'd.
Pur.: Mabery Hunter, Wm. Madden, Wm. Stone, Mabra Hunter, David
Madden, Joel Burges, Widow Hunter. Jno. Hunter, exr. Petition
of John Hunter for himself and guardian of Emeline and Caroline
Hunter, minors, Mabra Hunter, Elizabeth Hunter and Labun Hall
who married Salley Hunter for an order of sale which was grant-
ed 17 Dec. 1831. 2nd Sale Bill. Isaac Dial, Mabra Hunter, Ransom
Fuller, Albert Madden, Jno. Hunter, Wm. Davis, Jno. Fowler,
Allen Dial, Jno. L. Madden, Jno. Simmons, Wiley Milum, Haisten
Madden, James Collins, D. M. Winn, Elizabeth Hunter, L. Hall.

26 Dec. 1829. Adm. of estate of JAMES SOUTH, dec'd to Asa Forgey.
Thomas Lockhart and John Lockhart, sur.

21 Dec. 1829. Adm. of estate of JAMES BURNS, dec'd to Nancy
Burns. Samuel Lewars and Wm. Franks, sur.

12 Dec. 1829. Adm. of estate of ROBERT SHAW, dec'd to Martin
Shaw. Joel L. Anderson and Thomas Lockhart, sur.

29 Oct. 1829. Appraisal of estate of ELENOR HILL, dec'd by Jos.
Garrett, Linse? Whitten and Joseph Dollar. 25 Nov. 1829. Sale
Bill. Pur.: Isaac Hill, Benj. Hill, Lewis Conner, Mary Garrett,
James Flinn, Andrew Bobo, James Dillard, Jno. Garrett, Jno.
Miller, James Gaswick, John Norman, Jno. Hays, Wm. Robertson,
Enoch Garrett, Henderik Bobo, Jos. Dollar, Geo. Young, Jno.
Whitmore. Benj. Hill, exr.

31 Dec. 1829. Appraisal of personal est. of DANIEL DANDY, dec'd
by James Watts, Sr., Wm. R. Smith and Elihue C. Watts. Marcus
Dandy, exr. Certified 7 Jan. 1830.

(No date) Appraisal of estate of LANGSDON EAST, dec'd by W.
D. Watts, Wm. Neal and James Craford. Sale Bill (no date). Pur.:
Fredrick Foster, Wade Griffin, Saml. Neill, David Boyd, James
Stewart, Wm. East, Jr., Robt. Abel, Saml. Barksdill, James Lin-
sey, Jno. Luke, Wm. Johnston, Wm. Hewit, David Dalrymple, David
Enterkin, Robt. Long, Wm. Young, Lewis Jones, Saml. Young, John
Haney, Jesse? Lockeby, Andw. Monroe, Thos. Wilson, Wm. Neil,
Elizabeth East, Wm. Caldwell. Wm. East, Jr., adm.

14 Dec. 1829. Darby Nowland against Peter Gallihair, adm. of
PATRICK J. NOWLAND, dec'd - pay to sd Darby Nowland, Mikel Nowland, Ann Nowland (his wife), Catharine Nowland, John Hannon
and Mary Nowland, his wife. (N. B. Mikel Nowland has been marked
over what appears to be McFerson).

21 Dec. 1829. Appraisal of estate of DAVID MASON, dec'd by Fredrick Foster, Wm. Moore and Richd. Bonds. 21 Dec. 1829. Sale

MASON cont'd:
Bill of estate. Pur.: Abner Young, Hedley Davis, Saml. Jones, John Langston, John Deen, Andw. Hunter, Patrick Reeder, Fredrick Foster, Ezekiel Johnston, Thos. Wilson, Isaac Conner, Jeremiah Leek, Jno. Dreuson, Jno. Bonds, Jas. J. Carlisle, David Boyd, Wm. Smith, Jno. Murel, Jonathan Case, Saml. Young, Warner Meadors, Jno. Young, Carding Mesheen, James Mason, Jno. Luke, Andw. Chambers, Jno. Dillard, Jno. Dunken, Jno. Milum, Wm. Murkle, Jno. Beasley, Washington Meadors, Lofton Johnston, Jesse Dunken, Abraham Gray, Miles Furguson, Jno. Whitmore, Mrs. Mason, Richd. Bonds, Henry Langston, Jno. Holland, Lewis Jones, Even Linville, Jno. Horton, James Blackburn, Jno. Brown, Jno. Dalrymple, Jesse Bradley, Jefferson Dillard, Jno. Johnston, Robt. Adair, Jno. Bowling, Jno. Bell, James Niell, Jno. W. Tucker, Saml. Miller, Andy Monroe, Joel East, Robt. Duggan, Thos. Blakely, Bluford Griffin, Jno. Saxon, Thos. Leek, Pendleton Stokes, Danl. Lofton, Thos. Dalrymple, David Gambell, Jno. Epps, Robt. Long.

5 Nov. 1829. Appraisal of estate of DANIEL MARTIN, dec'd by Jno. Woody, Robt. Allison, Sr. and Collyar Barksdill. 6 Nov. 1829. Sale Bill. Pur.: Danl. Martin, Jr., Littel B. Martin, Carter Parker, Joseph Hopper, Drury Martin, Wm. Todd, L. B. Martin, Jas. S. Rodgers, Robt. Martin, Allen Deal, Jno. Dugless, Jno. Burress, Jr., Arnold Millener, W. D. A. Deen, P. D. A. Deen, Micajah Night, Callar Barksdill, Robt. Hopper, Lewis Deal.

9 Feb. 1826. Will of LUCY SMITH. Son Charles Allen; money due me in Virginia; Adkins, dau. of Lydral Allen; Frances and Cynthia Allen, daus. of Lydral Allen; grand son Joel Allen; dau. Sarah McNees; dau. Mary Harris; grand dau. Sarah Crisp and her dau. Lucy Crisp; Milley Allen, widow of Lydral Allen; grand dau. Lucy Brown Allen; grand dau. Harriet Saxon. Son Charles Allen, exr. Wit: Colville Abercrumbie, Jr., Mary Marshall and E. S. Rowland.

4 Dec. 1829. Sale Bill estate of BURQUIT DEVENPORT, dec'd. Pur.: Marstin Henderson, Ryley Milum, Lemorus Deal, Margret Devenport, P. G. Devenport, Jos. Abercrumbie, Andw. Todd, Henry Tompson, Jno. Todd, Chas. Brook, Wm. Todd, Jno. Henderson, Saml. Martin, Jno. Blakely, Elihu Pinson, Jno. Milum. Notes on Jacob Niswanger, Jno. Findley. Asa Forgey, adm.

28 & 29 Dec. 1829. 2nd Sale of property of JOHNSTON WEASON, dec'd. Pur.: Mrs. E. Weason, Edw. Weason, Jno. Whitmore, James Adaair, Thos. L. Leek, Moses Betty, Jos. Hughs, Jos. Abrahams, Claxdon Ray, Geo. Young, Jno. Richey, Jas. Challames, Saml. Pickering, Nancy Weason, Henry Bennet, Jas. Philips, Alex. Furguson, J. W. Tucker, Richd. Furguson, Geo. Abrahams, Wm. Presley, Nathan Whitmore, Julius Wison, Sarah Mathis, David Gambell, Reuben Anderson, Miles Furguson, Mrs. E. Dillard. James Blackburn, adm.

21 Oct. 1829. Appraisal of estate of ABRAHAM JOHNSTON, dec'd by A. B. Johnston, Robt. Hurt? and James Craford. 22 Oct. 1829. Sale Bill. Pur.: Saxon McCay, Anna Johnston, Henry Shell, Robt. Hunter, A. B. Johnston, Jno. Shepard, David Rooks, Wm. Farrow, Robt. Able, Jno. Johnston, Jno. McCay, Benj. Blakely, Geo. Johnston, W. D. Watts, Anderson Johnston, Andw. Monrow, Wm. Johnston, Elbert Linsey, Abraham Johnston, James Case, Jno. Willson, Wm. Hurt, Wm. Horne, David Vance. Ann Johnston, adm.

1 Feb. 1829. Jno. Mansfield Fowler, minor, chose Wm. Fowler,

FOWLER cont'd:
his guardian. William Holbert and Thomas Crymes, sur.

9 Feb. 1830. Will of JOSEPH NEELY, dec'd proven. Will dated
19 Oct. 1824. Dau. Rebeca Neely; son Young Neely; loving wife
Nancey Neely. Wife and and son, exrs. Wit: Robt. Campbell, Jos.
Willcutt and D. Anderson.

(No date) Notes, accounts, etc. due estate of DAVID MASON, dec'd.
Chesley Davis, Wm. Lord, Wm. Shepard, Wm. Vickery, Jno. Deen,
Stover Saxon, Jno. Linvell, Jno. Boyd, Linvell Stewart, Aron
Johnston, Jno. Cobb, Jno. M. Hunter, Andw. Monroe, Jacob Garey,
Thos. Willson, Jno. Saxon, Jno. Barksdill, Wm. Moor, Jos. Ramage,
Wm. Perchams, Mikel Sheldon, Even Linvell, Jno. Davis, black-
smith, Jno. Young, Richd. Davis, Saml. Hall, Abner Young, Wm.
Bennett, Robt. Philips, Danl. Conner, Jno. Chambers, Mikel Dal-
rymple, Jno. Enlow, Wm. Bandy, Robt. P. Keane, Jas. Copland,
Jas. Harding, Andw. Wheeler, Humphrey Linsey, Elbert Linsey,
Sr., Cullen Linsey, Jonathan Stanford, Jr., Isaac Finny, Eliza-
beth Williams, Margaret Leek, Wm. Cole, Jane Starks, Glenn Lin-
sey, Cornelius Bradley, Gabriel Cole, Casinder Williams, Eloner
Conner, Geo. Teague. Jno. Mason, exr.

2 Jan. 1830. Appraisal of estate of JAMES BURNES?, dec'd by
Wm. Franks, Jno. Franks and Martin Glidewell. 5 Jan. 1830. Sale
Bill of JAMES BURNS, dec'd. Pur.: Nancy Burns, Joseph Burns,
Beufort Burns, Alfred Barksdill, Alfred Jones, Jno. Simmons,
Jno. King, Wm. E. Linch, Jno. Vaughn, Jr., Jorden Burns, Bluford
Orsborn, Reuben Dollar, Jno. Orsborn, Sr., Bradock M. Burns,
Lewis Cargill, Wm. Franks, Matt Barksdill, Jno. Crisp, William
Powers, Saml. Franks, Kitt Burns, Geo. Vaughn, Chas. Knight,
Chas. Simmons. Note on Allen Burns and Nicklus Owens. Nancy
Burns, adm.

13 Feb. 1830. Will of THOMAS BURTON, dec'd proven. Will dated
12 Feb. 1827. Beloved wife RAchel Burton; sons William and Charles Burton; all my children (no names). Sons William and Charles,
exrs. Wit: Isaac J. Pinson, Jos H. Lowery and Augustin Marshall.

13 Jan. 1830. Appraisal of estate of JAMES SOUTH, dec'd by James
Henderson, Wm. H. Henderson and Jno. Fowler. 14 Jan. 1830. Sale
Bill. Pur.: Jno. Cannon, Nancy South, Jno. Todd, Jno. Fowler,
Saml. Morten, Thos. Williams, Starling South, Peggey South,
Newton South, Anthony South, Plesant Devenport, Jno. Burton,
Elias Brook, Aron Shirley, Turner Richardson, Harey Williams.
Asa Forgey, adm.

20 Feb. 1830. Adm. of estate of CHARLES BURTON, dec'd to William Burton. Jacob Elledge and John Burton, sur.

1 Mar. 1830. Will of JOHN ODELL, dec'd proven. Will dated 30
Jan. 1830. Wife Rebakey Odell; son Thomas Odel; son William
Odel; son John; dau. Elender Odell; dau. Margret Odell; dau.
Marthey Odell; Leave (Levi?) Rodgers. Friend Thomas Hendrick,
exr. Wit: K. L. Stephens, James Duncan and James J. Johnston.

1 Mar. 1830. Will of ISAAC GRAY, dec'd proven. Will dated 26
Mar. 1829. Dau. Salley Roundtree; John Taylor - land adj. Thos.
Farley and Salley Fowler and the heirs of Aberham Gray; Wm.
____; grand dau. Jenney Gray her husband John Gray; grand dau.
Eliza Gray; grand dau. Bathiah Meadors, wife of Thomas Meadors;
Aberham Gray to pur. for my grand dau. Mahla Meredith; grand-

GRAY cont'd:
children - Lesley Gray, Melepa Taylor, wife of John Taylor, Tollison Gray, Losina Gray, Poleskey Gray, Albelina Gray, Mekena (Melsena?) Gray, Madison Gray and Archer Gray. Friend John Taylor, exr. Wit: Starling Tucker, Saml. Parsons and Elias Cheek.

10 Nov. 1829. Appraisal of estate of JOHN C. MURREL, dec'd by Lewis Burk, John Boyce and George Dillard. 11 Nov. 1829. Sale Bill. Thos. J. Dillard, adm.

23 Jan. 1830. Appraisal of estate of LUCY SMITH, dec'd by Colvin A. Crumbie (Abercrumbie?), Aron Bolt and Jonathan Downs. Debts due est.: Saml. B. Lewars, Saml. Mills, Jonathan Downs, Jno. Bolt, Jr., Jno. L. Harris, Jno. R. Scrip, James McDowall, Wm. Lindly, E. L. Rouland. Chas. Allen, exr. 12 Feb. 1830.

24 Feb. 1830. Inventory of property of JOSEPH NEELY, dec'd by John Wait, John Sims and James Anderson. Notes due: Martin Shaw, Jonathan Downs, Jno. L. Harris, Saml. Downs, Hutsen Butler, Jno. Butler, Geo. Madden, Geo. Funk, Lewis Jones, Wm. Goss, Jno. Garlington, Wm. Young, Garlington Young, E. P. Fuller, Philip Wait, Jr., Wm. S. Campbell, Jno. Adams, Wm. Golding, Elizabeth Adams, Cristopher Watson, Wm. P. Gains, Wm. West, Wm. Crocker, James Wait; book acct's: James Anderson, Nathl. Rosemond, Josiah Anderson, Geo. Madden, Jno. Sims, James Wait, Thos. Wait, Elizabeth Creecy, Wade Sims, Polley Norman, Berry Watson, Wm. Graves, Wm. Burnside, Andw. Rodgers. Young Neely, exr.

15 Mar. 1830. James Crocker, exr. of JAMES CROCKER, SR., dec'd and his wife ELIZABETH CROCKER, now dec'd willed a life estate; now to be sold and divided. James Crocker, Jr. to sell, etc.

3 Mar. 1830. Appraisal estate of JOHN ODELL, dec'd by Benj. Duckett, Stephen Hill and Eli Odell. 19 Mar. 1830. Sale Bill. Rebacha Odell. Thos. Hendrick, exr.

8 Jan. 1830. Appraisal of estate of ROBERT SHAW, dec'd by Jno. Findley, Joseph Irby and Bluford Wells. 8 Jan. 1830. Sale Bill. Pur.: Martin Shaw, Wm. Bell, Polley Shaw, John Wood, Richd. Harris, Jno. Findley.

10 Mar. 1830. Appraisal of estate of CHARLES BURTON, dec'd by Jacob Eldridge, B. S. Saxon and Andw. Henderson. Sale Bill of CHARLES BURTON, dec'd amounts to $437.95½. Reference to the Sale Bill of THOMAS BURTON, dec'd. Wm. Burton, adm.

10 Mar. 1830. Appraisal of estate of THOMAS BURTON, dec'd by Jacob Eldridge, Andw. Henderson and Jno. Bolt, Jr. Sale Bill. Pur.: Elizabeth Burton, Wm. Burton, James Cunningham, Abt. Chamfried, John Bolt, Charles Irby, Wm. Prim, Augustin Martin, John Burton, Abel Campbead.

24 Mar. 1830. 2nd Appraisal of estate of JOHN BOYD, dec'd by Ferel Milum, Jno. Dandy and Thos. Nickles. Chas. Williams, J. P. John D. Boyd, adm. (Ferel also spelled Ferrell). 20 Jan. 1830. 2nd sale bill of property at the mill and mill house after the expiration of the rent. Pur.: Joel Allen, Thos. Nickles, Walter W. D. A. Dean, Saml. Powell, John H. Boyd.

31 Mar. 1830. Appraisal of estate of JAMES CROCKER, dec'd by Marsten Shaw, George Funk and Geo. Holdridge. Sale Bill. Pur.:

CROCKER cont'd:
Joseph Crocker, Asa Forgey, Robt. Morgen, Geo. Bowing, Elizabeth
Byrd, Stanford Glover, Alsa Fuller, Isaac Mitchel, Geo. Moor,
Paul Findley, Joel Hendrick, James Crocker, Robt. Willson, John
Crocker, Geo. Anderson, Hedley Davis, David Medlock, Wm. H.
Parsley, Joseph Irby, Sarah Fuller, Geo. Shirley, Melinda Crock-
er, Elihu Watson, Wm. Braxton, Austin Parsley, Lettey Shaw?.
James Crocker, exr.

23(28?) Apr. 1830. Adm. of estate of JOHN ABERSON, dec'd to
John Smith. Martin Shaw and Thos. Lockhart, sur.

18 Mar. 1830. Appraisal of estate of ISAAC GRAY, dec'd by Saml.
Parsons, Elias Cheek and R. Colbertt.

3 May 1830. Adm. of estate of WILLIAM PARK, dec'd to James Park.
James Park, Jr. and Andrew Park, sur.

17 May 1830. Adm. of estate of ROBERT TAYLOR, dec'd to John
and James Taylor. Wm. Taylor and Richd. Cotteral, sur.

17 May 1830. Will of JOEL PEARSON, dec'd proven. Will dated
17 Jan. 1830. Son William ; daughter Mary Pearson; wife Elizabeth; all my children - dau. Mahala Scrugs, wife of Marada Scrugs
and Nancy Coal wife of __lson Coal; Elizabeth Edwards wife of
Joel Edwards, Mendy Pearson, single, and my son Ephrum Pearson,
and William Pearson. Elizabeth Pearson and Ephrum Pearson, exrs.
Wit: Joseph Brown, Isaac Cooper and Nancy Cooper.

27 Nov. 1828. Sale Bill estate of HUNTER BRYSON, dec'd by Mary
Bryson, adm. Notes on hand: Robert Bryson, John Henery, Joseph
Rodgers and Hugh Logan.

17 May 1830. Petition for sale of estate of MORTEN BALL, dec'd
to meet debts as property left not enough to cover it. Thomas
Garrett, exr.

24 Nov. 1818. Sale Bill of estate of RICHARD GOLDEN, dec'd.
Pur.: Wm. West, John Watson, Jeremiah Warren, Reuben Powell,
James Glover, Wm. Golding, Robt. Delph, Geo. Adams, Wm. Jones,
Benj. Adkins, James Moor, Geo. Madden, James Sims, Henry Delph,
Willis Watson, Jno. Smith, Hudson Butler, Wm. Mormon, James
Golding, Thos. Redden, Wm. Goddard, John Lee, Jacob Niswanger,
Eligey Chism, James Rose, Austin ARnold, Sarah Golding. Jacob
Niswanger, adm. Notes/acct's: Wm. Alberson, Wm. Normon, Wm.
Golding, Robt. Golding, Geo. Goddard.

(No date) 2nd Sale of estate of DAVID MASON, dec'd by John Mason,
exr. Pur.: the widow Isbel Mason, Abner Young, Caney John Johnston, John Dalrymple, Wm. Lofton, John Dillard.

5 July 1830. Will of MARGRET TAYLOR, dec'd proven. Will dated
21 Nov. 1829. Son James Taylor; son James Taylor; will of husband; son Robert Taylor; dau. Jane Chambers - her husband;
dau. Catharine Roberson; Alender McCorley; daus.: Margret and
Hannah (Taylor). John and James Taylor, exrs. Wit: Robt. Cottrell, Saml. Parsons and Sterling Tucker.

5 July 1830. Adm. of estate of WILLIAM BELTON, dec'd to Daniel
Johnston. James Smith and Isaac Teague, sur.

5 July 1830. Adm. of estate of ROBERT PORTER, dec'd to Henry

PORTER cont'd:
H. Young. Samuel B. Lowers and David Anderson, sur.

24 May 1830. Appraisal of estate of JOEL PEARSON, dec'd by Benj.
Griffith, Charles Box and Isaac W. Cooper.

3 June 1830. Appraisal of estate of ROBERT TAYLOR, dec'd by
William Rose, Robert Mosley and Elias Cheek.

19 June 1830. Appraisal of estate of MARTEN BALL, dec'd by Harrey
Morton, William Asbey and Jeremiah Ball. 19 June 1830. Sale
Bill. (2nd). Pur.: Solomon Robertson, Charner Night, John Gar-
rott, Johnston Delong, James Higgins, Thos. Crook, Thos. Garrett,
James Higgins, Jr., John Garrett, Sr., Stephen Garrett, Ambrous
Garrett, John Robertson, Reuben Ball, Nimrod Pulmon, James Kene-
dy, Wm. Riddle, James Riddle. Thos. Garrett, exr.

18 July 1830. Will of MARY MC GOWING, dec'd proven. Will dated
27 Apr. 1829. Plantation lying on Mudlick creek to be sold and
divided between my four children: William, Elizabeth, Agness
and Sarah; six children of son William McGowing, namely William,
John, Samuel, Patrick, Martha and Mary; dau. Elizabeth Reed
and her children, namely Jonathan, David, Elizabeth and Martha
Jane Reed; my son and daughter, Andrew McGowing and SArah Mc-
Williams. Son Wm. McGowing and Jonathan Reed, exrs. Wit: James
Austin, Alexander Austin and John Champbell.

6 Sept. 1830. Will of ROBERT WORD, dec'd proven. Will dated
13 Jan. 1829. Wife Joice? Word; children: Eliza J., Elizabeth
A., Jane B., Mary, Thomas, William F. and Robert C.; land in
this state and in Georgia. Wife and son-in-law John N. Hooper?,
exrs. Wit: John Nickles, Nehemiah Franks and Demilian Deale.

22 Dec. 1829. Appraisal of estate of WILLIAM DILLARD, dec'd
by Thomas Prater, Lewis Jones and Joseph Dunkin. Notes on: James
Kennedy, Saml. McConnathy, James Jones?, John Dillard, Sarah
Simmons, Menassa Willson, Chas. A. Kerns, Mathw. Willson, Jose.
Greer, Wm. C. Persons, Wm. Maleen?, James Greer. 15 Dec. 1829.
Bill of Sale. Pur.: Henry Casey, Mathew Miller, John McDay,
John Dillard, Henry Clarey, Henry Garret, Martin Millar, John
McCray, Geo. Young, Geo. Dillard, Menassa Wilson, Thos. Prater,
Henry Gray, Micher Millar, James Hollis, Cheney Garrett, Wm.
Harris, Wm. Dillard, Joshua Dunkin, Miles Forgeson, Benj. Bishop,
Widow Dillard, Wm. Gibson, King Prater, Saml. McConatha, Henry
Dillard, Nathen Harris, James Reed, David Raiford, Joseph Jones,
Henry Bennet, James Smith, Caney Johnston, Wm. Beasley, Widow
Sims, Lewis Beasley, Leford Rodgers, Wm. Godfree, James Davis,
Jeremiah Philips, Thos. Dodd, David Sanders, John Forgeson,
John Whitmore, Richd. Ducket, Beheney Garret, Geo. Aberhams,
Joseph Aberhams, Henry Baldwin, William Eps, Jeremiah Jones.
Sale was on 15 & 16 Dec. 1829.
20 July 1830. Inventory of estate of WILLIAM BELTON, dec'd by
Isaac Teague, Joshua Pitts and D. McCullar. 20 July 1830. Return
of the personal property of Wm. Belton, dec'd. Pur.: Martha
Colier, John Culberson, Jehu Coats, Reuben Clemmens, Henderson
Waldrop, John Smith, Elisha Smith, James Durrow, James Moorhead,
Joshua Pitts, Mrs. E. Hannah Pitts, Mrs. Nancey Pitts, Josey
Belton, Isaac Teague, David McCullar, John Satorwhite, Saml.
Waldrop, Wm. Morgan, Thos. Morgan, Elihu Goggen, David McClure,
Saml. Saterwhite. Notes in the hand of estate: Bery Pitts, James
Morehead, Ruben Clemmons, John B. Pitts, Hannah Pitts, John
Neal, Reuben Pitts, John Coats, Elias Brook. Danl. Johnston,adm.

21 Sept. 1830. Adm. of estate of MARMADUKE JONES, dec'd to William Burnside. Joshua Teague and John D. Williams, sur.

27 Sept. 1830. Will of HENRY HITT, dec'd proven. Will dated 3 Mar. 1828. Wife Elizabeth Sereens? Hitt; three youngest sons Benjamin, Henry and Martin Hitts; land adj. Lewis Ball and Aberham Hollingsworth; son Jesse Hitt; land bought of Benjamin Hill; sons William and Henry Hitt; land adj. John Hitt; dau. Elizabeth Hollingsworth's children Mary, Elizabeth, Susanah and Rainey Hollingsworth. Sons Jesse Hitt, William Hitt and Lewis Ball, exrs. Wit: Martin Ball, Willis Ball and Peter H. Boyd.

4 Oct. 1830. Will of JOHN BARKSDALE, dec'd proven. Will dated 14 Apr. 1830. Sister Nancy (Barksdale); sister Martha Barksdale; sisters Polley and Leanah; brothers Collyer and Nathaniel. Allen BArksdale and Thomas F. Jones, exrs. Wit: Andrew Kennedy, Francis Ross and John Garrett.

4 Oct. 1830. Adm. of estate of SAMUEL BARKSDALE, dec'd to William D. Watts. John D. Williams and James Watts, sur.

4 Oct. 1830. Adm. of estate of JAMES FAREBARN, dec'd to Samuel M. Farebarn. Abner Rodgers, Robert Blakely and Josiah Niell, sur.

9 Oct. 1830. Estate of MARTIN MILLAR, dec'd. His sons Franklin and Albert Miller now aged 21 years; estate should be adm.; his wife Martha Miller has now remarried.

9 Oct. 1830. Adm. of estate of JAMES CROCKER, JR., dec'd to Jacob Niswanger. Elihu Watson and Bary Watson, sur.

15 Oct. 1830. Will of JUDY (JUDE) SHAIRS, dec'd proven. Will dated 22 June 1830. Son Samuel Shares; dau. Lettey Shairs(Shares). Dau. Lettey exr. Wit: Usyola Brooks, Milinda Crocker and Thos. Harris.

18 Oct. 1830. Will of ZACHARIAH TINSLEY, dec'd proven. Will dated 25 Mar. 1830. Beloved wife Betsey; my children when they come of age (none named). Wife Betsey and much respected friend John Dandy and William Simpson, exrs. Wit: Abner Pyles, Joel Dandy and Samuel Vance.

9 Nov. 1830. Will of JANE HOLLAND, dec'd proven. Will dated 23 Aug. 1830. Son Thomas; mentions land of Henry Shells and Henry Dunkens; land to be divided between children and grandchildren, Thomas excepted. Loving son-in-law John Leek and son Thomas Holland, exrs. Wit: John B. Kennedy, Thomas Wier and John Littel.

1 Nov. 1830. Adm. of estate of JOHN C. BEASLEY, dec'd to Joseph Harlen. William Blakely and James Hipps, sur.

2? Nov. 1830. Estate of WILLIAM PARK, dec'd. Adm. James Park.

23 Oct. 1830. Estate of JAMES CROCKER, SR., dec'd; Elhanion, William and James Crocker, his sons; Elhanioin and James qualified, William has removed out of the state; sd Elhanion Crocker and James (Crocker) deceased before adm.; Joseph Crocker has proven sd will. Henry C. Young and Jacob Niswanger, sur. Adm. to Joseph Crocker.

4 Oct. 1830. Will of JANE HOLLAND, dec'd. John B. Kennedy sworne

HOLLAND cont'd:
as being one who wrote will from notes taken by him at his own
house 3-4 weeks before she executed sd will; she came to his
house, stayed all night for purpose of getting him to write
sd will; he did not write it then but later from his notes;
was sent for, took notes with him, found dec'd very low and
appeared much afflicted; he doubted then if she was of sound
mind but thinks she understood what she was doing; read it to
her and she acknowledged it; two grandchildren mentioned in
the will to have their mother's part as the mother now dec'd.
Dr. Ware sworn as the attending "Fishion" (physician) to the
dec'd. Mr. Littel swore he saw dec'd make her mark to the sd
will sitting in her bed; read to her by Mr. Kennedy. Decree
in favor of sd will and order same recorded. D. Anderson, Ord.

10 Nov. 1830. Appraisal of estate of HENRY HITT, dec'd by Richd.
Watts, Andy Andrews and Isaac Grant.

15 Nov. 1830. Adm. of estate of MASTIN GLIDEWELL, dec'd to Nancy
Glidewell. Stephen Potter and John Dollar, sur.

15 Nov. 1830. Adm. of estate of JAMES V. CRAVEN, dec'd to Joseph
Sulavan. James S. Rodgers and B. L. Posey, sur.

15 Nov. 1830. Wesley Symouns, guardian of Dorotha Vaughn, minor;
dau. of Mary Vaughn, dec'd. John Simpson, adm. Citation of
accounting.

4 Oct. 1830. Appraisal of personal estate of MARMADUKE JONES,
dec'd by John D. Williams, Reuben Hitt and Joseph Lygon. Wm.
Burnside, adm.

15 Nov. 1830. Will of RICHARD CHILDRESS, SR., dec'd proven.
Dec'd did not appoint any exrs. Richd. Childress, Jr. and Robt.
Childress qualified. Wm. Crook and Mathw. P. Evans, sur. Will
dated 23 Mar. 1825. Wife "Marthew" (Martha?); oldest son (not
named); dau. Fanney; son John; dau. Nancy; dau. Sarah; dau.
Haner; son Robert; equally divided ... Aberham and Robert; dau.
Patsey; dau. Melindey; dau. Betsey; dau. Lucey. Wit: George
Fuller, Jr., Geo. Fuller, Sr. and Robt. Tuater?.

23 Oct. 1830. Appraisal of estate of JAMES CROCKER, JR.,dec'd
by Asa Forgey, Elihu Watson and John Sims. Sale Bill (No date)
Pur.: James Shirley, John Fowler, Wm. West, Geo. Shirley, Allen
Andrews, Elihu Watson, John Coats, Harey Hazel, Westly Savage,
John Watson, Robt. Wilson, Wm. McGowen, Alexander Winn, Young
Neely, Philip Cummeford, Wm. Burnside, John Henderson, Levi
Hill, Geo. Jowell, Barnes Mosley, Jacob Niswanger, John Milum,
A. G. Jones place, Richd. Harris, Jacob Brooks, Benj. Rosemond,
Elizabeth Wadkins, Dr. Anderson, Elizabeth Glover, Joseph Crock-
er, John Crocker, John Wadkins, Julius Glover, John L. Madden,
Chas. Brook, Saml. Martin, Zachariah Sims, Nathl. Rosmon, John
Findley, John Bell, Wm. Golding, Col.? Starnes, Thos. Pope,
Jno. Walker, Elias Brock, Joseph McCullar, John K. Moore, Nathl.
Nickles, Jacob Crocker, Thos. Washington, James Prymmy, Mathw.
Wilson, Thos. Adkins, Wm. Holms, Isaac Pitts, Barnes Mosley,
Shubal Starnes, Benj. Lucas?, Susah Crocker. Notes on: John
Adams, James Glover, Joseph Akin, Jos. Adkins, Geo. Jowell,
James J. Richardson, Wm. Crocker, Jno. R. Crocker, Benj. Norman,
James Shirley, Danl. South, Robt. Shirley, Jacob Fuller, Geo.
Elmore, James Wait, Lewis Watson, Wm. West, Jno. Wright, Joel
Weathers, Geo. Pope, Saml. Richey, Wm. Gofford, Geo. Madden,

CROCKER, cont'd:
Thomas Redden, Jno. Alberson, James Powell, James Brown, John
Rush, John McCann, Riall Jones, Lewis Jones, E. Starns, Jno.
R. Crocker, Shubal Starns, Elihu Shirley, Elias Brook, Jno. Milum
and Thos. Adkins, Jno. Moor, Wm. Savage, Milanda Crocker, Reuben
Arnold, Martin Shaw, Thos. Bell, Wm. Yager, David Andrus, Henry
C. Young, Reuben Powell, Adam C. Jones, Terrel Andres, James
Cook, Wm. Neal, Seaborn Jones, GAbriel Hand, Wm. Nickels, Thos.
Craford, Jno. Williams, Saml. Sprewell, Marthew Leak, Green
W. Smith, Aron Murphey, Elizabeth Crocker, Geo. Elmore, Gray
Elmore, Berrey Watson, Zachariah Arnold, Wm. Flin, Albert Wair,
James Richardson, E. Stains, Robt. Millar.

25 Oct. 1830. Acct. of property appraised of estate of JUDETH
SHAIRS, dec'd by Hancel Hendrick, Joseph Crocker and Joseph
Irby.

3 Nov. 1830. Appraisal of estate of ZACHARIAH TINSLEY, dec'd
by Abner Pyles, Hardey Davis and Saml. Vance. 4 Nov. 1830. Sale
Bill. Pur.: Sylus Dandy, Hardey Davis, Joshua Teague, James
Young, Esq., Capt. R. Milum, John Dandy, Sr., Henry Madden,
Capt. John Davis, James M. Pollard, John Young. Betsey C. Tins-
ley, adm.

4 Dec. 1830. Adm. of estate of SAMUEL ADKESON, dec'd to John
Cook. Faries? Hill and Charles Snowe, sur.

(No date) Appraisal of estate of SAMUEL BARKSDALE, dec'd by
Wm. Dunlap, Saml. Young and Fedrick Foster?. (No date) Sale
Bill. Pur.: Joshua Teague, Higgerson Barksdale, John Blakely,
Elihu Griffen, Elijah Teague, John Miller, James H. Lowery,
Saml. Copeland, William Dunlap, Wade Griffen, James Copeland,
John Littel, Wm. Enterkin, Jeremiah Leek, Jno. Simpson, Thos.
Enterkin, James Simpson, Wm. Gambell, John Linvell, Henry R.
Shell, Saml. Garey, Jonathan Case, Thos. Holend, Wm. East, Jno.
Dunlap, Jno. Gray, Raber Bell, David Boyd, Robt. Monroe, Margret
Hooker, Hezekiah Rice, Mideton Cobb, Miss B. S. Barksdale, Geo.
Johnston, James Bryson, John Johnston, John McCay, Geo. M. Young,
James M. Pollard, David Brooks, Wm. Aberanie, David Gambell,
Thos. Mitchell, James G. Corsline, Wm. Huet, Washington Meadors,
John Milum, Joseph Griffen, James McNeatre, James Neil, John
Copelan, John Saxon, Anthony Griffen, Jobe Johnston, Henry Shell,
Sr., Saml. Young, Benjamin Saxon, Joseph Young, Jno. H. Davis,
Elizabeth Copeland, Clark Baley, Joseph Young, Sr., Thos. Teague,
Saml. Enterkin, Jno. Hunter, Saml. Neil, W. D. Watts. Notes
on Saml. Neel, Jno. Johnston, Saml. Copeland. W. D. Watts, adm.

1 Dec. 1830. Appraisal of estate of MARTIN MILLER, dec'd by
Alsey Fuller, Henry H. Fuller, Jones Fuller, N.C., and Salam
Fuller. Franklin and Albert Miller, exrs.

11 Dec. 1830. Appraisal of estate of RICHARD CHILDERS, SR.,
dec'd (also spelled CHILDRESS), by Wm. Crooks, A. Owings, David
Studard and A. A'crumbie. Richard Childress, Jr., adm.

20 Dec. 1830. Will of DRURY BOYCE, dec'd proven. Will dated
31 July 1830. Debt due Anderson Arnold as his share of his father's estate by dec'd marriage to administratrix of sd estate;
my beloved wife; sons Drury G. Boyce and James M. Boyce; friend
Dempsey Nisbet; daus. Nancy C. Boyce and Polley C. Boyce. Wife
(not named) as exr. At her death, Dempsey Nisbet, exr. Wit:
John Armstrong, Nathan Nisbet and Thomas Nisbet.

31 July 1830. Codicil to will of DRURY BOYCE. James Graydon, son of Mathew Graydon land adj. Thos. Nisbet, Wm. Wood, Harris Thompson. Wit: (same as above).

20 Dec. 1830. Will of DRURY BOYCE proven by Mary Boyce, Nathan Nisbet and Thos. Nisbet. Mary Boyce, exr.

20 Dec. 1830. Will of DRURY COKER, dec'd proven. Menice Coker, exrtx. Will not dated. Land where Joseph Coker now lives (son); wife Betsey Coker; land adj. Nathen Henderson, Abner Putmon; dau. Menice Coker; dau. Polley Dial. Dau. Menice Coker, exrtrx. Wit: Saml. Downs, James Bruster and Wm. F. Downs.

3 Jan. 1831. Will of SAMUEL GOODMAN, dec'd by James G. Williams and E. D. Williams, wit. John D. Williams, exr.

16 Nov. 1830. Appraisal of estate of JOHN C. BEASLEY, dec'd by John Adair, Moses Leek and Geo. McCrary. Notes on Ephraim Pitts, Massum? Jones, James Fulton, Amos Prather, John Prather, G. A. gray, Lewis Hammond, A. A. Faireborne, Jhn. Holland. (No date) Sale Bill.

15 Feb. 1830. Return rec'd of estate of LANGSTON EAST, dec'd by William East, adm. Rec'd of Isaac Jones, John Garlington, Horis Rice acct against Eli'a. Glenn, dec'd.

9 Oct. 1829. Will of SAMUEL GOODMAN. Beloved wife; Gillum Goodman; Lewis Ball; son James Goodman; son Samuel Goodman; Mrs. Aston's field; Drewry Sims old field; son Gilliam Goodman; son David Goodman; dau. Rhoda, wife of James Nickles; dau. Maria, wife of James Cook; dau. Jemima, wife of William Cook. John C. Williams, exr. Wit: M. M. Christman, James G. Williams and E. D. Williams.

3 Jan. 1831. Adm. of estate of JOHN F. KERN, SR., dec'd to John F. Kern, Jr. Henry C. Young, John Garlington and John L.(S.) James, sur.

22 Nov. 1830. Appraisal of estate of JANE HOLLAND, dec'd by David Enterkin, Geo. McCrarey, Jhon Littel, Henry Shell and Chas. Littel, chosen by the children of dec'd. Note on Thos. Holland, Chas. Blakely.23 Nov. 1830. Appraisal of negroes willed by dec'd to her children. (No date) Sale Bill. John Leek and Thos. Holland, exrs.

10 Jan. 1831. Adm. of estate of ELIZABETH DAVENPORT, dec'd to Hanie Hendrick. Joel L. Anderson and Joel Hendrick, sur.

(No date) Sale Bill estate of MORTEN MILLAR, dec'd. Pur.: Zachariah Bailey, Wm. Ferguson, Jones Fullar, Joshua Teague, Haregrove Miller, Eilia Motes, Jno. Fendey, Peter Fullar, Hogen Motes, Philip F. King, John Felts, Jacob Miller, Ezekel Furgeson, Ezekel Purkison, Hillis Willcot, Jesse Motes, Wm. Bryson, Aa. D. Waldrop, Bird Roberts, John Kelley, Anthony G. Leek, Meredith G. Waldrop, Rignal Dunken, Celia Motes, Wm. A. Fullar, Ezekiel Millar, Geo. Wright, Bird G. Waldrop, Henry M. Pasley, Mrs. Hillis Waldrop, Jesse M. Fullar, Henry Fullar, Joseph Ligen, Danl. Carter. Franklin A. Miller and Albert Miller, exrs.

15 Sept. 1830. Appraisal of estate of ROBERT WORD, dec'd by W. W. Simpson, Wm. Lowe and James Davis. Shown by execturix; mention of JOHN JONES, dec'd will of Nov. 2, 1830. Notes on

WORD cont'd:
William Byn, James Bruster, John Tiner, Chesley Conant, Elias
Busy, John Boyd, P. Farrow, Isaac Mitchel; accounts: John Boyd,
Peggey Crocks, Wm. F. Downs, James Irby, Francis Medley, Clark
Bailey, Thos. Davis, Thos. Nickles, Margret Marten, Wm. Moor,
Sr., David P. Saxon, Elizabeth Word, Wm. Moor, Jr., Valentine
Hasting, David Craddock, Archey Holt, Saml. McDowell, Saml.
Low, Joseph Vance, Jr., James Edmonson, Joseph Travis, Wm. Kel-
lett, Stephen Tiner, John Simmons, Bluford Moor, Flemon Bettey,
Zimri Madden, James W. Craddock, Abner Teague, Batt Craddock,
Turner Richardson, John Bailey, Lewis Smith, John Templeton.
Joyce Word, exrtx.

17 Jan. 1831. Adm. of estate of WILLIAM J. YOUNG, dec'd to Blbu-
ford F. Griffen. John Odel and John Smith, Sr.?, sur.

17 Jan. 1831. Adm. of estate of ELIAS BROOK, dec'd to James
Brook. John Fowler, Chas. Brook and James Abercrumbie, sur.

17 Jan. 1831. Adm. of estate of RODEY KENEDY, dec'd to Allen
Barksdill. Pertillar Farrow and B. L. Posey, sur.

17 Jan. 1831. Will of WILLIAM HOPPER, dec'd proven. Will dated
19 Nov. 1830. Wife Lettuce Hopper; son Joseph Hopper; son Samuel
who is dec'd, to his children; dau. Polley Brown. Saml. G. Williams and James S. Rodgers, exrs. Wit: Saml. Irby, H. L. Beadel
and John S. Orsborn.

(No date) Appraisal of estate of MASTIN GLIDEWELL, dec'd by
Saml. B. Lewers, Stephen Potter and John Dollar. (No date) Sale
Bill. Pur.: Geo. Crook, John Dollar, Fowler Henderson, Saml.
Franks, Jesse Garrett, Thos. Garrett, Thos. Lockhart, Aron Moor,
Stephen Potter. Nancy Glidewell, adm.

28 Oct. 1830. Appraisal of estate of JOHN BARKSDILL, dec'd by
Arch'd Owens, John Garett and F. Ross. (Date not clear) Sale
Bill. Pur.: John Garrett, James Cargill, Richd. Childress, Stan-
ford McMiken, Francis Leverack, M. P. Evens, Rich'd B. Owens,
Arch'd Owens, Nathaniel Barksdill, Nathan Cassey, Sr., Hosa
Garrett, Martha? Nobles, Wm. Holbart, Joel Gentry, Lewis Cor-
gill, Thos. Waters, Jr., Evan Bell, West Ford, Thos. Helton,
Jesse Garrett, Saml. Barksdill, Cristepher Garlington, Reuben
Estes, Morten Kellett, Reuben Robertson, Warner R. Grasey, Wm.
Strange, John Cowan, Nathan Currey, Garrett Sullivan, Abner
Knight, Wm. B. Davis, Nancy Barksdill, Tulley Mosley, Philip
Gray, Thos. Goodwin, Collyar Barksdill, Mathew Barksdill, Alfred
Corgill, Chas. Corgill, Thos. Kellett, Hudson Moor, A. Barks-
dill, Nathan Barksdill.

22 Jan. 1831. Will of JAMES MC CLURKIN, dec'd proven. Will dated
26 Jan. 1828. Wife Catharine McClurkin; sons Samuel, John and
James (all under age of 21). Catharine McClurkin and friend
Thomas Cunningham, Jr., exrs. Wit: Saml. Cunningham, Mansel
Owens, Thos. Washington and Geo. G. Washington.

17 Jan. 1831. Joseph Baldin about 21 years of age, chose Menasse
Wilson guardian. James Milum and John Mason, sur.

7 Dec. 1830. Appraisal of estate of SAMUEL ADKISON, dec'd by
John Hitt, Francis Hill and Saml. Todd. John Cook, adm. 22 Dec.
1830. Sale Bill. No pur. named.

12 Feb. 1831. Will of HENRY B. ROWLAND, dec'd proven. Will dated

ROWLAND cont'd:
24 Apr. 1828. Beloved wife Lettece and children (not named).
Wife and friend John Whitmore, exrs. Wit: James Blackburn, Aron
Johnston and John Johnston. Signed: H. B. Rowland.

10 Feb. 1831. Adm. of estate of BARRUCH DUCKETT, dec'd to John
Odle. Jones Fuller, N. C. and Jacob Millar, sur.

21 Feb. 1831. Adm. of estate of WILLIAM HARRIS, dec'd to Nathan
Harris. Jesse Briggs and Thos. Duckett, sur.

21 Feb. 1831. Samuel Copeland, guardian of Thomas Littel, minor
who has become of lawful age. Accounts settled.

4 Jan. 1831. Appraisal of estate of DRUREY BOYCE, dec'd by Benj.
Arnold, Wm. Arnold and Jno. Hopkins. Notes due dec'd: Wm. Arnold,
Ira Arnold, Hendrick Arnold, Jos. Harris, Thos. Harris, James
Arnold, Thos. Grayham, Benj. Arnold, Eilus Arnold, Jonathan
Abercrumbie, Cabreble Abercrumbie, Wm. Boyes, Wm. Boyce, Drury
Boyce, Martin Nesbit, Abner Babb, Linsey A. Baker, Dempsey Nis-
bet, Saml. Barker, John Barker, Berrey Bowland, Wm. Babb, Lewis
Cargill, Gideon Thomas, James Cowan, Robt. Coker, Wm. Helum,
Nathl. Currey, Gideon Thomson, Wm. Crook, N. P. Evens, Mary
Cunningham, J. D. Cunningham, Richd. Childers, James Durrow,
Geo. French, Jos. Sulivan, Wm. C. Garey, Geo. F. Wallis, James
H. Grace, James H. Terrey, Tulley Bowling, Silus Gains, Nathl.
Gains, Jeremiah Hopkins, Shadrack Jamison, Danl. Johnston, Isaac
Teague, Chas. Saxon, Flemmon Hunter, M. Bryers, Hugh Mahaffey,
Allen Mahaffey, Baley Mahon, John Mayhan, R. B. Arnold, David
McHaffey, Aberham Nixon, Joseph Avery, Saml. Babb, Saml. Purkins,
John Pool, Wm. Pool, John Peden, David Peden, Robt. Peden, Richd.
Simpson, Henry Linsey, Thomas and Mary Morgen, Danl. Welch,
Wm. West, John F. Woolf, Geo. Jankially, Wm. Henderson, Wm.
Johnston, Geo .Jukesty, Gideon Thomas, Wm. and Judah McConahay,
Wm. Irby, Wm. Wood, Thos. Kirkpatrick, Wm. M'Cusahan, Geo. Tou-
kesty.

12 Jan. 1831. Appraisal of estate of SAMUEL GOODMAN, dec'd by
Joseph Babb, Richd. Sims, James Watts, Jr. and Joseph Ligon.
John D. Williams, exr. Mrs. Goodman, a lifetime estate. 28 Jan.
1831. Rec'd of John D. Williams, exr. of sd dec'd, property
loaned to dec'ds wife, Elizabeth Goodman according to his will.
Test.: Hanie Hendrick. Sale Bill (no date). Pur.: John D. Wil-
liams, William Austin, Thos. Speareman, Henry Hitt, Mrs. Ann
Owens, Robt. Walton?, Saml. Goodman, Jr., Wm. Philips, Jesse
Henderson, David Goodman, Mrs. Mariah Goodman and James Cook,
Ala Austin, Hugh Leeman, Chas. Egestun, Henry O'Neal, James
Goodman, John Hudley, Mathew Bryson, Johnston Reid, Gillum Good-
man, Jones Fullar, John McWilliams, Kellis Waldrop, John Arm-
strong, Wm. Sanders, Wm. Ligon, _.? N. Nickles, Thos. C. Reader,
Franklin Pollard, Danl. Winn, Wm. Thompson, James Busby, Chas.
M. King, James Wright, Joseph Cook, John Plant, James Watts,
Wm. McGowen, Elizabeth Goodman, Lewis Ball, James Criswell,
Delimion Deal, Horatio Wells, Larkin Millar, James Goodman,
Alen Kirkpatrick, Robt. Witiford, James Nickles, Nathan Proctor,
John White, Marshel Pollard, Polley Valentine, Luke Henderson,
Alex. Austin, Saml. Goodman.

18 Jan. 1831. Appraisal of estate of JOHN F. KERNE, SR., dec'd
by Robt. Owens, Geo. McCrary and John Boyce. 24 Jan. 1831. Sale
Bill. (also spelled KERN). Pur.: Suza Kern, Ugenia Kern, Widow
Kern, Alfred Kern, Joshua Saxon, Thos. Gore, Robt. Owens, George

KERN/KERNE cont'd:
Dillard, Eugenee Kern, Moses Leek, Luza Kern, Louis Kern, Richd.
Ducket, Saml. Young, Jno. Henderson, James Littel, Thos. Craig,
Ambrous Ray, Jno. F. Boyce, Louisa Kern, Edw. Stephens, Robt.
Adair, Joseph Piper, H. S. Neil, R. Haistingis, Thos. Dunken,
Peter Haisting, Wm. Gibson, Jno. Templeton, Jno. Fowler, Robt.
Owen, Mathew Millar, John Copelan, Hugh Saxon, Danl. Felder,
Jno. Crafton, Mason Jones, Ephraim Pitts, Thos. Leek, Jno. Mc-
Cay, Benj. Hill. (Long list) John F. Kern, adm.

8 Mar. 1831. Appraisal of estate of ELIAS BROCK, dec'd by James
Henderson, Sr., Thos. Goggins, Jno. C. Wadkins and Richd. Black-
well. James Brock, adm. 10 Mar. 1831. Sale Bill. Pur.: Susanah
Brock, widow, Charles Brock, James Brock, Austin Henderson,
Leroy Madison, Wm. Todd, Geo. Moor, Sr., James Morgen, Geo.
Elmore, Chas. Brook, Sr., Chas. Irby, Jno. Crocker, Wm. Holady,
James Henderson, Sr., Jno. L. Madden, Plesant G. Devenport,
Jacob Brock, Jno. Smith, Jno. Burton, Elizabeth Wadkins, Jno.
Cuberson, Thos. Coats, Robt. Stephens. Notes, judgements, etc.:
James Abercrumbie, J. A. Jowell, James McClurkin estate, Wm.
Hollady, John Brock (Brook?), Mastin Henderson, Jos. Blackwell,
Chas. Parks, David Parks, Thos. Goggins, Adam C. Jones, Grey
Elmore, Elijah Pinson.

10 Feb. 1831. Appraisal of estate of JAMES MC CLURKIN, dec'd
by Philip Wait, Sr., Mikel Clardy and Mansel Owins. Catherine
McClurkin, exrtx. 15 Feb. 1831. Sale Bill. Mrs. Catherine Mc-
Clurkin purchased most of estate; also Thos. Morgen, Jno. Coats,
Isaac Boyd, Adam C. Jones, Thos. Washington, Robt. Boyd, Philip
Cummeford, Elias Brock, Harrison Black. Jacob Wright his prop-
erty.

18 Feb. 1831. Adm. of estate of ALHANIEN CROCKER, dec'd to Milanda Crocker and Turner Richardson. Was adm. by James Crocker,
dec'd. Bond with Joel S. Anderson and Henry Thompson, sur.

21 Mar. 1831. Will of BENJAMIN BYRD, dec'd proven. Will dated
14 Nov. 1828. BENJAMIN BIRD (BYRD). Son Purnall J. Bird; son
William D. Bird; son George; Purral J. Bird and William Hill;
dau. Sarah Allen, wife of B. H. Allen; dau. Mary; grandson Benjamin Hill; dau. Leah. Sons Purrall J. Bird and Wm. D. Bird, exrs.
Wit: R. Criswell, Jno. Corgill and Robt. Horstin.

9 Feb. 1831. Appraisal of estate of RODY KENEDY, dec'd by Lemion
G. Williams, Lewis Bramblet and N. Barksdle (Barksdale?). Allen
Barksdill, adm. 9 Feb. 1831. Sale Bill. Pur.: Siminion Kenedy,
James Parks, James Garner, Saml. Thomas, James S. Rodgers, Wm.
Powers, Chas. Williams, Joseph Hopper, Nathen Barksdill, Walton
W. Wallis, Nehemiah Franks, Chaney Knight, William Moor, James
Kenedy. Note on Peter Gallihair and William Irby.

19 Mar. 1831. Adm. of estate of WILLIAM M. LOCKHART, dec'd to
William Ligon. Alexander Austin and Bluford Wills, sur.

28 Mar. 1831. Adm. of estate of JAMES HOLLINGSWORTH, dec'd to
Mary Hollingsworth. Saml. Rodgers and Wm. Hollingsworth, sur.

(No date) Sale Bill estate of MARMADUKE JONES, dec'd. Pur.:
Thos. Rodgers, Danl. Jones, Geo. Wright, Wm. Burnside, Jesse
George, Jno. Bailey, Bird Roberts, Bluford Wells, Willard Bone,
Jno. Hollingsworth, Reuben Hitt, Robt. Coleman, Bird Golding,
Lazarus Hitt, Wm. Farrow, Jno. D. Williams, Sarah Cane, Jacob

JONES cont'd:
Millar, Nehemiah Rodgers, Wm. Hollingsworth, Robt. Campbell, Allen Haregrove, William Bone, Saml. Rodgers, Mary Jones. Cash rec'd from Eliza Coffee, Wm. Fullar for Jason Fullar, James Merison and Bevely Walker.

21 Jan. 1831. Appraisal of estate of ELIZABETH DEVENPORT, dec'd by Joseph Crocker and Joel Hendrick. 21 Jan. 1831. Sale Bill. Pur.: Tempa Devenport, Zebulon West, Joel Hendrick, Rachel Hendrick, Bearns Mosley, Zachariah B. Sims, Rebeca Hendrick, Puggey? (Peggy) Willard, Brines Mosley. Hanie Hendrick, adm.

26 Feb. 1831. Appraisal of estate of HENRY B. ROWLAND, dec'd by Jno. Johnston, Richd. Bonds and Lewis Jones. Sale Bill (1st day of Mar. 1831). John Whitmore, exr.

16 Apr. 1831. Adm. of estate of JOSEPH YOUNG, dec'd to John Holland. John Young and Sarah Young, sur.

16 Apr. 1831. Will of ALEXANDER ABERCRUMBIE, dec'd proven. Will dated 28 Dec. 1830. Wife Susanah; son Lewis; land adj. to Wm. and Jno. Abercrumbie, Harris, Thompson, Graydon, Wm. Woods and Wm. Chaycee; dau. Susanah and Polley; my unfortunate son Jonathan as long as he may live; sons - Henry, Hugh, John, Alexander and Lewis; daus. - Hannah, Susana and Polley. Sons John and Alexander, exrs. Wit: John Harris, John Woods and Mathew P. Evens. 21 Jan. 1831. Codicil. Wit: John Abercrombie, John Woods and Mathew P. Evens.

16 Apr. 1831. Will of MARY REED, dec'd proven. Will dated 28 Mar. 1831. Grandchildren: Maryan and Caroline (no last names): sister Elizabeth Strain; brother William Reed. Wm. Reed. exr. Wit: J. M. H. Johnston, Catherine Whiteford and Kitey King.

2 May 1831. Estate of MARY FARLEY, dec'd, Thompson Farley against W. R. Farley, adm. James Hunter, Flemming Mosley and John A. Farley, sur. Thompson Farley now adm.

2 May 1831. Will of ISAAC COUCH, dec'd proven. Will dated 22 Mar. 1817. Isaac Couch, farmer. Loving wife Susanah Couch; children: Beckey Stroud, wife of John Stroud, Susana Roberson wife of Barruch Roberson and my son Samuel Couch. Son Samuel exr. Wit: John W. Young, A---(Anthony?) Young and Nancy Young.

23 Apr. 1831. Appraisal of estate of ALEXANDER ABERCRUMBIE, SR., dec'd by Wm. Crook, Richd. Childers, Robt. Woods and Jonathan Abercrumbie, Sr. (also dated 26 Apr.) 29 Apr. 1831. Amt. of money dec'd died possessed of. Alexander Abercrumbie, exr.

17 May 1831. Estate of WILLIAM DILLARD, dec'd, adm. Henry Gray, now dec'd. John Dillard now adm. Washington Meadors, Isaac Jacks and Saml. Young, sur.

13 Apr. 1831. Appraisal of estate of JAMES HOLLINGSWORTH, dec'd by Henry W. Pasley, Mathew Bryson, Jones Fullar, N. C. and W. Burnside. 14 Apr. 1831. Sale Bill. Pur.: Mary Hollingsworth, John Hollingsworth, Saml. Rodgers, Isaac Mitchel, William Hollingsworth, Andw. Rodgers, Wm. Bryson, Jones Fullar (N. C.), Danl. Jones, Jacob Millar, Wm. Rodgers, Wm. Burnside, Thos. Austin, Richd. Golding. Polley S. Hollingsworth, adm.

14 May 1831. Memorandum. Appraise bill of estate of ISSAC COUCH,

COUCH cont'd:
late of Laurens Dist. as shown by Samuel Couch, exr. Jeremiah
Ball, Lewis Cargill and Reuben Roberson, app'rs. 17 May 1831. Petition for order of sale of dec'd estate in order to pay debts.

7 Apr. 1831. Appraisal of estate of BENJAMIN BYRD, dec'd by
John Crig (Craig?), Walter Steward and Joshua Saxon. 28 Apr.
1831. 8 Apr. 1831. Sale Bill. Pur.: George Byrd, Robert Gilland,
John Adair, Thos. J. Dillard, James Burk, Wm. Hill, Noah Smith,
Lien? Gillum, Jno. S. Hutcheson, Robt. Pitts, Wm. Wallis, Shed-
rick Vance, Jno. Craig, Henry Harlan, Geo. Templeton, Wm. Good-
win, Simpson Hutcheson, James Blakely, Obediah Vier, Shedrick
Vier, Jos. Crocker, Geo. Gordin, W. W. Wallis, John Langston,
David Newman, Robt. Pucket. Notes on hand: James Irby, Joshua
Saxon, Joseph Crocker, William Hill, Henry Langston, James Liles,
Chas. Richardson. W. D. Byrd, exr.

2 May 1831. Appraisal of estate of MARY REED, dec'd by Andey
Andrews, Benj. Malden and Clemment Wells. 2 May 1831. Sale Bill.
Pur.: Bird Roberts, Wm. Winn, Clement Wells, Wm. McGowing, Eliza-
beth Strain, James Goodman, John P. Watts, John McWilliams,
Elizabeth Reed, John White, Plesent Saddler, John Beesley, John
Ling, Sarah McCreedy, Joseph Butler, Benj. Malden, Wm. Reed,
James F. Pinson, Katey Whiteford, Alfred Smith, Chas. King.
Note on Aron Pinson, James F. Pinson and Wm. Reed.

4 May 1831. Appraisal of estate of JOSEPH YOUNG, JR., dec'd
by Wm. Wright, Joseph Young and John Young. 4 May 1831. Sale
Bill. Pur.: Reason Young, John Young, Sarah Young. Notes on
Sarah Young, Wm. B. Sheldon and Joseph Young, Sr. John Holland,
adm.

1 Mar. 1831. Inventory of cash, notes and open acct's of estate
of JOHN F. KERN, SR., dec'd. Robt. Owen, Saml. Brigs, Geo. Mc-
Crary, Saml. Copland, David Gambell, Elexander Fillson, Mathew
Millar, Joseph Jones, Wm. Blackburn, Ward Forgeson, David Temple-
ton, Thos. Garrett, Menasse Willson, Menasse Leek, Jos. Garrett,
James Dillard, Elizabeth Bobo, Thos. Ducket, Danl. Owen, James
McLure, Jno. Davis, Jno. Dollar & Whitter, Jno. Whitmore, Isaac
Hill, Jno. Norman, Nelley Ramage, Julious Wesson, Jno. Templeton,
Jr., Henry McKelvey, Josiah Ramage, Jos. Hughs, Jesse Norman,
Joshua Gore, Wm. Musgrove, Jno. Templeton, Sr., Jno. Adair,
Sr., Francis Prator, Danl. Felder, Lyman Muslely (Mosley?),
Jno. Leek, Thos. Gore, Jos. McConathy, Mary Garrett, Enoch Gar-
rett, James Kenady, Wm. Melone, Elizabeth Jones, Wm. Musgrove,
Thos. Jones, Jno. Ramage, James Craddock, Loyed Jones, Jos.
Aberhams, Jos. Devalois, James Puckett, Jno. Whitter, Fielding
Foster, Elizabeth Green, Mason Jones & Boyd Craddock, James
Hannah, Wm. Cell, Jno. Adair, Saml. Forguson, Saml. Hunt, Geo.
McCrary, Drayton McCay, Allen Garrett, Wm. Simmons, Wm. Holland,
James Langston, Alexander Jones, Saml. Campbell, David Grayham,
Thos. Rains, Saml. Stone, John Corgill, Wm. Burk, Wm. Dillard,
Moses Garrett, Saml. Langston, Lewis Bobo, Arch'd Prator, Jno.
Craig Creek, Richd. Farrow, Richd. Ducket, Jno. Garrett, Thos.
Bishop, Solomon Bobo, Jno. F. Henry, Jno. B. Ford, W. W. Inlow,
Wm. Spark, Geo. Young, Jesse Ramage, Wm. Dollar, James Prater,
James Prater, Sr., Jno. H. Mulwee, Benj. Jones, Thos. Desheilds,
Jno. Jackson, Jno. Lamb, Jno. Dillard son of Squire, Wm. Abbrams,
Thos. Fraiser, Jno. Duckett, Philip Huff died insolvent, James
Bettey, James Brown, Andw. Gibson, J. H. Puckett died insolvent,
Robt. Pucket, Isaac Gambell, Jno. B. Bernet died insolvent,
Jos. Balden, Howel Allen, Johnston Martin, Thos. Adinson, Jones

Inventory cont'd:
Brown, Thos. Dandy, Mansfield Owens, John Cole, James Gambel,
Jno. Jones, Wm. Liles, B. H. Allen, Joel Kelley, Elisha Adair,
Wm. Hollis, Thos. Martin, Antony Foster, James Foster, Richd.
Butler, Josiah Gamble, Henry McCay, Robt. Templeton, Isaac Whit-
ton, Jesse Mabray, Jacob Hambliton, Wm. Jackson, Robt. C. Barrey,
James H. Hunter, Delyah Cambell, Bard N. Simpson, Isaac Wesson,
Stephen Johnston, Martin Hopkins, Joseph Keen, Jonathan Cooper,
Danl. C. Edwin, Jno. Lynch, Isaac Gambell, Celaha Adair, Jno.
Greer, James Ryley, Wm. Burrus, Henry Fuguson, Jno. Garret,
Jno. Craig, Thos. Aberhams, Jacob Bowle, Wm. Sheldon, Gideon
Gray, Henry Craddock, Wm. Glenn.

8 June 1830. Sarah Young, now Sarah Naylor, adm. of JOHN YOUNG,
dec'd; due to Washington Sample in right of his wife Judith.
Due to Martin C. Garey who married Eliza; guardian of Elizabeth
M. Young, 25 Oct. 1830 monies in trust for her from John Young,
dec'd. 17 May 1830, paid G. W. Young (also guardian of above
Elizabeth) his share of est. of his father John Young, dec'd.
John & James Young, minors, 17 Nov. 1830, paid to each $1562.04.

5 Feb. 1831. Inventory of estate of WILLIAM HOPPER, dec'd by
Saml. Irby, Jno. Crooks and Jno. Wood. Note due estate by A.
Hammond, Edgefield. 7 Feb. 1831. Sale Bill.

20 June 1831. Adm. of estate of ROBERT HAISTING, dec'd to James
S. Rodgers. James Hayden and H. C. Young, sur.

6 June 1831. Request of Frances Dobyns, formerly Frances Irby,
that Charles Irby be appointed guardian for her minor children:
Benjamin H. Irby and James Irby. Samuel Irby and James H. Irby,
sur.

4 July 1831. Adm. of estate of MAREY FARLEY, dec'd. Thomson
Farley, adm. not able to find any goods, etc. belonging to dec'd.
No appraisement made.

5 Apr. 1831. Appraisal of estate of WILLIAM MC G. LOCKHART,
dec'd by J. Findly, Jno. Lockert and Bluford Wells. Sale Bill.
(No date) Pur.: Thos. Lockhart, Wm. Ligen, Caty Nickles, Martin
Shaw, John Lockhart. Notes on Robt. Burns, Robt. Sales?, Saml.
Irby, Jno. H. Lockhart, Thos. Lockhart, Sr. Wm. Ligon, adm.

1 Aug. 1831. John Dillard, adm.; Fredrick Gray, adm. of HENRY
GRAY, dec'd, who was the adm. of WILLIAM DILLARD, dec'd (by
consent)...an accounting.

20 Mar. 1830. Sale Bill personal property of ISAAC GRAY, dec'd.
Pur.: Zeny/Zana Gray, Josiah Persons, Roberson Mosley, James
Hunter, Ellie? Gray, Eyre F. Farley, Calub Woodrough, Leslie
Gray, Thompson Farley, Flemming Mosley, Esley Gray, Thos. Park,
Saml. Park, Zachariah Gray, Thomas Farley, Benj. Griffen, Eyre
Mosley, Jobe Woodrough, David Patton, Nathan Bramblet, Joel
Fowler, John Taylor. Rec'd of William Hannah his note and of
Lesley Gray, his note in full. John Taylor, exr.

15 June 1831. Sale Bill goods of ISAAC COUCH, dec'd. Pur.: Barnet
Roberson, Richd. Owen, Wm. Travis, Charley Cargill, Reuben Roberson, Robt. Hand, Wm. Owens, Jno. Owings. Saml. Couch, adm.

1 Aug. 1831. Return of John Dillard, adm. of WILLIAM DILLARD,
dec'd. Rec'd of Fredrick Gray, adm. of HENRY GRAY, dec'd the

DILLARD cont'd:
former adm. of WM. DILLARD, dec'd. Notes and cash due estate.

4 Oct. 1831. Will of EDWARD PUGH, dec'd proven. Will dated 17
Jan. 1829. Son William Pugh; daughters - Polley Compton, Eliza-
beth Gilbert, the wife of William Gilbert, Nancy Spirgen, widow
(also spelled Spurgen), Salley Pugh, single woman. Son-in-law
William Gilbert, exr. Wit: Joseph Brown, Jacob Roberts and Joseph
Allen.

3 Oct. 1831. Adm. of estate of THOMAS GOODWIN, dec'd to Thomas
Goodwin, Jr. William Holbert and Thoplas? Goodwin, sur.

18 Oct. 1831. Citation by legatees of DAVID COWING, SR., dec'd
against James Cowing, adm. of dec'd.

18 Oct. 1831. James Burk and Saml. Dillard, former sur. of Thomas
J. Dillard for his adm. on estate of JOHN C. MURREL, dec'd...to
be released from sd sur. James Dillard and Thos. Duckett, new
sur.

18 Oct. 1831. Adm. of estate of PARLEY GROVENER, dec'd to James
W. Thompson. Thos. F. Jones and Jno. L.? James(Jones?), sur.

18 Oct. 1831. Petition of William Gilbert, exr. of EDWARD PUGH,
dec'd for order of public sale of est.

25 Oct. 1831. Petition of John Ball, Susana Ball, Henery Ball,
Thomas Ball, Reuben Ball, Martha Ball and John Ball guardian
of Joseph Ball, minor...GEORGE BALL, dec'd made a will...when
youngest child reached 21 lands should be sold and a division
made, etc.

8 Nov. 1831. Will of JAMES STRAIN, dec'd proven. Will dated
20 Oct. 1831. Sisters Susana Strain and Jane (Strain?). Susan
Strain, exr. Wit: Nathaniel Nickle, Andrew Rodgers and Wm. Green.

7 Nov. 1831. Will of MARY ANN GAREY, dec'd proven. Will dated
8 Jan. 1831. Mary Ann Gary...beloved aunt Isabella Mason all
my estate, etc. John Mason, exr. Wit: Abner Young, David Boyd
and Zebah? Young.

5 July 1831. Appraisal of estate of ROBERT HAISTON, dec'd by
Jos.? Byrd, Joshua Saxon and David Templeton. James L. Rodgers,
adm. 5 July 1831. Sale Bill of ROBERT HERSTON, dec'd. "sold
to sundry persons..."

11 Nov. 1831. Milland Crocker & Turner Richardson, adms. of
ELHANION CROCKER, dec'd, he being son of JAMES CROCKER, SR.,
dec'd..a citation to call Joseph Crocker, adm. of sd JAMES CROCK-
ER, SR., dec'd with the will of sd dec'd annexed to account
how he adm'd estate. Legatees summoned; Henry J. Bryon for himself and attorney for Whitfred Bryon, Elizabeth Byrd, Jacob
Niswanger, adm. of JAMES CROCKER, JR., dec'd & John Crocker.
Acct. of sales of estates, board for James Crocker's children,
rents, etc.

7 Nov. 1831. Adm. of estate of JAMES TAYLOR, dec'd to Elizabeth
Taylor. John Taylor and John McClintock, sur.

(No date) John Smith acct. with JOHN ABERSEN, dec'd. A. Pinson,
Charleston; notes due John Smith, etc.

7 Nov. 1831. Adm. of estate of CHARLES SAXON, dec'd to Hugh Saxon. William F. Downs and Samuel Downs, sur.

14 Nov. 1831. Adm. of estate of HARREY HAZEL, dec'd to John Smith. (also spelled Hazlet). John West?, Zebulon Savage and John Watson, sur.

14 Nov. 1831. Adm. of estate of ROBERT BRYSON, dec'd to Sarah Bryson. Mathew Bryson and John Felts, sur.

1 Nov. 1831. Joseph Ball, minor about 19 years of age, chose John Ball his guardian. Lewis Ball and Thomas Hill, sur.

10 Nov. 1831. Will of JOSEPH JONES, dec'd proven. Will dated 3 Nov. 1831. Beloved wife Margret Jones; Rhoda Jones; son Samuel Jones. George Ball and James Neely, exrs. Wit: R. Leeke, John Ball, Nathaniel Nickle and Cornelius Puckett.

21 Nov. 1831. Request for sale of estate of DRURY BOYCE, dec'd by Mary Boyce, exr.

21 Nov. 1831. Life estate left to RUTH BRAZILE, dec'd wife of ENOCK BRAZILE, dec'd, legatees also dec'd and left issue. Property to be sold and divided among dec'd heirs children.

7 Nov. 1831. Adm. of estate of SAMUEL SAXON, dec'd to Lydral Saxon. Richd. F. Simpson and Henry C. Young, sur.

22 Nov. 1831. Adm. of estate of ABSALUM ANDRESS, dec'd to Samuel Beeks. Frances Beeks and Ferrel Andress, sur.

12 Nov. 1831. Appraisal of estate of DAVID STRAIN, dec'd by Zimry Carter, Benj. Malden and Wm. Reed.

7 Nov. 1831. Will of JOHN DAVIS, dec'd proven. Will dated 22 Apr. 1823. Dau. Mary Criswell; son John Davis land in Washington co., KY by titles of conveyance from Littel Buseby Sullivan to myself; son James Davis; beloved wife Anne Davis; unfortunate dau. Elizabeth Davis; friend Robt. Criswell, John H. Davis, Benjamin James, John McClennon and Doctor James Davis guardians and trustees of sd dau. Elizabeth; (son is also listed as John H. Davis). Sons John H. Davis and James Davis, Robt. Criswell and Dr. James Davis, exrs. Wit: Robt. Word, James Williamson, Frs. Medley. Codicil. Dau. Elizabeth remains under protection, etc. of son James on real estate in Laurens Dist.. 2nd Codicil. 6 Mar. 1826. Wit: James Williamson, Absolum Bayley, Wm. Martin and James Powell. (N. B. most of the long will is concerning the care, etc. of his dau. Elizabeth.) 20 Mar. 1829. Deed, other items to son James Davis and John H. Davis. 7 Nov. 1831. Deed of gift proven in court.

8 Nov. 1831. Appraisal of estate of JOHN DAVIS, dec'd by John Nickles, James McDowal and David Martin. James Davis, exr.

5 Dec. 1831. Will of CHARLES LITTEL, planter, dec'd. Will dated 19 Sept. 1831. Beloved wife Ann; Henry Bonds; Caroline Bonds, children of Ann and Mary Bonds now residing in Georgia; sons Robert Henderson Littel, James Clendenen Littel, Charles and David Littel; son-in-law James Kirk; grand-dau. Sarah Kirk, dau. of my dau. Catty; grand-dau. Margret Winn, the dau. of my dau. Jeen Taylor. Wife Ann, sons Robt. Henderson and Charles Littel, exrs. Wit: Robt. Criswell, Andw. Kennedy, Jer. Leek.

21 Nov. 1831. Appraisal of property of MARY ANN GARY, dec'd by Abner Young, John Hunter and Jeb Deen. John Mayson, exr.

1 Dec. 1831. Memorandum of property of JOSEPH JONES, dec'd. Wm. Tinsley, Saml. McWilliams and Cornelius Puckett.2 Dec. 1831. Geo. Ball and James Neely, Jr., exrs. request public sale of property to pay debts of dec'd.

19 Dec. 1831. Appraisal of estate of HARREY HAZEL, dec'd by Zebalum Savage, John Weit, Saml. Feeman? and Jno. Watson. (N. B. date also shown as 9 Dec.). 20 Dec. 1831. Sale Bill. Pur.: Elizabeth Hazel, James Redden, Jno. Smith, Mitchel Clardy, Mansel Owen, Wm. Moor, Leroy Madison, Wade Sims, Aaron Hill, Asa Forgey, Young Neely, Wm. Gafford, Wm. Moor son of Thomas, Thos. Goggins, Jno. Fowlar, Willis Watson, Wm. Groves, Hannah Brook, George Moor son of Wm., Zachariah Sims, Wm. South, Saml. Hall, Joseph Daniel, H. B. Kelsey, Geo. Tiree, Robt. Waters, Filley F. West, Jno. Hall, James Hazle, Walter Jones, Wiley Watson, Saml. Kinmon, Bery Watson, Geo. Tearce, Hardiman Rosemon, L. F. West, Burk Busbey, Jno. Cooks, Hardeyman Bammor, Lucey Sims, Wm. Daniel, Julius Glover, James Adkins, Mathew McDanniel, Hamon Collins, Hardiman Barmore, Hannah Brook, Jno. Culberson, James and John Hazle, Jno. B. Davis, Hemson Norris, Thos. Redden, L. M. Madison, Philip Cummeford, Wm. Moor son of Robt., Henderson Norris, Saml. Hambleton, Gabriel Thomas, Zebulon Savage, Rail Jones, Jefferson Moor. Jno. Smith, adm.

9 Oct. 1831. Appraisal of estate of THOMAS GOODWIN, dec'd by Wm. Holbert, Moses Holbert and Theoplus Goodin. Thos. Goodwin, Jr., adm. 26 Oct. 1831. Sale Bill. Pur.: Harris Bramblet, Jno. Clark, Wm. Holbert, Joshua Gilbert, Carter Johnston, Jno. Cargill, Robt. Hand, Hare Holcombe, Aberham Bramblet, Jno. Garrett, Thos. Stepp, Wm. Gilbert, Charley Cargill, Jno. Filler, Philip Goodwin, Reuben Jones, Jerry Collins, Wm. Qualls, Larkin Bramblet. Note on John Smith, Wm. Holbert, Ezekiel Dunlap. Cash to Enock Bramblet, Basdle Ginn, Thos. Gwin, Wm. Clardy, Presley Owens, Joshua Gilbert, Aberham Bramblet, Ruben Estes, Jno. Owen, Calvin Wallis, Zachariah Bruce, Jno. McPatton, James Moore, Danl. Roberson, Mrs. Franks Ross. Ceala Goodwin and Thos. Goodwin, Jr.

22 Nov. 1831. Appraisal of estate of JAMES TAYLOR, dec'd by Alexander McCarley, Wm. Mills and Jno. McClintock.

30 Nov. 1831. Appraisal of estate of SAMUEL SAXON, dec'd by Wm. Irby, Wm. Pinson and James Cunningham. Notes: Jno. Dial, Jno. Pool, Colmon C. Philips, W. G. Davis. SAMUEL B. SAXON, dec'd. Lyel P. Saxon, adm.
Sale Bill.(?) Pur.: Sarah McNees, Abel Campbell, Winfield R. Prim, Saml. L. Cunningham, Eliza Franks, Elisha Helmons, Wm. Burton, James H. Lowery, Jno. Bolt, Jno. Burns, Hirum Burton, James Homes, Mark Killingsworth.

2 Jan. 1832. Will of JOHN WHITTEN, dec'd proven. Will dated 3 July 1828. Children: Lyndsy Whitten, John Whitten, Jr., Salley Hinley, Amey Jacks, Fanney Ray and Susanah Kenedy. Son Lyndsay Whitten and Braxton Ray, exrs. Wit: Jno. F. Kern, Alfred A. Kern and Jno. Fredrick Kern, Sr.

26 Feb. 1831. Appraisal of estate of BARUCH DUCKETT, dec'd by Joseph Babb, Jones Fullar, N. C., and Benjamin Brown. John Felts, J. P. Sale Bill. (No date) Pur.: Joseph Ligon, James Watts,

DUCKETT cont'd:
Mary Duckett, Joseph Millar, Mathew Brown, Isaac Mitchel, Wm.
Burnsides, Wm. Austen, Merida Waldrop, Mardy Waldrop, Peter
Fullar, Jesse Fullar, Dandy Motes, James Hollingsworth, Jacob
Millar, Regal Duncan, Alsa Fullar, Kellet Waldrop, Austen Pres-
ley, Danl. Matisone, Jesse Henderson, Jno. Odle, Rignal Dunkin,
James Wells, Nancy Jones, Robt. Campbell, Danl. M. Winn, Thos.
Rodgers, Foster Nickles, Thos. Teague, Benj. Drummon, Lazarus
Hitt, Arthur Slendin, Pattey Duckett. Notes on Wm. Stone, A.
Stone, Richd. M. Owen, Peter Cubirson, Brexter Owens, Jacob
Muller, Lazarus Hill, Peter Fullar. Jno. Odle, adm.

(No date) Appraisal of estate of GEORGE BALL, dec'd by Jno.
Af. Watts, Jno. McClanahan, Richd. Watts and Lewis Ball. John
Ball, exr. Sadler's tract of land (135), Mill tract (147), Gold-
ing tract (266½). Sale Bill (no date) No purchasers named on
sale of $5739.35 est. Estate of WILLIAM BALL, dec'd to est.
of GEORGE BALL, dec'das of 1825. Notes/cash from A. G. Butler,
Gimiah Ball, Geo. Ball, Thos. Hill, Martin Ball, Henry Ball,
Joseph Ball, Jno. Ball.

29 Nov. 1831. Appraisal of estate of ROBERT BRYSON, dec'd by
Jones Fullar, N. C., Richd. Golding and Mathew Bryson. 30 Nov.
1831. Sale Bill. Pur.: Peter Fullar, Alexander Austin, Wm. Bry-
son, Mathew Bryson, Merideth Waldrop, Nancy Jones, Bird Roberts,
Robt. Moor, Danl. Beechum, Jane Bryson, Joseph McGowan, James
Roberts, Saml. Rodgers, Robt. Todd. Sarah Bryson, adm.

22 Nov. 1831. Sale Bill estate of JOSEPH JONES, dec'd. Pur.:
Isaac Grnt, Martin Ball, Saml. McWilliams, Saml. Jones, James
Long, Wm. Winn, Cornelius Puckett, Chas. King, Doctor B. Smith,
Kittey Whiteford, Harey Oneail. Geo. Ball and James Neely, exrs.

7 Dec. 1831. Appraisal of estate of ABERHAM ANDRESS, dec'd by
Jno. Walker, Jno. Milam and Mitchel Clardy. Saml. Beeks, adm.
8 Dec. 1831. Sale Bill. Pur.: Frances Beeks, Turrel Andress,
James Teague, John Smyth, Jno. Walker, Jno. Pitts, Widow Matilda
Andress, Jno. Milum, Saml. Hambleton, Jno. Moore, Chas. Smyth,
Chas. Kay, Saml. H. Owens, Saml. McClurkin, Danl. Jent, Saml.
Hall, David Andress, Allen Andress, Thos. Washington, Elisha
Yager, Danl. South, John Gent, David P. Posey, Isaac Pitts,
Thos. Andress, James Mitchel, David Goddard. Note on Thos. John-
ston; acct on Lilley F. Wait.

14 Jan. 1832. Adm. of estate of THOMAS HITT, dec'd to James
Wright. Abram Holingsworth and John Hitt, sur.

15 Dec. 1831. Appraisal of estate of CHARLES SAXON, dec'd by
Barnet Smith, Robt. Coker and Saml. Downs. Hugh Saxon, adm.
15 Dec. 1831. Sale Bill. Pur.: Ira Arnold, Lewis Allen, James
Johnston, Wm. Bolt, Abraham Bolt, Thos. Brown, Starback Coker,
James Cargill, Thos. Coker, Saml. Downs, Austin Diel, Elijah
Franks, Wm. Goss, Wm. Henderson, Jena Henderson, Mathew Johnston,
Haistin Johnston, James Johnston, Hosa N. Cahaffey, Mark C.
Owings, John Orsborn, Stephen Potter, Carter Coker, Isabella
Saxon, Richd. F. Simpson, James Saxon, Stewart Henderson, Wm.
Queales, Oney Saxon. Book acct's: Ira Arnold, James Boyd, Isaac
Dial, James Henderson, Saml. McClurkin, Free Bill Gradion, Robt.
Coker, Robt. Flemming, Tulley F. Sullavan, Henderson Coker,
Jno. Henderson, Wm. Simpson, Robert Paden, Jonathen Henderson,
Negro Harvey, Sam. Saxon, David Saxon, Harris Tompson, Robt.
McNees, Thos. Milum, Abner Mathes, Wm. Johnson, Robt. & Saml.

SAXON cont'd:
Flemming, Jno. Madden, Ransom Fullar, Wm. Hance, John Niel,
John Manley, John Crymes, Joel Allen, Wm. Irby.

16 Jan. 1832. Will and two codicils of ELIZABETH LONG, dec'd
proven. Will dated 9 Nov. 1831. Four daus.: Salley Gowin, Polley
Simpson, Nancy Long and Elizabeth Davis; all my children con-
sisting of two families - Madox and Long: John Madox, Wm. Madox,
Salley Guinn and Polley Simpson of the Mattox family and Ware
Long, Reuben Long, James Long, Daniel Long and the two sons
of my dec'd son Lamore? Long, Dery Long and Micajah Long, Nancy
Long and Elizabeth Davis. Thomas Garrett, exr. Wit: Ambros Gar-
rett, Halums Worthmartin and Barnet Garrett. 1st Codicil. 9
Nov. 1831. Same witnesses. 2nd Codicil. John Long, son of my
dau. Sally Gwinn. 30 Dec. 1831. Wit: Ambrose Garrett, Bennet
Garrett and Hollins Worthmartin.

16 Jan. 1832. Adm. of estate of CLACKSTON RAY, dec'd to Saml.
Young. John Whitmore and John Ferguson, sur.

16 Jan. 1832. Adm. of estate of THOMAS PARKS, dec'd to James
Parks and Saml. Parks. Thos. N. Young, Nathaniel Parks and Danl.
Wallis, sur.

14 Oct. 1831. Appraisal of estate of EDWARD PUGH, dec'd by Benj.
Griffith, Jacob Roberts and Joseph Allen. William Gilbert, exr.
Sale Bill. (No date) . Pur.: Salley Pugh, Nancy Spurgen, Wm.
Holbert, James Taylor, Wm. Cooper, Wm. Crumbton, Joseph Allen,
Micagah Crumton, Elijah Johnston.

6 Feb. 1832. Petition of John Whitmore, exr. of HENRY B. ROW-
LING, dec'd for sale of property.

6 Feb. 1832. Adm. of estate of ZEDICAH SOUTH, dec'd to Gabril
South. Wm. South and Archaball Norwood, sur.

6 Feb. 1832. Adm. of estate of JAMES OWENS, dec'd to Wiley Mylum. John Walker and Wm. Low, sur.

6 Feb. 1832. Adm. of estate of SARAHAN BENNET, dec'd to Thos.
Young. Jno. Whitmore and Lewis Jones, sur.

6 Feb. 1832. By request of their mother, Bevely Potter, Nancy
Potter and Sarah Potter, minors, chose Stephen Potter their
guardian. Allen Barksdill and Wm. Henderson, sur.

17 Dec. 1831. Appraisal of estate of CHARLES LITTEL, dec'd by
W. W. Simpson, Jno. Leake and Chas. Blakely. Robt. H. and Chas.
Littel, exrs. 20 & 21 Dec. 1831. Sale Bill. Pur.: Wm. Blakely,
Sr., Norman Garey, Saml. Vance, Thos. Milum, Thos. Holland,
James Little, Elihu Griffin, A. A. Fareborne, David Blakely,
Thos. Blakely, Josiah Freskey, Henry Shell, Saml. Neighbors,
Jno. Taylor, Jesse Johnston, Jno. Tigrett, Jr., Jno. Little,
Hedley Davis, Wm. Blakely, Jr., Saml. Taylor, Jeremiah Tribble,
James L. Crag, David Martin, Saml. Gray, Henry Clevlan, Chris-
topher Garlington, Jonathan Warping, Wm. Vance, Wm. Templeton,
Jno. McClintock, W. W. Wallis, Jno. Gary, Ann Little, widow,
David Little, Nancy Parke, Robt. Blakely, James Bryson, Jno.
Garlington, Jno. Luke, Chas. Blakely, Robt. Milum, Hugh Workman,
Alexander McKelvey, Thos. Ferguson, Thos. Little, Wm. Goodwin,
Jno. Simmons, Thos. Hannah, Wm. Rodgers, Chas. Rodgers, Geo.
McKendrick, Wm. Goss, Robt. Spears, Saml. Copland, Saml. Taylor,

LITTEL cont'd:
Jno. Davis, Wm. Simpson, Wm. Turner, Wm. Blakely. Robert H.
Little, exr.

20 Feb. 1832. Adm. of estate of HENRY REESE HALL, dec'd to widow,
Salley M. Hall. Anthony F. Golding and John G. Brown, sur.

10 Jan. 1831. Appraisal of estate of JAMES CRAVEN, dec'd by
Francis Beeks, David Simmons and S. Davis. (Also shown as JAMES
V. CRAVEN). Sale Bill. (No date). Joseph Sulliivan, adm.

22 Feb. 1832. Appraisal of estate of ZEDEKIAH SOUTH, dec'd by
Isaac Teague, Jesse E. Clardy and John Cook. 23 Feb. 1832. Sale
Bill. Pur.: Rutha South, Wm. South, Sr., James Mitchel, Gabriel
South, Daniel South, James Teague, James Simmons, John Gent,
Isaac E. Clardy, Isaac Teague, Danl. Johnston, James H. South.
Gabriel South, adm.

18 Jan. 1832. Appraisal of estate of ELIZABETH LONG, dec'd by
Ambros Garrett, Willis Cheek and Edw. Garrett. 3 Feb. 1832.
Sale Bill. Pur.: Wm. Powers, Stephen Garrett, Solomon Glaspy,
David Higgins, Robt. Hann, Jr., Starling Tucker, Jonathan Jones,
Jno. Garrett, Thos. Garrett, Stephen Garrett, Sr., Nancy Long,
Edw. Garrett, Carter Parker, Jemimah Martin, Jno. Maddox, Jno.
Garrett, Sr., Lauran Harris, James Nobles, Nimrod Putmon, Saml.
Flemming, Reuben Estes, Jno. Guinn, Danl. Long, Thos. Simpson,
Wm. Guinn, W. B. Davis, Ambros Garrett, Willis Cheek, Berry
Long, Elias Cheek, Jno. Meadors, Aron Moor, Reuben Long, Thomp-
son Fowler, Benj. Martin, J. T. Parsons, Martin Shaw, Saml.
Nabors, J. B. Higgins, Henry Martin, Hannah Garrett, Jno. Riddle,
Jr., Joel Maddox, Austin Gilbert, Guinn Anderson, Nathl. Gil-
bert. Thos. Garrett, exr.

31 Jan. 1832. Appraisal of estate of CLAXTON RAY, dec'd by Richd.
L. Ferguson, Jno. W. Ferguson and Luke Wesson. Notes on Benj.
Adair, James Gamble, Saml. Mathews, Jno. Robertson, Robt. Phil-
lips, James Ray, John Ray, Reuben Ray and Braxten Ray. 1 & 2
Feb. 1832. Sale Bill. Saml. Young, adm.

24 & 25 Nov. 1831. Sale Bill of estate of JAMES TAYLOR, dec'd.
Pur.: Jno. McClintock, Alexander McCurley, Wm. Flemming, Flemming
Mosley, Mathew Holledy, Andw. Park, Wm. Taylor, Alfred Jones,
Jno. Flemming, Jno. Deen, L. B. Posey, Wm. Ronson, Jno. Taylor,
Thos. McCurley, Wm. Power, Jno. Blakely, Nelson Meredith, Hannah
Garrett, Alfred Parsons. Elizabeth Taylor, adm.

(No date) Sale Bill of SAMUEL SAXON, dec'd. Pur.: Owney Saxon,
Mark Killingworth, Harrting Diel, Alfred Blackwell, Saml. Lowry,
Garlington Diel, Lewis Diel, Chas. Irby, Wm. D. Pinson, Isaac
S. Diel, Jr., Isaac Diel, Sr., Hambleton Lowery, Jno. Culberson,
Ambros Huggins, Wm. Bolt. Lyd. P. Saxon, adm.

23 Feb. 1832. 2nd Sale Bill of HENRY B. ROWLAND, dec'd. Jno.
Whitmore, exr.

22 Feb. 1832. Appraisal of estate of SARAH ANN BENNETT, dec'd
by Joseph Dunken, Jno. Addington and Jno. McCoy. 23 Feb. 1832.
Sale Bill. Thos. Young, adm.

27 Mar. 1832. Will of THOMAS BEESLEY, dec'd proven. Will dated
23 Feb. 1821. Betsey, my dearly beloved wife; land bought of
Wm. Bourland, Sr., Elmore & Saxon, Dillard, Rody W. Roberts,

BEESLEY cont'd:
Abraham Holland, Meadows estate, Benj. Wilson, Jr., my black-
smith shop; eldest dau. Polly Ferguson; grandson Edmond Holland,
in trust for my second dau. Nancy Holland, wife of Abraham Hol-
land; third dau. Elizabeth Ferguson; in trust to Dr. Alexander
Chambers for my fourth dau. Jenney Williams; fifth dau. Dolley
(Dorothy) Chambers. Son-in-law Dr. Alexander Chambers and Warner
W. Meadors, exrs. Wit: Perry Jones, Elizabeth W. Ferguson and
Sary Bell.

30 Dec. 1831. Property sold of estate of DRURY BOYCE, dec'd,
Mary Boyce, exr. Pur.: Wm. Nash, David Peden, Robt. Willis,
Joseph Good, Edmond Nash, Joseph McCullar, Joseph Crook, Henry
Johnston, Jno. Owens, Jno. McHarrison, Jno. Standhouse, Silys
Arnold, Wm. West, Wm. Thompson, Martin Ball, Dempsey Nisbet,
James Martin, Nathan Nisbet, Geo. Thomson.

2 Feb. 1832. Appraisal of estate of THOMAS PARKS, dec'd by R.
Criswell, Thos. M. Young and Benj. Griffith. 29 Dec. 1831. Inv.
of ready money, notes & acct's of estate, being the day after
the decease of sd Thomas Parks. Saml. Parks, James Parks, Jesse
Wallis, Jacob Roberts, Mrs. Roberts, Lucy Meador, Charitate
Gray, Wm. Wallis, Nathl. Parks, David Gilbert, Amelia Campbell,
Nancy Parks, Lewis Bramblet, Jency Davis, Grif Pucket, Jacob
Brown, Saml. Henderson, Edw. Waddle, Caller Waddle, Zach. Gray,
Joel Fowler, Mrs. Powell. James Parks, adm.

15 Dec. 1831. Adm. of estate of REUBEN G. CASE, dec'd to Draten
Nance. Robt. Dunlap and Fredrick Nance, sur.

8 Feb. 1832. Sale Bill of estate of THOMAS PARKS, dec'd. Pur.:
Jacob Meador, Thos. Parks, Jr., Edmund (Emmanuel?) Lyons, Nathan
Parks, Lesley Gray, Wm. Parks, Gueler Lindy, Thos. Helton, James
Parks, Jno. Deen, Geo. Fowler, Elijah Johnston, Jas. Hughs,
Thos. Woodruff, Jon'h. Gilbert, Jno. Harris, Jno. Taylor, Nathan-
iel Parks, Jno. Cooper, Richd. Owens, Danla. McKee, Lewis Sand-
ford, F. Ross, Richd. K. Owing, Jno. Flemming, Henry Brockman,
Harrison Woodruff, Jacob Roberts, Jonathan Huresk, Noel Waddel,
Benj. White, Wm. Chandler, Isaac Cooper, Wm. Quals, Lucey Mead-
ors, Mary Parks, Garred Drumens, Thos. Garrett, Jed Dean, Hart-
ing Jester, Jeremiah Creek, Roland Hand, Thos. Blackburn, Thos.
Chappel, Thos. Hudson, Thos. Campbell, J. B. Wallis, Wm. Cen-
nady, Nehan Muada(Meorady), Jno. Balding, Mrs. H. Whitemartin,
Thos. H. Westmoreland, Thos. Wright, Joel Allen, Chas. Petty,
Jno. Hand, Benj. Griffith, Jno. Peaden, Lesley Gray, Henry Thomp-
son, Wm. Halbert, Robt. Holland, Jno. C. Fowler, Jesse Wallis,
Robin Hand, Wm. Bonner, Wm. Holland, Alford Deen, Seaborn Parks,
Garner Roberts, Lebon Parks.

16 Apr. 1832. Adm. of estate of SOLLOMON MEHAFFY, dec'd to
Hosa Mahaffy. Danl. Johnston and James S. Rodgers, sur.

3 Dec. 1830. Sale Bill estate of WILLIAM PARKS, dec'd. Pur.:
James Parks, Robt. Taylor, Jr., Wm. Blakely, Jr., James Blakely,
Christopher Garlington, Wm. Sims, Jno. Garlington, Rachel Parks,
Jane Parks, Robt. Spence, Wm. Mills, Sr., Jno. Sneed, Jules
Martin, James S. Hutcheson, Chas. Smith, Barnet Parsons, Whit-
bury Wallis, Chas. Simmons. James Parks, adm.

22 Feb. 1832. Appraisal of estate of JAMES OWENS, dec'd by Jehu
Nickles, Jno. Walker and Wiley Hill. Wiley Milum, adm. Sale
Bill. (No date). No purchasers named.

4 (No month) 1830. Sale Bill of ROBERT TAYLOR, dec'd. Pur.:
James Hunter, Jno. Taylor, Joel Fowler, James Rodgers, James
Taylor, Alexander McEarley, Saml. Mills, Elijah Johnston, Emuel
Lyon, Pasley Owens, Aron Moor, Wm. Brown, Wm. Henderson, James
Moor, David Higgins, Tulley E. Mosley, Saml. Flemming, James
Williams, Jno. Gray, Elias Cheek, Jonathan Abercrumbie, Jose.
Brown, Peter Pool, Calup Woodruff, Wm. Powers, Hamton G. Parson,
Even Beal, Stephen Garrett, Alexander Powers, Chas. Allen, Wm.
Cowan, Danl. P. McKee, James Garner, Wm. Ross, James B. Fleming,
Flemming Mosley, Benegah Cennedy, Alexander Mills, Sr., Jno.
Wallis, Abraham Garrett, Wm. Sims, Wm. Hill, Fowler Roberson,
Roberson Mosley, Abraham Crow, Abraham Arnold, Mathew Holland,
Mathew Holliday, Anderson Brown, Wm. Mills, Sr., James Rhodes,
Robt. Flemming, Harmon Garrett, Edw. Fowler, Ey-- F. Forley.
Property willed to Robert Taylor by his mother Margret Taylor
and sold on 6 Nov. 1830.

14 Apr. 1832. Will of JAMES AUSTIN, dec'd proven. Will dated
30 Mar. 1832. Son James; beloved wife Henerata Austin and my
children. Alex'r. Austin, exr. Wit: R. C. Austin, Jno. Moore
and Thomas Austin.

3 Nov. 1826. Sale Bill of estate of CATHERINE ROSS, dec'd. Pur.:
Sarah B. Ross, Elizabeth Glenn, Walter A. Dean, Lydral Williams,
James Fleming, Wm. Ross, A. G. Williams, Benj. B. Dall, Thos.
Deen, Chas. Williams, Nancy Parks, Joseph Vance, Jno. Nabours,
Nimrod Ross, Wm. Cowen, Frances Ross, Saml. Fleming, Raney Ball,
Walter A. Dean, Abner Wright, Gideon Owens, James Garner, Jr.,
Wm. Hunter, Andw. Park, Robt. Franks, Jno. Cowen, Sarah Hutche-
son, Wm. Ashby, Joel Allen, Jno. Todd, Stephen Garrett, Alexander
McDaniel, James Riddle, Wm. Mills, Sr., Aney Gant, John Gant,
Benj. B. Hall. Wm. Cowing, exr.

(No date) Appraisal of SOLLOMON MEHAFFEE, dec'd by Thos. Gradon,
Joseph Avery and Edw. H. Garrett. Sale Bill. (No date) Hoseaa
Mehaffee, adm. Pur.: Martin Ball, Lewis Mehaffee, Martin Babb,
James Tramen, Wm. Mehaffee, Nancy Mehaffee, Jno. Nash, James
Durrough, Jeremiah Hopkins, Jno. Helloms, Edw. H. Garrett, Lewis
Benham, Thos. Moses.

5 Dec. 1825. Mathew Scott, Sarah Ann Scott, Patrick Scott, Thomas
Scott and Margret Scott, minors, chose James Scott, guardian.
Patrick Scott and William Fullton, sur.

30 Apr. 1832. Appraisal of estate of JAMES AUSTIN, dec'd by
Joseph Owens, Jno. Moore and Thos. Ligon. 1 May 1832. Sale Bill.
Pur.: Wm. Austin, Larkin Colemon, Albert Miller, Woodson Ligon,
Thos. Austin, Anthony Griffen, Jno. Moore, Jno. White, Robt.
Campbell, Wm. Thomson, James Austin, Isaac Grant, Danl. Jones.
Alexander Austin, exr.

7 Nov. 1831. Probate renounced will of RUTHA BREAZEALE, dec'd
by James Davis, wit. 6 July 1832. Henry W. Paisley took oath
as adm. with will annexed. Zachariah Bailey and Edmond Paisley,
sur. (Also spelled Parsley). Will dated 3 Aug. 1831. She was
then residing in Anderson Dist., S. C. but her effects and place
of residence being Laurens Dist. Dau. Hulda Johnston, wife of
Geo. W. Johnston; grand-daus. Frances and Hemmeltal Johnston;
grand-dau. Frances Emeline Hill; grand-dau. Caroline Elizabeth
Hill; Eunice Hollingsworth. James Davis, exr. Wit: Mathew Gambrell, James Davis and Barbra Casey.

13 July 1832. Leminion Dillard, guardian of John Boling, minor,

GUARDIANSHIP cont'd:
for settlement of legacy. John <u>Balling</u> now of lawful age. (also
spelled Bouland).

13 July 1832. Adm. of estate of JANE BRYSON, dec'd to Mathew
Bryson. Jones Fuller, N. C. and John Felts, sur.

1 Aug. 1832. Will of JAMES NEELY, SR., dec'd proven. Will dated
19 July 1824. Beloved wife Mary; daus. Nancy and Betsey; son
Samuel; son James; Newbury tract of land; son-in-law Joseph
Jones, son George. Sons George and James Neely, exrs. Wit: Wm.
Tinsley, Wm. W. Pollard and Jab. W. Johnston. 1 Aug. 1832. Jabez
W. Johnston was requested by James Neely, dec'd to write his
will and requested him to make this addition to same. (Codicil).

6 Aug. 1832. Will of JOHN CUNNINGHAM, dec'd proven. Will dated
27 June 1832. Beloved wife Mary Louise Cunningham; beloved son
Samuel Jones Cunningham; brother Thomas Cunningham; brothers
and sisters (not named). My <u>only</u> brother Thomas Cunningham,
exr. and also guardian of my son who is under 21 years. Wit:
H. C. Young, R. Campbell and A. Kenedy.

6 Aug. 1832. Jackson Coley, minor, about 15 years, chose John
Culberson, guardian. Saml. Rodgers and Jacob Elledge, sur.

6 Aug. 1832. Adm. of estate of JEMIMAH GRIGGS, dec'd to Sterling K. Smith. Wm. S. Puckett and Joseph Avery, sur.

20 Aug. 1832. Will of SARAH RODGERS, widow, dec'd proven. Will
dated 1 June 1832. Son James S. Rodgers; dau. Tabitha; debt
due Albert Madden; children but names only these two. Friend
Richard F. Simpson, exr. Grand-dau. <u>Mimima</u> Morten. Wit: Saml.
Downs, C. W. Allen and Jonathan Allen.

3 Nov. 1831. 2nd appraisal of estate of ENOCK BRAZELE, dec'd
by Alsey Fuller, Jno. Nickles and David Mortin. Wm. Hill, exr.
(also shows 30 Nov. and surname spelled Breazell. Signed: John
Felts, J.P.) (No date) Sale Bill. No pur. named.

1 Sept. 1832. Adm. of estate of WILLIAM BRYSON, JR., dec'd to
Robert Nickles. Marshal Starnes and James Nickles, sur.

14 Aug. 1832. Appraisal of estate of JANE BRYSON, dec'd by Alsey
Fuller, Joseph Ligon, Jones Fuller, N. C., and Wm. Thompson.

8 July 1832. Adm. (will annexed) of estate of WILLIAM BRYSON,
SR., dec'd to Mathew Bryson. Joseph Ligon, sur. 14 Aug. 1832.
Appraisal of estate by Alsey Fuller, Joseph Ligon, Jones Fuller,
N. C. and Wm. Thompson.

(No date) 1832. Will of RICHARD BLACKWELL, dec'd proven. Will
dated 25 July 1832. Son Alfred Blackwell; son James Blackwell;
son David Blackwell; wife and children; lower plantation purchased from John Simmons and Jno. F. Gray; wife Margret Blackwell;
children: Elizabeth Blackwell, Nancey Blackwell, David Blackwell,
Rebeca Blackwell, Joel Blackwell, Hanah Blackwell, Margret Blackwell, Caroline Blackwell, Richard Blackwell and Susanah Frances
Blackwell. Charles Brook, Jr., exr. Wit. S. Cunningham, Jas.
Abercrumbie, Sr., Jno. Coats and Jno. Morgan.

17 Sept. 1832. Will of JANE GORDON, dec'd proven. Will dated
29 June 1832. To William Dunlap in trust for the use and benefit

GORDON cont'd:
of my sister Charlot Fuylton; two sisters Cally Alexander and
Charlota Fulton (later writtene Catty and Caralin). Wm. Dunlap,
exr. Wit: Edw. Jones, Robt. Johnston and James R. Sips.

14 Aug. 1832. Appraisal of estate of JAMES NEELY, dec'd by Wm.
Tinsley, Anthony Golding and Isaac Grant. Mentions Mason Maney.
Sale Bill. (No date) Pur.: Miss Elizabeth Neely, Abraham Gallit
(also Gullet), Major Wright, Betsey Neely, Samuel Neely. Geo.
Neely, exr.

6 Mar. 1832. Appraisal of estate of HENRY REASE HALL, dec'd
(then signed 16 July 1832) then certified on 27 Sept. 1832
by A. Griffin, Benj. William. Daniel Williams, one of the ap-
praisers was deceased before business finished. 8 & 9 Mar. 1832.
Sale Bill. Pur.: David Caldwell, G. F. Wells, Capt. Anthony
Griffin, J. W. Roazmon, Anthony F. Golding, Jno. Armstrong,
Jno. Simpson, Benj. Williamson, Danl. Pitts, James Watts, Mrs.
Salley M. Hall, Richd. Golding, Jno. Hall, Fredrick Nance, James
Criswell, Patrick Todd, Allen Andrews, Thos. C. Reeder, Wm.
Fuller, Alexander Austin, Wm. R. Smith, Moses Pitts, Jno. G.
Brown, Martin Langston, Wm. Croswhite, James Davis, Nathan Proc-
tor, James Burton, B. F. Griffin, Johnston Lowry, Wm. Atwood,
Patrick Lynnett, Anthony McFall, Jno. Beekeborger, Jonathan
Devenport, Anthony G. Luke, Jesse Goggins, Jno. D. Williams,
Danl. Hitt, James Watts, Cheney McClure, Chas. Flowed, Drury
Vaughn, David C. Bozamen, Elihu Pain. Sally M. Hall, adm.

28 Sept. 1832. Appraisal of estate of JOHN CUNNINGHAM, dec'd
by Geo. Bowen, Jno. Garlington and J. James. Thos. Cunningham,
exr. 8 Aug. 1832. Jno. Garlington, Geo. Bowing and W. G. Davis.
Accepted by Louisa Cunningham. Test. L. Cunningham. Sale Bill
agreeable to his will. Store goods sold to Kirkpatrick & Kenedy.
Rest to sundry persons. Notes belonging to the firm of Cunningham & Sharp, when collected will be equally divided between
them. A. W. Arnold, Abraham Andrews, Allen Andrews, Terrel And-
rews, Thos. Adkins, Lewis Alison, Henry F. Alison, Robt. Alison,
Joel Allen, Stephen Allen, John L. Adkeson, Johnston Allen,
Edw. Anderson, John Bennium, David Bell, Wm. Burgess, Wm. Blake-
ly, Hugh Bruster, Capt. Jno. Blakely, Thos. Blakely (son of
Thos.), James Bond, Jno. G. Baker, James Cunningham, Jr., John
D. Cunningham, Rubin Clement, Jno. Culberson, Edw. Edwards,
Elizabeth Burton, Capt. Jno. Davis, Thos. Davis, Jr., Thos.
Davis, Sr., Hardyman Duke, Lewis Daniel, Jno. Daniel, Wm. F.
Downs, James Ensley, N. Franks, Robt. Franks, Saml. Flemming,
James Garner, Wm. Goss, Christopher Garlington, Simon Garrett,
Ambros Garrett, Henry Grimes, Wm. Hosey, Newton Higgins, Jno.
Hunter, Edw. Hix, Wm. Henderson, Sr., Wm. Hardy, Andw. Henderson,
A. S. Hutcheson, Estes Hunter, Wm. Hudgins, A. Hudins, Robt.
B. James, Alfred James, Danl. Johnston, Jonathan Allen, Wm.
Johnston, Haisting Johnston, Chas. Irby, Joseph Irby, Jno. G.
Black, James Loveless, James H. Lowery, Saml. B. Lowery, Wm.
Leake, John Leek, Thos. B. Lockert, Aquillia Lindley, Wm. E.
Lindley, Bennet Lee, Diall Martin, Bailey Mehon, Jno. Mehon,
Drury Mastin, James Morgen, Wm. Morgen, Saml. Morgen, Jonathan
Motes, James McGowan, Geo. McNight, Henry Madden, David Madden,
Capt. Jno. Madden, Mrs. Maden, Sr., Jno. Mitchell (RR), Andw.
McKnight, Marshal Martin, Capt. Geo. Moor, Mrs. Madden, Jr.,
Capt.A. Mixon, Alexander Nabours, Re__ Orsborn, M. D. Pinsen,
Jno. Pinson, Whitfiel Primer, Jno. B. Pits, Wm. Park, David
Park, Wm. Potter, Jno. Pool, Wm. Quales, Wm. Ransam, Saml. Rod-
gers, Maj. Francis Ross, E. B. Ridgey, James Riddle, Elijah

CUNNINGHAM cont'd:
Sanders, Jno. Simmons, E. G. Smith & S. Murphey, Wm. Sumervill
& Owens, Wm. South, Simon Spruel, W. W. Simpson, Mickel Smith,
Elijah Smith, James Smith, Jno. Smith (son James), R. B. Saxon,
R. F. Simpson, Wm. Sulevan, Chas. Saxon, Davis Shockley, Pleasant
Sulivant, Jarrett Sulivant, James Teague & E. Smith, Elias &
Isaac Teague, Wm. Teague & McM. D. A. Davis, Saml. Taylor, Hams-
ton Taylor, John Twedy, Capt. Jno. Templeton, Jno. Tod & J.
Young, Jno. Todd, Thos. Wood, Joel Wood & Thomas, Mathew White,
Saml. Wallis, James Wilson, Jno. Word, Hugh Wilson, Wm. Wilson,
Thos. Wilks, Thos. Wilks & S. Rodgers, Henry C. Young. List
of open acct's belong to firm of Cunningham & Sharp: Robert
Allison, Absolum Andrews, Milly Allen, Henry Allison, Johnston
Allison, Wm. Allison, Jno. Alison, John L. Adkeson, James Alex-
ander, Jno. Burton, Stanmore Brooks, Wm. Bird, Jno. H. Bird,
David Bell, Wm. Bruce, Thos. Blackley, James Brown, Robt. Blak-
ley (son Wm.), James A. Blakley, Pinckney Bobo, Wm. Burnside,
Jehu Coats, Mathew Cunningham, Martin E. Cunningham, James Duke
Cunningham, Wm. Cunningham, Saml. Cunningham, Elihu Cunningham,
James Cunningham, Sr., Jeremiah Cobb, James Clark, Jno. Culber-
son, W. L. Cobb (free negro), Lemareus Deale, Isaac Dial, Sr.,
Isaac P. Boyd, Jonathan Davis, Jno. Dunlap, Alexander Deale,
Wm. R. Farley, Wm. Farrow, Robt. Franks, Sr., Forrest Farley,
Joshua Franks, Harmon Garrett, Warren George, Davis Garlington
& Spencer(N. B. this may be Garlington, Davis & Spencer), Nimrod
Gent, Elizabeth Gaines, Asa Garrett, Benj. Groves, Wm. Goss,
Danl. Gent, Jos. Hill & J. H. Byrd, Mary Ann Hutcheson, Ambrose
Hutcheson, Col. James Hunter, Col. Wm. Hill, Wm. Hardy, James
Hall, Andw. Henderson, Jno. Hudgins, Jno. Hitch, James Hunter
(blind), Wm. Irby, Henderson Johnston, Jabuz (a free negro),
Allen Johnston, Nancy James, Dial Johnston, Wm. Johnston, Haist-
ing Johnston, Jno. G. Black, Andw. Kenedy, Wm. Lefoy, Thos.
B. Lockhart, Jno. Leek (son of Wm.), Wm. Lindley, Jonathan Lind-
ley, Chartila Lowery, Albert Madden, Wm. Madden, Jr., Jno. L.
Madden, Maj. Jno. Milam, Wm. Mehan, Mathew McDaniel, James Mor-
gin, Capt. Geo. Moor, Wm. Madden, Sr., Jacob Niswanger, Jno.
B. Pitts, Elihu Pinson, B. L. Lowery, Jno. Pool, Hannah Pitts,
Wm. Potter, Capt.Abner Rodgers, Saml. Rodgers, Anne Rodgers,
Wm. Ranson, Wm. J. Stephens, Thomson Swena, R. F. Simpson, Robt.
Spruel, Joshua Saxon, Jno. R. Stephens, Jas. L. South, Owens
Sumerall?, Chas. Saxon, Reuben Stephens, Chas. Stuart, Robt.
H. Spears, Sul_orn Sumner, Chaney Stone, Robt. Stephens, James
Simmons, Zachariah Taylor, Joshua Teague, Elijah Tribble, N.
V. Vanpatton, Maren Timmens, Lydrall Williams, Mathew White,
Robt. Wilson, Jane Wilson, Jno. Wilson, Danl. Winn. List of
Negro acct's belong the firm: (name and who belongs to): Henry
(Thos. A. Sharp), Peter (Robt. Brock), Charles (Mark Killings-
worth), Brumus (Mary Cunningham), Daniel (H. C. Young), Jesse
(Robt. Ellison), Peter (Chas. Smith), Davy (W. F. Simpson),
Absalum (Mrs. Kenedy), Viney (H. C. Young), Maggy (D. P. Saxon),
Henry (Jno. S. James) also Cyrus, Eleck (James H. Irby) also
John. Judgements belonging to firm: Ransom Fuller, Elizabeth
Word, Jos. H. Prichards, J. W. Craddock, Thos. Goggins, Jas.
Moats, H. F. Allison, J. L. Gains, Wm. B. Grey, A. C. Jones,
Saml. Boyd, Wm. Johnston, Jno. Miller, Jno. Allison son of Joel,
Wm. Holmes, Shubal Starns, Jno. Hunter, Henry Lindley, James
Henderson, Jr., Stephen Folly?, Stanmore Brooks. Notes belonging
to estate of JOHN CUNNINGHAM, dec'd. Garlington, Davis and Simp-
son, Wm. Leek, Jno. Leek, Sr., Henry C. Young, B. Holdridge,
J. Stanford, Wm. D. Allen, Andw. Thomas, Jno. Benjamin, Edmund
Roberts, Hezekiah Chesure, Robt. Criswell, Jno. Dunlap, Thos.
Deen, Thos. Gray, Christopher Garlington, Campbell Mehaffey,

CUNNINGHAM cont'd:
Edw. Hix, Newton Higgins, Jno. Hunter, James Hardy, Stirling
Gradon, Haiston Johnston, Allen Kelly, Geo. McKnight, Wm. Morgen,
Jno. Martin, Tully E. Marley, Capt. Jno. Madden, Wm. E. Lynch,
Chas. Saxon, W. W. Simpson, Plesant Sulivan, Elijah Smith, Jr.,
Hunsford Tremens, Geo. Williams, Henry Williams, Elizabeth Word,
Devall Morten, James McNeales?, Thos. S. Wilks. Acct's cont'd:
Thos. Blakely, son of Jas., Edw. Hix, Abner Pyles, Thos. Andrews,
Clerey Stone, Chas. Williams, Esq., Chas. Littel, Jr., Mrs.
Jane Willson, B. L. Posey, Wm. Leek, Saml. Cunningham, Esq.,
Cristopher Garlington, Allen Kelley, N. V. Vapatton (Vanpatton),
Thos. Lockert, Sr., Jno. Hunter, Capt. L. K.? Saxon, Jno. S.
James, Nancy Park, David Bell, Maj. Thos. S. Wilks, Jane Park,
Edw. Anderson, James Hardy, Jno. Pool, Saml. Anderson, Wm. Park,
Newton Higgens, Wm. Hanie, Elijah Smith, Jr., James Smith, Wm.
Patten, Repts. Tisborn, Danl. Martin, Col. Wm. Farrow, Mason
Sammons, Israel Holt, Wm. Lindey, Starling Graden, Wm. Morgen,
Jno. Garlington, Danl. Johnston, J. D. _. Simpson, M. E. Cun-
ningham, James Cunningham, Geo. Tompson, Nancy Jones, Mitchel
Smith, Jno. B. Stephens, Jno. Stephens, Elisha Watson, Thos.
Davis, Sr., Nimrod Putmen, Wm. Blakely, son of James, Mrs. John
Barros, Jos. Vance, Susan Wilson, Andw. I. Wilson, Robt. Lenie,
Jno. Bolt, Capt. Jas. Templeton, M. D. Pinson, Peggey Crooks,
Jno. Simmons, Jr., Jno. Martin, Sr., Henry Williams, Wm. Madden,
Jr., Wm. Ransom, S. B. Lewars, H. C. Young, Lydral Williams,
James Jensey, Henderson Johnston, Susana Crocker, Wm. Burgess,
Elihu Burgess, Elizabeth D. Wallace, Hugh Mayhaffey, Allen Ma-
haffey, Jno. M. C. Glenn, Cristopher Burn, Wm. Burnside, Jno.
Shell, Robt. Stephens, Jno. Culberson, Dr. Wm. Irby, Jno. Walker,
Maj. James Clardy, Thos. E. Moor, Elihu Cunningham, Jacob El-
lege, Jas. Henderson, Sr., Jeremiah Cole, Susan Garrett, Chas.
Simmons, Sr., R. F. Simpson, Wiley Hill, Henry Madden, Geo.
McClintock, Wm. Boyd, Valentine Harling, Elizabeth Wilks, Wm.
Blakely, son of Wm., Dr. Robt. Campbell, Mabra Madden, Sr.,
Chas. G. Franks, Thos. Hood, Richd. Denton, Robt. Spears, Jno.
Leek, Jr., son of Wm., Wm. Adams, Alfred Jones, Laborn Summer,
David Delong, Elizabeth Garner, Harmon Duke, Langston Orsborn,
Jno. H. Coleman, Edw. H. Garrett, Jno. Todd, Elizabeth Nabours,
Elizabeth Pinson, Purcivell J. Boyd, Dr. Jno. H. Davis, Elizabeth
B. Ridgeway, Jas. F. Foster, Wm. R. Farley, Luerens Deal, Mrs.
Harriet Caldwell, Jno. Simmons, son of Alick, Sarah McNees,
Wm. Todd, son of Patrick, Ira Potter, Jeremiah Hopkins, Hannah
Brooks, Harsting Deal, son of Isaac, James Martindill, Jos.
Hopper, Mrs. Mary D. Reynolds, Mrs. Sarah Young, Geo. Moor,
widow's son, Mrs. Andw. Todd, Geo. W. Swindle, Richd. Cotterell,
Polly Smith, Caty Pinson, Jas. Shockley, Jno. Rupel, Moses Mad-
den, Jane McDowell. Negro acct's belonging to estate of JNO.
CUNNINGHAM, dec'd. (Name and owner): Jack (Saml. Cunningham,
Esq.), Peter (same), Josa? (F. F. Jones), William and Peter
(J. Cunningham), Daniel (Nat. Day), Winney (Thos. Wood), Ceasor
(old free man), Joel (Jno. Garlington), Frank (Robt. Todd),
Squire (R. F. Simpson), Peter (Jno. Garlington), Pompy (Jno.
Cunningham), Henry (Jno. Garlington), Ira (S. Cunningham).

25 Sept. 1832. Appraisal of estate of JANE GORDON, dec'd by
David Grayham, Jno. Blakley and Jno. Adair.

1 Oct. 1832. Will of RICHARD BLACKWELL, dec'd proven. Will dated
25 July 1832. Son Alfred Blackwell; son James Blackwell; son
David; lower plantatioin purchased from John Simmons and Jno.
F. Gray; wife Margret Blackwell; children - Elizabeth Blackwell,
Nancy Blackwell, David Blackwell, Rebacha Blackwell, Joel Black-

BLACKWELL, cont'd:
well, Hannah Blackwell, Margret Caroline Blackwell, Richard Blackwell, and Susanah Frances Blackwell. Chas. Brook, Jr., exr. Wit: S. Cunningham, Jas. Abercrumbie, Sr., Jno. Coats and John Morgen.

22 Oct. 1832. Will of ISAAC GRANT, dec'd proven. Will dated 6 Sept. 1832. Son Marion Grant land adj. James Lowe; wife Jane Grant; other children (not named-moved and left); dau. Arianah. Son Marion Grant and Wm. Austin, exr. Wit: Jno. Boyd, Sr., Thos. Salman and Salley Golding.

5 Nov. 1832. Letters test. on estate of THORNEBURY BOWLING, dec'd to Josiah N. Bowling, exr.

5 Nov. 1832. John H. Coleman, adm. of WILLIAM COLEMAN, dec'd.

5 Nov. 1832. Adm. of estate of WILLIAM CLARDY, dec'd to Jesse E. Clardy. Jno. Smith and Jas. S. Rodgers, sur.

19 Nov. 1832. Adm. of estate of HOSA HOLCOMB, dec'd to Nathan Holcomb. Thos. Wright and Wm. Hobert, sur.

22 Nov. 1832. Ainah Grant, minor about 17 years, chose Lewis Ball, guardian. aWm. Austin and Zimri Carter, sur.

21 Nov. 1832. Sale of part of estate of ISAAC GRANT, dec'd by Jean Grant. Wit: Thos. Salman and Andy Andrews. Wm. Austin, exr.

25 Sept. 1832. Appraisal of estate of WILLIAM BRYSON, dec'd by Wm. C. Nickles, Geo. Nickles and Wm. Hollingsworth. Sale Bill. (no date) Pur.: Catharine Bryson, Jas. Nickles, Alex. Austin, Robt. Nickles, Kellis Waldrop, Robt. McCreedy, Geo. Roberts, Geo. Nickles, Jesse W. Fuller, Nathl. Nickles, Wm. Thompson, Mathew Bryson, Isaac Mitchel, Jas. McMahon, Thos. Rodgers, Danal. McWinn, Wm. Austin, Jos. Ligon, Wm. Bryson, Elisha Waldrop, Elias Waldrop, Wm. C. Nickles, Jones Fuller, Saml. Workman, Thompson Creson, Wm. Ferguson. Pattey Guin, Jno. Monroe due estate. Robt. Nickles, adm.

3 Dec. 1832. Will of SARAH DUCKETT, dec'd proven. Will dated 13 Jan. 1832. Children: John Duckett, Geo. Young, Jr., Thos. Duckett, Leddey Dillard, Alsey Roberson, and Martha Duckett. John Duckett and Geo. Young, Jr., exrs. Wit: Jno. Whitmore, Jesse P. Garrett and Geo. Dillard.

10 Dec. 1832. Adm. of estate of SAMUEL B. LOW, dec'd to Wm. Low. Jno. Lockhart and Wiley Milum, sur.

3 Dec. 1832. Will of DAVID GARY, dec'd proven. Will dated 23 Sept. 1832. Wife Sarah; son Warner (also Warron); son Joseph. Wife Sarah Gary, exr. Wit: Saml. Downs, Henry P. Bruster and Wm. F. Downs.

16 Nov. 1832. Appraisal of estate of ISAAC GRANT, dec'd by Jno. Ball, Lewis Ball and Bluford Willis. 23 Nov. 1832. Sale Bill. Pur.: Jno. Ball, Wm. Grant, James Wright, Wm. Hill, Richd. Griffin, Alex. Austin, Richd. Sims, Wm. Fuller, Lewis Dandy, Jas. Low, Thos. Smith, Wm. Austin, Anthony Golding, Marion Grant, Wm. Pollard. Notes due: Janey Whiteford, Rodey Valentine, Elizabeth Runalds, Clemment Wells, Bluford Wells, Plesant Sadler,

GRANT cont'd:
Jno. Pinson, Jesse Henderson, Wm. Tinsley, Thos. Salmon, Drury
Sims, Elizabeth Reed, Cornelius Puckett, Wm. W. Pollard, David
Owen, Wm. McGowing, Jas. Low, Jno. Boyd, Dandy Anderson, Jas.
Austin, Saml. McWilliams, Jno. McWilliams, Edw. Creson, Wm.
Austin, Jno. Austin. Wm. Austin, exr.

28 Sept. 1832. Appraisal of estate of SARAH RODGERS, dec'd by
Robt. Allison, Jno. Woody, Sr., and Colyar Barksdill. R. F.
Simpson, exr. 28 Sept. 1832. Sale Bill. Pur.: Jno. Allison,
Wm. Bright, Thos. Brownlee, Allen Dean, Robt. Allison, Haistene
Johnston, Jno. Duglass, Berry Morton, Robt. Morton, J. S. Rodg-
ers. R. F. Simpson, exr.

20 Nov. 1832. Sale Bill estate of JOHN CUNNINGHAM, dec'd (2nd
sale). Pur.: Robt. H. Littel, Cornelius Wilks, Wm. P. Milum,
Saml. Cunningham, Saml. Taylor, Jesse Moore, Jno. Blakely, B.
L. Posey, White Wilks, Wolff Benjamin, Robt. Allison, Thos.
Wilks, Lydral P. Saxon, Jno. McClintock, Jno. G. Klink, Wm.
Goss, Geo. Bowing, B. L. Posey, Sanford Powell. Notation: Nancy
the mother of George died before sale.

27 Oct. 1832. Appraisal of estate of RICHARD BLACKWELL, dec'd
by Robt. McNeese, Jno. Coats and Andw. Henderson. Includes property given to Alfred Blackwell and David Blackwell. Test.: Alfred
Blackwell. 8 Nov. 1832. Sale Bill. Tract of land. Chas. Brook,
Jr., Exr.

7 Jan. 1833. Barbary J. Barksdill, minor of 17 years, chose
Saml. Copeland guardian. Wm. East and Jas. Copeland, sur.

7 Jan. 1833. Nancy L. Barksdill, minor of 15 years, chose Hicksen Barksdill, guardian. John Hunter and Jesse Johnston, sur.

7 Jan. 1833. James Kenedy Barksdill, minor of 15 years, chose
William East, guardian. Saml. Copeland and Thos. C. Reeder,
sur.

7 Jan. 1833. Estate of JOHN YOUNG, dec'd. Sarah Young, widow
has married James Nalor. John & James Young, now minors. Adm.
revoked and given to John Black and made sur. with James H.
Irby and James Wright.

24 Nov. 1832. Appraisal of estate of WILLIAM CLARDY, dec'd by
James Jones, Gabriel South and Seaborn Jones. 24 Nov. 1832.
Sale Bill. Pur.: Mahala Clardy, Thos. Ware, Henry Johnston,
Silus Medlock, James Clardy, Sr., James Clardy, Jr., James Gains,
Mansfield Simmons, Aron Clore, Jno. South, David Simmons, Mitch-
el Clardy, Chas. Jones, James Medlock, Abner Noble, A. C. Jones.
Notes on: Caty Simmons, Wm. Lowery, Stephen Allen, David Med-
lock, Sanders Williams, Abner Ware, David Wright, Reuben Carter,
Jno. Hall, Manassa Culberson, Jno. Coats, Abner Freeman, Wm.
Freeman, James Clardy, Jesse Daniel. Jesse E. Clardy, adm.

12 Dec. 1832. Appraisal of estate of RICHARD BENNET, dec'd by
Hicks Weasem. David S. Raiford and Wm. Hendricks. 29 Dec. 1832.
Sale Bill of household property. Thos. Hendrick and James Jones,
exrs.

3 Jan. 1833. Adm. of estate of RICHARD BUTLER, dec'd to Wm.
Glenn. Jno. Crage and Alexander Feltson, sur.

(No date) Appraisal of estate of HOSA HOLCOMB, dec'd (rest too

HOLCOMB cont'd:
dim to read). 2nd page: 13 Dec. 1832. Sale Bill of estate of
HOSA HOLCOMBE, dec'd. Nathan Holcombe, adm. No purchasers named.

(No date) Sale Bill estate of JANE BRYSON, dec'd. Pur.: Geo.
Nickle, Henry Bryson, Jones Fuller, N. C., Jos. McGowen, Mathew
Bryson, Silus Waldrop, Wm. C. Nickles, Albert Miller, Roberts
Miller, James Roberts, Saml. Flemming, Wm. H. Motes, Danl. Car-
ter, Henry O'Neel, Jos. Ligon, Jno. Kelley, Sarah Bryson, Nancy
Jones, Bethain Bryson, Bird Waldrop.

20 Jan. 1833. John Stroble of Colleton Dist., Josiah Goggen
of Newbury Dist. and John F. Kerns of Laurens Dist. citation
to have will of JOHN MIMS, dec'd proven. Will dated 2 Oct. 1831.
Wife Martha Mims; only child Charles Allison Mims; John Strobel,
(may be Shoble) of Colleton Dist., Josiah Goggens of Newbury
Dist. and John F. Kerns of Laurens Dist. trustees for sd son;
nephew Josiah Goggens; Sally, dau. of Richard and Frances Sims;
John Stroble, Jr. Thomas Dalsheilds not to have anything to
do with my estate. Above named trustees my exrs. (N. B. name
may also be Dashields, not clear). Wit: Danl. Felder, Jesse
Felder and Rachel Felder.

10 Jan. 1833. Appraisal of estate of SAMUEL B. LOWE, dec'd by
Jno. Nickles, J. H. Lockert and Wiley Milum. William Lowe, adm.
27 Jan. 1833. Sale Bill. James Lowe, Plesent Lowe, Jno. Young,
M. C. Lowe.

30 Jan. 1833. John N. Golden, Cristena Golden and Sarah Golden,
minors, chose Bery Watson of Laurens Dist. guardian. Westly
Savage and John Addems, sur.

7 Feb. 1833. Will of NANCY MAHAFFEY, dec'd proven. Will dated
7 July 1832. Son William; dau. Polly Babb; dau. Sally Cunningham; dau. Cynthia Nesbit; dau. Nancy Babb; son Lewis Mahaffey;
son Hosea Mahaffey who is also exr. Wit: James G. Coker, Wm.
F. Downs and Edw. H. Garrett.

4 Feb. 1833. Will of ALEXANDER KIRKPATRICK, dec'd proven. Will
dated 27 Dec. 1832. Wife Susan; my children as they come of
age (not named). Wife and brother Susan Kirkpatrick and Thomas
Kirkpatrick, father-in-law William Ligon, exrs. Wit: R. Cunningham, R. Hooker and E. Kirkpatrick.

8 Feb. 1833. Accounting by John Chappell, adm. of estate of
LEWIS DAY, dec'd.

28 Jan. 1832. Appraisal of estate of THOMAS HITT, dec'd by Richd.
Watts, Elihu _____ and Danl. Foshee. 30 Jan. 1832. Sale Bill.
James Wright, adm.

29 Jan. 1833. Appraisal of estate of RICHARD BELTON(BOLTON?),
dec'd by Alex. Fulton, Wm. Dodd and _____. 29 Jan. 1833. Sale
Bill. Wm. Glenn, adm.

___ Jan. 1833. Appraisal of estate of SARAH DUCKETT, dec'd by
J. Garett, Ab. Ray and Benj. Hill. (also dated 19 Sept. 1832.
Sale Bill dated 20 Dec. 1832). Geo. Young, exr.

12 Feb. 1833. Return of Robert Wells, guardian of Clemment Wells
and Harrison Wells, minors. John W. Anglin, adm. of SENER WELLS,
dec'd.

(No date) Appraise bill of negroes disposed of by THOMAS BEASLEY, dec'd by will to: Mary Ferguson, Nancy Holland, Elizabeth Ferguson, Jane Williams, A. W. Chalmers in right of Dorothy Chalmers. Signed: Jno. Boyce, Robt. Owen and Washington Meadors. 4 Jan. 1833. Appraise bill of estate of THOMAS BEASLEY, dec'd. (by same signers as above). 8, 9 & 10 Jan. 1833. Sale Bill. Pur.: Robt. Owens, Jno. Horton, Thos. Fergeson, Paskel Meadors, Warner Meadors, E. W. Holland, Saml. & Jerah Jones, A. W. Chambers, F. _. Chambers, Mary Ferguson, Jno. McCay, Richd. Bonds, James Littel, B. E. Williams, Wm. Mitchel, Thos. Wier, Stephen Braddock, Word Ferguson, Jno. Henderson, Washington Meadors, Wm. Gambell, Mathew McCrary, H. L. Neel, Elizabeth Dillard, Robt. Littel, Jno. Davis, Jno. Flemming, Wm. Ferguson, Henry Ferguson, Geo. Dillard, Wm. Dillard, James Glenn. A. W. Chalmers, exr. Book Acct's belonging to estate: Jefferson May, Saml. Ferguson, Dugless Puckett, Jesse Hill, Sarah Bennet, Geo. Ferguson, Wade Shettel, Horice Bennet, Jno. Roberson, Rimer Prather, Reuben Adair, Robt. and Jno. Rammage.

19 Jan. 1833. 2nd Appraisal of estate of JOHN RODGERS, dec'd by Wm. Pitts and Collyer Barksdill. Sale Bill same date. James S. Rodgers, exr.

10 Nov. 1832. Appraisal of estate of SAMUEL BOULING, dec'd by Bailey Mahon?, Thos. ___, Jno. Terrey and Willis Benham. 18 Dec. 1832. Sale Bill of SAMUEL BOLLING, dec'd. Pur.: J. N. Bolling, Wm. Babb, Jno. Terey, Isaac Devenport, David Cowen, Wm. Tompson, Saml. Bolling, James Anderson, Nathan Nisbet, Tulley Bolling, Alfred Barrett, Jno. Hopkins, Alfred Bennett, Nimrod Nabours, Thos. Mahon, Wm. Hatcher, Edw. Nash, Ezekiel Wadkins, Jno. Nash, Plesant Shaw, Jno. McDavid, Thos. Grayham, Garland Sims (also Garlin and Garlington), Abner Nixon, Lewis Pyles, Robt. Bolling, Henderson Sulivant, Baley Mahon, Wm. Devenport.

19 Jan. 1833. Stephen Potter, guardian of Bevely, Nancy and Sarah Potter, minor children of ADAM POTTER, dec'd...return on Collar (Colyar) Barksdill bond.

20 Mar. 1833. Appraise bill estate of WILLIAM TAYLOR, dec'd by J. Park, Andw. Park and Alex. McArley.

5 Mar. 1833. Return of adm. Robt. Campbell, of NANCY MC MAHON, dec'd.

25 Mar. 1833. Adm. of estate of ABRAHAM B. JOHNSTON, dec'd to John Hunter. Jno. Black and Jno. Odle, sur.

9 Feb. 1833. Appraise bill estate of JOHN MIMS, dec'd by Edw. Jones, Jno. Boyce and David Felder.

22 Feb. 1833. Appraise bill estate of NANCY MEHAFFEY, dec'd by Jesse Garrett, Barnet Smith and Willia Benham. 22 Feb. 1833. Sale Bill. Pur.: Lewis Mehaffey, Jonthn. Abercrumbie, Sampson Babb, Jno. Cunningham, Barnett Smith, Jeremiah Hopkins, Martin Ball, Wm. Mehaffey, Aberham Nixon, Wm. Nisbet, Lindley Crumbie, E. S. Roland, Plesant Shaw, Jno. Lowery, Allen Mehaffey, Willis Benham, Moses Kellet, Wm. Ridgeway, Alex'r Nixon, Jno. N. Nash, Standback Coker, "Free" Silus. Hosa Mehaffey, exr.

20 May 1833. Adm. of estate of MARY CUNNINGHAM, dec'd to Wm. Leek. David McCullar and Wm. Irby, sur.

16 Feb. 1833. Appraisal of estate of ALEXANDER KIRKPATRICK,

KIRKPATRICK, cont'd:
dec'd by Wm. Lygon, Henery Oneall and Solomon Fullar. John Felts,
J. P. Cash rec'd from Jesse Henderson, Jno. Mitchel, Jno. Mc-
Gowan, James Ligon, Littel River Congaration and Wm.? Nickle.
Debts paid to: Bailey Coleman, Wells & Carter, Burrel Leek,
blacksmith's acct., Jesse Motes, Ruth Harris. Notes on Wm. Scarfe
of Georgia and James Nailar and Jno. Black. Amt. due to the
Liberty Spring Congregatioin, Cuffeltown Congregation and the
Littel River Congregation. Thos. and Susan Kirkpatrick, exrs.

10 Apr. 1833. Appraisal of estate of ABERHAM B. JOHNSTON, dec'd
by David Vance, Saml. Vance and James Young. Shown by Jno. Hunt-
er, adm. and signed 16 Apr. 1833. 11 Apr. 1833. Sale Bill. Pur.:
Robt. Hunter, Dr. Thomas Teague, James Godfree, David Vance,
Wm. East, Sr., Cain Jones, Saml. Vance, Jesse Enterkin, Wm.
Young, Fedrick Foster, Wm. Hurt, Sr., Wm. East, Jr., F. C. Reed-
er, H. Johnston, Esq., Widow Rachel Johnston, Jno. Miller, Peter
Sadler, Wm. Abernathey, Jno. Johnston, Higgsen Barksdill, Robt.
Monrow, Thomas C. Reeder, J. H. Davis, Davis Johnston, Fedrick
East, Dr. Elijah Watson, Edw. Orsborn, Stephen Hudgens, James
Jones, Hosa Johnston, James Linsey, Jno. Dalrymple, Jno. Boyd,
Thos. Harris, Andrew Monrow, Wm. Linsey, Brigdel Dunken, Jno.
Black, Anthony Griffen, David Greer, Dr. Jno. Gary. John Hunter,
adm.

25 May 1833. Adm. of estate of WILLIAM BURNSIDE, dec'd to George
Burnside. Andw. Burnside, Israel Holt and Nathan Sims., sur.

6 May 1833. Return of Starling K. Smith, adm. of GIMIMA GRIGGS,
dec'd. Rec'd from Wm. R. Farley; paid to J. H. Irby. Wm. R.
Farley, J. P.

2 May 1833. Will of THOMAS NORRIS, dec'd proven. Will dated
12 Mar. 1833. Dau. Matilda Sadler; son Cristopher Norris; son
Felix Norris; all my children by my first wife $1.00 each with
the exception of above Malinda Sadler; my wife Sarah Norris;
children: Cristopher Norris, Felix Norris, Jemna? Norris, Cla__-
visd? Norris, Azel Norris. Wife and son Cristopher named exrs.
Wit: Saml. Cunningham, J. A. Cheek and Alfred Blackwell. 24
May 1833. Appraisal of estate by Jas. Irby, James Cheek and
Andw. Henderson.

2 June 1833. Will of JOHN TAYLOR, dec'd proven. Will dated 6
Apr. 1833. Beloved wife and all my children (also 'either' of
my children) no names given. I appoint no executor. Wit: Nathaniel Day, Saml. Templeton and Saml. Taylor.

3 June 1833. Saml. McClurkin, Jno. D. Cunningham, Thos. Cunning-
ham, Shubal Starnes, James Hall, Saml. Cunningham, David Mc-
Cullough, Wm. Williamson and Wm. Cunningham, each rec'd of Mary
Cunningham, extrx. of THOMAS CUNNINGHAM, dec'd our legacies.
Signed: James Crocker, test., dec'd, by Joseph Crocker who swore
the handwriting was the sd. James Crocker, dec'd. W. R. Farley.
4 June 1833. Appraisal of estate of MARY CUNNINGHAM, dec'd by
Thos. Cunningham, Wm. Irby, Mark Killingsworth and James Durrow.
Sale Bill. Pur.: Danl. Gent, Wm. Holady, James Teague, Alfred
Blackwell, James Durrow, Wm. Cunningham, Elijah Smith, Jno.
Hambleton, Saml. Waldrop, James Blackwell, Saml. Cunningham,
Jehu Pitts, Thos. Cunningham, Danl. South, Danl. Mitchel, David
McCullor, Saml. Waldrop, Mrs. Catherine McClurkin, Shubal Starnes,
Jno. Bolton, Jno. Morgen, Mathew Johnston, Jos. Sullivan, Jno.
Culberson, Chas. Smith, Mrs. Malinda Cunningham, Mrs. Brook,

MARY CUNNINGHAM, cont'd:
Haisten Johnston, Francis Bealk, John Burton, Jno. Henderson, Thos. Andrews, Mrs. Margret Blackwell, Saml. Martin, John Pitts, Thos. Goggins, Elisha Smith, Sr., James Durrough. William Leek, adm.

29 July 1833. Appraisal of estate of JOHN TAYLOR, dec'd (will annexed), Jane Taylor, adm., by Saml. Taylor, Wm. Speer? and N. Day.

1 July 1833. Adm. of estate of HEDLY DAVIS, dec'd to William Blakely, Jr. Wm. Blakely, Sr. and Jno. Young, sur.

5 June 1833. Appraisal of estate of WILLIAM BURNSIDE, dec'd by Jno. Felts, Saml. Rodgers and Benj. Brown. 10 July 1833. Sale Bill. Pur.: Nathan Sims, Mary Ducket, Andw. Rodgers, David L.? Burnside, Geo. Burnside, Saml. Rodgers, Henry Fuller, Danl. Jones, Geo. Holdridge, Allen Deal, Jno. Odle, Allen Walker, David Glenn, Alsey Fuller, Jno. Felts, Geo. Anderson, Thos. Reeder, Mary Burnside, Geo. Anderson, Barruch Dunken, Elizabeth Hopper, Wm. Golding, Jno. Millar, Robt. Moor, Andw. Burnside, Hanah Burnside, Riegal Dunkin, Thos. Gill, Thos. Hill, Thos. Wilks, Thos. Austen, F__ Mylum. Notes/acct's due est: Hannah Burnside, Martin Shaw, Geo. Funk, Wm. A. Young, Thos. Gray, Haisten Madden, Turner Richardson, James Machon, Wm. Bone, Chesley Bone, Sarah Fuller.

_ Aug. 1833. Sale Bill of part of estate of JOHN TAYLOR, dec'd. Jane Taylor, adm. (will annexed). Pur.: Robt. Littel, Thos. McDowal, Wm. W. Simpson, D. Clark Templeton, Robt. Slone, Nat. Day, Mrs. Jane Taylor, Jonathan Blakely.

10 Aug. 1833. Will of JOHN DEAN CUNNINGHAM, dec'd proven. Will dated 13 Dec. 1832. Wife Mahala Cunningham; son Thomas Wilhite Cunningham; children - Mary M. Cunningham, Elvirey Cunningham, Sintha A. Cunningham, Margret R. Cunningham, Thomas W. Cunningham, Laurrsay W. Cunningham and Nancy E. Cunningham. Wife Mahala Cunningham, exr. Wit: Philip Wait, J. Culberston and Allen Johnston.

27 Aug. 1833. Adm. of estate of JAMES WATTS, dec'd to William D. Watts. Jno. D. Williams and Anthony Griffin, sur.

17 July 1833. Inventory of estate of HEDLEY DAVIS, dec'd late of Laurens Dist. by Abner Pyles, Saml. Vance, James McCullum amd Wm. Blakely, Sr. 18 July 1833. Sale Bill. aWm. Blakely, Jr., adm. Pur.: Allen Dial, Robt. Vance, Dr. Jno. H. Davis, James N. Pollard, Thos. F. Swann, Henry Cleaveland, Dr. H. Paisley, Wiley Milum, Wm. Nuget, Wm. W. Wallace, Capt. Robt. Milum, Andw. Rodgers, Jno. Cunningham, Esq., Sampson Brooks, Wm. Park, James Park, John Langston, Hugh Tolen, James Brown, W. W. Simpson, Saml. Taylor, Sr., Jno. Young, Jno. Garlington, Jno. Simmons, Wiley Hill, Danl. M. Winn, Capt. Jno. Davis, Robt. Blakely.

2 Sept. 1833. Will of ABNER YOUNG, dec'd proven. Will dated 20 Mar. 1833. Beloved wife Rebecca; children-Dorothy, Isabella M., James Mason, Emma E., Florella E. Young. Wife exr. Wit: Jno. Mason, Jno. Hunter and Wm. Hunter.

19 Aug. 1833. Samuel M. Murrell, minor, about 19 years, and chose Thos. Duckett, guardian. Jno. Templeton and Nathan Harris, sur. D. Anderson, Ord.

21 Sept. 1833. Order of public sale of estate of ALEXANDER KIRK-PATRICK, dec'd. Susanah Kirkpatrick, exr.

17 Oct. 1833. Adm. of estate of SAMUEL NABOURS, dec'd to John Nabours. Wm. Powers and Robt. Franks, sur.

26 Oct. 1833. Adm. of estate of JOSEPH OWENS, dec'd to David Owens. Elizabeth Owens, Richard Sims and John Hitt, sur.

26 Oct. 1833. Adm. of estate of BURREL LEEK, dec'd to William Ligon. Thomas Ligon and James Rowland, sur.

4 Oct. 1833. Inventory of estate of JOHN D. CUNNINGHAM, dec'd by James Dorrah, Wm. Morgen and Jno. Walker.

22 Oct. 1833. Mary Prator and Josiah Prator, minors over twelve years and chose Fransian (also Transina and Traslina) Prater, guardian. Thos. Gore and Danl. Felder, sur. (N. B. guardian is female).

4 Nov. 1833. Adm. of estate of JOHN DUNLAP, dec'd to John W. Simpson, with Richd. F. Simpson and Jno. Garlington, sur.

4 Nov. 1833. Will of GEORGE YOUNG, SR., dec'd proven. Will dated 21 Feb. 1826. Beloved dau. Lettice Rowland; son Thomas Young's two surviving children: George and Thomas (Jr.); beloved dau. Jane Whitmore; beloved son George Young; beloved dau. Mary Young; beloved dau. Elizabeth Young. Andrew McCrary, my bro. Cristopher Young and my son George Young, exrs. Wit: Thos. Young, Jr., Jno. Boyce and Cristopher Young, Jr. (N. B. dau. Lettice's surname also spelled Bowland.)

12 Nov. 1833. Will of JOHN MC GOWEN, dec'd proven. Will dated 4 June 1833. Beloved wife Jane; grandchildren (not named except John McWilliams. Wit: Wm. McGowen, Jonathan Reed and Wm. Mc-Gowen, Jr. Codicil dated 11 Oct. 1833. Appoint Wm. McGowen, Sr. and Jonathan Reed, exrs. Test.: Robt. Cunningham, Louisa (Leorisa?) Cunningham and Wm. McGowen, Jr.

23 Oct. 1833. Adm. of estate of JEREMIAH TRIBLE, dec'd to Nathaniel Day. Jno. S. James and Wm. Ransom, sur.

11 Nov. 1833. Petition for sale of estate of JAMES BAILEY, dec'd, Rebecah Bailey, wife of sd dec'd and Silus Bailey, exr. for division among legatees.

4 Dec. 1833. Will of HENRY TOMPSON, dec'd proven. Will dated 17 Feb. 1825. Dau. Rebecah Richey; son John Tompson; daus.: Polley, Nancy and Jenny? James Tompson; wife Catharine Tompson. Wife and son exrs. Wit: Martin Shaw, Joseph Irby and Menoah Forgey.

19 Oct. 1833. Appraisal of estate of SAMUEL NABOURS, dec'd by Lem'l (Sam'l?) G. Williams, Wm. Power and Robt. Franks. 25 Oct. 1833. Sale Bille. Pur.: Alexander Nabours, Chas. Franks, Barnet Parsens, Jacob Brock, Meredith Griffen, Wm. Power, Wm. Power, Jr., Wm. Thompson, James Mills, Mansfield Owens, Jno. Nabours. Acct's: Reuben Estes, Jno. Brock, Orsborn Garrett, Wm. Owens, James Garner, Jas. H. Irby, Alfred Jones, Jesse Garrett, Jas. Nabours, Wm. Nabours, A. S. Hutcheson. Jno. Nabours, adm.

2 Dec. 1833. Sarah Bell, mother of Ruth Ann Bell and Martha

BELL, cont'd:
Susan Bell, made choice of Thomas Weir be their guardian. Robt.
Long and Sarah Bell, sur.

2 Dec. 1833. Adm. of estate of JOHN D. BOYD, dec'd to Joseph
Vance. Saml. Vance, Robt. S. Vance and Elygah Tribble, sur.

2 Dec. 1833. Adm. of estate of WILLIAM DILLARD, dec'd to James
M. Dillard. Manessa Williamson and Ransom Johnston, sur.

(No date) Martin Ball, guardian of Evy Hitt, minor rec'd of
Lazarus Hitt, $48.09.

26 Nov. 1833. Appraisal of estate of JOHN MC GOWEN, dec'd by
Wm. Ligon, Clemment ____ and Jonathan ___. Signed and dated:
4 Dec. 1833. Property sold 27 Nov. 1833. Clemment Wells, Wm.
McGowen, Jr., David Whitford, Bird Roberts, Henry Austin, Jno.
McWilliams, Jno. Bell, Jno. Chappel, Henry Ball, Wm. Braxter,
Reuben Ball, Patrick Todd, Abram Hollingsworth, Bailey Coleman,
Dandey Snow, Wm. W. Pollard, Isaac Mitchel, Bluford Wells, Robt.
Whiteford, Jos. Ball, Jno. Findley, Jas. Rowland, Catharine
Whiteford, Martin Wells, Robt. Carter, Redden Puckett. Notes:
J. Roland, B. Leek, Marshel Starnes, Robt. Whiteford, J. F.
Pinson, Jno. McWilliams. Jesse Hitt. John Jones acc't; Henry
Johns. Wm. McGowen, Exr.

11 Nov. 1833. Appraisal of estate of BURREL LEEK, dec'd by Jas.
Rowland, Bluford Wells and Thos. Ligon, signed and dated 4 Oct.
1833.

17? Nov. 1833. 2nd appraisal of estate of HARDY DAVIS, dec'd
by Abner Pyles, Wm. Blakely, Sr., Saml. Vance and James Callum.
20 & 21 Nov. 1833. 2nd sale of est. of HEDLEY DAVIS, dec'd.
Wm. Blakely, Jr., adm.

4 Jan. 1834. Adm. of estate of RANDOLPH S. MURFF, dec'd to Elizabeth Murff and Wiley Murff. Jas. Gains and Jno. Rusell, sur.

6 Jan. 1834. Adm. of estate of THOMAS FULTON, dec'd to John
Holland. Joel S. Foster and Henry Strand?, sur.

6 Jan. 1834. Adm. of estate of WILLIAM DILLARD, dec'd to Saml.
Dillard, Jno. Langston and Henry Harley?, sur.

6 Jan. 1834. Adm. of estate of JOHN MARTIN, dec'd to Hollingsworth Martin and Glesing Martin. Wm. Power and Benj. Martin,
sur.

19 Nov. 1833. Inventory of estate of GEORGE YOUNG, dec'd by
Jno. Boyce, Jno. Henderson and Jno. F. Kern. (N. B. this is
George Young, Sr.)

4 Nov. 1833. Return of Wm. East, guardian of James K. Barksdill, minor for years 1831,32 and 33. W. D. Watts, adm. of the
personal est. of the dec'd minors father.

20 Nov. 1833. Sale Bill of the estate of GEORGE YOUNG, SR.,
dec'd. Geo. Young, Jr., exr.

8 Nov. 1833. Appraisal of estate of JOSEPH S. OWENS, dec'd by
Jno. Cook, Richd. Sims and Saml. Goodman. David Owen, adm. (No
date and too dim to read page). Sale Bill. Notes due, acct's.

23 & 24 Dec. 1833. Sale Bill estate of JOHN DILLARD, dec'd.
Wm. Dillard, adm.

20 Jan. 1834. James M. Bell, minor, chose William Gambell, his
guardian. Jno. Mason and Jno. Finney, sur.

12 Dec. 1833. Appraisal of estate of HENRY TOMPSON, dec'd by
Asa Forgey, Jno. Fowler and Lemarsus Deale. 19 Dec. 1833. Sale
Bill. James McFerson, Nancy Tompson, Elizabeth Shirley, Saml.
Martin, Jno. Fowler, Menoah Forgey, Geo. Shirley. Jno. Tompson,
adm.

(No date) Inventory of estate of JOHN MARTIN, dec'd by Henry
Martin, A. G. Parsons, Stephen Garrett and Benj. Martin. Sale
Bill (no date). Elizabeth Martin, Henry Martin, Reuben Ball,
Elihu Garrett, Glasgien Martin, Jas. Fench, Hollilngsworth Mar-
tin, Gasingin Martin, Founten Martin, Reuben Martin.

18 Dec. 1833. Appraisal of estate of JAMES BAILEY, dec'd by
J. H. Coleman, Alsey Fuller and James Young. Alloted to each
legatee according to will (negroes to legatees) who are Benjamin
Brown, Heirs of William Bailey, Sarah Ducker, John Hollings-
worth, James C. Bailey, Silus M. Bailey, Wineford Bailey, Eliza-
beth Bailey and Suse (or Luvi?) Bailey. 19 Dec. 1833. Sale Bill.
Jno. Cunningham, Isaac Mitchel, Austin Pasley, James C. Bailey,
Felix C. Bailey, Lewis? M. Bailey, Salley Ducker, Benj. Brown,
Allen Vance, J. H. Coleman, Wm. Milum, Sr., Tompson Swan, Winne-
ford Bailey, Franklin Miller, Larkin Coleman, James Bailey,
W. W. Wallis, Thos. Wilks, Jno. Young, Jas. M. Pollard, Wesley
W. Wallis, William P. Milum, Saml. Young, Saml. Rodgers, Hagen
Walker, Jno. Black, Elijah Tribble, Allen Dial, Wm. Todd, Thos.
McDowell, Lewis Smith, Saml. Brooks, Robt. Simmons, Jno. God-
free, Jno. Davis, Henry Madden, Cornelius Tribble, Ransom Fuller,
Haregrove Miller, Edmond Pasley, Jno. Bailey, Burrel Dunken,
Zachariah Bailey, Thos. G. Wilks. Silas M. Bailey, exr.

(No date) Appraisal of estate of ABNER YOUNG, dec'd by Wm. Young,
David Martin and Jno. Hunter. 7 Nov. 1833. Sale Bill. Rebecah
Young, exr. Notes and acct's due.

3 Dec. 1833. Inventory of estate of JEKENIAH TRIBBLE, dec'd
by Saml. Vance, Sr., Wm. Blakely and Jas. McCalum. (Person-
al estate). Nathaniel Day, adm. 4 Dec. 1833. Public auction
of personal estate. Robt. Littel, Widow Tribble, Elijah Tribble,
Cornelius Tribble, W. W. Simpson, Chas. Littel, Jno. Taylor,
Elihu Griffen, Wm. Blakely, Wm. Bowland, Jno. A. Tribble, Henry
Franks, Jas. Rodgers, Saml. and Robt. Vance, Alexander Simpson,
Jas. McCollums, Jno. Luke, David C. Templeton, Jno. Young, Joel
Dandy, Henry Taylor.

3 Feb. 1834. Will of CHARLES PARK, dec'd proven. Will dated
26 Apr. 1833. (Also spelled PARKS). CHARLES PARKS, SR.-loving
sister Lusinday Parks; brother Samuel Parks and his children:
Henry Parks, Sarah Parks and Bluford Parks. Bro. John Parks
and James Boyd, exrs. Wit: James Boyd, Jno. Coats and Elizabeth
Boyd.

2 Jan. 1834. Appraisal of estate of BENJAMIN F. CLEAVLAND, dec'd
by Wm. Irby, Jno. Yagers? and Mark Killingsworth. 3 Jan. 1834.
Sale Bill. H. Cleaveland, adm. of B. F. CLEAVELAND, dec'd. Mrs.
McNeese, Wm. Irby, Jurden Burns, Aron Burton, M. Cleaveland,
James Lowery. Notes and acct's.

17 Feb. 1834. Adm. of estate of ELISHA BROOKS, dec'd to Stanmore
Brooks. John Brooks and John Young, sur.

20 Jan. 1834. Appraisal estate of THOMAS FULTON, dec'd by H.
R. Shell, Saml. Crage, Jno. and Jos. Young. 21 Jan. 1834. The
Sale Bill with John Holland, adm.

17 Feb. 1834. Estate of JAMES A. WILLIAMS, dec'd. Elihu D. Williams new exr. as former exr. dec'd.

24 Jan. 1834. Appraisal of estate of RANDOLF MURF, dec'd by
James Gains, Cornelius Cook and Jno. Rusel. (also spelled MURFF).
28 Jan. 1834. Sale Bill. Pur.: Widow, Wm. Murff, Nathan Davis,
Thos. Carter, Malinda Murff, David Mitchel, Saml. Kinmon, Wm.
South, Wm. McClure, Jas. Knight, Danl. South, Geo. Brownlee,
Mahala Murff, W. G. Johnston, Joel Stone, Moses Miyers, J. W.
Studards, G. Southwood, Silus Medlock, Thos. Carter, M. M. John-
ston, James Pills, F. E. Ware, Henry P. Gains, Lewis Pyles,
David Medlock, Thos. Weir, Geo. G. Johnston. Notes: Elias Teague,
Jno. Morrison, Reuben Arnold, Reuben Hannah, Thos. Donaldson,
Benj. Miller, Jno. Blackstock, Wm. Purkins, Wm. Cook, Jno. Cra-
ford, Flemming Sallemore, Robt. Stephens. Elizabeth Murph, Adm.

3 Mar. 1834. Will of ELIZABETH KERN, dec'd proven. Will dated
23 Mar. 1833. Dau. Luisa Lucy Kern (11 shares in S. C. Bank),
dau. Eugenia Caroline Kern (10 shares in S. C. Bank), dau. Eliza
Amelia Saxon (12 shares in Platers & Muannai?-Planters & Merchants? Bank of S. C.), dau. Mary Ann Perry (12 shares in Planters
Mechanics Banks of S. C.) same to be held by my son John F.
Kern in trust during the life of her husband James L. Perrey
and not to go to sd hus.; son Jno. F. Kern (13 shares in same
bank), son Alfred A. Kern (13 shares in same bank). Gifts of
negroes to each child. Grand-dau. Elizabeth Susan, dau. of my
dec'd son Peridon Daniel Kern and his son, Benjamin Daniel Kern.
My dec'd husband John F. Kern. Sons John F. and Alfred A. Kern,
exrs. Wit: Jno. Whitmore, Thos. R. Ferguson and Benj. Hill.

9 Sept. 1833. Appraisal of estate of JAMES WATTS, dec'd by Jno.
D. Williams and Saml. Goodman. 11 Sept. 1833. Sale Bill. Pur.:
N. C. Watts, Jno. Chappel, Richd. Sims, Robt. C. Morgen, Danl.
Jones, Chas. Egurton, Saml. Rodgers, Nathl. Proctor, Benj. Grigs-
by, Willis Waldrop, A. G. Lockes, Wm. Cook, Elihu Watts, James
Goodman, Franklin Cook, Fredrick Nance, Dr. Jno. P. Watts, Jno.
Watts, Jno. K. Griffen, Nathl. Nickles, E. B. Waldrop, Chas.
Snow, B. F. Griffen, Willis Brown, Danl. Pitts, Isaac Mitchel,
Edw. Jones, Jas. Criswell, Saml. Austin, Foster Nickles. Sale
cont'd on 23 & 24 Dec. 1833. W. D. Watts, Jas. Criswell, Elijah
Watson, David Owens, Jas. Vaughn, Wm. Atwood, Thos. Lockhart,
Richd. Sims, Dr. Nathl. Nickles, Wm. E. Black, Geo. Adams, Chas.
Dandy, Jas. M. Golding, Philis Reeder, Patrk. Todd, Robt. Cole-
man, E. M. Watts, Sarah Williams, Wm. E. Caldwell, Nancy C.
Watts. Notes due estate. W. D. Watts, adm.

7 Jan. 1834. Appraisal of estate of JOHN D. BOYD, dec'd by
Jno. Cunningham, Robt. Vance and Saml. Vance. Joseph Vance,
adm. 8 & 9 Jan. 1834. Sale Bill. Pur.: Luray (or Susan) Boyd,
widow, Thos. D. Stedman, Jno. Fowler, Thos. Milum, Jno. Reed
Griffen, Jno. Cunningham, Col. Wm. Hill, Jos. D. Hopper, Danl.
Morten, Jno. Higgen, Miss Eliott Boyd, Jno. Simons, Hagen Dandy,
Wm. Simpson, Wm. G. Vance, Jno. Yager, Robt. Elison, Wm. Madden,
Robt. Vance, Jesse W. Fullar, Wm. Glen. Notes due est.: Phips
Campbell, Jas. B. Moore, Arch McClurkin, Jno. Snead, Solomon

BOYD cont'd:
Cole, Robt. Cennard, Joel Carter, Chesley Connant, Jeremiah
Cole, Jos. Cole, Levi Chapman, Henry Allison, Herley Adkerson,
C. J. Allen, Wm. Boyd, Reuben Brownlee, Thos. Babb, Thos. Bull,
Jno. Bailey, Wm. Bailey, Jno. Blakely, Abraham Boyd, Wm. Bryson,
Jno. C. Burges, Jno. Bryson, Wm. Brownlee, Richd. Duty, Thos.
Gray, Lenard Gray, Chas. W. King, Jno. Hetzag, Wm. Hughs, Valen-
tine Horten, Richd. Hodge, Zimry Madden, Wm. Madden, David Mad-
den, Chas. Madden, Henry Madden, Chas. Martin, Jas. M. Norrell,
Eldridge Full, Robt. Culbertson, aWm. Nelson, Jno. Pinson, Aron
and Isaac Pinson, Wm. Winn. Another long list of bad and out
of date accounts. (2 more pages). Jos. Vance, adm.

22 Feb. 1834. Appraisal of estate of CHARLES PARKS, dec'd by
M. D. Pinson, Isaac P. Boyd and Jno. Coats.

21 Jan. 1834. Appraisal of estate of WILLIAM DILLARD, dec'd
by Jno. Adair, Jas. L. Craig and Moses Leek. Saml. Dillard,
adm. Sale Bill (no date)

4 Mar. 1834. Adm. of estate of JANE COWAN, dec'd to Wm. Cowan.
Ross and Jno. Hunter, sur.

3 Mar. 1834. Will of THOMAS POWELL, SR., dec'd proven. Will
not dated. Wife Lucinda; youngest child Margaret Delia; sons
Thomas and Samuel; dau. Marietta Goodman wife of David Goodman;
land bought of Chas. Dickerson in Anderson Dist.; dau. Elizabeth;
dec'd dau. Nancy Baley's children; five children-Thomas, Elizabeth, Samuel, William and Robert (also Margaret Delia). Sons
Thomas and Saml. Powell, and friend R. F. Simpson, exrs. Wit:
Hugh Bruster, John Teedy? and Thos. P. Williamson.

2 Mar. 1834. Margaret Starnes, minor, chose Thos. Andress her
guardian. Also guardian of Milton Starnes, minor. Terrel Andress
and Saml. Beeks, sur.

17 Mar. 1834. Will of RICHARD OWINGS, dec'd proven. Will dated
13 Aug. 1828. Wife Sarah; daus. Rachel and Nancy Owings; Polley
Thompson; Elizabeth Studdard; sons Richard, William, Archabald
and John Owings (Owens). Richd. and Wm. Owings, exrs. Wit: A.
R. Owings, Turner Goldsmith and Lavina Owings.

11 & 16 Dec. 1833. Appraisal of estate of JOHN DUNLAP, dec'd
by Jas. Young, Jno. Blakely, Jno. Gall___ and Thos. Reeder.

22 Mar. 1834. Thos. Starnes and Davis? Starnes, minors, chose
Thos. Andrews (Andress), guardian. Shubel Starnes and Terrel
Andress, sur.

14? Dec. 1833. Sale Bill estate of JOHN DUNLAP, dec'd. Jno.
W. Simpson, adm. (3 pages of sale very dimly written.)

7 Mar. 1834. Return of Stephen Potter, guardian of minor children
of ADAM POTTER, dec'd, to wit: Bevely, Nancy and Sarah Potter.

(No date) Return on appraise bill property of WILLIAM DILLARD,
dec'd from B. Johnston, Sheriff of Union Dist. Signed: Wm. Gambell, Robt. Owings and Z. Sparks. Note on Joshua Wadkins.

4 Apr. 1834. Adm. of estate of ANN PRATOR, dec'd to Israel Prator. Wade Johnston and Lemuel Dillard, sur. 4 Mar. 1834. Will was
proven. Will dated 12 Jan. 1834. Son Israel; husband dec'd;

PRATER cont'd:
note on Moses Beaty; Mr. Young's estate; Nancy Odle (Odel).
Son Israel Prater and John Alan?, exrs. Wit: Saml. Young, Moses
Baty, Jno. Roberson and Margery McMillen.

21 Mar. 1832. Sale Bill of estate of WILLIAM TAYLOR, dec'd.
Pur.: Jas. Parks, Jno. Flemming, Jas. Mills, Jno. Taylor, Oswell
Richardson, Henry Jones, Chas. Simmons, Jane Taylor, Free Dub-
lin, Thos. McCurley, Wesley W. Wallis, Wm. Rose, Silus Dandy,
Elizabeth Wallis, Jas. Bramblett, Lewis Powers, Solomon Goodwin,
Jno. S. Hutchison, Edw. Anderson, Jno. Langston, Jos. Prichard.
Jno. Taylor, adm.

7 Apr. 1834. Adm. of estate of WILLIAM CUNNINGHAM, dec'd to
Wm. Holladay. Mathew Holladay and Jno. Burton, sur.

5 Mar. 1834. Appraisal of estate of ELIZABETH KERN, dec'd by
Jno. Boyce, Jno. Whitmore and Benj. Hill.

14 Nov. 1833. Sale Bill estate of BURRELL LEEK, dec'd. Pur.:
Wm. Ligon, Jesse Henderson, James Neely, Bird Roberts, Clement
Lowe, Bailey Coleman, Wm. Tompson, Jno. Busby, Wm. Winn, Bird
Waldrop, Saml. Vance, Saml. Asten, Wiley Hill, Sarah McCreedy,
Washington Winn, Jas. H. Irby, David Martin, Thos. Ligon, Jno.
Chappell, Jno. Findley, Alex. Austin, Thos. Todd, Anthony C.
Leek, Jas. Rowland, Hagen Walker, Miles Williams, Clement Wills,
Mary Hill, David Ball, Marshal Starnes, Jno. F. West, Henry
Oneall, Mary McCreedy, Robt. P. Smith, Jno. Couch, Lewis Salmon,
Andw. Nelson, Anny Jones, Patsy Leek, Bryant Leek (several pages)
listing goods. Notes belonging to dec'd. (4 two column pages).

17 Apr. 1834. Appraisal of estate of ANN PRATER, dec'd. Israel
Prater, exr. Willed property of dec'd. Appraised by J. Low,
Saml. Young and Waid Johnston. Sale Bill of property. Saml.
Prater, Jno. Odle, Alex. Mitchel, Israel Prater, Saml. Young,
Benj. Burk, Magra McMillen, Jas. Grayer, Jno. F. Collumes, Thos.
Prater. 5 May 1834. Sale Bill of property left by will to be
sold-negro man.

24 Apr. 1834. Return of Samuel Copeland, guardian of Barbary
G. Barksdale, Wm. D. Watts, adm. of SAMUEL BARKSDALE personal
est., paid James Godfree and Byrd Johnston.

(No date) Return of Thomas Andress, guardian of Milton Starnes
and Margret Starnes, minors; also guardian for Thomas Starnes
and Davis Starnes. Later notice dated 8 May 1834.

END OF BOOK

START OF BOOK 1834-1838

29? Mar. 1834. Appraise bill of JOSIAH PRATER, dec'd by Richd.
Furguson, Isaac Jacks and J. McCay. Lists of property of dec'd
with purchasers: Israel Prater, Isaac Jacks, Wm. Dunkin, Gideon
Cannon, Micagah Bennet, Wm. Prather, Thos. Prather, Jos. Dunkin,
Jno. Ray, Israel Prather, Elizabeth Johnston, Edw. Wesson, Geo.
Aberham, Jas. Pucket, Julius Wesson. Thomas Prather, exr.

18 Mar. 1834. Appraisel of estate of THOMAS POWELL, dec'd by
Silus Bayley, Thos. C. Reeder and Newman Gary. Appraisal of
certain property left as security for debt due dec'd. 19 Mar.

POWELL cont'd:
1834. Sale Bill of property of THOMAS POWELL, dec'd. Pur.: Allen
Dial, Capt. Jno. Davis, Jno. Blakely, Elisu Griffen, Hagen Mets,
Geo. Johnston, Elijah Teague, Cristopher Garlington, Thos. Henderson, Saml. Bryson, Thos. Wilks, Thos. Powell, Elijah Griffen,
Wm. Templeton, Wm. F. Burnsides, Thos. Powell, Jr., Austin Porsley, Wm. Milam, Jno. Bailey, Jno. Young, James Dickerson, Capt.
G. E. Hutcheson, Jno. Hutcheson. 5 May 1834. R. F. Simpson,
as the exr.

22 Apr. 1834. Appraisal of estate of WILLIAM CUNNINGHAM, dec'd
by Thos. Cunningham, David Bell and James Cunningham, Jr. Wm.
Holiday, adm. Sale Bill (not dated). David Bell, David McCullar,
Danl. South, Wm. Leek, James Durrow, Wm. Holladay, Mahaley Cunningham, Wm. Morgen, David Mitchel.

_____1834. John F. Kern, exr. in acct. with estate of ELIZABETH
KERN, dec'd. Note on John and Alfred Kern. Shares in Planters
and Mecanics Bank of Charleston. Shares in S. C. Bank of Charleston.

2 June 1834. Return of Hickerson Barksdill, guardian of Nancy
Barksdill, minor, W. D. Watts, adm.

18 Mar. 1834. John Odle, guardian of Sarahann E. Odle, rec'd
from Wm. Wilson, Ord. for Newbury Dist. ..from her father's
estate; rec'd from Andw. Turner; John Odle, guardian for Nancy
E. Odle, rec'd of Thos. Prater, exr. of estate of JOSIAH PRATER,
dec'd....to Nancy E. Odle ..her grandfather's estate.

21 July 1834. Will of MARY DEALE, dec'd proven. Will dated 9
Apr. 1834. Son Demarius? Deale; son Marcus Deale; son James
Deale and dau. Polley Cason?. Son Demilian Deale; Alexander
Deale. Negro woman Delia be emancipated and be taken by my dau.
Sally Hitt. Son Marcus Deale and nephew John Hitt, exrs. Wit:
Richd. F. Griffen, Jno. Hitt, James Wright. 22 July 1834. Inv.
and Appraisal of Mary Deale, dec'd by Lewis Ball, Willis Cook
and Bluford Wells.

11 Oct. 1833. 2nd appraisal of bal. of estate of WM. BURNSIDE,
dec'd by Jno. Felts, Benj. Brown and Saml. Rodgers. 26 Dec.
1833. 2nd Sale Bill. Pur.: David Burnside, Andw. Burnside, Dillion Wharton, Saml. Rodgers, David S. Burnside, Mary Burnside,
Geo. A. Burnside.

4 Aug. 1834. William Taylor, minor about 17 years, chose James
Blakely guardian. Wm. Blakely and Robt. Blakely, sur.

4 Aug. 1834. Est. of JANE COWAN, dec'd, Wm. Cowan, adm. ...found
no goods, etc. belonging to sd dec'd.

5 Aug. 1834. Estate of JOHN PINSON, dec'd, Howard Pinson, exr.,
dec'd's wife Elizabeth Pinson now dec'd.....sale of negroes
left to Elizabeth. 19 Aug. 1834. Appraisal of negroes of sd
John Pinson, dec'd. James Rowland, Geo. Funk and Richd. Harris,
appr. 19 Aug. 1834. Sale Bill. Pur.: Geo. Bowing, Bleuford Wells,
Wm. Runnalds, Seth Welbare.

19 Aug. 1834. Adm. of estate of FRANCES RAY, dec'd to Saml.
Young. Jno. Garlington and Jno. Holland, sur.

1 Sept. 1834. Sale. Est. MARY DEALE, dec'd, Lemarus Deale, exr.

12 Sept. 1834. Adm. of estate of NATHANIEL NICKLES, dec'd to William C. Nickles. Jessey W. Fullar and George Nickles, sur.

27 Sept. 1834. Adm. of estate of JOHN BALL, dec'd to Richard Watts. James Wright and Jno. P. Watts, sur.

14 Oct. 1834. Appraisal of estate of FRANCES RAY, dec'd by Luke Wesson, Hannon G. Dillard and Isaac Parks. Note on Jesse Ramage and Sarah Bennet.

20 Oct. 1834. Adm. of estate of SUSANAH CRAGE, dec'd. to Saml. Crage. Saml. and James Copeland, sur.

30 Sept. 1834. Appraisal of estate of NATHANIEL NICKELS, dec'd by Jesse W. Fullar, Geo. Nickle, James Nickle and Joel? L. Anderson. 16 Oct. 1834. Notes belonging to est. Jno. Felts-paid; Wm. Bryson, Plesent Neely, Mathew Hunter, Andw. Rodgers, Wm. Motes, Walton Procter, Silus Sadler, Alex. Smith, Danl. M. Winn, Robt. Miller, Robt. Means, Robt. Todd, Henry Johns, Andw. Snow, Jno. Bailey, Virgal Owens, Jno. Hazlet. Wm. Nickle, adm. Medical Books of the estate: Wm. Ligon, Sr., Wm. Runch, Wm. Miller, Jno. Nickels, Jesse W. Fuller, Zimry Carter, Robt. Carter, Wm. Carter, James Leaman, Jno. Henderson, Jas. Goodman, Virgill Owens, Jas. Roberts, Jno. Starnes, Chas. King. 1 Oct. 1834. Sale Bill of property of estate. Pur.: Jno. P. Watts, Saml. Jones, Jno. Moor, Sr., Wm. Reed, Geo. Nickle, Marshel Starnes, Alex. Austin, Wm. W. Harris, Wm. Asten, Geo. Funk, Bluford Watts, Jno. Watts, J. W. Fuller, Geo. W. Ware, Isaac Mitchell, Wm. Nickle, Jno. Coleman, Geo. Anderson, Eliza Nickle, Leaven W. Dall, Israel Holt, Jaustion Henderson, Elisha Waldrop, Bird Roberts, Wm. C. Nickle, David Owens, Howell Ling, Bignal Duncan, Larken Coleman, Silas Sadler, Jno. D. Williams, Jno. Fowler, Brint Leak, Allen Deal, Chas. Jones, Jno. Felts, Jno. Chapell, Jno. Odel, Jno. West, Dr. A. Watson, Wm. Green, H. W. Parsley, Allen Watson, Elizabeth Nickles, Bulis Sims, Charley Snow, Benj. Malden, Chas. W. King, Geo. Grant. Land, cash, medical books, medical accounts, etc. accounted for.

20 Oct. 1834. Will of WILLIAM CANADY, dec'd proven. Will dated 14 Sept. 1834. Dau. Nancy, wife Elizabeth. Dau. Nancy exr. Wit: Jno. Gwin, Jesse Davis and Seybern Hand. (Also spelled Cenedy).

25 Sept. 1834. Appraisal of estate of JANE GORDON, dec'd by David Grayham, Jno. Blakely and Jno. Adair.

1 Nov. 1834. Adm. of estate of THOMAS ANDRESS, dec'd to Mary Andress. Shubal Starnes and Terrel Andress, sur.

1 Nov. 1834. Adm. of estate of THOMAS C. REEDER, dec'd to David Martin. Jno. H. Davis and Jno. S. James, sur.

1 Dec. 1834. Adm. of estate of WILEY JONES, dec'd to John Whitmore. Joseph Dunken and Benj. Hill, sur.

1 Dec. 1834. Adm. of estate of ROBERT TOMPSON, dec'd to Gideon Tompson. James Dunlap and Wm. Tomson, sur.

1 Dec. 1834. Adm. of estate of REBECAH JONES, dec'd to Lewis Jones. Wm. Adair and Jno. Jones, sur.

19 Mar. 1834. Appraisal of estate of RICHARD OWENS, dec'd by Francis Ross, R. Owens and Robt. Ward. 4 Apr. 1834. Sale Bill.

1 Dec. 1834. 2nd Appraisal of estate of JAMES A. WILLIAMS, dec'd by Joel Allen, Aberham Bolt and Robt. McLane. Same day, the land of dec'd sold. E. D. Williams, exr.

6 Dec. 1834. Will of ZACHARIAH BAILEY, SR., dec'd proven. Will dated 17 June 1833. Dau.: Rebecah Motes; sons & daus.: Zachariah Bailey, Jr., Absalum Bailey, William Bailey, John Bailey, James Bailey, Polley Chandler, Wineford Walker, Sarah Chandler, Rebecah Motes and Coleman Bailey whose share is to be equaly divided between his three children: James A. Bailey, William L. Bailey and Lueasy Bailey. Beloved sons Zachariah Bailey, Jr. and William Bailey, exrs. (Tombstone and graveyard to be purchased out of each share for "your mother". Wit: Alsey Fullar, James Fullar and W. A. Waldrop.

15 Dec. 1834. James Blakely, guardian of William Taylor, Jr., being about to remove from the sate, sd minor chose William Taylor, Sr. his guardian. James Park and R. H. Spear, sur.

12 Nov. 1834. Appraisal of estate of WILLIAM CENNADAY, late of Laurens Dist., dec'd by Jno. Gowan, Jesse Davis and Robt. Hand, Jr. Notes: Austen Gilbert, Joel Gentray, B. Cennaday, W. Cennaday, Zachariah Bruce, Dr. Jno. Hand and James Cergill. 14 Dec. 1834. Sale Bill. Pur.: Nancy Cennaday, Jno. Guin, Davis Garrett, Wm. Holbert, L. Harris, Jno. Hand, Stanten Hendbark, Mica'h Crumton, Robt. Hand, Jr., Martin Willis, Robt. Hand, Cleaveland Wallis, Jno. Harris, Thos. Right, Simien Higgan, Thos. Garrett, Thos. Knight, Jno. Rowings, Zachariah Bruce, Absolam Harris?, Jesse Davis, Nancey Kennaday of Collier?, Jno. Grant, James Cunningham, Abner Knight, Alford Cargill, Hezekiah Gray, Richd. R. Owings, Saml. Couch, Thos. Cryms, Wm. Davis, Wm. Riddle, Elihu Garrett, Jno. Owens, Reuben Long. Nancey Cennady, exr. and Jno. Gowing, clerk.

24 Nov. 1834. Appraisal of estate of JOHN BALL, dec'd by James Wright, Andy Andrews and Lewis Ball. Richd. Watts, adm. Sale Bill. (No date). Pur.: Narissa Ball, Austin Box, Richd. Watts, Bird Roberts, David Cureten, Henry Hill, Netren Ball, Jno. Austin, Jesse Hill, Jesse Hitt, Wm. Hitt, Danl. Foshee, Benj. Owens, Foster Nickle, J. Pollard, Alex Austin, Saml. Jones, Wm. Mc-Gowan, Anthony Golden, B. F. Watts, Wm. Aston, Abraham Hollingsworth, Jos. Ball, J. W. H. Johnston, Mitchell Hill, Bluford Wills, James Braxter, Henry Ball, Wm. Cook.

24 Dec. 1834. Adm. of estate of BARTLET L. SATERWHITE, dec'd to Isaac P. Boyd. James Boyd and Jno. W. Simpson, sur.

1 Oct.? 1834. Appraisal of estate of SUSANAH CRAIGE, dec'd by James Copland, Jno. Finney and Wm. Gamble. Samuel Craig, adm. 3 Dec. 1834. Sale Bill.

13 Dec. 1834. Appraisal of estate of WILEY JONES, dec'd by Luke Weasan, Word Furgeson and Minial Dillard. 16 Dec. 1834. Sale Bill. Jno. Whitmore, adm.

17 Dec. 1834. Appraisal of estate of REBACK JONES, dec'd by Thos. Adams, Richd. Bonds and Thos. Dalrymple. Lewis Jones, adm. 18 Dec. 1834. Sale Bill.

19 Jan. 1835. Adm. of estate of MARY HOLCOMB, dec'd to Nathaniel Holcomb. Jacob Meadors and Wm. Holbert, sur.

19 Jan. 1835. Adm. of estate of JOHN DOLLAR, dec'd to Nancy

DOLLAR cont'd:
Dollar. William James? and George Cook, sur.

25 Nov. 1834. Appraisal of estate of THOMAS ANDRESS, dec'd by
Mansfield Owens, Thos. Washington and Mikel Clardy. Mary Andress,
adm. 25 Nov. 1834. Sale Bill. Pur.: Chas. Brock, Mansfield Owens,
Turel Andress, Lewis Arnold, Elizabeth Wadkins, "widow", Thos.
Washington, Wm. Cooper, Starling Smith, Robt. Box, David Mitchel,
Cranes Jones, Wm. Moor, Saml. Beck, Saml. Studdard, Geo. Wash-
ington, Danl. Goddard, Ansel Godfree, Artis Cook, Wm. Howell,
Jefferson Arnold, Geo. Brownlee. Notes on Wm. Yager, Wm. Leek,
Jno. Norwood.

(No date) Appraisal of estate of BARTLETT S. SATERWHITE, dec'd
by W. D. Watts, Wm. N. Vance, Wm. Hiran and Jno. Boyd. Isaac
P. Boyd, adm. Sale Bill. (No date). Pur.: Margret Saterwhite,
Jno. Vance, Wm. D. Watts, Hugh Wallace, Wm. Leawell?, Jno. Luke,
Wm. Vance, Wm. Saterwhite, Jesse Entriken, Aron Johnston, James
Boyd, Saml. Caldwell, Wm. Linsey, David Brooks, Jno. Johnston,
Wm. Abernathy, Ephrum Dalrumple, Humphra Linsey, Ann Horn, Robt.
Gray, Oser Blake, James Craddock, R. F. Griffen. Notes due in-
testate: David Pitts, Duke Goodman, Wm. Allen, Drurey S. Allen,
James Loyd.

2 Feb. 1835. William C. Teague, minor about 19 years, chose
Thos. Teague, guardian. David Martin and James M. Pollard?,
sur.

24 Jan. 1835. Adm. of estate (will annexed) of MATHEW HUNTER,
dec'd to John Hunter. Henry Shell? and Joseph Young, sur.

2 Feb. 1835. Adm. of estate of JAMES CROCKER, JR., dec'd to
Susanah Crocker. Chas. Brock, Jr. and Chas. Brock, Sr., sur.

___ Nov. 1834. Sale Bill estate of FRANCES RAY, dec'd. Saml.
Young, adm.

11 Feb. 1835. Will of ALLEN WATSON, dec'd proven. Will dated
11 Jan. 1835. Accounts be collected except David Cureton, Esq.;
brothers and sisters and their heirs; father; sister Martha
Burnside. Dearly beloved father my exr. Wit: A. Griffen, G.
W. Young and Elihu Watson. Elijah Watson, exr.

17 Nov. 1834. Appraisal of estate of THOMAS C. REEDER, dec'd
by Jno. H. Davis, Norman Gary and Saml. Gary. David Martin,
adm. 21 Jan. 1835. Schedule of acct's, etc. Home place at Littel
River. Thos. L. Wilks, Hezekiah Chesure, Elijah Teague, White-
head Wilks, Geo. Johnston, James M. Pollard, Jno. Garey, Thos.
Teague, Wm. G. Wright, Abner Teague, Free Allen, Robt. Coleman,
Free Cain* (* both freed persons), Thos. Gill, Robt. Campbell,
Wm. Watson, Reuben Hill, Isebell? Reder (Reeder), Wm. Hays,
Wm. Logan, Col. J. Williams, Shedrick Waldrop, Dr. Elijah Watson,
Jesse Moats, Miss Milley Hall, Peter Fullar, Wm. Farrow, Jno.
Odel, Isaac Whiteworth, Nancy Roberts, Abner Teague, Henry Rob-
erts, Sarah Cone, Jno. Cobb. Signed: James M. Pollard, Samuel
Gary and Newmen Gary. Schedule of acct's due dec'd No. 2. David
Martin, adm. 21 Jan. 1835. Schedule of acct's No. 3. Names:
Oswell Reeder, Robt. Campbell, Wm. D. Jones, Jesse George, Meri-
dith Waldrop, Isaac Motes, (others named above). 21 Jan. 1835.
Sale Bill of estate. Pur.: Mary Reeder, Geo. Johnston, Elijah
Teague, James M. Pollard, Mary B. Dunlap, Thompson Swan, Danl.
P. Milone, Jno. Gray, Danl. Jones, Jno. Black, Jno. Davis, Elisha

REEDER cont'd:

Teague, F. F. Jones, Abner Gary, Wm. W. Simpson, Thos. F. Jones, Jno. H. Harris, James Littel, Jno. Gary, Norman Gary, Wm. Bryson, Franklin Miller, Mary B. Duckett, Jno. Bouland, James Craford, Robt. H. Littel, Hagen Walker, Jno. Black, Jno. Young, Wm. Brown, Benj. Brown, Saml. Coplen, Davis Williams, Manning Reeder, Wm. Cobb, Andw. Johnston, Thos. Oswell, Wm. Vance, Jeremiah Leek, Henry Reeder, Geo. Johnston, Thos. Wilson, Free Reuben, Henry Cleveland, Jno. Tinsley, Andw. F. Gary, Jno. Simpson, Hamon Millar, Philip King, Whitehead Wilks, Jos. Vance, Nemiah Dumas, Jno. West. 18 Nov. 1834. List of notes due: Elisha Teague, W. W. Wallis, Wm. Swet, T. S. Bechum, Jr., Dr. Elijah Watson, Wm. Mitchel, Jno. Black, Hannah Burnside, Wm. F. Burnside, Manning Reeder, Saml. Gary, Jno. Odle, Abner F. Gary, Stephen Rodgers, Jno. Gary, Silus Dandy, Robt. P. Hunter, Anthony Leek, Robt. P. Smith, Benj. Simmons, R. B. Smith, Jno. B. Rollin, Jno. B. Stanley, James Cook, Franklin Cook, Zachariah Chesure, White Wilks, Daniel Magum, Wm. Goss, Edw. F. Cargill.

22 Dec. 1834. Appraisal of estate of Col. ZACHARIAH BAILEY, dec'd by Jno. Felts, Danl. Carter and Jos. Willert?. 24 Dec. 1834. Sale Bill. Pur.: Jno. Bailey, Geo. Nickle, Zachariah Bailey, Wm. Bailey, Wm. H. Motes, Henry Fullar, Cornelius Wilks, Danl. Carter, Barthalumas Craddock, Bailey Coleman, Absolum Bailey, Jos. Willent?, Wiat Chandler, Austin Bailey, Haman Millor, Azeriah Walker, Allen Vance, Benj. Brown, Richd. Golden, Albert Millor, Andw. Snow, Jno. Young, Jno. Davis, Jno. Findley, Asa Chandler, Jesse Motes, Richd. Owens, Seth Willbar, James M. Pollard. Note on Absalum Bailey.

7 Feb. 1835. Adm. of estate of JACOB NISWANGER, dec'd to Elihu Watson. Jno. Sims and Barry Watson, sur.

2 Mar. 1835. Adm. of estate of SARAH WESON, dec'd to Thos. K. Whitmore. Jno. Whitmore and Wm. Hill, sur.

2 Mar. 1835. Edward Weson, minor over 14 years, chose James Blackburne, guardian. Davis Williams and Jno. Fels?, sur.

2 Mar. 1835. Washington Wesson, minor over 14 years, chose Thos. K. Whitmore, guardian. Jno. Whitmore and Wm. Shell, sur.

16 Feb. 1835. Marey Tribble, mother of Elizabeth Tribble, Andrew K. Tribble, Jane R. Tribble, Ezekiel H. Tribble, Susanah M. Tribble, minors of JEKENIAH TRIBBLE, dec'd..petition for guardianship. Wm. Blakely and Nathaniel Day, sur.

7 Mar. 1835. Adm. of estate of DEMILIAN DEALE, dec'd to Lemarus Deale. Asa Forgey and James Scott?, sur.

24 Mar. 1835. Adm. of estate of JOHN HUNTER, dec'd to Nancy Hunter. Chas. Fowler, Wm. Hunter "B"? and Oswell Richardson, sur.

5 Feb. 1835. Appraisal of estate of MARY HOLCOMB, dec'd by Thos. M. Young, Jacob Meador and Emmson Lyon. Nathan Holcomb, adm. 21 Feb. 1835. Sale Bill. Notes: John Holcomb, Hyrum Holcomb, Nathan Holcomb, Jacob Meadors.

10 Mar. 1835. Appraisal of estate of SARAH C. WEASON, dec'd. Goods and chattels to be found 2 Mar. Rec'd of James Blackburn, adm. of JOHNSTON WEASON, dec'd. 11 Mar. 1835. Sale Bill. James

WEASON/WESSON cont'd:
Blackburn is the guardian of Edward Weason. Thomas R. Whitmore, adm.

15 Dec. 1834. Appraisal of estate of ROBERT TOMPSON, dec'd by M. P. Evans, Wm. Crook, Richd. Childress and Gideon Tompson. Property of Martin Gwennt advertised by R. Thomson 28 Feb. 1835. All of Vincent Roberson also advertised and appraised 28 Feb. 1835. 15 Dec. 1834. Sale Bill. Gideon Thompson, adm. of ROBERT THOMPSON, dec'd.

10 Feb. 1835. 2nd Appraisal of estate of MATHEW HUNTER, dec'd by Henry Shell, Hickerson Barksdill and James H. Harden. 12 Feb. 1835. Sale Bill. John Hunter, adm. with the will annexed.

6 Apr. 1835. Adm. of estate of JOHN HOLLAND, dec'd to James M. McElery. Andrew McElery, Saml. Crage, Thos. Crage and Joel F. Foster, sur.

11 Apr. 1835. Adm. of estate of THOMAS ANDERSON, dec'd to Henson Norris. Jesse Danniel and Lendrus Williamson, sur.

6 Apr. 1835. Will of ISAAC DIAL, dec'd proven by Haisten Dial, Sr. Garlington Dial, exr. Will dated 4 Mar. 1835. William Henderson who married my dau. Polley (land bounded by Robt. Coker and the sd Henderson); son Haisten; Garlington Dial in trust for the children of my son Isaac Dial that he had or may have by Jane Patton with whom (he) now lives in the character of a wife; son Garlington; wife Polley Dial (land bounded by Jno. Smith, G. Cook, Abner Putman and Chas. Edmonds); note due me on John Coker; son James and these children: Henry, Frankling, Heriet, Harrison, Nancy, Martha, Isabella, Drury and the child my wife is now pregnant with. Sons Garlington and Henry Dial, exrs. Wit: M. D. Pinson, F.? Richardson and Haisting Dial, Sr.

26 Feb. 1835. Appraisal of estate of DR. ALLEN WATSON, dec'd by Jno. D. Williams, A. Griffen and Ro. M. Young. Elijah Watson, Esq., exr. 28 Feb. 1835. Sale Bill. Pur.: Elijah Watson, Fedrick Vance, Elihu Watson, Edw. _. Burnside, Willard Watson, Robt. Nickle, Jno. Fels, Robt. Austen, Thos. Austen, Maj. Jno. D. Williams, Jno. P. Watts, James Burnes, Geo. Young, Capt. Wm. D. Watts. Elijah Watson, exr.

20 Apr. 1835. Will of JOHN TODD, SR., dec'd proven by Jno. S. Todd and Saml. Hunter. Will dated 11 Feb. 1835. Beloved wife Eliza Julia Todd; children-Permelia, Joseph, Maria and James; son James R. Todd; 3 eldest sons; sons William and Joseph; daus. Polley and Matilda; dau. Eliza. Son John S. Todd and friend Saml. Hunter, exrs. Wit: Wm. Rose, Saml. Mills and Wm. Sims.

5 May 1835. Adm. of estate of URSLA BROOKS, dec'd to Bartla Brooks. Robt. Nickle and James Nickle, sur.

4 May 1835. Adm. of estate of THOMAS FULTON, dec'd to Henry Stroud. James Henry and A. P. Fulton, sur.

31 Jan. 1835. Inventory of goods of JOHN DOLLAR, dec'd by Collar Barksdill, Geo. Cook and Wm. Franks. 3 Feb. 1835. Sale Bill. Pur.: Geo. Cook, Spencer Celey, James Burk, Harum Morgen, Wm. Knight. Nancey Dollar, adm.

21 May 1835. Appraisal of estate of ISAAC DIAL, dec'd by M.

DIAL cont'd:
D. Pinson, H. Dial, Sr. and Robt. Allison. Garlington Dial,
exr. Judgements in favor of dec'd: Isaac Dial vs John Coker;
Isaac Dial vs Jno. Arnold; Isaac Dial vs Garlington Coker. Notes
due dec'd: N. E. Lynch, Charlota B. Lowrey, Ransom Fuller, James
J. Lowrey, Drury Coker.

4 May 1835. Sarah Fox, minor about 18 years, chose Ebenezer
Hammond guardian. Wm. Henderson and Joshua Franks, sur.

4 May 1835. Catherine Mathis and Nancy Mathis, minors and chose
Elijah Teague guardian. Jno. Hunter, Sr. and Jno. Dalrumple,
sur.

10 Apr. 1835. Appraisal of estate of JOHN HUNTER, dec'd by Saml.
Hunter, Fleming Mosley and Wm. Mills. 14 Apr. 1835. Sale Bill.
Pur.: J. H. Byrd, Joshua Saxon, Nat Vance, Jno. Blakely, Wm.
Power, Saml. Mills, Wm. Cowen, Bery Powell, James Park, Toliver
Roberson, Mark Noble, Alex. Power, Wm. Hunter, Jr., Alex. Power,
Jr., Wm. Power, Jr., Thos. McCarley, Wm. Power, Sr., Hara Gar-
rett, Anderson Brown, Robt. Spence, Lauson Harris, Jesse Gray,
Jesse Gray, Sr., O. Richardson, Drury Clark, Stephen Garrett,
Hosa Garrett, Chas. Smith, Jesse Roberson, Saml. Flemmon son
of James, Saml. P. Fleming, Thos. Pool, Robertson Owing, Lewis
Abercrombie, Elias Crooks, R. H. Day, Jno. S. Hutcheson, Andw.
Brown, Pleskey Gray, Cristopher Garlington, Chas. Littel, Wm.
Hunter, Wm. Simpson, Jesse Pool, Reuben Thomas, Thos. Deen,
Saml. Fleming, Jr., Palaska Grey, Jen Fowler, Reuben Putman,
Even Bell, Saml. Meredith, Wm. Hunter, Jr., Wm. Todd, Benj.
Higgins, Thos. McCrary, Jno. Kinedy, Francis Glenn, Jno. Fowler,
Boyce Garrett, Reuben Thomas, Elias Cheek, Saml. Martin, Andw.
Park, Jr., J. S. Hutcheson, Nancy Hunter, Meredith Fowler, Chas.
Williams, Alex. McCarley, Robt. Campbell, Jno. McClintock, Saml.
Parson, Jr., Free Dublin, Nath. Simmons, Jno. E. Clink, Jno.
Cunningham, Jno. G. Klink, Danl. Dandy, Zachariah Edwards, Joshua
Saxon, Henry Garlington, Saml. Morten, Aron Moore, Alex. Nab-
ours, Aron Starnes, Jno. W. Cargill, Hubert Hutcheson, Brown
Moore, Wm. Mills, Nath. Gilbert, Hensley Garrett, Jonathan Jones,
Toliver Roberson, James Ridle, Nimrod Putman, Bruce Garrett,
Boyce Garrett, Jno. Atwood, Henry Toland, Lewis Bramblet, Jere-
miah Mortin, Thos. G. Wilks, James French, Saml. G. Williams,
Wm. Cowing, Stirling Jones, Reuben Estes, Elihu Pool, Robt.
Hann, Jno. Delong, James Crumpton, Solomon Goodwin, Jonathan
Delong, Wm. Rose, Benj. Baulden, Bery Pool, Sr., Bery Pool,
Jr., Wm. Knight, Jno. Knight, Ambros Garrett, Harrison Garrett.
Book acct's. - Mathew Holaday, Mark Noble, Frances Glen, Hugh
Toland, Saml. Parsons, Jr., Benj. Baldwin, Sarah Brown, Nehe-
miah Franks, Alford Cargill, Jesse Godfree, F. E. Mosley, James
Putman, Thos. Cowan, Wm. Fowler son of William, Saml. Rose,
Lewis Bramblet, Chainey Farrow, James Garrett, Heman Garrett,
James Flemon, Sr., Alex. Noble, Jas. Garner, Jno. Sullivan,
Palaskie Gray, Hezekiah Chesher, Levina Tucker (widow), Jno.
Taylor, Pleasent Sullivan, Elizabeth Pool, Jno. Crooks, Davis
Garrett, Bery Pool, James Crumpton, Jno. Fleming, Sr., Robt.
Slone, Jr., Jno. Knight, James Higgins, Jr., Elihu Garrett,
Reuben Ball, Jeremiah Power, Jas. Bramblet, Wm. Rose, Reuben
Bramblet, Wm. Crumton, Jno. Simons, Nancy Pool, Elizabeth Glen,
Jas. Taylor, Jr., Wm. Garrett, Thos. McCrary, Robt. Pool, Har-
vest? Millar, Jno. Bell, Bryum Knight, Jno. Pool, Benj. Simons,
Free Hillidy (negro), Haney Toland, Danl. Robeson, Seaborn Moor,
Alex. McCrary, Jno. Harris, Sr., Ebenezer Hammens, Drury Moor,
Jackson Griffin, Catharine Cowen, Seaborn Garrett, Saml. Gray,

HUNTER cont'd:
Sarah Power, Wm. Park, Jane Sloan, Housley Garrett, Thos. Power,
Melmeth? Riddle, Daulien? Hunter, Fleming Mosley, Chas. Knight,
Zach. Davis, Elihu Pool, Saml. Workman, Nancy Crow, Saml. Flem-
ming, Sr., Jas. Kenedy, Sr., Wm. Slown, Thos. G. Wright, Young
Turrey?, Creswell Knight, Robt. Fleming, Louisa Simpson, Vinein?
Knight, Boyce Garrett, Robt. Parson?, Presley Owing, Jno. Harris,
Jr., Wm. Riddle, Abner Owen, Wm. Knight, Jr., Jno. Putman, Jno.
A. Farley, Thos. Sloan, Jno. Kenedy, Jas. S. Smith, Simien Gar-
rett, Jas. Power, Archebald Slone, Elihu Simpson, Mathew Knight
son of Wm., Robt. Hutcheson, Jno. Nabours, Capt. Saml. Person,
Susan Brown, Greenbury Garrett, Jno. J. Atwood, Alex. Power,
Sr., Robt. R. Hunter, Benj. F. Garrett, Joel Dandy, Jr., Drury
Cheek, Robt. Franks, Jno. Power, Jas. Langston, Chas. A. Crisp,
Hervest? Cleaveland, Sarah Franks, Morten Garrett, Jno. Crumton,
Bill Knight Baney, Reason Bell, Lawson Harris, Catherine John-
ston, Mathew Gorden, Jas. Gant, Jno. Hutcheson, Jr., Thos. F.
Farrow, Wm. Hunter, Sr., Saml. B. Martin, Thos. Crooks, David
Higgins, Jr., Nicklus Garrett, Jas. Riddle, Reuben Estes, Miss
E. Sulivan, Polley Suliven, Sarah Power, Alfred Jones, Mitchel
Smith, Jr., son of James, Fountain Moor, Richd. Cheek, Mary
M. Mills, Wm. S. Fowler, Joel Allen, Alex. Mills, Jr., Sarah
Moor, Sarah Suliven, Anderson Brown, Wm. Crooks, Louisa Moor,
Mehatey Moor, O. Richardson, Wm. Knight, Sr., Jno. Asby, Gorden
Riddle, Gini Wright, Mora Paterson, Aron Moor, Miss Nancy Gant,
Nancy Glidewell, Tucker Riddle, Zach. Nabours, Eunety Power,
Alex. Nabours, Jno. Nabours, Elizabeth Glen, Polley Smith, Carter
Parker, Free Doublin (negro), Mary Golden, Rebecah Elmore, Polley
Moor, Thos. Adkins, Jeremiah Power, Jno. Blakely, Jesse Bell,
Trasey Martin, Easter Elmore, Sarah Hughs, T. Devenport, Sarah
Bailey, Jr., Catey Bailey, Mary Davis, Sarah Davis, Elizabeth
Pool, Sarah Franks, Elizabeth Collins, Jas. Crumbie, Robt. C.
Simmons, Henry Meredith, Elizabeth Garner, Jos. Prichard, Nancy
Glidewell, Anna Smith, Robt. Fleming, Arch. Slone, Frances Jones,
Anne Simmons, Jos. Irby, Wm. Crumton, Edw. Anderson, Haisting
Dial, Ann Richard (runaway to Georgia), Thos. Todd (runaway
to Alabama), Haisten Dial (runaway not known where), Elizabeth
Fowler, Salley Danlin?, Jobe Holliday, Edw. Hicks, Wm. Mills,
Henry Toland, Elizabeth Nabours, P. J. Byrd, Elender Corkrum
(been away to Georgia), Mirimen Cowan, Jas. Kenedy, Alex. Mills,
Jr., Saml. Hunter, Wm. Riddle, Silus Knight, Seaborn Moor, Jacob
Brock, Meridith Fowler, Benj. Knight, Nehemiah Franks, Simion
Garrett, Hollingsworth Morton, Tompson and Jno. Farley, Lemual
and Luke Crumton, Marshal Martin, David Enterkin, Robt. Pucket,
Mathew H. Henry, Dinsey Cheek, Mitchel Smith, Abraham Crow,
Mordica Ferguson, Wm. Asbery, Jacob Fuller, William Asbey, dec'd.
(N. B. About 15 pages in all.)

25 Apr. 1835. Appraisal of estate of JOHN HOLLAND, dec'd by
Jno. Godfree, Saml. Crage and Wm. Gambell. Sale Bill. James
McElery, adm. Notes on: Jno. Holland vs Saml. Enterkin, Jno.
Holland vs Thos. Fulton, Thos. R. Adair, Thos. Holland, James
Copeland, David Enterkin.

(No date) Appraisal of estate of DEMILION DEAL, dec'd by Danl.
Foshee, Anthony Golding and Willis Cook. Sale Bill. (No date).
Pur.: Wm. Atwood, Demarus Deal, Danl. Foshee, Tandy Turner,
Anthony Golding, Jas. Wright, Jno. Hitt, Willis Cook, Bluford
Watts, Jno. Hill.

20 June 1835. Martha Ball, guardianship of Susanah Ball, minor.

22 May 1835. Appraisal of estate of URSALA BROOKS, dec'd by

BROOKS cont'd:
Robt. Nickle, Moses Griffin and James Nickle.

28 Apr. 1835. Appraisal of estate of THOMAS ANDERSON, dec'd
by Sandres? Willisom?, Harison Daniel and A. C. Jones. 29 Apr.
1835. Sale Bill. Pur.: Wm. W. Anderson, Henry Johnston, L. W.
Anderson, Jefferson Arnold, Reuben Stephens, Jno. Smith, Sal.
Kinman, A. C. Jones, Thos. Pope, Mrs. Grayman, Lewis Arnold,
Sandes Williamson, David McCullor, James Killingsworth, H. Nor-
ris, Wm. Moor, Wm. Wilson, Thos. Washington, Jno. Adams, Jno.
Smith, Benj. Jones, A. L. Anderson, A. J. Anderson, Jno. Grey-
ham, Philip West, Wm. Stephens, Zachariah Carewile, Jno. Pitts,
Thos. Kindman, Geo. Washington, B. G. Gary, L. W. Matterson.
Henson Norris, adm. Cash, notes, & acct's: cotton sold in Ham-
burg; James Greyham, Hinson Norris, Sandes Williamson, Saml.
H. Owens, Valentine Jones, Wm. Goggens, Wm. Yager, Jos. McWil-
liams, James Moor, Artis Cook, Jas. Watson, Jno. W. Hodges,
Walter Anderson, Jos. Hall, Wm. Bradon, Aron Mullinox, Jno.
Nash, Benj. Cooper, David Anderson, Thos. Anderson, Wiley Cum-
ming, Robt. Golding, Benj. R. Mitchel, Geo. West, Jno. Cumming.

13 May 1835. Appraisal of estate of JOHN TODD, dec'd by Wm.
Rose, Saml. Mills and Elias Cheek. 15 May 1836 (1835). Pur.:
Saml. Flemming, Abner Gidins, W. Syms, Wm. Terry, Lemuel Par-
sons, Stephen Garrett, Edw. Garrett, F. Langston, R. Campbell,
Fleming Mosley, Wm. Cowing, Berrey Pool, Austin Moor, Saml.
Mills, Anderson Brown, Danl. Mekie, Elizabeth Todd, Wm. Todd,
Jno. Todd, Saml. Todd, Jno. Fleming. Notes, etc. due estate:
Sampson Bobo, Absalum Bobo, Geo. Bobo, Even Bell, Jno. Atte-
way, Edw. Fowler, Zach. Gray, Mathew Holladay, Jno. Hannah,
S. F. Higgins, Jno. Hannah, James Layton, Tuley Mosley, Robt.
Patterson, Jos. Patterson, Sterling Tucker, Jonathan Crow, Jno.
Saml., Robt. and Wm. Todd, Wm. and Young Terrey, Saml. Workman,
Richd. Woodruff, Henry Langston, Thos. Strand, Foster Bobo,
Richd. Cahill, Wm. Watson, Gideon, Wm. and Abner Carey, Henry
Miller, Zach. Davis, Wm. Whitmore, Allen Grantrey, Willis Strand,
David Wells, Jno. Whitfield, Willis Bobo, Wm. Bobo, Anteney
Hand, Wm. and Jas. Watson, Ann Morgen, Alfred Crow, Robt. Slone,
Wm. and Elisha Watson, Thompson Farley, Peter Towns, Nancy Stone,
Harrison and Anderson Brown, Merston Pool, Wm. Noble, Jno. Rober-
son. Jno. S. Todd and Saml. Hunter, exrs.

7 July 1835. Will of JOHN BLACK, dec'd proven. Sarah C. Black
and James Caldwell (exr. and wit. to will).

15 Apr. 1835. Will of THOMAS BLAKELY, SR., dec'd proven. Thos.
Blakely, Jr., exr. Will dated 2 Aug. 1826. Son John; son Samuel;
son Thomas; dau. Elizabeth Ann Bryson; dau. Jane Adair; Jno.
Blakely Carpenter who married my dau.; my wife Margret; son
Charles. Sons John and Thomas Blakely, exrs. Wit: James Watts,
Jr., Hedley Davis and J. E. Hutcheson.

29 Dec. 1834. Will of JOHN BLACK, merchant. Beloved wife Sarah
Conaway Black; 3 youngest children Cresa?, Franson? and Hariet;
dau. Agatha (who is married but no name given); Jno. & Wm. Black
(firm) and mentions her first husband; son William Ewell Black;
land in Spartenburg (Attorney Foster, Sr. for which dec'd is
security); dau. Elizabeth Henderson; sons: John Blair Black,
Richd. ___ Black, Trenmon F. Black; dau. Harriet Melvine. Wife
sole exr. (Mentions oldest sons and two sons-in-law). Wit: James
J. Bailey, James Caldwell and Wm. Milligan.

18 July 1835. Will of ELIZABETH GLOVER, dec'd proven by Geo.

GLOVER cont'd:
Anderson, exr. Will dated 11 Oct. 1832. Children: Stanford Glover, Susanna Savage, Nathaniel Glover, Desey Jones, Julis Glover, Misilla M. Glover, James A. Glover; dau. Mimmy Glover; dau. Catey C. Glover; dau. Luesanny Glover; William A. Glover. Friend George Anderson, exr. Wit: Wm. Groves, Y. Neely and P. W. Sims.

8 Aug. 1835. Will of REUBEN GOLDING, dec'd proven. Will dated 25 Oct. 1830. Loving wife Peggey Golding; loving children: Molly Tinsley, Anthony Foster Golding, Nancy Golding (now dec'd), Reuben Golding, Elizabeth Ordrey?, Anteney Golding, Richard G. Golding, Salley Jones and Susey Wood; son-in-law James Golding and grandsons William Golding and Ira Golding, children of dec'd dau. Nancy; grandchildren, children of my grand-dau. Rachel Henry now dec'd; grandsons Wm. and Ira, sons of James Golding and dau. Nancy. Loving son Richard G. Golding and trusty friend Nimrod Obevy? (also appears to be Oveby, hus. of dau. Elizabeth), exrs. Wit: Joel W. Pinson, Nathaniel Nickele and Anthony F. Golding.

22 July 1835. 2nd Appraisal of estate of JOEL PERSONS, dec'd by Isaac Cooper, Berey Edwards and Benj. Griffith. (also shown as JOEL PEARSON). Sale Bill, 23 July 1835. Pur.: Mary S. Hughs, Lowery Griffith, Menody? Sughs (also Meardy Shugs), Elisha Mehugh, Saml. Parks, Mesideth Scrugs, Jno. Connant, Merady Scrugs (see above also), Jno. Cole, Henry Pearson, James Cooper, Jno. Maddox, Osborn Cole, Chas. Cox, Kevel Roberts, Jno. F. Bennet, Jno. Rashell, Joel Edwards, Menda Pearson, Jonathan Cooper, Drury Cox, West Wood Foret, Wm. Haisten, Thos. Roberts, Nancy Spurgin, Andw. Massey, Jesse Brown. Ephrum Pearson, exr.

8 Aug. 1835. Appraisal of estate of THOMAS BLAKELY, SR., dec'd by Wm. Blakely of Wm., Robt. Bell and Hugh Workman.

5 Oct. 1835. Mary Cunningham, about 18 years old, Eleanor Cunningham, about 16 years, and Syntha Cunningham, about 14 years of age, and chose Fielding Jent (Gent?), guardian. Wm. Morgen, Mahaley Cunningham and Jno. Cunningham, sur.

1 Oct. 1835. Nancy Jones and Elizabeth Jones, minors, chose Samuel Jones, guardian. Wm. McGowing and James Low, sur.

20 Sept. 1835. Adm. of estate of JAMES ADKISON, dec'd to Samuel Todd. Nathan F. Proctor and Thos. Todd, sur.

21 Sept. 1835. Adm. of estate of ISRAEL PRATER, dec'd to Wade Johnston. Aron and Fedrick Johnston, sur.

14 Oct. 1835. Appraisal of estate of ELIZABETH GLOVER, dec'd by Wm. Groves, Jno. Waitt and Jno. Sims.

19 Oct. 1835. Adm. of estate of JESSE AVERY, dec'd to Barrington Avery. Joseph Avery and Richd. F. Simpson, sur.

11 Sept. 1835. Appraisal of estate of JOSEPH JONES, dec'd by Thos. Hitt, Wm. McGowen and Alexander McWilliams. James Neely, exr. James Wright, J. P. 11 Sept. 1835. Sale Bill. Pur.: Jesse Hitt, Jno. McClennahan, David Owen, Saml. Jones, Thos. Butler, P. R. Sims, James Braxter, Elihu Watts, Jno. Sims, James Neely, Nancy Jones, Radey Jones, James Wright, E. D. Jones, B. F. Watts, James Strain, Elias Jones, Eliza Jones, W. J. Johns, R. Whiteford. James Neely, exr. of JOSEPH JONES, dec'd.

1 Oct. 1835. 2nd Sale Bill estate of DAVID MASON, dec'd. Jno. Mason, adm. Pur.: Gideon Cannon, Ezekiel Johnston, Nathan Cain, Elbert Lindsey, Wm. Gamble, John Langston.

2 Nov. 1835. Adm. of estate of ELIZABETH NICKLE, dec'd to John Boyd. Alexander Austin and Thomas Austin, sur.

16 Nov. 1835. Adm. of estate of ARTHUR FULLER, dec'd to Henry Fuller. Wm. C. Nickle and Jno. Felts, sur.

16 Nov. 1835. Adm. of estate of RIGNOL DUNKIN, dec'd to Baruch Dunkin. John Odle and John Felts, sur.

22? Sept. 1835. Return of Saml. Todd, adm. for estate of JAMES W. ADKESON, dec'd, to certify· that dec'd had no goods or chattels to his knowledge. Had his share of his mother's estate with interest for six years to to 2 Nov. 1835; due dec'd bal. of settlemtnt; rec'd from sale of cotton from Marcus Dandy; expenses paid Henry Young, counsel. Pd. David Anderson, ord. fee.

6 Nov. 1835. Appraisal of estate of JOSIAH PRATOR, dec'd by Robt. Owen, Benj. Hill and Jno. Ramage. 16 Nov. 1835. Sale Bill. Alfred Kern pur. 3 slaves.

29 Sept. 1835. Appraisal of estate of REUBEN GOLDING, dec'd by James Rowland, Hamton Fendley, Sr., John Fendley, Sr.

19 Nov. 1835. James Cheek ask for guardianship of his two daus. Catherine C. Cheek and Susannah Cheek. Chas. Smith and Jos. Irby, sur. (also shows Catherine G. Cheek).

31 Oct. 1835. Mahaley Cunningham, mother of Margret Cunningham, Thomas Cunningham, Lisa Cunningham and Elizabeth Cunningham, minors for Fielding Jent be guardian. Elias West and Jno. Culberson, sur.

26 Jan. 1835 (1836?). Sale Bill estate of ALEXANDER KIRKPATRICK, dec'd. Pur.: Jno. Milum, Andy Nelson, Jno. Climens (also Climes), Wm. Tompson, Robt. Todd, Husten Parsley, M. F. Kirkpatrick, Jno. Felts, Jno. Campbell, (2nd page-ink smeared).

7 Dec. 1835. Will of CAIN JONES, dec'd proven. Adm. to John B. Black with will annexed. Will of CAIN JONES, free man of color, dated __ May 1826. Wife; daus. Pl___? and Rachel; there sister already married (not named); dau. Charlotta and her bro. Daniel and Elliott; wife Sarah (mentions "unfortunate Charlotta") and he asks John and William Black, merchants, to be exrs. Wit: Minor Walker, James Crawford, Chas. Furguson and Wm. Tasner?.

7 Dec. 1835. Adm. of estate of DAVID GREER, dec'd to John Greer. James Crawford and Benj. Blakely, sur.

7 Dec. 1835. Will of AGNES MAHAN, dec'd proven by Mary and Elizabeth Mahan. Will dated 23 May 1833. Daus. Mary and Elizabeth; dau. Rachel. Daus. Mary and Elizabeth, exrs. Wit: John Stewart, Henry Langston and John Couch.

3 Aug. 1835. Elenor Davis and Emely Davis, minors, chose James Crawford, guardian. Both over 15 years. John Meyson and G. W. Young, sur.

2 Dec. 1835. Appraisal of estate of JESSE AVERY, dec'd by Joseph

AVERY cont'd:
Sulivan, James Durrow and Aberham Bolt?. 19 Nov. 1835. Sale
Bill. Pur.: Elizabeth Avery, Barington Avery, Thos. Manley,
Jos.? Avery, Wm. Hill, James Durrow, Henry Pitts, Kindred Vaughn,
Lewis Mahaffey, Joseph Avery, James Small, Saml. Waldrop, Jas.
Wilson, Henry Hill, Absalum Mixon, Jas. Watson, Asa Garrett,
Nimrod Nabours, Wm. Manley. Barrington Avery, adm. Notes due:
Elijah Smith, E. H. Garrett, Joel Avers, Enoch Hill, Wm. Hill,
Sr., Ransen Fuller, Mathew Avery, James Sandres (Sanders?),
Barrington Avery, James M. Sanders, Harris Hill, William Avery.

28 Dec. 1835. Will of ELIJAH WATSON, dec'd proven. (also codicil)
by Jas. H. Beechum. John Felts, exr. Will dated 1? Apr. 1835.
ELIJAH WATSON, JR. will. Land formerly of Benj. Cheshure, Sr.;
(where he died) and land formerly of Benj. B. Cheshure, Jr.;
son Casper Watson; land formerly of Thos. C. Reeder; dau. Amelia
Caroline Watson; dau. Laura Lew__ns? Watson; dau. Bephamia Wat-
son; wife Nancy. Worthy friends Gen. John R. Griffin, Dr. G.
Washington Young and John Felts, exrs. Wit: Danl. G. Beechum,
Wm. A. J.? Brown and James H. Beachum. 3 Apr. 1835. Codicil.
Same witnesses.

24 Sept. 1835. 2nd Appraisal of estate of JAMES AUSTIN, dec'd
by Jno. H. Coleman, Thos. Ligon, Blufort Wells and James Austin.
Alex. Austin, exr. Sale Bill. (No date). Pur: Wm. Austin, Alex-
ander Austin, Samuel Austin, Allen Dial, Mrs. Jane Goodman,
Bird Robert, Miss Chang? Snow, Wm. Rodgers, Thos. Rodgers, John
C. Coleman, Allen Vance, James Austin, Thos. Todd, Wm. Braxter,
James Braxter, Mrs. Thos. Snow, J. F. Nickle, J. Armstrong,
Sarah Astin (Austin?), Anthony Cook, Wm. Bryson, Wm. McGowen,
B. Gill, Melton Mote, Elijah Watson, Esq., J. Moor, Saml. Good-
man, R. C. Astin (Austin?), Solomon Fuller.

21 Dec. 1835. Appraisal of estate of DAVID GREER, dec'd by David
Vance, Peter Sadler and Benj. Blackeby. (Also dated 22 Dec.).
22 Dec. 1835. Sale Bill. Pur.: Allen Andrews, Mrs. Nancy Greer
(widow), Jno. B. Blach, Silus Cain, Miss Ann Horan, Thos. Wilson,
Jesse Enterkin, Saml. Vance, Geo. Johnston, Benj. Blackely,
Wm. Hays, Jno. Miller, Saml. Caldwell, Jno. Dalrymple, David
Vance, Jno. Luke, Anderson Johnston, Larken Monroe, Peter Sad-
ler, Johnston Gaggard, Wm. Neal, Humphrey Linsey, David Brooks,
Willard Boon, Wm. Abernatha, Cullen Tinsley, Elihu Watson, James
S. Godfree, Wm. Devanl, Ephrum Dalrymple, Wm. Johnston, James
Carter, Chas. Jones, Thos. Teague, Shadrick East, Jno. H. Davis,
Mrs. Sarah Black, Green Vickery, Jos. Hips. Notes due: Benj.
Blackeby, Henry Jones, Elizabeth Land, Elizabeth Smith, Willers?
Barun, Elihu Watson. John Greer, adm.

9 Dec. 1835. Appraisal of estate of RIGNAL DUNKIN, dec'd by
John Odell, Benj. Brown, Joseph Babb and John Felts. Notes due:
Wm. Williams, Jno. Roberson, Wm. Wilson, Jno. Odle. 10 Dec.
1835. Sale Bill. Barruch Dunkin, adm. Pur.: Fedrick Nance, Thos.
Rodgers, Wm. Wilson, Danl. Cureton, Elizabeth Dunkin, Jesse
G. Watson, Benj. Brown, Jesse Young, Danl. Winn, Danl. Jones,
Isaac G. Weason, C. M. Wilks, Mary Hollingsworth, Silus Motes,
Elijah Trible, Hannah Burnside, David Littel, Elizabeth Hill,
John Odle. Note on Jno. Odle. Note on Felden Bailey and Mary
Duckett.

6 Jan. 1836. Martha Morehead, minor, about 19 years, chose John
B. Pitts, guardian. Elijah Smith and Jehu Pitts, sur.

4 Jan. 1836. Luisa Ray, minor about 14 years, chose Miles Bennet,

RAY cont'd:
guardian. Benjamin Brook and Manning E. Jones, sur.

4 Jan. 1836. Adm. of estate of WILLIAM JACKSON EAST, dec'd to William East. Saml. Copeland and Jesse Enterkin, sur.

1 Nov. 1835. Appraisal of estate of ARTHUR FULLER, dec'd by Jno. Felts, Hagen Motes and Albert Miller. (also dated 17 Nov.). 12 Dec. 1835. Sale Bill. Henry Fuller, adm. Pur.: Wm. Brownlee, Geo. Roberts, Henry Fuller.

9 Dec. 1835. Appraisal of estate of USLEY BROOKS, dec'd by Robt. Nickle, Moses Griffin and James Nickle. (also spelled URSALY). Sale Bill (No date). Pur.: Mrs. Brooks, James Goodman, Allen Coleman, Mariah Brooks, Jas. and Robt. Nickle, Moses Griffen, Ranson Fuller, Bird Waldrop, Alex. Astin, Wm. Green, Joel Anderson, N. B. Coleman. 2nd sale (not dated). Wm. Brooks, Jas. Rowland, Jno. Walker, Jno. Findley. B. Brooks, adm.

(No date) 2nd sale bill estate of DAVID MASON, dec'd by James Mason, exr. Pur.: Gideon Cannon, Ezekiel Johnston, Jonathan Cain, Robt. Linsey, Wm. Gamble, John Langston.

6 Dec. 1836(1835). William S. Thorneton, minor about 15 years, chose Martin Sadler, guardian. Plesant Sadler and James McFerson, sur.

11 Jan. 1836. Adm. of estate of JOHN BOYD, dec'd to Wm. D. Watts. Anthony Griffen and Jno. C. Watts, sur.

18 Jan. 1836. Will of JAMES CUNNINGHAM, SR. proven by James Cunningham, Jr. Will dated 13 July 1835. Wife Molly; heirs of dau. Catherine Cooper; son John P. Cunningham; dau. Marget Allison; dau. Polley Pinson; Kitty Cunningham, Marima Cunningham; Polly Adams, dau. of son Samuel Cunningham, dec'd; dau. Salley Holliday wife of Wm. Holliday; Wm. Hudgens; son William; son James; son Thomas; dau. Jane; dau. Be___am? Puckett; dau. Permelia Dial. Wife Molley and son James, exrs. Wit: Jno. Cunningham, Wiley Yagin and Nancy Yagin.

18 Jan. 1836. Adm. of estate of JOSEPH YOUNG, dec'd to Sarah Young. Joseph Young and Robt. Liles?, sur.

18 Jan. 1836. Adm. of estate of WILLIAM PUCKETT, dec'd to Alfred Puckett. G. W. Sullivan and C. P. Sullivan, sur.

4 Dec. 1835. Appraisal of estate of JOSIAH PRATOR, dec'd by Saml. Young, Isaac Jacks and Jno. Forgison. (JOSIAH PRATER, SR.). 5 Dec. 1835. Sale Bill. Pur.: Richd. Bonds, Joseph Dunkin, Joseph Jones. Thos. Prator and Jos. Dunkin, exrs.

19 Nov. 1834. Appraisal of estate of THOMAS POWELL, dec'd by (no names). 24 Nov. 1834. Sale Bill. Pur.: (2 pages very dim). Thomson Vance, Martin Bailey, Wm. Milum, Sr., Thos. Powell, Jr.

23 Jan. 1836. Return of Martin Sadler, guardian of William S. Thorneton, minor. Rec'd of Cristwell Moor.

1 Feb. 1836. Will of GEORGE GORDON, dec'd proven. Will dated 6 Dec. 1835. Son Alfred George Washington Gordon; sued William Musgrove for 12 acres; dau. Charlotta Fulton; Thomas Fulton;

GORDON cont'd:
and son Alfred George Washington Gordon, sole exr. Wit: Thos.
L. S. Fraser, Bird Hill and Anders Floyd.

18 Feb. 1836. 2nd Appraisal of estate of ZACHARIAH ARNOLD, dec'd
by Elihu Watson and Wm. Graves. 7 Mar. 1836. Sale Bill. Note
on Lewis I. Arnold. John West, exr.

16 Nov. 1835. 2nd Appraisal of estate of ALEXANDER ASTIN (AUSTIN)
SR., dec'd by Bluford Wells, Jno. Vance and Mathew Bryson.
16 Nov. 1836. Praise bill of property of AGNES AUSTIN, dec'd
wife of ALEXANDER AUSTIN, SR., dec'd. 17 Nov. 1835. Sale Bill.
Pur.: I.? P. Austin, R. C.? Austin, Saml. Austin, J. F. Camp-
bell, Allen Colmon, Marcus Dandy, Alex. Austin, J. P. Austin,
C. Snow, P. Newby, A. Griffin, Sarah Austin. 23 Mar. 1827. Deed
of life assignment by Agnes Austin. Wit: Jno. F. Coleman, Robt.
Campbell, Dr. Names children: Alexander Austin, Samuel Austin,
James? H. Austin, Matt E. Austin, John Austin and Sarah Austin.

10 Dec. 1835. 2nd Appraisal of estate of JOHN HOLLAND, dec'd
by Wm. Gamble, Saml. Craig and Jno. Godfrey. 15 Dec. 1835. Sale
Bill. Pur.: Mary Ann Holland, John P. Holland, Lucretia Holland,
Jno. G. Couch, signed by James M. McElroy, adm.

18 Jan. 1836. Adm. of estate of JOSEPH YOUNG, dec'd to Sarah
Young. Joseph Young and Robert H. Little, sur.

18 Jan. 1836. Adm. of estate of WILLIAM PUCKETT, dec'd to Alfred
Puckett. G. M. Sulivant and P. Sulivant, sur.

1 Feb. 1836. Adm. of estate of ELIZABETH NICKLES, dec'd to James
McDowal. William Blakely and James Templeton, sur. Inventory
and sale (no date). Inventory made by John Boyd. Pur.: Jean
Boyd, T. Nickle, Jane Boyd. Notes due est.: Nathan Nickle, Geo.
Nickle, Jesse W. Fuller. James McDowal, adm. de, bonis, now,
of Elizabeth Nickles.

11 Jan. 1836. Adm. of estate of JOHN BOYD, dec'd to William
D. Watts. Anthony Griffin and J. P. Watts, sur.

29 Dec. 1835. Appraisal of estate of AARON HARLAN, dec'd and
sale bill. No names of appraiser or purchasers.

23 Jan. 1836. Appraisal of estate of WM. J. EAST, dec'd by Thos.
Teague, James Crawford and Ashley Willson. Pur.: Elizabeth East,
Thomas Neill, Jno. Young, Thos. Teague, Ashley Wilson, Larken
Monroe, Wm. Memsestree?, Bethiah S. East. Wm. East, adm.

29 Dec. 1835. Appraisal of estate of CAIN JONES, dec'd by Wm.
Young, Benj. Blackaby and David Vance.

2 Mar. 1836. Adm. of estate of JAMES CALDWELL, dec'd to David
R. Caldwell. Joseph Dickson and H. M. Wardlaw, sur.

15 Oct. 1835. List of estate of JOHN BLACK, dec'd by James Young,
David Vance, and Saml. Vance. 1 Oct. 1835. Appraisal of est.
of JOHN BLACK, dec'd Spartanburg Dist., S. C. by Jno. Murph,
Jno. Wells and A. Foster, Jr. (1st list made in Laurens Dist.).
17 Dec. 1835. Articles sold at JOHN BLACK's plantation by Sarah
C. Black, exr. Pur.: Saml. Austin, Alexander Austin, Wm. E.
Black, Sarah C. Black, Wm. Burnsides, James J. Bailey, Silus
Bailey, John Bailey, James Caldwell, Dr. John H. Davis, Newton

BLACK cont'd:
Fowler, Wm. Goulding, Richd. Goulding, John Godfrey, Chas. Jones,
Federick Nance, Newton Pyles, David Martin, Wm. Thompson, Saml.
Vance, Jno. Vance, Jno. D. Williams, Jno. D. Williams. Sarah
C. Black, exr. Widow's share list; minor children's share: Rich-
ard Oscar Black, F. F. Black, Harriet W. Black.

7 Jan. 1836. Appraisal of estate of DR. ELIJAH WATSON, dec'd
by G. W. Young, J. P. Watts and F. Nance, Jr. 12 Jan. 1836.
Sale Bill. Pur.: Thos. Rodgers, Capt. A. Griffen, Allen Vance
(Nance?), David S. Beachm, Fed. Nance, Elihu Watson, Jas. Crad-
dock, Shade East, Wm. Cole, Geo. Holdrick, Nimrod Stewart, Saml.
Vance, Dr. G. W. Young, Danl. Jones, Isaac Mitchell, Elijah
Watson, Dr. T. Teague, Jno. Black, James J. Bailey, Jno. D.
Williams, James Wright, Dr. J. P. Watts, Saml. Workman, Dr.
Griffen, Dr. R. Austin, Saml. Bryson, Capt. A. Griffen, Chas.
Jones, Geo. Roberts, Marcus Motes, Saml. Rodgers, E. J. Burn-
side, Daniel S. Beachum, Danl. M. Winn, James Wright, Dr. G.
W. Young, Wm. Hays, W. E. Black, Jacob Miller, Sanford Powell,
A.G. Cook, Mauris Motes. John Felts, adm.?

22? Mar. 1836. Will of JOHN BEASLEY. Dau. Nancy Nichols; child-
ren named Ransom Beasley, Levi? Beasley, Matilda Gullett? and
Lucy Buzbee. Friend Nimrod Ob__(part of page not copied), exr.
Wit: J. F. Pinson, Thos. J. Butler and Mecajah Busby.

29 Oct. 1836. Appraisal of estate of JOHN NICKLES, dec'd by
Jno. Armstrong, Richd. Sims and Jonathan Reed. 4 Nov. 1836.
Sale Bill. Jno. F. Nickles, adm. Pur.: Alexander Austin, Allen
Vance, Anthony Golding, Chas. Haigwood, Elizabeth N. Nickles,
Edw. Cason, Jno. F. Nickles, A. F. Golding, Dr. Watts, Robt.
Nickles, Libby Nickles, Thos. Rodgers, Thos. Gill, Thos. Moore,
Wm. Bryson, Jno. D. William guardian for Wm. Nickle, Wm. Samuels,
Robt. Coleman, James Goodman, Jonathan Reed, Lewis Ball, Robt.
Moore, Richd. Golding, James Baxter, Matthew Bryson, H. M. Nick-
les, Isaac Mitchell, Andw. Johnson, Jno. Milam, Pleasant Foster.
Note on Elizabeth Nickles. Jno. F. Nickles, adm.

_ Jan. 1836. Appraisal of estate of JOHN BOYD, dec'd by Allen
Andrews, Danl. Vance and Peter Sadler. W. D. Watts, adm. Sale
Bill-Jan. (no date). Pur.: Isabella Boyd, Jno. D. Williams,
David Vance, Anderson Johnson, Robt. Nickles, Allen Andrews,
Saml. Vance, Wm. Jones, Jno. Shepherd, Aaron Brooks, Fred. Nance,
Jno. Vance, Chesley Butler, J. W. Johnson, Wm. Bryson, Cullen
Lindsey, Thos. Rodgers, Wm. Johnson, Wm. Horan, Humphrey Lind-
sey, Elbert Lindsey, Abram Thompson, David Little, Dr. G. W.
Young, James B. Little, Jas. H. Boyd, Edw. Burnsides, Capt.
A. Griffin, Moses Anderson, James Craddock, Thos. Wilson, Jno.
Miller, Saml. Money, Wm. Vaughan, Pinckney Bullock, Danl. Jones,
Jno. Young, Benj. Black, Robt. Hunter, Jno. G. Plant, Elijah
Tribble, Job Dalrymple, Wm. C. Boom, Geo. Johnson, Jno. D. Wil-
liams, Jno. Lindsey, Saml. Caldwell, Wm. East, James Crawford,
Aaron Johnson, H. Barksdale, Jane Boyd, Peter Sadler, Jno. &
W. D. Watts, Saml. Boyd, Elihu Watson. Note on Wm. Lenvil, A.
G. Leek, Jas. B. Little, Alex. Austin, Jno. Gray.

21 Oct. 1836. Appraisal of estate of WILLIAM L. CRAIG, dec'd
by John Boyce, John Henderson and John Craig. 26 Oct. 1836.
Sale Bill. Pur.: Jno. Boyce, Jno. Craig, Jno. Little, Robt.
Pitts, Jas. Little, Britton Wiggins, Jacob Wiggins, Thos. En-
terkin, Park Meadows, Dr. Thos. Weir, John Templeton, James
Adair, John Henderson, Nathaniel Vance, James Burk, Jno. Luke,

CRAIG cont'd:
Jno. Dalrymple, Jno. Bowling, Alfred Kern, Saml. Wiggins, Jno.
Kern, Joshua Saxon, Byrd Hill, Stephen Yarborough, D. J. Puckett,
Geo. Bowing, Jno. West, Henry McKelvy, Hiram Yarbrough, Martin
Huckanly, Jno. Fowler, Joseph Abrams, Wm. Adams, James McCrary,
Phillimon Hinds?, Geo. Dillard, Issac Briggs, Wm. Malone, Thos.
Blakely, Robt. Blakely, M. Hartford, Robt. Little, Thos. Whit-
more, Turner Ferguson, Thos. Gore, Jno. Willard, Wm. Bobo, Wm.
Alexander, A. G.? Bell, Edwin McCrary, Benj. Adair, Jno. Davis,
Thos. Lamb, Robt. Martin, A. A. Fairborn, Ross? Young, Danl.
Felder, Giles Goodwin, Robt. Owen, Jno. Norman, Danl. Hasmining?,
Thos. J. Ray, Geo. Byrd, Wm. Dodd, Chany Farrow, Jno. Craig,
Wm. Byrd, Gillam Huckaby, Thos. Holland, Ephraim Pitts, Saml.
Ferguson, Robt. Gilliland, James Lambright, Joel Dean, James
Dillard, Chas. Dillard, Geo. Templeton, Allen Puckett, Benj.
Nix, Jonathan Bailey, Aaron Starnes, Wm. Starnes, Joseph Mc-
Conathy, Thos. Craig. Personal est. sold 20 Dec. 1836. John
Craig, Jacob Wiggins, A. A. Fairborn, E. Campbell, Geo. Gordon,
Thos. Young, E. D. Williams, Saml. Young, John Whitton, Berry
Jeans, Benj. Hill, Thos. Whitmore, Thos. Powell, E. Adair, Geo.
Byrd, A. A. Kern, Wm. Hunter, Nat Vance, Jno. Dalrymple, M.
Mims, L. Whitten, Joseph West, Jno. Finney, Wm. Blackburn, Wm.
Simpson, Joshua Gore, W. G. Davis, Thos. Potter, Levi Burke,
Alex. Glenn, Thos. Wier. Notes due est.: Richd. Starnes, Benj.
Lamb, Wm. Lamb, W. J. Bobo, James Lambright, Robt. Martin, Jesse
Dodd, Jr., Byrd Hill, Wm. Langston, Jacob Wiggins, Joshua Smith,
T. W. Waters, W. W. Casey, Wm. M. Inlow, D. J. Pucket, Allen
Pucket, Davis Newman, W. A. Templeton, Wm. Huff, Robt. Hannah,
Fielding Foster, Abram Holland, Jos. Cooper, (list identical
to list of purchases above), Sarah Puckett, Martha Mims.

(No date) Appraisal of estate of ELLIS DENDY, dec'd by James
Watts, Jno. Grant and E. C. Watts. 9 Feb. 1837. Sale Bill. Pur.:
Robt. Gates, Wm. R. Smith, Patrick Todd, James Watts, Sr., Isaac
Whitworth, Jno. Hitt, Jno. Grant, Marcus Dendy, Willis Dendy,
Arianner Dendy, Archy Todd, Thos. Spearman, Chas. Eagarton,
Wm. Atwood, Abraham Hollingsworth, Rhoda Valentine, Richd. Grif-
fin, Robt. P. Smith, Squire Jones, Foster Wills, Eli Valentine,
Andy Andrews, James Wright, James Goodman, Wm. Austin, James
Wallace. Note on Marcus Dendy (also adm.).

28 Sept. 1836. Appraisal of personal estate of JAMES KINMAN,
dec'd by Wm. Arnold, Jno. Loveless and G. W. Brownlee. 29 Sept.
Sale Bill. Pur.: Geo. Brownlee, Jno. Mormon, L. R. Smith, James
Thomas, Jesse Gent, Jno. Bagwell?, Stother Flowers?, Joseph
McCullough, James Kinman, Thos. Carter, Lindsey Hand, Gabriel
Hand, Wm. Maddox, Winniford Kinman, James Kinman, Thos. Kinman,
Sarah Kinman, Quinton Kinman, Jno. Mahon. (N. B. This belongs
to heirs of Thos. Kinman, dec'd.). Sale Bill of goods going
to heirs of Elizabeth Cook - Rachel Williamson. Names: Lewis
Pyles, Jno. Cook, Strother Flowers, James Kinman, Elisha South,
Geo. Brownlee, Mastin Nabors, Edw. Howard, Gabriel Hand, Thos.
Carter, Edw. Howard, Vincent Austin, Thos. Kinman, Moses Myers,
Winniford Kinman, James Trainham, Jas. Kinman, Jno. Padget,
Peggy Kinman, Wm. Nix, Lewis Pyles, B. L. James, Wm. Purl, Eliza-
beth Mahan, Jefferson Arnold, Chas. Kay, Thos. Taylor, Wiley
Davis, Jno. Williamson.

23 Aug. 1836. Estate of HUGH LEMON?, dec'd. Pur.: Madison Milam,
Jesse Hill, B. Wills, Isaac Mitchell, Minor Winn, Alex. Winn,
Thos. Moon, Jno. Kelly.

(No date). Appraisal of estate of JOHN MC COY, dec'd by Isaac
Jacks, Thos. Rather and Richd. S. Fergeson. Willed property:
Bell? McCoy, J. L. McCoy, Eligah Godfrey, Charity Anderson,
David B. McCoy. Sale Bill (Dec. 1836). Pur.: Isaac Jacks, Jno.
M. Fergerson, Barnet McCoy, Thos. Whitman, Isaac Whitten, Thos.
Garrett, Lewis Anderson, Isaac Hill, Mathew McCrary, Jno. Nor-
man, Jos. Abrams, Miles Fergerson, Jos. Duncan, Claxton Ray,
Asa Dodd, Edmond Adair, Mannon Dillard, Jno. L. McCoy, Wm. Adair,
Jno. Whitmon, Chas. Miller, Jno. Harmon, Richd. Fergerson, Geo.
Abrams, Wm. Young, Geo. Young, Lewis F. Jones, Jas. S. Godfrey,
Henry Rodgers, Danl. Cornelius, Ed. Phillips, Reuben Sims, Jno.
Ray, Wm. Jacks, Geo. Rowland, Isaac Cox, Rachel Riley, Stephen
Hill, Nathan Gossit, Miles Bennet, Nathan Whitmon. Jno. L. Mc-
Coy, exr. Note on Jos. Shettlesworth, Henry McCoy and Benj.
Adair.

21 Dec. 1836. Appraisal of estate of WILLIAM M. VANCE, dec'd
by Jos. Caldwell, Jas. G. McClarkin?, Jno. Godfrey, Wm. P. Cook,
Wm. East and Lewis Young, cont'd on 27 Dec. at the farm in New-
bury Dist., Laurens. Sale Bill 22 Dec. 1836. Pur.: N. C. Vance,
Elizabeth Vance (widow), James McCollum, Jno. H. Hatten, Jos.
Caldwell, Wm. Harris, Chas. F. Slike, Richd. P.? Brown, Wm.
Cates, Wm. Hipp, Arthur Dugan, Wm. McCraken, Saml. Hutchinson,
Joel East, B. D. Durwill?, T. B. Rutherford, Saml. Hipp, James
Cannon, David Vance. Cont'd 28 & 29 Dec. Saml. & Allen Vance,
the widow, Jno. Vance, Nathaniel Vance, Wm. Horan, B. F. Griffin,
Frederick Nance, Cullen Lindsey, Elbert Lindsey, James Lindsey,
Dr. Wm. Rook, Dr. Jno. H. DAvis, Moses Anderson, Jno. Plant,
Wade Dalrymple, C. B. Griffin, J. A. Egleberger?, Humphrey Lind-
sey, Jno. Lindsey, Jno. Miller, Saml. Neel, Wm. Abernathey,
Wm. Green, Edw. Foster, Dr. G. M. Young, Jas. Craddock, Wm.
E. Black, Wm. East, Jno. Luke, and "Free" Jesse. John Vance,
adm. Inventory of notes due est.

16 Feb. 1837. Appraisal of estate of MABERRY GARRETT?, dec'd
and sale bill. Pur.: Wm. Manley, Peter Touns, Wm. Boult, Asa
Boult, Asa Garrett, Richd. Tiere, Allen Mahon, Lewis Garrett,
Peter Towns, Barrington Avary, Chas. Avary, Jonathan Abercrombie,
Stephen Garrett, Kellet Crombie, Polly Garrett, Lewis Garrett,
E. H. Garrett, Tira Manley, Allen Mahaffey, Robt. Manley, Mathew
Avary, Colvil Abercrombie, Jno. Glenn, Starling Garrett, Jno.
Watkins, Eli Hardin, Orsamus Mahaffey, Hannah Johnson. E. H.
Garrett, adm.

(No date). Appraisal of estate of JAMES BLAKELEY, dec'd by Jno.
Clark, Jno. Stewart and W. W. Hitch.

15 Sept. 1836. Appraisal of estate of JAMES PARK, B., dec'd
by Chas. Fowler, Andw. Parks and James Park. (N. B. Throughout,
this is written James Park B. No explaination). 5 Sept. 1836.
1st Sale. Saml. Hunter, adm. Pur.: Thos. Parks, G. C. Dial,
James F. Parks. 2nd sale.14 Dec. 1836. Mrs. N. Park, Wm. G.
Bryson, Wm. R. Fairly, Jas. Bramblett, A. McCarley, Peter Poole,
Robt. Parks, Jas. Garner, Jno. Smith, D. C. Templeton, D. Dendy,
Rachel Parks, Geo. Ross, Wm. Mills, Wm. Hunter, Jr., Seth Pool,
Jas. M. Pollard, Andw. Park, Jno. Compton, Wm. Robertson, Saml.
Mills, Maj. S. F. Farrow, Jas. Flemming, Jacob Brock, Nehemiah
Franks, N. Simmons, Wm. Fowler, Geo. Abrams, Jno. McClintock,
Thos. Langston, Geo. McKitrick, Jno. Hutchinson. Notes: W. Wal-
lis, Jno. Hitch, Clark Templeton, Nancy Park, Wm. Goss, Andw.
Park, Geo. McKitrick, John Compton.
24 Sept. 1836. Appraisal of estate of AARON STARNES, dec'd by

STARNES cont'd:
James Rowland, Asa Forgie and Thos. Lockhart. 1 Dec. 1836. Sale
by Martin Shaw for est. Pur.: James Hill, Jno. Walker, Jas.
Anderson, Jno. Fowler, Wm. Cobb, Silus Fuller, Aaron Hill, Mary
Ann Starnes, Asa Forgie, John Luke, Hinson Norris, Chas. Irby,
Jno. Brownlee, Chas. Brock, Geo. Shirley, Isaac Mitchell, Jno.
K. Moon, Jno. Fowler, Richd. Harris, Alsey Fuller, Wm. Moore,
Geo. Moore, Elihu Burgess, Wm. Nickles, Jno. Todd, Julius Glover,
Philip Wait, Wm. Vernell, Geo. Elmore, Amos Roberts, Wm. Savage,
Jno. Willard, Jas. McPhearson, Martin Shaw, Chas. Irby, Saml.
Lockhart, Alfred Milam, Nathan Sims, James Rowland. Martin Shaw.,
exr.

1 Dec. 1835. Appraisal of estate of ISRAEL PRATHER, dec'd by.
F. F. Calmes, Moses Beaty and James Blackburn. Notes on Levin
G.? Stewart, Thos. Fuller. 3 Dec. 1835. Sale Bill. Wade Johnson,
aadm. Pur.: Martha Prather, William Scott, Josiah Duncan, Saml.
Young, Geo. Abrams, Gideon Cannon, Jno. Fergeson, Jno. Cald-
well, Moses Beatty, James Abrams, Wade Johnson, Richd. Fergeson,
Thos. J. Dillard, James D. Sims, James Blackburn, Stephen Hill,
and notes above mentioned.

3 Feb. 1837. Appraisal of estate of MARY COLE, dec'd by Wm.
Boazman, Saml. Caldwell and Jno. Mangram. 3 Feb. 1837. Sale
Bill. Pur.: W. D. Watts, James Black, Allen Andrews, Nathan
Whitman, John Feltz. Allen Andrews, exr.

13 Feb. 1837. Appraisal of estate of BEAUFORT WELLS, dec'd by
Allen Coleman, James L___ amd Jesse Hill. 14 Feb. 1837. Sale
Bill. Widow Elizabeth Wells, Wm. Ligon, Benj. M. Wells, Wm.
Carter, Allen Coleman, Clement Wells, Amos Roberts, Alexander
Austin, Foster Nickles, Jesse Hill, Martin Ball, Wm. Hitt, Henry
Hitt, Benj. Hill, Jno. Milam, Andy Nelson, David Owens, Thos.
Austin, Allen Vance, Alsey Coleman, Jas. Wells, Wm. Cook, Mar-
shall Starnes, Jabez W. H. Johnson, Martin Shaw, Jas. Lowe,
Justinion Henderson, Wm. Green, Saml. Jones, Jno. Campbell,
Isaac Box, Willis Dendy, Nancy Valentine, Wm. Wells. Note on
Geo. Anderson, Wm. Samuel. Wm. Hitt, adm.

22? Dec. 1836. Appraisal of estate of JAMES DILLARD, Esq., dec'd
by Geo. Dillard, Nathan Harns? and Jno. Craig. 28 Dec. 1836.
Sale Bill. Jno. Dalrymple, Mary Garrett, Chas. H. Dillard, Thos.
Duckett, James Dillard son of John, Jason Davis, Geo. Dillard,
Mary Dillard, Wm. Adair, Giles Goodwin, Jno. Whitton, Robt.
Pitts, Aaron Starnes, Jos. Garrett, Geo. Young, Danl. Felder,
Jno. Whitmore, Jno. Boyce, Elijah Wilbourn, Jno. Norman, Wm.
Langston, Robt. Gilliland, Jno. Miller, Jno. Craig, Robt. Martin,
Britton Wiggins, Jno. Henderson, Edw. B. Phillips, Amos Prather,
Martin Hopkins, Wm. D. Byrd, Henry Garrett, Jefferson Turley,
Isaac Whitton, Jno. Templeton, Ephraim Pitt, Nathl. Vance, Jno.
Langston, Hugh Toland, Thos. Craig, Jas. Burk, Geo. Byrd, Jno.
F. Kern, Lindsey Whitten, Jas. H. Dillard, exr.

2 Feb. 1837. Sale Bill of estate of ISAAC GRANT, dec'd. Wm.
Austin, Duke Goodman, Marion Grant, Jas. Lowe, Arianna Dendy,
Andy Andrews, Alex. McWilliams, Alex. Weston?, Dr. Jno. P. Watts,
Robt. Whiteford, Lewis Ball, Jas. Wells, Marcus Dendy, Geo.
Grant, Benj. Hitt, Jas. Baxter, Richd. Griffin, Jas. Watts,
Allen Vance, Franklin Cook, Benj. Foshee, Thos. Moon, Beaufort
T. Watts, Lewis Salmon, Jno. Austin, Pleasant Newbey, Wm. Mc-
Gowan, Jas. Wright, Chas. Eagarton, Thos. Butler, Jno. Grant,
David Whiteford, Jas. Goodman, Jos. Ball, Richd. Watts, Squire

GRANT cont'd:
McClelen, Willis Dendy, Jas. Austin, David Cureton, Jno. Chapell,
Wm. Neely, Jonathan Reed, Jas. Todd, Elihu Watts, Jno. Hitt,
Thos. Todd, Wm. Hitt, Richd. Sims, Martin Ball, Wm. Nickles,
Anthony Golding, Wm. Carter.

17 Feb. 1837. Appraisal of estate of MOSES LEEK, dec'd by Jno.
Little, A. A. Fairbarn and Thos. Craig. 20 Feb. 1837. Sale Bill.
Jno. Leak, Jno. Little, Lowther D. Hitch, Allen Kelly, Robt.
Tucker, James Langston, Jno. Dalrymple, Wm. S. Leak, Jno. W.
Leak, Marthann Leak, Jas. McKelvy, Thos. Gray, Jas. Duvale,
Jno. Duvale, Thos. Blakely, Wm. D. Sheldon, Armstead Leak, Jno.
Templeton, Jno. Higgins, Jno. Blakely, Jno. McClintock, Cristo-
pher Garlington, B. B. Gaines, Robt. Pitts, Jno. Clark, Geo.
McCrary, Jas. Dillard, Robt. Gilliland, Jesse Couch, Wm. Starnes,
Jno. Couch, Elihu Fairbarn, Robt. Adair, Henry Stroud, Jno.
Flemming, Jas. G. Rogers, Thos. S. Leak, Saml. McKelvy, Presley
Craig, Robt. H. Little, Newton Higgins, Robt. Pucket, Danl.
Bailey, Byrd Hill, Jas. Leak, some notes due est. Jno. Leek,
adm.

11 Feb. 1837. Appraisal of estate of DAVID P. SAXON, dec'd by
G. W. Sullivan, W. G. Davis, J. M. Pollard and Thos. E. Her-
bert. 13 Feb. 1837. Sale Bill. Geo. Bowen, C. P. Sullivan, Chas.
Irby, Edw. Hix, Robt. Allison, W. F. Downs, A. Barksdale, H.
C. Young, Willis Wallace, W. R. Fairly, Jno. Osborn, Jno. Alli-
son, Hugh Saxon, Mark Killingsworth, Saml. Vance, Robt. Little,
Lewis Ellison, Wm. Motherall, Berry Martin, Christopher Gar-
lington, Wm. Cornwell, Wm. Caldwell, Jos. Spencer, Willis Benham,
A. C. Jones, Wm. McNeese, L. G. Williams, Jos. Vance, G. W.
Sullivan, Jno. D. Williams, Tyra Walker.

21 Feb. 1837. Appraisal of estate of JAMES WILLIAMSON, dec'd
by Jno. Nickles, Jas. McDowall and Willis Benham. 22 & 23 Feb.
1837. Sale Bill. Agnes Williamson, Hamon Miller, Allen Dial,
Willis Benham, Edw. Martin, Jos. McCollum, Capt. Jno. Davis,
Wm. Ranson, Wm. Templeton, Thos. Milam, Wm. Waldrop, Jno. Young,
Jesse W. Moon, Elijah Tribble, Wm. S. Blakely, Walter D. A.
Dean, Doc. Jno. Nickles, Doc. Wm. Williamson, Sanford Powell,
Mrs. Margarite Martin, Miss Jane Williamson, Doc. Thos. William-
son, Abram Cook, Jas. McDowal, Wm. Hardy, Doc. Jno. Williamson.
Jas. Davis, adm.

10 Aug. 1836. Appraisal of estate of JAMES JOHNSON, dec'd by
Wm. Irby, Saml. Downs, Jas. Nelson and Jas. Dorroh. Notes due
estate. Hannah Johnson, adm. 1 Sept. 1836. Sale Bill. Jas. Henderson, Elijah Franks, Jno'th Abercrombie, Henry Lindley, Jas.
Wilson, Hannah Johnson, Jas. Cunningham, Jas. Dorroh, Thos.
Morgan, Jno. Hudgins, Stephen Garrett, Wm. Pitts, Alex. Abercrombie, Wm. Qualls, Albert Madden, Wm. Holliday, Hastings Johnson, Walter Dean, Jno. S. James, Jas. J. Lowry, Wm. Lindley,
Abner Nobles, Jno. L. Madden, Jas. Dial, Harrison Johnson, Saxon
Wilson, Wm. P. Boult, Lewis Allen, Jno. G.? Shell, Carter Parker, Jas. Eledge, Jonathan Johnson, Jas. A. Blackwell, Jas. Coker,
and on 3 Feb. 1837, remainder of personal est. sold.

27 Mar. 1837. Appraisal of estate of ELI BEARDEN, dec'd by Elihu
C. Watts, Marcus Dendy and Jas. Watts. 28 Mar. 1837. Sale Bill.
Matilda Bearden, Cason Hill, Benj. Foshee, Drury Vaughan, Jas.
Vaughan, Wm. Smith, Jas. Clark, Richd. Watts, Patrick Todd,
Danl. Proctor, Jno. Chapell, Jas. Goodman, Jas. Burton, Geo.
Adams, Jas. Wallace, Wm. Simpson, Zachariah Proctor, Jno. Plant,

BEARDEN cont'd:
Wm. Caldwell, Lewis Ball, Marcus Dendy. Zachariah Proctor, adm.

4 Mar. 1837. Appraisal of estate of H. A. DIAL, dec'd by W.
G. Davis, Thos. E. Herbert and Saml. R. Todd. (Also spelled
DEAL). 7 Mar. 1837. Sale Bill. Notes due estate. G. C. Dial,
adm. of estate. Note on Isaac S. Dial.

(No date) Appraisal of estate of BARNETT ROBERSON, dec'd shown
by Saml. Roberson, exr. to Reuben Roberson, Solomon Galispee
and Jos. A. Moore.

(No date) Appraisal of estate of GEORGE T. SLOAN, dec'd by Zador
F. Smith, Wm. Gilbert and Jno. Hughs. Sale Bill (no date). Jos.
Brown, Brinkley C. Clifton, Thos. Edwards, Jno. Edwards, Westwood
F. Fort, Beverly B. Garrett (Garnett?), Wm. Gilbert, Lucy Grif-
fith, Samnl. B. Hill, Jno. Hughes, Wm. Houston, Durham Johnson,
Thos. Parks, Jacob Pennington, Wm. Roberts, Thos. R. Roberts,
Geo. A. Sloan, Alfred Sloan, Mary Sloan, Thos. Sloan, Jno. Smith,
Z. F. Smith, Richd. Woodruff. Wm. A. Sloan, adm.

(No date) Sale Bill estate of ISAAC DIAL, dec'd. Wm. Irby, Chas.
Irby, Chas. Brock, Jas. Lowry, Wiley Young, Wm. Henderson, Chas.
Franks, J. L. Dial, Mary Dial, Hastings Dial, Danl. Bell, H.
A. Dial, Thos. F. Jones, Dr. J. W. Simpson, G. C. Dial, B. F.
Dial, Wm. Henderson, J. Blackwell, Alsey Coleman, Jas. Brown,
Sampson & Wm. Babb, Wm. R. Farley, Andw. Winn, Wm. Burton, Jr.,
H. Burton. G. C. Dial, exr.

(No date) Appraisal of estate of WILLIS COOK, dec'd by Richd.
Watts, Richd. F. Griffin and Richd. Golding. Sale Bill. Richd.
Golding, Jno. D. Williams, Wm. R. Smith, Anthony Golding, Jas.
Goodman, Jno. Cook, Anthony Griffin, Jno. Austin, Thos. Austin,
Isaac J. Whitworth, Franklin Cook, Mrs. Nancy Owens, Elihu C.
Watts, Jas. Cook, Mrs. Jane Cook, Robt. Coleman, Wm. Atwood,
Allen Vance, Dr. Wm. H. H. Griffin, Mrs. Susan Waldrop, Edw.
Ward?, Martin Ball, Marcus Dendy, Richd. Watts, Danl. Owens,
Jno. and Alex. Hitt. A. Griffin, adm.

(No date) Appraisal of estate of JAMES NICKLES, dec'd by Jno.
Wood, Robt. McCrary? and Matthew Hunter. Sale Bill. (No date).
Widow Nickles, Anthony Campbell, Jno. Todd, Jno. B. Simpson,
Widow Bryson, Jno. Bailey, Tyree Walker, Jno. Finley, Thos.
Greer, Martin Shaw, Wm. Ligon, Nathan Sims, Wm. Green, Wm. C.
Nickles, Mrs. Susan Boyd, Richd. Sims, Alex. Nickles, Elizabeth
Nickles.

29 ____ 1837. Sale Bill of JOHN BEASLEY, dec'd. Robt. Coleman,
Alex. McWilliams, Wm. Nichols, Henry & Jesse Hitt, Redden Pucket,
Jno. H. Williams, Wm. Baxter, Chas. Brock, Jno. Pinson, Jno.
D. Pattison, Joel L. Anderson, J. W. H. Johnson, David Stewart,
Hampton Finley, Saunders Brownlee, Chas. Simmons. Nimrod Overby,
exr.

10 & 11 Aug. 1836. Sale Bill estate of DAVID ANDERSON, dec'd.
21 Oct. 1836. Sale Bill of goods & chattels. 20 Jan. 1837. Sale
cont'd. List of notes due estate. List of judgements. Magistrates
executions: Jno. Lee, Larkin Gaines, Thos. Harris, Moses Cole,
Jas. Golding, Thos. Sims, Peggy Willard. Acct's due dec'd: Ann
Johnson, exr. of Thomas Johnson, Jos. Blackerly adm. of Jos.
Blackerly, Milly Vickery adm. of Christopher Vickery, Phebe
Lewis adm. of Crawford Lewis, Chas. Saxon exr. of Chas. Saxon,

ANDERSON cont'd:

Sr., W. F. Downs exr. of T. Saxon, Joseph Owen exr. of John
Owen, Saml. B. Lewis adm. of Thos. Lewis, Josiah Box adm. of
Joseph Box, Elizabeth Wescoat adm. of Joel Wescoat, Saml. J.
Kern adm. of John Kirk, Cisley Rodgers admx. of Jno. Rodgers,
Mary Nisbet exr. of James Green, B. B. Chisher adm. of G. Winn,
Ann Estes admx. of Moses Smith, Wm. Fulton, Sr., adm. of Wm.
Fulton, Francs Medley admx. of Edw. Medley, Margarite Hatcher
admx of Felt Hatcher, Robt. Creswell adm. of James Criswell,
Wm. Brown, exr. of James Brown, Moses Garrett adm. of Levi Gar-
rett, Hasting Dial and Isaac Dial exrs. of J. Dial, Wm. Abrams
adm. of P. Noland, Wm. Lara adm. of T. Green, Jas. Blackely
adm. of ___McClary, Benj.? Brown exr. of Roger Brown, Richd.
and H. R. Allen, exrs. of John Wilson, Jonathan Jones adm. of
Thos. Jones, Wm. R. Farley adm. of A. Farley, Reuben Meadors
adm. of James Meadors, Jas. Copeland adm. of Jno. Copeland,
Reuben Meadors adm. of Susan Meadors, Reuben Roberson adm. of
Micajah Robinson, Drury Boyce adm. of B. McPherson, Henry Martin
adm. of Jas. Martin, Wm. Green exr. of Wm. Green, Danl. Osborn
adm. of D. Osborn, Jane Middleton admx. of James Middleton,
Peter Hammond exr. of John Rodgers, James S. Rodgers exr. of
John Rodgers, Wm. and J. H. Irby exrs. of Wm. Irby, Benj. Hill
exr. of Eleanor Hill, Wm. Burton adm. of Chas. Burton, Joicy
Word admx. of Robt. Word, Saml. M. Fairborn exr. of Jas. Fair-
born, Manisy? Coker admx. of Drury Coker, Jas. S. Rodgers, adm.
of Wm. Hopper, Malinda Crocker and A. T.? Richardson, adms.
of Elkanan Crocker, Mary Hollingsworth, admx. of Jas. Hollings-
worth, Thompson Farley adm. of Mary Fenley (Farley?), Thos.
Goodman adm. of ___ Goodman, J. W. Thompson adm. of Farley
Grovner, Wiley Hill exr. of E. Brazeal, Jno. Hunter exr. of
Thos. Hunter, Jas. Wright adm. of Thos. Hill, Henry W. Pasly
adm. of Ruth Brazeale, Josiah N. Bowlin exr. of Thos. Bouling,
Sarah Gray exr. of David Gray, Wm. Glenn adm. of Richd. Bullen,
Rebecca Young exr. of A. Young, Tabitha Prather guardian of
Mary Prather, Jos. Vance adm. of J. D. Boyd, Jas. Boyd and J.
Parks exrs. of Edw. Parks, Jno. F. Kern exr. of E. Kern, Wm.
Holliday adm. of Wm. Cunningham, Gideon Thomason adm. of R.
Thomason, Z. Bailey exr. of Z. Bailey, Susannah Crocker exr.
of Jas. Crocker, Elihu Watson adm. of J. Niswanger, Nancy Hunter
admx. of Jno. Hunter, Henson Norris adm. of T.? Anderson, G.
C. Dial exr. of J. Dial, Jno. Todd and S. Hamilton exrs. of
J. Todd, Bartlett Brooks adm. of Uslay Brooks, Henry Stroud
adm. of Thos. Fulton, Nathaniel Glover exr. of E. Glover, Richd.
Golding and Nimrod Overby exrs. of Reuben Golding, Sarah C.
Black exr. of Jno. Black, Saml. Jones guardian of N. E. Jones,
Wade Johnson adm. of Israel Prather, Alexander Austin exr. of
Jas. Austin, also exr. of A. Austin, Sr., Jno. Boyd adm. of
E. Nickle, Henry Fuller adm. of A. Fuller, Jno. B. Black adm.
of Karn Jones, Jno. Feltx exr. of Elijah Watson, Wm. East adm.
of W. J. East, W. D. Watts adm. of Jno. Boyd, Jas. Cunningham
exr. of Jas. Cunningham, Alfred Puckett adm. of Wm. Puckett,
Elijah Watson exr. of Allen Watus?(Watts, Watson?). 21 Dec.
1836. 2nd appraisal of estate of DAVID ANDERSON, dec'd. by
David Madden, Jas. McPherson and Richd. Harris.

17 Feb. 1837. Appraisal of estate of SUSANNAH DILLARD, dec'd
by Jno. Bouland, Saml. Young and Jos. Duncan. Notes on Lewis
Jones, Jesse Garrett, John and Ellen Garrett, Joshua Davis,
Joseph Suttle. 21 & 22 Feb. 1837. Sale Bill. Pur.: Elizabeth
Ellen (Allen), Jos. Abrams, Geo. Young, Greenberry Jeans, Jno.
Garrett, Thos. Garrett, Elvisa Gray, Enoch Garrett, Jos. Duncan,
Elizabeth Wesson, Isaac Hill, Jno. Whitmon, Martin Miller, Reuben

DILLARD cont'd:
Anderson, Lewis Anderson, Jas. Dillard, Dr. Vanleer, A. King,
Geo. Dillard, Reuben Sims, Peter Davis, Levi Rodgers, Henry
Rodgers, Henry Neel, Wm. Abram, Richd. Ferfeson, Luke Wesson,
Jno. Hefferman, Jas. Pucket, Jno. Huston, Edw. Wesson, Richd.
Fergeson (see Ferfeson above), Nathan Garrett, Jno. Garrett,
Joshua Whitman, Wryman Roberts, Benj. Hill, Lindsey Whitten,
Jas. Watson, Alfred Kern, Fed. Wesson, Jos. Phillips.

8 Feb. 1837. Appraisal of estate of MRS. SARAH SIMPSON, dec'd
by Jno. Godfrey, Newman Gary and Saml. Gary. 9 Feb. 1837. Sale
Bill. Pur.: Wm. Dunlap, Capt. Jno. Davis, Tandy Walker, Wm.
Goss, Col. Jno. D. Williams, Mrs. Sarah Creswell, Geo. Higgins,
Frances Parks, Jno. Black, Danl. M. Winn, Wm. Dunn, Saml. Neel,
Wm. E. Black, Thos. G. Wilks, Jno. Garlington, Jno. Watts, Robt.
Bell, Jno. Godfrey, Mathew Simpson, Jno. Luke, L. S. Monroe,
Jefferson May, Henry Milum, Andw. Johnson, Lina Cobb, Tom Cobb,
Robt. H. Little, Hillary Foster, Chas. Little. Jno. Garlington,
exr. Negro property division according to will: Henry W. Garling-
ton, Sarah Creswell, Jno. Garlington and Wm. Dunlap, trustees
for Dr. Edw. Foster in right of his wife Sarah Foster and Wm.
Caldwell, Maj. Wm. Dunlap and Margaret his wife. 7 Feb. 1837.
Jno. Godfrey, David Martin and W. D. Watts.

17 May 1837. Appraisal of estate of JAMES MEDLOCK, dec'd by
Jno. Knight, Chas. Jones and Reuben Williamson. 18 May 1837.
Sale Bill. Pur.: John Knight, Wm. Arnold, Wm. Saxon, Wiley Murff,
Thos. Crawford, Wilson Cooper, Wm. Weatherall, Widow Saxon,
Pleasant Saxon, Jno. Padgett. Sarah Medlock, admx.

(No date) Appraisal of estate of MARGARETT GOLDING, dec'd by
Geo. Funck, Hampton Finley, Sr., and Joel W. Pinson. Richd.
Golding, adm. 5 May 1837. Sale Bill. Pur.: Nimrod Overby, Anthony
Golding, Jno. Word, Richd. G. Golding, Sarah Williams, Robt.
E. Campbell, James Copeland.

15 Feb. 1837. Appraisal of estate of W. W. SIMPSON, dec'd by
N. Day, Wm. Blakely and Robt. Vance. 16 Feb. 1837. Sale Bill.
Deed of trust by Jno. Garlington, Dr. Jno. W. Simpson and Richd.
F. Simpson assigning...to me as trustee for my mother, brothers
and sisters.....sale of negroes. Jno. W. Simpson, Jr., trustee.
Mrs. Nancy Simpson, (who pur. most of est.), Allen Vance, Jno.
Garlington, Dr. Jno. W. Simpson, Thos. Parks, Saml. Rodgers,
Jas. M. Pollard, Robt. S. Vance, Wm. Blakely son of Wm. Blakely,
Jas. Parks, Saml. Bryson, Wm. P. Milam, Jno. Lockhart, Wm. Ran-
son, Henry Milam, T. T. Levan, Chas. and Jas. Little, Jno. S.
Hutchinson, Chas. Todd, Robt. H. Little, Christopher Garling-
ton, Wiley Hill, W. D. A. Dean, E. G. Simpson, Julius Martin,
H. W. Garlington. List of accts in ordinary's office due est.

2 June 1837. Sale Bill of estate of SQUIRE JONES, dec'd. Pur.:
Elizabeth W. Jones, Francis Hill, Duke Goodman, McA. Jones,
Marcus Dendy, Susan Jones, Chas. Eagarton, Dr. W. Phillips,
Duke Gates, Robt. Gates, Jno. Grant. William Phillips, adm.

1 Nov. 1835. Sale Bill of ELIZABETH GLOVER, dec'd. Pur.: Stan-
ford Glover, Chas. Simmons, Capt. Jno. West, Jno. Jas. Readin, Wm.
Watson, Jackson Glover, Julius Glover, Thos. Greer, Jno. Smith,
Wm. West, Joel Anderson, Danl. Watson, Jno. Moon, Jesse Daniel,
N. Glover, Wm. Savage, Polly Norman, T. G. Nealy, Wesley Savage,
Starling Smith, Polly Simmon, Aaron Hill.

15 Sept. 1837. Appraisal of estate of WILLIAM GOODWIN, dec'd

271

GOODWIN cont'd:
by John Clark, Wm. Brown and W. W. Hitch.

6 June 1837. Appraisal of estate of JOHN E. BURNSIDE, dec'd
by John Watts, J. D. Williams and Jas. Young. Capt. Robert Milam,
adm. 16 June 1837. Sale Bill. Pur.: John Watts, Madison Milam,
Robt. Milam, W. Johnson, Jesse Fuller, J. D. Williams.

(No date). Appraisal of estate of R. B. COKER, dec'd by Austin
Moon, Reuben Thomas and Abner Putman. Notes due: John Henderson,
Standback Coker, James Henderson, Thomas Coker, Henderson Cokekr,
Wm. F. Downs by James Bruster for crop.

(No date). Appraisal of estate of MICAJAH COMPTON, dec'd by
H. Thompson, Jas. Parks and Wm. Halbert. 28 & 29 Nov. 1837.
Sale Bill. Pur.: Mrs. Nancy Compton, Jno. D. Bennett, Robt.
Hand, Capt. Wm. Halbert, Edmond Crimes, Jonathan Owing, Jno.
M. Potter, Hutson Moon, Thos. Hitton, Alford Cargill, Hazekiah
Bruce, A. G. Owings, Wesley Compton, Wm. Owings, Thos. Halbert,
Joshua Halbert, Scarlet Robinson, Abner Knight, M. Thompson,
Mrs. Nancy Parks, Mrs. Jane Brown, Thos. Parks. Alford Compton,
adm.

15 Nov. 1837. Sale Bill of RICHARD M. OWEN, dec'd. Pur.: Alex.
Austin, Richd. Sims, Jno. Sims, Isaac Mitchell, Geo. Funck,
Francis Hill, Briant Leek, Thos. Todd, Fields Rudd, Benj. Hitt,
David Owen, Wm. Heto, Jno. S. Jones, Elizabeth Owen, Andrew
Nelms, Jno. D. Williams, Cason Hill, Rebah Hill, Jas. Vaughan,
Wm. McGowen, Jr., Wm. Owen, Henry Hitt, Thos. Rudd, Jno. Black,
Thos. Moore, Jas. Wills, Jas. Stephens, Lewis Salmon. Richd.
Sims, exr.

15 Nov. 1837. Sale Bill of ANN OWEN, dec'd. Pur.: Richd. Sims,
Foster Nickles, Jno. Williams, Alex. Austin, Anthony Cook, Jno.
Hitt, Elizabeth Owen, Pleasant Newby, Wm. Hitt, Jas. Stephens,
Jno. Grant, Saml. Austin, Wm. Atwood, Jno. Sims, Andy Andrews,
Narcissa Owen, Danl. Beacham, Jno. Burton, Benj. Foshee, Jas.
Wells, E. C. Latimer, Franklin Arnold, Isaac Mitchell, Wm. C.
Owen, Isaac Whitworth, Wm. Austin, Jno. H. Coleman, Danl. Foshee,
Jno. Wood, Drury Sims, Jas. Goodman, Willis Mounce, Thos. Moon,
Tandy Turner, Anthony Golding, David Carenten, Robt. Whiteford,
David Owen, Benj. Hitt, Allen Coleman, Benj. Owen, Braxton Owen.

8 Dec. 1837. Sale Bill of GEORGE THOMASON, dec'd. Pur.: Elizabeth
Thomason, James Thomason, Thurman Coker, Wm. Thomason, Washington
Thomason, George Thomason, Gideon Thomason, Abner Babb, Silus
Arnold, Enoch Hill, Yancy Helms, Titus Arnold, Masten Armstrong,
Standback Coker, Wm. Curry, Philip Garey, Frances Thomason,
BArnett Smith, Jonathan Johnson, Harper Coker, Zachariah Gray,
Lewis Owings, Jno. Harris.

(No date). Appraisal of estate of THOMAS MOORE, dec'd by Jos.
Sullivan, Abraham Meachim and Jas. Riley. 28 Sept. 1837. Sale
Bill. Pur.: Jno. Flowers, Alfred Puckett, Wm. Motherall, Jas.
Dorroh, Francis Beaks, Jas. Grimes, Gabriel Hand, Jos. McCul-
lough, Henry Pitts, Saml. Moon(also Moore), Thos. T. Taylor,
E. W. South, Jos. Sullivan, Jno. Simmons, Tyree Manley, Wm.
Weatherall, Zion Smith, Harvey Nabors, Thos. Manley, Abraham
Machin, Alfred Perrett, Bery L. James, Jas. Riley, Jas. Cheek,
Osborn Taylor. Samuel Moore, adm.

(No date). Appraisal of estate of SETH P. POOLE, dec'd by J.

POOLE cont'd:
H. Boyd, Roberson Manley and John Attaway.

(No date). Appraisal of estate of GEORGE THOMASON, dec'd by
B. Smith, Robt. Willis and Francis Thomason. Mentions: Washington Thomason, James Thomason, George Thomason, Sarah Willis.

(No date). Sale Bill of ROBERT B. COKER, dec'd. Elizabeth Coker,
adm'x. Sale Bill. (No date). Elizabeth Coker, Elisha   Freeman,
Saxon Coker, Standback Coker, Jonathan Henderson, Barnett Smith,
Washington Thomason, John Hellams.

(No date). Appraisal of SQUIRE JONES, dec'd est. by Travis Hill,
A. Griffin and Willis Brown.

(No date). Appraisal of estate of WILLIAM REED, dec'd by Manhall?
Starnes, Jos. Butler and Jno. White.

24 June 1837. Appraisal of estate of ABRAHAM HAROLD (also HARNEL)
dec'd by John Deen, Jacob Souter and John Mason. 24 June 1837.
Sale Bill. Pur.: Dr. Wm. Rook, Jno.Miller, Geo. Metly, Wm. K.
Wills, Levin Y. Stewart, Jno. Johnson, Wm. Rook, Sr., Davis
Williams, Jno. Deen, David Martin, Wm. Yarborough, Ezekiel John-
son, Danl. Cannon, Abraham Wilkes, Wm. H. Logan, Richd. Meltz,
Byrd Cromer, Jacob Souter, Jno. Bond, H. Simpson, Josh Horton,
Levi L. Young, Jno. H. Hatten, Thos. Deen, Wm. Neel, Henry Meltz,
Jno. Jones, Wade Johnson, Saml. Neighbours. Note on Elizabeth
East, Lemuel Dillard, Jas. Denson, Wade Johnson, Wm. Harnel,
Byrd Cromer, Elijah Cromer, David Meltz, Abraham Wicker, Nathl.
Enterkin, Saml. Copeland.

(No date). Appraisal of estate of DR. GEORGE MC CRARY, dec'd
by A. A. Fairborn, Jno. Little and Jas. McKelvey. Sale Bill.
Pur.: Saml. McKelvey, Matthew H. Henry, Elizabeth McCrary, widow,
Elihu Fairborn, Caroline McCrary, Beverly Martin, A. A. Fairborn,
Robt. Cunningham, Jos. D. Hopper, Wright Cunningham, Joshua
Brown, Washington Duvall, Thos. Craig, Jas. Wright, Dr. J. Dil-
lard, Wm. Starnes, Noah Fairborn, John Duvall, Christian B.
McCrary, Saml. S. Fergeson, Wm. Wright. Saml. W. Fergeson, adm.
(N. B. the next pages show return of notes with no indication
if it is still part of the above estate). Named: Jno. D. Bailey,
Alexander Jeans, M. H. Henry, Saml. Stone, Henry Cunningham,
Jas. Powell, Jas. Tinsley, Mary Studdard, Wm. Blakely of Jas.,
Jas. F. Blakeley, Chas. Little, Robt. Blakeley, Lilly Farbarne,
Jas. Henry, Noah Farbarne, Jas. Little, Jas. Blakeley, Sr.,
Newton Higgins, Matthew E. Cunningham, Jas. Leek, Jr., Jas.
Leek (Little), Saml. Leek, Jas. Duvall, Wm. Starnes, W. E. Henry,
Hansey Godfrey, Saml. Godfrey, Danl. Edmonson, Saml. Martin,
Thos. Holland, Wm. Wright, Jas. Hanna, M. H. Henry, Jno. Higgins,
Sr., Jos. Harlan, Sarah Higgins, Jno. Glenn, Wm. Craig, Thos.
R. Adair, Wm. Langston, Masson Jeans, Jno. Higgins, Jr., Henry
& Ephraim Pitts, David Bailey, Elihu & Ransom Golightly, Jas.
Duvall, Julius Martin, Elizabeth Cole, Alexander McKelvy, Wm.
Tinsley, Jno. Hanna, Jas. McKelvy, Thos. Craig, Roddy Woodruff,
Wm. Henry, Geo. McKitrick, Wm. Sheldon, Lewis Duvall, Jno. Dal-
rymple, Jno. Young (Little River), Wm. & Martha Starnes, Jas.
Duke, Jno. D. Bailey, Wm. & Fanny J.? Brock, Jonathan Blakeley,
Jeremiah Leek, Noah Smith, Saml. Fergerson, Jr., Robt. Milam,
Chas. Blakeley, A.a A. Farbarne, Mrs. P. Studdard, Dorcus Leek,
Andw. Studdard, Joel Dendy, Henry Cunningham, Wm. Cooksey, Widow
N. Blakeley, Jas. McGowan, Cheston B. McCrary, Armstead Leek,
Henry Stroud, Wm. & Widow Goodwin, Jno. Tygart, Uriah or Nancy

Acct's cont'd:
Davis, James Little for Watson, Wm. Godfrey, Jacob Cockran, James Tinsley.

(No date) Appraisal of estate of JAMES NIX, dec'd by E. McHugh, F. Smith and Thos. S. Sloan. 7 Nov. 1837. Sale Bill. Pur.: Jos. Brown, Jno. Bennett, W. Blankenship, West Ford, Wm. & B. B. Garrett, W. H. Gilbert, Moses Hughs, Jno. Jones, Josiah Kilgore, Joel Leagen, Elizabeth Nix, W. W. Nix, Jacob Peyten, H. G. Pearson, W. G. Roberts, Z. F. Smith, S. K. White, Jno. Wallis. J. Kilgore, adm.

1 Jan. 1838. Appraisal of estate of SAMUEL JONES, dec'd by Alexander McWilliams and Geo. Neely. 2 Jan. 1838. Sale Bill. Pur.: Sarah Jones, Lewis Ball, Alexander Weston?, Saml. Caldwell, Wm. Austin, Wm. McGowen, Amos Roberts, Anthony Golding, Henry Hitt, Wm. Nealy, Lewis Salmon, Marshall Pollard, Jno. D. Puttman, Wm. Green, Isaac Mitchell. Wm. McGowen, adm.

3 Apr. 1838. Appraisal of estate of B. F. HUTCHESON, dec'd by Jas. B. Martin, A. S. Hutchinson and John Taylor. 14 Apr. 1838. Sale Bill of B. F. HUTCHINSON, dec'd. Pur.: Mary A. Hutchinson, John S. Hutchinson, Jas. Glenn, Saml. Martin.

(No date) Appraisal of estate of MILLEY ALLEN, dec'd by Jesse Garrett, Sr., Saml. & Wm. F. Downs. 20 Feb. 1838. Sale Bill. Pur.: James Wilson, John Crysp, Jesse Garrett, Sr., Thos. Lindly, Titus Arnold, Asa Bontt?, Matthew Johnson, Wm. F. Downs, Anderson Arnold, Wm. Pitts, Reuben Flowers, Asa Garrett, Jonathan Johnson, Joseph Gourganis. Jonathan B. Allen and Anderson Arnold, exrs.

11 Apr. 1838. Return on estate of SETH P. POOLE, dec'd. Pur.: Saml. Mills, Jesse Brown, Berry Pool, Wm. A. Todd, Jno. Dean, Jas. Higgins, Jas. B. Higgins, Jas. _.? Burke, Martin Poole, J. W. Wallis, Jos. Patterson, Peter Pool, Ephraim Campbell, Anna Cottrell, Robinson Mosely, Davis Newman, Thos. F. Stone, Elihu Poole, Robt. Gilliland, Jno. Poole, Silas Woodruff, Nathan Bramblet, Jno. Langston, Bartlett Coleman, Edw. Garrett, Silas Dendy, Wm. H. Farrow, Taylor Goodwin, Margarett Poole, Betty Poole, Ellis Cheek, Nat. Vance, Wm. Cunningham, Robt. Coleman, Drury McDaniel, Jane Martindale, Jackson Casey, Jesse Couch, David Glenn, Alex. Alexander, Jas. Burke, Shadrick Waldrip, Jno. Sloan, Jno. H. Byrd, Stephen Tally, R. B. Hall, Thos. Park, Wm. Sims, Wm. Rose, Richd. Cheek, Wilson Harris, Jas. Harlan, Andw. Park, Mas. F. Manley, Anderson Brown, Saml. F. H. Todd, A. P. Bobbo, Martin Huckerby, Thos. Gore, Jno. Miller, Jas. Sloan, Robt. Patterson, Wm. Terry, Sr., Jas. Alexander, Saml. Meredith, Dr. Peter Wallis, Chany Farrow, David Sloan, Allen Gentry. Notes on James Compten, Shadrick Waldrip, Wm. Robertson, Wm. Pearson. John P. Poole and Peter Poole, exrs.

11 Jan.? 1838. Appraisal of estate of JAMES KINMAN, dec'd by H. G. Johnson, John Loveless and C. T. Latimer. 12 Jan.? 1838. Sale Bill. Pur.: Gabriel Hand, Benj. Arnold, Thos. Mahon, G. W. Brownlee, Widow Kinman, Thos. T. Taylor, Edw. F. Lattimer, Pleasant Saxon, Joel Stone, Robt. Scott, Thos. Carter, Reuben Stephens, Timothy Stephens, Saml. Downs, Squire Calhoun, A. C. Jones, L. W. Madison, Tully Bowling, Vincent Shaw, Chester Kingsley, Wm. Mitchell, Nimrod Donalson, Walter Johnson, Washington Youngblood, Wyatt Norwood, Edw. Nabors, Jefferson Arnold.

(No date). Appraisal of estate of RANSOM FULLER, dec'd by Jno.

FULLER cont'd:
Nickles, Wm. Lewis? and Martin Shaw.

(No date). Inventory of notes due estate of D. P. SAXON, dec'd. (six pages in length)

3 Feb. 1838. Appraisal of property of JOHN HOLLAND, dec'd brought from Alabama and sold as part of his estate by Jas. Henry, Thos. Holland and Jno. Little. 3 Feb. 1838. Sale Bill. (These were slaves). Pur. by Joel L.? Foster. James McLeroy, adm.

8 Sept. 1837. Appraisal of estate of EEAN BEAL, dec'd by Wm. ___?, Jos. Patterson and Saml. Mills.

29 Nov. 1837. Appraisal of estate of REBECCA SWAN, dec'd by Chas. Fowler, Alex. Powqers and W. W. Hitch.

END OF BOOK

START OF VOL. E
1836-1839

28 Feb. 1836. Will of DAVID ANDERSON. Children already rec'd real & personal property; grandchildren (3 children of my son); (N. B. this is son Wade, dec'd); note on Thos. Lockhart; trustees of sd children: Geo. Anderson, Turner Richardson; (children named: George, Joel and Mary Richardson; grandson David Anderson, son of Wade Anderson, dec'd and 2 sisters; son George Anderson; dau. Mary L. Richardson; son Joel Anderson; son George Anderson; land of Aaron Sherley, John Middleton, Jos. Crocker; M. L. Richardson; son-in-law Turner Richardson. Sons George and Joel Anderson and son-in-law Turner Richardson, exrs. Wit: Lemarcus Deale, Saml. T. Lockhart and Asa Forgy. 28 July 1836. Will was proven on 18 July 1836 before W. W. Simpson, J.C.O.

5 June 1836. Will of HUGH LEEMAN. Beloved wife Elizabeth; sons Samuel, William and Hugh; daus. Nancy Hunter, Mary Ann and Isabella Leeman. Bro. James Leeman and wife Elizabeth Leeman, exrs. 26 July 1836. Will proven. Wit: Wm. Thompson, Sr., Matthew Bryson and Anthony F.? Golding.

3 Dec. 1831. Will of SARAH SIMPSON. Dau. Margarett wife of Wm. Dunlap; dau. Sarah wife of Elihu Criswell; grandson Henry William Garlington, son of John Garlington?; grand-dau. Sarah Caldwell; grandson William Caldwell; family burying ground at Little River Meeting House. Wm. Dunlap and Jno. Garlington, exrs. Wit: Jno. Dunlap, Jno. Blakely, (B.F.) and Middleton Cobb. Will proven before W. D. Watts, J.C.O. on 22 Jan. 1837.

19 Feb. 1832. Will of MARY COLE. Dau. Nancy Pearson; grandchildren: William Andrews, Polly Feltz, Allen Andrews, Ephraim Andrews, Nancy Williams, Elizabeth Blackburn, Edney Andrews, Young Andrews. Beloved grandson Allen Andrews, exr. Wit: Anthony F. Golding, B. F. Griffin and Wm. Plant. Will proven 18? Jan. 1837?

17 Jan. 1837. Will of BARNET ROBERTSON, farmer. Loving wife Susanna; loving son Samuel; son John; other four sons (not named) and dau. Rebecca Owings. Saml. Robertson, exr. Wit: Milly Robertson, Cassy Hiller and Wm. Owings. Will proven 20 Feb. 1837.

29 Oct. 1836. Will of WILLIAM REED. Wife Nancy; dau. Elizabeth; land on Puckets Creek adj. Wm. McGowen and Saml. McWilliams;

REED cont'd:
children of my brothers and sisters. Jabez W. Johnson, exr.
Wit: John White, Jas. Lowe and R. Campbell. Will proven 1 June
1837 before W. D. Watts.

3 Nov. 1835. Will of JOHN MC COY. Son Drayton McCoy; dau. Eliza-
beth; son Barnett McCoy; sons Micajah and John; son-in-law John
Fergerson and his dau. Eliza Alburton?; dau. Eliza Godfrey;
dau. Charity; son David McCoy. Sons John and Micajah McCoy and
John Fergerson, exrs. Wit: Jno. Hitch, W. W. Hitch and Nancy
Hitch. Will proven 4 Feb. 1837.

28 Mar. 1829. Will of JOHN WAIT. Beloved wife Frances; dau.
Mariah wife of James Sims being dead and left children named
John and Rhoda Sims; sons Philip and Franklin Wait; daus. Peachy,
Polly and Fanny. Philip and Franklin Wait, exrs. Wit: Jedakiah
South, Moss Myers and Michael Clardy. Will proven 15 Feb. 1837.

26 Feb. 1834. Will of JAMES BLAKELY. SR. Beloved wife Nancy;
son Jonathan Blakely and son William; sons James and George;
son Thomas; daus. Sarah and Catharine; daus. who are married;
children: Polly Cunningham, Margarite Hutcherson wife of Robt.
Hutchinson, Agnes Blakely; grand-dau. Martha Blakely dau. of
my dec'd son Matthew Blakely. Exrs. not named. Wit: Jno. D.
Williams, H. C. Young and Robt. Creswell, Jr. Will proven 11
Feb. 1837.

1 Dec. 1825. Will of WILLIAM GOODWIN. Wife Jane (also exr.);
children (not named). Wit: Jno. Stewart, Math. Cunningham and
Robt. Taylor. Will proven 7 Aug. 1837.

31 Nov. 1836. Will of EVEN BEAL. Wife Polly; children: David,
Reason, John (gets nothing), Nancy Sullivan, Rachel Robeson,
Polly Knight. Wife Mary Beal, exr. Wit: Wm. Ross, Saml. H. Ross
and Jas. L. Hill. Will proven 4 Sept. 1837.

3 Nov. 1837. Will of REBECCA SWAN. Children of Timothy Swan;
children of Barbara Sloan; dau. Ann Simmons wife of John Simmons;
dau. Molley (also exr.). Wit: Jno. Hitch, Wm. Compton and Chas.
Fowler. Will proven 21 Nov. 1837.

13 May 1837. Will of DAVID BELL. Beloved son Adam Bell; beloved
son Robert J. Bell; land formerly John Bell; land of Dr. F.
F. Calwell?. Beloved nephew William Adams agent or guardian
for Adam Bell, or in his place, Richard Fergerson. Robt. J.
Bell, exr. Wit: Jas. Blackburn, Lewis Jones and Edw. Wesson.
Will proven 8 Nov. 1837.

7 Jan. 1838. Will of MILLY ALLEN. dau. Frances; dau. Lucy Arnold;
grandson Allen Atkins; son Jonathan Allen; dau. Sarah (in trust).
land of W. F. Downs. Son Jonathan Allen and son-in-law Anderson
Arnold, exrs. Wit: Wm. F. Downs, Jas. Bruster and Garland Sims.
Will proven 31 Jan. 1838.

27 Sept. 1837. Will of SETH P. POOLE. Son Martin Poole and balance of my children. Sons John and Peter Poole, exrs. Wit. Wm.
Cowan, Lucy and Emily Poole. Will proven 28 Oct. 1837.

_____ 1836. Will of MARTHA MC CLINTOCK. Children: Robert and
Mary; land pur. of Elizabeth Copeland. Wit: Wm. Thompson, Mary
Bryson and Elizabeth A. Thompson. Will proven 19 Feb. 1838.

21 Sept. 1836. Will of ABRAHAM RIDDLESPERGER. Beloved wife Molny?

RIDDLESPERGER cont'd:
(or Molsey); dau. Purches B. wife of Hezekiah Gray; children:
Ann Gouch and Samuel Riddlesperger and children of my dec'd
dau. Elizabeth Gouch. Henry C. Young, exr. Wit: Jno. N. Young,
Jno. H. Coleman and Thos. M. Young. Will proven 2 Jan. 1838.

25 Apr. 183_. Will of WILLIAM PITTS. Wife Sally; son Reuben
Griffin; son William Pitts; son Daniel Pitts; dau. Nelly Frasher;
son David Pitts; sons Jesse J., Thomas and John; children: William, Daniel, Nella, David, Reuben Griffin, Jesse J., Thomas
and John. Friend John Boult, Esq., exr. Wit: Meredith Griffin,
Henry Simpson and Canada Henderson. Will proven 2 June 1838.

12 Jan. 1838. Will of ELLIS CHEEK. Children: William Cheek,
Richard Cheek, Sally S___tell, Mary Rhodes, Jane Rhodes, Cassy
Farrow, Willis D. Cheek, Linney Riddle. Son Willis D. Cheek,
exr. Wit: Jas. B. Higgins, Saml. Mills and Benj. B. Higgins.
Will proven 17 Sept. 1838.

2 Mar. 1839. Will of EDWARD JONES. Bro. and sister Anderson
McAnderson and Elizabeth Jones. Bro. sole exr. Debts I owe:
John Cook and last physician's bill. Wit: Wm. Phillips, Rebecca
Y.? Hale and Clementina B. Phillips. Will proven 1 July 1839.

19 Mar. 1834. Will of JANE HAMILTON. Dau. Elizabeth Taylor;
son-in-law William Mills and my dau. Margarette Mills; dau.
Nancy McClintock; son John McClintock; in trust for Nancy Mc-
Clintock; grand-dau. Jane Taylor; grand-dau. Elizabeth Taylor;
(next part is faded beyond reading). Son John McClintock, exr.
Wit: Jno. Dean, Herbert Hutchinson and S.? Dean. Will proven
16 Apr. 1839.

14 Mar. 1836. Will of WILLIAM DUNLAP. Son Robert land in village
of Newberry; grandchildren: Sarah, William, Mary, Robert, Richard
and James and Sophia Dunlap, childred of my son John Dunlap;
dau. Nancy (in trust with Wm. W. Simpson, Henry C. Young and
Henry W. Garlington). dau. Margarett Dunlap; life est. of wife
Margarette Dunlap (entire page faded). Wife Margarette Dunlap
and friend John Garlington, Dr. John W. Simpson, Henry C. Young
and Henry W. Garlington, exrs. Wit: J. M. Fairborn, Wm. Dunn
and Jno. Godfrey. Will proven 29 June 1839.

30 Mar. 1833. Will of ROBERT MC NEESE. Wife Sarah; son Samuel;
dau. Susannah wife of John Milner; children or child of my dec'd
dau. Margarett Babb; son Richard; children of my dec'd son James;
dau. Agnes wife of Joshua Teague; dau. Sabra White. Friends
Joseph Babb and Jno. S. Lewis, exrs. Wit: David R. Dorroh, Jno.
Phillips and Elijah Saunders. Will proven 23 Jan. 1840.

2 Jan. 1839. Will of JOHN CUMMINGS. Nephew John Cummings son
of my bro. Thomas; nephew John Cummings son of my bro. James;
beloved sister Peggy Henderson; beloved sister Mary Youngblood;
niece Elizabeth dau. of my bro. James Cummings; niece Peggy
Simpson. Anthony F. Golding, exr. Wit: Benj. Williamson, Caroline
M. Golding and Christiana N. Golding. Will proven 28 Nov. 1839.

18 Feb. 1837. Will of BRYANT LEEK. Son Anthony G. Leek; land
to his exrs.; slaves also held in trust; dau. Sarah wife of
William Atwood; son James Leek; grandson William B. Leek son
of Burrell Leek; grandson Bryant Leek; grand-dau. Martha Leek;
son James to be trustee for grandchildren. Sons are to be exrs.
Wit: Willis Brown, Daniel Gates and John D. Williams. Will was

LEEK cont'd:
proven 19 Sept. 1839. Codicil attached. Signed by same wit.

31 May 1838. Will of JOHN CALHOUN. Grandsons: John A. Atkins
son of Polly Atkins, John A. Posey son of Matilda Posey and
John C. Calhoun son of Squire Calhoun; wife Sarah Calhoun and
children: Margaret wife of James Kinman and Clarissa the wife
of Hirum? Pitts, Lucinda wife of Barnes Walker, Kizziah wife
of Russell Briggs, Nancy wife of Washington Henderson, Harriett
Calhoun, Emaline Calhoun and Squire Calhoun (who is also exr.).
Wit: Barrington Avery, Jno. Phillips and Wm. F. Downs. Will
proven 17 Dec. 1838.

REST OF BOOK EMPTY. END OF BOOK.

VOL. A 1839-1862

30 Mar. 1833. Will of ROBERT MC NEES. Wife Sarah; dau. Susannah
wife of Jno. Milner; children of dec'd dau. Margaret Babb; son
Richard; children of dec'd son James; dau. Agnes wife of Joshua
Teague; dau. Sabra White. Joseph Babb and Jno. S. James, exrs.
(N. B. see page 277).

23 Sept. 1836. Will of WILLIAM THOMPSON. Beloved wife Jane;
children: Sarah Ann, Isabella, Elizabeth D., Nancy, Jane and
Mary. Wife Jane Thompson and John W. Perry, exrs. Wit: Jno.
H. Coleman, Allen Coleman and Wm. G. Coleman. Will proven 18
June 1840.

9 May 1840. Will of AMBROSE GARRETT. Wife Nancy; my children
(not named). Wife and friend Fountain Martin, exrs. Wit: Stephen
Garrett, Jesse Davis and Baesden Davis. Will proven 9 July 1840.

17 June 1840. Will of RACHEL OWINGS. Sister Nancy Childs and
her son Richard; bro. William Owings; mentions Granberry Willis
and John Garrett, Jr.; brothers: Wm., Richard, Archebald and
John Owings. Wit: B. K. Owings, James Owings and H. E. Owings.
Will proven 12 July 1840.

25 Aug. 1834. Will of MARTHA BOWLAN. Sons William H. and Albert
D.; daus. Elizabeth, Patsy and Matilda; two married daus. Nancy
and Polly. Son Wm. H. Bowlan and bro. William Green, exrs. Wit:
Elisha Watkins, Franklin Glenn and Jno. C. Watkins. Will proven
2 Nov. 1840.

4 Aug. 1837. Will of JOSEPH GOODGOINS. Wife and children (not
named). interest of Wm. Allen in sd lands, Wm. F. Downs, his
agent. Appoint Micajah Berry agent for business of est. Mentions
book acct's. Wit: Garland Lewis, Thomas Peden and Jonathan Downs.
Will proven 7 Dec. 1840.

13 Dec. 1839. Will of THOMAS MC CARLEY. Wife Martha; grandson
Thomas Augustus McCarley; son Alexander McCarley (also exr.).
Wit: C. Williams, Wm. and Alex. Powers. Will proven 23 Mar.
1840.

5 Aug. 1840. Will of WILLIAM AULD. Beloved wife Sarah E.; John
Garlington, trustee; my children. Wife is exr. Wit: Jno. Wm.
Simpson, Wm. M. Garlington and Richd. Denton. Will proven 11
Sept. 1840.

9 Nov. 1827. Will of ROBERT HAND. Wife Elizabeth; dau. Polley

HAND cont'd:
and her children: Sally, Polly, and Nancy Thomason, daus. of
Robert Thomason; son Robert Hand. Son Robert Hand and friend
Reuben Burditt, exrs. Wit: Archd. Young, Thos. Wright and E.
Young. Will proven 24 July 1840. 8 Oct. 1838. ROBERT HAND, SR.
codicil: Revokes exr'ship of Reuben Burditt and nominates wife
Elizabeth Hand. Wit: Jno. N. Young, Arch. Young and Thos. Wright.

31 Aug. 1838. Will of AVENT FULLER. Niece Rebecca A. Fuller;
John Friesan? Fuller, son of my niece Delphy Fuller. Delphy
Fuller and Henry O'Neal, exrs. Wit: Justinian Henderson, James
Leamon and Jas. P. Perry. Will proven 6 Sept. 1841.

(day and month?) 1840. Will of MARY VANCE. Son John; son James
W. Vance; son Joseph H. Vance; children: Samuel, Nathaniel,
Allen, David, John, James Washington, Joseph H., Frances Green,
and children of my dec'd son William. Joseph H. Vance, exr.
Wit: Jno. Watts, Elihu Alton? and J. W. Watts. Will proven 16
Nov. 1841.

26 Oct. 1841. Will of SARAH DOLLER. Dau. Susan Coley; my hus-
band, dec'd.; son William; rest of children: Reuben Doller,
Rhoda Begles?, Elizabeth Barker. Chas. G. Franks, exr. Wit:
J. D. Hopper*, Joshua Burns and Thos. Lewis. (*Joseph D. Hopper).
Will proven 18 Feb. 1842.

25 Jan. (year cut off). Will of JAMES DORROH. Son William M.
Dorroh; son David; daus. Margaret, Nancy and Martha; dau. Mary;
beloved wife Sarah; son Lewis C.. Wife and son David Dorroh,
exr. Wit: Jno. B. Simpson, Jane M. Todd and Saml. R. Todd. Will
proven 5 Mar. 1842.

11 Mar. 1839. Will of NATHAN BRAMBLE (BRAMBLETT?). Beloved wife
Elizabeth; Wm. M. Kennedy, Henry Bass and David Derroh, trustees;
Missionary Society of S. C. Conference, Methodist Episcopal
Church; (N. B. Most of his estate was appropriated for the use
of church and preachers, widows and orphans of preachers); four
Societies of the S. C. Conference. Thos. Brownlee and Wm. Hender-
son, exrs. Wit: D. Higgins, Jas. French and Jas. B. Higgins.
Codicil 11 Mar. 1839. Will proven 16 Mar. 1842.

1

Andw.Jr.,074, Andy,014,
186, Charity,266, D.,016,
023,028,068,073,091,092,
095,113,118,122,129,130,
142,144,164,206,209,212,
217,243, Dandy,239
ANDERSON, David,004,005,007,
016,019,022,023,025,029,
034,036,050,065,068,079,
080,089,104,109,114,127,
144,147,155,174,180,198,
215,258,260,269,270,275,
Dr.,217, Edw.,235,237,249,
257, Eli,107, Eliz.,088,
Elizabeth,088, Ephraim,051,
101
ANDERSON, G.,193, Gabriel,020,
Geo.,005,007,016,019,135,
158,162,167,169,194,195,
198,201,207,214,243,251,
259,267,275, George,002,
019,206,259,275, Guinn,231,
James,089,181,186,196,213,
241, Jas.,019,113,135,267,
Jno.,087, Joel,262,
Joel L.,207
ANDERSON, Joel L.,210,219,
251,269, Joel S.,222, Joel,
262,271,275, John,064,
Josiah,213, Killis,150,
L.W.,258, Lewis,088,266,
271, Lucy,088, Lydia,019,
Maria L.,158, Maria S.,169,
Molley,019, Molly Sr.,074,
Molly,022, Moses,264,266,
Ned,088
ANDERSON, Philip,072,088,
Polly,074,106, Rachel,033,
034,131,206, Reuben,088,
211,270, Robt.,017,034,
Saml.,017,019,036,051,076,
104,135,237, Saxon,109,
T.(?),270, Thomas,255,258,
Thos.,068,113,145,161,258,
Wade(Dr.),169, Wade,135,138
ANDERSON, Wade,157,158,275,
Walter,258, Watt,088, Wm.,
007,011,019,037,087,089,
093,098,101,135,150,195,
196, Wm.W.,258
ANDRES, Allen,198, Ephraim,
030, Ezekiel,045, Terrel,218
ANDRESS, Aberham,229, Absalum,
227, Allen,229, David,229,
Ferrel,227, Jno.,087, Mary,
251,253, Matilda,229,
Terrel,248,251, Thomas,249,
251,253, Thos.,229,248,
Tirel,186, Turel,253,
Turrel,229, Wm.,087
ANDREWS, Abraham,235, Absolum,
236, Allen,129,149,159,160,
198,217,235,261,264,267,
275, Andey,224, Andw.,207,
Andy,217,238,252,265,267,
272, E.,130, Edney,275,
Efrum,130, Elizabeth,125,
Ephraim,149,275, Ezek.,095,
Ezekiel,045,086, Francis,
160
ANDREWS, Leonard,130,149,
Teril,113, Terrel,069,235,
Thos.,237,243,248, William,
275, Wm.,160, Young,275,
Zezekal,137
ANDRUS, David,218
ANGLIN, Jno.,043, John W.,240,
John,038,039, Kerenhappcuh,
038, William,038, Wm.,039
ANSLEY, Jas.,189
ARCHABALD, Wm.,134
ARCHEBEL, Thos.,143
ARCHIBALD, Thos.,125,141
ARLING, James,162
ARMSTRONG, Cyntha,196, Eliz.,
096, Elizabeth,094,096,
Geo.B.,168, J.,172,261,
James,005,056,062, Jas.,
040, Jno.,040,100,101,102,
105,108,174,185,188,190,
191,235,264, Jno.H.,152,
John,005,017,056,064,072,
094,096,150,218,221, Jos.,

005
ARMSTRONG, Joseph,039,040,
Mary Ann,005, Masten,272,
Mr.,099, Rebekah,005,
Rhebeckah,005, Sarah,196,
Wm.,099
ARNAL, Zachariah,046
ARNALL, Joshua,004, Leanna,
004, Martha,004
ARNOLD, A.W.,235, Abraham,233,
Anderson,005,038,086,087,
089,102,218,274,276, Arthur,
126, Austin,147,214, Benj.,
013,117,146,147,148,221,
274, Eilus,221, Franklin,
272, Geo.,093, Hendrick,013,
034,221, Henry,187, Ira,013,
034,090,106,109
ARNOLD, Ira,118,127,147,148,
150,152,207,221,229,
James M.,184, James Mc.,
188, Jas.,221, Jefferson,
207,253,258,265,274,
Jeremiah,120, Jno.,207,
John,007,063,070,207,
Joshua,004, Lewis I.(?),
206, Lewis I.,263, Lewis,
195,253,258, Lucy,276
ARNOLD, Mary,013,086,089,102,
206, Nancy E.E.,206, Nancy,
013,094,117, R.B.,221,
Reuben,071,078,090,193,
206,218,247, Ruth,013,
Saml.,063,107, Sarah,206,
Silas,196, Silus,188,272,
Silys,232, Sims F.,166,
Titus,136,272,274, Willis,
189
ARNOLD, Wm.,010,013,034,051,
070,075,087,088,090,109,
113,117,133,146,150,164,
169,193,207,221,265,271,
Wm.A.,206, Wm.Anthony,206,
Z.,192, Zach.(Rev.),193,
Zach.,079,087,096,107,113,
120,158,173, Zachariah,051,
145,173,190,193,206,207,218
ARNOLD, Zachariah,263
ARNOLDS, Jos.,056
ARON, Casey Jr.,189
ARROWWOOD, Sarah,016
ASBERY, Wm.,257
ASBEY, William,257, Wm.,215
ASBY, Jno.,257
ASHBY, Wm.,233
ASHLEY, Eliz.,156, Jno.,155,
Jno.Jr.,156, John Jr.,148,
John Sr.,148, John,010,
012,033,063,106, Thos.,055,
Wm.,148,156,201
ASHLY, John,010
ASHMORE, Nathan,098
ASTEN, Alex.,101, Saml.,249,
Wm.,251
ASTIN, Alex.,262, Alexr.Sr.,
263, R.C.,261, Sarah,261
ASTON, David,012, Mrs.,219,
Wm.,252
ATCHESON, John,154, Jos.,154
ATCHISON, Saml.,133
ATEWAY, Jno.,161, Wm.,146
ATKINS, Allen,276, Benj.,092,
Elizabeth,008, Hillary,105,
John A.,278, Polly,278,
Thos.,082,095, Wm.,090
ATKINSON, Henry,020, John,020,
Mary,020, Wm.Alexr.,020
ATTAWAY, Chesley,180, Harley,
006, Isaac,180, Jas.,047,
Jesse,180, Jno.,040,081,
180,208, John Jr.,176,178,
180, John Sr.,178, John,006,
059,179,273, Mrs.,180, Wm.,
093
ATTEWAY, Elisha,122, Isaac,
169, Jesse,169, Jno.,205,258
ATTOWAY, E.,141, Isaac,169,
John Jr.,176, John Sr.,176
ATWOOD(?), John,071
ATWOOD, Ann,105, James,048,
058,066,099,101, Jas.,036,
077,079,109,110, Jas.Wm.,
051, Jno.,164,256, Jno.J.,

257, John,033,038,184,193,
Polly,099, Sarah,277,
William,099, Wm.,099,131,
160,185,187,190,191,195,
196,235,247,257,265,269,
272,277
AULD, Sarah E.,278, William,
278
AUSTEN, ,191, Jno.,131, John,
006, Nancy,144, Robt.,255,
Saml.,131, Samuel,191,
Thos.,243,255, Wm.,191,229
AUSTIN(?), Alexr.,084
AUSTIN, A.Sr.,270, Agnes(Mrs.),
187, Agnes,184,187,263, Ala,
221, Alex'r.,233, Alex.,080,
094,095,109,174,187,221,
238,249,251,252,261,263,
264,272, Alexander,185,260,
261,263, Alexd.,140, Alexr.,
080,101,130,157,184,187,
194,197,198,215,222
AUSTIN, Alexr.,229,233,235,
263,264,267,270, Alexr.Sr.,
184,263, Caroline,187, Edw.,
133, Elex(?),187, Hareata(?),
184, Harriet(?),184,
Henerata,233, Henretta,187,
Henry,245, I.P.(?),263,
J.P.,263, James H.,263,
James,174,184,185,187,191
AUSTIN, James,194,215,233,
261, Jane,187,197, Janet H.,
184, Jas.,102,239,268,270,
Jno.,186,187,239,252,267,
269, Jno.Alexr.,191, John,
184,263, Matilda,109,
Matt E.,263, Nathl.,117,
Nelley,191, R.(Dr.),264,
R.C.(?),263, R.C.,233,261,
Robt.,184
AUSTIN, Robt.,187,194, Saml.,
101,129,140,184,187,247,
263,272, Samuel,191,194,
197,261,263, Sarah,184,261,
263, Thomas,191,194,233,
260, Thos.,077,185,223,233,
267,269, Vincent,265,
Walter,109, Widow,194,
William,197,221, Wm.,184,
187,198
AUSTIN, Wm.,205,233,238,239,
261,265,267,272,274,
Wm.Henry,191
AVARY, Barrington,266, Chas.,
266, Mathew,266
AVERS, Joel,261
AVERY, Barington,261, Barrington,
259,261,278, Elizabeth,261,
Jesse,259,260, Joel,188,
Jos.,026,261, Joseph,221,
233,234,259,261, Mathew,261,
William,261
BABB, Abner,007,026,221,272,
Ahaiel,040, Alsey,206,
James,057,166,188, Jno.,
163, Jno.Jr.,178, Jos.,092,
103,105,113,117,119,136,
171, Joseph,120,171,221,
228,261,277,278, Lettey,135,
137,141, Letty,149, Marey,
103,105, Margaret,278,
Margarett,277
BABB, Martin,126,166,233,
Mary,171, Mercer,027,
Nancy,240, Polley,120,
Polly,240, Rhoda,053,
Saml.,221, Sampson,241,
269, Samson,026,030,188,
Thomas,002,037,054,117,
119, Thos.,039,040,046,051,
065,092,103,105,120,135,
137,147,177,188
BABB, Thos.,206,248, Thos.Jr.,
117,119, William,135,136,
Wm.,117,118,119,120,137,
152,166,188,221,241,269,
Young Thos.,118
BAGNEL, Isaac,149
BAGNELL, Isaac,186,188,189,
John Sr.,195
BAGWELL(?), Jno.,265
BAILEY, ,191, A.,169, Abraham,

065,146, Absalom,118,
Absalum,144,252,254,
Absolum,065,254, Ann,006,
Austin,254, Beath(?),182,
Betsy,182, Catey,257,
Clark,220, Coleman,144,
146,252, Danl.,268, David,
006,006,008,040,189,273,
Eliz.,162
BAILEY, Elizabeth,246, Fanny,
169, Felden,261, Felix C.,
246, Isaac,007,009
BAILEY, James A.,252, James C.,
246, James J.,263,264,
James,006,029,041,052,065,
162,169,182,186,244,246,
252,258, Jas.,022,103,113,
146, Jas.M.,182, Jno.,122,
145,173,222,246,248,250,
251,254,269, Jno.D.,273,
John,006,074,220,252,263,
Jonathan,040
BAILEY, Jonathan,265, Jos.,
169, Levicey,006, Leviney,
182, Lewis M.,246, Lucey,
006, Lueasy,252, Luvi,246,
Maddison,182, Margaret,085,
Marjary,006, Martin,262,
Mary,006,020, Rebecah,244,
Saml.,169, Sarah Jr.,257,
Silas M.,246, Silus M.,162
BAILEY, Silus M.,182,246,
Silus,182,244,263, Susana,
182, Suse,246, William L.,
252, William,006,246,252,
Wineford,246, Winneford,
182,246, Wm.,007,016,027,
028,029,031,041,075,077,
091,102,118,120,182,248,
254, Wm.Jr.,075, Wm.Sr.,075,
Z.,019
BAILEY, Z.,085,165,169,270,
Z.Sr.,064, Zach,016, Zach.,
007,018,040,065,088,091,
092,106,188, Zach.Jr.,065,
075,077,146,169,185,188,
Zach.Sr.,144, Zachariah Jr.,
181,252, Zachariah Sr.,252,
Zachariah,006,007,008,021,
090,144,162,163,167
BAILEY, Zachariah,169,182,
219,233,246,254
BAILY, Absalom,151, Wm.,091,
151, Wm.Jr.,151
BAIN, James,157, Thos.,098
BAIR(ADAIR?), Alexr.,011
BAIRD, Mary,020
BAKER, Jno.,092, Jno.G.,235,
Linsey A.,221
BALD(BOLD?), Wm.,001
BALDEN, Jno.,156, Jos.,224
BALDIN, Joseph,220
BALDING, Jno.,232
BALDWIN, Benj.,256, Henry,215,
Isaac,105
BALEY(BAILEY), Coleman,169
BALEY, Clark,218, Elie,142,
Elizabeth,248, James,041,
Jas.,042, Jno.,073,099,
101,141, John,042,064,114,
Margaret D.,248, Nancy,248,
Robert,248, Samuel,248,
Thomas,248, William,248,
Wm.,041,042,099, Zach.,042,
064, Zachariah Jr.,12%
BALEY, Zachariah Jr.,151,
Zachariah,064
BALL, David,249, Geo.,054,
057,124,196,228,229, George,
058,109,111,226,227,229,
Gimiah,229, Hannah,200,
Henery,226, Henry,229,245,
252, James,052,066,124,168,
Jas.,109, Jemima,054,109,
Jemimah,195, Jeremiah,058,
103,156,168,200,201,215
BALL, Jeremiah,224, Jinney,
195, Jno.,133,160,191,196,
229,238, John,109,124,128,
150,159,168,169,184,195,
226,227,229,251,252,
Johnston,029, Jos.,252,
267, Joseph,226,227,229,

Lewis,052,058,063,064,106,
109,124,127,150,152,185,
195,203,205
BALL, Lewis,216,219,221,227,
229,238,250,252,264,267,
269,274, Lillian,052,053,
056,058, Marta(Martha),195,
Marten,215, Martha,195,
226,257, Martin,156,161,
166,168,169,197,200,201,
216,229,232,233,241,245,
268,269, Mathew,094,195,
Morten,214
BALL, Narcissa,120, Narsissy,
120, Netren,252, Permela,
052, Peter,052,054,124,168,
Raney,238, Reuben,168,200,
201,215,226,245,246,256,
Susana,226, Susanah,257,
Thomas,226, Thos.,103,
William,052,058,136,195,
229, Willis,216, Wm.,023,053
BALL, Wm.,056,060,094,099,
112,151,155, Wm.C.,111,
Wm.P.,140, Wm.Sr.,054
BALLENGER, Bat.,063
BALLING, John,234
BALLON, Mathew,167
BAMMOR, Hardeyman,228
BANDY, Wm.,212
BANEY, Bill K.,257
BANKS, Frank,195, Rachel,133
BANTON(?), Lewis,002,004
BANTON, Lewis Sr.,030, Lewis,
007,013,016,022
BARD, Wm.,018
BARDE, Thos.,020
BARDLEY, Bryson(?),072
BARDOE, James,150
BARKER, Abby,055, Aggy,055,
Catherine,055, Elizabeth,
279, James,055, Jesse,050,
055, John,055,221, Laurens,
050, Lawrence,012,055, Liza,
166, Margaret,050, Saml.,
221, Wm.,101,105,108,144,156
BARKSDALE, A.,082,159,171,
268, Allen,081,082,083,084,
104,107,108,116,159,216,
B.S.(Miss),218, Barbary G.,
249, Collar,106, Collier,
116, Collyer,107,159,216,
Colyar,082,083,084, Colyer,
109,115, Danl.,083, H.,264,
Higgerson,218, Jno.,083
BARKSDALE, Jno.,102,108,174,
John,082,216, Leanah,216,
Leanna,082, Martha,216,
Mary,082,083, Nancy,082,
122,216, Nathan,004,082,
083,107,108, Nathaniel,082,
216, Nathl.,082,108,159,
173, Polley,216, Saml.,100,
104,216, Samuel,081,082,100
BARKSDALE, Samuel,129,218,
249, Susannah,082, Wm.,009,
015,021,032,066,086,104
BARKSDIL, Collar,255, Jno.,
143
BARKSDILL, ,196, A.,220,
Alfred,212, Allen,153,205,
220,222,230, Barbary J.,239,
C.,200, Callar,£11, Cally,
196, Collar,241, Coller(?),
153, Collyar,211,220,
Collyer,241, Colyar,239,
Hickerson,132,250,255,
Hicksen,239, Higgsen,242,
Hikeson,168
BARKSDILL, James K.,245,
Jas.Kenedy,239, Jno.,160,
167,179,200,212, John,157,
220, Mary(Mrs.),151, Mathew,
220, Matt,212, Nancy L.,239,
Nancy,220,250, Nathan,220,
222, Nathl.,151,178,196,
220, Saml.,132,160,205,210,
220, Samuel,157
BARKSDLE(BARKSDALE?), N.,222
BARMORE, Hardiman,228, Peter,
082,113
BARNES, Zach.,052
BARNET, Saml.,044

BARNETT(?), Jno.,011
BARNETT, Elizabeth,130
BARON, James,151
BARRETT, Alfred,147,241, Byrd,
151, Joshua,103, Robt.,071
BARREY, Robt.C.,225
BARRON, James,151, Jas.A.,151
BARROS, John(Mrs.),237
BARROW, Jas.,124
BARTEN, Wm.,206
BARTEY, Jno.,143
BARTON, Alas(Alice),005,
Rebacker(?),005, Reuben,
058, Thomas,026, Wm.,207
BARUM, Willers,261
BASLEY, James,188
BASS, Henry,279
BASWELL, John,071
BATEY, James,054
BATH, Aberham,161
BATTEY, Jas.,061
BATTY, David,008
BATY, Chas.,173, Mary,011,
015, Moses,249
BAUGH, Agness,003, David,003,
Elizabeth,003, John Sr.,
009, John,003,063, Jonathan,
003, Margaret,003, Mary,003,
William,003
BAULDEN, Benj.,256
BAULL, Narsisey,119, Wm.,119
BAXTER, James,264, Jas.,267,
Wm.,140,269
BAYLEY, Absolum,227, Eliz.,
175, Silus,249
BAYLIS(?), Lewis,002
BEACHAM, Danl.,116,272
BEACHM, David S.,264
BEACHUM, Daniel S.,264, Danl.,
124, Danl.S.,157, James H.,
261
BEADEL, H.L.,220, Henry S.,
199
BEAKS, Francis,272
BEAL, David,276, Eean,275,
Even,233,276, John,276,
Mary,276, Polly,276,
Reason,276
BEALK, Francis,243
BEALY, Jno.,172
BEARD, Mary,020, William,020
BEARDEN, Eli,268, Matilda,268
BEASLEY(?), Thos.Y.,163
BEASLEY, Jno.,108,160,207,
211, John C.,216,219, John,
038,050,057,124,264,269,
Levi(?),264, Lewis,215,
Ransom,264, Thomas,241,
Thos.,048,060,063,076,079,
086,110, Wm.,206,215
BEASSLEY, Chainey,023,
Jene(Jean),023, John,023,
Nancy,023
BEATTY, Moses,267
BEATY, James,158, Moses,249,
267
BEAVENS, Wm.L.,184
BEAVERS, Jinny,185
BEAVOURS, Saml.,186
BEAZLEY, David,006, Wm.,031
BECHUM, T.S.Jr.,264
BECK(?), Frank,192
BECK, Frances,176, Frank,195,
Henry P.,174, Saml.,253
BECKNEL, Thos.,190
BEECHAM, Danl.,187
BEECHUM, Danl.,120,131,157,
185,229, Danl.G.,261, Henry,
157,185, Isaac,144, Jas.H.,
261, Saml.,131, W.,133
BEEDLE, Thos.,034
BEEKEBORGER, Jno.,235
BEEKS, Frances,227,229,
Francis,231, Saml.,229,
248, Samuel,227
BEESLEY, Betsey,231, John,224,
Thomas,231
BEEZLEY, Jonathan,019
BEGLES(?), Rhoda,279
BEGLEY, Thos.,162
BEHAM, Willis,241
BELCHER, Frances,157
BELEC(?), Martha,119

3

BELL(?), J.W.,170
BELL(BALL?), Wm.,018
BELL, A.G.,265, Adam,006,020,
  054,055,162,276, Danl.,269,
  David,030,031,054,113,117,
  125,128,132,135,142,151,
  235,236,237,250,276, Dr.,
  128, Eliz.,054, Ester,054,
  Evan,220, Even,161,191,
  256,258, Hannah,060,
  Isabela,054, Isabella,006,
  022
BELL, James Jr.,162, James M.,
  246, James,005,021,026,031,
  054,129,162,163,192,201,
  Jas.,096,129, Jesse,257,
  Jno.,079,101,211,245,256,
  John Jr.,186, John,036,
  048,054,056,162,182,217,
  276, Marey,054,055,130,
  Martha,244, Mary,054,
  Raber,218
BELL, Reason,257, Richard,006,
  020,022,030, Robert J.,276,
  Robert,006,022,030,162,
  206, Robt.,054,123,168,194,
  259,271, Ruth Ann,244,
  Samuel,208, Sarah,129,162,
  244,245, Sary,232, Susan,
  245, Susana,162, Thos.,218,
  Wm.,151,213
BELT, Jno.Jr.,179
BELTON, Jesse,076, Josey,215,
  Richard,240, William,214,
  215, Wm.,215
BEMARE, Peter,162
BENHAM, Elizabeth,201, Lewis,
  233, Willia,241, Willis,241,
  268, Wm.,166
BENJAMAN, James,207
BENJAMIN, Jno.,236, Wolf,180,
  Wolff,239, Woolf,202
BENNET, Delia,210, Henry,211,
  215, Horice,241, Jno.F.,259,
  John,020,072, Joseph,049,
  Micagah,249, Miles,266,
  Richard,136,239, Sarah Ann(Mrs.),
  210, Sarah,047,241,251,
  Sarahan,230
BENNETT, Alfred,241, Anna,136,
  Jennette,136, Jno.,137,
  274, Jno.B.,136,139, Jno.D.,
  272, John,088, Miles,136,
  Richard,137, Richd.,055,
  061,136, Sarah Ann,231,
  Sarah,136,137, Wm.,212
BENNIUM, John,235
BENSON, Wm.,151
BERD, Thos.,020, Widow,020
BERK, Martin,118
BERNET, Jno.B.,224
BERREY, Jno.,190
BERRY, Edey,056, Geo.,002,
  012,046,047,050,056, George,
  006,045,059, Hudson,013,
  Hutson(Hudson),005, James,
  188, Mary,004, Micajah,194,
  278, Thos.,047, Usley,006,
  William,045,057, Wm.,006,
  045,047,056, Wm.Sr.,050
BET--(?), Bev.,111
BETEY, Moses,210
BETTEY, Flemon,220, James,224
BETTY, Moses,211
BEVARD(?), Thos.,044
BEVIS, Orzel,043
BEVOURS, Saml.,188
BIGGS, John,011
BILLUPS, Wm.,063
BINGHAM, Robt.,137
BINNION, Willis,187
BIRD, Benj.,098,102,103,121,
  160,181, Benjamin,222,
  George,222, J.H.,206, Jno.,
  146, Jno.H.,236, John,206,
  Leah,222, Mary,222,
  Purnall J.,222, Purral J.,
  222, Purrall J.,222, Sarah,
  222, William,151, Wm.,098,
  236, Wm.D.,222
BISHOP, Benj.,215, David,062,
  John,054, Joshua,043,
  Nathan,161,169, Saml.,010,

011,021, Samuel,054,165,
  Thos.,224, Verlinda,054,
  165, Wm,165, Wm.,043,055
BLACH, Jno.B.,261
BLACK(?), Aaron,074
BLACK, Agatha,258, B.B.,126,
  Benj.,264, Cresa,258,
  David,193, F.F.,264,
  Franson,258, Hariet,258,
  Harriet W.,264, Harrison,
  222, J.,105, James,047,267,
  Jane,047,163, Jno.,088,
  095,098,101,103,104,105,
  111,112,115,120,125,126,
  129,157,167
BLACK, Jno.,174,178,179,183,
  185,189,193,194,241,242,
  246,253,254,258,264,270,
  271,272, Jno.B.,270, Jno.C.,
  235, Jno.G.,236, John B.,
  260, John Blair,258, John,
  030,051,062,066,073,091,
  110,124,127,129,176,191,
  194,197,239,258,263, Richd.,
  258
BLACK, Richd.Oscar,264,
  Robert,029, Robt.,014,198,
  Sarah C.,258,264,270,
  Sarah,261, Thos.,008,
  Trenmon F.,258, W.E.,264,
  William,260, Wm.,062,102,
  124,127,142,152,177,179,
  185,193,258, Wm.E.,247,263,
  266,271, Wm.Ewell,258
BLACKABY, Benj.,263
BLACKBURN, Eliz.,275, James,
  160,199,209,210,211,254,
  255,267, Jas.,221,276, Jno.,
  036, Stephen,209, Thos.,232,
  Wm.,006,224,265
BLACKBURNE, James,254
BLACKEBY, Benj.,261, Jos.,034,
  068,089
BLACKELY, Benj.,261, Jas.,270
BLACKERBY, Wm.,129
BLACKERLY, Jos.,269
BLACKEY, Josiah Sr.,051
BLACKLEY, Thos.,236
BLACKSTOCK, Jno.,115,118,188,
  247, John,071, Wm.,118,151
BLACKWELL, Alfred,231,234,
  237,239,242, Caroline,234,
  David,234,237,239, Eliz.,
  234,237, Hanah,234, Hannah,
  238, Isabella,125, J.,269,
  James,234,237,242, Jas.A.,
  268, Joel,234,237, John,012,
  044, Jos.,222, Josiah,012,
  042, Margret C.,238
BLACKWELL, Margret,125,234,
  237,243, Nancey,234, Nancy,
  237, Pleasant,071, Rebacha,
  237, Rebeca,234, Richard,
  108,234,237,238,239, Richd.,
  094,100,114,119,128,186,
  222, Susanah F.,234,238
BLADON, Jno.,144
BLAKE(?), Jno.,089
BLAKE, Jane,163, Jannete,038,
  Jenet,038, Jno.,095, John,
  018,038, Oser,253, Robert,
  038, Robt.,018
BLAKELEY, Chas.,273, James,
  266, Jno.,128, Jonathan,273,
  N.(Wid.),273, Thomas,123,
  Thos.Sr.,123, Wm.,123
BLAKELY, Agnes,276, Benj.,031,
  194,211,260, Catharine,276,
  Charles,258, Chas.,138,
  195,219,230, David,230,
  George,276, Ginny,090, J.,
  174, James F.,176,178,
  James,027,041,066,145,151,
  152,161,178,180,224,232,
  237,250,252,276, Jas.,076,
  084
BLAKELY, Jas.,098,124,142,
  146,183,237, Jas.F.,273,
  Jas.Sr.,141,273, Jesse,160,
  Jno.(Capt.),235, Jno.,097,
  098,117,141,145,151,159,
  178,183,187,205,211,231,
  239,248,250,251,256,257,

268,275, John,068,071,134,
  147,149,150,154,157,172,193
BLAKELY, John,196,197,218,
  258, Jonathan,058,065,074,
  091,243,276, Jos.,076,087,
  088,098,179, Joseph,033,
  087, Margret,258, Martha,
  098,276, Mathew,178,196,
  197, Matthew,276, Nancy,276,
  Nathen,168, Robert,108,
  216, Robt.,146,152,178,195,
  230
BLAKELY, Robt.,243,250,265,
  273, Samuel,258, Sarah,276,
  T.,174, Thomas Jr.,258,
  Thomas Sr.,258,259, Thomas,
  152,195,258,276, Thos.,151,
  176,178,189,197,205,211,
  230,235,237,265,268,
  Thos.Jr.,122, Thos.Sr.,122,
  W.,174, William,159,216,276
BLAKELY, Wm.,029,064,074,104,
  117,134,137,143,153,157,
  171,182,189,197,231,235,
  237,243,246,246,250,254,
  259,263,271,273, Wm.Jr.,230,
  232,243,245, Wm.S.,268,
  Wm.Sr.,182,230,243,245
BLAKLEY, James A.,236, Jno.,
  237, Robt.,130,236, Wm.,236
BLANE, Danl.,007
BLANKELY, Jas.,141
BLANKENSHIP, Wm.,274
BLANKS, Robt.,167
BLEW, Hosa,136
BOAZMAN, Wm.,267
BOBBO, A.P.,274
BOBO, Aaron,109, Absalom,004,
  042,089, Absalum,258, Amey,
  089, Andrew,210, Burrel,042,
  Burrum,186, Chany,109,
  Elizabeth,224, Foster,258,
  Geo.,258, Hendrik,210,
  Kindred,061, Lewis,224,
  Mr.,061, P.,206, Pinckney,
  236, Sampson,011,258,
  Solomon,098
BOBO, Solomon,188,224,
  Spencer,164, Stephen,047,
  Timon,122, W.J.,265,
  Willis,258, Wm.,164,258,265
BOC, Jonah,113
BOHANNON, A.,132
BOHANNOR, Jno.,045
BOLAND, Adam,167, Catharine,
  200, Jacob,168, Jane,135,
  Saml.,148, William,164
BOLDEN, Jno.,120, John,150
BOLDON, Marey,135
BOLEN, James,022, Jean,022
BOLING, Abel,002, Henry F.,
  166, John,042,233, Robert,
  194, Thornbury,067, Tully,
  090, Valentine,151
BOLLING, Abie,067, J.N.,241,
  John,067, Lucinda,067,
  Polley,067, Polly,067,
  Robert,067, Robt.,241,
  Saml.,007,026,067,241,
  Samuel,067,194,241,
  Thornberry,194, Thornbury,
  067, Tulley,067,241, Tully,
BOLT, Aberham,135,163,252,
  261, Abraham,005,032,078,
  084,120,121,134,171,229,
  Abrha.,101, Abrum,054,
  Aron,213, Edmond,118, J.,
  124, Jas.,102, Jno.,178,
  228,237, Jno.Jr.,213, John,
  013,072,123,133,213, Lewis,
  013, Margaret,032, N.B.,100,
  Nancy,073
BOLT, Peggy,013, Polly,013,
  Robert,032, Robt.,026,
  Robt.Jr.,013, Sally,013,
  W.P.,096, Wm.,100,116,229,
  231, Wm.P.,100
BOLTON, Jesse,065, Jno.,242,
  Jos.,061,067,069,076,083,
  087, Mathew,069,083,137,
  Matt.,095,113, Matthew,097,
  Richard,240, Wm.,113
BOMMAY(?), Elenor,156

4

BOND, Adam,167, James,014,
235, Jno.,273, Patty,027
BONDS, Ann,227, Calvin,129,
Caroline,227, Dudley,028,
Eliz.,069, Elizabeth,069,
Henry,227, James,129,130,
Jas.,119,120,146, Jesse,
129, Jno.,211, John,061,
069,129,130, Mary,227,
Rhode,129, Richard,129,
158, Richd.,120,130,131,
163,167
BONDS, Richd.,186,192,197,
210,211,223,241,252,262,
Wm.,069,084,096,128,166
BONE, Chesley,243, Willard,
222, William,223, Wm.,243
BONHAM, Arnold,132
BONHUM, Rebecah,127
BONNER, ,012, Jos.,009,013,
Wm.,232
BONTT, Asa,274
BOOK, James,207
BOOM, Wm.C.,264
BOON, Willard,261
BOOZER, Henry,183
BORLAND, Wm.,040
BORLING(?), Geo.,127
BOSEMAN, Jno.,167
BOSLEY, John,134
BOSTICK, Littleberry,019,
Stephen,039
BOULAND, (Will),127, Charlot,
127, Charlota,133, James,
127, Jane,127, Jno.,168,
254,270, John,127,128,175,
234, Martha,164, Mary,127,
Robt.,127,128, Sarah,127,
Thomas,127,133,135,
William,173, Wm.(Son?),127,
Wm.,133,135
BOULING, Miss(?),148, Robt.,
105, Samuel,241, Thos.,270
BOULT, Asa,266, John,277, Wm.,
266, Wm.P.,268
BOURLAND, Andrew,044, James,
045, Jas.,044, John,043,
044,045,054, Marey,044,045,
Wm.,020,045,056, Wm.Sr.,
044,231
BOURLANDE, Wm.,003
BOWEN, Geo.,173,174,235,268,
George,127, Jacob,201,
John,010, Nancy,002,
Rebeca,140, Rolley,010,
Rolly R.,002, Rolly,013,
Wm.,013,031,058,173
BOWES, Jas.,043
BOWIN, Saml.,151
BOWING, Geo.,149,167,169,214,
235,239,250,265, Wm.,201
BOWLAN, Albert D.,278,
Elizabeth,278, Martha,278,
Matilda,278, Mrs.,174,
Nancy,278, Patsy,278,
Polly,278, William,174,
Wm.,087, Wm.H.,278
BOWLAND, Berrey,221, Charlotte,
132, John,051,054, Lettice,
244, Thos.,132, Wm.,132,
202,246
BOWLDING, Charlotte,135
BOWLE, Jacob,225
BOWLIN, Josiah N.,270
BOWLING, Henry R.,198, James,
187, Jno.,043,211,265, John,
026,194, Josiah N.,238,
Nathan B.,128, Robt.,126,
Sam.,187, Samuel,070,194,
Thornebury,126,238, Tulley,
221, Tully,109,194,274, Wm.,
087
BOWLLING, Abigail,194, John,
194
BOWMAN, Jacob,019
BOX, Abraham,071,133, Austin,
252, Benjamin,133, Charles,
215, Chas.,093, Hennery,033,
043, Henry,012,036,067,068,
069,071,092, Isaac,267,
Jacob,042,071, James,012,
Jas.,042, Jemiah,132, John,
020,044,132,134

BOX, Jos.,071,075,083,094,
Joseph,014,115,270, Josiah,
082,087,095,115,118,145,
270, Luisa,132, Michael,015,
Nancy,092, Rachel,132,
Robert,133, Robt.,071,253,
Shadrick,133
BOYC, Jas.,095
BOYCE, ,125, D.,128, David,
072,123,127,133,137,159,
195, Drurey,221, Drury G.,
218, Drury,007,026,072,094,
163,166,182,184,192,218,
219,221,227,232,270,
Elizabeth,079,093, Geo.,
164, J.,078,184, James M.,
218, James,007,051,052,053,
057,059
BOYCE, James,062,064, Jas.,
146, Jesse,007, Jno.,168,
170,175,181,183,199,241,
244,245,249,264,267, Jno.F.,
222, John,007,068,071,075,
076,078,079,087,093,188,
198,199,213,221,264, Mary,
219,227,232, Nancy C.,218,
Polley C.,218, Saml.,164
BOYCE, Thomas,007,013,014,
018,021, Thos.F.,007,016,
William,192, Wm.,006,221
BOYD, Abigail,106,108,
Abraham,098,248, Abrhm.,
099, Agess,045, Benj.,199,
David,163,176,204,210,211,
218,226, Eliott(Miss),247,
Elizabeth,246, Isaac Dial,
130, Isaac P.,236,248,252,
253, Isaac,222, Isabella,
264, J.A.,124, J.D.,270,
J.H.,273
BOYD, James,025,065,066,106,
108,125,130,147,160,163,
166,174,175,178,179,194,
195,203,204,229,246,252,
253, Jane,263,264, Jas.,102,
108,128,131,132,134,146,
270, Jas.H.,264, Jean,263,
Jno.(Capt.),109,187, Jno.,
034,043,094,095,101,108,137
BOYD, Jno.,142,155,185,187,
207,212,239,242,270, Jno.D.,
141,170, Jno.Sr.,238, Jo.,
253, John D.,132,155,201,
213,245,247, John H.,213,
John Sr.,206, John,007,
016,037,039,045,048,049,
057,073,201,213,220,260,
262,263,264, Laird,034,
Lard(Laird),034
BOYD, Luray,247, Nancy,034,
Peter H.,216, Purcivell J.,
237, Robt.,096,163,222,
Saml.,055,066,101,102,105,
106,108,141,151,152,236,
264, Samuel,155, Saray,094,
Susan(Mrs.),269, Susan,247,
T.D.,114, Wilson(?),094,
Wm.,014,055,101,176,177
BOYD, Wm.,200,204,237,248
BOYES, Wm.,221
BOYSE, John,156
BOZAMEN, David C.,235
BRACKMAN, Henry,184
BRADBERRY, Thos.,020
BRADDOCK, Francis,060,
Stephen,241
BRADEN, Betsey,143, David,018,
068,095,097,107,113,143,
145, Isaac,143,145, Isack,
143, Jno.,145, Margaret,069,
Margret,143, Peggey,143,
Polley Ann,143, Reuben,143,
145, Sary,143, Susan,143,
Thos.,070, William,143,
Wm.,107,113,117,143
BRADEN, Wm.,145,186
BRADEY, Andrew,066, Geo.,078
BRADFORD, Chas.,006, Robt.,
034
BRADLEY, Cornelius,212, David,
076,077, Eliz.,077, Iscm,
061, Jane,077, Jesse,211,
Jno.,165, John,061, Nancy,

077
BRADOCKS, James,197
BRADON, David,041, Isaac,137,
Wm.,176,186,258
BRADY, Alex.,041, Alexr.,052,
Charles,052, Chas.,052,
Geo.,052, James,168, John,
041,052, Wm.,052
BRAGG, Catherine,094, Daniel,
092, Danl.,075, Eliz.,094,
Elizabeth,092, Rody,094,
Zebulon,094
BRAGNEL, Isaac,160,164
BRAMBLE, Elizabeth,279,
Nathan,279, Reuben,256
BRAMBLET, Aberham,228, Enock,
228, Garnet,186, Harris,228,
Jas.,256, Larkin,228,
Lewis,222,232,256, Nathan,
225,274, Reuben,082, Wm.,
044,196
BRAMBLETT(?), Nathan,279
BRAMBLETT, Jas.,249,266,
Larkin,197, Nathan,208,
Wm.,197
BRAMLETT, Ambrose,117, Nathl.,
094, Reuben,103
BRANDON, Thomas,008
BRANES(?), Margaret,063
BRANNON, James,171
BRATCHER, Saml.,009
BRAXTEN, Wm.,194
BRAXTER, James,252,259,261,
Wm.,187,245,261
BRAXTON, James,187, Wm.,140,
202,206,214
BRAY, Benj.,040
BRAZEAL, E.,270
BRAZEALE, Ruth,270
BRAZELE, Enock,234
BRAZILE, Enock,227, Ruth,227
BREADY, Chas.,052, Elinor,052
BREAZEAL, Enoch,181,185,
Rutha,181
BREAZEALE, Caroline,181,
Rutha,233
BREAZELL, Enock,234
BREWTON, Geo.,094, Jno.,094
BRIANT, Patrick,015
BRIFFEN, R.F.,253
BRIGGS, Isaac,265, Jesse,221,
Jno.,086,139, John,086,
Kizziah,278, Russell,278,
Wm.,139
BRIGHS, Jesse,164
BRIGHT, James,001, Wm.,088,
239
BRIGS, Saml.,224
BRION, Henery,144, Meredith,
144, Sarah,144, Whitfield,
144
BRIRE, Wm.,180
BRISON, Hunter,198, James,023,
Jane,023, Jas.,098, Jno.,
098, John,023,062, Robert,
023, Sarah,023, Wm.,023,171
BRITON, Jno.,092, Joseph,028
BROADY, Alexr.,043
BROCK(BROOK?), John,222
BROCK, Charles,222, Chas.,079,
253,267,269, Chas.Jr.,253,
Chas.Sr.,253, Elias,105,
109,128,207,217,222,
Fanny J.,273, Geo.,041,
098, Jacob,222,244,257,266,
James,222, Jno.,244, Robt.,
236, Susanah,222, Thos.,076,
079,092,097,109, Wm.,273
BROCKMAN, Amelia(?),028,
Amelia,063, Emily,028,
Henery,045, Henry,028,038,
063,077,104,232, J.,093,
John,002,005,009,010,013,
028,031,063, Wm.,063
BRONLER, George,148
BRONN, Benj.,261
BROOK, (Mrs.),242, Benjamin,
262, Charles,129, Chas.,177,
180,211,217,220, Chas.Jr.,
234,238,239, Chas.Sr.,222,
Elias,125,175,178,212,215,
218,220, Frances,116,
Hannah,125,228, James,220,

Wm.,156
BROOKS, Aaron,264, B.,036,
262, Bartla,255, Bartlet,
036, Bartlett Jr.,174,
Bartlett,037,270, Bartley,
033,035,050,051,059,
Bluford,096, Chas.,094,
David,166,193,203,218,253,
261, Elisha,099,247,
Frankey,156, Hannah,237,
Jacob,217, John,247
BROOKS, Mariah,262, Miecas(?),
176, Mrs.,262, Richd.,101,
Saml.,170,246, Sampson,243,
Sarah,204, Stanmore,236,
247, Ursala,257, Ursaly,262,
Ursla,255, Ursula,051,
Uslay,270, Usley,059,262,
Usyola,216, Wm.,055,262
BROUGH, Alex.Rodger,014
BROWLEE, G.W.,274
BROWN, Aaron,117, Abby,187,
Alex.,085,105, Allimon(?),
058, Anderson,146,161,208,
233,256,257,258,274, Andrew,
122, Andw.,133,256, Anne,
208, Anney,177, Bailey,149,
Bard R.,096, Benj.,029,
050,061,072,085,086,110,
182,186,205,228,243,246
BROWN, Benj.,250,254,261,270,
Benjamin,246, Bexey,208,
Bexy,177, Brexey,177,
Clabourn,037,041,046,048,
Claybourn,022,047, David,
079,134,146,151, Efron,117,
Eliz.,085,149, Ellender,
109, Esq.,021, Fanney,177,
Fielder,109, Fielding,085
BROWN, Foley,205, Francess,
116, Geney,177, Geo.,040,
046,048,051,185, Ginney,177,
Harling,169,208, Harrey,
151, Harrison,258, Isaac,
028,201, J.A.(Dr.),027,
J.R.,001,022, Jacob R.,027,
039,054, Jacob,028,093,232,
James,027,029,059,065
BROWN, James,072,086,149,150,
159,172,180,184,185,204,
206,208,218,224,236,243,
270, Jane,149,172,272, Jas.,
031,044,045,047,093,094,
098,102,269, Jeremiah,108,
Jesse,177,259,274, Jno.,
079,098,099,116,117,128,
131,146,151,160,167,173,174
BROWN, Jno.,179,180,203,211,
Jno.G.,235, John G.,231,
John,001,038,061,063,116,
206,208, Jones,224,225,
Jos.,058,074,093,104,115,
116,117,131,165,183,269,
274, Jose.,233, Joseph,028,
116,163,186,214,226, Joshua,
189,273, Judy,177, Levie,122
BROWN, Lyda,177, Mary,149,
177, Mathew,172,229, Matty,
177, Mrs.,062,208, Nancey,
208, Nancy,085,086, Nathan,
103, Nicholas,006, Nicklus,
208, Peby(Pheby),177,
Peggey,177, Peggy,149,
Polley,182,220, Polly,048,
Rachel,149,177,208, Rebaca,
177
BROWN, Rebecka,046, Rebeckah,
048, Richd.P.(?),266, Robt.,
040,048,189, Rodey,103,
Rodger,025,033,099,177,188
BROWN, Roger,004,015,020,049,
083,084,177,270, Ruth,085,
Salley,161,208, Sarah,256,
Spencer,040,081, Susan,208,
257, Susanah,161, Thos.,039,
104,229, Vinson,047, W.,
174, William,117,177,208,
Willis,101,247,273,277,
Wm.,007,022,025,028
BROWN, Wm.,050,051,063,066,
073,083,084,093,097,098,
099,101,103,104,123,149,
150,156,168,178,184,185,

203,204,233,254,270,272,
Wm.A.J.,261, Wm.Jr.,116,
Wm.Sr.,116
BROWNLEE, Easter,055, Esther,
206, G.W.,163,265, Geo.,109,
126,176,207,247,253,265,
James,188,206, Jno.,128,
267, Jos.,039,046,047,048,
052,055,057,099,105, Joseph,
037, Lucinda,199, Reuben,
248, Ruben,151, Saunders,
269, Thomas,199, Thos.,193
BROWNLEE, Thos.,239,279,
Thos.A.,143, Wm.,120,248,
262
BRUCE, Wm.,236, Zachariah,228,
252
BRUSTER, Henry P.,238, Hugh,
235,248, James,219,272,
Jas.,120,220,276, Jno.,120,
Louisa(?),120, Phebe,120
BRUTON(?), James,190
BRUTON, Geo.,092, Jno.,094
BRYANT, Jno.,096, Meredith,
036, Patrick,022, Wilson,007
BRYCE, John,025
BRYERS, M.,221
BRYON, Henry J.,226, Whitfred,
226
BRYONS, Jno.,137
BRYSON, Bethain,240, Bob,187,
Catharine,238, Elizabeth Ann,
258, Elizabeth,064, Henery,
120, Henry,114,240, Hunter,
114,120,140,203,214, James,
029,058,064,114,168,180,
218,230, Jane,064,114,229,
234,240, Janney,065, Jas.,
102,123,145, Jno.,132
BRYSON, Jno.,248, John,045,
046,064, Margaret,114,
Martha,045, Mary,114,214,
276, Mathew,120,203,221,
223,227,229,234,238,240,
263, Matt.,106, Matthew,114,
141,264,275, Philace,203,
Robert,114,135,214,227,
229, Robt.,064,071,120,131,
151
BRYSON, Robt.,160,199,203,
Saml.,250,264,271, Sarah,
064,227,229,240, Vinson,114,
Widow,269, William Sr.,234,
William,074,238, Wm.,029,
037,045,064,085,095,114,
164,177,187,198,199,203,
219,223,229,238,248,251,
254,261,264, Wm.G.,266,
Wm.Jr.,114
BRYSON, Wm.Jr.,194,234,
Wm.Sr.,065,114,115
BRYSONS, Wm.Sr.,065
BUCHANE, Willis,166
BUCKEL, Thos.,040
BUCKHANNON, Jane,053
BUCKNER, Philip,042
BUDD, Jno.,191, Thos.,185
BULGER, John,062
BULL, Thos.,248
BULLEN, Richd.,270
BULLER(?), A.G.,207
BULLOCK, Pinckney,264
BUMPASS, James,015,019,023,
030,032,054,065, Jas.,016,
Robt.,050,095
BUNTON, James E.,186
BURCHFIELD, Jos.,005, Rebacah,
144, Thos.,077
BURDITT, John,169, Reuben,279,
Reubin,169
BURGE, Wm.,199
BURGES, Jno.C.,248, Joel,210
BURGESS, Betsey,037, Elan,037,
Elen,037, Elihu,237,267,
Elijah,037, Elizabeth,016,
Ellen,055, Jenney,037,
Jno.,128,138,152, Jno.G.,
151, Joel Jr.,034, Joel Sr.,
034, Joel,019,027,036,037,
039,055,099,105,120,136,
166,193, John,037, May,015
BURGESS, Nelley,037, Rowland,
167, Rowling,037, Salley,

037, Thomas,037, Thos.,040,
Walker,034, Walter,037,
107, Wm.,008,037,040,055,
235,237
BURK, Benj.,249, James,047,
048,178,182,189,209,224,
226,255,264, Jas.,145, Jas.,
043,267, Levi,165, Lewis,
213, Martin,076,103,
Rebecca,047,048, Wm.,224
BURKE, J.,184, Jas.,274, Levi,
165,265
BURKES, John,037
BURKET, B.,182
BURKHALTER, Elizabeth,201
BURKS, Jas.,038
BURLAND, Wm.,011
BURN, Cristopher,237
BURNES(?), James,212
BURNES, James,131,255, Jas.,
034, John,024
BURNETT, Jno.,011
BURNS, Aaron,151, Allen,151,
212, Beufort,212, Bradock M.,
212, David,151, Francis,168,
Henry C.,173, James,101,
210,212, Jeremiah,159, Jno.,
228, Jorden,212, Jos.,151,
Joseph,212, Joshua,279,
Jurden,246, Kitt,212,
Laird,026, Mary,094
BURNS, Mary,209, Nancy,210,
212, Robt.,043,225
BURNSIDE, A.,059, Andrew,005,
017,067,090,181,202, Andrw.,
182, Andw.,177,205,242,243,
250, Ann Jane,177,181,202,
205, Ann,017, Anna,037,
Augustin,059, David L.,243,
David S.,250, David,250,
E.J.,264, Eliz.,017,
Elizabeth,177,181,202,204
BURNSIDE, Elizabeth,205, Geo.,
243, Geo.A.,250, George A.,
202, George,202,205,242,
Hanah,243, Hannah,017,177,
181,202,205,243,254,261,
J.,022, James,005,017,037,
040, Jane,017, Jas.,099,
Jas.Sr.,017, Jno.,101,131,
160, John E.,272, John,037
BURNSIDE, John,044, Marey,070,
182, Margaret,017, Martha,
017,177,181,202,205,253,
Mary,205,243,250, N.C.,223,
Nancey,070, Thomas,177,
181,182,202, Thos.,012,016,
017,019,035,037,042,051,
065,066,074,085,106,110,
111,117,125,135,141,142
BURNSIDE, Thos.,177,186,197,
W.,045,223, William,177,
202,205,243, Wm.,141, Wm.,
017,037,039,040,041,044,
046,049,051,058,060,064,
065,067,071,073,085,092,
098,099,111,114,141,151,
205,213,216,217,222,223,
236,237,242,250, Wm.F.,071,
254
BURNSIDES, Edw.,264, Thos.,
171, Wm.,229,263, Wm.F.,250
BURNY, Jno.,123
BURRELL, Z.,080
BURRESS, Jno.Jr.,211
BURREY, Wm.,122
BURROW(?), Henry,092
BURROW, Henery,146, Henry,201,
James,121, John,070
BURRUS, Wm.,225
BURTON, Allen,056, Amely,028,
Anna,033, Aron,246, Benj.,
033,034, Charles,212,213,
Chas.,098,105,270, Eliz.,
235, Elizabeth,213, H.,269,
Hirum,228, Hutchens,022,
Jacob,084, James,191,235,
Jas.,097,268, Jno.,084,
175,178,212,222,236,249
BURTON, Jno.,272, John,091,
193,212,213,243, Jos.,016,
020, Joshua,093, Judah,033,
Lillian,033,043, Rachel,

084,212, Reuben,081, Robert,
038,045, Robt.,028,031,033,
039,043, Saml.,033,043,
Sarah,038,045, Thomas,027,
033,034,043,212,213, Thos.,
029
BURTON, Thos.,046, William,
212, Wm.,005,081,086,136,
149,213,228,270, Wm.Jr.,269
BUSBEY, Burk,228, Jno.,202
BUSBY, James,221, Jno.,249,
Mecajah,264
BUSH, Geo.,008,011,015,
George,018
BUSY, Elias,220
BUTLAR, Thomas,192
BUTLER, A.G.,229, Anthony,120,
133, Betty,017, Chesley,150,
166,264, Henry,101, Hudson,
137,214, Hutsen,213, Hutson,
173, Jno.,087,213, John,005,
056,062,108, Jos.,273,
Joseph,157,224, Moses,037,
093, Richard,239, Richd.,
225, Samson,005
BUTLER, Thos.,259,267,
Thos.J.,264, Wm.,159,203
BUTTON(?), Dr.,035
BUZBEE, Lucy,264
BYN, Wm.,220
BYRAM, Jesse,034
BYRD, Benj.,015,026,061,068,
098,104,120,149,161,168,
178,183, Benjamin,158,222,
224, Eliz.,130, Elizabeth,
214,226, Geo.,224,265,267,
J.H.,236,256, Jane,120,
Jno.,155,159,174,195,
Jno.H.,161,169,187,274,
Jos.(?),226, P.J.,257,
Saml.,119
BYRD, W.D.,224, Wm.,015,102,
130,162,164,169,265, Wm.D.,
267
BYRUM, Jas.,041,042, Thos.,
042
BYSHOP(BISHOP), Boling,005
CABANESS, Elijah,156, Martha,
077
CABERNESS, Eliz.,086
CABINESS, Eliz.,154
CABNESS, Aime,156, Aimy,154,
Amey,154, Elijah,079,154,
Elizabeth,156
CAESAR, Free,116
CAHAFFEY, Hosa N.,229
CAHILL, Richd.,258
CAIN, Danl.,141, Free,253,
Jonathan,262, Mary,048,
Nathan,260, Silus,261
CAINE, Jas.M.,042, Jno.,043
CAISEY, Levy,001
CALAHAN, John,006,011
CALDWELL, David Jr.,123,
David R.,263, David Robt.,
194, David,009,014,034,050,
053,057,062,068,080,124,
128,129,131,235, Eliz.,046,
Geo.F.,194,198, Harriet(Mrs.),
237, James,002,054,056,057,
059,060,072,194,198,206,
258,263, Jas.,009,036
CALDWELL, Jas.,039,062,079,
096, Jno.,267, John G.,061,
068, John,049,050, Jos.,266,
Margret,191, Mary Ann,197,
Mary,059, Moses,019, Mrs.,
194, P.C.,194, Rebecca,059,
Robt.,044, S.,131, Saml.,
056,060,063,066,067,068,
072,101,159,198,253
CALDWELL, Saml.,261,264,267,
Samuel,063,072, Sarah,275,
William,197,275, Wm.,001,
019,036,059,062,066,090,
140,161,163,210,268,269,
271, Wm.E.,247
CALEMIES, F.F.,135
CALHOON, Anne,079, Cracey,079
CALHOUN, Emaline,278, Jno.,
151, John C.,278, John,278,
Sarah,278, Squire,274,278
CALLAGHAN, John,014

CALLAHAN, John,020
CALLUM, James,245
CALMES, F.F.,267
CALMOS, F.F.,210
CALWELL(?), F.F.,276
CALWELL, David,051, James,054,
Jas.,040
CAMBELL, Anguish,056, David,
177, Delyah,225, James,149
CAMMACK, Jas.,043
CAMMEL, Archbd.,102
CAMP, B.,016, Benj.,005,008,
016, Joseph,147, Nathan,013
CAMPBEAD, Abel,213
CAMPBELL, Abel,228, Amelia,
232, Anguish Jr.,148,
Anguish Sr.,062, Anguish,
025,031,036,042,046,056,
073,088,139, Angus Jr.,044,
Angus Sr.,067, Angus,002,
003,013,022,039,071,096,
097,118, Anthony,269, E.,
265, Elisha,189, Ephraim,
274, Green Lee B.,181
CAMPBELL, Greenlee B.,183,
J.F.,263, James,172,183,
188, Jas.,113,188, Jno.,260,
267, John,150, Jos.,184,
Lewellen,071, M.,046,
Milley,071, Pheabah,183,
Philip,169, Phillip,160,
Philup,188, Phips,247, R.,
083,234,258,276, Rebecah,183
CAMPBELL, Robert,071,097,
Robt.(Dr.),237, Robt.,071,
088,096,100,107,108,109,
111,118,132,139,140,148,
181,184,194,212,223,229,
233,241,253,256,263,
Robt.E.,271, Saml.,224,
Thos.,075,094,104,183,184,
205,232, Wm.,248, Wm.S.,213
CAMPBLE, Saml.T.,002
CANADA, Wm.,196
CANADY, Benaiah,117, Beneniah,
165, Elizabeth,251, Nancy,
251, Robt.,095, Roday,131,
Rodey,100,119,141, Rody,
108, Saml.,069, William,251
CANE, Danl.,171, Sarah,222
CANEDY, Rodey H.,113
CANNADY, Rody,098,103,152
CANNEDY, Rodah,083
CANNON, Burrell,157, Danl.,
273, Gideon,204,210,249,
260,262,267, James,174,266,
Jno.,212, Joel,146,
Nathaniel,006, Rebecca,004,
Richd.L.,192, Thos.,093,
Wm.,038,039
CANON, Jabuz,128
CARDES(?), Nancy,191
CARE, Sarah,025, Wm.,025
CARELISLE, Coleman,147
CARENTEN, David,272
CAREWILE, Zachariah,258
CAREY, Abner,258, Wm.,258
CARGILE, Danl.,157, John,066
CARGILL, Alford,252,256,272,
Charley,225,228, Chas.,104,
196, Cornelius,014,079,081,
086,111, Danl.,096,112,116,
185, Edw.F.,254, James,229,
Jno.,183,186,228, Jno.W.,
256, John A.,029, John W.,
188, John,007,017,026,029,
047,057,058,060
CARGILL, John,067,068, Lewis,
072,103,193,196,201,212,
221,224, Rachel,058, Thos.,
019,024,025,199
CARGLE, Lewis,156
CARLETON, Elender,195
CARLISLE, Coleman,102,103,
115,116,122,164,165,
Colemon,192, Eliz.B.,122,
Eliza L.,164, Gideon N.,
164, Gideon,192, Jas.G.,164,
Jas.J.,211, Jno.Abel,164,
Joanna Lewis,122, Jonna L.,
164, Sarah H.,164, Sarah,
164,208, Thos.A.,164, Wm.H.,
164

CARNEY, Jno.,043
CARNS, Saml.L.,119
CARPENTER, Jno.B.,258
CARR, Wm.,099
CARSLILE, Coleman,164,167,
F.F.,135, Gidion N.,167,
Sarah H.,167, Thos.A.,167,
168
CARSON, Wm.,018
CARSWELL(?), Coleman,108
CARTER(?), George,002
CARTER, Ann,016, Bailey,085,
Baley,100,107, Benj.,085,
Benjamin,005, Betsey,064,
203, Cornelius,153, Danl.,
203,219,240,254, Eliz.(Betsey),
175, Elizabeth,020,202,
Frankey,020, George,014,
016, Henry N.,205, J.,113,
James,154,175,207,261
CARTER, Jno.,081, Joel,040,
065,068,074,079,085,107,
169,248, John R.,205, John,
009,013,014,016,017,053,
084,085,086, Mary,025,
Nancy,175, Rachel,017,
Reuben,045,076,239,
Richard,175,205, Richd.,
014,099,162,165,177,202,
207, Robert,175
CARTER, Robert,177,202,205,
206, Robt.,014,017,104,128,
151,153,162,245,251,
Robt.Jr.,077,079,175,
Robt.Sr.,077, Thomas,153,
154, Thos.,027,185,247,265,
274, Wm.,017,029,044,050,
051,057,101,191,251,267,
268, Zebiah(Keziah?),053,
Zebiath,053
CARTER, Zimri,120,153,154,
238, Zimrie,202,207, Zimry,
025,175,177,205,227,251
CARWILE, Zach.,014,018,035
CARYTH(?), Jno.M.,123
CASA, Isaac,101
CASE, Anne,166, Anora,166,
Chas.,169, Isaac,036,083,
128,136,162,166,189, James,
211, Jonathan,211,218,
Reuben C.,131, Reuben G.,
232, Reuben,128,162,166,
Robt.,179, Thos.,105,176,
Willey,176
CASEY, Abner,042,043,048,
Aron,188, B.,088, Barbra,
233, E.,071, Elisha,008,
084, Henry,215, Jackson,274,
Jesse,189, Jno.,088,
Jno.A.,183, Moses,188,
Syntha,189, Thos.,076,101,
111,118,120,137,151, W.W.,
265
CASH, J.P.,242
CASHBURN, Wm.,085
CASON, Benj.,009,050,058,
Edmond,190, Edw.,264,
Giles,030,035,038, Isaac,
133, James,048,132, Jas.,
039,108, Jeremiah,201, John,
014,015,025,132,202, Jonah,
133, Jos.,048,051,074,120,
190,195, Joseph,160, Josha,
161, Josiah,120,131,133,158
CASON, Mary,132,134,202,204,
Nancy,132,201, Polley,250,
Rebecah,201, Saml.,132,
Samuel,202, Silas,025,
Thomas,021,033,201, Thos.,
001,004,018,051,061,132,
201,202, William,201,202,
Wm.,011,012,018,019,027,
132,133,201, Wm.Jr.,011
CASSEY, Nathan Sr.,220
CASTELS, Susannah,185, Wm.,
185
CATES, Wm.,266
CATINLINE, Rhoda,160
CATO, David,210, Jesse,032
CATON(?), Wm.,049
CAUDER, Wm.,174
CAULDWELL, David,007
CAYDON(?), Thomas,126

7

CELEY, Spencer,255
CELL, Wm.,224
CENNADA, Benches(?),165
CENNADAY, B.,252, Nancy,252,
W.,252, William,252
CENNADY, B.,165, Beneah,147,
Nancey,252, Rody,151, Wm.,
232
CENNARD, Robt.,248
CENNEDY, Benegah,233
CERGILL, James,252
CHALLAMES, Jas.,211
CHALMERS, A.W.,241, Dorothy,
241
CHAMBERS, A.W.,241, Alexr.(Dr.),
232, Alexr.,150, Andw.,211,
Dolley,232, Dorothy,232,
F.,241, Jane,214, Jno.,212
CHAMFRIED, Abt.,213
CHAMP, Robert,018
CHAMPBELL, John,215
CHANDLER(?), Ann,092
CHANDLER, ----,144, A.,149,
169, Asa,065,114,118,143,
169,173,185,188,201,205,
254, Ase,167, David,155,
Israel,166,167, Isral,162,
Joel,027, John II,205,
John,023,143,144,201,
Josha,036, Mary,143,144,
Polley,252, Sarah,252,
Wait,205, West,205
CHANDLER, Whit,169, Wiat,254,
Wiett,143, Wm.,117,232
CHANLER, Asa,092
CHANLETON, Danl.,023
CHAPELL, Jno.,251,268
CHAPMAN, Benj.,048,063,
Charles,150, Chas.,138,
Enoch,055, Jno.,112,120,
133,138,161,195,209, John,
150,158, L.,161, Levi,248,
Nathan,133, Thos.,080
CHAPNEL, Thos.,232
CHAPPEL, Jno.,158,187,245,247
CHAPPELL, Jno.,133,160,184,
191,195,196,249, John,150,
184,196,202,203,240,
Martha S.,196, Thos.,203
CHARDY, Ellis,145
CHARLES, Jas.,039, Jno.,039,
John,051,067,068, Margaret,
067, Tom,127
CHATWELL, Jas.,039
CHAYCE, William,192
CHAYCEE, Wm.,223
CHEAKE, Willis,075
CHEEK, Catherine C.,260,
Dillis(Willis?),148,
Dinsey,257, Drury,257,
Elias,044,081,094,136,141,
145,161,178,180,205,213,
214,215,231,233,256,258,
Elis,166, Elisha,047,
Eliss(?),004, Eliz.,018,
Elizabeth,022, Ellis,077,
092,104,107,159
CHEEK, Ellis,173,274,277,
Frances,201,208, J.A.,242,
James,208,242,260, Jas.,
043,107,272, Jno.,096,
Richard,277, Richd.,257,
274, Susannah,260, William,
277, Willis D.,277, Willis,
055,094,195,231, Wm.,008,
032,040,197
CHESER, H.,157
CHESHER, Benj.,151, H.,171,
174, Hezekiah,256
CHESHIR, Benj.B.,127
CHESHIRE, B.B.,100,126,127,
Benj.,085,101,103, H.,136,
Hezehiah(?),129, Hezekiah,
129
CHESIRE, Benj.,083
CHESURE, Alexd.,140, B.,140,
B.B.,140, Benj.,131,
Benj.B.,132, Benj.Jr.,261,
Benj.Sr.,261, Danl.S.,148,
Ezekiah,148,157,160,169,
H.,130,131,187, Hez.,131,
Hezekiah,152,157,236,253,
Jack(?) H.,131, O.,140,

Ob'h.,140, Sheldon,140,
Zachariah,157
CHESURE, Zachariah,254
CHEW, Samuel,032
CHILD, Rebeckah,111
CHILDERS, Jesse,016,059, Jno.,
131, John,059, Richard,059,
147, Richd.,221,223,
Richd.Sr.,218, Thos.,074,
136
CHILDRESS, Aberham,217,
Betsey,217, Fanney,217,
Haner,217, Jesse,086,087,
102,115, Jno.,117, John,002,
010,217, Lucey,217, Martha(?),
217, Marthew(?),217,
Melindey,217, Nancy,217,
Patsey,217, Peter,002,
Richard Jr.,217, Richard Sr.,
217
CHILDRESS, Richd.,220,255,
Richd.Jr.,218, Richd.Sr.,
218, Robt.,217, Sarah,217,
Thos.,115
CHILDS, James,009, Jonathan,
009, Nancy,278, Richard,278,
Thos.,100, Wm.,058,085,
110,112
CHILES, Judah,057, Wm.,057,
063,101,120
CHISHER, B.B.,270
CHISHIRE(?), Benj.B.,120
CHISM, Eligey,214, Elijah,075,
145, Ezekiel,102, Jas.,096,
Jno.,087,095,097,113,117,
145
CHISUM, Elisha,105, John,147,
Zach.,102
CHISURE, Philip,133
CHOICE, Sophia,194, Tully,067,
Wm.,007,067,070,188
CHRISTEN, Wm.,063
CHRISTIAN, John,087, Lewis,
087, Wm.,096
CHRISTMAN, M.M.,219
CHRISTOPHER, Amy,171, Ephraim,
172
CLARDEY, James,123, Mikel,137,
Polley,143, Susanah,123,125
CLARDY, Archd.,098, Chas.,051,
Eliz.,137, Isaac E.,231,
J.,095, J.E.,126, James Jr.,
239, James Sr.,239, James(Maj.),
237, James,020,023,024,051,
062,068,109,125,162,191,
206,239, Jas.,045,076,082,
095,097,098,105,116,118,
145, Jas.Jr.,113
CLARDY, Jesse E.,113,143,231,
238,239, Jesse,176,178,
Lucy,042, Mahala,239,
Michael,276, Mikel,222,
253, Mitchel,113,186,228,
229,239, Patsy,042, Sarah,
020, Susannah,100,109,
William,238,239, Wm.,113,
176,228
CLAREY, Henry,215, Sarah,015
CLARK, Allen,126, Drury,256,
Hirum,178, J.,094, James,
191,236, Jas.,096,268, Jno.
,152, Jno.,094,121,184,228,
266,268, Jno.R.,161, John,
272, Nancy,203, William,158,
Wm.,038,098,126,134,141,
146,155,158,160,161
CLAYTON, Wm.,094
CLE--, Harvy,169
CLEAR, Ransom,108
CLEAVELAND, B.F.,246, Benjamin F.,
246, H.,145,184,246, Henry,
243, Hervest,257, M.,246
CLEAVLAND, Harvey,172
CLELAND, Robt.,017
CLEMANS, Mary,122
CLEMENT, Reuben,176, Rubin,
235, Wm.,102
CLEMENTS, Reuben,163
CLEMMENS, Reuben,215, Ruben,
215
CLEMMONS, Fanney,079, Jacob,
079, James,053, Jas.,121
CLEMONS, Jacob,015, Jas.,019,

Jno.,099, John,122, Mary,
122
CLERKERSON(?), John,154
CLEVELAND, F.,194, Franklin,
176, Harvy,196, Henry,145,
190,208,254
CLEVLAN, Henry,230
CLIFTON, Brenchley,164,
Brinkley C.,269
CLIMENS, Jno.,260
CLIMES, Jno.,260
CLINK, ,201, Jno.E.,256
CLOFTON, David,070,073,085,
086, Eliz.,086, Jno.,167,
179, Priscilla,085,086,087
CLORE, Aaron,019,021,036,075,
076,077,082,094,097,119,
121,126,145,203, Aron,135,
139,197,239
COACHMAN, Wm.,124
COAL, Ison,214, John,001,027,
Nancy,214
COATS, Jehu,215,236, Jesse,
109, Jno.,042,172,222,234,
238,239,246,248, John,215,
217, Thos.,222
COB(COLB), Thos.,127
COB, James,168, Midleton,168
COBB, Anderson,208, Charles,
181, James,011,012,047,181,
Jas.,103,108,115, Jeremiah,
236, Jno.,212,253, John,181,
Lina,271, Mena Ann,074,
Middleton,275, Mideton,218,
Thomas,181, Tom,123,271,
W.L.(Free Negro),236, Wm.,
254,267
COCHRAN, Alex.,008, James,027,
Jno.,046, John,012,014,
016,021,027,052,070,073,
116, Margaret,014, Mary,116,
Nancy,014,116, Phebe,027
COCKHAM, Alex.,151
COCKRAN, Jacob,274, Timothy,
172
COCKRIM, Faney,190
COCKS(COX), Wm.,038,039
COFFEE, Eliza,223, Thos.(Dr.),
018
COFFEY, Alan,049
COGGANS, Johnston,111
COIL, Polley,152, Robt.,034
COINNE, Agnes,183, John,183
COKER(?), Robt.,185
COKER, Betsey,219, Bob,109,
Calvin,005,007, Carter,229,
Casandry,056, Drury,007,
056,080,081,219,270,
Elizabeth,273, Francis,081,
156, Garlington,103,256,
Harper,200,272, Henderson,
229,272, James G.,240,
James,156, Jas.,081,268,
John,002
COKER, John,007,010,056,255,
Jos.,081,103,156, Joseph,
007,219, Manisy(?),270,
Mary,007, Menice,219,
Milley,056, Mrs.,081, R.,
135,200, R.B.,272, Robert B.,
273, Robert,032, Robt.,002,
055,059,081,084,133,200,
221,229,255, Saxon,273,
Silas,156
COKER, Stanback,272, Standback,
241,272,273, Starback,229,
Thomas,272, Thos.,007,229,
Thurman,272
COLB, Lind.,127, Mary,171
COLBERTT, R.,214
COLCOCK, Chas.J.,089
COLE, David,096, Elizabeth,
273, Gabriel,212, Henry,117,
J.,105,117, James,086,
Jeremiah,152,237,248,
Jesse,098, Jno.,084,098,
111,259, John Sr.,017, John,
070,225, Jos.,063,084,248,
Marey,149, Mary,015,149,
267,275, Moses,079,112,201
COLE, Moses,202,269, Osborn,
259, Robt.,050, Solomon,042,
097, Terry,097, Wm.,071,

113,128,166,212,264
COLEMAN, Absalom,051,091,094,
Alfred,091, Allen,092,106,
262,267,272,278, Alsey,091,
267,269, Bailey,242,245,
249,254, Bartlett,274,
Deborah,091, J.H.,207,246,
Jno.,113,156,251, Jno.F.,
263, Jno.H.,139,237,261,
272,277,278, Jno.W.,203,
John C.,261
COLEMAN, John H.,200,238,
John,091, Larken,251,
Larkin,091,203,246, N.B.,
262, Polly,203, Robt.,157,
167,174,187,222,247,253,
264,269,274, Sarah,091,139,
William,139,200,203,238,
Wm.,007,034,037,058,091,
114,117,140,151,172,173,
Wm.G.,203
COLEMAN, Wm.G.,278
COLEMON, Larkin,233
COLES, Jno.,096
COLEY(CORLEY), Jas.,127
COLEY, Charles,119,120,
Honaretta,119,121, Honarita(?),
119, Jackson,119,234, James,
119, John,119, Joice,119,
Spencer,119, Susan,279
COLIER, Martha,215
COLLIER, Benj.,022, Jno.,185,
187
COLLIN, Martin,140
COLLINS, Chas.,041, Eliz.,144,
Elizabeth,257, F.F.,210,
Hamon,228, James,159,210,
Jas.,114, Jer.,063, Jere.,
109,113, Jeremiah,042,087,
089,118,135, Jerm.,104,
Jerry,228, William,172,173
COLLUMES, Jno.F.,249
COLMON, Allen,263
COLWELL, John,038
COMBS, Thos.,053
COMMER, Thos.,047
COMPTEN, James,274
COMPTON, Alford,272, Jno.,266,
John,266, Jos.,088,
Micajah,272, Nancy,272,
Polley,226, Wesley,272,
Wm.,169,276
CONALEY, Edw.,017
CONANT, B.,117, Burrel,098,
117, C.,117, Chesley,151,
220, Hardy,019,111,120,170,
Jer.,099, Jere.,112, Jerm.,
098,103, Nelley,117
CONE, Sarah,253
CONNANT, Allen,151, B.,117,
129, Burrel,152,160, Chas.,
152, Chesley,120,138,248,
Curtis,163, Eliz.,169,
Hardey C.,162, Hardey,145,
Hardy,029,040,065,169,
Jer.,111, Jeremiah,073,
Jerm.,103, Jno.,259, Thos.,
063
CONNELL, Polley,147
CONNENT, Burrel,151
CONNER, Danl.,128,212, Eloner,
212, Gideon,199, Isaac,211,
James,201, Jos.,041, Lewis,
135,210, Thos.,041, Uriah,
011,020
CONNOR, F.(Dr.),193, Geo.Jr.,
193, Jno.W.,193
COOK, A.B.,202, A.G.,264,
Abraham,116, Abram,043,
268, Anthony,261,272, Artis,
074,128,192,253,258, Caty,
017, Clayton,105, Cornelius Jr.,
146, Cornelius Sr.,146,
Cornelius,117,207,247,
Daniel,020,105,131,142,
148, Danl.,118,135,141,142
COOK, Danl.,145,151,167,171,
185, Elijah,092, Eliz.,265,
Eliza.,126, Franklin,184,
247,254,267,269, G.,255,
Geo(?),142, Geo.,202,255,
George,253, Henretta,201,
Isaac,012, J.,070,093,

James,008,017,023,035,037,
051,060,064,066,105,107
COOK, James,111,126,147,157,
177,197,203,205,218,219,
221,254, Jane,269, Jas.,009,
100,102,106,111,269, Jemima,
219, Jno.,079,080,082,117,
121,137,145,152,155,185,
190,245,265,269, John,036,
038,039,054,056,057,059,
062,064,065,066,069,070
COOK, John,073,074,076,081,
087,105,106,108,120,126,
148,154,155,184,218,220,
231,277, Jos.,080,101,221,
Maria,219, Mitchel,105,
107,111,115,142, Mitchell,
105,110,111, Mr.,088, Nancy,
117, Randal,015, Richd.,140,
S.R.(?),203, Saml.,116
COOK, Thos.,063,116,126,203,
Tobias,099,105,130,131,
142,148,160,181, Ursula,105,
219, Willie,250,257,269,
Wm.,131,155,187,203,205,
207,247,252,267, Wm.P.,266
COOKS, Jno.,228
COOKSEY, Wm.,273
COOPER, Amos,164, B.,100,
Benj.,097,113,258, Catherine,
262, Charles,099,101, David,
088, Eli,169, Eliz.Ann,099,
Elizabeth,199, Isaac W.,
215, Isaac,169,183,214,232,
259, Jacob,073, James,259,
Jno.,184,232, John,093,
Jonathan,225,259, Jos.,181
COOPER, Jos.,188,265, Josiah,
105, Lewis,201, Mary Amanda,
199, Mr.,071, Nancy,152,
167,214, Reuben,099,199,
201, Robt.,128,180, Saml.,
122, Sarah,099, Temple M.,
181, Wilson,271, Wm.,093,
117,176,178,230,253
COPELAN, John,218,222
COPELAND(?), John,073
COPELAND, Eliz.,200,218,
Elizabeth,276, James,186,
200,218,251,257,271, Jas.,
132,239,270, Jno.,045,085,
097,101,102,123,186,270,
John,051,066,073,074,138,
186, Margret,186, Nancy,154,
Saml.,199,209,218,239,262,
273, Samuel,208,249, Susan,
270
COPELAND, Wm.,132,150,170
COPELIN, Jno.,107, Wm.,108
COPLAND, Elenor,168, James,
182,189,252, Jas.,212, Jno.,
182, John,182, Saml.,182,
189,224,230, Wm.,177,188
COPLEN, John,137, Saml.,254
COPLIN, Jas.Park,135
COPLING, Jas.,138, Jno.,167,
Saml.,138
CORDER, Danl.,026
CORE, Joshua,224
CORGILL, Alfred,220, Chas.,
220, Jno.,222, John,224,
Lewis,220
CORKRUM, Elender,257
CORLEY(?), James,124
CORLEY, Elihu,141, James,127
CORNELIUS, Danl.,266
CORNWELL, Wm.,268
CORSLINE, James G.,218
COSON, Wm.,060
COSTEN, Henry,020
COSTIN, Henry,011
COTTERAL, Richd.,214
COTTRELL, Richd.,237
COTTRELL, Anna,274, R.,205,
Richard,205, Robt.,214
COUCH, Anna,078, Anny,078,
Beckey,223, Bevister(?),
103, David,061, Deliliah,
189, Drury,077,078,081,094,
098, Isaac,078,100,103,223,
225, Israel,079,100, Issac,
223, James R.,158, James,

161,172, Jas.,078, Jesse,
268,274, Jno.,116,169,249
COUCH, Jno.,268, Jno.G.,263,
Jobe,166, John,260, Jos.,
078, Joseph,077,078, Nancy,
077, Nathan,169, Nelly(Mrs.),
078, Saml.,100,225,252,
Samuel,223,224, Susana,223,
Susanah,223, Wm.,164,169
COUTH, Wm.,197
COWAN, Ann,187, Anna,188,
David,019,032,037,041,043,
087,094,102,116,185,186,
187,188, Frances,187,188,
James,187,221, Jane,248,
250, Jno.,155,173,185,187,
188, John,220, Leila,188,
Mirimen,257, Rebecah,187,
Thos.,256
COWAN, Wm.,081,104,121,131,
140,155,169,182,233,248,
250,276
COWELL, Geo.,178
COWEN, Catharine,256, David,
035,071,078,181,182,241,
Geo.,173, James,182, Jno.,
104,156,159,161,163,196,
233, John,197, Leila,181,
Richd.,051, Wm.,169,178,
192,196,233,256
COWIN, James,148, John,148
COWING, David Sr.,226, David,
068, James,226, Wm.,035,
233,256,258
COX, Allen,047,100,150, Baley,
128, Chas.,073,094,164,165,
169,183,186,259, Danl.,018,
047,048,063,066, Drury,259,
Edw.,047, Elizabeth,052,
Isaac,266, Jno.,076,161,
Jno.S.,173, Robt.,048,066,
William,032
CRACKER, Athanion,144,
Athenion,144, Eliz.,144,
James Sr.,144, James,144,
145, John,144, Jos.,144,
Sarah,144
CRADDOCK, ,139, Ann,006,
Archabel,158, Archalus,126,
Archelus,160, B.,117,141,
Ba't.,204, Barth,099,
Barthalomew,206, Barthalumas,
254, Barthol.,145, Bartholomew,
020, Bat.,143, Batholume,
206, Batt,220, Boyd,224,
Daniel,160,161, David,034
CRADDOCK, David,101,124,151,
152,220, Edmd.,040, Edmond,
006,047,053,190, Edmund,169,
Edw.,047, Henry,198,225,
J.,190,204, J.W.,236,
James W.,220, James,253,
264, Jas.,264,266, Jno.A.,
152,190, John A.,124,140,
Mary,160, Sarah,160,161
CRADDOCK, Sidney,189
CRADOCK, B.,048, Barth,098,
Barth.,098, David,098,
Edmon,151, Edmond,178,185,
James,224, Jno.A.,141,151,
Wm.,189
CRAFFORD, Esther,084, Jno.,
191, Wm.,084
CRAFORD, James,179,180,194,
210,211,254, Jas.,131, Jno.,
140,142,161,162,166,247,
John,154,176,193,194,
Saml.,207, Saml.B.,207,
Thos.,218, Wm.,084
CRAG, James L.,230
CRAGE(CRAIG), Elenor,008
CRAGE, Elizabeth,086,088,118,
James,008,086,088,118,
Jno.,239, John,008, Robt.,
118, Saml.,247,251,257,
Susanah,251, Thos.,098,
145,149,255, William,008,
Wm.,016,081,088,112,118
CRAGILL, James,220
CRAIG & MARTINDALE, ,189
CRAIG(CRAGE), Wm.,086
CRAIG, Danl.Hirum,183,
Eleanor,165, Isabella,006,

9

James,008,089,165,168,184,
188,189, Jas. L.,248,
Jas.L.,189, Jno.,086,160,
165,168,178,189,224,225,
264,265,267, John,006,165,
264,265, Lewis,183, Presley,
268, Robt.,157,165,168,
Saml.,164
CRAIG, Saml.,166,181,183,263,
Samuel,252, Thomas,184,
188, Thos.,156,165,168,172,
177,181,182,183,188,189,
208,222,265,267,268,273,
William,164,166,168, Wm.,
001,006,007,011,012,018,
020,033,075,089,103,112,
139,160,165,188,273, Wm.L.,
168
CRAIG, Wm.L.,264, Wm.Sr.,026
CRAIGE, John,188, Susanah,252,
Thos.,156
CRAIGHEAD, Frances,070
CRAIN(?), Sarah,053
CRAMTON, Wm.A.,105
CRANSHAW, A.,176, Abner,201
CRARY, Thos.,081
CRAVEN, James V.,217,231,
James,231
CRAWFORD, ,184, Charles,128,
G.H.,207, James,128,183,
185,189,260,263,264, Jas.,
111, Jno.,076, John,018,
185,193, Thos.,271
CREASY, John,010
CRECY, Jno.,144, John,031
CREECY, Doc,040, Dr.,018,
Eliz.,079, Elizabeth,080,
213, Jno.,029,040,078,079,
John(Dr.),053,079, John,
005,014,016,029,036,051,
061,076,080, Moses,081
CREEK, Jeremiah,232, Jno.Craig,
224
CREMSHAW, Wm.,122
CRENSHAW, Abner,108,172
CRESON, Jos.,190, Thompson,
238
CRESWELL, Agness,023, E.,056,
082, ELihu,063, Elihu,034,
063,066,101, James,009,018,
Jas.,027, Jno.S.,101, Mary,
038, R.,087,095,149, Robert,
038,149, Robt.,029,032,033,
034,043,046,051,066,068,
086,088,090,095,096,098,
099,100,103,114,119
CRESWELL, Robt.,125,133,172,
270, Robt.Jr.,276, Sarah,
271, Wm.,125
CRESWILL, Robt.,154
CREWELL, Sarah,271
CRIG(CRAIG?), John,224
CRIMES, Edmond,272
CRISP, Chas.A.,257, Jno.,098,
212, Jno.R.,159, John,082,
Lucy,211, Manfil,032,
Mansfield(?),032, Sarah,
211, Wm.S.,040
CRISTAN, Jas.,113
CRISTEN, Jno.,137
CRISTIAN, Jane,167, Jno.,165,
167,178, John,176, William,
165,167, Wm.,113
CRISWELL, E.,148, Elihu,164,
275, Eliz.,037, James,146,
148,190,203,221,235,270,
Jas.,247, Mary,147,227,
R.,192,222,232, Robt.,033,
058,124,129,145,146,148,
150,153,176,191,204,227,
236, Sarah,275,Wm.,129
CROCKER, Alhanan,110,112,
Alhanien,222, Alhanon,114,
Elhanion,145,161,162,169,
216,226, Elhannon,106,
Elhanon,111,117, Elizabeth,
100,213,218, Elkanan,270,
James Jr.,213,216,217,226,
253, James Sr.,213,216,226,
James,050,068,105,145,180
CROCKER, James,186,192,193,
196,198,206,213,214,216,
222,242, Jas.,052,087,114,

118,161,270, Jas.G.,156,
Jno.,162,222, Jno.R.,169,
196,217,218, John,214,217,
226, Jos.,171,223,224,275,
Joseph,169,214,216,217,
218,226,242, Malinda,169,270
CROCKER, Melinda,214, Milanda,
218,222, Milinda,216,
Milland,226, Robt.,180,
Samuel,217, Susana,237,
Susanah,253, Susannah,270,
William,216, Wm.,052,068,
071,075,076,079,093,113,
135,145,162,169,173,213,217
CROCKS, Peggey,220
CROFFORD, Moses,030
CROFORD, Jno.,102
CROMBIE, Kellet,266
CROMER, Byrd,273, Elijah,273
CROMWELL, Hugh,007
CROOK, Geo.,220, H.,174, Hugh,
175, John,147, Joseph,232,
Thomas,195, Thos.,215, Wm.,
217,221,223,255
CROOKS, ELias,256, Hugh,116,
121,133,151,153, Jas.,043,
Jno.,034,040,225,256, Jos.,
097, Margret,190, Peggey,
237, Thos.,106,173,197,257,
Wm.,218,257
CROSBY, Thomas,004
CROSEN, Wm.,187
CROSON, ,191, Benj.,038,
Hana M.,191, Julian,191,
197, Martha,125,191,
Melidon,197, Permela A.,
191, Permila,197, Thomas,
125,197, Thos.B.,191, Wm.,
125,133,160
CROSS, Wm.,080,105,156
CROSSMORE, Thos.,080
CROSSON, Benj.,027, Martha,
024,096, Thomas,096, Thos.,
024,025,026,080,098,
Thos.Jr.,025, Wm.,096,100,
157
CROSSWHITE, Jacob,029
CROSWHITE, Jacob,149, Wm.,235
CROW(?), Burns,180
CROW, Abraham,233,257, Alfred,
258, Chas.,096, Isaac,122,
Jno.,094,146, Jonathan,258,
Nancy,257, Wm.,010
CROWDER, Geo.,072, John,072
CROWTHERS, Geo.,156
CRUGGS, Merit L.,184
CRUMBIE, Colvin A.,213, Jas.,
257, Lindley,241
CRUMBLEY, Thos.,141
CRUMBTON, Wm.,230
CRUMBY, Thomas,160
CRUMLEE, Alex.,147
CRUMP, Aaron,082,146, Aron,
142, Wm.,082
CRUMPTON, James,256, Jas.,044,
077, Jno.,077,119, Levi,044,
068, Lewis,044
CRUMTON, ,122, E.,055, J.,
016, Jno.,133,190,257, John,
008, Lemual,257, Luke,257,
Mica'h,252, Micaagh,230,
Saml.,028, Thos.,190,
William,202, Wm.,256,257
CRYMES, John,230, Thomas,212,
Thos.,162,165,183,186
CRYMS, Thos.,252
CRYSP, John,274
CUBERSON, Jno.,222
CUBIRSON, Peter,229
CULBERSON, Ester,085, James,
065,163,176, Jas.,034,040,
074,106,120, Jno.,176,228,
231,235,236,237,242,260,
John,215,234, Jos.,098,
Manassa,239, Peter,136,
Porter,106, Robt.,109, Wm.,
007,014
CULBERSON, J.,243
CULBERTSON, Alex.,109, Hiram,
099, Jas.,040,058,088,092,
103,105,111,112, Peter,105,
Porter,099, Robt.,046,092,
248, Young Jas.,118

CUMINS, Jas.,057, Thos.,057
CUMMEFORD, Philip,217,222,228
CUMMING, Jno.,258, Wiley,258
CUMMINGS, Elizabeth,277,
James,277, John,056,059,
277, Robt.F.,098, Thomas,
277, Thos.,059,101
CUMMINS, John,062,064, Thos.,
044,072
CUNINGHAM, Geo.,003, Jas.,003,
John,003, Patrick,002,
Patrk.,007, Samuel,003,
Thos.,003, Wm.,003
CUNNINGHAM & SHARP, ,235,236
CUNNINGHAM, Ann,014, Capt.,
175, David,013, Eleanor,259,
Elihu,236,237, Elizabeth,
260, Elvirey,243, Geo.,050,
Henry,273, J.,084,090,237,
J.D.,221, J.P.,071,084,
086,091, J.W.,019, James Jr.,
235, James,021,032,054,213,
237,252,262, Jane(Mrs.),151
CUNNINGHAM, Jane,109,262,
Jas.,032,091,120,124,228,
268,270, Jas.Duke,236,
Jas.Jr.,109,161,250,262,
Jas.Sr.,236,262, Jenny,021,
Jno.,079,080,098,117,141,
163,170,201,208,237,241,
243,246,247,256,259,262,
Jno.D.,090,186,242, Jno.P.,
082
CUNNINGHAM, Jno.P.,098,104,
109, John B.,092, John D.,
056,071,235,243,244,
John P.,262, John Sr.,071,
John,014,015,046,047,056,
080,090,091,092,126,127,
144,149,234,235,236,239,
Kelly,021, Kitty,262,
L.(S?),144, L.,146,235,
Laurrsay W.,243
CUNNINGHAM, Lisa,260, Louisa,
235,244, M.,076, M.E.,208,
237, Mahala,243, Mahaley,
250,259,260, Malinda,242,
Margaret,260, Margret R.,
243, Marima,262, Martha,144,
149, Martin E.,236, Mary Louise,
234, Mary M.,243, Mary,015,
032,056,221,236
CUNNINGHAM, Mary,241,242,259,
Math.,276, Mathew E.,151,
Mathew,077,078,109,130,
134,176,178,236, Matthew E.,
208,273, Matthew,076,093,
Mitchel W.,084, Molley,262,
Molly,262, Mrs.,078,
Nancy E.,243, Nancy,090,
091,208, Patrick,013,014
CUNNINGHAM, Patrick,015,019,
021, Polley,178, Polly,276,
R.(Capt.),158, R.,174,240,
Robert,126,206, Robt.,015,
019,071,079,080,097,098,
127,134,144,145,149,169,
172,176,178,183,197,198,
244,273, Robt.A.,127, S.,
130,144,234,237,238, Sally,
240
CUNNINGHAM, Saml.,220,236,
237,239,242, Saml.Jones,234,
Saml.L.,228, Samuel,056,
262, Sarah,071, Sintha A.,
243, Susannah,076,078,093,
109, Syntha,259, Thomas,234,
242,260,262, Thos.(Mrs.),
152, Thos.,003,056,090,235,
242,250, Thos.Jr.,220
CUNNINGHAM, Thos.W.,243,
Widow,047, William,144,
249,250,262, Wm.,014,015,
056,071,080,090,101,109,
125,145,149,151,176,236,
242,270,274, Wright,273,
Zach.,096,099,109, Zachariah,
100
CUNNINS, Thos.,056
CURENTON, David,160
CURETEN, David,252
CURETON, Daniel,035, Danl.,
261, David,035,150,161,162,

253,268, Edw.,035, Eliz.B.,
035, Geo.Wash.,035, Hannah,
035, Jno.,131, John,024,
035,037, Nathl.,035,
Susannah,035, Thomas,035,
Thos.Taylor,035
CURINGTON, David,120,133
CURITON, Chas.,191, David,190,
203,205
CURNAL, Moses,072
CURNANT(?), Jeremiah,024
CURREY, Nathan,220, Nathl.,
221
CURRY, Nathan,098, Wm.,091,
272
CURTIS, Betsy,051
DABBS(?), Wm.,035
DACUS, John,007,020
DAIS, Wiley,030
DALL, Benj.B.,233, Leaven W.,
251
DALRUMPLE, Ephrum,253, Jno.,
256
DALRYMPLE(?), John,006, Mikel,
025, Sarah,010
DALRYMPLE, Ann,064, Anna,060,
061, David,150,166,203,210,
E.,204, Ellinor,003,
Ephraim,203,204, Ephrum,
261, Geo.,003,055,074,
George,064, J.,011,014,
James,061, Jno.,146,203,
211,242,261,265,267,268,
273, Job,147,166,264, Jobe,
204, John,003
DALRYMPLE, John,014,015,016,
036,055,060,061,189,204,
214, Lewis,163,166,179,193,
Michael,204, Mickel,028,
Mikel,167,212, Mikl.,051,
Mitchel,166, Nancy,189,
Rosanna,003, Saml.,003,
076, Sarah,166, Susanna,061,
Thomas,036,061,150,163,166
DALRYMPLE, Thos.,018,019,028,
036,060,072,076,079,084,
096,131,134,146,203,204,
211,252, Thos.Jr.,066,068,
Thos.Sr.,025,066,068, Wade,
266
DALSHEILDS, Thomas,240
DANDAY, Cornelius,023, John,
029, Mary,023, Thomas,023,
Thos.,023, Wm.,023
DANDEE, Chas.,247, Hagen,247
DANDEY & REED, ,151
DANDEY, Cornelius,043,044,
045, Jas.H.,045, John,030,
048,122, Polley,043, Polly,
045, Thomas,043, Thos.,007,
Wm.,036,043,044,045,145
DANDY, Cornelius,024, Daniel,
209,210, Danl.,152,161,256,
Jenne,209, Jno.,141,151,
152,213, Joel Jr.,257, Joel,
151,152,216,246, John Sr.,
218, John,025,151,206,216,
Lewis,238, Marcus,209,210,
260,263, Martha,151,
Marthey,152, Patsey,161
DANDY, Pattey,149, Silus,249,
254, Sylus,218, Thomas,024,
Thos.,024,025,151,225,
Thos.C.,152, William,148,
150,209, Wm.,024,149,150,
151,152,161
DANIEL(?), Jas.,141
DANIEL, Harison,258, Harrison,
076,137,139, James,163,
Jas.,145, Jesse,126,176,
239,271, Jno.,235, Jos.,176,
178, Joseph,228, Lewis,235,
Wm.,146,228
DANLIN, Salley,257
DANNIEL, Jesse,255
DARD(?), James,123
DARD, Robt.,123
DARUMPLE, Mikel,025
DASHIELDS, Thomas,240
DASHILL(?), Thomas,126
DAVENPORT, Burket,102,139,
D.,062, David,063,064,
Eliz.,107,219, Francis,166,

Jas.,040, John,018,022,
026,063,064, Lettice,102,
Michael,092, Mildred,063,
Ransom,063,079, Ranson,173,
Richd.,063,064,065, Salley,
102, Thomas,104, Thos.,018
DAVENPORT, Thos.,026,032,036,
040,042,043,046,063,076,
079,097,101,102,107, Wm.,063
DAVID, Hardy,167, Hyrum,204,
Wm.G.,201
DAVIDSON, Thos.,018
DAVIS & SIMPSON, ,236
DAVIS, ,236, Ann,088, Anne,
227, Baesden,278, Chesley,
096,209,212, Clardy,205,
Clement,008, Daniel,006,
028, Elenor,260, Elizabeth,
227,230, Ellinor,003, Emely,
260, H.,117,149, Hardey,218,
Hardy,150,168,206,245,
Harely,151, Hedley,117
DAVIS, Hedley,148,208,209,
211,214,230,243,245,258,
Hedly,204,243, Hency,232,
Henery,152, Henry,014,049,
056,061,088, Hirum,162,
J.H.,242, James,008,215,
219,227,233,235, Jane,008,
010, Jas.(Dr.),018,227,
Jas.,141,268, Jason,267,
Jesse,156
DAVIS, Jesse,165,196,251,252,
278, Jno.(Capt.),235,268,
Jno.,098,104,124,128,162,
167,174,179,183,208,212,
224,231,241,243,246,250,
253,254,265,271, Jno.B.,228,
Jno.H.(Dr.),158,237,243,
266, Jno.H.,154,174,178,
218,251,253,261, Jno.Jr.,143
DAVIS, John H.(Dr.),263,
John H.,123,227, John(Capt.),
218, John,003,015,020,065,
070,103,149,150,154,197,
205,227, Jonathan,236,
Jonth,077, Jonth.,096,
Jos.,080, Joshua,088,183,
270, Martin,147, Mary,257,
McM.D.A.,236, Nancy,175,
273,274
DAVIS, Nathan,006,247, Oneall,
134, Peter,271, Richd.,111,
164,189,212, S.,231, Samuel,
134, Sarah,257, Stealy,117,
Thorton,162, Thos.,003,
098,141,146,174,220,
Thos.Jr.,235, Thos.Sr.,235,
237, Uriah,099,157,273,274,
Vann,096,101,111, W.B.,231
DAVIS, W.C.,269, W.G.,192,
228,235,265,268, Wiley,031,
265, William,008, Wm.,005,
066,096,120,160,167,196,
203,210,252, Wm.B.,220,
Wm.F.,157, Wm.G.,201,
Wm.R.,196, Zach.,257,258,
Zachariah,156,197
DAWES, John,070
DAY, Amry,011, Anna,058,
Avery,112, Bacy.,011,048,
057,058, Claxton,156,
Daniel,011,066,191, Danl.,
048,050,112,133, Drummond,
072, Elizabeth,011, Emry,
063, Frances,011, Jemima,
011,161, Jno.,112,190, John,
011,018, Lewis,184,191,
Mansfield,112
DAY, Mary,011,063, N.,090,
188,243,271, Nancy,011,
Nat.,148,161,237,243,
244,246,254, Nathl.,011,
065,066,081,111,152,153,
154,158,159,160,161,188,
201, Phileah(?),154,
Philip Sr.,158, Philip,011,
012,014,112,133
DAY, Philip,190, Philup,161,
R.H.,256, Ransom,133,150,
Reason,120, Wm.,011,054,160
DAYLEY, Vines,070

DEAL, Alex.,140, Alexr.,003,
012,039, Allen,211,243,251,
Clement,003, Damilion(?),
121, Delimion,221, Demarus,
257, Demilion,257, Ellexander,
039, Haistings Sr.,191,
Harsting,237, Isaac,237,
James Sr.,159, Jno.,110,
John,039,124, Leamanus,152
DEAL, Lemorus,211, Lewis,211,
Luerena,237
DEALE, Alex.,187, Alexander,
250, Alexr.,013,036,048,
108,190,191,236, Demarius,
250, Demilian,215,250,254,
Demilion,108,121,187,
Denialion,157, James,250,
Jas.,108, Jno.,106, John,
036,048,070,087,108,
Lamurus,177, Lemarcus,275,
Lemareus,208
DEALE, Lemareus,236, Lemarius,
187,207, Lemarsus,246,
Lemarus,175,176,250,254,
Marcus,250, Marey,036,
Mary,250, Polly,048,
Richd.S.,110, Sim.(?),081
DEAN, Alex.,034, Allen,239,
Anna,178, Catharine,141,
178, Catherine,003, G.,094,
Hannah,047, Henry,160,164,
James,047, Jas.,093, Jed,
232, Jno.,096,141,174,178,
274,277, Joel,010,265, John,
040,144,178,205, Jos.,039,
040,045,047,056,057
DEAN, Jos.,083,116, Joseph,
002,003,046,141, Mary,028,
Polley,178, S.(?),277,
Sarah,144, Thos.,141,178,
192, Thos.Jr.,046,047,
Thos.Sr.,046,047, W.D.A.,
271, Walter A.,233, Walter D.A.,
268, Walter W.D.A.,213,
Walter,268
DEAS(?), Jesse,155
DEASON(?), Edw.,127
DEASON, Benj.,137, David,128,
Edw.,127,128, Johnston,159
DEEN, A.,196, Alford,232,
Catharine,175, Hannah,090,
Isaiah,073, Jas.,081, Jeb,
228, Jno.,102,128,143,166,
169,180,212,231,232,273,
Joel,063, John,063,072,
128,146,159,175,178,205,
211,273, Jonathan,072,
Jos.(Est.),151, Jos.,056,
071,073
DEEN, Jos.,081,091,115,133,
137, Joseph,006,139, Josiah,
041,063,109, P.D.A.,211,
Polley,109, Thos.,233,236,
256,273, W.D.A.,211, Walter,
206
DEERE, Watts,154
DELFH, T.,146
DELONG, David,237, James,012,
Jno.,256, Johnston,215,
Jonathan,156,256
DELOREY, Jonathan,151
DELPH(?), Robt.,078
DELPH, B.P.,158, Henry,108,
113,126,214, Polly,089,
Robt.,082,214, Robt.P.,113,
117,121,126, Sherman,082
DEMPSEY, Luke,024
DENDEY, Chas.,065, Danl.,063,
065,066, F.,063, Jno.,143,
John,063, Thos.,023,063,
065, Wm.,045,051,062,065,
Wm.Sr.,063
DENDY(?), John,030, Rodey,094
DENDY, Arianna,267, Arianner,
265, Betsy,030, Charles,122,
Chas.,045,073,098,122,
Clary,030, Cornelius,099,
122, D.,266, Danl.,030,133,
138,203, Ellis,265, Francis F.,
173, Harriet,122, Janny,112,
Jas.H.,030,041,099, Jno.,
098,111,112,114
DENDY, Jno.,115,116,117,118,

151, Joel,030,031,056,057,
098,111,117,205,273, John,
007,009,012,030,057, Marcus,
265,267,268,269,271, Mary,
023,045,122, Nancy,122,
Patsey,110, Patsy,112,
Pattey,121, Patty,121,122,
Polley,114, Polly,045,059
DENDY, Polly,098, Sally,114,
Silas,274, Silus,205,
Thomas,058,059,061,099,
122, Thos,122, Thos.,030,
045,051,057,065,074,098,
111, Thos.Jr.(?),122,
Thos.Jr.,045, Thos.Sr.,019,
023, William,110,121,122,
Willis,265,267,268, Wm.,
006,023,030
DENDY, Wm.,045,058,059,060,
061,095,099,101,112,122,
143, Youngset(?),098,
Youngset,099
DENNENTON, Wm.,098
DENSON, Jas.,273
DENTON, Richd.,237,278
DERN, L.D.,154
DERROH, David,279
DESCHAMPS, H.W.,037
DESHEDDS, Thos.,160
DESHIELD, Thos.,189
DESHIELDS, Jno.,156, Thos.,
106,224
DESHIELS, Thos.,106
DESON, Hicks,159
DESSON, Edw.,132
DEVALL, James,195
DEVALOIS, Jos.,224
DEVANL, Wm.,261
DEVAUL, James,178,188, Jas.,
146, Saml.,149
DEVAULE, Lewis,033
DEVAULL, James,197
DEVENPORT, Burguet,179,180,
Burket,179,180,207,
Burquet,207,208, Burquit,
211, Chas.,180, Eliz.,223,
Francis,121,191, Isaac,241,
Johnston,191, Jonathan,235,
Jos.,190,191, Margret,211,
P.G.,191, Peggey,179,180,
207, Plesant G.,222,
Plesant,212
DEVENPORT, Ransom,187,
Stephen,176, T.,257, Tempa,
223, Thos.,191, Wm.,241
DIAL(DEAL), Isaac S.,237
DIAL, Allen,210,243,246,250,
261,268, B.F.,269, D.,133,
Drury,255, Eliz.(Miss),152,
Eliz.,070, Frankling,255,
G.C.,266,269,270, Garlington,
255,256, H.A.,269, H.Sr.,
256, Haisten,092,255,257,
Haisting Sr.,255, Haisting,
257, Haistings,191
DIAL, Haistings,269, Haiston(?),
070, Harrison,255, Hasting,
172,270, Hastings,070,073,
116,187, Henry,255, Heriet,
255, Isaac Jr.,152, Isaac Sr.,
236, Isaac,070,092,099,104,
105,130,132,171,172,173,
210,229,255,256,269,270,
Isabella,255
DIAL, J.,095,270, J.L.,269
DIAL, James,070,171, Jas.,268,
Jas.Jr.,151, Jno.,228,
John,071, Jos.,151, Joseph,
163, Martha,255, Martin,005,
007,008, Mary,190,269,
Nancy,255, Permelia,262,
Polley,219,255, Rebecah,
171, Rebecca,171,172,173,
Rebekah,070, Widow,116
DICE, ,201
DICKERSON, Chas.,248, James,
250
DICKESON, Wm.,163
DICKS, Robert,007
DICKSON, Joseph,263, Michel,
163
DIEL, Austin,229, Garlington,
231, Harrting,231, Isaac S.Jr.,

231, Isaac Sr.,231, Joel,
088, Lewis,231
DIEL/DIAL/DEAL, ,191
DILL, Geo.,173, John,201,
Nancy,201
DILLARD, (Maj.),103, (Wid.),
215, ,231, Ann,054,055,139,
141,159, Asa,061, Betsy,186,
Chas.H.,267, E.(Mrs.),211,
Eliz.,184, Elizabeth,158,
159,241, F.J.,210, G.W.,164,
Geo.,026,043,054,058,103,
118,139,141,158,159,164,
188,195,203,215,221
DILLARD, Geo.,238,241,265,
267,271, Geo.W.,160, George,
055,156,182,184,213,222,
Hannon G.,251, Henry,215,
J.,184,273, J.F.,184,
James M.,245, James,010,
011,022,043,047,048,051,
054,061,076,139,164,183,
188,210,224,226,265,267,
Jas.,011
DILLARD, Jas.,015,020,043,
075,088,131,160,268,271,
Jas.H.,267, Jefferson,211,
Jno.(?),139, Jno.,106,108,
110,120,130,139,156,158,
159,162,163,164,186,188,
189,198,199,211,224, John,
021,023,025,026,055,061,
069,095,158,159,192,203,
214,215
DILLARD, John,223,225,246,
267, Leddey,238, Leminion,
233, Lemuel,248,273, Lyda,
126, Mannon,266, Mary,164,
267, Minial,252, Ruth,021,
Saml.,011,015,018,049,054,
126,164,172,182,184,186,
209,210,226,245,248, Samuel,
055,139,175, Sarah,139
DILLARD, Siminion,159, Squire,
224, Susannah,270, Thos.J.,
209,213,224,226,267,
William,156,208,215,225,
245,248, Wm.,011,021,043,
049,054,056,060,061,064,
069,078,085,086,116,123,
125,137,141,164,174,183,
189,195,215,223,224,225,
226,241
DILLARD, Wm.,246
DILRUMPLE, John,060
DINES(?), Jos.,174
DOBYNS, Frances,225
DODD, Asa,266, Jesse Jr.,265,
Jesse,015,018,189, Mary,
184,186, Thos.,215, Wm.,240,
265
DOGHARTY, Jane,006
DOLFF, F.,124
DOLLAR & WHITTER, ,224
DOLLAR, Eliz.,135, Elizabeth,
135, Hancel,123, Hansel,123,
124, Jno.,224, John,124,
133,134,135,196,217,220,
252,255, Jos.,168,189,190,
210, Joseph,185,210, Nancey,
255, Nancy,252, Reuben,124,
196,197,212, Sarah,123,124,
196, Solomon,247, Wm.,049
DOLLAR, Wm.,124,224
DOLLER, Reuben,279, Sarah,279,
William,279
DONAHO, Cornelius,037, Elnah,
032, John,032,034, Timothy,
037, Wm.,037
DONAHOE, Eleanor,032, Eliza Sarah,
032, John,032
DONAL, Henry,044
DONALD, James,067
DONALDSON, Thos.,022,247
DONALSON, Nimrod,274
DONNEL, Archd.Jr.,042
DONOHEW, Wm.,007
DOOLAND, Jennet,044
DORAN, Henry,102, Jacob,096,
097,101,104,111, Nancy,101
DORRAH, Anne,130, James,071,
244, Jas.,018,129, Jas.Jr.,
130, Jas.Sr.,129,130, John,

071, N.,071, Nancy,071, Wm.,
018,071
DORROCK(DORRACH), Jas.,003
DORROH, David R.,277, David,
279, James,056,279, Jas.,
268,272, Lewis C.,279,
Margaret,279, Martha,279,
Mary,279, Nancy,279, Sarah,
279, Wm.,070, Wm.M.,279
DORROUGH, James,071, Jas.Jr.,
068, Wm.,068
DOTSON, Charles,134, E.,136,
Elihu,150, Jno.,120, Lewis,
041,120, Stephen,057, Wiley,
186
DOUBLIN, Free,257
DOWNAN(?), Jane,008
DOWNEY, Jas.,005, Jos.,075
DOWNING, James,071, Wm.,071
DOWNS, Danl.,122, Frances,120,
Jane,120,122, Jonathan,005,
034,078,106,120,122,213,
278, Jos.,005,015,016,021,
027,034,070,122, Joseph,005,
013,026,032,124, Joshua,006,
Louisa(?),120, Maj.,019,
Mary L.,122, Milly,120,
Phebe,120, Saml.,082
DOWNS, Saml.,095,116,120,134,
142,178,179,213,219,229,
234,238,268,274, Samuel,227,
Sarah,120, Thos.,033, W.F.,
141,170,185,268,270,276,
Wm. F.,184, Wm.,071,079,
087,098,107,122, Wm.D.,172,
Wm.F.,081,086,087,088,095,
099,104,106,108,109
DOWNS, Wm.F.,113,120,127,129,
137,141,146,148,159,168,
176,184,196,197,219,220,
227,235,238,240,274,278,
Wm.P.,119,272, Wm.T.,122,
Zachariah,162
DRAKE, B.,088, Benj.,025,033,
051,076,111, Edmond,027,
033, Jno.,101,110,111,112,
174,179, John,128,129,185,
193, Mitchell,110, Richd.S.,
139, Sarah,164,193, Wm.,101
DRAPER, Green B.,188
DREUSON, Jno.,211
DREW, Elizabeth,001, Langston,
001, Lucy,001, Paul,001,
Polly,001, Sarah,001,
William,001,007
DRUMENS, Garred,232
DRUMMON, Benj.,229, Milley,
077, Norman,077
DRUMMOND, Benj.,029,111,
Danl.,078,082,191, Milley,
078, Milly,082, Nath'l.,157,
Nathan,103, Nathl.,007,
093,098,111, Norman,078,
North(?),129, S.,129,
Saml.,071, Warren,165, Wat,
171, Wm.,040,082
DRUMMONS, Norman,076
DRYMPLE(?), Thos.,128
DUBLIN, Free,249,256
DUCKER, Enoch,156, Salley,246,
Sarah,246, Wm.,151
DUCKET, Allen,149, Barach,174,
Barruch,154,171, Benj.,149,
Jacob,041,049, James,011,
015, Jas.,043, John,043,
Jos.,088, Josha(?),043,
Mary,243, Richard,215,
Richd.,011,043,222,224,
Thomas,171, Thos.,174,224
DUCKETT, Alsey,126, B.,061,
Barruch,111,157,221,
Baruch,092,111,228, Baruck,
144, Benj.,181,183,200,213,
Burket,106, Geo.,183,
Henry,168, Isaac,055,
Jacob,020,049,055,061,183,
James,054,058,060,061,126,
161,183, Jas.,055, Jno.,123,
224
DUCKETT, John,055,061,125,
126,156,238, Jos.,049,056,
183, Joseph,183, Josiah,049,
061,079, Lyda,126, Marey,

126, Martha,125,238,
Mary B.,254, Mary,229,261,
Pattey,229, Richard,156,
Richd.,049, Robt.,157,
Sarah,060,061,126,195,238,
240
DUCKETT, Thos.,098,126,158,
183,184,186,188,221,226,
238,243,267, Thos.Jr.,181,
Thos.Sr.,181, Wm.,098,156,
181
DUDLEY, Chas.,101, Danl.,133
DUFF, Robt.,148
DUGAN, Arthur,266
DUGGAN, Robt.,211
DUGLASS, Jno.,128,151,239
DUGLESS, Jno.,211
DUKE, Hardaman,143, Hardeman,
142, Hardiman,188, Hardyman,
235, Harmon,237, Henderson,
055, Henry,189, James,051,
Jas.,273, N.,190, Sallamon,
183, Wm.,048
DUKES, John,013, Wm.,106
DUMAS, Betsy,168, Danl.,203,
David,168, Eleline,168,
Fanney,149, Lucy,168, Mary,
149, Nancy,168, Nathl.,168,
Nemiah,254, Polley,168,
Sarah,168, Stephen,092,
141,144,149,168, Tilda,168
DUN-GH, Mitchel,145
DUNCAN(?), Joseph,156
DUNCAN, Bignal,251, James,200,
212, Jane,047, John,017,
019, Jos.,137,154,158,183,
266,270, Joseph,049,158,
201, Joshua,156, Josiah,267,
Margret,183, Martha,049,
Regal,229, Robt.,017, S.,
055, Sarah,048, T.L.,055,
Thos.L.,033, Wm.,017
DUNKEN, Barruch,243, Brigdel,
242, Burrel,246, David,200,
James,200, Jesse,211,
Jnathan,200, Jno.,211,
Jos.,088,089,154,231,
Joseph,200,251, Josiah,183,
Marah,088, March,183, Mary,
200, Rignal,219, Thos.,222,
Wm.,183
DUNKEN/DUNCAN, Irby,201
DUNKENS, Henry,216
DUNKIN, Barruch,261, Elizabeth,
261, James,090, Jas.,055,
Jos.,055,088,249,262,
Joseph,154,175,182,215,
262, Joshua,215, Josiah,156,
Leander,181, Leonard,032,
Riegal,243, Rignal,229,
261, Salley,182, Wm.,249
DUNKLIN(?), Jas.,076, Jno.,
116
DUNKLIN, Eliz.,067, Jas.,096,
Mary,005, Wm.,098
DUNKLING, Elizabeth,194,
Irby J.,201
DUNLAP & UNDERWOOD, ,122
DUNLAP, Agnes,089, Brice,071,
Cathern,005, Christen,062,
David,003,016,018,020,038,
062, Dehditell(?),141,
Eliz.,062,090,091, Elizabeth,
085, Ezekiel,228, J.,087,
204, James,005,028,048,062,
068,190,251,277, Jane,062,
Jas.,074,137, Jno.,087
DUNLAP, Jno.,104,139,142,143,
145,153,154,155,159,161,
164,169,172,173,176,179,
180,182,188,192,218,236,
John,005,014,021,038,062,
123,125,126,144,147,149,
152,168,244,248,277, Maj.,
051, Margaret,002,271,
Margarett,275,277, Margarette,
277
DUNLAP, Martha,062, Mary B.,
253, Mary,005,062,277,
Mathew,190, Michael,174,
Michel,138, Mitchel,062,
169,175,200, Mr.,014,
Nancey,005, Nancy,277,

Price,062, Rebecca,174,
Richard,277, Robert,062,
126,277, Robt.,097,123,232,
Saml.,002
DUNLAP, Saml.,003,071,074,
091, Samuel,005,085,086,
090, Sarah,005,277, Sophia,
277, Suzanna,005, William,
234,277, Wm.,014,017,021,
024,027,031,032,033,038,
059,060,062,065,066,068,
074,075,076,087,088,099,
100,102,107,120,123,127,
136,139
DUNLAP, Wm.,143,144,150,177,
178,180,194,204,205,206,
218,235,271,275
DUNN, Wm.,271,277
DUNNAHO, Timothy,029
DUPREE, Drury,020,021,023,
Lewis,021,023
DUPREY, Danl.,009
DURAM, Peggy,007
DURHAM, Mary,014, Peggy,007,
014
DURKEY, N.(Maj.),081
DUROUGH, James,149
DURRAH, James,171, Jas.,109,
Jas.Jr.,109
DURROH, James,163,198
DURROUGH(DORRAH), Jas.,130
DURROUGH, James,233,243,
Jas.Sr.,130
DURROW, Henry,130, James,162,
215,221,242,250,261, John,
149
DURWILL(?), B.D.,266
DUTY, Richard,077, Richd.,039,
040,248
DUVALE, Jas.,268, Jno.,268
DUVALL, Jas.,273, John,273,
Lewis,013,273, Washington,
273
DYLRUMPLE, Thomas,128
Ducket, Barrch,171
EAGARTON, Chas.,267,271
EAGERTON, Chas.,265
EAKINS, Lewis,002,007, Saml.,
006,007
EARBY(IRBY?), Polley,031
EARBY, Nancy,031, Ritter,031
EARP, Caleb,062
EAST, Allen,008,074,075, Ann,
008, Bethiah S.,263, Eliz.,
263, Elizabeth,210,273,
Fedrick,242, Isaiah,051,
Isham,011,020, Israel,065,
Joel,017,066,211,266, John,
008,027,074,075, Jos.,011,
Josiah,003,006,017,020,
163,164,165,181, Landsdon,
189
EAST, Landston,092, Langsdon,
164,179,193,194,210,
Langston,101,104,111,128,
163,166,179,181,208,209,
219, Mary,008, Nancy,164,
Ob.,094, Rebecah,164,
Shade,264, Shadrach,008,
009, Shadrick,261, Tarleton,
011,020,026, Thomas,008,
Thos.,005
EAST, Thos.,011,020,054,101,
Thos.Jr.,006, Thos.Sr.,006,
W.J.,270, William,009,219,
262, Wm.,026,136,166,209,
218,239,242,245,263,264,
266,270, Wm.J.,263, Wm.Jackson,
262, Wm.Jr.,210,242, Wm.Sr.,
008,066,166
EASTER, F.,126
EASTRIDGE, Reuben,117
EASTWOOD, Elizabeth,008
EATHERS, Thos.,042
ECKISON, Jos.,056
ECTERKEN, Jas.,128
EDDINS, Abraham,021, William,
036, Wm.,044
EDMONDS, Chas.,255
EDMONSON, Danl.,273, James,
220
EDWARDS, Andrew,131, Andw.,

077,093, Berey,259, Charles,
001, Chas.,152, Edw.,235,
Elijah,030, Eliz.,214,
Ginney,088, James,048,051,
057,058, Jas.,050,061, Jno.,
088,131,165,269, Joel,214,
259, John,038,088,131, Mary,
049, Mr.,019, Thos.,269
EDWARDS, Widow,131, Zachariah,
256
EDWIN, Danl.C.,225
EGERTON, Chas.,190,195,196
EGESTUN, Chas.,221
EGGERTON, Chas.,202
EGLEBERGER(?), J.A.,266
EGURTON, Chas.,247
ELDRIDGE, Ephrum,129, Jacob,
213
ELEDGE, Jas.,268
ELISON, Joel,152, Robt.,247,
Thomas,149, Thos.,126
ELLEDGE, Jacob,212,234
ELLEGE, Jacob,237
ELLEN(ALLEN), Eliz.,270
ELLING, Joel,193
ELLIOT, Isum,026, Rebacca,026,
Thos.,011
ELLIOTT, Isum,050, Rubin,050,
Thos.,015,050, Wm.,208
ELLISON, Joel,147, Jos.,010,
Lewis,268, Robt.,163,236,
Wm.,084
ELMORE & SAXON, ,231
ELMORE, Easter,257, Elijah,
170,206, Geo.,104,217,218,
222,267, George,170, Graham,
170, Gray,218, Grey,222,
Huldy,170, J.A.,015,027,
043,045,047,054,067,078,
103, Jas.,042, Jno.A.(Col.),
119, John A.,006,014,047,
John,010,011,016, Polly,170
ELMORE, Rebecah,257, Rebecca,
170
ELPHANT, Cesar,152
EMBREY(?), Stephen,022
EMBREY, Stephen,015
EMMORY, Margaret,022, Mrs.,
022, Stephen,022,028
EMRY(EMBRY?), Stephen,016
EMSLEY, Rachel,154
ENDLSEY, Jas.,104
ENLOW, Jno.,212, Wm.,167
ENSLEY, James,026,161,235,
Jas.,101,141,145, Thos.,027
ENTEKIN, Thos.,160
ENTERKEN, David,141, Jas.,128,
141
ENTERKEN, David,167,192,210,
219,257, James,160,166,
Jesse,204,242,261,262,
John,157,160, Nathl.,273,
Polly,160, Saml.,203,204,
218,257, Thos.,166,167,179,
200,204,218,264, Thos.Jr.,
203, Thos.Sr.,203, Wm.,218
ENTRACAN, Thos.,066
ENTRAKIN, James,174
ENTREKEN, Jas.,146
ENTREKIN, James,051,068, Jas.,
097,128, Jno.,146, John,019,
020, Mercer,079, Thos.,020,
032,051
ENTREKING, Thos.,055
ENTRICAN, Jno.,011, John,002,
Thos.,006,011
ENTRIBAN, John,002
ENTRIKEN, Jesse,253
EPPS, Jno.,211
EPS, William,215
ERBY, Carter,051
ESON, Sarah,254
ESTES, Ann,095,119,270, Joel,
108,155, Kesiah,121, Nancy,
155, Obediah,095,096,108,
119, R.,094, Reuben,094,
103,108,121,196,197,220,
231,244,256,257, Ruben,228,
Susanah,155, Wm.,101,108
ESTRAGE(?), Reuben,081
ESTRAGE, Obediah,081
EVANS(?), D.,130
EVANS, ,013, Deidamia,027,

13

FORLEY, Ey-- F.,233
FORREST, Geo.,019
FORT, Westwood F.,269
FORTER, Mr.,118
FOSHEE, Benj.,101,267,268,
  272, Benj.Jr.,161,162,184,
  Benj.Sr.,162,184, Benjamin,
  161,190, Daniel,161,190,
  203, Danl.,133,240,252,257,
  272, Nancy,161, Susanah,161,
  190, Susannah,184
FOSTER(?), Fedrick,218
FOSTER, A.Jr.,263, Anthony,
  188, Antony,225, Edw.,266,
  271, F.,184, Fedrick,137,
  150,160,242, Felding,189,
  Fielding,224,265, Frederick,
  204, Fredk.,101,116,
  Fredrick,210,211, Fredrk.,
  068,069,096,134,136,201,
  202, Hillary,271, James,188
FOSTER, James,225, Joel F.,
  255, Joel L.(?),275,
  Joel S.,245, Joel,189,
  Jones,077, Moses,077,
  Nancy,149, Pleasant,264,
FOUNTAIN, Moses,094, Stephen,
  074
FOWLAR, Chas.,178, Davis,183,
  Jno.,228, John,188,192,
  193, Polley,157, Richard,
  157, Sarah,157, Thos.,157,
  Wm.,157
FOWLER, Agnes,041, America,
  004, Andrew,122,166,
  Charles,041,122,132,153,
  166, Chas,266, Chas.,098,
  113,116,119,140,146,159,
  175,187,208,254,275,276,
  David,041,091,092,130,132,
  Deborah,004, Edw.,233,258,
  Elias,207, Elizabeth,005,
  113,257
FOWLER, Geo.,117,232, Henry,
  189, Hugh,178, Isabel,071,
  Isabella,116,129,131,133,
  Israel,151, James,004,041,
  049,072,091,113,115,116,
  Jane,132, Jas.,042,043,
  075,092,093, Jen,256, Jesse,
  004, Jno.,083,105,146,177,
  210,212,222,246,247,251
FOWLER, Jno.,256,265,267,
  Jno.C.,232, Jno.Mansfield,
  211, Joel,004,063,094,225,
  232,233, John,004,041,047,
  071,131,132,217,220, Jones,
  132, Jos.,107, Joshua,005,
  Josiah,081,085,105,106,
  110,111,114, Leahala(?),116,
  Levi,060,061,078,089
FOWLER, Levi,111,123,125,126,
  194, Lewis,061, Martha,194,
  Marthey,171, Mary(?),071,
  Mary(Mrs.),160, Mary,092,
  094,115, Menoah,246,
  Meredith,256, Meridith,257,
  Molly,004, Mose,004, Nancy,
  041, Nathan,123,125,175,
  Nathen,194,195, Newton,110
FOWLER, Newton,263,264, Peter,
  174, R.,131,136, Rich.,111,
  Richard,005,110,111,171,
  Richd.,106,110,111,125,
  127,129,153, Roadey,132,
  Salley,212, Sarah Ann,194,
  Sarah,091,110,130,132,169,
  170,171,174, Solomon,047,
  Tabitha,004, Thomas,110
FOWLER, Thompson,231, Thos.,
  110,111,169,185, Thos.M.,
  004, Wade N.,137, William,
  094,115, Wm.,004,008,041,
  047,059,060,061,067,081,
  083,092,093,094,099,104,
  117,132,137,156,205,211,
  254,256,266, Wm.S.,257
FRAISER, Thos.,224
FRANKLIN, Asa,082, James,186,
  Matthew,142
FRANKLING, Jas.,135, Matthew,
  141
FRANKS, Allen,084,085, Chas.,

116,244,269, Chas.C.,196,
  Chas.G.,237,279, Elijah,
  229,268, Eliza,228, Elizabeth,
  107, Geo.,169, Henry,246,
  Jane(Simmons),155, Jane,
  152, Jno.,173,212, Joshua,
  004,085,107,108,134,174,
  196,197,236,256, M.,124
FRANKS, Marshal,043, Marshall,
  008, Martha,107, Mary,196,
  Merrion,151, N.,004,143,
  235, Nancy,023,084,085,145,
  Nehemiah Jr.,159, Nehemiah,
  023,048,098,107,115,133,
  145,151,152,155,197,215,
  222,256,257,266, Poley,004,
  Robert,004,106, Robt.,017
FRANKS, Robt.,043,050,069,
  107,136,159,173,180,233,
  235,244,257, Robt.Sr.,236,
  Saml.,054,065,084,085,101,
  116,151,201,212,220, Samuel,
  004, Sarah,069,072,257, Wm.,
  043,048,055,069,070,072,
  103,106,107,108,116,133,
  134,172,210,212,255
FRASER, Thos.L.S.,263
FRASHER, Nella,277, Nelly,277
FREEMAN, Abner,239, Elisha,
  273, Robt.,009,016,018,044,
  139, Saml.,018,027,069,095,
  104,113,190,207, Wm.,006,
  017,018,239
FRENCH, Geo.,207,221, James,
  256, Jas.,279
FRESKEY, Josiah,230
FRIER, Anna,137, Bery,137,
  Grace(?),137, John,132
FROST, Jacob,014
FRYER, John,076
FUGUSON, Henry,225
FULL, Eldridge,248
FULLAR, A.,149,191, Alsa,229,
  Alsey,133,165,179,191,252,
  Arch,188, Archey,188, G.,
  149, H.,149, Hamon,188,
  Henry,188,219,254, Israel,
  182, James,149,252, Jason,
  223, Jesse M.,219, Jesse W.,
  247,251, Jesse,163,229,
  Jessey W.,251, Jones,157
FULLAR, Jones,182,188,219,
  221,223,228,229, Peter,141,
  157,188,219,229,253, Posey,
  162, Ransom,230, Sarah,188,
  Solomon,242, Wm.,149,179,
  223, Wm.A.,182,219
FULLEN, Wm.,190
FULLER, A.,270, Abner,085,
  Alex.,098, Allen,171, Alsa,
  214, Alse,110, Alsey Jr.,
  174, Alsey,134,139,140,167,
  169,170,171,174,180,181,
  184,194,195,203,205,207,
  218,234,243,246,267,
  Archbd.,078, Archd.,092,
  Aron(?),123, Arthur,260,
  262, Asey,206
FULLER, Aug.F.,113, Avent(?),
  138, Avent,279, Benj.,027,
  Britton,075,077, Ch.,093,
  Charlota,140, Charlotte,
  090,139, Danl.,037,105,160,
  Delphy,075,279, E.P.,213,
  Eldridge,027,105,120,
  Geo.Jr.,217, Geo.Sr.,217,
  Gilley,138, Harmon,203
FULLER, Henry H.,218, Henry,
  036,045,051,053,055,061,
  074,090,091,093,098,167,
  199,204,206,243,260,262,
  270, Isaiah,142, Isam,052,
  Isham,029,042,174, Iscm,
  055,078,206, Israel,111,
  167,199, Isum,051,053, J.S.,
  068, J.W.,261, Jacob,128,207
FULLER, Jacob,217,257, James,
  042,065,171,174, Jas.,029,
  111,114, Jas.Sr.,169,
  Jesse W.,238,251,263,
  Jesse,272, Jno.,140,
  John F.,279, John,138,167,
  170, Jones,029,036,040,073,

074,078,079,088,090,091,
  092,101,106,111,127,151,
  165,167,171
FULLER, Jones,173,185,188,
  198,199,202,203,204,206,
  207,209,218,221,234,238,
  240, Jony,158, Martha,198,
  Mary Ann,078, Peter,078,
  103,106,111,155,167,169,
  171,173, Posey,085,169, R.,
  088, Ransen,261, Ransom,085,
  091,092,094,101,104,105,111
FULLER, Ransom,113,120,124,
  136,138,140,145,201,206,
  210,246,256, Ranson,262,
  Ranssom,236, Ransum,151,
  Rebecca A.,279, Salam,218,
  Sally,027, Sarah,051,055,
  111,152,207,214,243, Silus,
  267, Sollomon,134,187,
  Solomon Jr.,105,115,138,
  Solomon,018
FULLER, Solomon,021,040,042,
  065,085,087,091,094,101,
  106,111,138,139,140,171,
  173,194,199,204,261, Sylus,
  170, Thomas,126, Thos.,267,
  Wm.,088,106,111,113,138,
  141,167,198,200,202,203,
  235,238, Wm.A.,199, Wm.Arthur,
  198, Wm.S.,140
FULLER, Jas.,151
FULLTON, Wm.,233
FULOR, Jonas,151
FULTON, A.P.,255, Agness,141,
  Alex.,240, Caralin(Catty),
  235, Charlett C.,134,
  Charlota,235, Charlotta,
  262, Charlotte,177, James Sr.,
  151, James,183,219, Jno.,
  178,183, M.H.,174, Marey,
  141, Thomas,134,245,247,
  255,262, Thos.,083,123,140
FULTON, Thos.,141,143,178,
  183,189,210,257,270,
  Thos.Jr.,134,152,168,183,
  Thos.Sr.,141, William,188,
  Wm.,009,025,039,044,045,
  060,062,067,071,098,100,
  107,125,134,141,167,168,
  172,178,180,189,270, Wm.H.,
  172,210, Wm.Jr.,139,141,
  151, Wm.Sr.,139
FULTON, Wm.Sr.,141,270
FUNCK, Geo.,271,272
FUNK, Geo.,158,162,174,181,
  193,195,213,243,250,251,
  George,213
FUQUA, Seth,062
FURGASON, James,171
FURGESON, Charles,198, Ezekel,
  219, Saml.,200, Word,252
FURGUSON, Chas.,260, Miles,
  211, Richd.,211,249, Wm.,152
FUSHEE, Danl.,161
FUYLTON, Charlot,235
GADBURY, Allen,140, Chas.,140
GAFFORD, Wm.,165,228
GAGGANS, Polly,111
GAGGARD, Johnston,261
GAINES, B.B.,268, Betsy,089,
  David,009, Edmond P.,161,
  Edmond,113, Elizabeth,236,
  Henry,113, James A.,016,
  James,161, Jas.,118,
  Jas.A.,015, Joel,145,
  Jona.,076,082, Jos.,145,
  187, Julian,161, Larkin,076,
  089,110,113,117,118,145,
  269, Richard,015
GAINES, Richard,037, Richd.,
  075,078, Robt.,061,064,078,
  116, Sarah,061, Steph.,076,
  Stephen,082, Thomas,037,
  Thos.,015,016,061,113, Wm.,
  186
GAINS, Abner,147, B.B.,210,
  Benj.,195, Betsey,146,
  Edmond P.,162, Gracy Adline,
  206, H.P.,162,203, Henry P.,
  162,203,247, J.L.,236,
  James,162,210,239,247,
  Jas.,082,095,126,137,139,

245, Jno.,162, John,195,
Jonadal,162, Julian,162,
July Ann,206
GAINS, L.,147, Larken,169,
Larkin,124,126,135,139,
146,193, Nathl.,221, Richd.,
021,181, Robt.,036,080,082,
Silus P.,203, Silus,207,
221, Stephen,069, Thos.,101,
Wm.,140,162, Wm.P.,173,213
GALAHAR, Peeler,176
GALISPEE, Solomon,269
GALL----, Jno.,248
GALLAGA, Wm.,150
GALLAHAIR, Peter,191
GALLAHER, Peter,186
GALLBGLY, Garner,061, George,
066, Hannah,044,045, James,
028, John,018,028, Jos.,011,
016,036,060,061, Joseph,019,
027,064,066, Robt.,028,051,
064,066, Sarah,064, Wm.,015,
022,028,035,044,045
GALLEHAIR, Peter,191
GALLIGA, John,030
GALLIHAIR, Peter,210,222
GALLIT(GULLET), Abraham,235
GAMBEL(?), Jno.,080
GAMBEL, Geo.,073, James Sr.,
020, James,225, Jas.Jr.,020,
John,073
GAMBELL, David,211,218,224,
Isaac,224,225, John,200,
William,208,246, Wm.,140,
143,166,168,170,179,186,
218,241,257
GAMBLE, Christopher,083,
David,079,096,168, Elias,
083,157, Elizabeth,083,
George,083, Haney,083,
Isaac,083, James,025,083,
131,157,231, Jno.,012,079,
116,167, John,021,025,039,
083,143, Josiah,083,225,
Patsey,185, Rachel,083,
Sarah,143
GAMBLE, Wm.,083,085,116,131,
189,252,260,262,263
GAMBRELL, David,102,110,
Mathew,233
GAMLEN, John,014
GAMMEL, James,011, Thos.,015
GAMMELL, Wm.,132
GAMMER, Jas.,001
GANES, Justian,161
GANT(GRANT?), Jesse,142
GANT, Almon,055, Almond,063,
Aney,233, Jas.,257, John,
233, Nancy,257
GANTT, Ludy,183
GARCE, Thomas,033
GARETT, Enoch,054, J.,240,
John,220
GAREY, Eliza,179,225, Jacob,
103,212, Janes,150, Jesse,
150, Jno.,098,103,253,
Joshua,097,176, Martin C.,
225, Martin,179, Mary Ann,
226, Newman,143, Norman,230,
Philip,272, R.,097, Rachel,
094,097, Saml.,218, Samuel,
080,122,126, Thos.,166
GAREY, William,094,095,097,
Wm.,102, Wm.C.,221
GARLAND, Henry,149
GARLING, Henry Jr.,202
GARLINGTON, ,236, --,155,
Christop.,235,236,237,268,
Christopher,230,232,256,
271, Cristepher,220,
Cristopher,250,268, Davis,
236, Edwin,155,160, Eleanor,
155,160, Elender,196, H.W.,
271, Henry W.,271,277,
Henry Wm.,275, Henry,256,
J.,090
GARLINGTON, Jno.,101,144,145,
151,153,154,157,159,160,
161,162,173,213,230,232,
235,237,243,244,250,271,
275, John,033,086,147,149,
151,152,155,176,204,206,
219,275,277,278, Joseph,160,

Wm.M.,278
GARLINTON, John,142
GARMAN, Charles,034
GARMON, Adam,072,097, Geo.,
044
GARNER, Benj.,036,040,053,
059,079,084,085,135,173,
Benjamin,005, Eliz.,085,
237, Elizabeth,005,257,
James,150,222,233,235,244,
Jas.,016,256,266, Jas.Jr.,
233, John,005,043, Matilda(Mrs.),
151, Sally,005, Sarah,005,
Thomas,005,016, Thos.,082
GARNER, Thos.,087
GARNET, Isaac D.,184
GARNETT(?), ,269
GARRET(?), Stephen,080
GARRET, Anna,033, Beheney,215,
Chas.,064, Enoch,042,
Harasha,033, Henry,215,
Herusha(?),033, James,032,
Jesse,032, Jno.,173,225,
271, John,031,033, Nathan,
271, Nickles,031, Nicklus,
033, Silas,011, Stephen,038,
Wm.,033
GARRETT(?), Maberry,266,
Robt.,071
GARRETT, Abraham,233, Alice(Abbie),
058, Allen,224, Ambros,230,
231,235,256, Ambrose,201,
230,278, Ambrous,215, Ann,
011, Anna,147,148, Anney,
010, Asa,178,179,236,261,
266,274, Asley,197, B.B.,
274, Barnet,230, Benj.F.,
257, Bennet,230, Betsy,100
GARRETT, Beverly B.,269,
Boyce,256,257, Bruce,256,
Chaney,215, Charles,058,
136,162, Coleman,152, Danl.,
163, David,106,148, Davis,
252,256, E.,055,094, E.H.,
261,266, Ed.,148, Edmond,
161,197,201, Edw.,075,081,
155,197,205,231,258,274,
Edw.H.,179
GARRETT, Edw.H.,233,237,240,
Edward,010, Edwd.,011,012,
Elihu,246,252,256, Elisha,
058,136, Eliz.,048,064,
Ellen,270, Enoch,048,049,
061,088,210,224,270,
Greenbury,257, Hannah,058,
090,136,231, Harmon,075,
103,156,196,201,205,233,
236, Harrison,256
GARRETT, Heman,256, Henry,058,
267, Hensley,256, Homer,201,
Hosa,197,220,256, Hosea,
156, Housley,257, Isaac,131,
197,201, J.,055, Jacob,049,
James,010,011,012,048,058,
080,186,256, Jas.,055,092,
093,117,131,138,164,
Jas.Sr.,178, Jesse Jr.,178
GARRETT, Jesse P.,238,
Jesse Sr.,135,141,142,274,
Jesse,011,022,058,073,077,
082,084,147,148,156,162,
164,178,179,188,196,197,
201,220,241,244,270,274,
Jessey,148, Jno.,088,094,
106,156,164,179,184,195,
196,210,224,228,231,270,
Jno.Sr.,231
GARRETT, John Jr.,049,278,
John Sr.,215, John,007,
010,011,031,049,050,053,
057,058,061,125,148,192,
197,201,216,220,270,
Jonathan,105, Jonth.,094,
Jos.,058,064,084,141,159,
164,183,184,188,210,224,
267, Joseph,156,175, Levi,
162,164,270
GARRETT, Lewis,266, M.,094,
Margaret,049, Margret,125,
Martha,125, Mary(March?),
010, Mary,049,164,210,224,
267, Morten,257, Moses,162,
164,195,224,270, Nancy,148,

278, Nathan,103, Nathl.,075,
Nicholas,011,082,169,
Nicklas,103, Nickles,148
GARRETT, Nicklos,058, Nicklus,
031,077,153,257, Noah,188,
Norman,197, Orsborn,244,
Polly,266, Rebecca,058,
Salley,081,178, Sally,100,
Saml.,121,161, Seaborn,256,
Silas,049,050,139, Silus(?),
125, Simien,257, Simion,257,
Simon,235, Starling,266
GARRETT, Steph.,094,155,201,
Stephen Jr.,201, Stephen Sr.,
141,231, Stephen,010,011,
024,052,055,058,080,081,
101,102,106,107,133,142,
146,147,148,156,163,173,
186,194,197,215,231,233,
246,256,258,266,268,278,
Stepn.,075, Susan,237,
Thomas,153
GARRETT, Thomas,214,230, Thos.,
161, Thos.,081,093,097,103,
138,148,161,168,179,186,
200,201,202,215,220,224,
231,232,252,266,270, W.,
105, Wm.,011,043,074,094,
103,105,121,148,181,256,
274, Wm.Jr.,094
GARREY, Robt.,163
GARROT, Edw.,010
GARROTT, John,215
GARRY, David,178
GARSONS(PARSONS?), Jos.,002
GARY, Abner F.,254, Abner,254,
Abraham,082, Andw.F.,254,
B.G.,258, Chas.,056,096,
Chas.F.,147, David,056,
238, Jacob,102,170, Jno.(Dr.),
242, Jno.,096,230,254, John,
010, Joseph,238, Juda,075,
Martin,111,150,165,170,
Mary Ann,226,228
GARY, Newman,051,065,101,150,
249,271, Newmen,253, Norman,
253,254, Saml(Gen.),,114,
Saml.,065,253,254,271,
Samuel,081,253, Sarah,122,
238, Stephen,075, Thos.,096,
111, Warner,238, Warron,238,
Wm.,019,056
GASTON, John,050
GASWICK, James,210
GATES, Alexr.,191, Daniel,277,
Duke,271, Jas.,039, Jno.,
090,120,129,185,187, John,
030,064,072,203, Jos.,191,
Robt.,265,271
GAUTIER, Peter Wm.,119
GAXSTON, Robert,028
GAY, Jno.,191
GEAR, Natty,067
GENT, Daniel,147, Danl.,090,
109,236,242, Fielding,259,
Jesse,265, John,229,231,
Nimrod,236
GENTRAY, Joel,252
GENTRY, Allen,274, Joel,220,
Saml.,205
GEORGE, Alexr.,026,032,048,
061, Ambrous,034,035,
Elijah,050,058,070,072,
Isaac,034,079, Israel,059,
Jesse,157,222,253, John,
004, Nancy,070, Warren,236,
Wm.,029,050,072,097,113
GETHARD, Jno.,173
GIBBS, John,073
GIBSON, Andw.,224, David,012,
Jacob,002, James,011,060,
061, Jas.,021, Mary,002,
Wm.,215,222
GIDDEN, James,008
GIDDENS, Edw.,021, Mr.,011,
020
GIDINS, Abner,258
GILBERT, A.,140, Austen,252,
Austin,231, Cassey,058,
Catharine,144, David,232,
Eliz.,092,226, James,144,
Jas.,057, Jeremiah,093,144
GILBERT, Jno.,092,093,094,

104,109, John,144, Jon'h.,
232, Jos.,104, Joshua,093,
144,165,228, Lucinda,109,
Lucindy,058, Lucy,116,
Matilda,109, Matildy,058,
Nath.,256, Nathl.,231,
Saml.,108, Sarah,058,109,
144, Thos.,093, W.H.,274,
William,145
GILBERT, William,226,230, Wm.,
073,077,088,092,093,116,
117,164,169,226,228,269,
Wm.Jr.,144, Wm.Sr.,144
GILBREATH, Jno.,113
GILDEWELL, Martin,021,152
GILES, John,057
GILL, Anna,045, Annaritter,
046, B.,261, Benj.,076,082,
083, Benjamin,084, Chas.,
203, Elizabeth,177, Jacob,
065,066,076, Jas.,133, Mary,
076, Robert,045, Robt.,046,
106,111,140,157, Thos.,092,
126,129,132,143,145,157,
171,243,253,264
GILLAM, Robt.,001,005,019
GILLAND, James,026, John,189,
Nancy,188, Robert,224,
Robt.,149,157,158,183,188,
189, Saml.,149, Wm.Jr.,156,
Wm.Sr.,156
GILLESPIE, Edw.,078,098,101
GILLIAM, Robt.Jr.,039,
Robt.Sr.,005
GILLILAND, Robt.,265,267,268,
274
GILLUM, James,191, Lien(?),
224, Robt.,040, Wm.,165
GINN, Basdle,228, John,027
GLADWELL, Martin,196
GLASBY, Solomon,197
GLASPEE, Moses,161
GLASPY, Solomon,231
GLAZE, John,048
GLAZEBROOK, Mary,077,088,
Nancy,077, Wm.,073
GLEN, David,035,115, Elizabeth,
256,257, Frances,256, Wm.,
247
GLENN, Alex.,076,101,112,265,
Alexander,166, Alexr.,066,
068,074,110,111,165,169,
176,179,180, Ann,164, Anna,
137,171, Anne,092,191,
Annie,070, Bernard,086,
Black G--,151, Blackgeorge(?),
063, Blackgrove,045,051,
055,059,063,070,074,092
GLENN, Blagrove(?),035,
Catharine,171,191, Catherine,
104, D.J.(?),169, David,043,
081,087,094,098,104,137,
138,168,169,203,243,274,
Eli'a.,219, Eliz.,169,
Elizabeth,068,104,137,138,
167,169,174,233, Frances,
151,176,179, Francis,037,081
GLENN, Francis,104,137,169,
256, Franklin,278, G.,092,
Geo.,126,137,141,155,164,
165,187, Geo.M.,169,175,
Geo.W.,167, George M.,168,
James E.,186, James,055,
081,104,105,124,137,169,
174,187,241, Jane,137, Jas.,
040,081,087,088,094,274
GLENN, Jer.,074, Jere.,111,
Jeremiah,036,065,070,072,
073,074,085,092,101,164,
171,191, Jno.,094,096,196,
266,273, Jno.M.C.,237, John,
104,137,171, Jos.,081,
Margaret,089, Margret,176,
179, Rebecca,137, Reuben,
068,069, Riley,121, Thomson S.,
186
GLENN, Thos.,098, Tiree,070,
Tyre,074, Tyree,074, Widow,
095, William,148,152,155,
191, Wm.,065,070,073,074,
088,092,101,103,110,111,
115,141,149,151,152,156,
171,189,225,239,240,270

GLIDEWELL, Martin,108,212,
Mastin,217,220, Nancy,217,
220,257, Robt.,029
GLLOVER(GLOVER?), B.,150
GLORE, Aaron,071, John,057
GLORUR, Geo.,137
GLOUR, Jas.,135
GLOVER, Benj.,095, Benjamin,
155, Catey C.,259, E.(Mrs.),
207, E.,270, ELizabeth,259,
Elizabeth,198,217,258,271,
Jackson,271, James A.,259,
James,095,186,195,198,214,
217, Julis,259, Julius,217,
228,267,271, Luesanny,259,
Mimmy,259, Misilla M.,259
GLOVER, N.,271, Nathaniel,259,
Nathl.,270, Standford,198,
Stanford,196,214,259,271,
William A.,259
GLOWER, Benj.,142
GLURE, Aaron,137
GODD, Wm.,246
GODDARD, Danl.,137,253, David,
137,229, Geo.,047,063,068,
097,137,214, George,135,
Wm.,137,214
GODFREE, Ansel,253, James S.,
261, James,242,249, Jesse,
256, Jno.,189,246,257, Rich,
200, Wm.,215
GODFREY, Ansel,035, Eligah,
266, Eliza,276, Hansey,273,
Jas.,078, Jas.S.,266,
Jat.(?)S.,209, Jesse,103,
Jno.,179,263,266,271,277,
John,070,193,264, Saml.,
273, Thos.,078, Wm.,034,274
GOFF, Hugh,090,150,152,
Rebecah,150,152, Rebeckah,
150, Thos.,150
GOFFORD, Wm.,217
GOGGANS, James,128, Jno.,097,
Saml.,110,111,129, Samuel,
128, Thomas,128,129
GOGGEN, Elihu,215, Josiah,240
GOGGENS, Anderson,131, Jno.,
176, Josiah,240, Wm.,258
GOGGIN, Rachel,036
GOGGINS, Jas.,036, Jesse,235,
Jno.,160,201, Jonathan,179,
Mary,036, Rachel,034,036,
Saml.,137, Thos.,036,222,
228,236,243, William,036,
Wm.,034
GOLDEN, Andw.H.,098, Anthony,
023,195,205,252, Cristena,
240, James,064,072, Jas.,
062, John Jr.,089, John N.,
240, John,089,149, Mary,257,
Reuben,057,072, Richard,
214, Richd.,076,096,205,
254, Robt.,096, Sarah,240,
Thos.,083
GOLDING, ,229, A.,108, A.F.,
198,264, Anteney,259,
Anthony F.(?),275, Anthony F.,
029,139,196,198,199,231,
235,259,275,277, Anthony G.,
198, Anthony,029,030,032,
106,120,133,150,158,161,
185,203,235,238,257,264,
268,269,271,272,274, Benj.,
124
GOLDING, Bird,222, Caroline M.,
277, Chas.,021, Christiana N.,
277, Elisha,160, Elizabeth,
029, Foster(?),172, Foster,
207, Geo.,188, Ira,259,
Isabel,029, James,029,095,
214,259, Jas.,269, Jas.M.,
247, Jas.N.,207, Jno.,186,
John R.,029, John,021
GOLDING, John,095, Margarett,
271, Nancy,259, Peggey,259,
Permelia N.,029, R.,149,
Rachel,029, Reuben,106,
108,124,133,160,191,259,
260, Richard G.,259,
Richard,095,120, Richd.,
113,173,174,185,198,223,
229,235,264,269,270,271,
Richd.G.,271

GOLDING, Robert,095, Robt.,
032,160,214,258, Salley,238,
Sarah,214, Thomas,029,
Thos.,099, Thos.W.,107,
109,110, William,259, Wm.,
095,145,203,213,214,217,
243,259
GOLDNG, Reuben,270
GOLDSBY, Byrd,008
GOLDSMITH, Thos.,166, Turner,
248
GOLIGHTLY, Elihu,273, Ransom,
273
GOMER(?), Benj.,128
GOOD, Joseph,232
GOODEN, Solomon,172
GOODGOINS, Joseph,278
GOODIN, Theoplus,228
GOODLEY, Chas.D.,140
GOODMAN, ,270, Benj.,056,062,
Charles,012,035, Chas.,051,
085,104,105,106,111,
Clabourn,009,016,035,048,
Claiborn,012, Clarband,012,
Claybourn,013,027,035,
David,187,219,221,248,
Duke,129,159,187,203,253,
267,271, Eliz.,221, Gilliam,
219
GOODMAN, Gillum,187,219,221,
James,005,009,012,014,016,
019,022,157,174,191,203,
219,221,224,247,262,264,
265, Jane,261, Jas.,019,
251,267,268,269,272, Jemima,
219, Jon.,019, Jos.,012,
014, Joseph,035, Maria,219,
Mariah,019,035,221,
Marietta,248
GOODMAN, Mary,009, Meriah,014,
019,027,035,037, Mrs.,221,
Nancy,064, Rhoda,219,
Saml.,005,046,051,068,070,
080,084,106,114,138,153,
185,187,221,245,247,261,
Saml.Jr.,221, Samuel,035,
080,199,219, Starling,173,
Thos.,270, Timothy,012,022
GOODMAN, Timothy,035, William,
009, Wm.,013
GOODSON, Wm.,143
GOODWIN, (Wid.),273, Ceala,
228, Cealey,195, Cealia,197,
Celey,197, Eliz.,085,
Giles,265,267, Hannah,106,
Harris,195,197, Hiram,106,
Jane,276, Mark,008,058,
Peter,043,060, Philip,228,
Solomon,159,180,249,256,
Taylor,274, Theophilus,071
GOODWIN, Thomas,037,085,226,
228, Thoplas(?),226, Thos.,
025,028,043,050,057,074,
077,100,115,145,220,
Thos.Jr.,226,228, William,
271,276, Wm.,002,098,124,
143,197,224,230,273
GOODWYN, Wm.,145
GOOSMAN, Chas.,036, Clabourn,
036, Jos.,036, Meriah,036,
Nancy,036, Saml.,036
GOR, Thos.,183
GORDEN, Mathew,257
GORDIN, Geo.,224
GORDON, Alfred Geo.W.,263,
Ann C.,178, Ann G.,177,
Ann J.,177, Drury,166,
Geo.,168,177,265, Geo.Wash.,
262, George,004,262, Jain,
177, James,065,066, Jane,
234,237,251, Jno.,076,
Lydall,062, Rubin,047, Wm.,
194
GORE, Joshua,265, Thomas,036,
Thos.,221,224,244,265,274
GOSS, Jos.,060, Thos.,239,
Wm.,213,229,230,235,236,
254,266,271
GOSSIT, Nathan,266
GOUCH, Ann,277, Elizabeth,277
GOULDING, Richd.,264, Wm.,264
GOURGANIS, Joseph,274
GOW, Stephen,060, Thos.,060

GOWAN, Jno.,252
GOWEN(?), Mrs.,171
GOWIN, Salley,230
GOWING, Jno.,252
GOZA, Aron,122
GRACE, Cassa,044, Geo.,088,
117,119,121,138, George,147,
Jas.H.,221, Sarah,044
GRADBURY, Chas.,140
GRADEN, Starling,237, Thos.,
094
GRADION, Free Bill,229
GRADON, Drury,188, Mathew,148,
Nathen,166, Stirling,237,
Thos.,118,146,148,166,185,
233
GRAFORD(?), Jno.,101
GRAFTON, Jno.,222
GRAGE, Wm.,109
GRAHAM, David,041, Jno.,173,
Wm.,164,170,188
GRANGER, Edmond,016
GRANSHAW(?), A.,162
GRANT(?), Jesse,142
GRANT, Ainah,238, Almon,043,
105,136, Arianah,238, Geo.,
160,251,267, Isaac,005,133,
185,217,233,235,238,267,
Jane,238, Jean,238, Jeane,
027, Jno.,196,252,265,267,
271,272, Marion,238,267,
Mary,130, Wm.,238
GRANTREY, Allen,258
GRASEY, Warner R.,220
GRASS, Wm.,038
GRAVES(GROVES), Martin,176
GRAVES, Amos S.,102, Fanney,
076, George,130, Lewis,004,
015,015,019,049,053,071,
075,076, Martin,076,207,
Rebecah,076, Wm.,076,117,
195,213,263
GRAVESS, Jos.,123
GRAY(GAREY), Lesley,183
GRAY, ,090, Aberham,212
GRAY, Abraham,001,002,020,
083,156,203,205,211,
Absalom,001,004, Albelina,
213, Andrew,028, Andrw.,027,
Archer,213, Catherine,025,
Charitate,232, Charles,028,
Chas.,027, David,036,270,
E.,056, El,071, Eliz.,094,
Eliza,205,212, Elizabeth,
010
GRAY, Elizabeth,027, Ellie(?),
225, Elvisa,270, Esley,225,
Fredrick,225, Fredrk.,096,
G.A.,219, Gideon,225,
Henry,108,151,208,215,223,
225, Hezekiah,156,183,252,
277, Isaac,004,026,043,051,
075,079,096,125,128,135,
212,214,225, Isabel,018
GRAY, Isabel,025, Isabele,024,
Jacob,036, James,010,018,
027,028,169, Jane,094, Jas.,
036, Jenney,212, Jesse Sr.,
256, Jesse,205,256, Jno.,
100,109,153,218,233,253,
264, Jno.F.,234,237,
John Jr.,011, John Sr.,011,
John,008,014,024,025,027
GRAY, John,028,057,065,071,
148,212, Lenard,248, Lesley,
213,225,232, Leslie,205,
225, Losina,213, Madison,
213, Mary Ann,209, Mary,001,
004,020,058, Mekena(Melsena?),
213, Palaskie,256, Phebe,
027, Philip,136,152,220,
Pleskey,256, Poleskey,213
GRAY, Purches B.,277, Rebecca,
061,071, Robt.,027,071,095,
106,108,123,124,253,
Roger(?),095, Saml.,065,
085,156,230,256, Sarah,027,
270, Thomas,207, Thos.,025,
055,061,083,236,243,248,
268, Tolletason,205, Tollison,
213, West,055, Wm.,006
GRAY, Wm.,010,011,014,022,
026,043,051,054,060,061,

066,068,076, Z.,061, Zach.,
232,258, Zachariah,165,205,
225,272, Zana,205, Zeny/Zana,
225
GRAYDON, ,223, James,219,
Mathew,219, Matthew,026,
Thos.,186
GRAYER, Jas.,249
GRAYHAM, David,021,108,143,
224,237,251, Geo.,151,
James,186, Jas.,087, Jos.,
135, Susannah,083, Thos.,
221,241, William,154, Wm.,
076,083,108,129,130,132,
135,154,158,166
GRAYMAN, (Mrs.),258
GREEK(?), Jas.J.,003
GREEN(?), Jno.,125
GREEN, Agnes,164,167, Casey,
165,167, Danl.,109, David,
008,020,028,066,087,095,
136, Eliz.,105,108, Elizabeth,
224, Frances,279, Gilley A.,
139,140, Henry,076, James,
008,102,119,270, Jeremiah,
007, Jno.,174, Jos.,189,
Mrs.,008,206, Nathl.,050
GREEN, Robert,062, Saml.,074,
091,097,098, T.,270, Thomas,
176,179, Thos.,020,095,
William,139,164,278, Wm.,
012,018,051,057,063,064,
080,101,107,108,120,160,
165,166,167,179,206,207,
226,251,262,266,267,269,
270,274, Wm.Jr.,164,
Zachariah,008
GREENE, Wm.,013
GREER, David,018,036,038,050,
055,067,068,074,090,106,
132,137,150,199,242,260,
261, Henry,104, James,215,
Jane,008, Jas.,011,020,
Jno,168, Jno.,043,101,120,
225, John,008,010,020,135,
260,261, Jonas,010, Jos.,
055,110,166,168, Jos.Sr.,010
GREER, Jose.,215, Joseph,156,
Josiah,010, Mary,060,
Nancy,261, Robt.,010,021,
Saml.,104, Thos.,011,269,
271
GRENNAGE, Edmond,007
GRESON, Edw.,239
GREY, Palaska,256, Wm.B.,236
GREYHAM, James,258, Jno.,258
GRFFIN, John R.,149
GRIER, David,135, John,011,
Jos.,010, Joseph,010,
Susannah,198, Wm.,132
GRIFFEN, A.(Capt.),264, A.,
253,255,264, Anthony,218,
233,242,262, B.F.,247,
Benj.,225, Bluford F.,220,
Dr.,264, Elihu,218,246,
Elijah,250, Elisu,250,
James,199, Jno.K.,247,
Jno.R.,247, Joseph,218,
Meredith,244, Moses,262,
Richd F.,250
GRIFFEN, Wade H.,199, Wade,
218
GRIFFIN, (Capt.),102, A.(Capt.),
187,203,264, A.,054,056,
131,132,203,235,263,269,
273, Ab.,036, Abe,056, Abia,
017,051,054,056,062, Ad.,
057, Adi,044, Adin(?),057,
Adinda,056, Aelius(Alice?),
057, Anth.,066, Anthony(Capt.),
235, Anthony,005
GRIFFIN, Anthony,006,017,057,
062,064,069,095,100,101,
102,103,108,111,127,129,
132,140,141,148,152,157,
158,160,190,191,196,207,
243,263,269, Asa,017,054,
056,062,108, B.F.,235,266,
275, Benj.,081,097,113,132,
141,161,166,205, Benjamin,
111
GRIFFIN, Betsey,113, Bleuford F.,
174, Bleuford,209, Bluford,

211, C.B.,266, Caty,006,
Charles,006,029,057,
Charter,101, Chas.,024,
051,054,057,101,149,
Christopher,085,108,
Cristopher,159, D.H.,167,
Daniel,018, David,053,064,
066,073
GRIFFIN, E.,090, Elender(?),
054, Elihu,113,203,205,230,
Elijah,160,203, Elinor,057,
Eliz.,110,113, Ellinor,054,
Ezekiel,007, F.,269,
Frances,074, Francis,087,
093, Ira,056,057, Jackson,
256, James Sr.,021, James,
006,017,027,035,042,051
GRIFFIN, James,057,066,199,
207, Jane,006, Janet,027,
Jas.,029,031,131,137,147,
Jno.,100,101,110, Jno.B,
151, Jno.B.,159, Jno.D.,129,
Jno.R.,140,160, John K.(R?),
149, John R.,095,209,261,
John,007,039,056,057,059,
083, Jos.,024,114, Jos.L.,
026
GRIFFIN, Joseph,001,006,056,
177, Kitty,095, Larkin,057,
161, Lewis,042, Mary Ann,
017,056, Mary,001,027,095,
Meredith,277, Moses,111,
161,204,258,262, Nancy,066,
Patsey,143, Peggy,006, R.,
101, Rachael,006, Reuben,
083,095,111,113,157,159
GRIFFIN, Reuben,160,277,
Reubin,030, Richard,002,
005,006,017,018,022,054,
056, Richd.,001,012,013,
028,039,050,057,238,265,
267, Richd.S.,207, Richd.Sr.,
056, Robt.,018, Steph.,063,
Sucky,017, Thos.,137,
Wade H.,167,208, Wade,160,
207,210
GRIFFIN, Wm.,011,048,050,056,
057,105,110,113, Wm.H.H.,
269, Wm.Sr.,006
GRIFFITH, Benj.,163,164,180,
181,183,184,215,230,232,
259, Ezekiel,012,058,
Lowery,259, Lucy,269,
Milla(Milia),183
GRIGBY, John,009
GRIGGS, Gimima,242, Jemimah,
234
GRIGSBY, Benj.,190,247, John,
027, Sarah S.,190, Solomon,
196
GRIMES, Henry,235, James Sr.,
162, James,191, Jas.,113,
272, Jno.,186, Thos.,097,
Wm.,061,113
GRIZEL, Eliz.,115, Elizabeth,
075, John,075, Nancy,075,
Stephen,075, Wm.,075
GRIZZEL, Thos.,111
GRNT(GRANT?), Isaac,161
GRNT, Isaac,229
GROOMS, Richd.,013
GROSVENOR, Parley,162
GROVENER, Parley,226, Peter,
192
GROVES(GRAVES?), Martin,180
GROVES, Benj.,236, Martin,169,
176, Wm.,228,259
GROVNER, Farley,270
GRULD(?), Geo.,151
GRUMBLY, Thos.,098
GRY, John,021
GUGHAN, Geo.,041
GUIN, Bacon,033, Danl.,012,
Jno.,197,252, Martha,125,
Pattey,238, Thomas,125
GUINN, Basden,105,115, Bosden,
197, Jno.,231, Martha,191,
Salley,230, Wm.,231
GULLET, Abraham,196
GULLETT(?), Matilda,264
GUNDIFF, Geo.,166
GURDON(JURDON), Mildred,139
GUTHERY, John,008

GUTHREY, Dudley,098, Eliz.,
017
GWENNT, Martin,255
GWIN, Jno.,251, Thos.,228
GWINN, Sally,230
HAIGWOOD, Chas.,264
HAISEL, Harey,176
HAISTEN, Wm.,259
HAISTING, Peter,222, Robert,
225
HAISTINGIS, R.,222
HAISTINGS, Robt.,188, Wm.,187
HAISTON, Robert,226
HALBERT, Joshua,272, Thos.,
272, William,194, Wm.,104,
195,196,202,232,272
HALBURT, Wm.,145
HALCOM, Elisha,050, Jos.,104,
Marey,050, Obediah,104
HALCOMB, Ob.,057, Posel,144
HALE, Rebecca Y.,277
HALIDA, Wm.,137
HALL(?), Wm.,072
HALL, Abram,020,099, Alex.,
133, Alsey,133, Anne,057,
Benj.B.,233, Drury,136,
Elizabeth,057, H.B.,148,
Hennery,024, Henry R.,150,
231,235, Henry,020, James,
057,236,242, Jno.,162,228,
235,239, Joel,188, John,007,
Jos.,048,071,088,258,
Joseph,056
HALL, Joseph,072,083, L.,210,
Labun,210, Margaret,003,
071,083, Marton,166,
Mary Ann,171, Mary,020,
Milley,253, R.B.,274,
Salley M.(Mrs.),235,
Salley M.,231, Salley,210,
Sally M.,196,235, Saml.,
128,137,178,212,228,229,
Samuel,015, Susanna,065
HALL, Thos.,077, William,020,
133,134,136, Wm.,002,003,
022,023,034,066,107,124,129
HALLADAY, Robt.,163
HALLAMS, Jno.F.,185, Wm.,007
HALLEMS, David,073
HALLUMS, John,008, Wm.,008
HALUMS, David,063
HAMBLETON, Eliz.,080, James,
066,067,068,072, Jane,153,
155, Jas.,025,042,080, Jno.,
242, Robert,080, Robt.,067,
068,072,085, Saml.,228,229,
Wm.,081,098,122,139,153,155
HAMBLITON, Jacob,225
HAMES, Jesse,069
HAMILTON, James,029,059,155,
Jane,155,171,277, Jno.,155,
John,155,171, Martha,171,
Robertson,155, Robt.,061,
S.,270, Samuel,171, Thos.,
013, Wm.,151
HAMMENS, Ebenezer,256
HAMMOND, A.,225, Ann,100,
Ebenezer,256, Elisha,096,
Isam,196, Iscm,100,103,
Isum,193, James,156,196,
Jno.,196, John,115,196,
Joseph,115, Lewis,219,
Mackey,115, Nancy,103,193,
194,196, P.,196, Peter Sr.,
196, Peter,030,038,077,091,
100
HAMMOND, Peter,103,155,156,
193,194,196,208,270,
William,100
HAMOND, Martin,189
HAMONS, Peter,169
HANAH, Thos.,142
HANCE, Wm.,230
HANCOCK, Clement,049,051,
Isabella,051, James,049,
051, John,049, Jos.,049,
Patsey,049, Richd.,007,
016, Wm.,017,021,031
HAND, Anteney,258, Elizabeth,
278,279, Gabriel,218,265,
272,274, Jno.,117,232,252,
Lindsey,265, Polley,278,
Robert Sr.,279, Robert,278,

279, Robin,232, Robt.,010,
013,090,094,103,164,196,
197,201,205,225,228,252,
272, Robt.Jr.,104,252,
Robt.Sr.,190
HAND, Roland,232, Seybern,251
HANDBY, John,127
HANDCOCK, Jas.,024, Jos.,049,
Wm.,049,051
HANDLEY, John,126
HANEY, John,210
HANIE, Wm.,237
HANN, Robt.,256, Robt.Jr.,231
HANNA, David,112, James,026,
065,144, Jas.,273, Jno.,119,
273, John,004,048,058, Robt,
009, Robt.,004,008,013,026,
112, Wm.,014,021,029,144
HANNAH, David,145, James,063,
144,224, Jas.,008,097,098,
103,134,145, Jas.Littel,189,
Jno.,205,258, Jos.,145,
Reuben,247, Robt.,098,145,
178,188,265, Thos.,230,
William,225, Wm.,093,098,
145,155, Wm.Jr.,145,
Wm.Robt.,189
HANNER, Thos.,041
HANNON, John,210, Mary,210
HANSEL, John,010
HARDEN, Henry,050, James H.,
255, James,168, Jas.H.,115,
Mark,050
HARDIN, Eli,266, Geo.,070,
James,096, Mark,088,
Nicholas,070, Nick.,096,
Sarah,070, Thomas,070,
William,070, Wm.,018
HARDING, Aaron,099, Abner,070,
Abraham,070, Abrum,036,
Chas.,073, Chr.,096,
Elizabeth,070,103, George,
070, Henry,070, James,073,
097,103, Jas.,098,102,107,
212, Jas.H.,115, Jno.,097,
108, John,103, Mark,096,
097, Matthew,103, Nicholas,
036
HARDING, Nicholas,070,084,
Sally,070, Sarah,073,098,
101,103, Susannah,070,
Thomas,072, Thos.,073,
Valentine,116, William,070,
Wm.,019,036,060,072
HARDY, James,237, Kitt,159,
Wm.,235,236,268
HAREGROVE, Allen,223
HAREY(?), John,190
HARINGS, Jno.F.,188
HARLAN, Aaron,060,061,263,
Eliz.,060, George,060,
Henry,224, Isaiah,060,
James,060,172, Jane,060,
Jas.,274, Jos.,060,273,
Joshua,060, Mary,060,
Rebecah,060, Saml.,060,
HARLAND, Jos.,188
HARLDAN, Valentine,145
HARLEN, Cinthia E.,165,
Joseph,216, Valentine,123,
Wm.C.,165
HARLEY, Henry,245
HARLIN, Hugh,134
HARLING, Valuntine,098,187,
237, Valuntine,143
HARLINGONE, Valuntine,145
HARLINGS, Jane,168, Wm.C.,168
HARLON(HARTON?), Jas.,134
HARLON, Elizabeth,134, James,
161,172, Joseph,149,
Valentine,134, Wm.,134
HARMING, Jno.,188
HARMON, Danl.,187, Jno.,190,
266, Thos.,190,191, Wm.,191
HARNEL, Abraham,273, Wm.,273
HARNS(?), Nathan,267
HAROLD, Abraham,273
HARPER, Isabel(?),044, Jno.,
034, Wm.,055
HARREY, Jane,193, John,192
HARRINGTON, G.L.,127
HARRIS, ,223, A.,117, Absolam,
252, Benj.,097, Braddock,

024,042, Chas.,024,040,065,
066,087, Ebenezer,076, Edw.,
038, Ginny,105, Jane,036,
Jas.,102, Jinney,074, Jno.,
029,045,088,093,101,173,
232,252,272, Jno.H.,254,
Jno.Jr.,257, Jno.L.,172
HARRIS, Jno.L.,213, Jno.Sr.,
256, John G.,062, John L.,
188, John(?),147, John,006,
021,023,024,029,031,034,
048,062,072,073,074,205,
223, Jos.,113,164,221, L.,
252, Lauran,231, Lauson,256,
Lawson,257, Lucy,102,
Margaret,106, Martha,049
HARRIS, Mary,211, Minnard,063,
105, Minyard,024,036,081,
098,099, Mrs.,024, Nathan,
136,164,182,221,243, Nathen,
215, Overton,069, Peggy,062,
Richd.,188,213,217,250,
267,270, Robt.,097, Ruth,
242, Stephen,012,016,023,
Thos.,021,024,048,054
HARRIS, Thos.,064,099,111,
117,171,216.221,242,269,
William,221, Wilson,274,
Wm.,019,024,034,040,103,
136,164,186,199,215,266,
Wm.W.,251
HARRISON, Danl.,101
HARRISS, Archbd.,139, Jane,
123, John,133, Jos.,136,
Nathan,136, Wm.,141
HARRON, John,092
HARROWS, Wm.,099
HARRY(?), Davis S.,152
HARRY, Chas.,097, Jno.,097
HART, W.,013
HARTEN, Jos.,200
HARTFORD, M.,265
HARTING, Robt.,188
HARTLEY, Tabitha,067
HARTON, Jos.,200, Valentine,
124
HARVEY, Chas.,007,079, Jno.,
104, Joel,010, Littleberry,
022, Philip,022
HARWELL, Absalom,052
HASEL, Henry,045
HASLET, Jno.,022, Nancy,016,
Robt.,016
HASMINING(?), Danl.,265
HASTING, Valentine,220
HATCHER, Fell(?),144, Felt,
144,147,270, Felt.,072,
Fleming,074, John,188,
Margaret,144,147, Margarite,
270, Wm.,126,147,241
HATHORN, E.,135, Edney,113,
Edny,135, J.L.,135, James,
089,095,112,113,114,134,
135, Jas.,108, Jas.,135
HATTEN(?), Abraham,121
HATTEN, Jno.H.,266,273
HATTER, Benj.,009,164, David,
060, John,065,066, Rich.,
009, Richard,008,100,
Richd.,012,018,046,047,
048,057,063,066,100,
Richd.Sr.,066
HATTON, Francis,167
HAULE, Wm.,027
HAWLER, Jos.,042
HAY, Thomas,148
HAYDEN, James,162,225
HAYNES, Isaac,019
HAYS, Jno.,210, John,125,128,
130, Jonathan,128, Joshua,
191, Susana(?),010, Wm.,149,
160,193,253,261,264
HAZEKIAH, Bruce,272
HAZEL, Danl.,139, Eliz.,063,
228, Harey,217, Harrey,227,
228, Harry,097, Henry,019,
040,087,113, Honey,186,
Jno.,161,205, John,019,
069, Wm.,040
HAZLE, Harrey,068, Harry,063,
Henry,018,062, James,228,
John,228
HAZLET, Grizzel,107, Harrey,

19

227, Henry,041,178, Jno.,
251, John,013,203
HAZLETT, Grizlet(?),102,
Grizzell,104, Grizzle(?),
102, John,102, Nancy,102,
Robt.,102
HEDLEY, Allen,139
HEFFERMAN, Jno.,271
HELLAMS, Ann,006, Constant,
002, David,044, Dempsey,102,
Geo.,084, Jno.,188, John,
002,273, Jonathan,002,
Nancey,002, Rachael,002,
Thos.,071, William,002,
Wm.,005,006,013,072
HELLOMS, Jno.,233
HELMONS, Elisha,228
HELMS, Andw.,170, David,046,
171,172, Wm.,170, Yancy,272
HELTHAN, Jno.,183
HELTON, Thos.,165,220,232
HELUM, Wm.,221
HEMPHILL, Dr.,040,045, John,
033
HENDBARK, Stanten,252
HENDERSON, Andrew,136, Andw.,
042,213,235,236,239,242,
Ann,017,021,031,032,
Archd.,063, Austin,222,
Canada,277, Charles,059,
Chas.,060, D.,114, Daniel,
121,122, David,069, Elizabeth,
258, Fanney,031, Fowler,220,
Frances,077,082, Frankey,
060
HENDERSON, Geo.,017, James,
002,009,021,027,152,197,
199,200,206,212,229,272,
Jas.,017,029,031,036,038,
042,055,079,084,087,097,
114,174,189,268, Jas.Jr.,
021,236, Jas.Sr.,222,237,
Jaustion,251, Jena,229,
Jesse,221,229,239,242,249,
Jno.,081
HENDERSON, Jno.,098,151,189,
200,211,222,229,241,243,
245,251,267, John,009,055,
060,111,154,217,264,272,
Jonathan,273, Jonathen,229,
Justinian,111,279, Justinion,
267, Luke,221, Marey,063,
Marstin,211, Mastin,222,
Nancy,111,278, Nathan,043
HENDERSON, Nathen,219, Noah,
208, Patsey,031, Peggy,277,
Polley,255, Sally,111,
Saml.,008,009,017,027,029,
031,032,043,063,065,075,
080,086,092,099,102,232,
Saml.C.,076, Samuel,021,
031,074,110,111,112,174,
Sarah,031,060,063, Sarey,
062
HENDERSON, Stewart,229,
Susan(Mrs.),151, Susannah,
088,110,111, Thomas,059,
060, Thos.,055,059,158,250,
Washington,278, William,
062,197,255, Wm.,017,031,
042,051,060,098,108,109,
113,116,129,136,141,152,
174,178,193,221,229,230,
233,256
HENDERSON, Wm.,269,279, Wm.H.,
212, Wm.Sr.,235
HENDLEY(?), John B.,127
HENDLEY, Jno.,139, Wm.,043,
050
HENDRICK, H.D.,137, Hancel,
218, Haney,207, Hanie,169,
219,221,223, Hanna,174,
Honee,185, Jeremiah,061,
Joel,214,219,223, Joshua,
183, Margret,015,016,
Micajah,015,018, Rachael,
015, Rachel,223, Rebeca,223,
Tabitha,037, Thos.,041,
052,056
HENDRICK, Thos.,136,137,183,
189,212,213,239, Wm.Win,015,
037
HENDRICKS, Mrs.,051, Thos.,

049,086,088, Wm.,144,239
HENDRIX, Abner,117, Jno.B.,
164, Larkin,093
HENERY, Jas.,137,141, John,
214, Mathew,137,145, Robt.,
097
HENLEY, Gennet,010, Jas.,029,
John,189, Wm.,056
HENNERY, Alexr.,097, Nelley,
097
HENRY, Alex.,076,104,106,113,
Alexr.,029,099,100,107,
114, Elenor,189, Eliz.,087,
Ibby,087, James,087,137,
255, Jane,087, Jas.,273,
275, Jno.F.,224, M.H.,174,
273
HENRY, Mathew H.,168,257,
Mathew,137,149,150,
Matthew H.,273, Matthew,
087, Nancy,087, Nelley,107,
Nelly,100,114,119, Polley,
193, Rachel,259, Robert,087,
Robt.,084,099,104, Sarah,
087, W.E.,273, Wm.,273
HENSLEY, Saml.,090,117
HENSON, Thos.,043
HERBERT, Thos.E.,268,269
HERRING, Jno.,093,116,117
HERSTON, Robert,226
HETO, Wm.,272
HETZAG, Jno.,248
HEWART, Jno.,190
HEWIT, Ashley,100, Catherine,
100, Charles,100,102, Chas.,
093, Jno.,100,104,179, John,
100,127,147,208, Ruth,100,
Susanna,100, William,100,
Wm.,111,167,210
HEWITT, Jno.,138
HICKS, Edw.,192,257, Jno.,133
HIFFS, James,150
HIGENS, Jno.,178
HIGGAN, Simien,252
HIGGEN, David,205, James B.,
201, Jno.,247
HIGGENS, J.F.,122, James,072,
Jno.,178, Mark,191, Newton,
237, Parmer,189, Tucker,178,
Wm.,122,141
HIGGINS, Benj.,256, Benj.B.,
277, D.,279, David Jr.,257,
David,081,132,133,146,156,
169,201,233, Geo.,271, J.B.,
231, James Jr.,201,215,256,
James,013,044,059,060,215,
Jas.,133,274, Jas.B.,274,
277,279, Jno.,082,083,099,
134,141,142,268
HIGGINS, Jno.Jr.,273, Jno.Sr.,
273, John,055, Newton,010,
075,082,084,099,235,237,
268,273, O.B.,194, Palmer,
151, Parmer,133, Reuben,010,
S.F.,258, Sarah,273,
Serena,044, Thos.,012,094,
Tireana,044, Tucker,155,
Wm.,006,044,053,060,063
HIGGINS, Wm.,081,094,103,132
HIGGNS, David,231
HIGH, Richd.,052
HILBORN, Levy,028
HILL(?), David,080
HILL(HALL?), ,077
HILL(HITT?), Henry,023,
Marshall,080
HILL, Aaron,228,267,271,
Abner,203, Anne,209, Benj.,
124,209,210,222,240,247,
249,251,260,265,267,270,
271, Benjamin,209,216,
Bennett,030,077, Bird,263,
Byrd,265,268, Caroline Eliz.,
233, Casen,203, Cason,190,
268,272, Danl.,046,047,
David,165
HILL, David,209, Dennett,077,
Eleanor,270, Elenor,210,
Eliz.Emeline,209, Elizabeth,
261, Ellender,041,043,208,
Enoch,261,272, Fanney,159,
Fanny,158, Faries(?),218,
Faris,191, Frances E.,233,

Frances,190, Francis,203,
205,220,271,272
HILL, Harris,261, Haruntal(Hamulal
181, Hennery,042,043, Henry,
041,132,133,186,190,252,
261, Isaac,164,189,209,210,
224,266,270, Jacob Wm.,209,
James,131,158,182,267,
Jas.,120,130, Jas.L.,276,
Jer'y,124, Jesse,241,252,
265,267, Jno.,097
HILL, Jno.,098,100,114,116,
133,167,190,206,257, John,
003,126,203, Jos.,043,133,
236, Joseph,153, Jusey,080,
Larkin,191, Laurens,053,
Lazarus,229, Levi,063,176,
178,182,184,186,217, Martha,
164, Mary,133,136,140,158,
159,164,190,191,209
HILL, Mary,249, Mitchell,252,
Moses,076,188, Peter,048,
Polley,131,158, Ray,240,
Rebah,272, Reuben,198,253,
Robert,158, Robt.,043,077,
131, S.S.,159,190, Sally,
158, Saml.B.,269, Sarah Fanny,
131, Steph.,200, Stephen,
137,209,213,266,267
HILL, Susey,209, Thomas,131,
133,150,158,227, Thos.,048,
063,065,066,077,100,110,
112,120,121,133,190,196,
229,243,270, Travis,190,
203,273, Wiley,167,188,232,
237,243,249,270,271, Willey,
181,185, William,155,159,
Wm.(Col.),236, Wm.,044
HILL, Wm.,055,072,074,085,
123,131,133,158,159,160,
164,166,184,222,224,233,
234,238,247,254,261,
Wm.Hendrick,209, Wm.Jr.,
133, Wm.P.,191, Wm.Sr.,261
HILLER, Cassy,275
HILLIDY, Free,256
HILITON, Rebeca,200, Thomas,
200
HINDS(?), Phillimon,265
HINLEY, Salley,228
HINSLEY, James,194
HINSON, James,022, Thos.,139
HINTON, Elander,017, Elizabeth,
017, Jno.,040, John,017,
018,019,036,068, Robert,017,
Robt.,017,018, Thomas,017,
Wm.,098
HIPP, Saml.,266, Wm.,266
HIPPS, Elizabeth,178, James,
216, Joseph,178,204
HIPS(?), James,168
HIPS, Jos.,261, Joseph Jr.,
203
HIRAN, Wm.,253
HISTELOE, Iscm,012
HITCH, J.,137,171,187, Jno.,
095,138,187,236,266,276,
John,035,065,068,155,172,
188, Jos.,134, Jos.N.,177,
195, Joseph N.,197, Joseph,
177, Joshua,065,068,
Lowthen D.,142, Lowther D.,
268, Luther D.,195, Luther Sr.,
177, Luther,099, Nancy,276
HITCH, Rosannah,177, Sarah,
177, W.D.,197, W.W.,174,
266,272,275,276, Wm.D.,187,
Wm.W.,195, Wm.Winder,172
HITT, Abner,056,058,066,110,
124,203, Alex,269, Ben.,058,
Benj.,053,056,080,110,124,
128,267,272, Benjamin,216,
Danl.,009,235, David,044,
057,058,093,094,101,110,
111,124,128, Eliz.,052,
Eliz.S.,216, Elizabeth,203,
Evy,245, Geo.,052, Henry,
009
HITT, Henry,038,050,058,109,
124,152,160,187,203,216,
217,221,267,269,272,274,
Jesse,085,187,203,216,245,
252,259,269, Jno.,085,165,

167,185,257,265,268,269,
272, John Jr.,203, John,052,
126,152,216,220,229,244,
250, Larkin,058,110,112,
Laurene,023
HITT, Lazarus,012,057,058,
063,072,080,127,152,190,
222,229,245, Martin,216,
Mary,058, Peter,009,057,
058,203, Reuben,080,085,
100,217,222, Sally,250,
Stephen,052, Thomas,229,
240, Thos.,057,058,066,108,
259, Wm.,195,216,252,267,
268,272
HITTON, Thos.,272
HITTS(?), Efrum,130
HIX, E.,149, Edw.,141,151,
152,159,179,235,237,268
HOBBS, Chas.,105, John,135
HOBBY, Jno.,094
HOBERT, Wm.,238
HODGE, Benjamin,054,056, John,
054, Jos.,120, Richard,054,
Richd.,248
HODGES, Jno.W.,258, Jos.,139,
Joseph,016, Naomi,016,
Richard,062,065, Richd.,
074, Wm.,113
HODGINS, Ambrose,159
HOG, Willis,167
HOGG, Lewis,041, Willis,151
HOKINS, Solomon,094
HOLADAY, Janney,186, Mathew,
143,163,178,256, Matthew,
141, Robt.,124,161,187,
William,186, Wm.,141,186,
222
HOLADY, Wm.,242
HOLAY, Wm.,149
HOLBART, Wm.,220
HOLBERT, Moses,228, William,
212,226, Wm.,155,156,205,
228,230,252
HOLCOM, Elias,042, Elisha,025,
051, Jos.,051, Mary,051
HOLCOMB, David,165, E.,137,
Elisha,010,013,029,031,
037, Elizabeth,178, Hosa,
168,173,180,183,186,197,
206,238,239, Hose,153,
Hosea,165, Hyrum,254,
James,073, John,254, Jos.,
074, Mary,252,254, Molly,
156, Moses,013,172,173,
Nathan,168
HOLCOMB, Nathan,197,238,254,
Nathaniel,252, Nathl.,165,
Richard,010, Sarah,010
HOLCOMBE, Hare,228, Hosa,240,
Hosea,156, Nathan,240
HOLCUM, Elisha,028, Joshua,
028
HOLCUMB, Hoss,202
HOLDEN, James,157
HOLDER, Delilah,020, Elizabeth,
020, Jeremiah,020, Jesse,
020, John,020, Martha,020,
Mary,020,171, Rebecka,020,
Sarah,020, Solomon,020,
047, Thos.,013, Willie,020
HOLDMAN, Thorton,158
HOLDRICH(?), Wm.,041
HOLDRICH, Wm.,091,118
HOLDRICK, Geo.,264
HOLDRIDGE, B.,236, Geo.,181,
195,213,243, Wm.,006,117,
Zach,117
HOLDRITCH, Geo.,041, Jas.,041,
042, Lelline,041, Lucy,041,
Polly,041, Wm.,029,042,
118, Zachariah,041
HOLEND, Thos.,218
HOLIDAY, Jenney,183, Margret,
183, Mathew,183, Robert,183,
Robt.,180, William,183,
Wm.,091,250
HOLINGSWORTH, Abram,229, Jno.,
097
HOLINGWORTH, Jas.,144
HOLLADAY, Martha,192, Mathew,
193,249,258, Robt.,145, Wm.,
249,250

HOLLADY(?), Hiram,027
HOLLADY, Wm.,222
HOLLAN, Jane,097, Richd.,097,
Thomas,097
HOLLAND, A.F.,188, Aberham,
189, Abm.,086,098, Abraham,
011,025,026,027,060,079,
184,188,232, Abram,069,073,
078,173,265, Alexr.,073,
Assena,046, Bas'c(?),011,
Basil,020,021,027, Baswell,
025,026, Baswill,026,
Bessie(?),011, E.W.,241,
Edmond,232
HOLLAND, Eliz.,034, Eliz.Low,
165, Esenor,026, James,216,
Jane,083,099,216,219,
Jeremiah,011,034,168, Jno.,
096,132,145,167,206,211,
219,250,257, Joh,257,
John P.,263, John,034,192,
223,224,245,255,263,275,
Lucretia,263, Marah,034,
Mary Ann,263
HOLLAND, Mary,034, Mathew,233,
Nancy,011,232,241, R.,093,
Rachel,034, Reason,026,
Rezin,034,035, Richard,011,
026,034,046,099, Richd.,035,
082,083,085, Robt.,206,232,
Sarah,034, Thomas,099,
Thos.,025,026,027,034,035,
083,216,219,230,257
HOLLAND, Thos.,265,273,275,
Wm.,011,026,046,056,068,
098,224,232
HOLLANDS, A.,188
HOLLARD, John,247
HOLLEDAY, Robt.,159
HOLLEDY, Mathew,231
HOLLEN(HOLLAND), Reason,126
HOLLEN, Aseneth,047,048,
Reason,127, Wm.,047
HOLLEY, James,048,056,057,
058,064,065,067,068, Jas,
101, Jas.,024,039, Thos.,057
HOLLIDAY, Jobe,257, Mathew,
098,233, Robt.,098, Salley,
262, Wm.,098,262,268,270
HOLLINGSWORTH, Aberham,216,
Abraham,252,265, Abram,245,
Abrm.,002,203, Eliz.,062,
Elizabeth,216, Eunice,233,
Geo.,003,012,025,037,040,
Isaiah,165, J.,141,169,205
HOLLINGSWORTH, James,071,155,
171,177,180,186,197,202,
205,223, Jane,001, Jas.,098,
130,154,182,222,229,270,
Jas.Jr.,138, Jeremiah,095,
Jerm.,100, Jno.,114,138,
222, John,071,223,246,
Jonath.,040, Jonathan,186,
Jos.,009,012,013,025,037
HOLLINGSWORTH, Jos.,046,065,
099,117,154,164,177,180,
195, Josiah,165, Mary,216,
222,223,261,270, Moses,169,
Polley S.,223, Rainey,216,
Richd.,052, Robert,197,
Robt.,080,085,110,127,167,
182,185,187, Sarah,140,
Susana,197, Susanah,216
HOLLINGSWORTH, Unisa,197, Wm.,
180,186,195,222,223,238
HOLLINGWORTH, Geo.,001, Henry,
001, John,001
HOLLINWORTH, Jos.,142
HOLLIS, James,215, Joshua,191,
Wm.,225
HOLLNGSWORTH, Jas.,270
HOLLY, Thomas,192
HOLMANS, Polly,198
HOLMES, J.B.,019, Wm.,236
HOLMS, Wm.,217
HOLOMAN, Thorington,156
HOLT(?), Israel,204
HOLT, Archbd.,123,124,128,
Archey,220, Israel,149,
203,237,242,251, James,133,
134, Jas.,101, Jno.,128,
Joab,138, John,090, Sarah,
090,140

HOLTE, Archibald,123
HOMES, Hanah,084, James,228
HONOR, Thomas,021
HOOD, Jane,021, Robert,021,
Thomas,021, Thos.,087,183,
186,237
HOOKER, Edw.,013, Margret,150,
218, R.,240
HOOPER, John N.,215, Wm.,055
HOPE, Jno.,133
HOPKINS, F.,126, Frances,126,
Francis,093,124,163,
George,126, James,093,
Jeremiah,093,126,160,163,
187,188,221,233,237,241,
Jno.,160,163,221,241, John,
093,126, Martin,225,267,
Samuel(?),124, Samuel,126,
Sollomon,126, Solomon,026,
070
HOPKINS, Solomon,093,098,124,
126
HOPPER, Elizabeth,243, J.D.,
279, Jas.,135, Jos.,220,
237, Jos.D.,247,273,
Joseph D.,279, Joseph,211,
222, L.J.,135, Lettuce,220,
Robt.,211, Saml.,135,220,
Saml.J.,113, William,225,
Wm.,101,220,270
HORAN, A.(Mrs.),208, Ann,089,
261, Wm.,208,264,266
HORLING, Jno.H.,178
HORN, Ann,253
HORNE, Wm.,211
HORNER, Ann(Wid.),160, Geo.,
034, Thos.,016,018
HORSEY, Daniel,017, Danl.,041,
Jno.,042
HORSTIN, Robt.,222
HORSTING, Saml.,183
HORTEN, Benjam,201, Valentine,
248
HORTON, Chas.,054,096,128,
Enos,094,129,130,132, Ens,
094, James,130, Jno.,211,
241, John,129,200, Josh,273,
Margret,146, Mary Ann,129,
Peggey,130, Pheabey,130,
Phebey,129, Pheby,094,
Raughley,129, Reughly,129,
Wm.,096,184
HOSEY, Wm.,235
HOUGHS, Wm.,147
HOULDITCH, Geo.,103
HOULDRITCH, Wm.,041
HOUSE, Denis,117, Dennis,093,
131, Jno.,088,165,169,183,
186, John,072, Jos.,117,
Philip,072, Thos.,072
HOUSTON, Robert,158, Robt.,
158,160,161, Wm.,269
HOWARD, Edmond,187, Edw.,265,
Jeremiah,165,186, John,028,
072,147, Thos.,117,164, Wm.,
077
HOWARTON, Eliz.,140, Elizabeth,
143, Grasey,143, James,140,
143, Westly,143
HOWEL, Absalom,072, Geo.,047,
Jas.,040,043, Jos.,040,
Joseph,010, Winney,042,
Wm.,099
HOWELL, Elias,147, Elijah,069,
113, Mary,069, Wm.,043,253
HOWERTON, Jas.,061
HOWL, Wm.,048
HUBBS(?), Wm.,073
HUCKABEY, Wm.,188
HUCKABY, Gillam,265
HUCKANLY, Martin,265
HUCKERBY, Martin,274
HUDDLESTON, James,001,032,
Jos.,006,011,014,021
HUDGENS, Ambrose,016,021,097,
John,020, Mrs.,116, Patsy,
108, Saml.,076, Stephen,242,
William,108, Wm.,045,051,
078,096,097,099,100,105,
109,262
HUDGINS, Jno.,236,268, Saml.,
192, Wm.,002,235
HUDINS, A.,235

HUDLEY, John,221
HUDSON, Jas.,087, John,047,
    Thos.,232
HUET(HEWETT?), Chas.,074
HUET, Wm.,218
HUETT, Jno.,195
HUEY, Martin,003
HUFF, Henry,061, Philip,224,
    Wm.,265
HUGENS(?), Ambrose,011
HUGGENS, Ambrose,187, James,
    193
HUGGINS, Ambros,231, James,
    125, John,061, Wm.,037,040,
    045,061
HUGHES, Aaron,059, Caleb,029,
    Elijah,059, Elizabeth,020,
    Geo.,012, George,011,
    James,019, Jas.,005, Jno.,
    269, Joel,040,042,079, John,
    007,009,020,034,039, Joseph,
    005,020, Margaret,059, Mary,
    029, Moses,117, Sally,020,
    Thomas,020, Thos.,022
HUGHES, Wm.,007,020,034,059,
    098
HUGHS, Ann,059, Caleb,031,
    073, Chas.,104, Chesley,120,
    Curtis,189, Danl.,104,
    Eliz.,042, Elizabeth,079,
    080, Esau,165, Isaac,172,
    173, James,197, Jas.,055,
    232, Jesse,056,093, Jno.,
    088,093,165,269, Joel,022,
    068,097,131,177, John,036,
    040
HUGHS, John,045,046,055,063,
    Jos.,211,224, Mary S.,259,
    Mary,031, Moses,117,172,
    173,274, Nancy,187, Rachel,
    034, Rebecca,069, Rodey(Roda),
    148, Sarah,138,257, Stephen,
    188, Thos.,022,040,042,046,
    Wm.,042,248
HUGINS, Ambrose Jr.,179,
    Ambrose,179
HULSEY, Saml.,166
HUMPHRIES, Wm.,088
HUNT, Elisha,007,009, Israel,
    043, S.,184, Saml.,186,224,
    Saml.F.,186
HUNTER, (Capt.),081, Abigail,
    035, Andrew,013,084, Andw.,
    139,141,151,211, Betty,095,
    Caroline,210, Coleman,159,
    Daulien,257, Dublin(Black),
    149, Dubling,155, Easter,
    141,176,177,190, Elizabeth,
    013,087,095,141,157,210,
    Emeline,210, Estes,235
HUNTER, Flemmon,221, Francis,
    093, Henry,037,038,065,066,
    081, Isabela,134,190,
    Isabella,172,174, J.,094,
    James H.,225, James Jr.,
    159,166,178, James,013,037,
    068,071,087,088,121,151,
    153,155,157,161,166,167,
    168,175,177,186,190,223,225
HUNTER, James,233,236, Jane,
    013, Jas.(Capt.),151,
    Jas.(Col.),236, Jas.,040,
    041,043,047,048,081,094,
    098,116,119,139,141,145,
    Jas.Jr.,140, Jean,095,
    Jno.,001,011,040,043,081,
    104,115,116,141,142,163,
    166,168,177,189,210,218,
    235,236,237
HUNTER, Jno.,242,243,246,248,
    270, Jno.Jr.,093, Jno.M.,
    212, Jno.Sr.,087,256,
    John B.,037,121, John Jr.,
    065, John Sr.,121, John Wm.,
    020, John,013,020,023,024,
    027,031,032,033,037,038,
    047,049,051,058,062,066,
    072,073,087,092,115,121,123
HUNTER, John,124,155,158,190,
    195,210,228,239,241,242,
    253,254,255,256, Joshua,037,
    Laughlin,035,036,038,
    Mabery,210, Mabra(?),193,

Mabra,210, Marey,032,
    Margaret,011,095, Margarett,
    035, Margret,191, Mary,033,
    035,051, Maryum,163,
    Mathew(Est.),151
HUNTER, Mathew,011,033,067,
    106,126,127,128,134,139,
    147,157,190,251,253,255,
    Matt,095, Matt.,098,104,
    108, Matthew Sr.,095,
    Matthew,013,017,018,026,
    038,064,072,079,086,087,
    090,095,101,102,104,113,
    134,141,269, Meryam,207,
    Nancy,037,095
HUNTER, Nancy,121,141,254,
    256,270,275, Nathan,133,
    Peggy,040, Rebecca,089,
    Rebekah,088, Robert,134,
    135,161, Robt. R.,257,
    Robt.,013,102,108,131,138,
    141,166,172,190,211,242,
    264, Robt.P.,254, Ross,248,
    Salley,210, Saml.,086,107,
    121,132
HUNTER, Saml.,153,155,167,
    168,176,180,188,201,203,
    255,256,257,258,266, Samuel,
    121, Sarah,037,065,066,067,
    095, Thomas,163,166,210,
    Thos.,042,073,097,270,
    Widow,191,210, William,037,
    121, Wm.,004,006,010,011,
    016,020,028,029,030,032,033
HUNTER, Wm.,051,166,173,208,
    233,243,256,265, Wm.Jr.,256,
    266, Wm.Sr.,257
HURESK, Jonathan,232
HURT(?), Robt.,211
HURT, Wm.,211, Wm.Sr.,242
HUSE, Jacob,173
HUSKERSON, John,015, Mary,015,
    Robt.,015
HUSKESON, Elias,193
HUSTON, Alexr.,053, Jno.,271,
    John,006,022
HUSTONS, Robert,188
HUTCHERSON(?), Jas.E.,159
HUTCHERSON, Jas.,119,121,
    Margarite,276, Wm.,007,
    008,133
HUTCHESON, A.,189, A.S.,235,
    244, Ambrose,236, Angess,
    141, B.F.,274, Elenor,153,
    G.E.,250, Hubert,256, J.E.,
    258, J.S.,256, James,041,
    049,153,179, Jas.,030,043,
    047,081,116,130,142, Jas.E.,
    141,143,153, Jas.S.,232,
    Jno.,043,130,178,250
HUTCHESON, Jno.Jr.,257,
    Jno.S.,141,178,224,256,
    John,045,046,047,059,119,
    139,144,146,153,178,
    Mary Ann,236, Mary,089,
    Nancy,178, Robert,119,139,
    142, Robt.,029,041,046,072,
    140,141,143,151,153,178,
    257, Sarah,233, Simpson,224,
    William,049
HUTCHESON, Wm.,046,098,116,
    140,141,142,153,166, Wm.Jr.,
    049
HUTCHINSON, A.S.,274, B.F.,
    274, Herbert,277, J.E.,174,
    James,056, Jas.,116,
    Jas.Jr.,170, Jno.,171,266,
    Jno.S.,173,271, John S.,
    274, Mary A.,274, Robt.,056,
    276, Saml.,266, Wm.,170,171
HUTCHISON, Abner,187, Catharine,
    187, J.E.,192, J.S.,174,
    James Sr.,187, James,176,
    Jane,187, Jas.,106,115,
    119, Jas.E.,187,190, Jno.S.,
    249, John,007,014,056,064,
    068,193, Mary Ann,187,
    Nancy,187, Robt.,013,016,
    048,053,068,071,187,
    William,183
HUTCHISON, Wm,183, Wm.,065,
    068,117,187,190,196, Wm.Sr.,
    187

HUTSON, Elizabeth,083, Jas.,
    096,113, Jno.,083, John,069,
    Marey,055
INGRAM, Charles,150
INLOW, W.W.,224, Wm.,160,
    Wm.M.,265
INMAN, Benj.,061, Rufus,041
IRBY, Benj.H.,225, C.,149,
    Carter,021, Charles,134,
    182,187,213,225, Chas.,116,
    141,152,159,163,172,187,
    195,222,231,235,267,268,
    269, Frances,187,225,
    Henderson,142, I.H.,153,
    J.H.,208,242,270, James H.,
    152,158,159,201,209, James,
    180
IRBY, James,182,184,187,195,
    204,220,224,225, Jas H.,249,
    Jas.,114,145,242, Jas.H.,
    225,236,239,244, Jos.,081,
    098,101,105,108,123,133,
    141,151,257,260, Joseph,162,
    193,196,201,207,213,214,
    218,235,244, Moses,090,099,
    Mr.,118, Polly,021
IRBY, Saml.,124,128,163,187,
    208,220,225, Samuel,149,
    150,201, W. James,200,
    William,155,162,201,208,
    Wm.(Capt.),169, Wm.(Dr.),
    237, Wm.,002,017,021,057,
    081,086,097,100,104,107,
    115,116,124,129,162,163,
    172,187,192,208,221,222,
    228,230,236
IRBY, Wm.,241,242,246,268,
    269,270, Wm.Jr.,182, Wm.Sr.,
    152
JACKS, Amey,228, Isaac,088,
    158,175,223,249,262,266,
    John,049, Robt.,007, Wm.,
    266
JACKSON, Abrham,101, B.,043,
    Jno.,224, Wm.,225
JAMES(JONES?), Jno.L.,226
JAMES, Alfred,235, B.L.,265,
    Benj.,074,081,111,112,115,
    148,150,158,162,163,
    Benjamin,173,227, Bery L.,
    272, Danl.,110, Eliz.,096,
    Elizabeth,018, J.,235,
    J.S.,026, Jno.L.(?),158,
    Jno.L.,152, Jno.S.,153,
    157,169,173,236,237,244,
    251,268
JAMES, Jno.S.,278, John L.(S),
    219, John S.(L.?),158,
    John S.,148,152,201, John,
    061,103, Jonathan,156, Jos.,
    011,063, Larkin,121, N.,
    149, Nancy,236, R.,149,
    R.B.,158, Robt.B.,235,
    William,253
JAMISON, Jno.,160
JAMISON, Jno.,096, Shadrack,
    221
JANES(JONES?), Thos.,152
JANES, Benj.,150, James,043,
    Jos.,159, R.(Capt.),150,
    Tabitha,154
JANKIALLY, Geo.,221
JASON, Lana,042, Laney,067,
    068,072, Robert,042, Robt.,
    009,042,044, Sarah,044
JEAMS, Edw.,061, Jesse,061,
    John,061
JEANES, Berrey,182, Edw.,061,
    John,200, Jos.,015,182,
    Margret,200
JEANS, Alexander,273, Berry,
    265, Greenberry,270, Joseph,
    210
JEFFRIES, Nathan,087,113
JENAS, Masson,273
JENNINGS, Antony,004, Mily,
    122, Patsey,004
JENSEY, James,237
JENT, Danl.,229, Fielding,259,
    260
JESSE, "Free",266
JESTER, Harting,232
JEWELL(?), Geo.,121

JNOISS(?), Richd.,152
JOEL, Gabl.,036, Gabriel,040,
041,044,069,092,109, Geo.,
068,071,079, John,072,
Polly,182
JOHNS, Henery,129,140, Henry,
056,111,131,151,157,251,
W.J.,259
JOHNSON, Aaron,264, Agnes,009,
Ambrose,011,021, Anderson,
264, Andw.,264,271, Ann,086,
269, Bill,109, Douglas,009,
Durham,269, Ezekiel,174,
273, Geo.,264, H.G.,274,
Hannah,266,268, Harrison,
268, Hasting D.,173,
Hastings,268, Henry,012
JOHNSON, Henry,074,085, J.W.,
264, J.W.H.,269, Jabez W.,
276, Jabez W.H.,267, James,
171,268, Janet,009, Jas.,
012,083,109, Jno.,174,273,
Joel,008, John,009,013,
Jon.,046, Jonathan,002,
012,013,017,053,080,268,
272,274, Margaret,009, Mary,
009
JOHNSON, Mary,038, Matthew,
017,274, Rebecca,171,173,
Thomas,086,269, W.,272,
Wade,267,270,273, Walter,
274, Wm.,150,229,264
JOHNSTON, A.B.,193,211, Aaron,
146, Abel,179, Aberham B.,
242, Aberham,129,166,167,
203, Abner B.,193, Abner,
076,192,193,195, Abraham B.,
193,241, Abraham,017,076,
102,193,194,204,208,211,
Abram,137, Adey,208, Allen,
236,243, Ambrose,020
JOHNSTON, Ambrous,039,
Anderson,211,261, Andrew,
208, Andw.,183,254, Ann,086,
098,151,211, Anna,208,211,
Annouta,146, Aron,212,221,
253,259, B.,248, Benj.,028,
030, Benjamin,192, Byrd,249,
Caney John,214, Caney,215,
Carter,228, Catherine,257
JOHNSTON, Chas.,131, Crow,189,
Daniel,214,215, Danl.,146,
163,198,201,221,231,232,
235,237, Danl.C.,152, David,
178, Davis,242, Dial,236,
Douglas,029, Elijah,230,
232,233, Elizabeth,192,249,
Ethalinday,130, Ezekiel,
211,260,262, Fanney,146
JOHNSTON, Fedrick,259,
Frances,233, Geo.,166,167,
179,188,194,204,211,218,
250,253,254,261, Geo.C.,247,
Geo.W.,181,185,203,233,
Geo.Wash.,192, George,208,
H.,242, H.G.,147, Haisten,
243, Haistene,239, Haistin,
229, Haisting,235,236,
Haiston,237
JOHNSTON, Hemmeltal,233,
Henderson,236,237, Heney,
200, Henry,019,020,086,167,
199,200,200,232,239,258,
Hosa,198,242, Hulda,181,
233, Huzen,207, J.,070,160,
199, J.M.H.,223, J.W.H.,175,
252, Jabez W.,108,234,
Jabus W.H.,133, Jabuz,192,
James J.,212
JOHNSTON, James,026,130,134,
136,168,229, Jane,071, Jas.,
032,043,055,080,082,097,
109,116,132, Jehue,166,
Jeremiah,192, Jesse,029,097,
058,073,083,085,095,097,
103,110,116,123,127,132,
137,138,141,144,153,155,
157,168,186,193,195,199,
200,208
JOHNSTON, Jesse,230,239, Jno.
083,085,096,101,105,128,
130,142,146,164,167,199,
211,218,223,242,253, Jno.W.,

165, Job,200, Jobe,079,103,
203,218, Joel W.,150, Joel,
073, John,036,055,058,061,
125,128,200,208,218,221,
Jon.,077,118, Jonathan Sr.,
164
JOHNSTON, Jonathan,046,051,
057,071,083,096,097,120,
142,165,167,175,177,
Jonothan,138, Jonth..,063,
097, Jonth.Jr.,097, Jonthn.,
104, Jos.N.,194, Joseph,061,
062,063,192, Lofton,211,
Lucinda,194, Lynl,124,
M.M.,247, Margret,208,
Mary,054
JOHNSTON, Mary,062,063,
Mathew,163,229,242,
Matthew,063,130,136,
Mehalaha,192, Polly,086,
Rachel,242, Ransom,245,
Rebecah,192,195, Robert,
063, Robt.,036,086,200,235,
Salley,017, Saml.,128,
Stephen,225, Thomas,086,
130, Thos.,062,063
JOHNSTON, Thos.,076,086,096,
229, W.G.,247, Wade,199,
248,259, Waid,249, Wm.,017,
018,019,027,061,074,087,
128,130,137,162,164,166,
186,200,208,210,211,221,
235,236,261, Wm.G.,131
JOHNSTONO, Jonth.,105
JOINER, James,170, John,147
JONAS, Jno.,156
JONES(?), Henry,066
JONES, ,044, A.C.,117,126,
137,176,236,239,258,268,
274, A.G.,217, Aaron,028,
071,103, Abel,186, Adam C.,
113,139,218,222, Adam Craine,
121, Alexr.,224, Alfred,212,
231,237,244,257, Ann,033, Anny,249, Barey,
189, Benj.,047,055
JONES, Benj.,087,101,113,224,
258, Betsey,044, Betsy,160,
Cain,242,260,263, Charles,
140,141,157, Charlotta,260,
Chas.(Est.),151, Chas.,106,
117,118,162,239,251,261,
264,271, Cranes,253, Dan,
160, Daniel,156,158,193,
260, Danl.,078,110,112
JONES, Danl.,120,131,133,171,
202,222,223,233,243,247,
253,261,264, David,076,086,
179, Desey,259, Dr.,048,
Dred,047,049,052,072, Duke,
110,157,171,174, E.,204,
E.D.,259, Edw.,043,061,
064,185,187,190,196,200,
235,241,247, Edward,022,044
JONES, Edward,070,277, Elias,
259, Elie,186, Eliz.,044,
070,200,224,259, Eliza,259,
Elizabeth W.,271, Elizabeth,
072,277, Ellen,096, Elliott,
260, Ephraim,199,202,203,
Ephrum,146, F.F.,237,254,
Frances,186,187,257,
Frederick,200, Fredk(?),072
JONES, Gabriel,002,044,070,
Harrison,078,193,208,
Henry,186,189,245,249,261,
Hiram,164, Isaac,055,219,
James,047,048,049,070,072,
136,180,181,186,190,191,
215,239,242, Jas.,026,041,
076,087,096,097,110,113,
118,142, Jerah,241, Jeremiah,
215
JONES, Jesse,047,052,054,061,
064,072, Jno.,088,118,162,
166,173,174,185,225,251,
273,274, Jno.S.,272,
John S.,149, John,009,013,
018,022,034,044,049,055,
056,061,070,072,077,082,
150,158,160,170,181,196,
203,219,245, Johnston,160,
Joice,057

JONES, Jonathan,148,179,187,
231,256,270, Jos.,043,044,
047,049,055,061,072,088,
106,124,159, Jos.Jr.,181
JONES, Joseph,048,170,174,
175,181,182,195,215,224,
227,228,229,234,259,262,
Josiah,070, Joyce,077,078,
079, Karn,270, Lewis F.,266,
Lewis,088,089,130,136,137,
186,199,202,203,204,210,
211,213,215,218,223,230,
251,252,270,276, Loyed,224
JONES, Lucey,056, Lucy,047,
070, M.Duke,120, Manning E.,
262, Margaret,170, Margret,
070,150,227, Marmaduke,053,
064,126,216,217,222, Mary,
170,186,223, Mason,222,224,
Massum(?),219, Mathew,044,
066, McA.,271, Micajah,090,
Miles,047,049
JONES, Miles,061,072, Milley,
186, Mrs.,101,186, N.E.,270,
NAncy,140, Nancey,142,
Nancy,141,170,174,186,202,
229,237,240,259, Ned,064,
087, Patty,171, Perry,168,
189,232, Polly,029, Poston(?),
158, Rachel,260, Radey,259,
Rail,228, Reback,252
JONES, Rebecah,251, Reuben,
228, Rhoda,227, Riall,218,
Richard,017, Robt.,113,
151, Robt.L.,188,189,
S.S.(?),158, Salley,114,
259, Saml.,094,117,128,146,
150,166,199,202,211,229,
241,251,252,259,267,270,
Samuel,154,227,259,274,
Sarah L.,158
JONES, Sarah,044,070,200,260,
274, Seaborn,218,239,
Seybourn,176, Squire,265,
271,273, Stephen,035,053,
Stirling,256, Susan,271,
Thomas,031,052,070,118,
179,180,188, Thos.,029,045,
061,104,110,116,117,121,
169,186,187,224,270,
Thos.D.,170
JONES, Thos.F.,155,172,178,
201,208,216,226,254,269,
Tobiah,160, Toleson,160,
Valentine,258, Walter,228,
Weldon,193, Whitman,200,
Whitmore,047,048,049,052,
Wiley,251,252, Wm.,027,
093,103,113,117,137,149,
151,186,188,189,198,214,
264, Wm.D.,253
JONES, Wm.F.,162
JORDON, Chas.,043
JOWEL(JOEL), Jno.,104
JOWELL(?), Gabriel,125,
Rebecah,125
JOWELL(JOEL?), Gabriel,125
JOWELL, Gabriel,128,132, Geo.,
217, J.A.,222, Rebeca,128
JUKESTY, Geo.,221
JURDON, Reuben,139
JUREY(?), Eliphus,128
K--(?), Jno.,044
KANNADY, Rodey,153
KAY, A.,184, Chas.,229,265
KEANE, Robt.P.,212
KEARNAGHAN, Agnes,027
KEEN, Joseph,259
KELLET, Ann,001, Anna,012,
Esther,001, Hannah(?),012,
James,001,026,030, Jane,
012,026,185, Jennet,001,
012, Jno.,166, John,001,
012,065,126, Joseph,001,
Margaret,012, Martha,001,
Martin,001,012,025,026,
030,185, Mary,001,032,
Moses,241
KELLET, Wm.,001,005,012,118
KELLETT, Eliz.,188, James,147,
188, Jane,188, Martin,188,
Morten,220, Thos.,220, Wm.,
092,105,118,166,220

KELLEY(?), Stephen,122
KELLEY, ,122, Allen,151,152,
155,237, Betsy,168, Edmond,
017, Frances,120, Garaham,
026, James,017, Jno.,133,
240, Joel,225, John,149,
168,203,219, Jos.,081, Mary,
043, Moses,030, Nelson,029,
030, Reuben,019,029,053,
Thos.,092, Wm.,043,054
KELLEY, Wm.,061,064,120
KELLY, Allen,152,237,268,
Jno.,172,265, John,012,
Nelson,010,011
KELSEY, H.B.,228, Henry B.,
203, Henry D.,200
KENADY, James,224, Rody,159,
191
KENDRICK, Jas.,113
KENEDY, A.,234, Andy,236,
Faney,193, James,205,215,
222, Jas.,257, Jas.Sr.,257,
Jno.,257, John,148, Mody,
151, Mrs.,236, Polley,193,
Rodey,220, Rody,222,
Siminion,222, Susanah,228
KENELSON, Wm.,104
KENION, Frances J.,186
KENNADA, Jno.B.,177
KENNADAY, Nancey,252
KENNEDY, Andrew,216, Andw.,
172,227, J.B.,035, James,
215, Jh.L.,209, John B.,032,
033,216, Mr.,217, Rody,096,
109, Wm.M.,279
KENNERY, Jemimah,015, John H.,
015
KENNEY, Edw.,078
KER--(?), Curtis,112
KERN, A.A.,265, Alfred A.,209,
228,247, Alfred,175,221,
250,260,265,271, Benj.Danl.,
247, E.,270, Eliz.Susan,247,
Elizabeth,247,249,250,
Eugene,222, Eugenia C.,247,
J.,184, J.D.,014,020,028,
105,109, J.F. & Sons,184,
J.F.,183, Jno.,265
KERN, Jno.F.,180,183,186,228,
245,247,267,270, Jno.F.Jr.,
175,181,184, Jno.F.Sr.,183,
184, Jno.Fredrick Sr.,228,
Jno.L.,183, John F.,013,
198,209,222,247,250,
John F.Jr.,199,209,219,
John F.Sr.,219,224,
John J.P.,198, John,027,
041,180
KERN, John,250, L.D.,154,
Louis,222, Louisa,222,
Luisa Lucy,247, Luza,222,
P.D.,189, Peridon D.,183,
184, Peridon Danl.,180,
Perridon D.,247, Saml.J.,
270, Sarah P.,183, Sarah,
183, Suza,221, Ugenia,221,
Widow,221
KERNALL, Barnet,003
KERNE, John F.Sr.,221
KERNEL, Barnet,063, Curtis,
128, Gracey,063, Marey,063
KERNELS, Barnet,063
KERNS, Chas.A.,215, David,034,
John F.,240
KERR, Wm.,111
KEVIL, Agga,088, Benjamin,005,
088, Thomas,005,088, Thos.,
073,077
KEY, Charles,147
KIE, David,161
KIERK, James,023, John,023,
Sarah,023
KIERN(KERN), Peridon D.,181
KIGHT, Vinein,257
KILE, Jeremiah,101
KILGORE, Allen,104, Benj.,131,
J.,274, James,011, Jas.,
077, Josiah,274
KILLET, John,147
KILLETT, Wm.,151
KILLINGSWORTH, Chas.,145,
James,258, Manning,109,
Mark,091,092,098,101,116,

136,160,228,236,242,246,268
KILLINGWORTH, Mark,231
KIMBLE, Charles,107, Chas.,
101
KINCAID, Alex.,096, Wm.,096
KINDERMAN, Barbary,014
KINDMAN, Thos.,258
KINDRED, Jas.L.,088
KINEDY, Jno.,256
KING, A.,271, Charles,001,
Chas.(?),151, Chas.,152,
195,224,229,251, Chas.M.,
221, Chas.W.,163,248,251,
James,019,020, Jno.,212,
John,126,196, Kitey,223,
Margaret,175, Mary,020,
Philip F.,219, Philip S.,
203, Philip,254, Polly,020,
Sally,020
KING, Wm.Jr.,175
KINGSBOROUGH, Wm.,065,068
KINGSLEY, Chester,274
KINMAN, (Wid.),274, James,265,
274,278, Jas.,265, Margaret,
278, Peggy,265, Quinton,265,
Sal.,258, Sarah,265, Thos.,
265, Winniford,265
KINMON, Elizabeth,117, James,
117,118,147, Saml.,109,137,
147,148,228,247, Thomas,146,
147, Thos.,117, Winiford,
147, Winneford,146
KIRK, Catty,227, Dr.,018,
Elizabeth,027,029,031,045,
118, James,023,037,227,
John Jr.,119, John Sr.,119,
John,026,027,028,029,031,
037,045,052,110,118,270,
Sarah,023,227
KIRKPATRICK & KENEDY, ,235
KIRKPATRICK, A.,148,150, Alen,
221, Alex.,121, Alexander,
240,241,260, Alexr.,124,
130,146,147,153,244, E.,
240, James,130,147,148,
Jno.,148, John,124,130,
M.F.,260, Susan,240,242,
Susanah,244, Thomas,148,
240, Thos.,221, Wm.,146,
147,148
KLINCK, Jno.G.,208
KLINK(?), Jno.G.,145
KLINK, J.G.,208, Jno.G,239,
Jno.G.,256, Sarah,201
KNIGHT, Abner,055,173,196,
197,202,220,252,272, Benj.,
257, Betay,142, Bryum,256,
Chaney,222, Chas.,212,257,
Creswell,257, David,151,
156,202, Ephraim,039,182,
184, Ephram,161, Ephrum,161,
Jas.,247, Jno.,113,142,
146,256,271, John,142,146
KNIGHT, John,271, Lucinda,182,
Mathew,257, Polly,276,
Silus,257, Thos.,156,252,
Wm.,156,182,193,255,256,
257, Wm.Jr.,257, Wm.Sr.,257
KUMTON, Wm.,045
L--, James,267
LACEY, Wm.,006
LACK, Sarah C.,263
LAIRD, Archebald,189, Jas.,
021, Peggy,189, Saml.,026,
041, Samuel,020, Wm.,200
LAMB, Benj.,265, Jno.,224,
Thos.,265, Wm.,265
LAMBLING, Martin,183, Wm.B.,
183
LAMBRIGHT, James,265
LAND(?), Hirum,138
LAND, Elizabeth,261, John,020,
Thos.,068
LANDES(?), Nathl.,138
LANFORD, Wm.,094
LANGSFORD, Wm.,161
LANGSTON, Bennett,026,060,
171, Eliz.,044, F.,258, H.,
134, Henry,020,039,047,061,
068,134,155,169,171,172,
188,189,211,224,258,260,
Jacob,189, James,172,178,
224,268, Jas.,116,134,189,

257, Jno.,245,249,267,274,
John,211,243,260,262, Jos.,
169
LANGSTON, Martin,235, Nancy,
185, Nathan,109, Saml.,172,
224, Sarah,020,171, Solomon Jr.,
171, Solomon,020,039,068,
171,172, Thos.,266, Wm.,265,
267,273
LARA, Wm.,270
LARD(LAIRD?), Sarah,027
LATIMER, C.T.,274, E.C.,272
LATTIMER, Edw.F.,274
LAUGHRIDGE, Jas.,097,104,116
LAURENS, Abram,043
LAVENDER, Siminion,164
LAW, James,055,156, Saml.Jr.,
043
LAWENS, Eliz.,045, George,045
LAWINGS, Eliz.,052, Geo.,057,
George,052
LAWLER, Chas.,155
LAWLESS, Jas.,137
LAWSON(?), Geo.,045
LAYCE(LACEY?), Danl.,029
LAYRENS, ,019
LAYSON, Jos.,029, Morgan,025,
026
LAYTON, James,258
LEA, Marshall,087, Saml.,103
LEAGEN, Joel,274
LEAGON, Wm.,042
LEAGUE, Jacob(Joab?),089,
Jacob,077,088, Joab,005,010
LEAK(?), James Jr.,188
LEAK, Anthony,174, Armstead,
268, Barnet,108, Brint,251,
Burell,182, James Jr.,189,
James,192, Jas.,268, Jno.,
268, Jno.W.,268, John,138,
Josiah,012, Marthann,268,
Marthew,218, Moses,118,
144,208, Saml.,099, Thos.S.,
268, William,101, Wm.S.,268
LEAKE, Armistead,093, Geo.,
103, George,031, Jas.Sr.,
164, Jeremiah,031, Jno.,230,
John,091,093,102,192,
Martha,030, Mathew,093,
Moses,091,093,208, Providence,
101, Saml.,029,097,103,
Samuel,101, Sarah,093,
William,091,093, Wm.,030,
235
LEAKE, Wm.Sr.,101
LEAMAN, Hugh,095, James,251,
John,067, Saml.,025,026,
035,095,097,115
LEAMEN, Hugh,194
LEAMON(LEEMAN), Hugh,138,
James,138, Saml.,138
LEAMON, Hugh,138, James,279,
Jas.,138
LEAN(?), Jno.,178
LEARWOOD, Edmond,027, Ma--?,
027
LEARY(?), Wm.,152
LEATHERWOOD, James,072, Jas.,
081
LEAVELL, Edw.,019, Wm.,199,
207
LEAWELL, Wm.,253
LEDFORD, Simon,010
LEE, Bennet,235, Gimima,188,
James,151, Jno.,081,116,
269, John,214, Marshall,082,
Wm.,014, Wm.Jr.,151
LEEGON, Wm.,036, Woodson,036
LEEK(?), Narsissy,131
LEEK, A.G.,264, Alzira,126,
Anne,126,143, Anthony C.,
219,249, Anthony G.,277,
Anthony,185,191,195,254,
Armested,142,192, Armistead,
103, Armisted,150, Armstead,
181,273, Avery,037, B.,140,
245, Barnet,150, Bassell,
136, Branch,140, Briant,133
LEEK, Briant,272, Bryant,249,
277, Burrel,140,160,161,
185,242,244,245, Burrell,
140,249,277, Burwell,150,
Davis(?),208, Dorcus,273,

Eliz.,143, Eliza,143,
Foryphina(?),140, Geo.,100,
101,102,107,151, George,123,
126,127,143,150, James Jr.,
167
LEEK, James,066,126,143,167,
168,277, Jane,143, Jas.,141,
143,273, Jas.Jr.,273, Jenny,
126, Jer.,026,102,227,
Jeremiah,023,066,108,126,
205,211,218,254,273, Jerry,
147
LEEK, Jno.,137,167,181,224,
236,268, Jno.Jr.,237,
Jno.Sr.,236, John,023,180,
216,219,235, Margaret,103,
126,212, Margret,126,143,
Martha,167,277, Melelenda,
126, Menasee,224, Moses,141,
142,143,156,172,177,184,
219,222,248,268, Moss,142
LEEK, Obriant,191, Patsy,249,
Salley,103, Saml.,023,065,
143,273, Samuel,126,143,
150, Sinda,143, Sl.,138,
Susannah,204, Thos.,189,
211,222, Thos.L.,185,211,
William,103,243, Wm.,126,
132,143,236,237,241,250,
253, Wm.B.,277
LEEKE, Brian,056, Geo.,079,
Jane,051, John,102,
Margret,150, R.,227
LEEKS, Jas.,143
LEEMAN, Elizabeth,196,275,
Hugh,187,198,221,275,
Isabella,275, James,187,
198,275, Mary Ann,275,
Saml.,084,085, Samuel,275,
William,275
LEFAN, James,025, Jas.,112
LEFANN, James,066
LEFFAN, James,006,026, Jas.,
024
LEFON, Jas.,036
LEFOY, Matthew,014, Nancy,099,
Wm.,236
LEGIN, Joseph,171
LEMAN, Saml.,091
LEMON(?), Hugh,265
LENDORE, Jesse,184
LENIE, Robt.,237
LENVIL, Wm.,264
LENVILL, Lewis,128
LEONARD, Betsey,149, Fran.Elijah,
149, Golding,149, Jno.,029,
090,095,157, John,028,063,
064,066,130,149,159, Nancy,
149,160, Reuben,101,149,
Richard,149
LEOPARD, John,036
LEREEL(?), Wm.,199
LESLEY, Thos.,072
LESLIE, ,205
LESTER, Francis,036,039,065,
103,116, Hartwell,117,144,
156,164,173, Jno.,096,183,
John,115,116
LEVAN, T.T.,271
LEVEARS, Saml.B.,190
LEVEL, Noah,170
LEVERACK, Francis,220
LEVIL(LINVELL), Wm.,166
LEVY, Danl.,014, Jacob,019
LEW--NS, Laura,261
LEWARS, S.B.,237, Saml.B.,213,
Samuel,210
LEWERS, Mary,027, Saml.B.,113,
114,116,171,220, Thomas,027,
113, Thos.,028,043,081,082,
098
LEWIS, Annabella,122, Benj.,
039,043,051,065,077,079,
086,095,099, Crafford,077,
079, Craford,078, Crawford,
051,269, Day,240, Drewry,
133, Ellinor,003, Garland,
278, Jno.S.,277, John,066,
Lin,109, Phebe,079,269,
Phebey,077, Saml.B.,270
LEWIS, Thos.,041,043,270,279,
Widow,079, Wm.(?),275
LEWISTON, Jacob,167

LIGEN, Joseph,219, Wm.,225
LIGON, (?),075, B.,117,
Blackmon,164, Branch,116,
Chas.,064, Eliza,198,
F.Woodson,185, James,152,
167,242, Jas.,090,140, Jno.,
083, John,053,056,057, Jos.,
185,194,201,221,228,238,
240, Joseph,198,234, Miller,
118, Old Missis,140, Peter,
078
LIGON, Reuben,084,090,091,
Susan,185, Susanah,185,
198,199,205, Thomas,090,
181,185,244, Thos.,061,065,
073,091,100,102,121,139,
174,185,198,205,233,249,
261, Thos.Jr.,187, Thos.Sr.,
152, Virgil,185, W.,117,
William,197,198,222,240,
244, Wm.,039
LIGON, Wm.,066,075,088,117,
138,139,140,153,165,181,
182,185,187,199,221,225,
245,249,267,269, Wm.A.,185,
Wm.H.,194,198,199, Wm.Sr.,
185,251, Woodson,065,080,233
LIGTON, Thos.,245
LILES(?), Robt.,262
LILES, James,161,224, Jas.,
134, Thos.,169, Wm.,043,
049,225
LINCH, Wm.E.,212
LINDEY, Wm.,237
LINDLEY, Aquilla,073, Aquillia,
235, Eliz.,073,102, Hanna,
073, Henry,073,236,268,
James,003,028,073, John,
051,073,135,137, Jonathan,
073,236, Ruth,135,137,
Sarah,073, Thomas,003,073,
Thos.,028,102, Wm,073, Wm.,
236,268, Wm.E.,235
LINDLY, Jno.,118, Thos.,274,
Wm.,213
LINDSEE, James,007
LINDSEY, Cullen,264,266,
Dennis,013, Edw.,012,
Elbert,260,264,266,
Humphrey,174,264,266,
James,011,266, Jas.,021,
Jno.,264,266, John,002,
LINDVELL, Lewis,138
LINDY, Gueler,232
LINES, S.,149, Sarah,168,
Stephen,168,170,174
LING(?), John,051
LING, Howell,251, John,057,
224
LINSEY, Cullen,212, Denis,010,
Dennis,094, Elbert Sr.,212,
Elbert,211, Glenn,212,
Henry,221, Humphra,253,
Humphrey,204,212,261,
Jacob,055, James,203,204,
210,242, Robt.,262, Wade,
191, Wm.,117,164,242,253
LINULL(?), Lewis,127
LINVELL(?), Lewis,146
LINVELL, Evan,028, Even,212,
Iven,166, Jain,146, Jno.,
146,166,212, John,218,
Lewis,152, Mary,146,152,
Menaassa,146
LINVILL, Wm.,150
LINVILLE, Evan,174, Even,173,
211, Jno.,174, Lewis,078,
Marey,173, Mary(Mrs.),174,
Silvey,174, Wm.,174
LITTEL, Agnes,067, Ann,227,
C.,058,082,123, Catty,227,
Charity,082,083,184,
Charles,067,082,150,188,
208,227,230, Chas.,064,091,
098,104,135,138,141,142,
143,162,168,184,189,200,
204,219,230,246,256,
Chas.Jr.,237, David,025,
026,067,076
LITTEL, David,082,083,184,
189,208,227, H.,178, Hollen,
188, Isabel,067, James C.,
227, James,025,055,064,067,

068,167,186,209,222,230,
241,254, Jas.,137,141,189,
Jno.,189, John,216,218,
219, Mary,067, Mr.,217,
Nancy,189, R.D.,082,
Robert,067
LITTEL, Robert,204, Robt.,128,
241,243,246, Robt.D.,137,
Robt.H.,137,227,230,239,
254, Robt.M.,200, Samuel,
241, Thomas,067,189,208,
Thos.,221, William,067
LITTLE, Ann,230, C.,074,
Charles,059, Chas.,145,
159,192,271,273, David,230,
261,264, Fredrk.,045,
James B.,264, James,014,
274, Jas.,264,271,273,
Jas.B.,264, Jno.,230,268,
273,275, Robt.,096,265,268,
Robt.F.,159, Robt.H.,231,
263,268,271
LITTLE, Thos.,230
LIVELY, Thos.Fowler,174
LOCHEBY, John,063
LOCHRIDGE, Jas.,081,119
LOCKEBY, Jesse(?),210, John,
026, Wm.,043
LOCKERBY, Jas.,111
LOCKERT, J.H.,240, Jno.,225,
Thos.B.,235, Thos.Sr.,237
LOCKES, A.G.,247
LOCKHART, H.,171, Jno.,145,
172,238,271, Jno.H.,207,
225, John,210,225, Saml.,
267, Saml.T.,275, Thomas,
207,210, Thos.,162,179,208,
214,220,225,247,267,275,
Thos.B.,236, Thos.Sr.,225,
Wm.,151, Wm.M.,222,
Wm.McG.,225
LOCKHAT, Jno.,145
LOCKRIDGE, Jas.,136,141,145
LOFTON, Daniel,156, Danl.,143,
146,174,211, Wm.,103,143,
146,174,214
LOGAN, Cate,002, David,002,
Hugh,214, John,010,
Polly Hannah,002, Thos.,
008,009, Wm.,253, Wm.H.,273
LONG, Berry,231, Dan.C.,081,
Daniel,230, Danl.,086,196,
197,231, Dery,230, Elizabeth,
230,231, James,185,203,229,
230, Jas.,104,105,107, Jno.,
108, Jno.B.,079, John,050,
230, Joseph,156, Lamore(?),
230, Mary,077, Micajah,230,
Nancy,230,231
LONG, Reuben,230,231,252,
Robert,003, Robt.,010,021,
022,033,044,045,047,054,
060,083,129,154,162,210,
211,245, Wair,075, Ware,230
LONGSTON, John,224
LOOK, Jno.,173
LORD, Jno.,160, William,176,
Wm.,160,167,179,204,212
LOVE, Matthew,010, Wm.,040
LOVELAND(?), Wm.,097
LOVELESS, James,235, Jno.,265,
John,195,274
LOVING, Danl.,196
LOW, J.,249, James,158,259,
Jas.,043,137,238,239,
Saml.,220, Samuel B.,238,
Wm.,060,102,167,230,238,
Wm.Sr.,206
LOWE, Clement,249, James,238,
240, Jas.,267,276, M.C.,240,
Plesent,240, Saml.,040,
Samuel B.,240, William,240,
Wm.,007,036,046,073,104,
105,120,140,188,219, Wm.Sr.,
138
LOWERS, Saml.B.,215
LOWERY, B.L.,236, Bob,109,
Chartila,236, Chas.H.,097,
Geo.,107, H.,097, Hambleton,
231, James H.,179,235,
James,246, Jas.,108,092,
111, Jas.A.,104, Jas.H.,086,
129,131,218,228, Jno.,241,

Jonathan,108, Jos.H.,212,
  Larken,207, Robt.,086
LOWERY, Robt.,091,097,
  Saml.B.,235, Wm.,239
LOWES, Wm.,069
LOWREY, Charlota B.,256,
  James J.,256, Jas.H.,128
LOWRY, Jas.,269, Jas.J.,268,
  Johnston,235, Robert,063,
  Robt.,071,084, Saml.,231
LOYD, James,253, Wm.,044
LSNGSTON, Saml.,189
LTTLE, Jno.,264
LUCAS(?), Benj.,217
LUCAS, John,001,014, Sarah,
  014
LUKE, Alex.,149, Alexr.,156,
  157,189, Anthony G.,235,
  Isaac,149, James,149,
  Jas.Jr.,150, Jno.,182,188,
  210,211,230,246,253,261,
  264,266,271, Jno.Sr.,199,
  John Sr.,203, John,149,
  157,181,188,267, Martha,149,
  181,182, Samuel,147,149
LUKER, Jas.,108
LUMPKINS, Jno.,097
LUSKEY, Hugh L.H.,188
LUTTRELL, Robt.,043
LYGON, Jno.,080, Jno.Mamanuel,
  165, Joseph,217, Wm.,131,242
LYLES, James,152, Thos.,152
LYNCH, Aaron,050,170, Archbd.,
  169, Jno.,225, Jos.,170,
  Jos.A.,177, Joseph,038,
  168,169, Milanda,188, Mrs.,
  170, N.E.,256, Nancy,189,
  Naomi,189, Sarah,169,188,
  Thos.,169,189, W.E.,170,
  175, Wm.E.,168,170,182,237
LYNES, Stephen,170
LYNNET, Patrick,205
LYNNETT, Patrick,235
LYNSEY, Bailey,010
LYON, Emmson,254, Emuel,233,
  John,035,186, Jos.,050,
  058,072,085,100, Joseph,002,
  057, Wm.,117,186
LYONS, Edmund,232, Emmanuel(?),
  232, Jos.,010,013, Joseph,
  010, Sophia,066
M'CLAN, Jno.,193
M'COLLOUGH, David,178
M'CUSAHAN, Wm.,221
MABERRY, Jesse,103
MABRAY, Jesse,225
MABURY, Eton,113
MACHIN, Abraham,272
MACHON, James,243
MACPHARLON, L.D.,173
MADDEN(?), Sarah,145
MADDEN, A.,163, Abraham,013,
  070,097,171,195,207,
  Absalum,051, Albert,210,
  234,236,268, Ann,013,095,
  Charles Sr.,150, Charles,
  013, Chas.,073,097,138,143,
  248, David,005,013,019,034,
  040,041,042,063,097,138,
  163,166,210,235,248,270,
  Elihu,193
MADDEN, Elina,042, G.D.,186,
  Geo.,007,036,043,054,076,
  095,097,099,102,135,196,
  198,213,214,217, George,013,
  127, Gina,034, Haisten,210,
  243, Haiston,193, Harley(?),
  145, Henery,138, Henry,138,
  218,235,237,246,248,
  Hoisten,180, Hosten Jr.,180
MADDEN, Jacob,079,113, Jerob,
  128, Jno.(Capt.),235,237,
  Jno.,041,104,105,114,116,
  143,156,230, Jno.L.,193,
  210,222,236,268, John L.,
  217, John,013,059,073,076,
  095,097,099,138,155,193,
  Mabra Sr.,237, Mabra,019,
  070,104,116, Mabry,105,
  Mabury,171
MADDEN, Madson(?),013, Moses,
  007,009,029,051,052,059,
  069,076,237, Mrs.(Jr.),235,

Phebee,143, Phebey,127,
  Pheby,193, S.L.,207,
  Salley,152, Sally,155,
  Saml.,207, Sarah,138,155,
  Susan,143, Susannah,013,
  042, Wm.,013,059,073,097,
  116,130
MADDEN, Wm.,132,143,163,166,
  193,210,247,248, Wm.Jr.,166,
  236,237, Wm.Sr.,236, Zimri,
  220, Zimry,178,248
MADDOCKS, Mrs.,135
MADDON, David,016
MADDOX, Benj.,147, J.L.,150,
  Jesse,051, Jno.,076,231,
  259, Joel,231, John L.,150,
  John,051,063,068, Juda,075,
  Judah,035,051,076,091,
  Judith,034, Justian,034,
  Justinian,035,087,088,091,
  Letty,082,114, Mary,114,
  S.L.(L.L.?),152, Saml,147
MADDOX, William,115, Wm.,146,
  147,152,265
MADEN, Mrs.(Sr.),235
MADISON, L.M.,228, L.W.,274,
  Leroy,222,228
MADOX, John,230, Wm.,132,230
MAEDORS, Warner W.,232
MAGOWEN, Wm.,160
MAGUM, Daniel,254
MAHAFFEY, Allen,221,266,
  Hoses,240, Hugh,109,221,
  Lewis,240,261, Martin Sr.,
  007, Martin(Jr.),007,
  Martin,009, Mary,007,
  Nancey(Mrs.),126, Nancy,
  240, Orsamus,266, Solomon,
  141, William,240
MAHAFFY, Hosa,232
MAHAN, Agnes,260, Eliz.,265,
  Elizabeth,260, Mary,260,
  Rachel,260, Wm.,144,147
MAHON, Allen,266, Bailey,079,
  082,118,146,171,184,241,
  Baley,147,151,221,241,
  Jno.,265, Jos.,084, Nancy,
  103, Thos.,241,274
MAIRES, John,070
MAJOR, Susanna,066
MAJORS, John,015
MALCOLM, Saml.,029
MALCOMB, Joseph,007
MALDEN, Benj.,064,185,203,
  224,227,251, Thos.,004
MALDING, Benj.,207, James,171
MALKEN, Wm.,215
MALONE, Jno.,133,196, Jno.D.,
  133, R.A.,159, Robert,131,
  158, Robt.,130,133,160,162,
  185,190,191,203, Robt.A.,
  185, Wm.,265
MAMXFIELD, John,019
MANDLEY, Jeremiah,163, Mr.,
  074
MANEY, Mason,235
MANGRAM, Jno.,267
MANGRUM, Danl.,166, Wm.,142,
  146
MANGUM, David,150
MANLEY(?), Jas.,111
MANLEY, Christian,067, Eliza,
  084, Elizabeth,027, Ephraim,
  027, G.W.,084, James,067,
  082,084,151,201, Jno.,034,
  John Sr.,019, John,028,
  067,230, Jos.,027, Mas.F.,
  274, Nancy,027,084, Roberson,
  273, Robt.,266, Thos.,261
MANLEY, Thos.,272, Tire,266,
  Tyree,272, Vincent,027,
  Wash.,063, Washington,027,
  044,082,084, William,067,
  082,084, Wm.,027,046,097,
  201,261,266
MANLY, Jno.,098, John,090
MAOTES, Jesse,087
MARCH, D.W.,082
MARCHBANKS, Joel,028, Marah,
  058, Mary,117, Polly,057,
  Sally,100, Stephen,012,
  057,058

MARE(MORE?), Wm.,027
MARES(?), James,147
MARES(MARIS?), Saml.,015
MARKS, Robt.,057
MARLEY, Tully E.,237
MARLOW, Mikel,069, Nathl.,002
MARLY(?), Thomas,124
MARSHALL, Augustin,212, G.,
  204, Mary,211, Thos.,200
MARTEN, Henry,190, Jenana(Mrs.),
  190, John,133,134, Margret,
  220, Wm.,134
MARTENDILL, J.,184
MARTIN, Alfred,096, Andw.,205,
  Anne,176, Augustin,213,
  Benj.,081,138,168,169,200,
  231,245,246, Berry,109,116,
  143,199,268, Beverly,273,
  Chas.,054,248, Currey,151,
  D.,174, Daniel,209,211,
  Danl.,029,048,101,116,141,
  145,146,151,190,205
MARTIN, Danl.,237, Danl.Jr.,
  034,141,211, David,137,150,
  159,170,179,188,206,208,
  227,230,246,249,251,253,
  264,271,273, Diall,235,
  Drury,187,211, Edw.,268,
  Elizabeth,246, Fountain,
  278, Founten,246, Frances,
  052, Gasingin,246, Glasgien,
  246
MARTIN, Glesing,245, H.,094,
  Harberiot(?),124, Harburt,
  143, Harebert,084, Hennery,
  032, Henry,047,055,058,080,
  081,082,165,201,231,246,
  270, Herbert,107,116,
  Hollingsworth,245,246, J.,
  016, James,232, Jas.,270,
  Jas.B.,274, Jemimah,231
MARTIN, Jenna,190, Jeremiah,
  034,052, Jno.,040,045,084,
  138,206,237, Jno.Sr.,237,
  John Jr.,034, John,014,
  016,036,081,176,245,246,
  Johnston,224, Jos.,081,
  094, Joseph,153, Julas,143,
  145, Jules,232, Julius,109,
  271,273, Justonion,124,
  Justus,084
MARTIN, Katherine,168, L.B.,
  211, Littel B.,211, Marey,
  033, Margerite,268, Marshal,
  235,257, Martin,027, N.,
  067, Nancey,143, Nancy,153,
  Nathl.,067, Persila,178,
  Philip,200, Polley,176,
  Reuben,011,012,019,044,
  052,063,077,080,081,082,141
MARTIN, Reuben,168,173,246,
  Robt.,081,098,211,265,267,
  Ruben,141, S.B.,132, Saml.,
  018,084,211,217,243,246,
  256,273,274, Saml.B.,257,
  Samuel,005,081, Stephen,
  081,188, Tabitha,199, Thos.,
  078,225, Trasey,257, Wm.,
  040,044,051,052,057,076
MARTIN, Wm.,098,136,176,227,
  Wm.Jr.,034, Wm.Sr.,034
MARTINDALE(?), Jos.,049
MARTINDALE, Jane,274, Mary,
  189
MARTINDELL, John,021
MARTINDELL, James,188,237,
  Jno.,189
MASFIELD, Edw.,141
MASON, Archey,057, David,003,
  015,019,026,032,051,064,
  068,074,079,086,094,095,
  096,128,130,131,132,135,
  140,143,147,152,166,174,
  176,201,204,209,210,212,
  214,260,262, Dorritha,209,
  Elener,209, Isabel,066,
  Isabella,226, Isbel,209,
  214, Jacob,019
MASON, James,209,211,262,
  Jas.M.,027, Jas.R.,009,
  Jno.,094,102,108,212,243,
  246,260, Job,051,078,096,
  Jobe,102, Joel,072, John,

028,043,072,209,214,220,
226,273, Mary,070,209, Mrs.,
211, S.,138, Saml.,172,
Samuel,033, Wm.,009
MASSEY, Andw.,259, Bradock,
151, Jeremiah,117
MASSY, Nathan,147
MASTERS, Hillary,043, Jacob,
043
MASTIN, Drury,235
MATHENY, Danl.,036,040
MATHES(MATHIS), John,178
MATHES, Abner,229, Betsey F.,
179, Danl.,178, Ezekiel,106,
Hettey,178, Hetty,178,
John,178,179, Polley,178,
Thos.,178,179, Zebulon,092
MATHESS, Daniel,138, Ezekiel,
106, Rebecka,106
MATHEWS, ---,134, Andw.,161,
B.,210, Ezekiel,090, Isaac,
156, John,072, Joseph,032,
Julyather,134, Saml.,160,
210,231, Wm.,072
MATHIS, Andrew,147, Andw.,071,
072,103, Catherine,256,
Chas.,070, Daniel,127,128,
152, Danl.,085,111, Elizabeth,
128, Ezekiel,077, Jacob,111,
Jas.,098, Jno.,098, John,
041, Nancy,256, Robt.,069,
071, Saml.,037,051, Sarah,
211, Thomas,026
MATHIS, Thos.,025,030,072,
Wm.,044, Zeb.,029, Zebulon,
092, Zeln.,040
MATHISON, Geo.,147
MATHISS, Daniel,143
MATISONE, Danl.,229
MATTERSON, L.W.,258
MATTHEWS, Saml.,014, Suzanah,
125, Thos.,008
MATTHIS, Thos.,094
MATTISON, Benj.,142, Geo.,142
MATTOCKS, James,203
MATTOX, (Family),230
MAULDIN, Benj.,025, James,027
MAXFIELD, Geo.,082
MAXWELL, Mr.,112
MAY, Jefferson,241,271, Saml.,
050, William,192
MAYBERRY, Eaton,096
MAYBUM(?), Bartlet,147
MAYBUM, Ferrel,147, John,147
MAYBUN, Wm.,147
MAYERS/MEYORS, John,208
MAYHAFFEY, Allen,237, Hugh,
237
MAYHAN, John,221
MAYHON, Bailey,109, Baley,126,
148, Jno.,195, John,148,
Thos.,147
MAYHONE, Joseph,121
MAYHORN, Jno.,207
MAYORS, John,208
MAYSON, Jno.,117, John,228
MC-NN, David,139
MCADAMS, Catharine,178, Mary,
066, Robt.,019,028, Sarah,
178
MCANDERSON, Anderson,277
MCARLEY, Alex.,241
MCC--, Saml.,095
MCCAA(MCCADE?), Mary,005
MCCAA, D.,073,074, David,007,
016,034,048,054,055,057,
059,061,069,101,105,128,
155, Jno.,097, Polley,155
MCCAIN, James,001, John,001,
Mary,001
MCCAINE, Jas.,044
MCCALL, A.,196, Andrew,150,
195,196, Andw.,160, Thomas,
007
MCCALLISTER, Danl.,019
MCCALUM, Jas.,246
MCCAN, Jno.,177,207
MCCANATHEY, Jas.,131, Martha,
131
MCCANEHY, Jas.,119, Jos.,119,
Samuel,119
MCCANN, John,218
MCCANNAHA, Jos.,154, Margret,

154
MCCANNAHEY, Martha,132
MCCANTER, Jos.,041
MCCAREY, John,123, Jos.,117,
Robt.,010
MCCARLEY, A.,266, Alex.,256,
Alexr.,140,228,278, Danl.,
011, Martha,278, Thomas,278,
Thos.,094,256, Thos.Aug.,
278
MCCARLY, Thos.,087
MCCARRY, Jas.,117
MCCARTEY, James,203
MCCARTNEY, John,006
MCCARTY(?), Wm.,032
MCCARTY, Danl.,011,015,020,
Jno.,172
MCCARY(?), Jas.,125
MCCASH, John,009,013
MCCAUL, A.,090, Andrew,090,
Andw.,191
MCCAULL, Andw.,187, Wm.,034
MCCAY, Archd.,029, Drayton,
224, Henry,225, J.,249,
Jno.,153,211,222,241, John,
218, Nathl.Sr.,179, Saxon,
203,204,211
MCELVEY, Henry,091,177, Jas.,
141, Jno.,141, Jno.Jr.,141,
John,064
MCELVY, John,074
MCCLAHAN, Catharine,150,
Jennet,194, Jno.,151,193,
John,145, Samuel,145,
Samuel,194, Wm.,150,152
MCCLAIN, Agness,021, Andrw.,
021, Elinor,054, Geo.,021
MCCLAN, Jno.,165
MCCLANAHAN(?), ,183
MCCLANAHAN, Jane,146, Jennet,
201, Jno.,229, John,014,
035,065,146,193, Jones,146,
Mary,146, Nancy,146, Saml.,
014,146,201,204, Wm.,014,
084,097,135
MCCLANNA, Jno.,157
MCCLANNAHAN, Wm.,150
MCCLANNING, Jno.,199
MCCLARKIN(?), Jas.G.,266
MCCLARY, ,270, William,138
MCCLASKEY, Eliz.,065
MCCLAY, Saxon,203
MCCLEHAN, Jno.,188
MCCLELEN, Squire,267,268
MCCLELLAN, Benj.,015, Bridget,
112, Jno.,153,170, John,112,
Squire,208
MCCLELLAND, Saml.,148
MCCLENNAHAN, Jno.,259
MCCLENNING, Elias,152, Jno.,
143
MCCLENNON, John,227
MCCLERKEN, Saml.,102
MCCLERKIN, Jas.,109
MCCLINTICK, John,008
MCCLINTOCK, G.,009, Geo.,134,
140,141,190,237, James,004,
040,043, Jane,046, Jas.,008,
039,040,041,044,046,047,
048,141, Jno.,087,115,116,
130,133,134,141,161,173,
175,178,179,180,183,187,
208,228,230,231,239,256,
266,268, John,039,040,041
MCCLINTOCK, John,046,122,155,
226,277, Jos.,081, Margaret,
040,046,121, Margret,048,
Margt.,037, Martha,040,
204,276, Marthew,041, Mary,
276, Matthew,043, Nancy,040,
277, Peggy,155, Robert,276,
Robt.,041,043,044,116,
Saml.,141, Widow,040
MCCLINTOCK, Wm.,043
MCCLURE(?), Jean,024
MCCLURE, Alexr.,110, Ann,006,
Cheney,235, David,108,110,
215, Frances,109, Geo.,107,
James,109,139, Jas.,118,
Jesse Jas.,109, Jesse,103,
Jno.,108,110,118, John,028,
070,072,075,139, Rudy(?),
044, Ruth,139, Thos.,118,

William,139, Wm.,098
MCCLURE, Wm.,186,193,247
MCCLURKEN, Jas.,178, Saml.,
071
MCCLURKIN, Arch.,247, Catharine,
220, Catherine,222,242,
James,045,220,222, John,
220, Saml.,016,045,167,220,
229,242
MCCLUSKEY, ,143, Chas.,178,
Jeremiah,076
MCCOBB, James,030
MCCOLLUM, James,266, Jos.,268
MCCOLLUMS, Jas.,246
MCCON(?), Jno.,118
MCCONAHA(MCCONAY), Jas.,121
MCCONAHAY, Judah,221, Wm.,221
MCCONAHY, Jas.,120, Jos.,120,
Ruth,120, Samual,121,
Samuel,120
MCCONATHA, Jos.,189,198,
Saml.,198,215
MCCONATHEY, James,132
MCCONATHY, Jos.,182,224,265
MCCONEHEY, Saml.,006,010,011
MCCONEHY, James,119, Joseph,
119, Margaret,119, Ruth,119,
Samuel,119
MCCONNATHY, Margret,158,
Saml.,215
MCCONNEL, Isabella,094
MCCONNETHY, Saml.,010
MCCONTHAY, Jos.,158
MCCORELEY, Thos.,155
MCCORLEY, Alender,214
MCCORMICK, Mary,143
MCCOY, Barnet,266, Barnett,
276, Bell(?),266, Charity,
276, David B.,266, David,
276, Drayton,276, Elizabeth,
276, Henry,266, J.,078,
J.L.,266, Jno.,086,231,
Jno.L.,266, John,266,276,
Micajah,266, Nathl.,016,
Saxon,200, Wm.,015
MCCRACKEN, Acher,055
MCCRACKENS, Robt.,111
MCCRADA, Wm.,180
MCCRADY(?), Wm.,180
MCCRADY, Caroline,179, James,
179, Jane,179, John,179,
Mary,179, Morgan,179,
Robt.Carter,179, Wm.,179
MCCRAKEN, Wm.,266
MCCRAREY, Geo.,131,219, John,
130, Saml.,133
MCCRARY(?), Geo.,069, Robt.,
010,269
MCCRARY, Andrew,006,008,043,
244, Andrw.,011,018, Andw.,
020,043,045,054, Benj.Lewis,
011, Capton,139, Caroline,
273, Casey,083, Catherine,
008, Charles,008, Cheston B.,
273, Christian B.,273,
Christop.,048, Christopher,
008,011, Edwin,265
MCCRARY, Elizabeth,273,
Frankey,067, Geo.,011,018,
063,067,069,083,085,099,
133,143,156,157,160,164,
166,167,170,188,189,199,
219,221,224,268, George,008,
048,062,076,273, Isaac,043,
JOhn,168, James,017,053,
055,265, Jas.,018,021,025,
Jno.,137
MCCRARY, Jno.,173, Jno.W.,165,
John,017,043,050,055,061,
166, Lettice,011,014,018,
020, Lettie,008, Marey,042,
043, Mary,008,043, Mathew,
015,166,168,173,198,241,
266, Matthew,008,011,014,
018,021,043,175, Moses,008,
011,014,018,021,043,062
MCCRARY, Moses,063, Mr.,083,
Nancy,132, Polley,139,
Robert,042, Robt.(Col),020,
Robt.,043, Thomas,008,139,
Thos.,010,011,018,048,061,
082,083,097,098,099,132,
152,256, Thos.A.,022, Wm.,

017,061,064,108,173
MCCRAY, Alex.,256, John,215,
 William,193
MCCREA, Wm.,155
MCCREEDY, Mary,249, Robt.,238,
 Sarah,224,249
MCCRELESS, Geo.,135
MCCULAH, Jos.,138
MCCULLAH, Joseph,147
MCCULLAR, D.,215, David,187,
 215,241,250, Joseph,217,232
MCCULLARS, Jos.,187
MCCULLOCH, David,009,010,013,
 020
MCCULLOR, David,242,258
MCCULLOUGH, D.,163, David,163,
 242, Jas.,098,272, Jos.,084,
 090,094,098,109, Joseph,265
MCCULLUM, James,243, Jas.,143
MCCURLEY, Alex.,205, Alexr.,
 231, George,175, James,002,
 050, Jas.,047,081,098, Jno.,
 128, John,175,176,177,
 Margaret,036, Polley,175,
 177, Robt.,013,036, Thos.,
 081,133,187,231,249
MCDANIAL, Richd.,132
MCDANIEL, Adam,102, Alexr.,
 233, Archbd.,017, Archbd.Jr.,
 125, Archd.,044,087,118,
 Archebald,178, Archibald,
 175, Danl.,028, Drury,274,
 James,067, Jas.,142, Joel,
 175, John,037, Margret,017,
 Margt.Wade,175, Mary,044,
 Mathew,175,236, Matthew,017
MCDANIEL, Matthew,102, Pinson,
 130, Thomas,175, Wm.,044,
 066,102
MCDANNEL, Archebal,128, Mary,
 043, Mathew,042, Wm.,043
MCDANNIEL, Mathew,228
MCDARRALL, Patrk.,178
MCDAVID, ,005,101, James,013,
 071, Jas.,021,092, Jas.Jr.,
 082, Jno.,118,241, John,062,
 071, William,148, Wm.,147
MCDAY, John,215
MCDOLE(MEDOLE?), Wm.,002
MCDOLE, John,048
MCDONAL, Jos.,027, Mary,027,
 Thomas,025,027, Thos.,027,
 159, Wm.,027
MCDONALD, Abner,167, Jas.,093,
 John,070, Thos.,015, Wm.,
 003,093
MCDONNAL, John,072
MCDONNALD, Eliz.,030, Thos.,
 030,035
MCDONNEL, Eliz.,024, Thos.,
 024
MCDOUGAL, Allen,102
MCDOWAL, James,046,227,263,
 Jas.,268, Thos.,243
MCDOWALL, Esther,035, James,
 193,213, Jas.,268, John,179
MCDOWEL, Jas.,143, John,013,
 047
MCDOWELL(?), Patrk.,178
MCDOWELL, Benj.,004, Eliz.,
 004, James,090,091,180,
 Jane,237, Jas.,098,143,
 Jno.,121,145, John,007,
 082,180, Patrick,027, Saml.,
 220, Thos.,246
MCDOWL, Jno.,159
MCEARLEY, Alexr.,233
MCELERY, Andrew,255, James M.,
 255, James,257
MCELROY, James M.,263, John,
 004
MCEWEN, Jos.,133
MCFALL, Anthony,205,235
MCFAUL, Andw.,133, Anthoney,
 133
MCFEARSON, Wm.,007
MCFERSON, Burgess,184,191,
 Da--,177, James,104,173,
 184,192,206,207,246,262,
 Jas.,104,107,131, Lorenzadow,
 207, Rachel,206, Wm.,051,
 076,104,105,107,207
MCGEE, Ansel,007,015, Chas.,

077, Jesse,062, John,060,
 062,068,069,086
MCGIN(?), Danl.,016
MCGIN, Catherine,059, Daniel,
 036,059,060, Danl.,019,039,
 James,059, Mrs.,060, Wm.,
 059
MCGINN, Daniel,030, Danl.,023
MCGLADERY, David,005,018,045,
 Eliz.,046, Margret,046,
 Saml.,046,062,063,071
MCGLALDERY, David,046
MCGOWAN, James,235, Jas.,273,
 Jenet,196, Jno.,094,140,
 185,207,242, John,019,050,
 197, Joseph,229, Wm.,140,
 158,185,187,252,267
MCGOWEN, Jane,244, Jno.,096,
 181, John,030,244,245, Jos.,
 240, Wm.,165,181,217,221,
 244,245,259,261,274,275,
 Wm.Jr.,244,245,272
MCGOWING, Agness,215, Andrew,
 215, Elizabeth,215, Jno.,
 133, John,185,215, Martha,
 215, Mary,215, Patrick,215,
 Samuel,215, Sarah,215, Wm.,
 215,224,239,259
MCGOWN, Jno.,153, John,154,
 Jos.,194
MCGRARY, Geo.,076
MCGUMERY, Wm.,168
MCHAFFEE, Alex.,082,084,
 Martin,082,084, Nancy,082,
 084
MCHAFFEY, David,221, Hugh,001,
 008, John,003, Martin,001,
 Nancy,084
MCHAFFIE, Nancy,102
MCHARDEN, James,200
MCHARG(?), John,054
MCHARG, John,055, Susannah,
 013
MCHARRISON, Jno.,232
MCHERG(?), Archbd.,012
MCHERG, Alex.,071, Arch.,054,
 Elenor,055, John,032,054,
 055, Polly,055, Susannah,
 032,054,055, Wm.,054,055
MCHUE, Elisha,186
MCHUGH, E.,274
MCHURG, Arch'd,005, Nancy,100
MCJUNKENS, Aquillar,158
MCJUNKIN, Aquillar,169
MCKAY, Archbd.,030
MCKEE, Danl.P.,233, Danld.,
 232, Wm.,158
MCKEES, ,151, Robt.,171
MCKELEVY, George,189, James,
 189, John,189
MCKELVEY, Alexr.,189,230,
 Anna,189, Henry,224, Hugh,
 189, Isaac,189, Jabez,189,
 Jas.,273, Jno.,167,
 Jno.Jr.,151, John,188,189,
 192, Mary,188,189, Nelly,
 189, Polley,189, Rachel,189,
 Saml.,134,273, Samuel,189,
 Thomas,189, Wm.,189
MCKELVY, Alexander,273, Henry,
 108,265, Jas.,268,273, Jno.,
 138, Saml.,268
MCKENDRICK, Geo.,230
MCKINLEY, Jos.,072
MCKINSEY, Littleberry,008
MCKINTRICK, Geo.,142,146,157,
 James,150, Jas.,140,142,
 143, Priscilla,142, Priscilla,
 146, Saml.,140,142, Samuel,
 146
MCKITRICK, G.,174, Geo.,142,
 152,168,266,273, James,150
MCKNIGHT, Andrew,171, Andrw.,
 001, Andw.,072,172,194,201,
 207,235, Elizabeth,172,
 Geo.,237, James,008,172
MCLAIN, Geo.,011, Jno.,104
MCLANE, Robt.,252
MCLAUGHLIN, J.,016, John,024,
 029,034,048
MCLEROY, James,275
MCLURE, James,224
MCMAHAN, Danl.,096, James,042,

064,095,102, Jas.,036,092,
 111,117, Jas.Jr.,138,197,
 Jas.Sr.,197, Jno.,040,
 John,007,042, Wm.,072
MCMAHEN(MCMAHON), Jas.,154
MCMAHEN, Jno.,196
MCMAHON, Cornelius,001, James,
 144,171,180, Jas.,238,
 Jas.Jr.,138,144, John,154,
 Nancy,154,241, Wm.,114,
 147,154
MCMAKIN, Jno.,165
MCMANIS, John,155
MCMICKEN, Esther,206, John,
 206
MCMIKEN, Stanford,220
MCMILLAN, Archd.,096
MCMILLEN, Magra,249, Margery,
 249
MCMILLIAMS, Jos.,258
MCMORRIS, Jas.,096, Jno.,096
MCMURTON, James,063
MCMURTREE, Marey,068, Mathew,
 068, Wm.,068
MCMURTREY, Betsy,066, Cambell,
 065,066, Janney,066, M.,
 066, Mary,065,067, Mathew,
 076, Matthew,065,066,
 Rebecah,131, Rebecah,131,
 William,065, Wm.,067,068,
 076,131
MCMURTRY, Mary,012, Wm.,012,
 013,102,116
MCNABB, James,030,031
MCNARY, Gilbert,006,048
MCNEALES(?), James,237
MCNEATRE, James,218
MCNEEL, Arthur,151, Jno.,186
MCNEELY, Jas.,119, Jno.,186,
 Wm.,164
MCNEES, Dick,109, James,278,
 Richard,278, Richd.,098,
 105,116, Robert,278, Robt.,
 078,096,098,101,102,119,
 120,129,130,208,229, Salley,
 130, Sally,106,119, Saml.,
 031, Sarah,211,228,237,278
MCNEESE, (Mrs.),246, James,
 277, Richard,277, Robert,
 277, Robt.,239, Samuel,277,
 Sarah,277, Wm.,268
MCNEIR(?), Robt.,023
MCNEIR, Patsey,028, Robert,
 026
MCNEISE, Robt.,015
MCNESS, Robt.,054
MCNIGHT, A.,170, Abigail,002,
 003, Andrew,003,069,102,
 148,170, Andw.,070,093,138,
 Andw.Sr.,002, Archibd.,003,
 Eliz.,170, Geo.,235, Hiram,
 170, James,026,030,148,
 Jennet,002, Jno.,084, John,
 026
MCNORTON, Wm.,040
MCPATTON, Jno.,228
MCPHEARSON, Jas.,267
MCPHERSON, B.,270, Jas.,270,
 Sarah,170, Wm.,012,101,
 118,170
MCQUAY, Alex.,077, Alexr.,060
MCQUERNS, Jas.,038
MCTEER, Betsy,028, Eliz.,024,
 Elizabeth,024, Frances,024,
 042, Frankey,028, Margret,
 024, Nathl.,024, Widow,028,
 Wm.,024,026,028,170
MCVICKERY, Adam,074
MCWILLIAMS, Alex.,160,267,
 269, Alexander,259, Alexr.,
 084,085,091,274, Andrew,084,
 Andw.,079,140, David,084,
 097, Jane,084, Jno.,079,
 140,182,185,207,239,245,
 John,084,150,221,224,244,
 Mary,084, Robt.,084, Saml.,
 185,228,229,239,275, Sarah,
 215
MCWILLIAMS, Wm.,167
MCWINN, Danal.,238, David,151
MEACHIM, Abraham,272
MEADOR, Eliz.,109, Jacob,164,
 232,254, Jason,076, Jno.,

28

077,085,088,093,104,116,
117,164, John,005,025,050,
058,073,076,162, Lucey,164,
Lucy,232, Thos.,164,
William,162, Wm.,107,131,
172,173
MEADORS, Anne,180, Bathiah,
212, Eliz.,058,196, Hannah,
185,209, Henry,196, Jacob,
252, James A.,209, James,
047,181,182,270, Jas.,048,
Jason,047,120,153,154,156,
158,164,165,167,170,180,
Jehu,047, Jno.,109,131,
167,231, John,163,167,180
MEADORS, John,181,196, Lucey,
232, Marey,196, Martha,209,
Mary,197, Morris,196, Oney,
209, Paskel,241, Polley,196,
Preskal,209, Reuben,047,
061,078,167,179,180,181,
182,189,209,270, Rueben,130,
Susan,192,196, Susanah,180,
182, Susannah,047
MEADORS, Thomas,212, W.,197,
Warner W.,209, Warner,196,
199,211,241, Warren W.,196,
Wash.,130, Washington,164,
167,170,180,181,182,196,
211,218,223,241, William,196
MEADOW, Jno.,116, John,029
MEADOWS(?), Eliz.,058
MEADOWS, (Estate),232, John,
058, Park,264
MEANS, Robt.,251, Saml.,002
MEAR, William,192
MEARS, Cristan,150
MEDLEY, Edw.,092,270, Edw.Newton,
139, Edward,139, Fienus,162,
Frances,074, Francis,111,
139,171,220, Francs,270,
Frs.,227, Isaac,024,036,
058, James,058,065,139,151,
160, Polly,064, Sarah,058,
139, Whitehead,065
MEDLOCK, David,011,214,239,
247, James,162,239,271,
Reuben(?),195, Sarah,271,
Silus,239,247, Thos.,082,
147
MEDORS, Washington,199
MEDOW(MEADOR), Wm.,165
MEED, Isaac,151
MEEK, Betsey,038, Elinor,038,
Ellenor,038, James,038,
Jas.,119, Jinney,038, Jno.,
119,160, John,022,038,039,
136,144,150, Nancy,038,
Samuel,038, Wm.,038
MEEKEY, Danl.P.,156
MEER(?), Moses,126
MEHAFFE, Lewis,163, Solomon,
166
MEHAFFEE, Hosea,233, Lewis,
233, Nancy,233, Sollomon,
233, Wm.,233
MEHAFFEY, Allen,241, Campbell,
236, Hosa,241, Lewis,241,
Nancy,241, Varnel,147, Wm.,
163,166,241
MEHAFFIE, Alex.,147
MEHAFFY, John,003, Sollomon,
232
MEHAN, Jno.,183, Wm.,236
MEHANAHAN, ,183
MEHON, Bailey,235, Jno.,235
MEHUGH, Elisha,259
MEKIE, Danl.,258
MELONE, Wm.,224
MELTZ, David,273, Henry,273,
Richd.,273
MELVINE, Harriet,258
MEMSESTREE(?), Wm.,263
MENARY, Alex.,016, Gilbert,
016
MENDLEY, Jeremiah,134
MENG, Clough S.,179, Patsey,
179
MENOAH, Forgey,244
MERCEY, Garey(Dr.),189
MERDITH, Henry,039
MEREDITH, Henry,047,056,072,
091,161,257, Mahala,212,

Nelson,205,231, Saml.,205,
256,274
MERISON, James,223
MERIWETHER, Zach.,078
MERON(?), Nancy,100
MERRIL, Chas.,020
MERRILL, Chas.,021
MERTON, James W.,203
MESHEEN, Carding,211
MESHURE, Obediah,185
METHANY, Danl.,014
METHENEY, Danl.,007
METHENY, Danl.,016,021
METLY, Geo.,273
METS, Hagen,250
MEYRES, John,208
MEYSON, John,260
MICHAUX, Ob.,101
MICHEL, Elisha,040, Isaac,029,
Joseph,026, Moley,023,
William,062, Wm.,023,040
MICKELFORD, Jas.,042
MIDDLETON, Ainsworth,011,012,
014,020,045,047,073,079,
085,086,107,108, Andrew,011,
032,045,047, Andrw.,016,
033, James,011,169,270,
Jane,011,047,108,270, Jno.,
016,080,092,100,108,112,
John,007,011,014,015,019,
022,024,037,045,050,064,067
MIDDLETON, John,079,096,105,
107,275, Judith,011, Peggy,
033,034, Sarah,011, Thos.,
011
MIDDORS, Parshel,189
MIDLETON, Ainsworth,192,
Allen,168,204, Andrew,192,
196, James,196, Jane Jr.,
192, Jane,167,192,194, John,
193,196, Margret,196
MILAM, Alfred,267, B.,174,
Bartlet Sr.,148, Bartley,
098, Benj.,159, Elizabeth,
148, Ferrel,148,159, Henry,
271, Hettey,148, Isham,185,
Jno.(Maj.),236, Jno.,095,
116,143,229,264,267,
John Jr.,024, John,007,
127,148, Joshua,159, Judah,
148
MILAM, Madison,265,272,
Nancey,148, Riley,148,
Robert,272, Robt.,029,174,
273, Thos.,037,268, Wm.,113,
250, Wm.A.,159, Wm.P.,271
MILAN, Jno.,145
MILELR, Jacob,174
MILENER, A.,178, Arnold,178
MILES, John,038, Wm.,043
MILL, Isaac,164
MILLAM, John,175
MILLAR, Anderson,132, Ezekiel,
219, George,032, Hamon,254,
Hanner,157, Harvest,256,
Henry,183, Jacob,036,037,
198,221,222,223,229, James,
051, Jas.Hunter,190, Jno.,
128,131,157,161,178,179,
180,188,243, John,032,046,
061,062,068,132, Jos.,229
MILLAR, Larkin,221, Martha,
013, Martin,157,182,215,
216, Mathew,222,224, Micher,
215, Morten,219, Morton,182,
N.C.,221, Robt.,141,218,
Sarah,132, Wheate,189,192,
Wm.,132, Wm.Park,141
MILLENDER, Jno.,156, Thos.,
177
MILLENER, Arnold,211
MILLENOR, Joseph,004
MILLER, Albert,198,216,218,
219,233,240,262, Alex.,133,
Avant,141, Benj.,113,247,
Betsey,001, Chas.,266,
Ellinor,001, Franklin A.,
219, Franklin,198,216,218,
246,254, Fredrk.,103, Geo.,
033,051,087,088,089,092,
096,136, Hamon,165,268,
Hance,022
MILLER, Hanse(Hannce),001,

Haregrove,219,246, Harmon,
074, Harvest(?),151,
Harvest,172, Harvy,172,
Hayman,111, Haymon,167,
Haymun,167, Henry,258,
Hirum,141, Isaac,081,104,
Israel,043,098, Jacob Jr.,
165,167,209, Jacob Sr.,167,
209, Jacob,001
MILLER, Jacob,021,029,065,
066,074,093,098,111,142,
149,171,199,203,219,264,
James L.,151, James,203,
205, Jesse,001, Jno.,128,
167,204,210,236,242,261,
264,266,267,273,274, Jno.J.,
161, John,001,003,012,017,
021,026,034,042,051,065,
087,089
MILLER, John,125,128,201,202,
203,204,218, Jos.,042,169,
Joseph,001, Margret,125,
Martha,167,199,216, Martin,
048,085,111,140,171,174,
198,199,218,270, Mathew,215,
Morten,188, Roberts,240,
Robt.,134,188,207,251,
Saml.,043,152,165,211
MILLER, Sarah,171,172,201,
202,204, Seth,202, Susanna,
001, West,160, Wheat,098,
168, Wheate,140,152,157,
181, Wheet,172, William,201,
Wm.,062,074,251
MILLIGAN, Wm.,177,258
MILLIGEN, Wm.,194
MILLNER, Arnold,043, Jas.,108,
Jno.,174, Joshua,108,
Richd.,043,050, Wm.,075,
103,104
MILLOR, Albert,254, Haman,254
MILLS, Alex.,008,040,043,046,
047,085,087,094,104,105,
107,116,155, Alex.Jr.,257,
257, Alexr.,039,081,122,
123, Alexr.Sr.,183,233,
Andw.Jr.,133, Humphrey,093,
James,041,044,053,056,058,
081,087,088,089,183, Jas.,
008,039,040,043,046,249
MILLS, Jesse,117, Jno.,161,
Mamon,157, Margaret,008,
Margarette,277, Mary M.,
257, Mary,040,087, Nancy,
087, Rebecah,087, Rebecca,
089, Rebekah,081,088, Saml.,
094,116,121,131,141,155,
159,161,180,213,233,255,
256,258,266,274,275,277,
Samuel,008
MILLS, Samuel,157,159,
William,277, Wm.,008,087,
228,256,257,266, Wm.Sr.,232,
233
MILLWEE, Arnold,123, James,
002, John,002, Sarah,002,
William,002, Wm.,020,071
MILNER(?), John,074, Richard,
074
MILNER, Arnold,084, Eliz.,134,
152, Jas.,080, Jno.,081,
278, John,059,277, Joshua,
080,081, Richard,080,081,
Royal,136, Susannah,277,
278, Thos.,136, Wm.,109
MILONE, Danl.P.,253
MILUM, Allen,198, Almon,200,
Aron,198, Bartlet,130,198,
200, Bartlett,134, Bartley,
029, Benj.,134, Eliz.,153,
198,200, Elizabeth,153,162,
Emely,198, Emity(Emily?),
200, Feral(?),098, Ferel,
213, Feril,206, Ferrel,153,
Henry,271, Isham,209
MILUM, Ishum,197,209, James,
220, Jane,130,134,198, Jno.,
092,101,153,211,229,260,
John,024,025,036,065,134,
217,218, Joshua,153, Judah,
153, Judy,260, July Ann,198,
Kittey,153, Mary,117,153,
Polley,198, Polly,198,

29

R.(Capt.),218, Rachel,177
MILUM, Rebeca,198, Riley,173,
Robt.,205,230,243, Ryley,
134,211, Sally,198, Thos.,
098,229,230,247, Wiley,151,
210,232,238,240,243,
William P.,246, Wm.,065,
134,153, Wm.P.,239, Wm.Sr.,
246,262
MILWEE, Jno.,116, Wm.,011,027
MIMS, Charles A.,240, John,
240,241, M.,265, Martha,240,
265
MINAR, John,189
MINEWEATHER, Dr.,062, Zach.,
066
MINTEN(?), Wm.,102
MIRPHEY, Milly,033
MISHEEN, Cotten,187, Manoah,
187
MISHER, Obediah,169
MISHURE, Obediah,198
MITCHEL, Alex.,249, Benj.,135,
Benj.R.,113,258, Danl.,106,
242, David,247,250,253,
Elisha,031, Isaac,031,042,
113,151,167,214,220,223,
229,238,245,246,247, Israel,
151, James,031,158,164,167,
229,231, Jas.,113,120,133,
138, Jno.,136,242
MITCHEL, John,045,164, Judith,
181, Judy,162,169, Martha,
162, Wm.,062,241,254
MITCHELL, A.,097, Allen,090,
Banister,096,115, Benj.R.,
108, D.,090,111,112, Danl.,
065,074,099,111, Druscilla,
090, Drusilla,090, Harris,
109,113, Henry,071, Isaac,
052,060,065,073,087,109,
110,117,251,264,265,267,
272,274, Jas.,110,120
MITCHELL, Jas.L.,095, Jno.,
137,235, John,018,105,
Judith,186, Lewis,060,112,
113,135, Martha,118, Mary,
060, Randolph,019, Sinthey,
060, Thos.,060,218, Thos.D.,
095, William,060, Wm,051,
Wm.,002,009,101,110,274
MITCHERSON(?), Wm.,013
MITCHERSON, J.D.,077
MITCHESON(?), Edwd.,004
MITCHESON, Clarissa,109, Jno.,
088, Jno.A.,152, Jno.D.,109,
117
MITCHISON, John D.,151
MITCHUSON(?), Edw.,020
MIXON, A.(Capt.),235, Absalum,
261
MIXSON, Wm.,179
MIYERS, Moses,247
MOATES, Isaac,085, Joseph,143
MOATS(MOTES), Betsy,087,
Isaac,085
MOATS, Betsy,088,092, David,
085,104,105,106, Elisha,101,
Isaac,087,088, Jas.,
236, Jesse,085,101,106,253,
Jno.,101,102,132, Jonathan,
143, Silas,101,104,174, Wm.,
174
MONEY, Saml.,264
MONFORD, Easter,078, Johnston,
078
MONGRUNE, Wm.,142
MONRO, Andrew,136,208, Andw.,
137, Betsey,135, Carton,136,
Catharine,137, David,137,
Jno.,137, John L.,137,
John S.,136, John,135,136,
137, Larken,136, Nancy,136,
137, Robt.A.,137, Robt.Alexr.,
135, Sally,135, Sarah,137,
Widow,137
MONROE, Alex.,026, Andw.,179,
210,212, Andy,211, Jno.,076,
085,086,102,131,187,238,
John Sr.,191, John,015,
016,017,018,019,028,055,
067,074,127,130, L.S.,271,
Larken,261,263, Mr.,111,

Robt.(Dr.),174, Robt.,157,
160,179,189,194,218,
Robt.A.,187
MONROE, Robt.A.,194, Salley,
017, Wm.,080
MONROW, Andrew,242, Andw.,211,
Jno.,101,129, Robt.,106,
242, Sarah,208
MONTGOMERY, James,006, Jas.,
003, Margaret,006, Margt.,
035, Wm.,099
MOODIE, John,171
MOON(?), Mr.,025, Wm.,092
MOON(MOORE?), Wm.,074
MOON, Austin,272, Dr.,062,
Hutson,272, Jesse W.,268,
Jno.,271, Jno.K.,267,
Martha N.,070, Saml.,272,
Thos.,265,267,272
MOOR, Alexr.H.,129,130, Aron,
220,231,233,257, Austin,258,
Bluford,220, Cristwell,262,
Drury,256, Elizabeth,175,
Fountain,257, Geo.(Capt.),
235,236, Geo.,151,214,237,
Geo.Sr.,222, George,228,
Hudson,220, J.,261, James,
093,161,196,214
MOOR, James,233,258, Jefferson,
228, Jesse,093,151, Jno.,
218, Jno.Jr.,185, Jno.Sr.,
187,251, Jos.,106, Joseph,
169, Louisa,257, Mehatey,
257, Polley,257, Robert,148,
Robertson,195, Robt.,106,
228,229,243, Sarah,257,
Seaborn,256,257, Thos.,137
MOOR, Thos.,228, Thos.E.,237,
William,193, Wm.,107,128,
133,134,138,143,150,167,
193,212,222,228,253,258,
Wm.Jr.,113,220, Wm.Sr.,192,
220
MOORE(?), Salley,017
MOORE, Aaron,043,069,103,
Anderson,034,205, Aron,256,
Asa,103, Austin,022,029,
030,156, Betsey,157, Brown,
256, Geo.,200,207,267,
Hannah,017, J.,183,202,
James,034,056,057,228,
Jane,133,183, Jas.(Dr.),
062, Jas.,074,099, Jas.B.,
247, Jenna,056
MOORE, Jesse,056,239, Jno.,
103,113,160,191,198,229,
233, John K.,217, John,034,
061,064,074,191, Johnston,
056, Jonth.,094, Jos.A.,269,
Mark,022, Mordicah,117,
N.,057, Obed.,040,043,
Rebecca,106, Roberson,081,
082,106, Robertson,194,
Robt.,018
MOORE, Robt.,055,264, Saml.,
272, Samuel,272, Seth,207,
Thomas,004,272, Thos.,018,
041,126,264,272, Tryparana,
020, Valley,056, Wm.,067,
072,075,076,082,089,101,
104,107,113,149,163,165,
170,173,187,204,210,267
MOORHEAD, James,215
MORE, Alexr.,129, Anderson,
031, Andrew,032, Austen,032,
Austin,031, James,177,
Jesse,117, John,029,031,
032, Marey,032, Mary,031,
033, Nancy,029,032, Saml.,
039, Wm.,051,178
MOREH, Jno.,179
MOREHEAD, James,215, Martha,
261
MORGAN, David,005, G.,016,
Geo.,004,007,018,019,040,
076, Henery,146, Henry,082,
098,109,149, Isaac,010,
Jno.,234, Robt.,037, Thos.,
215,268, Wm.,215
MORGEN, Ann,258, Harum,255,
Henery,144, Henry,160,161,
163, James,163,222,235,
Jno.,242, John,238, Jos.,

163, Mary,160,221, Polley,
163, Robt.,214, Robt.C.,247,
Saml.,163,235, Thomas,163,
Thos.,221,222, Wm.,126,
149,160,161,163,235,237
MORGEN,244,250,259
MORGIN, James,193,236
MORISON, Alexander,103
MORMON, Jno.,265, Wm.,214
MOROE, Jas.,113
MORRES, Jos.M.,129
MORRIS, Jas.W.,096, Jno.,105,
John,029, Stephen,023,
Thos.,105
MORRISON, Alexr.,004,021,102,
Jno.,247, John,071, Prior,
203
MORROW(?), John,051
MORROW, Jno.,036, Wm.,023,
107,151
MORSE, Ebenezer,040, James,
059
MORSS, Ebenezer,032, James,
032, Obediah,033, Wm.,032
MORTEN, Danl.,247, Devall,237,
Harburt,151, James,166,
Mimima,234, Saml.,151,212,
256, Stephen,186, Wm.,151
MORTIN, David,234, Jeremiah,
256
MORTON, Berry,239, David,003,
Harrey,215, Hollingsworth,
257, John,026, Robt.,239,
Wm.,147
MOSELEY, George,159
MOSELLY, Roberson,159
MOSELY, Asheal(?),051, Geo.,
029,034,046,087, Isaac,051,
076, Jno.,151, John,051,
Robinson,274
MOSES, Thos.,233
MOSLEY, Andw.,161, Austin C.,
157, Barnes,217, Bearns,223,
Braddock,196, Brines,223,
Buckner,207, Burrel,028,
Burrell,046, Eliza A.,157,
Eyre,225, F.E.,256,
Fleming,157,159,161,167,
168,169,178,201,208,256,
257,258, Flemmen,192,
Flemming,157
MOSLEY, Flemming,205,223,225,
231,233, Fountain,157, G.,
094, Geo.,046,047,081,116,
137,146, Geo.Jr.,157,
Geo.Sr.,157, George,161,
Howel,170, Isaac,046,047,
050,062,063, James,161,
Jas.,097, Jesse Brown,206,
Jno.,092,093,094,183, John,
047
MOSLEY, John,059,157, Jordon,
036, Jurden,117, Mark,206,
Mrs.,161, Nancy,157,161,
Polley,157,161, R.,208,
Roberson,157,161,174,178,
180,225,233, Robert,161,
215, Sophia,157, Thos.A.,
157, Tuley,258, Tulley E.,
233, Tulley,220, Tully E.,
MOSLEY, Wm.,047
MOSS, Ebenezer,012,047, Eliz.,
105, Geo.,061, Janah,105,
Mason,051,091,105, Obediah,
044,047
MOSSLEY, Geo.,033
MOTE, Melton,261
MOTES, Andw.,096, Betsy,088,
Celia,219, Dandy,194,229,
Dendy,173, Drury(?),143,
Eilia,219, Elihu,129,
Eliz.,164, Ellis,202,204,
Frederick,028, Hagen,194,
262, Hagin,167, Hogen,219,
Isaac,087,129,157,253,
Jacob,108, Jesse M.,194,
Jesse,017
MOTES, Jesse,085,087,105,160,
171,172,173,194,195,199,
204,219,242,254, Jno.,106,
129,143,157, John W.,172,
173,204, John(Mrs.),129,

John,022,104,127,129,
Jona.,111, Jonathan,022,
106,127,163,164,235, Jos.,
023, Joseph,022,142,
Macklin,194
MOTES, Madison,203, Marcus,
150,264, Mary,022, Mauris,
264, Morrice,151, Nancy,106,
Ordery,022, Rebecah,252,
Richd.,129, Robt.,129,
Sally,030, Sarah,194,
Silas,106,111,173, Silus,
261, Thomas,036,155, Wm.,
173,251, Wm.H.,164,203,240,
254
MOTES, Zachariah,022,027,028
MOTHERALL, Wm.,268,272
MOTTS, Jenna,057, Zach.,051
MOUNCE, Willis,272
MOUNTGOMERY, Wm.,210
MULANAHON, Polley,183
MULENAHAN, James,183
MULLER, Jacob,229
MULLINOX, Aron,258
MULLINS, Franky,028, Stephen,
010,011, Thomas,028
MULWEE, Jno.H.,224
MUNFORD, An,061, Anney,060,
Easter,079, Hugh,060,061,
James,060,061, Jas.,079,
137, Johnston,061,079,
Johnstono,060
MUNRO, John,035
MUNROE, Elizabeth,191, John,
025,066
MUNROW, David,068, Jno.,040,
104,128, John,031,036
MUNROWE, John,025
MURDAUGH, Thos.,022
MUREL, Jno.,211
MURF, Randolf,247
MURFF, Elizabeth,245, Mahala,
247, Malinda,247, R.L.,162,
Randolf S.,161, Randolf,
247, Randolph S.,245, Wiley,
245,271, Wm.,247
MURKLE, Wm.,211
MURPH, Elizabeth,247, Jno.,
263
MURPHEY, Aron,177,218, Chas.,
039, Henry,130, James,156,
174, Jas.,119,130,146, Jno.,
130,156,166,174, John,014,
Marey,129, Nancy,129, S.,
236, Siminion,164
MURPHY, James,154, Jas.,119,
Jno.,096, John,003,154,
Roger Jr.,004, Saml.,050,
Wm.,172
MURREL, Jno.C.(?),184,
John C.,209,213,226, Mary,
012, Samuel,012
MURRELL, Mary,012, Saml.,012,
Samuel M.,243
MURROW, John,051,056, Wm.,092,
098
MUSDA(MCRADY), Nehan,232
MUSGROVE, Ann,004, Edw.Beaks,
004, Edward,004, Hannah,004,
Leah,004, Liney,004,
Margarett,004, Rachael,004,
William,004, Wm.,188,189,
224,262
MUSLELY(MOSLEY?), Lyman,224
MYARS, Elizabeth,139, Moses,
139
MYERS, Jno.,082, Moses,076,
078,096,113,181,265, Moss,
276, Thos.W.,181
MYHON, John,147
MYLAM, Josiah,167
MYLUM, Bartlet Jr.,151,
Bartlet Sr.,151, F.,243,
Jane,134, Saml.,189, Wiley,
099,230
MYRES, John,071, Moses,137
NABERS, Jacob,155,159, Jno.,
159
NABORS, B.,081,088, David,129,
Edw.,274, Elizabeth,174,
Harvey,272, Jacob,121,173,
Mastin,265, Rebecca,174,
Saml.,133,231, Wm.,173

NABOURS, Abraham,027,118,
Alex.,256,257, Alexr.,235,
244, Allen,147, B.,078,084,
086,091,092,100,104,115,
Benj.,071,076,078,087,093,
099,101,103,105, Benjamin,
086, Cage,109, Eliz.,237,
Elizabeth,257, F.,048,
Fleet,097,109, Howey,201,
Isaac,043
NABOURS, J.,094, Jacob,033,
060,070,090,101,105,119,
133,161,173, James,148,156,
Jas.,244, Jno.,093,233,
244,257, John,032,048,071,
147,148,244, Margaret,111,
Nat.,044, Nathl.,071,
Nimrod,241,261, Robt.,118,
133, Saml.,090,104,109,147,
Samuel,244
NABOURS, Thos.,080,085,094,
107, Wm.,244, Zach.,257
NAILAR, James,242
NALOR, James,239
NAMES, Dr.,263
NANCE, Alfred,202, Draten,232,
F.Jr.,264, Fed.,264,
Federick,264, Fedrick,261,
Fred.,264, Frederick,266,
Fredrick,232,235,247
NASH, Edmond,232, Edw.,241,
Jno.,084,102,163,166,233,
241,258, Jno.N.,109,151,
169,241, John,072,084, Wm.,
232
NASON, David,180
NAYLOR, Sarah,225
NCCLELLAN, Bridget,112
NEAL, James,033,041,192,
Jno.(Capt.),109, Jno.,097,
John,215, Nancy,033, Wm.,
028,096,210,261, Zachariah,
142,146
NEALE, Benj.,036, Charles,038,
John,036, Saml.,036, Thos.,
036, Wm.,036,037,038
NEALY, James,058, T.G.,271,
Wm.,274
NEEL, Benijah,173, Benj.,034,
036, David,070,072, Eliz.,
196, Frances,070,072, H.L.,
241, H.S.,209, Henry L.,192,
Henry S.,132,154,175,186,
191,196,198, Henry,271,
James,034,194, Jno.,151,
John,125, Saml.,104,160,
168,179,194,203,218,266
NEEL, Saml.,271, Samuel,032,
Thos.,056, William,208,
Wm.,011,061,128,163,167,
176,179,218,273
NEELEY, Jas.,111,120, Jos.,
092,107,129,139
NEERLIE, Robt.,128
NEELY(?), Nimrod,195
NEELY, Agness,009, Ann,009,
Betsey,234,235, Elizabeth,
235, Geo.,108,124,158,160,
195,235,274, George,009,
150,234, Henry S.,158,
Jacob,085, James Jr.,228,
James,009,160,227,229,234,
235,249,259, Jas.,089,109,
133, Jas.Sr.,160,234, Joel,
099
NEELY, John,039,084, Jos.,018,
080,095,102,107,112,113,
134,135,173, Joseph,186,
198,207,212,213, Mary,234,
Nancey,212, Nancy,234,
Plesent,251, Rebeca,212,
Saml.,011,095, Samuel,234,
235, Wm.,268, Y.,259, Young,
212,213,217,228
NEGRO, (Woman & Child),134,
Absalum,236, Betty,154,
Brister,149, Brumas,236,
Cato(Free),127, Ceasor(Free),
237, Charles,236, Clarkey,
154, Cupit,148, Cyrus,236,
Daniel,236,237, Davy,236,
Eleck,236, Frank,237,
Harry,139, Harvey,229,

Henry,236
NEGRO, Henry,237, Ira,237,
Jabuz(Free),236, Jack,237,
Jane,125, Jesse,236, Jim,
151, Joel,237, John,236,
Josa(?),237, Maggy,236,
Mat,109, Nance,164, Peter,
236,237, Pompy,237, Sam,154,
Squire,237, Stephen,154,
Viney,236, William,237
NEGRO, Winney,237
NEIGHBORS, Chas.,048, Fleet,
095, Jacob,084, Jno.,087,
Nathan,040, Saml.,048,081,
230, Samuel,020, Thos.,116
NEIGHBOURS, Jacob,172, John,
172, Permely,192, Saml.,273
NEIL, H.S.,222, Henry S.,189,
James,218, Saml.,025,111,
128,167,204,218, Wm.,094,
210, Zach.,082
NEILEY, Jos.,127
NEILL, James,019, Saml.,204,
210, Samuel,020, Susannah,
100, Thos.,263, William,203,
Wm.,117,143,164,181,204,
Wm.Jr.,203
NELEY, John,036
NELMS, Andrew,272
NELSON, Andrew,084, Andrw.,
079, Andw.,085,249, Andy,
260,267, David Jr.,108,
David Sr.,108, David,022,
057,091,098,102, Jas.,268,
Lewis,105,120, Mary,085,
William,037, Wm.,092,102,
120,163,248, Wm.Jr.,151
NESBET, Dempsey,192, John,192
NESBIT, Cynthia,240, Martin,
221
NESBITT, James,166, Nathan,
166, Polly,166
NEVEL(NEVIL), Ann,005
NEVIL, Jno.,097
NEWBEY, Pleasant,267
NEWBY, P.,263, Pleasant,272,
Robt.,037
NEWMAN, Avary,189, David,224,
Davis,116,265,274, Jas.,
094, Jno.,040,043, John,036,
040,068,076, Reuben,189
NEWPORT, Jane,089,091
NICBET, Dempsey,236
NICHOLL, Wm.,016
NICHOLS, Charter,053, Chartis(?)
113, James,051, Julius,022,
Nancy,264, Thos.,099, Wm.,
012,269
NICKAL, Wm.,025
NICKEL, Joel,251, John,194,
Robt.,040,203
NICKELE, Nathaniel,259
NICKELL, Nathl.,025
NICKELS, Charter,035,046,053,
093,095, Charters,063,
Eliz.,046, Elizabeth,087,
088, Isabel,046, James,019,
026,051,057,063,064,067,
068, Jas.,046,093,141,
Jas.Jr.,182, Jno.,098,251,
John,046,068,071, Nathaniel,
087,088,251, Nathl.,040,
Nathnl.,046
NICKELS, Robt.,087, Thos.,046,
141, Wm.,024,026,046,048,218
NICKLE(NICHEL), Chas.,180
NICKLE, Betsey,180, Catharine,
180, Charles,181, Chas.,181,
E.,270, Eliza,251, Elizabeth,
260, Foster,252, Geo.,179,
180,240,251,254,263, Ginna,
180, J.F.,261, James,180,
191,251,255,258,262, Jas.,
262, John,180, Margrett,180,
Nathan,263
NICKLE, Nathl.,226,227,
Necmiah,180, Polley,180,
Robert,180, Robt.,255,258,
262, Salley,180, T.,263,
Thomas,180, Turner,180,
William,180, Wm.,206,242,
251,264, Wm.C.,251,260
NICKLES, Alex.,269, Anney,180,

Catherine,064,065,131,
Caty,225, Charles,102,195,
Charters,062, Chas.,170,
Chas.C.,157, Eliz.,184,
263,264,269, Eliz.N.,264,
Elizabeth,251, Foster,229,
247,267,272, Geo.,238,
George,251, H.M.,264,
James,067
NICKLES, James,077,083,091,
160,187,195,219,221,234,
269, Jane,095, Jas.,081,
083,096,238, Jehu,232,
Jno.(Dr.),268, Jno.,078,
096,097,160,187,191,234,
240,268,275, Jno.F.,264,
Jno.H.,131, John,071,095,
149,215,227,264, Libby,264,
N.,221
NICKLES, Nathaniel,251,
Nathl.,087,217,238,247,
Nathn.,007, Rhoda,219,
Robert,146,234, Robt.,079,
087,098,101,162,163,169,
238,264, Thos.,117,148,161,
213,220, Widow,269, William C.,
251, William,065, Wm.,007,
064,065,108,267,268, Wm.C.,
238
NICKLES, Wm.C.,240,269,
Zachariah,147
NICKLESS, Jno.,078
NICKOLS, Wm.,108
NICOLLS, Robt.,098
NIEL, John,230, Wm.,098
NIELL, Henery,127, James,211,
Josiah,216
NIGHT, Abner,152, Charner,215,
David,043,081,133, Jno.,
162, John,126,142, Mathew,
084, Micajah,211, Nancy,146
NISANGER, Jacob,047
NISBET, Dempsey,218,221,
Demsey,163, Eliz.,163,
James,163, Mary,119,163,
270, Nancy,163, Nathan,218,
219,232,241, Nathnl.,163,
Polley,163, Samuel,163,
Thomas,218, Thos.,163,219,
William,163, Wm.,163,241
NISBETT, Dempsey,166, Marey,
119, Nathan,188, Polley Sr.,
166, Saml.,166, Samuel,166,
Wm.,166
NISBITT, ,166
NISWANGER, J.,118,270, Jacob,
018,019,042,044,051,063,
071,075,076,079,080,087,
089,096,097,098,104,105,
107,113,114,118,135,137,
139,161,169,170,193,211,
214,216,217,226,236,254
NIX, Benj.,265, Edw.,088,
Elizabeth,274, James,164,
186,274, Jas.,093,117, John,
094, Susannah,116, W.W.,274,
Wm.,265
NIXON, A.,172, Abe,109,
Aberham,221,241, Abner,147,
187,241, Absalum,187,
Absolum,188,207, Alex'r.,
241, Alison,148, Ann,147,
Mansfield,201,203, Polley,
148
NOBELS, Joshua,018
NOBLE, Abner,239, Alex.,256,
James,196,197, Joshua,061,
Mark,184,193,196,256,
Thos.,196, Wm.,258
NOBLES, Abner,268, Giney,143,
James,148,231, Joshua,076,
Martha(?),220, Wm.,078
NOLAND, P.,270, Patrick J.,
191
NOLEND, Patrick J.,173
NORELL, James M.,188
NORMAN, Benj.,217, Jesse,224,
Jno.,164,224,265,266,267,
John,210, M.,107, Martin,
015,018,107,145, Mary,186,
Polley,213, Polly,271, Wm.,
173
NORMAND, Jesse,188

NORMON, Wm.,214
NORRELL, Jas. M.,248
NORRIS, Archabald,191, Benj.,
105, Christopher,242,
Cla--visd(?),242, Felix,
242, H.,258, Hemson,228,
Henderson,228, Henson,255,
258,270, Hinson,258,267,
Jemna,242, Nelson,176,
Sarah,242, Thomas,242,
Thos.,086,098, Wm.,020,
thos.,045
NORTH, Ezekiel,095,101,105,
127,129, Richd.,057,066,
101,157, Wm.,157
NORWOOD, Archaball,230,
Archebald,191, Archibald,
137, Jno.,253, Wyatt,274
NOTEMAN, James,011
NOWLAND, Ann,210, Catharine,
210, Darby,210, Mary,210,
Mikel,210, Patrick J.,210
NUGANT, S.,174
NUGENT, Saml.,152,187, Wm.,
098,141
NUGET, Wm.,243
NUN, Ingrum,191
O'DANIAL, Mary,125, Wm.,125
O'DONAL(O'DANIEL), M.,017
O'HARE, Patrick,207
O'HARRA(?)& JONES, ,125
O'HARRA(?), Danl.,125
O'NAIL, Hugh,076
O'NEAL, Ann Jane,118,121, Ann,
051, Barney,051, Chas.,038,
Henry,221,279, Hugh,027,
028,051,066, Jane,051, John,
051,053,118, Margret,051,
Thos.,028, Wm.,051,053
O'NEALL(NEEL), Chas.,027,
Hugh,027, Thos.,027
O'NEALL, Ann,027, Hugh,027,
John,064, Patience,027,
Rachel,027, Ruth,027,
Sarah,064, Wm.,064
O'NEEL, Ann Jane,118, Henry,
240
O'NEIL, Sarah,062, Wm.,062
OAKLEY, Thos.,060
OATES, Jacob,149
OB--, Nimrod,264
OBANNON, Wm.,003,018
OBERBY, Meshack,072, Nimrod,
072
OBEVY, Nimrod,259
OBRIAN, Patrick,007, Wilson,
007
ODDLE, March,183
ODEL, Jno.,251,253, John,220,
Nancy,249, Thomas,212,
William,212
ODELL, Branch,183, Elender,
212, Eli,213, Jno.,156,174,
John,212,213,261, Margret,
212, Marthey,212, Rebacha,
213, Rebakey,212, Thos.,158
ODLE, Branch,183, Jno.,169,
171,229,241,243,249,254,
261, John,015,055,061,169,
181,221,250,261, Mary,043,
044, Nancy E.,250, Nancy,
249, Sarahann E.,250, Wm.,
183
OLIVER, B.G.,166, Benj.,169
OLLIVER, G.,157
OLTON, Margret,042
ONEAL, Artha,193, Arthur,124,
127,129, Wm.,021
ONEALL & JOHNSON, ,170
ONEALL, Henery,242, Henry,249
ONEEL, John,025
ONEIAL, Harey,229
ONEIL, A.,149
ORDREY, Elizabeth,259
ORLIVER, Benj.,142
ORSBORN, Betsy,207, Bluford,
212, Daniel Sr.,176, Daniel,
192,193, Danl.,151, Edw.,
142,242, Eliz.,193, Jesse,
110, Jno.,083,104,123,
Jno.Sr.,212, John S.,220,
John,049,196,229, Langston,
098,133,138,192,193,237,

Patsey,175, Pattey,207
ORSBORN, Re--,235, Ross,176,
Wm.,097,098
ORSBORNE, Daniel Sr.,176,
Edward,110, Elisah(Elij.),
110, John,110, Langston,176,
Polly,110, Priscilla,110,
Ruthey,110, Sally,110, Wm.,
110
ORSBURN, Wm.,111
ORZBOURN, John,039
OSBORN, D.,270, Daniel Sr.,
177, Danl.,019,270, Jno.,
268, John,019,039,040,049,
071,073, Wm.,078,111,
Wm.Sr.,072
OSBORNE, Daniel,176, Edw.,111,
Elizabeth,176, Jno.,110,
Langston,176, Ross,176,
William,110,176
OSBOURN, Dan,021, Danl.,019,
Danl.Jr.,034, John,034,036
OSBURN, Daniel,001, Eliz.,001,
Sarah,001
OSORNE, William,110
OSTER, Jas.F.,237
OSTOM(?), Milley,042
OSTON(OLTON), Milley,042
OSWELL, Thos.,254
OTIS(OATES), Jacob,140
OTIS, Betsey,140
OTTEWAY, Isaac,151
OTTIS(?), Jacob,154
OVEBY, Elizabeth,259, Nimrod,
259
OVERBY, Benjamin,104,105,
Martha,023, Mary,104,
Meshack,023,048,050,072,
079,104,108, Nicholas,104,
Nimrod,031,048,071,079,
091,104,105,108,269,270,271
OWEN(?), Thomas F.,197
OWEN, Abner,257, Ann,052,100,
272, B.M.,058, Benj.,272,
Benjamin,100, Braxton,272,
Danl.,224, David,058,100,
108,239,245,259,272, Eliz.,
111, Elizabeth,272, Jas.,
018, Jno.,077,080,228, John,
018,059,100,111,112,114,
205,270, Jos.,085,097
OWEN, Jos.,111,112,190,270,
Jos.S.,052,100, Joseph L.,
152, Joseph,205, Mansel,228,
Mark,197, Michael,090,
Narcissa,272, R.M.,052,
053,063,118, Richard M.,272,
Richard,188, Richd.,058,
225, Richd.Jr.,203, Richd.M.,
009,052,100,229, Robt.,222
OWEN, Robt.,224,241,260,265,
Stephen,058,097,100, Thad.,
017, Thomas,059, Thos.,018,
Wm.,017,038,058,069,161,
272, Wm.C.,272
OWENS, ,236, Alfred,190,
Amelia,028,063, Ann(Mrs.),
221, Ann,060,077, Archd.,
012,220, Archebal,188,
Benj.,048,252, Betsy,028,
Brexter,229, Daniel,060,
077,078,079,086, Danl.(Dr.),
176, Danl.,210,269, David,
057,060,066,244,247,251,267
OWENS, Eliz.,059,077, Elizabeth,
060,188,244, Gideon,173,
233, James,065,230,232,
Jas.,143,145, Jennet,077,
Jennett,060, Jno.,077,079,
103,161,232,252, John A.,
068, John H.,028,063, John,
003,008,010,011,021,022,
025,026,028,035,047,048
OWENS, John,060,061,063,065,
066,203,248, Jonathan,072,
Jonathon,136, Jos.,151,
233, Jos.S.,097,100,102,
185,187, Joseph S.,245,
Joseph,160,244, Lucy,028,
Mansel,220, Mansfield(Mrs.),
176, Mansfield,225,253,
Martha,060, Mary,003,060,
077

OWENS, Maxfield,145, Mensil,
186, Mensill,206, Nancy(Mrs.),
269, Nancy,136,158, Nicklus,
212, Pasley,233, Presley(?),
156, Presley,172,173,228,
Pursley(?),156, R.,251,
R.H.,099, R.M.,050,
Richard M.,100,102,
Richard,103,136,251,
Richd.,057
OWENS, Richd.,156,174,203,
232,254, Richd.B.,220,
Richd.M.,040,051, Robert,
060, Robt.,077,079,086,154,
156,181,183,203,221,241,
Saml.H.,229,258, Stephen,
068,072, Thomas,060,194,
203, Thos.,077,078,079,086,
154,156,195, Virgal,251,
Virgil,187
OWENS, Virgill,251, Wm.,056,
062,069,225,244
OWING, Jonathan,272, Jos.,124,
Presley,257, Richd.K.,232,
Robertson,256
OWINGS(?), Eliz.,052, George,
052
OWINGS, A.,218, A.G.,272,
A.R.,248, Archabald,248,
Archebald,278, Archibald,
074, B.K.,278, H.E.,278,
James,136,278, Jas.,075,
Jno.,225, John,006,007,
136,248,278, Jonathan,074,
Lavina,248, Lewis,272,
Mansell,181, Mark C.,229,
Nancy,074
OWINGS, Nancy,248, Polley,136,
Rachel,248,278, Rebecca,
275, Richard,002,074,248,
278, Richd.,136, Richd.M.,
050, Richd.R.,252, Robt.,
248, Sarah,248, Susanah,181,
William,074,278, Wm.,074,
085,086,115,183,248,272,
275,278, Wm.Jr.,115
OWINS, Mansel,222
P'POOL, Geo.,178, Wm.,146
P-POOL, Allen,161, Jno.,161
PACE, Joshua,106
PACKER, ,179
PACKERD, Jas.,145
PADEN, Alex.,007,072, Robt.,
229
PADGET, Jno.,265
PADGETT, Jno.,271
PAGE & LEVEL, ,170
PAGE, Anna,044, Betsey,044,
Frances,044, Hannah,044,
James,044, Jenney,044,
John,044,045, Pendleton,
138, Robt.,063,094, Wm.,044,
199
PAILY, Clark,152
PAIN, Elihu,235, Jas.,109,
Jesse,097
PAINE, Jesse,071, Patsey,071,
Wm.,003
PAISLEY, Edmond,233, H.(Dr.),
243, Henry W.,233, James,
152, Jas.,151
PALMER(?), James,177
PALMER, Dabney,088, James,179,
Joshua,060
PALMORE, James,177
PAN=(?), Alex.,081
PARER, Jas.,043
PARK, A.(Capt.),174, Agnes,
071, Alex.,151, Alexr.,172,
Andrew,071,072,073,122,
166,172,175,214, Andrw.,046,
Andw.(Capt.),190, Andw.,
134,141,152,159,161,172,
174,178,189,190,231,233,
241,266,274, Andw.Jr.,256,
Betsey,071, Charles,246,
Chas.,190
PARK, David,235, J.,174,241,
James B.,266, James Jr.,
134,161,172,174,175,190,
214, James Sr.,171,172,
James,013,071,072,073,122,
141,152,161,164,166,175,

180,190,205,214,216,243,
252,256,266, Jane Eliz.,172,
Jane,237, Jas.(Capt.),141,
190
PARK, Jas.,088,135,140,141,
142, Jas.Jr.,141, Jas.Sr.,
146, John,172, Margaret,013,
N.(Mrs.),266, N.,174,
Nancy,071,115,237,266,
Rachel,172, Robt.,152,190,
Saml.,142,164,225, Sarah,
071, Thos.,081,164,225,274,
W.Jr.,174, William,172,174
PARK, William,175,214,216,
Wm.,071,115,124,135,137,
141,142,143,151,155,159,
175,178,187,190,200,208,
235,237,243,257, Wm.Sr.,141,
161
PARKE, Nancy,230
PARKER, Alexr.,141, Carter,
211,231,257,268, James,013,
071,178,194, Jas.,055,084,
095,097,139, Jim,109, John,
002,042,055,071,072,074,
Jos.,156, Sarah,071,072,
074, Thos.,013,081,084,
William,007, Wm.,010,071,
088,104,105,156
PARKES, Thomas,032
PARKS(?), Zachariah P.,191
PARKS, And.,101,116, Andrew,
071, Andw.(Capt.),159,
Andw.,094,098,133,134,266,
Andw.Sr.,197, Anney,028,
Bluford,246, Charles Sr.,
246, Charles,246,248, Chas.,
040,042,102,222, Danl.,166,
David,222, Edw.,270,
Frances,271, Henry,246,
Isaac,133
PARKS, Isaac,251, J.,270,
James F.,266, James Jr.,
159,187, James Sr.,152,159,
190, James,029,048,071,131,
133,151,159,163,169,178,
184,222,230,232, Jane,232
PARKS, Jas.,008,031,044,075,
094,098,101,104,107,116,
133,134,141,145,232,249,
271,272, Jas.Jr.,098,
Jas.Sr.,133,141,151, Jno.,
135, John,176,246, Jos.,010,
Lebon,232, Lusinday,246,
Mary,232, Nancy,104,133,
139,232,233,272, Nathan,104,
232
PARKS, Nathl.,162,165,173,
230,232, Peggy,041, Rachel,
232,266, Robt.,266, Sally,
201, Saml.,063,075,104,169,
230,232,259, Samuel,246,
Sarah,167,246, Seaborn,232,
Thomas,004,230,232, Thos.,
009,039,050,051,058,063,
075,076,091,093,094,101
PARKS, Thos.,103,104,162,186,
266,269,271,272, Thos.Jr.,
232, William,104,139, Wm.,
041,063,085,093,094,098,
107,116,134,174,232, Wm.Sr.,
133,159
PARKSON, Wm.,174
PARRETT, Alford,194, Polley,
194, Samuel,194
PARSENS, Barnet,244
PARSLEY, Austin,214, Edmond,
233, H.W.,251, Henry W.,185,
Husten,260, Jno.,133,
Lewis,210, Wm.H.,214
PARSON, Ephrum,259, Hamton G.,
233, Jas.(Capt.),081,
Polley,209, Robt.,257,
Saml.,201, Saml.Jr.,256,
Wm.,184,210
PARSONS, A.G.,246, Alfred,231,
Alsey,192, Archebald B.,
191,192, Barnet,192,232,
Bryant,180, Capt.,081,
H.B.,192, Hamton,180,
Isaiah,191,192, J.T.,231,
Jas.,142, Jno.,152, Jos.,
008,020,050, Jos.C.,161,

Jos.E.,192, Joseph,008,
Josiah,161
PARSONS, Josiah,169, Lemuel,
258, Mary,192, Milley,192,
Saml.,004,012,016,043,047,
081,083,123,141,151,181,
192,213,214, Saml.Jr.,191,
192, Saml.Sr.,191, Thompson C.,
201, William,191,192
PARTLOW, Jno.,102
PASCAL, Ezekiel,082, Wm.,082
PASLEY(?), Wm.,042
PASLEY, Austin,246, Edmond,
246, Eliz.,118, Elizabeth,
073, Frances,163, H.,149,
Henry M.,219, Henry W.,223,
James,073,114,118,122,
Jas.,092,099,122, Jno.,133,
Mary H.B.,089,092, Robert,
089,092,118,119,130, Robt.,
024,037,040,064,065
PASLEY, Robt.,070,073,074,092
PASLY, Henry W.,270
PATERSON, Jno.,138,151,187,
Mora,257
PATTEN, Wm.,237
PATTERSON, Isaac,140, James,
063, Jno.,151, Jos.,007,
057,258,274,275, Joseph,157,
Rebeca,157, Robt.,157,258,
274
PATTISON, Jno.D.,269
PATTON, David,225, Jane,255,
Wm.,152
PAUL, Saml.,042
PAYN, Elihu,161
PAYNE, Elihu,133, Wm.,148
PEADEN, Jno.,232
PEADON, John S.,192
PEARSON, Eliz.,214, Elizabeth,
214, Ephrum,214, H.G.,274,
Henry,259, Joel,214,215,
259, Mary,214, Menda,259,
Mendy,214, Nancy,275,
Thos.,006, William,214,
Wm.,214,274
PEDDEN, Wm.,075
PEDEN, Andw.,164, David,072,
166,221,232, James,147,
John F.,126, John,221,
Moses W.,166, Robt.,221,
Saml.,072, Thomas,278,
Thos.D.,166, Wm.,077
PEDON, John,192
PEEK(LEEK?), Geo.,081
PEEKE, David,055
PELSE(?), Rachel,115
PENDLETON, Zachariah,152
PENNINGTON, Jacob Jr.,001,
Jacob,001,004,010,011,013,
269, John,004,020, Neomi,
001, Ruth,001, Wm.,189
PERCHAMS, Wm.,212
PERKINS, Wm.(Capt.),179, Wm.,
106
PERKINSON, Wm.,111
PERRETT, Alfred,272
PERREY, James L.,247
PERRIMAN, Danl.,012
PERRY, Ephraim,096, Ephrum,
146, Jas.P.,279, John W.,
278, John,009,027, Mary Ann,
247, William,208
PERRYMAN, Danl.,013
PERSON, Hampton G.,169, Joel,
169,186, John,149, Jos.,173,
Joseph,174, Nancy,149,
Saml.,257, Wm.,027,159,
Wm.C.,159
PERSONS, Joel,259, Josiah,225,
Littleton,047, Wm.C.,215
PETERSON, Ann,024, Benj.,009,
024,047,048, James,024,
Jas.,046, Jno.,081,087,
John,046, Jon.,040, Patsey,
024, Susanah,024
PETTY, Chas.,232, Pattey,005,
Thos.,005, Wm.,005
PETTYPOOL, Seth,006,045,056,
Wm.,056
PEW, John,075
PEYTEN, Jacob,274
PHIFER, Saml.,135,139,176

PHILIPS, Colmon C.,228, Jas.,
211, Jeremiah,183,215, Jno.,
160,185,199, John,054,
Jonathan,117, Robt.,212,
Wm.,133,221
PHILLIP, Jas.,188
PHILLIPS, Angelica,047,
Clementine B.,277, D.,271,
Ed.,266, Edw.B.,267, Jno.,
157,271,277,278, John,056,
061, Jonth.,093, Jos.,110,
Robt.,231, Starling,056,
110, William,271, Wm.,277
PHILPOT, Edward,001
PHILPOTT, James,014
PHILUPS, John,155,192
PHINDLEY, James,011, Paul,002
PHINNEY, James,014
PHLINN, Wm.,192
PICKENS, Polley,175
PICKERING, Saml.,211
PICKETT, Chas.,007
PIDDLE, James,192
PIERCE, Benj.,113
PILLS, James,247
PINSEN, M.D.,235
PINSON, A.(?),145, A.,226,
Aaron Jr.,015,042, Aaron Sr.,
042, Aaron,015,040,041,042,
044,069,077,079,104,124,
127, Abigah D.,132, Abijah,
116, Aron,165,202,224,248,
Betsey,077, Bijah(?),130,
Catharine,201, Catherine(Mrs.),
176, Caty,237
PINSON, Chas.,115, D.A.,151,
Duke,101,176, Edatha,176,
Edee,130, Elihu,211,236,
Elijah,115,222, Eliz.,042,
079,237, Elizabeth,015,250,
H.,108, Howard,034,051,
063,077,079,085,102,107,
140,164,165,191,250,
Huldath,130, Isaac J.,212,
Isaac,015
PINSON, Isaac,041,042,130,
132,161,193,248, Isom(?),
107, J.F.,245,264, James F.,
224, James,202,206,207,
Jas.F.,224, Jesse,105,
Jno.,042,079,235,239,248,
269, Joel W.,162,259,271,
Joel,023,108,165,175,207,
John,003,012,015,023,041,
077
PINSON, John,079,176,250,
Jos.,012,015,042, Josiah,
161, Leonard,083,091, Lucy,
090,165, M.D.,237,248,255,
256, Margret,042,175,
Marmaduke Jr.,012,132,
Marmaduke Sr.,130, Marmaduke,
001,041,062,087,130,132,
151,193, Mary(Mrs.),012,
Molley,130
PINSON, Moses Jr.,042, Moses,
015,041,042,044,151, Polley,
262, Rethey,130, Ruth,130,
Sally,130, Saml.C.,130,
Susannah,023, Thomas,090,
Thos.,050,051,077,079,084,
086,088, Wm.,129,228, Wm.D.,
231, Zach.,042
PIPER(?), Wm.,107
PIPER, Jesse,152, Jos.,098,
099,222, Joseph,187
PITS, Jno.B.,235
PITT, Ephraim,267
PITTIS, Henderson,207
PITTS, Allen,105, Belton,176,
Bery,215, Caleb,160,
Clarissa,278, Daniel,277,
Danl.,039,160,235,247,
David,253,277, E.Hannah,
215, Edw.,056, Ephraim,147,
183,189,219,222,265,273,
Garey,176, Hannah(Mrs.),
176, Hannah,022,215,236,
Henry Jr.,189
PITTS, Henry,022,149,156,175,
176,198,261,272,273,
Hirum(?),278, Isaac,217,
229, Jehu,189,198,242,261,

Jehue,163, Jesse J.,277,
Jesse,101,161,277, Jno.,
083,101,145,146,163,191,
193,229,258, Jno.B.,236,
John B.,215, John,071,175,
176,189
PITTS, John,243,261,277,
Joshua,176,215, Moses,235,
Nancey,215, Nathan,101,
Ob.,101, Reuben G.,277,
Reuben,163,175,176,215,
Robt.,183,224,264,267,268,
Thomas,277, Thos.,101,176,
William,277, Wm.,144,149,
152,241,268,274, Wm.C.,170,
Wm.G.,150
PITTS, Wm.Jr.,199, Wm.Sr.,200
PLANT, Chas.,071, Jno.,109,
266,268, Jno.G.,264, Joel,
097, John,221, Saml.,101,
Stephen,041,042, Wm.,097,
098,160,275
PNSON, Howard,085
POLK(?), Wm.,011
POLLARD, Alfred,113, Eliz.,
190, Elizabeth,113, Franklin,
221, J.,252, J.M.,268,
James M.,218,253,254,
James N.,243, James,008,
009, Jas.M.,266,271, M.,
110, Marshal,110,113,114,
131, Marshall,101,274,
Marshel,120,133,221,
Martin,081, Matilda,113
POLLARD, Richd.,009, Robt.,
009,114,120,131,133,
Thos.B.,133, William,113,
114, Wm.,009,027,057,066,
077,080,099,101,112,149,
160,161,238, Wm.Jr.,149,
Wm.W.,234,239,245
POLLERD, Jos.,182
POLLEY, Jas.,024
POLLOCK, Ann,010, Isabelle,
010, James,006,010,011,020,
John,010,011, Mrs.,020,
Saml.,010, Wm.,010
POOL, Berrey,208,258, Berry,
146,274, Bery Sr.,256, Bery,
256, Betsey,122, Elihu,256,
257, Eliz.,121, Eliz.Hils(?),
119, Elizabeth,144,146,256,
257, Geo.,122,151, James,
148, Jesse,256, Jno.,122,
146,228,235,236,237,256,
John,221, Madten,146
POOL, Martin,208, Merston,258,
Nancy,146,256, Patty,122,
Peter,107,122,146,173,208,
233,274, Rebacha,146,
Robert,121, Robt.,116,122,
256, Saml.,203,205, Seth,
122,146,266, Thomas,122,
Thos.,122,171,256, Wm. Petty,
144, Wm.,040,122,221
POOLE, Betty,274, Elihu,274,
Emily,276, James,201, Jas.,
098, Jno.,274, John P.,274,
John,276, Lucy,276,
Margarett,274, Martin,274,
276, Peter,266,274,276,
Reuben,137, Seth P.,272,
274,276
POPE(?), John,133
POPE, Geo.,217, Henry,108,
113,207, Jno.,107,151,178,
John,136, Jonathan(?),124
POPE, Thos.,075,113,217,258,
Wm.,089,113,151
PORSLEY, Austin,250, James,
152
PORTER(?), Thos.,124
PORTER, Jesse,088, Robert,214,
Thomas,172, Thos.,073,081,
088,089,090,098,102,104,
108,112,115,124,152,156,190
PORTERFIELD, Jno.,090
POSEY, B.L.,159,169,173,174,
187,190,217,220,237,239,
B.Lain,207, B.Lane,174,
176, Blance,163, Bruce,076,
Charles,134, Chas.,087,
207, David P.,113,121,139,

207,229, David,087, Frances,
147, Francis,118,163, Frank,
207, Jas.,088, John A.,278
POSEY, L.B.,231, Lane,172,
Matilda,278, Peachy,089,
Robt.,113,162, Thos.,187
POTTER, Adam,105,133,136,159,
196,241,248, Asa L.,108,
Bevely,230,241,248, Dinah,
141, Eliz.,196, Ira L.,196,
197, Ira,197,237, J--(?),
123, Jemima,016, Jno.M.,272,
John,016,043, Nancy,230,
241,248, Sarah,230,241,248,
Stephan,015, Stephen,005
POTTER, Stephen,012,016,083,
107,134,141,151,174,196,
197,217,220,229,230,241,
248, Thos.,265, Wm.,016,
235,236
POTTS, Ephrum,145, Wm.,018
POUNDS, John,030
POWEL, Beaufort,170, Elizabeth,
023, Jno.,040, R.,173,
Saml.,023,047
POWELL, (?),162, Amy,089,107,
Anny,140, Belinda,089,107,
Bery,256, Bluford,140,
Capt.,163, Elijah,097,
Eliz.,107, Elizabeth,248,
Ezek.,095, Ezekiel,076,
078,087,113,126,139,145,
F.,149, Fanny,107, James,
019,062,075,076,107,124,
135,176
POWELL, James,218,227, Janey,
089, Jas.,021,095,107,113,
117,118,135,137,139,273,
Jas.Jr.,113,126, Jas.Sr.,
113, Jno.,040, John,042,
045, Leanna,062, Lucinda,
248, Lucy,168, Malachiah,
010, Margaret D.,248,
Marietta,248, Milley D.,
121, Milly,089
POWELL, Milly,107, Mrs.,232,
Nancy Eliz.,107, Oliver,
162, Peachy,107, Polly,107,
113,117, R.,095,097,135,
186, Reuben,075,076,096,
113,124,135,139,162,176,
186,191,192,206,214,218,
Reubin,121,152, Reuen,126,
Rhody,107, Robt.,189,
Rulum(?),151
POWELL, Sally,107, Sam.N.,148,
Saml.,007,045,051,057,099,
112,117,118,153,162,213,
248, Saml.N.,112,122,161,
162, Saml.Sr.,045, Samuel N.,
122, Samuel,162,163,248,
Sanford,239,264,268, Sarah,
089, Thomas,162,168,248,
249,250,262, Thos.,064
POWELL, Thos.,099,112,113,
122,124,150,162,250,265,
Thos.Jr.,250,262, Thos.Sr.,
248, Virginia H.,121,
Virginia,089,107, William,
107, Wm.,037,069,078,087,
089,095,107,113,117,
Wm.Wesley,107
POWER, Alex,040,055, Alex.,
085,256,257, Alex.Jr.,256,
Capt.,063, Elisha,105,
Eunety,257, Holloway,002,
004,010, Jas.,257, Jeremiah,
256,257, Jno.,257, Nathl.,
063, Sarah,257, Thos.,257,
Wm.,008,085,104,117,231,
244,245,256, Wm.Jr.,244
POWER, Wm.Jr.,256, Wm.Sr.,256
POWERS, Alex,275, Alex.,094,
136,155,173,278, Alexr.,233,
Holloway,013, Jno.,173,
Lewis,249, Nancy,173,
Nathl.,039, William,212,
Wm.,040,156,174,205,222,
231,233,244,278, Wm.Jr.,159,
201, Wm.Sr.,201
PRATER, Amos,154,158, Ann,154,
249, Archebald,209, Basil,
043,054,105, Bazel,079,165,

Bazzel,010, Elender,185,
Eliz.,156, Francina,173,
175, Hollway,054, Holway,
043, Israel,154,249,259,
James,156,192,224, Jas.Sr.,
224, Jesse,136,154,156
PRATER, Jno.,079, John Alan,
249, John,156,168, Josiah Sr.,
262, Josiah,054,079,105,
154,158,165,173,175,249,
250, Judith,154, King Jr.,
175, King Sr.,173, King,174,
215, Martha,175, Nancy,158,
Nelley,180, Polley,180,
185, Polly,154, Price,180
PRATER, Rice,185, Ruth,175,
Ruthy,175, Saml.,249,
Sinah(Mrs.),175, Susanah,
185, Thomas,154,156,158,
Thos.,154,159,210,215,249,
250, Wm.,166
PRATHER, Amos,219,267,
Archebald,210, Dorcas,002,
E.(Mrs.),210, Israel,249,
267,270, John,219, Martha,
267, Mary,002,270, Rimer,
241, Susannah,209, Tabitha,
270, Thomas,249, Thos.,199,
249, William,002, Wm.,249
PRATOR, Ann,248, Arch'd.,224,
Francis,224, Fransian,244,
Israel,248, Josiah,244,
260,262, Mary,244, Thomas,
215, Thos.,188,262, Transina,
244, Traslina,244
PRESLEY, ,191, Asten,229, Wm.,
211
PRICE, Ezekiel,112, Hezekiah,
112, John,083, Margaret,015,
021,032, Mary,015,032, Ruth,
015,032, Sarah,015,032,
William,021,032, Wm.,006,
010,015,022
PRICHARD, Jo.H.,169, Jos.,141,
152,249,257, Joseph,207
PRICHARDS, Jos.H.,236, Joseph,
169
PRIM, Chas.,082,083,107,116,
James,082, Jas.,083,096,
097,141,143, Whitfield R.,
145, Winfield R.,228, Wm.,
213
PRIMER, Whitfiel,235
PRINCE, Enoch,030
PRINGLE, Drusilla,127,
Dubeybella,197, Jno.,076,
John,026,049,127,130,
Saml.,050
PRIOR, Jno.,102
PROCTER, Walton,251
PROCTOR, Danl.,268, Jane,090,
196, Nathan F.,259, Nathan,
205,221,235, Nathl.,247,
William,090, Zachariah,268,
269
PRUDE, Sarah,058, Wm.,050,064
PRYMMY, James,217
PUCKET, Allen,265, Benj.,149,
C.,010, Chas.,047, Cornelius,
077, D.J.,265, Dabney,031,
050, Grif,232, James,012,
031,124,153, Jas.,249,271,
John,027,033,076,153,
Jonathan,012, Lucy,031,
Martha,031, Milly,031,
Nealey,050, Neely,031,
Redden,269
PUCKET, Richard,031, Richd.,
050,077, Robt.,183,224,257,
268, Wade Jr.,174, Wm.,183,
203
PUCKETT, Alfred,262,263,270,
272, Allen,265, B.,189,
Be--am(?),262, Chas.,098,
Cornelius,038,079,227,228,
229,239, D.J.,265, Dabney,
023,090, Dugless J.,075,
Dugless,241, F.R.,207, G.,
196, H.,157, J.,184, J.H.,
224, James,013,023,049,156
PUCKETT, James,188,224, Jas.,
079, Jno.,145,188, John H.,
156, John,023, Jonathan,007,

013, Lucy,023, Martha,049,
Nathan,207, Neeley,023,
R.,202,207, R.L.,195,
Redden,245, Richard,023,
090, Richd.,017,049,079,
Roberson,195, Robt.,188,190
PUCKETT, Sarah,265, W.W.,207,
Wade,187,202, William,262,
Wm.,137,142,207,263,270,
Wm.S.,234
PUGH, Betsey,069, Edw.,039,
070,093, Edward,010,092,
226,230, Jesse,092, Jno.,
077,109, John,038,070,073,
092,093, Martin,069, Mary,
014,071,092,093,168,169,
Nathan,115,164,186,202,
Nathl.,093, Richard,001,
014,035,095, Richd.,013,
Salley,226
PUGH, Salley,230, Wm.,063,
069,073,075,226
PULLIAM, John,009
PULLUM, John,057,058
PULMON, Nimrod,215
PURKERSON, Wm.,157
PURKESON(?), Wm.,114
PURKINS, Saml.,221, Wm.,152,
247
PURKINSON, Wm.,185
PURKISON, Ezekel,219, Wm.,182
PURKLE, Michael,005
PURL, Wm.,265
PURTZ, F.,091, Frederick,053,
057,080,081,104, Fredk.,054,
057,059,061,069, Fredrk.,
053,055,063,092, M.,053,
Michael,053, Mikel(Michael),
059, Mikel,076
PUTMAN, Abner,197,255,272,
Danl.,104, Dubybella,197,
Duleybella,197, Henery,106,
Henry,105,106, James,156,
256, Jno.,257, John C.,197,
Marey,103,105,107, Mary,
107, Mitchel,105,107,
Mitchell,103, Nimrod,156,
194,197,256, Reuben,105,197
PUTMAN, Reuben,256, Salley,
106, William,103,104,105,
107,194,195,197, Wm.,103,
148,156,159
PUTMEN, Nimrod,237
PUTMON, Abner,219, Daniel,138,
Nimrod,231, Wm.,138
PUTNAM, Reuben,173
PUTTMAN, Jno.D.,274
PYLE, A.(Dr.),101
PYLES, A,(Dr.),122, Abner,023,
029,031,032,036,049,051,
062,065,066,076,085,105,
106,107,110,139,178,206,
216,218,237,243,245,
Addison,176,178, Agatha,
176, Enoch,183, Lewis,241,
247,265, Ludey,176, Ludy(Dr.),
158,160,178, Ludy,160,179,
Newton,264
PYLES, Permelia,060, Reuben,
013,016,019,020,022, Reubin,
002,004, Wm.,147
PYLKES, Abner,179
QUALES, Wm.,235
QUALLS, Wm.,228,268
QUALS, Wm.,196,232
QUATZ, Wm.,196
QUEALES, Wm.,229
QUIN(?), Martha,197, Thos.,
197
RADEY, Alex.,063
RAGSDALE, Wm.,017,018
RAGSDELL, Edmon,148
RAGWELL, Burkely,147
RAIFORD, David S.,239, David,
215
RAINES, J.,016
RAINS, James,019,183, Thos.,
160,224
RAMAGE, Elenor,185, James,006,
Jas.,026, Jennet,044,
Jesse,189,224,251, Jno.,
043,128,224,260, John,127,
Jos.,212, Joseph,192,210,

Josiah,224, Martha,127,
Nelley,224, Robt.,127
RAMMAGE, Benj.,078,079,080,
Elender,078,080, James,006,
Jean,003, Jno.,045,241,
John,010,022,127, Jos.,018,
054,055, Josiah,010, Robt.,
127,241
RAMSEY, E.,013, Ephraim,016,
Mr.,012
RANES, James,018, Thomas,126
RANEY, B.Y.,063, Geo.,061,
Penny,021
RANSAM, Wm.,235
RANSOM, Jno.,159, William,029,
032, Wm.,018,030,108,169,
192,237,244
RANSON, Catharine,140,
Mary Ann,140, Wm.,022,116,
236,268,271
RANSUM, Wm.,143
RASHELL, Jno.,259
RATHER, Thos.,266
RAY, Ambrous,222, Braxten,231,
Braxton,228, Claxton,230,
Claxdon,211, Claxton,159,
231,266, Eliz.,109, Fanney,
228, Frances,250,251,253,
James,011,014,231, Jno.,
249,266, John,231, Reuben,
231, Thos.J.,265
READ, Even,208
READER, Charlota,154, Charlotte,
154, David,061, Patsy,154,
Polly,154, Sarah,154,
Simon,156, Thos.,154,
Thos.C.,221, Wm.,154
READIN, Jas.,271
READR, Simon,154
REAGAN, Chas.,080, James,080
REAL, Even,208
REASE, Jesse,075, Nancy,069,
070
RED, Jonathan,244
REDDEN, David,137, Geo.,195,
206, James,228, Jas.,113,
135, Johnston,124, Rebecca,
086, Roberson,050,087,089,
195, Robt.,080, Thomas,218,
Thos.,186,214,228, Wm.,080,
095,097,104
REDDING, Wm.,113
REDDON, Wm.,173
REDER, Isebell,253, Orsborn,
205
REDING, Thos.,022, Wm.,126
REED(?), Thos.,089
REED, Caroline,223, David,025,
051,084,096,097,215, Eliz.,
096,224,239, Elizabeth,194,
215,275, Jacob,113, James,
051,215, Jane,051, John Allen,
096, John,057, Jonathan,025,
051,151,215,264,268,
Martha Jane,215, Mary,223,
224, Maryan,223
REED, Matthew,096, Nancy,275,
Thos.,057,090, William,223,
273,275, Wm.,051,096,102,
104,120,164,165,167,177,
206,224,227,251
REEDER, Danl.,089,158, David,
050,054,060,061,064,089,
164, F.C.,242, Henry,254,
Isebell,253, Jonathan,151,
Manning,254, Mary,253,
Oswell,253, Patrick,211,
Philis,247, Richd.,160,
Simon,076,089, Thomas C.,
242,251, Thos.,171,185,243,
248
REEDER, Thos.C.,174,235,239,
249,253,261, Wm.,146,158,
Young,060
REESE, Jesse,075, Nancy,075
REGEN, Jas.,145
REID, Johnston,221, Jonathan,
051, Jos.,024, Thos.,118
REILEY, Jos.,026
REMAGE, Jno.,173, Joseph,173
RENALETT(?), Jos.,075
RENNALS, Jos.,066
RESE, Geo.,189

REUBEN, Free,254
REYNALS & MADDEN, ,040
REYNOLDS, Marey,199, Mary D.,
237
RHOADES, Christop.,146
RHODES, James,233, Jane,277,
Mary,277, Nicklus,146
RICE(RISE?), Hezekiah,180
RICE, Ezekiel,195, Hezekiah(Dr)
179, Hezekiah,218, Horis,
219, Nancy L.(?),179, Wm.,
104
RICHARDS, B.W.,098, Benj.,104,
108, Elizabeth,128,146,
Green,125,128, Harriet,077,
James,196, Jos.,141, Wm.B.,
081
RICHARDSON, (?),087, A.,127,
A.T.(?),270, Chas.,224,
F.(T.),159, F.,153,163,
190,206,255, J.J.,207,
James,218, Jas.J.,217,
M.L.,275, Mary L.,206,275,
Mary,275, O.,256,257,
Oswell,249,254, T.,158,
Thos.,021, Turner,067,100,
104,127,139
RICHARDSON, Turner,155,156,
158,159,162,163,175,177,
180,190,192,193,212,220,
222,226,243,275
RICHERDSON, Turner,119
RICHERSON, Jno.,139
RICHESON, G.F.,114
RICHEY(?), Wm.,125
RICHEY, Ellen,005, Ellinor,
003, James,105, Jno.,079,
105,128,211, John Jr.,091,
105, John Sr.,056,124, John,
003,007,016,036,050,053,
054,062,064,069,074,091,
105,123,128,131, Margaret,
002, Margret,123, Martah(?),
003, Mary,003, Rebecah,244
RICHEY, Robert,002,003, Robt.,
011,020,076, Saml.,123,128,
131,207,217, Samuel,105,
Wm.,079,105,123,124,128,
131,160
RIDDLE, Gorden,257, James,161,
215,233,235, Jas.,257, Jno.,
044,080, Jno.Jr.,231, John,
075, Linney,277, Melmeth,
257, Tucker,257, Wm.,215,
252,257
RIDDLESPERGER, Abraham,276,
Molny(?),276, Molsey,277,
Saml.,277
RIDGE, Jno.,111, John,127
RIDGEWAY, Eliz.B.,237, Jno.,
090, Richard,148, Richd.,
118, Wm.,241
RIDGEY, E.B.,235
RIDGWAY, E.,201, Wm.,163
RIDLE, James,256
RIGBY, Elihu,202
RIGHT, Danl.,058, J.D.,067,
James,157, Thos.,164,252,
Wm.,068,069,141,164,180,194
RILEY(?), Jas.,112
RILEY, Abraham,090,134, Ames,
166, Cornelius,165, Elihu,
207, Elihue,165, Eliphas,
049, Eliphat(?),048,
Eliphaz,043, James,054,
058, Jas.,272, Jno.,029,
Patrick,004, Polly,207,
Rachel,266, Salley,207,
Sarah(Salley),175
RILY, James,195
RITCHEY, John,018
RIVERS, Noah,147
ROADS, Christopher,081,
Clopton,180
ROADY, Mrs.,078
ROAZMON, J.W.,235
ROBARDS, Evan,006, Jacob,010
ROBERSON(?), Jno.,139, Reuben,
033, Toliver,033
ROBERSON, Alsey,126,238,
Barnet,225, Barnett,033,
103,269, Barret,033,
Barruch,223, Catharine,214,

Danl.,180,228, Elijah,113,
Eph.,152, Fanny,033,
Fowler,233, Geo.,041,
George,033, Isom,080,092,
Isum,128, J.,095,099,
James,152, Jesse,256
ROBERSON, Jno.,078,079,081,
097,100,107,113,114,118,
121,124,128,131,145,151,
159,241,249,258,261,
Jno.Jr.,079,113,114,
Jno.S.,113, Jno.Sr.,079,
John Jr.,125, John Sr.,033,
092,125, John(Capt.),063,
John,006,009,018,022,031,
033,036,040
ROBERSON, John,041,042,043,
045,046,050,051,053,054,
055,057,059,061,063,064,
065,066,068,069,071,074,
089,093,135,138, M.,090,
Manoah,033, Marah(?),033,
Marey,033,042, Menoah,042,
103, Milly,033, N.,071,
Nancey C.,069, Nancy,066,
Nathl.,071
ROBERSON, Peggy,033, Polly,
033, Reuben,100,106,137,
196,224,225,269,270, Roady,
100, Robt.,079,080, Saml.,
269, Susana,223, Thomas,125,
Thos.,080, Toliver,256,
Tollever,197, Towlar,201,
Vincent,255, William,065,
066,080,081,093, Wm.,024
ROBERSON, Wm.,033,040,063,
064,065,068,071,076,079,
081,105,113,145,177
ROBERT, Bird,261
ROBERTS, Absolum,045, Amos,
267,274, Annes,170, Benj.,
002, Bird,140,219,222,224,
229,245,249,251,252,
Bordewine,200, Brady W.,
201, Burd,167, Clearcy(?),
058, Coleman,157, D.,096,
Delila,146, Edmond,029,
105, Edmund,236, Evan,026,
Garner,232
ROBERTS, Geo.,029,045,074,
077,085,101,111,140,167,
185,202,238,262,264, George,
027, Henry,253, Isaac,058,
073,109, Jacob,031,058,073,
077,093,101,104,109,115,
165,168,230,232, James,027,
028,029,036,105,107,167,
229,240, Jas.,040,085,251
ROBERTS, Jesse,140, Jno.,077,
109,117, Joel,058, John,031,
058,073, Judiah,128, Kevel,
259, Mary Ann,027,029,
Mary(Wid.),109, Mary,029,
058,073, Molly,005,058,
Mrs.,232, Nancy,157,253,
Obediah,061,200, Patty Bond,
029, Peter,027,028,029
ROBERTS, Peter,032,040,062,
140,157,160, Richd.,085,
Rodey W.,128, Rody W.,231,
Ryland,200, Sarah,105,
Susanna,027, Thomas,058,
Thos.,011,092,093,109,169,
259, Thos.R.,269, W.G.,274,
Wm.,048,269, Wryman,271
ROBERTSON, Barnabas,038,
Barnet,275, Danl.,197,
Elender,194, Folver,183,
Jesse,167, Jno.,112,231,
John,009,022,038,075,183,
215,275, Manoah,183,184,
Milley,183, Milly,183,275,
Nath.,145, Peggey,183,
Reuben,156,183,220, Samuel,
275, Solomon,215
ROBERTSON, Susanna,275,
Tolliver,156, Vinson,183,
Wm.,210,266,274
ROBESON, Danl.,256, Rachel,
276, Wm.,087
ROBINSON, John,006,020,
Micajah,270, Scarlet,272
ROCKER, Jacob,217

RODER, ,016
RODGERS, A.,029,085,088,163,
A.Jr.,001,002,006,017,028,
029,042,058, Abner(Capt.),
152,236, Abner,099,136,137,
141,143,144,146,153, Andey,
149, Andrew Jr.,007,052,
064,065, Andrew(Jr.),053,
Andrew,007,030,031,034,
036,106,137,138,143,226
RODGERS, Andrw.,106, Andrw.Jr.,
050, Andrw.,036,092,117,137,
151,169,182,196,213,223,
243,251, Andw.Jr.,036,
Andw.Sr.,146, Andy,118,
Ann,143, Anne,236, Benj.,
040, Betty,106, Chas.,230,
Cisley,270, D.,109, Danl.,
040,066,072,099, Elihu,133
RODGERS, Elihu,141, Elihue,
151, Elisha,151, Gazaway,
007, Henry,266,271, J.S.,
239, James L.,199,226,
James S.,199,217,220,222,
232,241, James,233, Jane,
164,199, Jas.,082,246,
Jas.S.,209,211,225,234,
238,270, Jno.,034,078,084,
092,097,104
RODGERS, Jno.,109,111,116,
270, John Jr.,021, John O.,
181,183, John Sr.,021,067,
John,006,007,016,028,034,
036,040,050,053,064,070,
072,119,137,199,200,241,
270, Jos'h.,140, Jos.,007,
010,014,029,062,064,065,
080,085,106,129,149,154,169
RODGERS, Jos.,171, Joseph,157,
214, Leford,215, Letty,064,
065,115,117, Levi,271,
Lezve(Levi?),212, Matheny,
040, McNees,098, N.T.(Mrs.),
104, Nehemiah,223, Patrick,
029,042,050,053, Polly,050,
117, Pollyana,050, Robt.,
185, S.,236, Salley,199
RODGERS, Sally,049,106,117,
Saml.,065,092,099,105,106,
111,117,118,136,137,142,
149,151,167,174,186,199,
205,222,223,229,234,235,
236,243,246,247,250,264,
271, Sarah,164,234,239,
Seamon A.,140, Shelton,168,
Stephen,254, Tabitha,234,
Thomas,157
RODGERS, Thos.,006,021,044,
064,065,074,079,085,092,
098,101,103,106,107,111,
115,117,118,137,141,149,
151,157,174,189,222,229,
238,261,264, Thos.Jr.,021,
William,137, Wm.,005,013,
016,027,031,048,049,050,
057,065,068,098,106,115,
117,134
RODGERS, Wm.,135,140,141,149,
152,164,167,171,223,230,
261, Wm.A.,017,111,149,
Wm.F.,151
ROERSON, John Sr.,092, John,
092, Thomas,092
ROFS(ROSS?), George,002
ROGERS, James,207, Jas.C.,268,
Wm.,074
ROLAD, Reubin,003
ROLAND, E.S.,019,241, Ezekiel,
018, J.,245
ROLING, John,016,018,021
ROLLAND, Alex.,118
ROLLIN, Jno.B.,254
RONSON, Wm.,231
ROOK, Emanuel,070, Margaret,
036,039, Nathaniel,036,039,
068,070, Wm.(Dr.),266, Wm.,
273, Wm.Sr.,273
ROOKS, David,211, Elias,175,
Nathl.,039, Sarah,058
ROSE, Geo.,007,047, James,214,
Saml.,256, Samuel,157,
William,157,159, Wm.,081,
157,161,215,249,255,256,

36

258,274
ROSEBROUGH, Alexr.,014
ROSEMAN, J.(Col.),117, Nathl.,
087, Nathl.J.,121
ROSEMON, Hardiman,228
ROSEMOND, Benj.,113,217,
Nathl.,213
ROSMON, Nathl.,217
ROSMOND, N.P.,113
ROSS & CRAIG, ,188,189
ROSS(?), Christop.,047
ROSS, B.G.,148, Catharine,182,
186, Catherine,034,233,
Caty,121, David,012,013,
055,071,108,162,163, Dr.,
015, Eliz.,055,182, F.,132,
220,232, Frances Sr.,190,
Frances,151,205,233,
Francis Sr.,016, Francis,
021,034,035,036,055,062,
116,182
ROSS, Francis,206,216,235,
251, Franks(Mrs.),228,
Geo.(Dr.),033,086,109,112,
118,172,199, Geo.,010,020,
022,050,062,069,103,149,
172,266, George,006,032,
035,128,172, Isabel,032,
Isabella,006, Isabelle,035,
James,123,151,182, Jane,
055,182
ROSS, Jas.Sr.,087, Jno.,188,
John Sr.,034, John,033,
048,055,062,147,182,
Margaret,055, Margret,055,
Moses,167, Nimrod,233,
Robert,055, Robt.,008,011,
016,020,034,050,152,
Saml.H.,276, Sarah B.,233,
Sarah,182, Sophiah,189,
Thos.,019
ROSS, W.,208, Wm.,016,048,
055,132,136,233,276
ROSSMOND, Thos.,113
ROULAND, E.L.,213
ROUNDTREE, Salley,212, Wm.,
013,032
ROWE, Benj.,009, Wm.,038
ROWINGS, Jno.,252
ROWLAND(?), James,127, John,
127, Robt.,127
ROWLAND, Betsey,068,071,
Christop.,099, Christoph.,
014, Christopher,097, E.S.,
037,049,211, Eliz.,071,
Elizabeth,204, Ezekiel,032,
116, Geo.,266, H.B.,221,
Henry B.,220,223,231,
James,244,250,260,267,
Jas.,151,245,249,262,
Jesse,105
ROWLAND, John,017,051,052,
054,057,059,061,068,071,
Lettice,221, Lettice,244,
Mary,014, Richard,014,
Robert,206, Robt.,014,099,
165,204, S.,151, Tabitha,
099, W.B.,199, Wm.,151
ROWLING, Betsey,067,071,179,
Christop.,096, D.,043,
E.L.,040, E.S.,039,040,
042,068, Eliz.,068, Ezekiel S.,
040, Ezekiel,036,037,039,
Henry B.,230, John,067,
071,075, Robt.,096
ROWLINGS, John,036
ROWNTREE, Wm.,031
RUCKS, Joel,012,013, Wm.,012,
013,031, Wm.Jr.,105
RUDD, Fields,272, Jno.,190,
John,150, Susannah,040,
Thomas,150, Thos.,040
RUNALDS, Eliz.,238
RUNCH, Wm.,251
RUNNALDS, Eliz.,153,154, Wm.,
250
RUNNELS, Wm.,029,036
RUNNOLDS, Anna,106, Betsey,
106, Eliz.,106, Joseph,106,
Lucinda,106, Polley,106,
William,106, Yearby,106
RUNOLDS(?), Jos.,062
RUPEL, Jno.,237

RUSEL, Jno.,119,121,193,247,
John,136
RUSELL, Jno.,245
RUSH, John,218
RUSING, Aquila,052,053, John,
039,058,070, Keziah,052,
Mildred,052, Sarah,052,
Wm.,052,058
RUSON(?), Wm.,029
RUSSEL, Charles,011, Chas.,
020, James,010, Jno.,186,
Nancy,183, Robt.,017
RUSSELL, Benj.G.,148, Charles,
006, Percey G.,148
RUTHERFORD, T.B.,266
RUTLEDGE, Amy,146, Betsey,146,
Delila,146, Edwd.,019,
Fanny,146, Jos.,142,146,
William,142,146, Wm.,082,
088,142
RYAN, Jas.,096, John,055
RYLEY, Abe,109, Elihu,202,
Eliphas,050, James,147,
225, Jas.,110, John,162,
165, Mrs.,165, Patrick,027,
Wm.,055,071
S--TELL, Sally,277
SADDLER, Jeremiah,030,
Plesant,224
SADLER, ,229, Jer.,063, Jere.,
110, Jeremiah,065,066,124,
Jno.,195, Jno.C.,162, John,
072,111,124,128, Malinda,
242, Marey,124, Martin,262,
Mary,052,066,124, Matilda,
242, Nathl.,161, Peter,127,
132,159,166,198,242,261,
264, Plesant,124
SADLER, Plesant,128,238,262,
Sarah,128, Silas,251,
Silus,251, Thos.,062, Wm.,
108,124
SAFFOLD, Sarah,005
SAGUE(?), D.F.,208
SALES(?), Robt.,225
SALISBURY, Edw.,091, Saml.,
092, Samuel,091
SALLEMORE, Flemming,247
SALMAN, Thos.,238
SALMON, Jno.,140, Lewis,249,
267,272,274, Thos.,110,203,
239
SALSBURY, Paul,164, Wm.Y.,164
SAMMONS, Mason,237
SAMPLE, Jno.,085, John,012,
013, Judith,225, Washington,
025
SAMPLES, Alex.,135
SAMSON, Jno.,101
SAMUEL, Wm.,267
SAMUELS, Wm.,264
SANDERS, David,215, Eli,098,
Elijah,235, James M.,261,
James,261, Jesse,071,109,
Martha(Mrs.),151, Martha,
152, Moses,024,033, Nathl.,
148, R.W.,151, Robt.D.,152,
Wilson,009,058,062,103,
110,198, Wm.,203,221
SANDFORD, Jno.,205, Lewis,232,
Wm.,205
SANDRES, James,261
SANFORD, Lowery,205
SATERWHITE(?), Bartlet,157
SATERWHITE, Bartlet L.,252,
Bartlett S.,253, John,057,
062,148, Margret,253,
Mitchel,120, Saml.,215,
Wm.,253
SATEWHITE, Jno.,146,176
SATORWHITE, John,215
SATTERFIELD, Thos.W.,011
SATTERWHITE, Drury,040, John,
059, Mary,164,167, Wm.,018
SAUNDERS, Benj.,086, Elijah,
277
SAVAGE, John,018, Susanna,259,
Wesley,217, Westly,217,
240, Wm.,178,198,218,267,
271, Zabulon,207, Zeb.,096,
Zebalon,181, Zebalum,228,
Zebulon,063,096,227,228
SAWYERS, Jno.,145, John,126

SAXN, Hugh,222
SAXON, (Wid.),271, A.D.,134,
A.M.,201, A.W.,163,
Allen D.,145, Allen,106,
142,146,147,150,187,188,
195,205,207, Ann,102,180,
Athey,041,107, B.,016,
B.H.,102, B.S.,213, Benj.,
021,045,138,218, Bethiah,
107, C.,120,129, Charles,
106,109,148
SAXON, Charles,227,229, Chas.,
002,022,086,095,097,110,
120,122,151,200,221,236,
237,269, Chas.A.,110,
Chas.Jr.,106, D.P.,120,
151,208,236,275, David P.,
120,134,152,159,180,220,
268, David,092,104,110,148,
187,229, Eliza A.,247,
Harriet,211
SAXON, Hugh,134,163,184,190,
205,207,227,229,268,
Isabella,134,229, James,
004,010,016,039,040,041,
047,049,070,180,229, Jas.,
005,022,043,047,057, Jno.,
107,131,145,167,179,203,
211,212, John,028,041,051,
102,107,129,132,218, Joshua,
004
SAXON, Joshua,103,183,187,
190,221,224,226,236,256,
265, L.,070,082,086,
L.K.(Capt.),237, Lem,013,
Lewis(Widow),106, Lewis,
005,010,012,019,086,088,
109,148, Lucy,041,094,
Lyd.P.,231, Lydral P.,239,
Lydral,227, Lyel P.,228,
Manda,041, Marey,039
SAXON, Marey,041,107, Mary,
148, Molly,107, N.,063,097,
Nathl.,095, Oney,229,
Owney,231, Persilla,207,
Pleasant,271,274, Polly,
047, R.B.,236, Robt.,041,
Ruthah(?),132, Sam.,229,
Saml.,016,022,069, Saml.B.,
228, Samuel,016,227,228,231
SAXON, Sarah E.,177,209,
Sarah(Wid.),110, Senthey,
164, Stover,212, T.,270,
Will,011, William,103,107,
Wm.,034,041,069,082,086,
102,107,132,188,271
SAYERS, Archbd.,022,045
SCARBROUGH, Edw.,012
SCARFE, Wm.,242
SCEAN(?), Mary,133
SCHRAUM, J.J.,019
SCILLION(?), Amy,105, Hugh,
105, Jane,105, Patsy,105
SCOTT, Ann,010,094,198, Anny,
119, Isabella,022, James,
018,061,180,198,233,254,
Jno.,088, Jos.,088,128,
Margaret,060, Margret,198,
233, Martha,198, Mary,127,
Mathew,233, Patk.,108,110,
Patrick,006,010,015,020,
069,198,233, Patrk.,055
SCOTT, Robert,155, Robt.,010,
011,015,020,022,041,274,
Sarah Ann,233, Sarah,198,
Thomas,198,233, Thos.,040,
053, William,267, Wm.,173,
175
SCRAGE, Wm.,139
SCRIP, Jno.R.,213
SCRUGGS, Edw.,093
SCRUGHS(?), Edward,131
SCRUGHS, Edw.,165
SCRUGS, Edmund,117, Mahala,
214, Marada,214, Merady,259,
Mesideth,259
SCURLOCK, Ann,016,022, Dolly,
016,023,030, Frances,022,
023,030, Frankey,016,
Joshua,016, Reuben,016,
Wm.,067
SEAY, Marshal,098
SENCE, Mr.,020

SEYMORE, Middlebrook,096
SHACKELFORD, Geo.,040, James,
  065, Jas.,040, R.,029,
  Richard,070, Richd.,007,
  028,029,065,074
SHACKLEFORD, Jas.,101, Rich.,
  104, Richard,021, Richd.,027
SHAIRS, Jude,216, Judeth,218,
  Judy,216, Lettey,216
SHANLER, Ann,092
SHARES, Samuel,216
SHARP, Betsey,069, Betsy,072,
  F.A.,208, Frances,145,
  Isaac,069,070,072, Thos.A.,
  236
SHAW(?), Lettey,214
SHAW(SHEA?), Martin,114
SHAW, (Capt.),135, Green B.,
  113, Harley,007, Marsten,
  213, Marstin,195, Martin,
  075,076,079,080,087,091,
  093,104,108,121,123,125,
  128,135,173,181,206,207,
  210,213,214,218,225,231,
  243,244,267,269,275,
  Pleasant,102,207, Plesant,
  126,148,185
SHAW, Plesant,186,187,198,
  241, Polley,213, Pud,109,
  Robert,007,210,213, Robt.,
  016,063, Vincent,274,
  Vinsen,195, Wm.,028
SHAWE, Saml.,063
SHEA, Elizabeth,114, Patrick P.,
  114
SHEL, Henry R.,218
SHELDON, M.B.,208, Mikel,212,
  Wm.,225,273, Wm.B.,149,
  160,224, Wm.D.,268
SHELL, Danl.,208, Drury,151,
  H.R.,247, H.T.,102, Henery,
  143, Henry Jr.,204, Henry Sr.,
  218, Henry,061,086,096,097,
  103,107,132,138,153,155,
  157,167,208,211,219,230,
  253,255, Jno.,237, Jno.G.(?),
  268, Wm.,254
SHELLS, Henry,216
SHELTON, Claugh(?),086, Jos.,
  183
SHEPARD, Elijah,167, Jno.,128,
  131,211, Larkin,084,
  Saml.B.,077, Wm.,207,212
SHEPHARD, Larkin,017
SHEPHEARD, John,204
SHEPHERD, Jno.,264
SHEPPARD, Larkin,084
SHERLEY, Aaron,275
SHETTEL, Wade,241
SHETTLESWORTH, Jos.,266
SHIRLEY, Aaron,104,123, Aron,
  212, Birey,104, E.,192, Eli,
  192, Elihu,207,218, Elizabeth,
  104,207,246, Geo.,104,177,
  192,207,214,217,246,267,
  James,217, Jno.,042,104,
  114, Jno.Sr.,044, John,051,
  101,104, Jonathan,192,198,
  Peggey,175, Riley,169
SHIRLEY, Robt.,051,101,104,
  217, Thos.,019,042
SHOBLE, John,240
SHOCKLEY, Davis,236, Hannah,
  055, Jas.,055,237, Levi,173,
  S.,094, Salathiel Jr.,156,
  Salathiel,050,055,059,060,
  080,081,098
SHOCKWELL, John,050
SHOTWELL, John,029
SHUGS, Meardy,259
SHUREEN(?), Isaiah,013
SHURLEY(SHIRLEY), Jno.,170
SHURLEY, Aaron,170, Bunley(?),
  170, Bunley,170, Easter,170,
  Eliz.,170, Jane,170, John,
  170, Lydia,170, Rebecca,170,
  Richard,170
SHUTTLESWORTH, Jos.,111
SIBEALL(?), Mary,143
SIBELL(?), Lewis,143
SILES, Wm.,141
SILLS, Benjamin,109,110
SILUS, "Free",241

SIMMONS, Alick,237, Ann,276,
  Anne,257, Benj.,254, Catey,
  075, Caty,076,140,239,
  Charles,005,006,019,028,
  049,142,145,149,152,153,
  155, Chas.,004,034,037,039,
  049,082,097,101,112,115,
  124,140,145,152,190,196,
  212,232,249,269,271,
  Chas.Sr.,237
SIMMONS, David,028,049,176,
  231,239, Eliz.(Mrs.),155,
  Eliz.,098, Elizabeth,005,
  006,152, James,050,075,076,
  140,162,176,186,191,231,
  236, Jas.,121,139, Jean,005,
  Jerm.,098, Jno.,101,106,
  119,143,145,208,210,212,
  230,236,237,243,272,
  Jno.Jr.,237
SIMMONS, John Sr.,034, John,
  001,005,006,048,049,075,
  076,140,152,155,220,234,
  237,276, Joseph,001,
  Little Chas.,068, Mansfield,
  239, N.,266, Nancy,001,
  Nath.,256, Polly,271,
  Robt.,001,246, Robt.C.,257,
  Sarah,005,215
SIMMONS, William,005,152, Wm.,
  019,026,048,050,072,097,
  100,124,145,151,155,224
SIMMS, Absalom,066, Zachariah,
  004
SIMON(?), John,011
SIMONS(SIMMONS), John,142
SIMONS, Benj.,256, Jno.,207,
  247,256
SIMPSON(?), Zach.,079
SIMPSON, A.,174, A.A.,141,
  Agnes,095, Alex,095, Alex.,
  016,042,045,101,141,161,
  Alex.Jr.,170, Alexander,
  090,246, Alexr.,018,026,
  028,038,066,139,147,
  Bard N.,225, Charles,126,
  Chas.,093,094,101,102,112,
  141,168,177, David,012,020,
  E.C.,271
SIMPSON, Elihu,257, Eliz.,089,
  Elizabeth,012, H.,273,
  Hatty,035, Henry,107,277,
  Hosea,156, J.,083, J.B.,
  163, J.D.,237, J.W.(Dr.),
  269, James A.,148, James,
  028,042,054,059,067,068,
  089,123,135,136,152,155,
  200,218, Jane,012,095, Jas.,
  018
SIMPSON, Jas.,038,045,095,
  097,101,124,129,132, Jno.,
  012,045,076,083,087,090,
  104,121,129,155,160,168,
  179,185,196,200,218,235,
  254, Jno.B.,087,146,163,
  269,279, Jno.D.,142, Jno.M.,
  198, Jno.W.,095,101,248,
  252,271, Jno.W.Jr.,271,
  Jno.Wm.,278
SIMPSON, John B.,198, John D.,
  147, John R.,146, John W.(Dr.),
  277, John W.,095,194,244,
  John(Col.),136, John(Maj.),
  028, John,013,014,015,016,
  018,022,024,025,026,030,
  032,037,038,045,050,054,
  063,065,067,071,072,073,
  082,086,089,095,101
SIMPSON, John,102,153,155,
  156,200,217, Kitty,015,016,
  095, Louisa,257, Margaret,
  014, Mary,095, Mathew,271,
  Matthew,079, Nancy,095,
  271, Newman,189, Peggy,277,
  Polley,230, R.A.,151, R.F.,
  143,153,171,208,236,237,
  239,248,250, R.P.,236, R.W.,
  206
SIMPSON, Richard F.,147,234,
  Richd. F.,244, Richd.,101,
  221, Richd.F.,139,142,144,
  145,152,159,170,172,179,
  227,229,259,271, Robt.,015,

  016,152, Saml.,015,094,156,
  Sarah,089,095,271,275,
  Thos.,231, W.,172, W.D.,
  157, W.F.,236, W.W.,101
SIMPSON, W.W.,114,136,149,
  167,219,230,236,237,243,
  246,271,275, William,216,
  Wm.,085,095,101,104,105,
  106,134,200,201,229,231,
  247,256,265,268, Wm.D.,137,
  138,160, Wm.W.,095,103,111,
  129,167,176,177,206,243,
  254,277
SIMS(?), Jno.,081
SIMS, (Wid.),215, Abraham,058,
  Alfred,187, Ann,059,061,
  086, Anne,053, Belinda,100,
  Bulis,251, Charles,086,
  Chas.,069, Clabourn,071,
  Claugh,086, Clayborn,010,
  Claybourne,007, Danl.,122,
  David,156, Drewry,219,
  Drury Jr.,126, Drury,009
SIMS, Drury,038,058,063,080,
  100,102,112,126,239,272,
  Elizabeth,015, F.,055,
  Frances,240, Francis,055,
  084, Garland,241,276,
  Garlin,241, Garlington,241,
  Geo.R.,086, Hiram,102,109,
  Hiriam,151, James D.,183,
  267, James,031,147,214,276,
  Jas.,076
SIMS, Jas.,079,080, Jas.D.,
  086, Jas.Jr.,053, Jno.,040,
  042,079,080,103,114,118,
  135,161,195,198,213,254,
  259,272, Jno.Jr.,079,
  Jno.Sr.,079, Joel,036,079,
  080,109, John Jr.,059,
  John Sr.,061, John,031,
  036,052,053,054,059,061,
  065,068,213
SIMS, John,217,276, Judith,
  086, Kellet,074, Lin,109,
  Lucey,228, Lucy Ann,086,
  Mariah,276, Martin,076,
  Messer Babb(?),053,
  Micajah,082, Nathan,053,
  097,102,169,176,180,242,
  243,267,269, P.R.,259, P.W.,
  259, Rachel,054,061,
  Rebecca,053
SIMS, Rebeccah,034, Reuben,
  053,266,271, Rhoda Babb,053,
  Rhoda,276, Richard,097,
  100,150,203,240,244, Richd.,
  066,080,110,120,140,185,
  196,221,238,245,247,264,
  268,269,272, Robt.,027,
  Rodey Babb,083, Sally,240,
  Sarah,086,137, Simeon B.,
  083
SIMS, Simeon,097, Simon B.,
  053, Susannah,110,112,
  Thadeus,053,054, Thos.,050,
  054,061,079,080,090,269,
  Vid.S.,188, Wade,213,228,
  William,002,010, Wm.,009,
  036,040,053,054,057,166,
  232,233,255,274, Zachariah B.,
  223, Zachariah,079,217,228
SIMSON, Agnes,012, Alexr.,028,
  Benj.,045, David,011, Jas.,
  025, John Jr.,024, John,029,
  030,034,037, Saml.,011
SINCLAIR, John,021,026,051,
  099,103, Marey,103
SINCLEAR, John,104, Marey,104
SIPS, James R.,235
SKELTON, Hugh,010
SKERLOCK, Joshua,173
SLAVE, (Female),092, Delia,
  250
SLEDGE, Levi,137
SLENDIN, Arthur,229
SLIKE, Chas.F.,266
SLOAN, Alfred,269, Archibald,
  172, Barbara,276, David,133,
  190,274, Geo.,131, Geo.A.,
  269, Geo.T.,269, Jane,257,
  Jas.,274, Jno.,102,190,
  274, Mary,269, Robt.,145,

190, Thos.,257,269, Thos.S.,
274, Wm.A.,269
SLOANE, R.,174, T.,174
SLONE, Arch.,257, Archebald,
257, David,106, Robt.,196,
243,258, Robt.Jr.,256
SLOWN, Wm.,257
SMALL, James,261
SMART, Joseph,157
SMITH(?), Wm.B.,138
SMITH, (?),124, A.,141,
Aberham,148, Abner,077,
088, Alex.,251, Alford,207,
Alfred,187,224, Allen,131,
165, Anna,257, Archbd.,102,
141, Archebald,178, Archibald,
060, B.(Dr.),229, B.,273,
Barnet,229,241, Barnett,
241,272,273, Benj.,045
SMITH, Benj.,097,100,140,
Benjamin,099, Brooker,168,
Brooks,140, Byrum,050, C.,
174, Charles,004,015,041,
063,073,074,105,121,139,
140,151,159,179,183,187,
191,232,236,242,256,260,
Daniel,200,203, Drury,018,
022
SMITH, E.,236, E.G.,236,
Edward,137, Eligah,139,
Elihu,160, Elijah Jr.,237,
Elijah,193,236,242,261,
Elisha Sr.,243, Elisha,215,
Eliz.(Miss),155, Eliz.,140,
145, Elizabeth,099,100,151,
152,261, Ellinor,003,
Elliot,022, Elliott,018,
Eppy,169
SMITH, F.,274, Fanny,130,
Geo.,181, George,018,
Green W.,218, Hancock,151,
Hannah,151, Hariot,072,
Harriet(?),071, Harry,018,
Henry,009, Hiram,009, J.,
174, James D.,156, James Jr.,
197,198, James Sr.,197,198,
James,018,030,056,057,072
SMITH, James,176,189,190,191,
198,202,214,215,236,237,
257, Jas.,062,074,101,110,
111,112,151,163, Jas.H.,117,
Jas.S.,257, Jesse,050,058,
071,072, Jno.,093,112,120,
150,163,166,173,174,176,
178,207,214,222,228,236,
238,255,258,266,269,271
SMITH, Jno.G.,156, Jno.Jr.,
103, Jno.W.,117,209,
John Sr.(?),220, John,018,
019,022,038,040,056,057,
058,072,101,103,150,196,
198,207,214,215,226,227,
228, Jones,176, Jos.,145,
Joshua,098,134,141,143,
151,172,178,202,204,265,
L.R.,265, Lenard,047
SMITH, Levi,098, Lewis,160,
193,198,206,220,246, Lucy,
078,084,112,204,211,213,
Mary,192,201, Mickel,236,
Mitchel Jr.,257, Mitchel,
151,152,190,237,257,
Mitchell,151, Moses,270,
Noah,098,100,141,224,273,
Patrick,203, Peter,007,
009,058
SMITH, Polley,168,257, Polly,
237, R.B.,254, Rachel,003,
Robert,117, Robt. P.,249,
Robt.(Rev.),019, Robt.,012,
046,166, Robt.L.,011,
Robt.P.,254,265, Salley,
119, Saml.,098,099, Sarah,
018,019,022, Solomon,109,
160,172, Starling,242,253
SMITH, Starling,271, Stephen,
024, Sterling K.,234,
Susanna,103, Thos.,050,
133,158,238, Wesley,161,
Wiley,044, William,158,
159, Wm.,018,022,057,063,
066,069,080,090,098,100,

102,112,117,131,133,148,
150,158,160,169,174,183,
187,190,203
SMITH, Wm.,211,268, Wm.B.,131,
133,158,159,190,203, Wm.Jr.,
030,110, Wm.R.,138,150,185,
196,203,210,235,265,269,
Wm.Sr.,138,151,161,185,
Z.F.,269,274, Zador F.,269,
Zion,272
SMYTH, Chas.,077,229, Dr.,014,
Drury,019, John,229, Mrs.,
014, Sarah,019
SNEAD, Jno.,114,247, Philip,
114, Pleasant C.,093, Widow,
114
SNEED, Jemima,133, Jno.,098,
104,111,182,232, Philip,098,
102,111, Pleasant C.,045,
Pleasant G.,056, Pleasant,
051
SNELGROVE, Jno.,183
SNELL, Alexr.,002
SNELLEY, Jno.,173
SNOW, Andw.,251,254, C.,263,
Chang(Miss),261, Charles,
150, Charley,251, Chas.,138,
161,203,205,247, Dandey,245,
Thos.(Mrs.),261
SNOWE, Charles,218
SOLOMON, Thos.,161
SOONE, Robt.,145
SOUTER, Jacob,273
SOUTH, Anthony,212, Daniel,
231, Danl.,069,076,139,163,
176,201,217,229,242,247,
250, Denis,137, E.W.,272,
Elijah,109,113, Elisha,265,
Ezekiel,137,139, Gabriel,
231,239, Gabril,230,
James H.,231, James,069,
210,212, Jas.L.,236,
Jedakiah,276
SOUTH, Jno.,076,082,176,191,
239, John,090,119,121,122,
126,136,137, Jos.,069,076,
113,178, Jos.Jr.,109,
Little Bill,109, Molly,133,
Nancy,212, Newton,212,
Peggey,212, Rachel,122,
Rebecah,119,136, Rebeckah,
122, Rutha,231, Starling,212
SOUTH, Wm.,018,020,050,070,
087,095,096,113,126,139,
145,176,187,228,230,236,
247, Wm.Jr.,126, Wm.Sr.,137,
139,231, Zedekiah,113,231,
Zedicah,230
SOUTHWOOD, G.,247
SPAREN, Patric,137
SPARK, Stephen,077, Wm.,224
SPARKS, Wm.,060,188, Z.,198,
248, Zach.,079, Zachariah,
182,186
SPEAR, Andw.,141, R.H.,252,
Wm.,098
SPEARE, Andw.,142, Wm.,042,
143
SPEARMAN, Thos.,221
SPEARMAN, Edmond,190, Edw.,
187, Susanah,190, Thos.,190,
265
SPEARS, Andrw.,048, Andw.,140,
143,172, David,045,048,172,
Frances,042, John,127,
Robt.,048,230,237, Robt.H.,
236, William,158, Wm.,048
SPEARY, Andw.,172
SPEER, Andw.,098,135,161,
David,052,066,087,096,098,
110, Jno.,089,137, Margaret,
098, Wm.,042,098,145,243
SPEERS(?), David,125
SPEERS, Andrew,125, Andrw.,
055, Andw.,159, David,011,
013,016,041,051,076,091,
118, Jno.,102, W.,174, Wm.,
159
SPELLS, Jno.,098
SPELTS(?), Jno.,116
SPELTZ(?), Jno.,109
SPENCE(?), Arthur,145
SPENCE, Andw.,143, Arthur,141,

143,150,152, David,069, Mr.,
011, Patrk.,096, R.,174,
Robt.,065,111,142,143,173,
232,256, Robt.Jr.,141,142,
145,146,152,159, Robt.Sr.,
145, Wm.,188
SPENCER, ,236, Jos.,268
SPENSE, Arther,145, Robt.Jr.,
145
SPILLERS, Geo.,010
SPIRGEN/SPURGEN, Nancy,226
SPREWELL, Saml.,218
SPRINGFIELD, Leodocia,171,
Thos.,172
SPROUSE, Vinson,032, Wm.,036,
040
SPRUEL, Robt.,236, Simon,236,
Wm.,087,113
SPRUELL, Simmion,148, Wm.,148
SPURGEN, Drury,183, Jno.,077,
093, John,063,075,076,117,
Nancy,117,183,230
SPURGEON, Drury,169, Jno.,089,
Nancy,115,169
SPURGIN, John,070,073,115,
116, Nancy,115,259, Wm.,120
SPURGINS, Eliza,004
STAFF, Philip,103
STAIN(?), Jos.,102
STAINS, E.,218
STALLARD, McElanahn,029
STANDFIELD, John,007,018
STANDHOUSE, Jno.,232
STANDLEY, Jno.B.,193
STANDLY, James,160, Jno.,097
STANFIELD, Jno.,099, John,021
STANFORD, J.,236, Jonathan Jr.,
212, Peter,137
STANLEY, Jno.B.,179,254
STARK, Jeremiah,174
STARKS, Jane,212
STARLING, Eliz.,191, Henry,
191, James,189,191
STARNE, Shubal,207
STARNES, A.,117,187, Aaron,
004,033,034,035,036,040,
118,122,146,149,160,161,
172,265,266,267, Ann,033,
034, Anna,004, Aron,256,
Avery,147, Col.(?),217,
Davis,248,249, Ebenezar,
004, Ebenezer,033,036,040,
069,144, Jno.,169,251, Joel,
133
STARNES, John,004,033,036,
Manhall,273, Margaret,248,
Margret,249, Marshal,201,
202,234,249, Marshall,267,
Marshel,245,251, Martha,
273, Mary Ann,267, Mary,004,
Milton,248,249, Rebekah,
004, Richd.,265, Shubal,120,
196,217,242,251, Shubel,248
STARNES, Shubet,192, Thomas,
249, Thos.,248, Wm.,265,
268,273
STARNS, Aaron,033,098,103,
Andw.,170,183, Anna,036,
Aron,094, Baron,134, Danl.,
183, E.,218, Ebenezer,079,
104, Joel,068,079, Moses,
087, Richard,172, Shubal,
169,170,218,236
STEART, Eben(?),128
STEDMAN, ,012, J.C.,048,
Saml.,097, Thos.D.,247
STEEL, Abner,057, Thomas,057,
059, Thos.,039
STEP, Thos.,196
STEPHENS, David,063,079,092,
120, Edw.,222, Jas.,272,
Jno.,082,119,191,237,
Jno.B.,237, Jno.R.,236,
John,014,020, K.L.,212,
Larkin,072, Marey,135,
Molly,135, Reuben,176,236,
258,274, Robert,247, Robt.,
137,176,191,222,236,237,
Timothy,274
STEPHENS, Wm.,201,258, Wm.J.,
236
STEPP(?), Larken,206
STEPP, Larkin,145,195, Thos.,

39

40

128,149,150,153,157,161,
171,174,178,179,194,206,
209,216
TEAGUE, Joshua,218,219,236,
277,278, Mary,105, Matilda,
105, Rachel,178, Robert,178,
Robt.,128,138, Siminion,
157, Susanah,203, T.(Dr.),
264, Thomas,158, Thos.(Dr.),
242, Thos.,116,137,149,157,
171,178,199,203,204,218,
229,253,261,263, William C.,
253
TEAGUE, Wm.,066,163,236
TEARCE, Benj.,143, Benj.F.,
145, Geo.,228
TEEDY, John,248
TEFF(?), Frank,013
TELLY, Seth,146
TEMPLE, David Jr.,075,
David Sr.,075
TEMPLETON, Clark,266, D.C.,
266, D.Clark,243, David C.,
159,246, David,109,112,149,
158,160,178,224,226, Geo.,
224,265, J.,174, James Jr.,
158, James Sr.,158, James,
112,145,152,159,160,179,
183,187,190,263, Jane(Mrs.),
159, Jas.(Capt.),143
TEMPLETON, Jas.(Capt.),152,
159, Jas.,093,107,124,141,
151,237, Jas.Jr.,159,
Jas.Sr.,112,159, Jno.,106,
145,159,165,174,183,188,
189,222,236,243,267,268,
Jno.Jr.,224, Jno.Sr.,188,
224, John,012,112,145,179,
220,264, Jos.,174, Polley,
159
TEMPLETON, Robert,009, Robt.,
112,118,188,189,225, Saml.,
048,151,187,242, Taylor,152,
W.,174, W.A.,265, William,
158, Wm.,094,109,112,124,
133,143,151,159,179,180,
187,230,250,268
TEREY, Jno.,241
TERREY, Jas.H.,221, Jno.,166,
241, John,126, Wm.,122,258,
Young,258
TERRY, Jno.,180, John,072,
Jos.,103,169, Stephen,146,
Wm.,161,180,258, Wm.Sr.,
146,274
THAXTON, Wm.,186
THETFORD, Josiah,043, Mr.,020,
Nancy,044, Wm.,011
THEWETT, John,133
THOMAS, ,236, Abel,042,052,
Andw.,236, Benj.,167,
Delilah,154, Edward,052,
Evan,052, Gabriel,178,192,
228, Gamble,169, Gambrel,
201,202, Gambriel,202,
Gideon,221, Isaac,028,052,
148, James,265, Jas.,096,
Jno.,036,111, John Jr.,049,
John,001
THOMAS, John,028,052,147,148,
Mary,052, Nehemiah,052,
Phoeby,052, Reuben,132,
156,201,202,256,272, Saml.,
222, Sarah,052, Thomas,052,
William,201,202, Wm.,005,
052,172
THOMASON, Elizabeth,272,
Frances,272, Francis,273,
Geo.,109, George,272,273,
Gideoi,272, Gideon,085,
086,270, James,272,273,
Nancy,279, Polly,279, R.,
270, Robert,279, Sally,279,
Washington,272,273, Wm.,
272, Wm.Jr.,005
THOMISON, Wm.,038
THOMPKINS, Norward,145
THOMPSON, ,223, Abraham,196,
198, Abram,264, Burrel,013,
151, Eliz.A.,276, Elizabeth D.,
278, Gideon,251,255, H.,
272, Harris,219, Henry,013,
222,232, Isabella,278, J.W.,

270, Jane,278, Jas.W.,226,
Job,020, John,014, M.,272,
Mary,278, Nancy,196
THOMPSON, Nancy,278, Nelly,
146, Polley,248, Robert,251,
255, Saml.,010,013, Sarah Ann,
278, Stephen,010, Usley,116,
William,196,278, Wm.,151,
171,187,191,198,221,232,
234,238,264,276, Wm.Sr.,198,
275
THOMSON, Geo.,232, Gideon,136,
221, Henry,036, R.,255,
Robt.,115,136, Wm.,233
THORNETON, Frances,187,
William S.,262, Wm.S.,262
THREAT, John,151
THREATE, Wm.,190
THREET, Sarah,125,126
THREETT, Reuben,123, Sarah,
123, Tom,123
THRELKELD, Willis,104
THRELKELL, Henry,109
THUBER(THURBER?), L.C.,139
THURMAN, Jas.,019, Thos.,063
THWEATT, Edw.,035
TIERCE, Benj.,082,126,
Benj.F.,136, Geo.,126,140
TIERE, Richd.,176,266
TIGRETT, Jno.Jr.,230
TIMMENS, Maren,236
TIMMINS, John,126
TINCH, Wm.,074
TINER, John,220, Stephen,220
TINSLEY, Abraham,019,026,058,
059,074, Ann,028, Betsey C.,
218, Betsey,216, Bowfort,
202, C.,104, Catharine,193,
194, Catherine,018,019,
Cornelius,056,057,091,093,
115,117, Cullen,261, Isaac,
163,166, J.,099, J.W.,099,
Jabez,234, James,029
TINSLEY, James,064,074,274,
Jas.,039,273, Jno.,254,
Larkin,195, Lewis,111,
Mary,074
TINSLEY, Molly,259, Nancy,058,
059,074, Pusila,196, Sarah,
031,074, Sherard,099,
Shered,102,116,118,
Sherril,045, W.,099,
William,074, Wm.,018,019,
101,124,128,132,133,160,
167,195,228,235,239,273,
Z.,134, Zach.,098,116,118,
Zachariah,152
TINSLEY, Zachariah,216,218,
Zacheriah,145
TIREE, Benj.,162, Benj.F.,121,
178, Geo.,162,228, Wm.,162
TIREY, Jno.,187
TISBORN, Repts.,237
TOALS(TOLLS), Danl.,062
TOD, Jno.,236
TODD, Able,138, Andrew,066,
090,134,171, Andw.(Mrs.),
237, Andw.,133,211, Archbd.,
150, Archebald,202, Archey,
187, Archy,265, Charles,135,
Chas.,117,152,271, David,
090, Dr.,116, Eliza Julia,
255, Eliza,171, Eliza.,255,
Elizabeth,258, J.,270
TODD, JAs.,135, James Jr.,150,
152, James R.,255, James Sr.,
150, James,147,150,151,188,
255, Jane M.,279, Jane,171,
Jas.,117,268, Jno.,081,
120,132,141,155,161,166,
169,171,205,211,212,233,
236,237,258,267,269,270,
Jno.Jr.,180, Jno.S.,255
TODD, Jno.S.,258, Jno.Sr.,139,
166,208, John S.,255,
John Sr.,255, John,019,
131,132,135,152,171,193,
Joseph,255, Lititia,171,
Margaret,171, Maria,255,
Mary,135,171, Matilda,255,
Nancey,135, Nathan,090,
Patk.,120, Patrick,039,
058,063

TODD, Patrick,066,090,093,
190,196,203,235,237,245,
265,268, Patrk.,044,057,
133,247, Permelia,255,
Polley,255, Robert,021,
135,152, Robt.,071,229,237,
251,258,260, Saml.,098,104,
150,161,187,190,191,196,
202,205,220,258,260,
Saml.F.H.,274
TODD, Saml.R.,171,269,279,
Samuel,171,203,259, Thos.,
090,160,191,249,259,261,
268,272, William,255, Wm.,
185,205,211,222,237,256,
258, Wm.A.,274
TOLAND, Haney,256, Henry,256,
257, Hugh,141,155,172,189,
256,267
TOLBERT, Wm.,004
TOLEN, Hugh,189,243
TOM, Arnold,148
TOMPSON, Aberham,140,157,
Abraham,185,187,196,203,
Benj.,167, Catharine,244,
Geo.,237, Gideon,255,
Harris,229, Henry,075,211,
244,246, Hirum,166, Isaac,
188, James,244, Jenny,244,
Jno.,187,246, John,075,
244, Jos.,093, Molly,196,
Nancy,244
TOMPSON, Nancy,246, Polly,244,
Robert,255, William,196,
Wm.,108,121,161,185,194,
196,241,249,260
TOMS, Jas.,081, Saml.,081
TOMSON & HANCOCK, ,016
TOMSON, John,137, Wm.,251
TOOD(?), Patrick,080
TOOD(TODD?), James,177, Jno.,
180
TOOD, John,258
TORRANCE, Franky,149
TOUKESTY, Geo.,221
TOUNS, Peter,266
TOUSAND, Benj.,187, Marthan,
187
TOUSHEND, Thos.,194
TOWNS, Peter,258,266
TOWNSEND, Thos.,194
TRACE(?), Benj.,135
TRAINHAM, James,265
TRAMEN, James,233
TRAMUM, Jas.,109
TRAP, Wm.,036
TRAVIS, Joseph,220, Wm.,225
TREMENS, Hunsford,237
TRENTTEN(?), Gab'l E.,193
TRIBBLE, (Wid.),246, Andrew K.,
254, Betsy,116, Cornelius T.,
115,116, Cornelius,246,
Elijah,236,246,264,268,
Eliz.,115, Elizabeth,254,
Elygah,245, Ezekiel H.,254,
J.,099,117, Jane R.,254,
Jekeniah,246,254, Jepah,
152, Jeremiah,048,115
TRIBBLE, Jeremiah,116,230,
Jno.A.,246, John Allen,115,
Marey,254, Stephen,094,
036,045, Susanah M.,254
TRIBLE(?), Jeremiah,168
TRIBLE, ELijah,261, Jeremiah,
244, Stephen,029
TROUTMAN, Jno.,164
TRUE, Benj.,058
TUATER(?), Robt.,217
TUCKER, Jno.W.,211, Joel,172,
174, Levina,256, Miss,122,
Robt.,268, Starling,032,
044,047,058,061,077,081,
094,155,192,201,208,213,
231, Sterling,162,166,214,
258
TUDD, Thos.,272
TULLEY, Stephen,208
TURK, Mary,022,023, Rachel,
017, Wm.,014
TURLEY, Jefferson,267
TURNER, Abbey,161, Alexr.,102,
Andw.,250, Asa,044,070,
Dan'l.,161, David,095,

Fanny,015, Fielding,018,
065,066, Geo.,095, James,
065,066, Jas.,101,120,
Jenney,161, Jer.,062,
Josiah,187, Littel B.,198,
Lucy,018, Mary,209, Polley,
190, Richard,008
TURNER, Richard,017,018,
Richd.,183, Robt.,066,
Salley,065,066, Sally,066,
161,190, Sarah,066,190,
Tandy,257,272, Thomas,154,
Thos.,058,063,153, Wm.,006,
011,012,050,231, Zachariah,
011
TURREY, Young,257
TWEDY, John,236
TYGART, Jane,179, Jno.,179,
273
TYGERT, Jno.,101, Nancy,200
TYNER, John,004
UNDERWOOD, Isaac,101,102,123,
125,154, J.,116, James,127,
154,157,168, Jane,154,
Jas.(?),138, Jas.,012,037,
051,091,107,145, Jas.Jr.,
157, Jno.,097,107,123,132,
144,167, John,123,125,127,
147,154,155, Mary,154,
Mathew M.,154, Robt.,154,
Wm.,017
UNDERWOOD, Wm.,029,038,103,
154
UNKNOWN, Allen,130, David,090,
Hambleton,101, James,176,
Jas.,138, Nelly,170, Perry,
173, Thos.,088, Turner,138,
Wm.,212,275, Wm.Jr.,136
VALENTINE, Eli,265, Nancy,267,
Polley,217, Rhoda,265,
Robt.,195, Roda,161, Rodey,
238, Rody,205
VANCE(NANCE), Allen,264
VANCE, Allen,150,246,254,261,
264,266,267,269,271,279,
Betsy,072, Chas.,100,
Danl.,264, David,031,045,
083,101,160,166,193,194,
198,208,211,242,261,263,
264,266,279, Drayton,194,
Eliz.,266, Fedrick,255,
James W.,279, James,028,
036,066
VANCE, Jas.,024, Jas.Wash.,
279, Jno.,253,263,264,266,
John,057,266,279, Jos.,029,
031,051,059,098,124,134,
141,143,145,151,237,248,
254,268,270, Jos.H.,279,
Jos.Jr.,220, Joseph,233,
245,247, Mary,042,082,083,
279, Milley,160, N.C.,266,
Nat,256
VANCE, Nat,265, Nat.,274,
Nathan,166, Nathaniel,030,
082, Nathl.,024,026,028,
055,066,068,083,167,170,
206,264,266,267,279, Robt.,
243,246,247,271, Robt.S.,
245,271, Saml.,037,042,048,
065,083,091,098,115,116,
117,118,124,151,170,182,209
VANCE, Saml.,216,218,230,242,
243,245,246,247,249,261,
263,264,266,268,279,
Saml.Sr.,246, Shedrick,224,
Thomson,262, W.W.,208,
Widow,031, William,279,
Wm.,042,083,101,117,198,
207,230,253,254, Wm.D.,199,
Wm.G.,141,247, Wm.M.,207,
209,266
VANCE, Wm.N.,253
VANLEER, (Dr.),271
VANPATTON, N.V.,236,237
VAUGHAN, Drury,268, Jas.,268,
272, Nancy,183, Wm.,264
VAUGHN, Benj.,012, Cathy,106,
Clabourn,122,123, Clabourne,
123,140, Claiborn,086,122,
Dorotha,217, Drurey,133,
Drury F.,056,150, Drury,
048,062,066,101,132,161,

190,202,203,205,235,
Eliz.Chappell,202, Geo.,
212, George,202, Henry,018,
102
VAUGHN, Henry,156, J.,111,
James C.,203, James,033,
081,156, Jas.,077,247, Jno.,
098,107,128,156,202,
Jno.Jr.,202,212, Jno.Sr.,
202, John,022,105,106,112,
114,122, Jonathan,156,
Kindred,261, Lettey,117,
137, Martha,168, Martin,045,
Mary,067
VAUGHN, Mary,122,123,140,153,
155,217, Nicholas,009,
Nicklous,009, Nicklus,034,
Reuben,081, Saml.,031,038,
055,063, Samuel,035,
Thomson,105, W.P.,101,
Walter P.,161,190,196,202,
203, Watley,066, William,
199,200, Wm.,081, Wm.W.,117
VENABLE, Chas.,080
VENEBURNER, Elie,186
VERELL, Jno.,157
VERNELL, Wm.,267
VERRALL, Jno.,092
VICKERY, Chr.,097, Christop.,
095,269, Green,261, Jno.,
081, Mikel,039,043,166,
Milley,095, Milly,269,
Mitchel,167, W.,157, Wm.,
130,212
VIER, Obediah,224, Shedrick,
224
VIMS, Richd.,187
VINES, Jas.,103
VINYARD, John,018
VITELLO, John,038, Sarah,038,
Stephen,051
VITO, Thos.,190
VITTELO, John,038
VITTO, Jeremiah,190
VIVRN(?), John F.Jr.,154
VREVN(?), John F.Jr.,154
WADDEL, Noel,232
WADDLE, Caller,232, Edw.,232
WADKINS, Ann,052, Charles,116,
Eliz.(Mrs.),178, Eliz.,222,
Elizabeth,217,253, Ezekiel,
241, Henry,082, Jas.,128,
Jno.G.,222, John,217,
Joshua,248, Lewis,193, Wm.,
045,052,150,190
WADSWORTH & TURPIN, ,016,019
WADSWORTH, (School),128, ,
012, Mr.,007, Thos.,008,
021,027,028
WAFFORD, Isaac,165
WAIR(?), James,147, Wm.,147
WAIR(WARE?), Saml.,071
WAIR, Albert,218
WAISTCOAT(?), Joel,112,116
WAISTCOAT, Cynthia,116, Joel,
115
WAIT, Frances,079,276,
Franklin,276, James,213,
217, Jas.,089,138, Jno.,080,
113,118,135,145,195, John,
024,075,076,079,086,089,
213,276, Lilley F.,229, P.,
087,117,135, Philip Jr.,213,
Philip Sr.,222, Philip,080,
087,094,095,097,107,113
WAIT, Philip,118,124,127,139,
178,243,267,276, Thos.,213
WAITS, ,054, Jno.,114, Philip,
135, Rodey,089
WAITT, Jno.,259
WALDRIP, Shadrick,274
WALDROP, A.D.,219, Abrum,056,
Andw.,140, Asa,142,
Bird G.,219, Bird,240,249,
262, E.B.,247, Elias,238,
Elisha,238,251, Eliz.,069,
094, H.,141, Harmon,098,
169, Henderson,215, Hillis(Mrs.),
219, Ira,205, Isaac,126,
139,162,176, Jas.,134
WALDROP, Jas.,141, Kellet,229,
Kellis,221,238, Mardy,229,
Meredith G.,219, Merida,

229, Merideth,229, Meridith,
253, Mikel,048, Mordica,140,
Richd.,028,198, Saml.,161,
198,242,261, Samuel,215,
Shedrick,253, Silus,240,
Solomon,047, Susan,269
WALDROP, Susanna,062, W.A.,
252, Willis,247, Wm.,006,
081,268
WALDWELL, Saml.,274
WALKER, Allen,091,117,203,
243, Alpha,135, Azeriah,254,
B.A.,151, Barnes,278,
Betsey,140, Bev.,111,
Beveley A.,168, Beveley,
167, Bevely,223, Danl.,018,
065,098,108,145,151,171,
Elijah,075,119,123,124,
126, Eliz.,070,112,123,
Elizabeth,004
WALKER, Elizabeth,110,126,
139, Garland,092, Geo.,074,
H.,057,161, Hagen,246,249,
254, Harriot(Mrs.),140,
Harusha(?),045, Herusha,
007,040,048, Horatio,014,
065,066, James,026,060,
Jatthrow,004, Jethro,004,
026, Jno.,011,040,094,114,
119
WALKER, Jno.,121,137,139,152,
207,217,229,232,237,244,
262,267, Joel,036,040,046,
103,114,139,162, John,005,
006,007,024,026,053,054,
066,071,091,119,124,126,
130,147,230, Kerusha(?),007,
Lucinda,278, Lyl,149,
Malium(?),151, Manfield,020
WALKER, Mansfield,024,037,
Martha,023, Mary,140,
Menn.,015, Minor,260,
Moses,004,005, Nancy,126,
Patsy,023, Robt.,018,
Sarah G.,070, Silas Jr.,
031,036, Silas,051, Silv's Sr.,
014, Silvanus Jr.,044,059,
061,065,066, Silvanus,014,
045,051
WALKER, Silvanus,055,071,150,
157,167, Silvs.,024,036,
045,047,063, Silvs.Jr.,024,
037,040,053,056,067,068,
Silvs.Sr.,043, Susannah,
026, Tandy,006,007,014,019,
150,271, Thos.,110,111,118,
151,169, Thos.Milton,139,
Tyra,268, Tyree,269, W.J.,
152
WALKER, William,110, Wineford,
252, Wm.,040,055,073,091,
092,098,099,101,112,140
WALLACE, Eliz.D.,237, Hugh,
253, James,028,265, Jas.,
024,268, Jno.,281, John,002,
013,028,062, Jonathan,028,
Patsy,013, Willis,268,
Wm.W.,243
WALLAS, D.,133
WALLASS(WALLACE), Geo.,146
WALLASS, J.,131, John,132
WALLER(?), James,170
WALLES(?), Martin,171
WALLIS(?), Jos.,129
WALLIS, Ann,055, Anne,054,
Bluford,206, Calvin,228,
Cleaveland,252, Clement,
138, Danl.,197,230, Elijah,
117, Elizabeth,166,249,
Geo.F.,221, Isaac,164,
J.B.,232, J.W.,274, James,
054,055, Jesse,028,063,104,
165,183,232, Jno.,104,108,
233
WALLIS, Jno.,274, John Sr.,
157,159, John,162,166,
Jonathan,091,190, Jos.,101,
Joseph,160, Peter,274,
Saml.,236, Sylvanus,179,
W.,266, W.W.,166,190,224,
230,246,254, Walton W.,162,
222, Walton,159,205,
Wesley W.,249, Wesley,166,

42

Westley,166
WALLIS, Whitbury,232, Wm.,146,
163,224,232
WALLISS, Jno.,131
WALLS, James,066
WALSEY, Jno.,146
WALTON(?), Robt.,221
WALTON, Stuart,188, Zach.,187
WARD(?), Edw.,269
WARD(WORD?), Robt.,077
WARD, Coleman,108, Eliz.,124,
Frances,070, Giney,066,
James,057,059,064,070,071,
102,124,152, Jas.,062,081,
083,098,100,102,104,107,
108,110,121, Jno.,051,124,
134,138, Joyce J.,077,
Robert,066,206, Robt.,078,
098,115,124,251, Samuel,075
WARD, Samuel,076,078, Sarah,
189, Seth,098, Susan,185,
Susannah,075,078, Thos.,
008,098,102,104,145, Wm.,
047,072,081,087,098,104,124
WARDLAW, H.M.,263, Jas.,143,
Jos.,143,145, Joseph,176
WARE, A.N.,162, Abner,239,
Cooper,186, Dr.,217,
Easter,016, Edmond,082,
Edw.,076,078, F.E.,247,
Geo.W.,251, James,071,
Long,090, Mary Chandler,
201, Nicholas,113, Saml.,
051, Thos.,151,166,176,239,
Wm.(Col.),139, Wm.,082,
WARFORD, Benj.,010, James,063,
Wm.,010
WARPING, Jonathan,230
WARREN, Geo.,173, Jer.,096,
Jeremiah,087,158,214,
Jerm.,097, Zach.,080
WARTON, Saml.,009
WASHINGTON, Eliz.,176,178,
Geo.,087,137,139,145,178,
253,258, Geo.G.,220, George,
186, Thomas,176, Thos.,087,
113,137,167,176,178,181,
186,217,220,222,229,253,
258, Widow,087, Wm.,015,
019,039,041,060,062,086,
087,094,127
WASIN, Peter,187
WASON, David,067
WASSON, Jno.,187
WATE, Philip,176
WATERS(?), Landy,169
WATERS, Jno.,196, Lynsey,189,
M.,188, Philamon M.,188,
Philip,189, Robt.,228,
T.W.,019,265, Thos.,196,
Thos.Jr.,220, Thos.W.,188,
W.M.,188
WATKINS, Charles,116, Elisha,
278, Elizabeth,116, Henry,
096,109, James,172, Jno.,
266, Jno.C.,278, Wm.,012
WATOSN, Elihu,187
WATS, James,158
WATSON, A.(Dr.),251, Allen,
251,253,255, Amelia C.,261,
B.,192, Barry,254, Bary,
189,216, Benj.,026,180,
Berrey,192,218, Berry,207,
213, Bery,228,240, Bevely,
192, Casper,261, Charles,
025, Cristopher,213, Danl.,
271, Dillard,151, Dr.,174
WATSON, E.,131,149, Elihu,150,
157,173,192,193,207,214,
216,217,253,254,255,261,
263,264,270, Elihue(Dr.),
157, Elijah Jr.,261,
Elijah(Dr.),160,264,
Elijah,036,046,060,062,
064,065,069,076,077,128,
129,167,169,187,242,247,
253,254,255,261
WATSON, Elijah,264,270,
Elisha(Dr.),157, Elisha,
039,059,103,131,157,237,
258, Eliz.,187, Ellender,
192, James,186, Jas.,097,
104,258,261,271, Jesse G.,

261, Jno.,097,102,113,158,
173,181,182,183,184,190,
207,228, Jno.Sr.,207,
John(Capt.),192
WATSON, John,008,009,010,047,
180,181,193,214,227,
Lemuel(?),096, Lewis,063,
069,096,097,135,173,189,
190,192,217, Nancey,181,
Pheby,192, Phillip,192,
Ruth,192, Rutha,189,
Samuel,096,097, Stephen,
057, Suckey,059, Thos.,055,
Wiley,192
WATSON, Wiley,228, Willard,
129,157,255, Willis,097,
189,192,214,228, Wm.,027,
074,253,258,271
WATT, James,159, Jno.,080,
Richd.,080
WATTS & WILLIAMS, ,152
WATTS(?), Eliz.,198
WATTS, B.F.,252,259, Beauford,
133, Beaufort T.,267,
Beaufort,081, Bluford,251,
257, Braxton,081,110,113,
120,133,150,151,187,188,
194, Catey(Wid.),101,
Cornelia,081, Dr.,264,
E.C.,265, E.M.,247,
Elihu C.,203,268,269,
Elihu,133,161,190
WATTS, Elihu,196,247,259,268,
Elihue C.,210, Eliza,081,
Elvira,081, Geo.,016,036,
043, J.L.,201, J.P.(Dr.),
264, J.P.,203,263,264, J.W.,
279, James Jr.,152,162,258,
James Sr.,150,210,265,
James,048,066,133,148,151,
152,158,160,161,162
WATTS, James,190,195,196,203,
205,216,221,228,235,243,
247,265, Jane(Mrs.),160,
Janetta,190, Jas.,046,047,
048,079,080,082,090,092,
110,111,112,120,138,267,
268, Jas.Jr.,148,158,221,
Jennata(Mrs.),161, Jno.,
034,077,078,167,189,195,
247,251
WATTS, Jno.,264,271,279,
Jno.Af.,229, Jno.C.,262,
Jno.D.,243, Jno.P.(Dr.),
267, Jno.P.,203,247,251,
255, John P.,081,224,
John R.,184, John,009,011,
014,018,024,030,039,046,
048,050,057,065,081,082,
272, Louisa,081, M.D.,203,
Matilda,081
WATTS, N.C.,247, Nancy C.,247,
Narcissa,081, Peggy,081,
Priscilla,030, Richard,081,
150,251, Richd.,048,081,
110,205,217,229,240,252,
267,268,269, W.D.,203,206,
210,211,218,245,247,250,
253,264,267,270,271,275,
276, W.W.,174, Wm.,160,
Wm.D.,216
WATTS, Wm.D.,243,249,253,255,
262,263, Wm.W.,195
WATUS(WATSON?), Allen,270
WEASAN, Luke,252
WEASEM, Hicks,019
WEASON, E.(Mrs.),211, Edw.,
210,211, Edward,255,
Fredrick,210, Isaac G.,261,
Jehue,210, Johnston,209,
210,211,254, Mrs.,210,
Nancy,211, Sarah C.,254
WEASSON, Edw.,198
WEATHERALL, F.,057, Wm.,271,
272
WEATHERS, Jno.,108, Joel,175,
202,217, Richd.,202, Saml.,
014, Thomas,077, Thos.,079,
108, Wm.,098
WEIR, John,027, Thomas,245,
Thos.(Dr.),264, Thos.,247
WEIT(?), Philip,183
WEIT, John,228, Redah,183

WELBARE, Seth,250
WELBORN, Seth,207
WELCH, Danl.,026,043,061,221,
Geo.,013, James,128, Jas.,
130, Nicholas,015
WELDING, Danl.,058
WELLS & CARTER, ,242
WELLS & SONS, John,019
WELLS, Aaron,060,061, Abner,
133,190, Asenath,060,
Beaufort,267, Benj.M.,267,
Bleuford,185,250, Bluford,
112,120,213,222,225,238,
245,250,263, Blufort,261,
Brefort,185, Clement,053,
094,097,114,224,267
WELLS, Clemment,224,238,240,
245, David,258, Elisha,060,
110,127, Eliz.,267, G.F.,
235, Harrison,240, Horatio,
221, James,190,229, Jas.,
042,267,272, Jno.,081,263,
John,013,196, Martin,245,
Mary,105, Moses,048,060,
061,104,105,108, Rebecca,060
WELLS, Robert,240, Sener,240,
Umphrey,129, Washington,
195, Wm.,267
WELSH, James,129, Jane,130,
Jinna,129, Marey,129,
Nicholas,011
WESCOAT, Eliz.,270, Joel,098,
270
WESON(WEASON), Jesse J.,183
WESON, Edward,254, Jesse I.,
188
WESSON, Benj.,052,158, Edmond,
199, Edw.,061,249,271,276,
Eliz.,047,270, Elizabeth,
052, Fed.,271, Henry,052,
Hicks,052,072,089, Isaac,
225, Jno.,098, John,052,
Julious,224, Julius,056,
249, Luke,175,231,251,271,
Martha,052, Polly,052
WESSON, Sarah,052,175, Thos.,
056, Washington,254
WEST(?), John,227
WEST, Berry,012,036,042,173,
David,151, Elias,260,
Filley F.,228, Geo.,258,
Geo.B.,206, Geo.Berry,206,
Jno.,173,251,254,265,271,
Jno.F.,249, John,004,192,
193,206,207,263, Joseph,265,
Judy,173,206, L.F.,228,
Mary,206, Perry,158,
Philip,258
WEST, Robt.K.,134, Thos.,176,
Wm.,018,089,104,113,166,
173,186,213,214,217,221,
232,271, Zebulon,187,198,223
WESTBROOK, Thos.,169
WESTCOAT, Cynthia,115, Joel,
105,115
WESTMORELAND, Jno.,089,186,
Jno.Jr.,117, John,088,
Robt.,183, Thos.,164,
Thos.H.,232, Zach.,186
WESTON(?), Alex.,267
WESTON, Alexr.,274, Thos.,055
WHARTON, Clement,040,053,
Dilling,120, Dillion,250,
G.,042, Geo.,036,040,053,
064,069,079,119,120,151,
188, Joshua,040, P.G.,054,
059,076, Pleasant,053,
Saml.,002,004,007,014,016,
054, Samuel,026, Stephen,
073,102
WHEALER, Andrew,128
WHEAT(?), Bazzle,169
WHEAT, Basil,172, Bazil,172
WHEATE, Bassill,189
WHEELER, Andw.,212, Saml.,079,
Wm.,057
WHITE, Benj.,232, Eliz.,111,
112, George,161, J.,202,
James,053,111,112,114,
Jane,130, Jno.,177,233,
273, John,201,221,224,276,
Mathew,192,236, Richard,
123,124,148, S.K.,274,

066,085,110,121,171,210,
213,242,246,263,266, Wm.A.,
167,203,243, Wm.Agustin,163,
Wm.E.,135, Wm.J.,220,
Wm.Sr.,051, Zach.,043,
Zebah(?),226
YOUNGBLOOD, Mary,277, Washt.,
274
YOUNGHUSBAND, Jon.,019
YOUNT, Jas.A.,103
ZAINS, Pendleton,192
ZEASLEY(?), Thos.Y.,163